THE ROUTLEDGE HANDBOOK OF AFRICAN LINGUISTICS

The Routledge Handbook of African Linguistics provides a holistic coverage of the key themes, subfields, approaches and practical application to the vast areas subsumable under African linguistics that will serve researchers working across the wide continuum in the field.

Established and emerging scholars of African languages who are active and current in their fields are brought together, each making use of data from a linguistic group in Africa to explicate a chosen theme within their area of expertise, and to illustrate the practice of the discipline in the continent.

Augustine Agwuele is Professor of Linguistics. He integrates the conceptual rigors of theoretical linguistics with ethnographically grounded scholarship in socio-cultural anthropology, language and culture, and in the studies of the peoples and cultures of Africa to address common and habitual practices involved in encoding, transmitting, and decoding of messages.

Adams Bodomo is Professor of African Studies (African Languages and Literatures) at the University of Vienna. He specializes in formal theoretical linguistics, cross-cultural communication, digital humanities (languages and literatures in new media), Computer-Mediated Communication for Linguistics and Literacy: Technology and Natural Language Education, and international studies involving Africa and Asia.

ROUTLEDGE LANGUAGE HANDBOOKS

Routledge Language Handbooks provide comprehensive and state-of-the-art linguistic overviews of languages other than English. Each volume draws on an international team of leading scholars and researchers in the field. As reference works, the handbooks will be of great value to readers in many different fields; linguistic typology at all levels, general linguists, historical linguists, sociolinguists, and students of the individual languages or language families concerned.

THE ROUTLEDGE HANDBOOK OF CHINESE TRANSLATION
Edited by Chris Shei and Zhao-Ming Gao

THE ROUTLEDGE HANDBOOK OF ARABIC LINGUISTICS
Edited by Elabbas Benmamoun and Reem Bassiouney

THE ROUTLEDGE HANDBOOK OF AFRICAN LINGUISTICS
Edited by Augustine Agwuele and Adams Bodomo

THE ROUTLEDGE HANDBOOK OF
CHINESE SECOND LANGUAGE ACQUISITION
Edited by Chuanren Ke

THE ROUTLEDGE HANDBOOK OF
ARABIC SECOND LANGUAGE ACQUISITION
Edited by Mohammad T. Alhawary

For more information about this series please visit:
https://www.routledge.com/Routledge-Language-Handbooks/book-series/RLH

THE ROUTLEDGE HANDBOOK OF AFRICAN LINGUISTICS

Edited by Augustine Agwuele and Adams Bodomo

LONDON AND NEW YORK

First published 2018
by Routledge
2 Park Square, Milton Park, Abingdon, Oxon OX14 4RN

and by Routledge
711 Third Avenue, New York, NY 10017

Routledge is an imprint of the Taylor & Francis Group, an informa business

© 2018 selection and editorial matter, Augustine Agwuele and Adams Bodomo; individual chapters, the contributors.

The right of Augustine Agwuele and Adams Bodomo to be identified as the authors of the editorial material, and of the authors for their individual chapters, has been asserted in accordance with sections 77 and 78 of the Copyright, Designs and Patents Act 1988.

All rights reserved. No part of this book may be reprinted or reproduced or utilised in any form or by any electronic, mechanical, or other means, now known or hereafter invented, including photocopying and recording, or in any information storage or retrieval system, without permission in writing from the publishers.

Trademark notice: Product or corporate names may be trademarks or registered trademarks, and are used only for identification and explanation without intent to infringe.

British Library Cataloguing-in-Publication Data
A catalogue record for this book is available from the British Library

Library of Congress Cataloging-in-Publication Data
A catalog record has been requested for this book

ISBN: 978-1-138-22829-0 (hbk)
ISBN: 978-1-315-39298-1 (ebk)

Typeset in Times New Roman
by Swales & Willis Ltd, Exeter, Devon, UK

DEDICATION

This *Routledge Handbook of African Linguistics* is dedicated to Ayo Bamgbose. With over five decades of exemplary scholarship on African languages, the indefatigable professor remains very active in the field and exceptionally passionate about research into African languages.

Additionally, the *Routledge Handbook of African Linguistics* is specially dedicated to the following African scholars for their exemplary scholarship on African languages: Professors Florence Dolphyne, Salikoko Mufwene, Sam Mchombo, and Bokamba Eyamba. These renowned scholars have championed the course of linguistics on the continent, and they have been exemplary in their commitment to research, teaching and mentoring generations of student-scholars.

The field of African linguistics would not have been in existence without the selfless efforts of many researchers, fieldworkers, informants, and diverse scholars and students of African languages. To these innumerable important personalities we also dedicate this Handbook.

CONTENTS

Notes on contributors	*x*
Foreword	*xiv*
Acknowledgements	*xvii*

Introduction: African linguistics   1
Augustine Agwuele and Adams Bodomo

PART I
History, method, and typology   **13**

1 A short history of African language studies in the nineteenth and
early twentieth centuries, with an emphasis on German contributions   15
Sara Pugach

2 Historical linguistics in an African context: a brief state of the art   33
Gerrit J. Dimmendaal

3 Linguistic research in the African field   55
Bruce Connell

4 Tone and tonology in African languages   72
Constance Kutsch Lojenga

5 A system-based typology of MOOD in Niger-Congo languages   93
*Isaac N. Mwinlaaru, Christian M.I.M. Matthiessen, and
Ernest S. Akerejola*

vii

Contents

PART II
Sound and syllable system
119

6 Coarticulation: segmental and suprasegmental interactions in Yoruba 121
Augustine Agwuele

7 Labial-velars of Africa: phonetics, phonology, and
historical development 150
Michael Cahill

8 Syllable structure and vowel/zero alternations in Moroccan
Arabic and Berber 168
Mohamed Lahrouchi

9 Vowel harmony (beyond ATR) and its impact on
morphological parsing 181
John Rennison

PART III
Phrase and sentence system
205

10 West African serial verb constructions: the case of Akan and Ga 207
Dorothee Beermann and Lars Hellan

11 Logophoricity, long distance reflexives, and the Yoruba anaphor *Òun* 222
Nike Lawal

12 The encoding of information structure in African languages 243
Nana Aba Appiah Amfo

13 Bantu applicatives and Chimiini instrumentals 262
Brent Henderson

14 The form and function of Dagbani demonstratives 281
Samuel Alhassan Issah

15 Experiencer predications in Chadic: a study of the
semantics-syntax interface 297
Zygmunt Frajzyngier

Contents

PART IV
Language and society: theory and practice   **323**

16 Translation theory and practice past and present: applying the
Target Audience Criterion to some West African languages   325
Keir Hansford

17 The representation of African languages and cultures on
social media: a case of Ewe in Ghana   343
Elvis Yevudey

18 Sustainable language technology for African languages   359
Arvi Hurskainen

19 Language planning for sustainable development: problems and
prospects in Ghana   376
Paul Agbedor

PART V
Creative expressions and cultural life   **389**

20 The language of youth in Africa: A sociocultural linguistic analysis   391
Heather Brookes and Roland Kouassi

21 African youth languages: the past, present and future attention   409
Sandra Nekesa Barasa

22 Gestures and gesturing on the African continent   427
Heather Brookes

23 Tense and time-depth in the Mabia languages of West Africa:
testing the philosophy of linguistic relativity   438
Adams Bodomo

Index   *450*

CONTRIBUTORS

Nana Aba Appiah Amfo is Associate Professor at the Department of Linguistics, University of Ghana. Her research interests include grammaticalization, information structure, the communicative role of function words, and language use in specific domains such as politics and medicine. She has recently published in *Discourse & Society*, *Acta Linguistica Hafniensia* and *Studies in African Linguistics*.

Paul Agbedor had his first degree in Linguistics and Russian from the University of Ghana, Legon, an MPhil degree in Linguistics from Cambridge University in England, and a PhD in Linguistics from the University of Victoria, British Columbia, in Canada. His research interest is in language planning and language policy, and the syntax of Ewe.

Augustine Agwuele is Professor of Linguistics at the Texas State University. His research interests include phonetics with focus on coarticulation using the locus equations' approach, socio-cultural anthropology, and the study of peoples and cultures of Africa.

Ernest S. Akerejola is a Lecturer in the Department of Linguistics, Macquarie University, where he obtained his PhD degree. His research interests include systemic functional linguistics and language description. He has described the grammar of Ọ̀kó (Benue-Congo), spoken in Nigeria.

Sandra Nekesa Barasa is a senior lecturer at Radboud University In'to Language Centre in The Netherlands. She holds a PhD in Linguistics from the University of Leiden. Her research interests include sociolinguistics, language and communication in social media, youth language and slang, multilingualism, language contact, and intercultural communication, especially in relation to Africa.

Dorothee Beermann is Professor at NTNU, Trondheim, Norway. Her current interests include digital humanities and linguistic tool development. She is an advocate of Open Access to research data, and through the TypeCraft initiative she tries to make linguistic data more accessible for future research. Her fields of interest are formal syntax and lexical semantics.

She teaches constraint-based grammars, mainly lexical functional grammar. She has worked for many years with African languages, especially Kwa languages of West Africa and the Bantu language Runyankore Rukiga spoken in Uganda.

Adams Bodomo is Professor of African Studies (holding the Chair of African Languages and Literatures) at the University of Vienna, Austria. He is currently Head of the University's Department of African Studies and Director of the Global African Diaspora Studies (GADS) Research Platform at the university. He has done pioneering research in many disciplines including African linguistics, Afriphone literature, and Diaspora studies.

Heather Brookes is an Associate Professor of Linguistic Anthropology. She specializes in gesture. Currently she works on gesture and youth languages and gestures among Zulu- and South Sotho-speaking populations in South Africa. She is based at the University of Cape Town with the South African Research Chair of Professor Rajend Mesthrie on Migration, Language and Social Change.

Michael Cahill (PhD 1999, Ohio State University) worked in the Konni multidisciplinary language project for several years under the Ghana Institute of Linguistics, Literacy, and Bible Translation. He was SIL's International Linguistics Coordinator for eleven years, and currently is the Orthography Services Coordinator. His linguistic interests include tone and phonology.

Bruce Connell, BA (Ottawa), MSc (Alberta), PhD (Edinburgh). Bruce Connell is on the faculty at Glendon College, York University. His research interests include phonetics, language endangerment, and comparative historical linguistics. His focus has been mainly on the languages of the Nigeria–Cameroon borderland. He has conducted fieldwork there and in other parts of Africa for over 30 years.

Gerrit J. Dimmendaal is a linguist whose main interests are the description and documentation of lesser known African languages, mainly belonging to the Nilo-Saharan and Niger-Congo phyla, as well as historical linguistics and language typology. Recent monographs include *Coding Participant Marking – Construction Types in Twelve African Languages* (2009), *Historical Linguistics and the Comparative Study of African Languages* (2011), and *The Leopard's Spots: Essays on Language, Cognition and Culture* (2015).

Zygmunt Frajzyngier is Professor of Linguistics at University of Colorado, Boulder. His research and publication interests include: foundations of syntax and semantics in cross-linguistic perspective; typological explanations in grammar; grammaticalization; Chadic and Afroasiatic linguistics, and descriptive grammars and dictionaries of Chadic languages. His early work was on Awutu, a Kwa language. He is the author, co-author and editor of 25 books, one lexical database, and over 120 papers. His work has been supported by the NSF, NEH, Fulbright Grant, University of Colorado, ANR (France), and Humboldt Foundation.

Keir Hansford and his wife Gillian joined SIL in 1971. From 1976 they were assigned to the Ghana Institute of Linguistics, Literacy and Bible Translation to study the Chumburung language. They became consultants for the translation of the whole Bible into that language, dedicated 2010. Keir was also Editor of *The Journal of West African Languages* for 16 years from 1998–2014.

Contributors

Lars Hellan, Professor, NTNU, Trondheim, Norway. He has worked in formal grammar and semantics, in earlier years on Government Binding syntax and Montague semantics, later within head-driven phrase structure grammar, and in meta-grammar formalisms in the valency domain, both as theoretical/descriptive research and as computational implementation. Aside from Norwegian, he has worked with formal analysis of West African languages in all of these areas, and co-coordinated cooperation projects between his university and universities in Ghana and in Malawi.

Brent Henderson is Associate Professor at the University of Florida, Department of Linguistics. His research interests include theoretical syntax and morphology with a strong empirical basis, chiefly focused on Bantu languages, as well as language documentation, particularly the Chimwiini language of the southern Somali coast. He also works on issues of language and healthcare in Guatemala in association with Wuqu'Kawoq: Maya Health Alliance.

Arvi Hurskainen is Professor emeritus, University of Helsinki. He has worked on rule-based language technology since 1985, using Swahili as a test language. The research results include the Swahili spelling checker (in Windows applications), Helsinki corpus of Swahili 1.0 and 2.0, Swahili Language Manager (SALAMA) that includes the Swahili to English and English to Swahili machine translation, dictionary, and language learning applications.

Samuel Alhassan Issah holds an MPhil in Theoretical Linguistics from the University of Tromsø in Norway. He started his teaching carrier in October 2009 at the University of Education, Winneba, Ghana. He has since researched various syntactic issues of Dagbani and has a number of publications in both local and international linguistic journals. He is currently a PhD candidate in Linguistics (formal syntax) at the Goethe-Universität, Frankfurt am Main, Germany.

Constance Kutsch Lojenga has been active in the field of African Linguistics for over 40 years. She has served with SIL assisting groups to develop writing systems for their languages throughout Africa. At present, she is still active as an SIL Senior Linguistics Consultant. She wrote her PhD on Ngiti, a Central-Sudanic language spoken in the northeast of the Democratic Republic of the Congo. For many years she also held a position at the Department of Languages and Cultures of Africa at the University of Leiden, the Netherlands, while continuing her activities in Africa.

Roland R. Kouassi, PhD, is an Associate Professor of Linguistics and Communication at the FHB University of Cocody-Abidjan (Cote d'Ivoire). He was a visiting Fellow at the University of Lancaster (UK, 2008), and a Fulbright Fellow at the University of Michigan, Ann Arbor (USA, 2012–2013). His interests include discourse analysis, business discourse, pragmatics, youth languages, phonetics and anthropology.

Mohamed Lahrouchi is a researcher at the French National Centre for Scientific Research (CNRS), member of a joint laboratory with Paris 8 University (UMR 7023 – Structures Formelles du Langage). He works primarily on the interface between phonology and morphology, and he specializes in Berber and Semitic languages.

Nike Lawal is Professor and Chair of the Department of Linguistics and African Languages at the Kwara State University, Malete, Kwara State, Nigeria. Her areas of research are syntactic theory, comparative linguistics and African linguistics with a focus on Yoruba language. Her other areas of interests are translation and the promotion of African languages as medium of instruction in schools. She is the co-author of *Understanding Yoruba Life and Culture* (2004).

Christian M.I.M. Matthiessen is Chair Professor at the Department of English at The Hong Kong Polytechnic University and a leading scholar in systemic functional linguistics. He works on systemic typology and co-authored *Introduction to Functional Grammar* (4th Edn) with Michael Halliday.

Isaac N. Mwinlaaru obtained his PhD degree from The Hong Kong Polytechnic University, and is an Assistant Lecturer at the University of Cape Coast, Ghana. His research interests include systemic functional linguistics, language typology and grammaticalization, focusing on Niger-Congo languages.

Sara Pugach is Associate Professor of History at California State University, Los Angeles. She is the author of *Africa in Translation: A History of Colonial Linguistics in Germany and Beyond, 1814–1945* (Ann Arbor: University of Michigan, 2012), as well as many articles and book chapters. Currently she is working on a project about African students in the former East Germany.

John R. Rennison, Associate Professor, Department of Linguistics, University of Vienna, BA from Oxford University, PhD from Salzburg University, Habilitation at Vienna University. Strong ties to Burkina Faso, author of *Koromfe* (Routledge, 1997). General linguist working on phonological theory and lesser-known language structures. Also interested in computational linguistics, especially automatic speech recognition.

Elvis Yevudey is a Doctoral Researcher in Applied Linguistics at Aston University. He holds degrees in Linguistics, English and Applied Linguistics from the University of Ghana and Aston University. His research interests include sociolinguistics, language contact, discourse analysis, multilingual education, language planning and development, and minority languages.

FOREWORD

When I was invited to write a foreword to this book, I insisted on seeing the content of the chapters of the book rather than basing my observations on just the table of contents and the abstracts. In the event, I was able to read all the chapters on Facebook with the exception of one dealing with communication in Ewe, a small group language in Ghana. Considering the assumption in some circles that many African languages are endangered and destined for extinction, it is interesting to see how a non-major language is holding its own on the social media. My conclusion on reading this book is that the editors have done African linguistics a good turn by bringing together a compilation of scholarly chapters on a wide range of topics in the field.

Several years ago, in reviewing the state of African linguistics in West Africa, I had cause to observe as follows: "The nature of language studies is such that linguists have become specialists in a narrow area of study. You hardly meet a linguist, but rather a phonetician, a phonologist, a semanticist, a lexicologist, etc." Ayo Bamgbose (2000/2001) "New Directions in West African Language Studies" *The Journal of West African Languages* XXVIII:1, 115. Not that there is anything wrong with specialization, but the effect it has had is that many African linguists don't know or may not even understand what other specialists in their fields are doing. In bringing out *The Routledge Handbook of African Linguistics*, the editors of the volume have provided inspiration for us to revisit topics we might have encountered in the distant past and to learn some new things about the research our colleagues are engaged in.

The topics covered in this book are comprehensive, balanced and representative of the different areas in African linguistics. Beginning with the history of African linguistic research by German scholars and an informative review and update of comparative historical studies of African languages, the book traverses a wide range of topics including prerequisites and strategies for data gathering in fieldwork in language in general and in tone in particular, physiological and instrumental investigation and description of coarticulated phonetic segments, alternating vowel and null in syllable structure, vowel harmony, topics in syntax including MOOD systems, serial verbal constructions, local and long distance anaphors, information structure, applicatives, demonstratives, and experiencer coding and predication. Language in society is represented by language planning, particularly in education, types of translation, as

xiv

Foreword

well as statistically as opposed to rule-based approach in machine translation. To round off the rich collection, concluding chapters in the book explore the phenomenon of urban male codes, which are said to be developing into a marker of identity, a review of the literature on gestures and gesturing in African languages, and a resurrection and application of the Whorfian hypothesis of linguistic relativity to a group of languages spoken in Ghana. I used the term "resurrection" in relation to the concluding chapter intentionally for I erroneously thought it was going to be a rehabilitation of a dead concept, but my fears were dispelled by the argumentation and the conclusion that found the hypothesis untenable.

Either by accident or design, at least ten of the chapters in the book are paired in the presentation of the same or a similar topic. While Chapter 1 gives a history of African linguistic research from the perspective of the contribution by German philologists and linguists, Chapter 2 makes a historical survey of African language classification leading to an update of recent developments. Chapter 3 shows the need for a language survey preparatory to fieldwork and then gives detailed guidelines on the phonetic study of languages in fieldwork, while Chapter 4 focuses on how to record and analyze tones. Chapter 6 provides an extensive instrumental investigation of the way phonetic segments interact during articulation while Chapter 7 maintains the conventional use of the term "coarticulation" to cover labial-velars, the interaction between whose segments is then analyzed articulatorily as well as instrumentally. Both Chapters 16 and 18 handle translation from two different perspectives, the former in the conventional approach of types of translations and challenges of translation, particularly with data from Bible translation, the latter with the advantages of rule-based over statistically based approaches to machine translation with convincing illustrations. Chapters 20 and 21 are both a survey of urban male codes based mainly on the same codes and equally with little or no illustration. In spite of the inevitable overlap in the coverage of each pair, putting them side by side is still worthwhile for we are enabled to see two sides of the same coin, since each chapter in the pair complements the other.

The contributions by most of the authors are well-researched, informative and authoritative. This is not surprising since the authors are writing on the languages they know and have been working on, in some cases for decades. It is also good to note that most of the chapters are well illustrated with language data from one or more languages. Such illustration helps the reader to form an opinion about the validity of the arguments being put forward and its probable cross-linguistic application. In fact, the analysis of data goes beyond accounting for what is presented but often leads to the theoretical implications of the conclusions. Talking of theory, the contributors come from different theoretical backgrounds and it is a credit to the editors that they have been able to accommodate these differences.

A look at the list of contributors shows that some of them are veterans in African linguistic research, while some are younger scholars. In fact, one of the contributors is a graduate student working on his PhD dissertation. Also, while many of the scholars are non-African linguists working on African languages either in Africa or in the Diaspora, a good proportion of the authors of the chapters in this volume are either established or budding African scholars in the field of African linguistics. I cannot help but reflect on a comment made by the author of Chapter 1 of this book. She draws attention to the way many early German researchers failed to give credit to the contribution to their work by African assistants, either by not acknowledging them by name or derogatively consigning them to the nondescript category of mere informants. It is a measure of the great strides that we have made in linguistics that African scholars of African linguistics are now given deserved recognition.

Foreword

As I said in the opening paragraphs of this foreword, we have a lot to gain by reading *The Routledge Handbook of African Linguistics*. Personally, I have been refreshed by updates on topics that I was familiar with and learnt new things about others. I recommend it to all linguists, particularly those in the field of African linguistics.

Ayo Bamgbose
May, 2017

ACKNOWLEDGEMENTS

A work of this kind is only possible due to an intensive and extensive cooperation and participation of several collaborators. The first Editor and initiator of this Handbook, Augustine Agwuele, attracted diverse collaborators and provided the editorial, intellectual, and coordinative oversights that brought this Handbook to fruition. The second Editor of the Handbook, Adams Bodomo, an experienced editor of Africanist journals and book series, contributed experienced reviewers from his vast network to ensure high quality reviews.

Profound acknowledgement goes to the contributors to the Handbook for their dedication and hard work in meeting the deadlines and going through several revisions. Some of them were not deterred by personal and familial challenges.

Each chapter in the Handbook benefitted greatly from the insightful reviews and invaluable comments of several anonymous reviewers. Thank you all for your support and your strong commitments to the intellectual process.

A huge thank you to Andrea Hartill and Camille Burns for their support throughout the publication process.

INTRODUCTION
African linguistics

Augustine Agwuele and Adams Bodomo

Presented in this introduction is a very brief overview of some landmarks in the development of the study of languages in Africa. Specifically highlighted are some of the approaches to documenting and classifying the different languages, some basic research themes featured in the theoretical explication of the languages with aspects of their practical implementations, as well as the dynamism involved in the use of language as a socio-cultural capital. These themes circumscribe the scope of the Handbook.

Study of African languages

The different languages and their speakers on the African continent have for centuries attracted attention from different quarters; ranging from compendium compilers, to Arab scholars, economic prospectors, missionaries, colonialists, and contemporary professional linguists. The diverse engagements with African languages showcase different ideologies influencing the works produced by the different observers including their scope and foci. As will be shown in this introduction, the initial impetus in the study of African languages owes largely to the European[1] contemporary theorization in linguistics that, however, has profited significantly from African scholarship on African languages.

The late 18th-century and early 19th-century Europe witnessed a wave of ideology interlinking the development of language and thought. The growth of the study of individual languages became a part of growing nationalism experienced in Europe during this time.[2] Within this milieu, Williams Jones emerged to propose, in 1786, a connection between Sanskrit, Greek, and Latin unleashing the now popular comparative approach synonymous with historical linguistics.[3] Armed with this approach, many European scholars went about collecting lexical items to determine not only the relationship between languages but the connection between peoples following August Schleicher's 1853 (Stammbaum) stem tree theory, through which related languages can be grouped together and traced to their ancestral origin. Both the European ideology and methodology eventually carried to Africa and led to the initial wave of classification of the peoples and their languages, albeit within a schema that not only othered the people but devalued them, their culture, history, and achievements.

Whereas this early practice was conducted with minimal or no fieldwork, the emergence of the so-called salvage anthropology of around the late 1800s and early 1900s, which emphasized a focus on form and structure based on the view that linguistics provides a tool for the analysis of culture, ushered in fieldworks and language documentation. This was the era of colonial linguistics, a part of a larger colonial project, which, according to Sara Pugach (Chapter 1), naturalized differences, privileged European knowledge and unraveled and remade precolonial African social and ethnic formations (Errington 2001), privileged some, and relegated others. Many African scholars have rightfully been critical of some of the works of this era and the ideologies that propelled them.

Following, and in reaction to, the ethnographic approach, was theoretical linguistics that studies each language on its own merit. The goal of this approach is to understand language as a phenomenon, a system, and as a means of introspecting into the mind. This era, largely championed by the Generative Grammarians, motivated linguists to work on their own languages, adopting methodologies modelled after the hard sciences. This era of 'introspective' linguistics created a dichotomy between performance and competence. To this distinction linguistic anthropologists and sociolinguists reacted by focusing on the performative aspect of language, underlining the communicative function of language and its function as an instrument of socialization through which individuals become full-fledged functioning members of their speech community. The chapters in this Handbook encompass studies on both competence (theoretical) and performance (socio-cultural) linguistics themes.

Since the 1970s, due to a confluence of shifts in paradigms and interests in social institutions, the study of language not only included a focus on marginal and disparaged speech forms such as pidgins and creoles, but also involved such topics as language evolution (Mufwene 2001, 2011) and acquisition (Mufwene 2010), the use of language in context, the place of language in social dynamics such as gender, identity, inter-group relations, and language as a social force.

The concerted efforts of the various extant linguists as well as the cumulative work of the different historical players ultimately yielded the currently accepted understandings about the linguistic situation in the continent. For instance, there are 2,144 living languages in the continent, with a total number of 887,310,542 speakers.[4] This is 13.4 percent of the world's 7,099 languages. These languages are classified into four linguistic phyla with several families. The phyla include the Niger-Congo phylum that stretches from the Gambia, through central Africa to South Africa. It has about 1,400 languages and around 200 million speakers. The Afro-Asiatic phylum, with 241 languages and 230 million speakers, covers the whole of North Africa including some languages in the Middle East. The third phylum, Nilo-Saharan, as the name suggests, covers the Saharan deserts. It is encased between the Afro-Asiatic phylum in the north and Niger-Congo in the south. It has 150 languages and about 12 million speakers. The fourth phylum is the Khoisan. This is the smallest member of the group with about 30 languages and 120,000 speakers.

Across these various epochs and disciplines the themes of old are still present, but they are no longer under some of the derogatory assumptions that preceded the 1960s. Sara Pugach's exploration of the Germans' contribution to the study of African languages in Chapter 1 provides a glimpse of the zeitgeist of colonial linguistics. Thus, in classifying African languages, for example, the current goal is no longer to devalue their speakers. Different from the missionary linguists for whom literacy and study of languages were essential for proselytization, documentation of languages is now carried out in recognition of language as a cultural good, and with the consciousness that the interrupted transmission of an integrated lexical and grammatical heritage spells the direct end of some cultural traditions, and the unraveling, restructuring, and reevaluation of others (Woodbury 1993). The consciousness of the place of language in cultural transmission, maintenance, and expression entrenches language documentation and

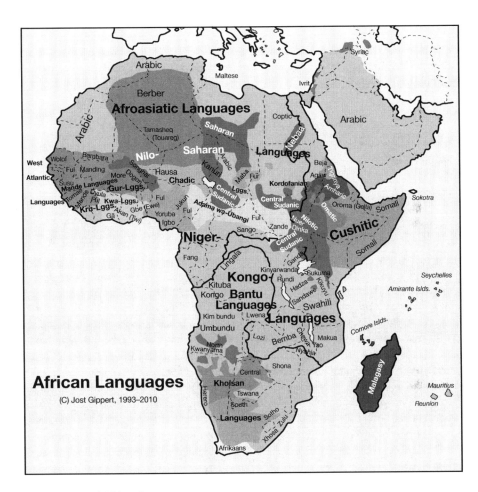

Figure 0.1 Map of African languages

Note: Used with permission of the author, Jost Gippert. Available online at: http://titus.uni-frankfurt.de/didact/karten/afr/afrikaf.jpg, (last accessed, May 16, 2017).

revitalization as a sub-discipline of linguistics, giving its practitioners on the continent the urgency that it rightfully deserves among scholars of African languages.

Our knowledge of the different languages in Africa has been expanding very rapidly, more so since the 1960s, when many African states began to gain political independence and had to make decisions on the adoption of a national language. At the time of independence, the reigning view was that African languages were poorly studied and the few that were described owed largely to the accounts of travelers, missionaries, agents of the colonialists and some sponsored western scholars. Since then, however, the study of African languages has effectively stopped being the sole prerogative of westerners. Many highly qualified and motivated Africans drawing from their academic trainings, native intuitions, and cultural heritages began to describe, explicate, and illuminate different aspects of their languages. Notable among these are Ayo Bamgbose, Florence Dolphyne, Salikoko Mufwene, Sam Mchombo, and Bokamba Eyamba whose notable works began to appear in the late 1960s and early 1970s. Younger scholars of African origin, some of whom are featured in this Handbook, have continued the tradition of excellence started by the first post-independence African scholars. Technological advances and innovations in different fields aid in furthering the scientific investigations of African languages. Increasing ease in traveling and better modes of transportation allow access to remote areas, making it possible for an increasing number of previously undocumented linguistic groups to be reached and studied.

Some issues in the study of African languages

In 2009 there were 6,909 known languages in the world. Out of these, 2,100 were in Africa (Lewis 2009). In 2017, 7,099 languages are recorded worldwide (Simons and Fennig 2017). Of these, 2,144 languages are in Africa. Just within a space of eight years, there is recorded an increase in the total number of languages existing in the world and in Africa. On a country level, 527 languages are listed for Nigeria in 2017. Seven of the attested languages are known to be extinct. Comparatively, there are now 520 living languages relative to the 521 listed for the country in 2009. An existing language could become moribund and eventually die out of use. Previously undocumented languages could be discovered as in the case of Nigeria. The dynamism involved in the life of language makes the quest to find, study, and describe them an ongoing concern of the linguistic community. No meaningful progress can be achieved in these efforts without a careful understanding of the historical dimensions to the earlier approaches and an appropriate grounding in contemporary scientific procedures inimical to making sense of the diverse issues that impinge on proper documentation of previously unstudied languages and yielding data for their theoretical analyses. Parts I, II, and III of this Handbook pertain to language documentation and theoretical descriptive analyses.

The activities of earlier European linguists and operatives across the continent were significant in their own right, although largely imbued with serious social, cultural and political flaws, the consequences of which are still being borne by Africa today. Some of the methodologies that they employed still remain useful to scholars working in the field today. Dimmendaal, in Chapter 2, instructively surveys the different methodologies that were employed to arrive at the classification of African language. They ranged from the large-scale word list comparisons approach of Wilhelm Koelle, to NeighborNet and rhizotic network currently in use, among others. By exploring the various practical approaches, the chapter presents us with an overview of the current language families of Africa, dialectical variations and language continuum, the dynamics involved in contact situations, the spread of language, that is, movement of people, and the connection of speech with groups' social identity.

While Dimmendaal's chapter explores the historical approaches employed in earlier description and classification of African languages, Bruce Connell in Chapter 3 presents modern and contemporary fieldwork tools invaluable to the scientific documentation and description of unstudied or understudied languages of Africa. The approaches highlighted are largely informed by recent developments in the field of documentary linguistics and a concern for language endangerment. He underlines, for instance, the sociolinguistics approach, which explores the knowledge and use of language. Different from the abstract formal approach of theoretical linguistics, the sociolinguistics approach allows for information on how the possible various groups that comprise a community may be obtained, and it provides insights that may allow subsequent aspects of the fieldwork to be better conducted. Information concerning language innovation and change, and language shift, can also be gleaned; this is of obvious importance when doing fieldwork on a threatened language. More generally, survey results can also be of use to local language committees, government, and non-government agencies, to inform language-planning policies and education policy. Additionally presented are a host of practical instruments of fieldwork; these range from community profile questionnaires, household, individual, and administrative survey, to self-reporting. Some of these instruments are used in studying, for instance, language use in the market place. He also describes and discusses the utility of phonetics, especially acoustic studies, for fieldwork with pertinent exemplifications from seminal applications of the same in presenting the structure of a language.

An important phenomenon in African languages is tone. The lexical manipulative of pitch contrastively employed by many languages in the continent, coupled with the dynamic changes that tones undergo in running speech, informed the formulation of the non-linear approach to phonology as contained in Autosegmental Theory (Goldsmith 1976). Recognizing the significant place of tone in African languages, Constance Lojenga, in Chapter 4, focused her discussion solely on grassroots fieldwork on tone and tonology, thereby giving prominence to this important but much neglected theme in the field. Tone may not be easily perceptible to those scholars whose first language lacks them, and for those that use languages where variation in pitch is lexical, making sense of the attested variations across languages may be inundating. Thus, there is the need for proper training to assure successful fieldwork and proper analyses. According to Lojenga, the training should include information about tone languages in general, typology of tone, and instructions on the methodology for doing fieldwork on tone. Fieldworkers are to be thoroughly equipped to develop skills in listening, hearing, and reproducing tones, in addition to being skilled in transcribing different tones. The provided theoretical discussion and practical guidelines of Chapters 4 and 5 continue the historical development of the study of African languages, showing contemporary scientific approaches as well as marking a change in the motivation and assumptions of fieldwork.

Language is one of the biological endowments of humanity. Linguistics, the scientific study of language, subsumes a wide range of subject matter purposefully deployed to explicate its universal properties and particular features as manifested in specific speech communities. Linguistics therefore includes not only the actual documentation, description and classification of existing languages, as shown in Part I, it also involves the quest to understand language as a phenomenon. Essentially, the goal of theoretical linguistics is to illuminate the language faculty (Chomsky 2000). Some of the issues involved in the theoretical explications of knowledge of language are often abstract in nature, since these issues target internalized rules common to speakers of a particular language. The explication of the internalized rules possessed by members of a language community include describing the rules and principles observed by speakers and hearers, as well as the form and structure of this common knowledge, that is the grammar of language. While it is stereotypically popular to look to African languages for 'exotic' linguistic features, such as tone, clicks, doubly articulated consonants or the famous Bantu noun (see Hombert and Hyman 1999), which are not peculiar to Africa, the ten chapters of Parts II and III of the Handbook elucidate the theory of grammar in general. They present some fundamental topics germane to exploring language as a system and that illustrate aspects of the thematic approaches relevant to understanding the workings of this system. Chapter 6 explores coarticulation, one of the oldest research inquiries in phonetics, pertaining to how hearers recover individual phonemes from speech sounds that are overlapped and fused in utterance. Thus, Agwuele studied the interaction of tone with the segments that bear it in Yoruba in order to understand if tone exerts influence on the segments, as observed when segments are perturbed by suprasegmental factors such as stress. Ultimately the study confirmed the tone vocalic feature in Yoruba. Another pervasive phonetic feature of the largest linguistics family in Africa is the presence of doubly articulated consonants. Labio-velar sounds are examined in Chapter 7 by Michael Cahil. The study of the structure of sounds, that is the patterns or distributions of the sounds of a language and how the different sounds interact, i.e., phonology, is the main focus of Chapters 8 and 9. Both further exemplify linguistic pursuits in the endeavor to uncover the knowledge of language possessed by its speakers, in this case, syllable structure vowel alteration, and vowel harmony. Going beyond the sound system to the level of phrase and sentence, Part III presents six chapters that provide additional data that show significant facts about human language. The themes explored include West African serial verbs, anaphors and Binding Theory, the encoding of information structure, applicatives, demonstratives, and experiencer predications. These topics present novel data that further showcase scientific approaches in the exploration of the language faculty, and, more significantly, they underscore the importance of African languages in theorizing about language.

Parts II and III exemplify some of the basic research on languages of Africa that generate knowledge about the phenomenon of language, and, quite importantly, they provide vital information necessary to address practical issues concerning the life of the people as contained in Parts IV and V. The fundamental issues involved, as carefully explored in both Parts, include that of representation of speech, thoughts and ideas; basic linguistic works thus feed into a whole lot of social and cultural matters including the use and representation of African languages in the social media. In a sense, the different themes of the 8 chapters that make up Parts IV and V rekindle the thoughts of the famous African writer wa Thiong'o, when he wrote; "This book, *Decolonising the Mind*, is my farewell to English as a vehicle of any of my writings. From now on it is Gikuyu and Kiswahili all the way" (Ngugi wa Thiong'o 1981). Language planning and language policy are two of the most important areas that have profited from continuous language documentation and basic research as these implicate nation building, economic, and educational development of independent African states, each of which is multilingual as well as ethnically and religiously diverse. The significance of language in the construction of a nation and in unifying people was a motivation for German involvement in language documentation in Africa, as shown by Sara Pugach in Chapter 1. In their efforts to seek 'national unity' in diversity, most independent African states adopted an exoglossic policy following independence. By maintaining and using the language of the ex-colonizer for official government business, education, and media, indigenous languages are not only suppressed and under-developed, but a large proportion of the people who do not speak these foreign tongues are effectively excluded from participating in the life of the state. Literacy in one's own language is not promoted, being related to mainly aural\oral language, most indigenous languages are not written so, therefore, they are undervalued. Above all, the people are denied their rights "to revitalize, use, develop and transmit to future generations their histories, languages, oral traditions, philosophies, writing systems and literatures".[5] Aside from this, several of the conflicts in the continent are ethnolinguistically centered. Thus, given the importance of language in forging unity and in resolving inter-ethnolinguistic conflicts, the various African states take seriously the issue of language planning and policy, relying on the works of linguists to make language policies and plan languages. Some of these linguists are Bamgbose (1999/2008; 2000), Koffi (2012) and Kamwangamalu (2016), among many others.

Whereas the poor state of research into African languages by the time of independence has often been seen as one of the reasons for maintaining the language of the ex-colonizer, the many linguistically informed positions of many African scholars on multilingualism and cultural pluralism not only nullify this old position, they also provide scientific basis for the value of all languages, not only as cultural heritage but also as cultural capital, thereby aiding the government of each country to come up with solutions that fit their specific situation. For instance, Ethiopia's official language is Amharic, South Africa operates 11 official languages, Tanzania recognizes Kiswahili, an indigenous lingua franca, as the official language, and Nigeria recognizes the three majority languages in the country (Hausa, Yoruba and Igbo) along with English as the official languages. Essentially, scholars, concerned with education, urge instruction in the mother tongue, presuming there to be an influence of the first language in perception and cognitive development. The scholarship in language documentation and education underscore the invaluableness of own language for educational and cognitive purposes, as well as how language implicates such socio-cultural factors as gender, individual and group identity, media and youth expressions. Focusing on the State of Ghana, Paul Agbedor, in Chapter 19, provides a good discussion of the problems and prospects of language planning for development. While he narrowly focuses on Ghana, some of the problems he noted are not confined to this country. With respect to Ghana, Bodomo (1996) proposed a trilingual model of education that he argues would ensure that Ghanaian/African children have a basic grounding in their mother tongues or first languages before learning to read and write in major African and world languages.

Beside the issues of national language and education, some contemporary scholars are exploring African languages for technological and forensic purposes, some others seek to apply linguistic knowledge to making possible machine reading for the blind. Regardless of the ends of these diverse linguistic works, gains are not possible without a careful understanding of the pertinent theoretical and conceptual issues such as are addressed by basic research studies in phonetics, phonology, syntax, and pragmatics. The diversity of approaches serves to make explicit the inter-relatedness of the sub-disciplinary perspectives in the scientific study of language, as well as the vast range of scholarship and literature of each sub-discipline. These differing and cohesive perspectives are also invaluable in showing the multiplex nature of language in relation to culture, society, and indeed civilization.

As a species-specific affair, language is a communal property, and an expressive socio-cultural product. It is a complex repository of knowledge, ideas, history, emotions, cultures and social dynamics of a people. It provides orientation to communal values; it indexes certain ethos, and, through its power to encode, it is the primary means of socializing a child into the society, and of transfer of cultural heritage inter-generationally. Thus, complementing theoretical linguists' quests to uncover the knowledge that speakers and hearers have of their language are efforts to empirically understand how users employ this knowledge across diverse communicative situations. Part V of the Handbook explores the verbal and non-verbal locutionary function of some African languages. This 'real world' (Sapir [1949] 1985: 162) orientation of the four chapters in this section underscores the fact that individuals and groups adjust to reality linguistically. The use of language is a local affair, it is specific to culture and responsive to social dynamics. Brookes and Kouassi (Chapter 20) and Barasa (Chapter 21) give comprehensive accounts of 'Youth language', a linguistic variety that, according to Brookes and Kouassi, emanated in urban centers, mainly among male groups on the periphery of society. These linguistic forms include Tsotsitaal spoken in South Africa, Sheng in Kenya, Nouchi in the Ivory Coast, and Indoubil in the Democratic Republic of Congo. Both chapters explore their origin, spread, structure, use, and future prospects. More pertinently, these 'spontaneous performative practices', which emerged as a social marker of identity and of social marginalization, have assumed mainstream economic and political significance analogous to the form of urban dressing explored for Sophiatown (i.e., Tsotsil, whose notoriety centered on internecine fights for street-corner dominance) by Sharp (2015).

Study of languages is not limited to the aural or spoken version as 65–70 percent of all communication is presumed to be non-verbal. Along with the documentation, description and theorization of African languages, there is a growing interest in the study of the non-verbal communicative strategies employed across the continent. For instance, Orie's (2009) description of Yoruba hand gesture, Brookes' (2001, 2004) repertoire of South African gestures, and Agwuele's (2014) documentation of Yoruba head and face gestures. These works focus not on sign language, but on quotable gestures (Kendon 1992). Heather Brookes in Chapter 22 provides an insightful panoramic overview of the study of non-verbal communicative gestures across the continent. This impressive work, which covers the typology of gesture, its theoretical underpinning with respect to the relationship between the nature of gestures and gestural behaviors, and the communicative ecology shaped by social and material environments among others, show the growing importance of documenting the various ways in which African people also 'speak without words'.

One of the persistent questions in language studies is the possible influence of language on its speakers.

> Everything humans perceive, think, value and feel are learned through their participation in a socio-cultural system, mediated by language. Language provides the mental categories through which experiences are categorized. Because different categories and conceptual schemes are found in different languages, it is presumed that speakers will be channeled to pay differential attention to aspects of the world that hold greater significance for them.
>
> *Agwuele 2016: 5*

The last chapter in the Handbook by Adams Bodomo addresses this primary question of linguistic philosophy. It is an inquiry into linguistic relativity using data from Dagaare and Dagbane, two Mabia languages of northern Ghana and adjoining areas of West Africa. The chapter uses the metrical tense structure of these languages to question the validity of the so-called Sapir-Whorf hypothesis. The main claim of the Sapir-Whorf hypothesis is that the language we speak determines, or at least influences, the way we view the world around us. The stronger version claims a determining relationship while the weaker version only claims that the relationship is one of influence and is not deterministic. Bodomo's study supports only a weak version of linguistic relativity, showing instead that, independent of the language they speak, all humans are capable of going through the same thought processes. Language does not determine or structure the logical thought process. What the structure of language does is to influence the way we express thought and not determine the way we reason about reality.

Why a handbook of African linguistics?

Already noted are the long and enduring interests in the different African languages and their speakers. Also noted is the uninterrupted growth in studying African languages. Keeping pace with this growth on the continent are the various outlets for the dissemination of the findings from these studies. There are different regional (e.g., West African Linguistic Association) and international (e.g., African Language Association) scholarly bodies and academic associations; local, national and international journals covering linguistics and sub-fields of linguistics; as well as the formation of different departments dedicated to the study of languages in a growing number of universities being created across the continent. Aside from these, there have been several landmark works. For instance, in 1995, Akinbiyi Akinlabi edited a very informative book entitled *Theoretical Approaches to African Linguistics*. This work, produced in commemoration of the 25th anniversary of the annual conference on African linguistics, contains 24 chapters covering syntax, phonology, and language acquisition and sociolinguistics. Heine and Nurse (2000) edited the anthology on *African Languages: An Introduction* which contains 12 chapters. The book covered four language phyla in Africa, it includes chapters on phonology, morphology, syntax and typology, and there is a section on comparative linguistics, on the history of African languages, and on sociolinguistics. This vast work is the closest thing to a Handbook. Perhaps as an addendum to it, Heine and Nurse in 2008 edited another book titled: *A Linguistic Geography of Africa*. It is a data-driven collection of essays that raised pertinent questions concerning the field of linguistics on the continent. Other works on African linguistics include *Studies in African Linguistic Typology* (Voeltz 2000). This collection of essays is aimed at providing a broad perspective of African linguistic typology, it has 21 chapters, each of which tried to produce data from a linguistic group on the continent. There is also *African Voices: An Introduction to the Languages and Linguistics of Africa* edited by Webb and Kembo-Sure in 2000. With contributions from scholars who are in African universities, the goals of this anthology were to introduce students to theoretical linguistics and to introduce language and linguistics in Africa. Finally, John Mugane edited in 2003 another anthology with the title: *Linguistic Typology and Representation of African Languages*. It comprised of 25 chapters selected from papers presented at the 33rd Annual Conference on African Linguistics. The three main sections, aside from the plenary papers, include chapters on phonetics, phonology and morphology, syntax and semantics, historical linguistics, and language and society. All the aforementioned works reveal the importance of language documentation, classification, and explication in Africa. They uncover data and observations that allow for conjectures on the origin of language; the relationship between languages and language change. Further, these works provide insights to how the different people employ languages in their everyday life as well as how language influences their institutions.

Despite all these, there is not in existence a single Handbook on African languages. This is a glaring gap yearning to be filled, especially given the enormous work on the different languages in the continent and the vibrancy that the field has experienced over the past 50 years. This present Handbook is an initial step towards filling this gap. The Handbook subsumes aspects of issues pertaining to language documentation and description, theoretical explications of the phenomenon of language, linguistic praxis, and socio-cultural dimensions. Notably missing in this first instalment of the Handbook are themes related to language origin, creoles, writing systems, forensics and computation. Subsequent editions will cover these and other issues.

African languages and the cultures associated with them require an interdisciplinary enterprise (Bodomo 2017). As such, there must be a serious agenda to describe, document and preserve them, not just for their own sakes, but for their important role in interdisciplinary scientific research. So, while the study of Africa (including its languages, literatures, histories, and societies) is important in itself (indeed, no university can claim to be a global university without a well-supported African studies program), the role of Africa in linguistics for any scholarly endeavors, especially in the humanities, remains invaluable. We therefore need resources such as this Handbook to provide reliable reference sources. It is hoped that this *Routledge Handbook of African Linguistics* will play such a role.

Why African linguistics?

The choice of the adjectivizing term, African, in the *Routledge Handbook of African Linguistics* is not to feed the evanescent othering of the continent and its people. There is no doubt of the reality of the burden of othering for Africans along the three dimensions eloquently described and elegantly demonstrated by Spivak in 1985. Be it in producing and reproducing Africa as the subordinate, or creating and making it the pathological, deviant and inferior, and seeing it as bereft of knowledge, science, creativity and advancement, this multidimensional process of othering is often reinforced and neophytes are socialized into it through a repetitive re-enactment of a single stereotype.

Rather than feed this insatiable appetite for infantilizing the continent, the adjective is mainly a geographical delimitation of the focus of the data being explicated, it is not to other, exoticize, or mark the linguists or the linguistic work on the continent. Linguistic scholarship on the continent is, in some cases, at the forefront of knowledge production in enriching the data that informs theories concerning language origin and diversification. This Handbook informs, educates, elucidates, and contributes new information to the field of linguistics in general, it does so decidedly in showcasing works that are based on data from languages in the continent. Rather than being subjected, and intensifying the line between us and them, the works on the languages of the continent become the objects of discourse, showing their invaluableness in linguistic theory and practice. The scholars, Africans and non-Africans alike, are not objects in colonial interpellations; they are active agents purposefully exploring different significant linguistic issues of universal import using diverse data from different language families in the continent.

Notes

1 For an overview of the history of European scholarship on the documentation and classification of African languages, see, for example, Agwuele, A. (2008); Nurse, D. (1997).
2 J.G. Herder in 1772 asserted that a nation cannot exist without its language, that is the language of its fathers. He considered language to be the collective treasure of a nation (see Herder, Johann Gottfried (1772) *Abhandlungüber den Ursprung der Sprache: welche den von der Königl. Academie der Wissenschaftenfür das Jahr 1770 gesezten Preiserhalten hat*. Berlin: Voss). For W. von Humboldt, language is the spirit of the nation, it is the mental exhalation of a nationally individual life (Humboldt, *On Language, On the Diversity of Human Language Construction and Its Influence on the Mental Development of the Human Species*, edited by Michael Losonsky. CUP 1999).
3 For thorough treatment of the practice of comparative linguistics in Africa with diachronic analyses, see Dimmendaal, G.J. (2011).
4 Simons, G.F. and C.D. Fennig (eds) (2017). *Ethnologue: Languages of the World*, Twentieth Edn. Dallas, TX: SIL International, online version: www.ethnologue.com.
5 E/CN. 4/sub. 2/1993/29. Part iii, Article 14 of the UN Sub-commission on Human Rights Declaration on the Rights of Indigenous Peoples.

References

Agwuele, A. (2008). "Practice of Historical Linguistics and Language Codification in Africa" *History Compass*, 6(1): 1–24.
Agwuele, A. (2014). "A Repertoire of Yoruba Hand and Face Gestures" *Gesture*, 14(1): 70–96.
Agwuele, A. (2016). "Culture Trumps Scientific Facts: Race in US American Language" *Social Analysis*, 60(2): 1–19.
Bamgbose, A. (1999). "African Language Development and Language Planning" *Social Dynamics*, 25(1): 13–30, DOI: 10.1080/02533959908458659 (published online May 2008).
Bamgbose, A. (2000). *Language and Exclusion: The Consequences of Language Policies in Africa*. Hamburg: LIT Verlag Munster.
Bodomo, A.B. (1996). "On Language and Development in Sub-Saharan Africa: The Case of Ghana" *Nordic Journal of African Studies*, 5(2): 31–53.
Bodomo, A.B. (2017). *African Languages, Linguistics, and Literatures: Exploring Global Interdisciplinary Research Trends in the Humanities*. Inaugural Lecture Monographs in the Humanities. Berlin, Germany: GALDA Press.
Brookes, H.J. (2001). "O clever 'He's streetwise.' When Gestures Become Quotable: The Case of the Clever Gesture" *Gesture*, 1(2): 167–184.
Brookes, H.J. (2004). "A Repertoire of South African Quotable Gestures" *Journal of Linguistics Anthropology*, 14(2): 186–224.

Introduction

Chomsky, N. (2001). *New Horizons in the Study of Language and the Mind*. Cambridge, MA: Cambridge University Press.

Dimmendaal, G.J. (2011). *Historical Linguistics and the Comparative Study of African Languages*. Amsterdam/Philadelphia, PA: John Benjamins Publishing Company.

Errington, J. (2001). "Colonial Linguistics" *Annual Review of Anthropology*, 30: 19–39.

Goldsmith. J.A. (1976). "Autosegmental Phonology." PhD Dissertation submitted to Department of Foreign Language, Literature and Linguistics, MIT.

Hombert, J.-M. and L.M. Hyman (1999). *Bantu Historical Linguistics: Theoretical and Empirical Perspectives*. Stanford, CA: CSLI.

Kamwangamalu, N.M. (2016). *Language Policy and Economics: The Language Question in Africa*. London: Palgrave Macmillan.

Kendon, A. (1992). "Some Recent Works from Italy on Quotable Gestures (Emblems)" *Journal of Linguistic Anthropology*, 2: 92–108.

Koffi, E. (2012). *Paradigm Shift in Language Planning and Policy: Game Theoretic Solutions*. Boston/Berlin: De Gruyter Mouton.

Lewis, M.P. (ed.) (2009). *Ethnologue: Languages of the World*, Sixteenth Ed. Dallas, TX: SIL International, online version: www.ethnologue.com/16.

Mufwene, S.S. (2001). *The Ecology of Language Evolution*. New York, NY: Cambridge University Press.

Mufwene, S.S. (2010). "Second Language Acquisition and the Emergence of Creoles." *Studies in Second Language Acquisition*, 32: 1–42.

Mufwene, S.S. (2011). "An Ecological Account of Language Evolution! Way to Go! Commentary on Luc Steel's 'Modeling the Cultural Evolution of Language'" *Physics of Life Reviews*, 8: 367–368.

Ngugi wa Thiong'o (1981). *Decolonising the Mind: The Politics of Language in African Literature*. Oxford: James Currey.

Nurse, D. (1997). "The Contributions of Linguistics to the Study of History of Africa" *The Journal of African History*, 37(3): 359–391.

Orie, O.O. (2009). "Pointing the Yoruba way" *Gesture*, 9(2): 237–261.

Sapir, E. ([1949] 1985). *Selected Writings in Language, Culture, and Personality*, ed. D.G. Mandelbaum. Berkeley, CA: University of California Press.

Sharp, M. (2015). "Dressed to Kill: Don Mattera's Sophiatown" in A. Agwuele (ed.), *Body Talk and Cultural Identity in the African World*. Sheffield, UK: Equinox Publishing Ltd.

Simons, G.F. and C.D. Fennig (eds) (2017). *Ethnologue: Languages of the World*, Twentieth Ed. Dallas, TX: SIL International, online version: www.ethnologue.com.

Spivak, G.C. (1985). "The Rani of Sirmur: An Essay in Reading the Archives" *History and Theory*, 24(3): 247–272.

Woodbury, A. (1993). "A Defense of the Proposition, "When a Language Dies, a Culture Dies." Proceedings of the First Annual Symposium about Language and Society – Austin (SALSA). *Texas Linguistics Forum*, 33: 101–129.

PART I

History, method, and typology

1

A SHORT HISTORY OF AFRICAN LANGUAGE STUDIES IN THE NINETEENTH AND EARLY TWENTIETH CENTURIES, WITH AN EMPHASIS ON GERMAN CONTRIBUTIONS[1]

Sara Pugach

Introduction: missionaries and the written word

This chapter provides a brief, non-exhaustive overview of the history of African language studies from the early nineteenth century. It will then narrow to focus on how scholars, particularly those from Germany, transformed the field from a humanistic pursuit to a discipline steeped in natural scientific methodologies. The transformation, which occurred around the turn of the twentieth century, shifted the discipline away from its roots in text-based, philological study, and towards an emphasis on the body's physical production and articulation of sound. I will examine this change using the example of the Phonetics Laboratory that officials at the Hamburg Colonial Institute established in 1910 at the request of Carl Meinhof, then Europe's foremost specialist in African languages. It was at the laboratory that Africans became Meinhof's main subjects. Meinhof and his colleagues, including phonetician Giulio Panconcelli-Calzia, examined Africans using mechanical equipment designed to capture sound. The experiments that were conducted were never benign; instead they were expressions of colonial power, as the experiments were used to "prove" the primitivity of African languages in comparison with those belonging to Indo-European and other language families. Further, the African participants were subordinated to scientific research led by Europeans, and had little input into the tests performed on them.

African/colonial linguistics were, moreover, generally part of the larger colonial project that naturalized difference while concealing the weakness of the power structures that undergirded European rule. At mission stations in Africa, where western African language studies were born, and in European universities, where the discipline was institutionalized, it was shaped by and embedded in a colonial matrix that privileged European knowledge and unraveled and remade precolonial African social and ethnic formations (Errington, 2001). Both the textual work of determining where linguistic territories started and ended, and the physical analysis of languages considered "primitive," fed into the wider objective of categorizing and controlling African peoples. As the late Patrick Harries pointed out, most African ethnic categories did not exist before the late nineteenth century, when missionaries researched and standardized their languages (Harries, 1988). Metropolitan sites of African language study continued this work by favoring certain languages over others, as well as by relegating them to the status of *Kolonialsprachen* (colonial or "primitive" languages), a category that implied they were underdeveloped in comparison with the mature European and Asian *Kultursprachen* ("civilized" languages).

This did not mean that European research on African languages remained static over the nineteenth and early twentieth centuries; the shift from a textual focus to a physical one, along with the emergence of a classificatory system that grouped African languages in terms of their supposed linguistic "maturity" and the growing influence of scientific racism as the nineteenth century wore on ensured that the discipline altered considerably through time (Irvine, 1993). Nevertheless, linguistics remained critical for colonization throughout, as it always helped determine the boundaries of African ethnic categories and reinforced hierarchies of difference.

Let us begin by looking concretely at how and why a field of African linguistics emerged in the west. European explorers, colonial officials, missionaries, and other visitors to Africa were the first westerners to take an interest in the continent's languages. The Portuguese, who interacted with and eventually colonized western and central African kingdoms such as Kongo and Angola, began to compile lists of words in various African languages in the early sixteenth century. Missionaries – in this case, Capuchins – were both learning the Kongo language and translating religious texts into it by the seventeenth century, primarily because they were frustrated with their inability to communicate without the aid of interpreters (Thornton, 2017). Around the same time, there was at least one "armchair" scholar, Hiob Ludolf, working on the extinct Ethiopian language of Ge'ez from his base in Germany; although not a missionary, his research was heavily influenced by his links to the Jesuits (Miehe, 1996; Uhlig, 1986). From this early period, Africans were also involved in linguistic research; the Capuchins in Kongo relied on the assistance of a Kongolese priest named Manuel Roboredo (Thornton, 2017), while Ludolf collaborated with Ethiopian priest Äbba Gorgoryos (Uhlig, 1986). Europeans could not conduct African language research without Africans, but nonetheless usually relegated them to ancillary roles, ensuring that Africans were not considered the primary authors of the Bible translations, grammars, and dictionaries that were produced (Pugach, 2007).

While the beginnings of African language studies do stretch back to the sixteenth century, it was in the nineteenth century that African language research really began to blossom. The amateur discipline was initiated largely, though not wholly, by German Protestant missionaries.[2] These missionaries first worked for British missionary societies, including the Anglican Church Missionary Society (CMS) and the Non-Comformist London Missionary Society (LMS). The CMS, in particular, became home to many Germans. William Wilberforce and other leading abolitionists had founded the CMS in 1799 (Hole, 1896). Its first station was in Sierra Leone, the British colony that had been designed as a haven for freed slaves. When the CMS was originally unable to find English missionaries for the enterprise, its leaders quickly drew on their continental contacts to recruit German-speaking, Lutheran pastors from Prussia and Württemberg, most of whom had trained in Berlin (Hole, 1896). Karl Friedrich Steinkopff, a one-time secretary of the *Deutsche Christentumsgesellschaft* (German Christianity Society) and pastor at St Mary's German Lutheran Church in London, was crucial in this regard (Kirchberger, 2007). This early cross-national collaboration was not without controversy; denominational disputes, such as whether the Lutherans would have to submit to the authority of an Anglican Bishop, troubled English and German alike (Kirchberger, 2007).

Nonetheless, since the Germans did not have the funds to go to Africa without British support, and the English did not have the personnel, an alliance was formed (Walls, 2001).

G.R. Nyländer, who had been educated in Berlin and arrived in Sierra Leone to work for the CMS in 1806, was the first German missionary to publish on an African language. This was the 1814 *Grammar and Vocabulary of the Bullom Language* (Anderson, 1999; Walker, 1847; Nyländer, 1814). In Sierra Leone Nyländer was soon followed by others, including C.F.C. Wenzel and J.S. Klein (Hair, 2014), who wrote on Susu, C.F. Schlenker, who worked on Temne (Schlenker, 1864), and S.W. Koelle, who compiled the *Polyglotta Africana*, an early classification of West African languages (Hair, 1967; Koelle, 1854), in addition to more specific work on Vai (Koelle, 1854). Other CMS missionaries from German-speaking Europe entered the service on different mission fields, such as J.L. Krapf in Ethiopia and Kenya (Pirouet, 1999), and J.F. Schön in Nigeria (Cust, 2002). Eventually, more Britons joined the CMS and German-speaking societies founded their own fields. The Berlin Missionary Society (BMS) established stations in East and South Africa (Wangemann, 1872), the Rhenish Missionary Society (RMS) settled in Namibia (Menzel, 1978), and the North German Missionary Society (NMS) moved into Togo (Schubert, 2003). German-speaking missionaries slowly began to shift from writing their dictionaries and grammars of African languages in English to composing them in German.

Why, though, were the bulk of the earliest missionary linguists German? And why did they take such a keen interest in the study of African languages? These are important questions, since missionary work set the tone for the future development of the African linguistics discipline. Practically, the missionaries hoped to dispense with interpreters and communicate directly with potential converts. Yet, on another level, the need for linguistic knowledge acquired more urgency. Nineteenth-century German missionaries were under the influence of a strong Pietist tradition. They believed that true conversion to Christianity could only be attained when the Christian message touched a person's heart in his or her native language. Following such late seventeenth- and eighteenth-century German Pietists as Philipp Jakob Spener and August Hermann Francke, these missionaries emphasized inner spirituality over strict church doctrine, a hallmark of German Pietism (Wallmann, 1995). Since the achievement of inner spirituality involved native language communication, transcribing unwritten languages became important, as did the production of dictionaries, grammars, Bibles, and other religious texts.

Theological issues initially sparked the missionary enthusiasm for language. Yet debates about national identity inside Germany – and the role of language in its construction – also contributed to the disproportionate involvement of German missionaries in African language research. There is an extensive literature on the significance of nationalism to the nineteenth-century German preoccupation with language study, which scholars such as George Mosse, Leon Poliakov, Suzanne Marchand, Douglas McGetchin, Tuska Benes, and George Williamson have all shown in different ways (Mosse, 1964; Poliakov, 1996; Marchand, 1996; McGetchin, 2009; Benes, 2008; Williamson, 2004). Germany was not politically unified until 1871, but had a strong contingent agitating for unification much earlier, indeed from the Congress of Vienna and the reconstruction of a Europe ravaged by Napoleon in 1815. For scholars such as J.G. Herder, Wilhelm von Humboldt and Jakob Grimm, language thus provided a common identity and awareness of nationhood well before a concrete German state actually existed (Köpke, 2009; Langham Brown, 1967; Roberts, 2010).

The argument further runs that German interest in linguistics is related to the early nineteenth-century Romanticism that connected a *Volk*, or people, both to the soil on which it lived as well as to the tongue that it spoke (Mosse, 1964; Poliakov, 1996). According to intellectuals such as Herder, language thus represented the spirit, or soul, of a nation (Herder, 1997; Benes, 2003).

Grimm's fascination with not only German itself, but also German literature – including the famous fairy tales – also demonstrates how a scholar came to associate culture with language, and to see the two as inseparable and intertwined (Grimm et al., 1812). This made sense, since again, before 1871, German identity had more of a linguistic than a political fixity.[3]

Missionaries and university philologists shared some common concerns about language. For example, both were inheritors of the seventeenth-century Pietist tradition that stressed a strong personal bond with Christ. Even so, before the late nineteenth century, the missionaries were largely uninterested in nationalism or German unification. Isolated from Germany, they identified mainly with other European Protestants. They considered themselves part of an international Christian community, not a national German one. Still, the CMS missionaries were educated in a milieu where texts by scholars such as Herder, Humboldt and Grimm were influential, and many had studied in German universities where their ideas were prominent. Some missionaries were also celebrated in the wider academic community, with the linguistic achievements of missionaries such as Krapf, Koelle, and Schön all fêted throughout Europe. Krapf received a PhD from the University of Tübingen in 1844 for his work on Ethiopian languages (Griefenow-Mewis, 1996), while his colleagues Koelle and Schön were both awarded the prestigious Volney Prize for comparative philology, as was Basel missionary J.G. Christaller for his work on Ghanaian languages (Leopold, 1999).

The transcription, creation and critique of texts in African languages was central to the work of these nineteenth-century missionaries. Their Pietist background encouraged this focus on text, especially when it was biblical. The biblical translations that German Pietists produced also led to a profoundly new way of envisioning the Bible itself, as Jonathan Sheehan has suggested (Sheehan, 2005). Pietists saw the Bible as a text for general consumption, and not the personal provenance of the learned elite. Consequently, the Bible was the crux around which Pietist life turned for all believers, regardless of social or class status, and certainly regardless of race. To missionaries raised in a Pietist framework, it was thus important that Africans be able to read biblical passages in their own languages, and in so doing make the texts their own.

Even though German missionary linguists did not think of themselves in nationalist terms, their work still contributed to the process of European colonization, in this case expressly British colonization. The CMS missionaries Krapf and Schön made their allegiance to Great Britain plain in their writings. Adrian Hastings has pointed out that Krapf proposed in 1841 that British political authority be established in Ethiopia to help secure the country for Christ, very specifically tying the success of Christianity to that of British colonialism (Hastings, 1996). Then, in an 1862 Hausa grammar, Schön went a step further. In the preface he quoted English abolitionist T.F. Buxton's assertion that "from the slave trade itself, a nation has been reclaimed, and now enjoys, in comparison with Africa, a blaze of light, liberty, religion, and happiness. That nation is Great Britain" (Schön, 1862, p. xiv). Their linguistic work was thus clearly carried out in the service of both British colonization and international Christianization, which were tightly entwined and reinforced the same European power structure (Pugach, 2012).

While German missionaries may have initiated nineteenth-century African language studies, many non-German Europeans also pursued and became distinguished for their linguistic research. As Viera Pawliková-Vilhanová has shown, the French Catholic White Fathers were extremely invested in learning and transcribing various African languages, to the extent that they were not allowed to speak any but the languages in which they preached after being in the field for a certain period (Pawliková-Vilhanová, 2007). Krapf was one of the founders of Swahili studies (Griefenow-Mewis, 1996; Pirouet, 1999), but the British Edward Steere, who missionized in East Africa from the 1860s and ultimately became Bishop of Central Africa, was also a pioneer in the discipline (Frankl, 1999), as were the French priest Charles Sacleux

(Ricard, 2007), and the British CMS Deacon William Edward Taylor (Frankl, 1999). A good discussion of the work of Protestant Swiss missionaries in South Africa in detail was made by Harries (1988). What all of these missionaries, and others, had in common was a commitment to colonization and Christianization, both of which contributed to the upending and reshaping of precolonial African societies. As per the Comaroffs (Comaroff and Comaroff, 1991), missionary linguistic interventions codified, ossified, and classified African languages, as well as the people who spoke them.

Colonial administrators worked as African linguists alongside missionaries. They also worked to reorganize African society to suit colonial needs – for instance, to bring Africans into a cash economy and reorient labor practices to benefit the mother country – and used language as a tool to do so. In the British context, some of the most well-known linguist-administrators were H.H. Johnston (Oliver, 1957), and Robert Needham Cust, the latter of whom was also an Anglican missionary (Cust, 2002). French administrators were involved in linguistic research as well, pursuing linguistic and anthropological research in tandem, as did most of those who conducted linguistic studies (Ginio, 2002).[4] In addition, from 1902 an entire series of books in Germany – the *Archiv für das Studium deutscher Kolonialsprachen* (Archive for the Study of German Colonial Languages) – were primarily composed by German colonial officials doubling as linguists (Pugach, 2012).

One of the other most pivotal figures in the development of African linguistics was Wilhelm Bleek, a German who was not a missionary but a scholar and librarian. Bleek was among the first to write a dissertation on African languages, and is renowned for having coined the term "Bantu" to describe the vast language family that dominates much of the African continent (Spohr, 1965).[5] His background in biblical criticism and theology was similar to that of his missionary colleagues, and he came of age intellectually in the same academic orbit (Bank, 2006). Bleek ultimately emigrated to South Africa, became librarian to Cape Colony Governor Sir George Grey, and continued his linguistic studies by meeting with and assessing the languages of local African populations, chief among them "Bushmen" (Bank, 2006).

Bleek's work with Africans again drives home the point that although Europeans considered themselves the primary "authors" of African language grammars, dictionaries, and Bibles, it is more apt to say that the texts were *co-authored* by Africans, since they supplied most of the raw data in their role as informants. Indeed, many scholars have addressed the significance of African participation in nineteenth- and twentieth-century ethnographic and linguistic research (Schumaker, 2001; Lawrance et al., 2006). This included many Africans who grew up on mission stations, became missionaries themselves, and conducted linguistic research. Akan minister C.C. Reindorf worked with Basel missionary Christaller on studies of Ghanaian languages (Bearth, 2000), and the celebrated West African Bishop Samuel Ajayi Crowther was a linguist as well (Hair, 1969). He and CMS missionary Schön recorded the languages they encountered while on a trip to the lower Niger. Crowther became the chief Yoruba specialist of the age, translating the Bible and other religious texts into Yoruba (Hair, 1987). He was indeed the first person to publish anything in Igbo (van den Berselaar, 1997).

Relationships between African and European missionary linguists were fraught with issues of power imbalance and white domination. Reindorf, for instance, ultimately had to yield to Christaller when they disagreed over issues related to their research (Bearth, 2000). The subject of power – and agency – in the study of nineteenth- and early twentieth-century African languages is extremely significant. Europeans could not conduct their linguistic research without Africans, but the names of many African researchers were never written down, and have been lost. Missionaries would often credit their African informants with having done more for their translations and vocabulary compilations than they had themselves (Pugach, 2012). Nonetheless, records on most of these Africans's lives are scarce, leading to an erasure of their presence at the site of linguistic production.

German colonialism, nationalism, and inherent racism

From the first publication of an African language grammar – Nyländer's 1814 work on Bullom – through the middle of the nineteenth century, the German missionaries at the forefront of African linguistics defined their identities through religion, not nationality. Above all else they were Christians. Later in the nineteenth century that changed. After German unification in 1871, missionaries were progressively swept up in the nationalist fervor that had gripped the country, especially as Germany began to compete with other European powers for African colonies (Stoecker, 1986).[6] While the Protestant missionary establishment in Germany was generally conflicted about whether to remain true to their ecumenical commitments or support German colonial ambitions, the most prominent missionary linguists were active proponents of German imperialism (Pugach, 2012). They followed the dictums of Rhenish missionary inspector Friedrich Fabri, who was never personally a missionary in Africa, but nevertheless became Otto von Bismarck's main adviser on colonial policy. Fabri was an avid colonialist who was convinced that Germany's success was dependent on its ability to participate in the colonial scramble (Fabri, 1884).

The main missionary behind this transformation, however, was Carl Büttner.[7] Büttner is central both to the history of African linguistics *and* to the history of German colonialism. Büttner was a member of the Rhenish Missionary Society (RMS), and went to South West Africa – what is now Namibia – in 1872. He remained there through 1880, both proselytizing to the local population and conducting research on local languages such as Herero. Büttner was originally in favor of the British expanding their dominion in the Cape Colony into South West Africa, thereby effectively placing the region under British imperial control. The British, however, were uninterested in annexing the territory, and Büttner ultimately concluded that Germany would be a better master.[8] Therefore, after he had been back in Germany for five years, Büttner returned once again to South West Africa, this time as an agent of the German imperial government. Büttner became one of the main participants in the negotiations that led to South West Africa officially becoming a German colony. His linguistic knowledge helped as he was able to negotiate treaties on Germany's behalf in South West African languages. Upon his final return to Germany in 1886, Büttner took on the role of Mission Society Inspector for the newly founded *Deutsche-Ostafrikanischer Missionsgesellschaft* (German-East African Missionary Society), a society that was expressly imperialist in nature (Menzel, 1978).

Büttner's enthusiasm for German colonization influenced his linguistic scholarship. Originally he wrote his work on Herero and other South West African languages in English. He later condemned himself and others for this. He argued that Germans had always been the most active Africanist scholars, and had diminished themselves by submitting to British domination through their use of English. This opinion that German linguists had been "slaves to a British master," carried over into what became the work of the rest of his life, a teaching position at the newly founded *Seminar für Orientalische Sprachen* (Department of Oriental Languages). The *Seminar* had been opened at the *Friedrich-Wilhelms Universität* (Friedrich-Wilhelms University) in Berlin for the express purpose of training Germans preparing for colonial careers in the languages they would need at their postings (Menzel, 1978).

At the outset, African languages were a minor consideration at the *Seminar*. Much more weight was given to Middle Eastern and East Asian languages, where it was assumed the bulk of the students would go. It did not take long, however, for African languages such as Swahili and Hausa to grow in popularity. As Germany's involvement in its colonies of German East Africa, German South West Africa, Togo, and Cameroon grew, so did the need for students who could communicate in their languages. These students were primarily civil servants (Pugach, 2012). Missionaries were no longer the primary audience for African languages studies and training. Accordingly, the Pietist goals of transforming a people by transforming their language diminished in importance, and an emphasis on practical speaking skills emerged.

At the same time, missionaries – or those with strong ties to the Protestant missionary community – remained crucial to the discipline as it underwent institutionalization. During his tenure at the *Seminar*, Büttner began to work with and mentor a pastor named Carl Meinhof, who would go on to become one of the most significant figures in early twentieth-century African linguistics. Meinhof, who was born in Pomerania in 1857, became interested in African languages during the 1880s. This was when a young Cameroonian, Njo Dibone (Dibone and Meinhof, 1889), lived with Meinhof briefly in order to study German. While Meinhof taught Dibone German, Dibone taught Meinhof his language, Duala. Already involved with Protestant missionary causes, Meinhof's encounter with Dibone radically altered his career path. Meinhof continued to research and write about African languages through the turn of the century, at first focusing largely on the Bantu group, to which Duala was classified. In 1899 he published the *Grundriss einer Lautlehre der Bantusprachen* (An Outline of Bantu Phonology) (Meinhof, 1899), which rocketed him to the apex of African linguistics. Ultimately, in 1903, Meinhof left his small country parsonage for Berlin and a position teaching Swahili and other Bantu languages at the *Seminar* (Pugach, 2012).

The growth of scientific racism, with an intensification of the belief that racial difference could be objectively measured by assessing physical criteria such as skull shape or skin shade, also had an increasing impact as the nineteenth century wore on, and certainly influenced linguists like Büttner and Meinhof. Linguistic phenomena were increasingly correlated with racial characteristics. For example, the languages of taller, lighter-skinned Africans were commonly classified as "Hamitic", whereas those of shorter, darker-skinned individuals were usually typed as "Nigritic" or "Sudanic." Anthropologists and linguists argued that the Hamites, a group that had migrated to Africa from Europe or the Middle East in the distant past, had conquered and suppressed Africa's original, "Nigritic" inhabitants. Once the Hamites had settled in Africa, they began to intermingle with the vanquished natives and lost many of their "superior" racial traits. Still, Meinhof – who published his *Die Sprachen der Hamiten* (Hamitic Languages) in 1912 (Meinhof, 1912), and had become the top scholar of Hamitic languages, as well as Bantu ones – maintained that the superior Hamitic languages, remarkable for inflection and the use of grammatical gender, were largely impervious to change. Therefore, even if a Hamitic group had blended in with its non-Hamitic neighbors, linguists would know from its language that the people in question were Hamitic (Meinhof, 1912).

When Meinhof published *Die Sprachen der Hamiten*, he was the acknowledged leader in the emergent field of *Afrikanistik* – African language studies. The only person who came close to matching him was former North German missionary Diedrich Westermann, the leading expert on non-Bantu West African languages and peoples at the beginning of the twentieth century (Stoecker, 2008). In 1912 Westermann took over from Meinhof at the *Seminar*, and Meinhof left for Hamburg's newly founded Kolonialinstitut. Meinhof left the *Seminar* because its leadership refused to grant him funding for a *Zeitschrift* and, more importantly, for a phonetics laboratory (Pugach, 2012).

The laboratory, as stated at the beginning of the chapter, was central to the development of African studies as the discipline was further institutionalized and moved increasingly away from the original missionary interest in language as a tool for religious conversion. At the laboratory, African language study was an "objective" science, with specific values to measure and quantifiable data to produce. Linguistic researchers continued to develop pedagogical techniques to expedite language learning. However, whether the linguists were missionaries or not, they were now equally preoccupied with uncovering structural patterns that European and African languages shared, with the hope that so doing would provide clues about not only the origins of specific African language groups, but German origins as well (Pugach, 2012).

While Meinhof and his colleagues searched for origins, the laboratory he had established also made it clear that African languages were fundamentally different from European ones. Indeed, Meinhof's insistence that the laboratory was crucial to African linguistics was rooted in the belief that African languages were exceptionally appropriate subjects for phonetic inquiry. The *Kultursprachen* – including most European and Asian languages – had lengthy written traditions that philologists had already examined, in some cases exhaustively. By contrast, because many African languages lacked written texts, they had hardly been touched by western scholars (Meinhof, 1910a). Further, African languages could not be illuminated using the literary techniques applied elsewhere. Instead, they required the careful phonetic analysis of "living speech" and the presence of either native speakers or well-made recordings of their voices.

While practical considerations were of principal importance to the Seminar and its Africa-bound students, Meinhof and his peers believed that their institution also had scientific obligations. Chief among these was, again, the responsibility to research the linguistic, and thus the cultural, religious, and biological origins of humanity, as well as of discrete racial groups. In this regard, Meinhof contended that *Kultursprachen* had usually altered so much since they were first uttered that it was impossible for science to recapture their original forms. Combined with the fact that ancient texts were composed in literary language and did not reflect the way people had really spoken, Meinhof felt that their value to the study of origins was limited. At the same time, he held that many African languages had remained practically untouched by history. Some of these groups, Meinhof maintained, lived in remote areas and had not come into contact with other people before Europeans arrived (Meinhof, 1936). Their languages had been preserved almost as if they were fossils, offering linguists a unique opportunity to explore the earliest structures of speech. With the sophisticated auditory, medical and transcriptive technologies available in the early twentieth century, those structures could be analyzed precisely, but only in a laboratory using newly developed methodologies to collect phonetic data.

The laboratory was originally founded principally for the study of African languages. Not long after it opened, though, Meinhof was besieged with requests to use the laboratory from professors in other departments, as well as the public. The laboratory was fast becoming recognized as a space to investigate all manner of languages and linguistic abnormalities (Pugach, 2012). Those who were interested in deaf-mute communications, stuttering, and deformities or injuries to speech organs all looked to the laboratory to conduct their research. In short order the laboratory turned into a locus for the construction of both the abnormal and the normal, defining what was "typical" for speech and what was not. Meinhof had begun with the assumption that European languages represented the pinnacle of linguistic sophistication, and that African languages were their stunted, underdeveloped cousins.

As the laboratory evolved, Africans continued to be the subjects of phonetic experiments, but were joined by others. For example, in 1913, linguists examined 400 "normal and deaf-mute children" with "anthropometric devices" such as the spirometer, which measured the volume of air coming in and out of the lungs (Panconcelli-Calzia and Körner, 1994). This meant that in the laboratory, African languages were ultimately located on an axis between primitivity and maturation, but also on a continuum between regular and aberrant. European languages were models of refinement, and the laboratory served as a chamber for exploring deviation within and outside them.

After Germany lost its colonies in World War I, the laboratory – which was founded in a specifically colonial context to advance the goal of imperial expansion – continued to branch out, increasingly moving away from its original purpose. Phoneticians studied veterans who had injured vocal organs (Göpfert, 1920), as well as twins and triplets. Panconcelli-Calzia brought three-year-old triplets Ursula, Erika, and Herma into the laboratory in 1935 to determine whether the register that they spoke in and the gestures they made while so doing were identical, thereby advancing the "science" of racial hygiene. He pointed to three "areas" of racial hygiene or genetic research, the "racial-biological, family-biological, and twin-biological," and held that phonetics was particularly suited to support the third. It was important to conduct experiments with children such as Ursula, Erika, and Herma at a young age because environmental factors had not yet altered their voices. Panconcelli-Calzia contended that research on the triplets and other *Mehrlinge* (multiples) would make a significant contribution to curing genetic diseases by unraveling the nature of biological inheritance (Schilling, 1950). What he did not mention, but which was surely the case, was that the laboratory also enhanced the wider Nazi project of classifying racial traits by adding phonological categories to the existing catalogue of racial characteristics.

That biological characteristics and the racial differences that could be attributed to them would become so relevant by the 1930s would not have been immediately apparent when the laboratory opened in 1910. While the laboratory defined the normal and abnormal, it was also envisioned as a site for the *effacement* of physical features and the abstraction of sound. Meinhof scoffed at anthropologists who claimed that African and European vocal organs were dissimilarly formed, and that this made them unable to pronounce certain sounds (Meinhof, 1910a; Müller, 1879, 1884). Biologically, the lips, larynx, and pharynx were constructed in the same way, and neither Africans nor Europeans had superior articulatory equipment. When Meinhof, Panconcelli-Calzia, and other Europeans working at the laboratory made phonographic recordings of Africans speaking, they often played them back later for purposes of assessment. The African bodies themselves disappeared, replaced by detached voices whose racial origins and identities remained obscure.

The turn to allegedly "objective" reality was part of the larger intent to model African linguistics after the physical sciences and to reject the humanistic philological traditions that applied to *Kultursprachen*. This entailed "reading" African languages in terms of physical, rather than cultural, texts. Indeed, while other fora, such as the various ethnological and geographical journals devoted to the study of the colonies, presented and interpreted the religious and social content of African oral history and folklore, articles that appeared in the laboratory's publication *Vox* emphasized topics such as sound shifts in African languages and the laws that governed them (Meinhof, 1918). Curiously then, although research coming out of the laboratory highlighted aspects of African languages that were foreign to Europeans, it also attempted to collapse difference and boil language down to a basic, unmarked series of combinations of consonants and vowels.

Pedagogy and research at Carl Meinhof's Phonetics Laboratory

This strange amalgam of emphasis on both difference and its dissolution, definitions of the abnormal and their negation, is what makes the history of Hamburg's Phonetics Laboratory so intriguing for the story of African linguistics. Psychological and physical characteristics all came under the laboratory's purview. During its first years the Phonetics Laboratory was part of Meinhof's *Seminar für Kolonialsprachen*. All research and teaching done in the laboratory was thus closely connected to the goals of instruction, and students who took classes in an African language often had to report for practical exercises at the laboratory. One of the most significant features in both classroom and laboratory was the division of workload between Germans and Africans. The Germans were the lecturers who "translated" African grammar and vocabulary into terms students could understand. The Africans' main job was to demonstrate correct pronunciation and elocution. Meinhof believed that their roles could not be reversed. He found it unlikely that even the best European instructor would be able to mimic "exotic" African sounds on a consistent basis. A European could not teach his or her students how to speak an African language correctly on a mechanical level. For that reason, while Europeans were used as test subjects for experiments on African languages when native speakers were not available, the distinct preference was always for Africans. The Africans at the laboratory shared some similarities with the informants who had worked with missionaries and administrators in the field, but this comparison can go only so far. In the field, Africans explained the particulars of their languages to the Europeans. In the laboratory, Africans did not comment on the grammatical or morphological characteristics of the languages, merely speaking words from them so that they could be repeated back (Pugach, 2012).

At the same time, Meinhof also believed that Africans could not teach Europeans grammar in terms that the latter could comprehend. As he explained in 1910,

> The native . . . is doubtless master of his material in the fullest sense, but he does not understand the European line of thought as it appears in the brain of the pupil. He is thus totally unable to supply the connecting links between European and non-European ideas . . . He who has ever interested himself in non-European languages knows . . . how great the gap is between these and our own. The discrepancy is based not only on the vocabulary or in a few deviations in the method of expression, but is founded on complete differentiation in the whole construction of the language, or in other words on quite another method of thought. What is plain to the one is unintelligible to the other, and what appears difficult to one is natural to the other. So, in African dialects, it is quite frequently the case that what the European calls the front, the African calls the back.
>
> *Meinhof, 1910b, p. 263*

According to Meinhof, thought itself was determined by grammatical structure. Therefore, Europeans and Africans, who spoke languages belonging to different families with what he considered different levels of sophistication, would not be able to describe their languages to each other.

Africans and Europeans also served different functions in the laboratory, even if the line between them was not always clear-cut. Students were encouraged not only to listen to Africans and repeat what they heard them say, but also to observe them with their eyes. Depending on how close they were to the African "test subject," this would allow them to see the exact place where articulation occurred and how speech organs moved. In order for students to be properly trained in the laboratory, African languages had to be absorbed visually before attempting to understand them aurally. Meinhof said that:

> first, the learner must be shown how he personally makes sounds. He is impelled to touch his own lips, to look in the mirror. Words are pronounced for him and he is required not to listen with his ear, but to observe the movement of the lips with his eyes. If he has understood how known sounds are produced, he can then be shown the way that unknown ones are, until he sees the difference. Then he must try to mimic these, and when he finally can do so, he can also learn to hear.
>
> *Meinhof, 1910a*

When British clergyman W.H.T. Gairdner visited the department in March 1912, he referred to the African teaching assistants at the laboratory as "living phonographs." He said that they stood "on the (European's) side" to be "cranked up" whenever there was need of demonstration (Gairdner, 1912). But he was only half right. For Meinhof, Panconcelli-Calzia, and other Europeans in the laboratory the African assistants were obviously much more than phonographs. They were literally "texts" to be "read" by students and studied by scholars.

This method of learning had roots in the training of *Taubstumme* (deaf-mutes), who would later become among the most important experimental subjects at the laboratory. Those who were deaf and mute could not learn to speak by listening to and repeating what they heard. They had to rely on visual cues, and in so doing demonstrated that language could be learned visually as well as aurally. Only when students were able to "think themselves into the position of a deaf-mute," would they become cognizant of the importance of phonetics to the study of African languages (Meinhof, 1910a). By extrapolating from the study of the "abnormal," students would arrive at an understanding of why they had to observe the way sounds were formed before personally repeating them.

In contrast to those who were deaf and mute, however, African difference had little to do with *physical* abnormality. Meinhof disparaged German scholars and missionary officials who maintained that "in spite of anatomy . . . the gums of the English are differently built," when they could not learn to speak English with the proper accent, and he felt likewise with respect to Africans and their languages (Meinhof, 1910a, p. 151). To Meinhof, African difference rested rather in psychology and culture. The missionary G.L. Cleve had made Meinhof aware of the ways in which custom could precipitate sound shift by demonstrating how sounds in some Bantu languages were transformed by the ritualistic wearing of lip pegs (*pelele* or *ndonya*) and mutilation of teeth:

> With these mutilated organs, a person can, naturally, not articulate all sounds as he can with healthy ones. As a result of the mutilation, a type of articulation thus becomes general. Even after the custom has disappeared, the articulation remains. This theory can also apply to specific cases. So, for example, Yao women wear a big piece of wood in their upper lips. They can't speak the letter f, and because the children learn to speak from the women, the f has disappeared from the language.
>
> *Cleve, 1903, pp. 681–701*

Meinhof's mentor Wilhelm Wundt, whose works on *Völkerpsychologie* had a marked influence on the linguist, had claimed that in the transition from countryside to city, sound shifts of a kind that Meinhof had noted for Swahili often began to occur:

> Wundt has made us aware of a process that is surely worth notice, namely that in the city, with increased contact, people speak more and more quickly than they do in the country with little contact . . . Naturally, in quick speech sounds will be more fleetingly pronounced and then disappear entirely. Thus, for example in Swahili, which as a coastal and trading language is spoken very quickly, the l after the stressed syllable has as a rule dropped away. Likewise the u after an m has mostly vanished, because both sounds, as lip sounds (bilabials) are very similar. People no longer say múti for tree, but rather m'ti, similar to how we still write "lesen" but actually say "lesn."
>
> *Meinhof, 1910a, pp. 59–60*

Language change was thus related to cultural and psychological phenomena, and students came to the laboratory not only to learn languages, but also to understand the African "mind."

Yet neither Wundt nor Cleve's theories sufficed to explain all sound shifts as historical or psychological phenomena. This was why the physical procedures conducted at the laboratory assumed such a central function. Although African pronunciation was still related to African psychology, the body, not the mind, was the object of investigation. Meinhof was convinced that the empirical observation of living beings would allow him the opportunity to train Germany's colonizers in proper pronunciation and, additionally, to uncover new sound laws. His approach and that of his students rendered Africans as objects who could be analyzed by a "professional." This kind of approach is similar to what Mary Louise Pratt has described in terms of travel writing, where Africans almost disappeared into the landscapes surrounding them, leaving only vestigial traces or "scratches" to indicate their existence (Pratt, 1992). The adopted approach or gaze to Africa in this case was, however, not located in the colonies, but rather in a laboratory environment in Germany, which was familiar to German teachers and students.

Meinhof indeed believed that it was only in the controlled setting of the laboratory that hypotheses could be tested and linguistic laws established. Knowledge of sounds and sound shifts had been significant to the categorization of African languages since the middle of the nineteenth century. The CMS missionary Koelle had prepared his *Polyglotta Africana* in 1854 with hopes of transcribing 200 or so African languages and comparing sounds across them (Koelle, 1854), and in 1863 the German Egyptologist and philologist Richard Lepsius had created a standard script for representing all the languages of the world, which also emphasized the importance of sound (Lepsius, 1863; Meinhof, 1913). Yet nineteenth-century linguists were, "dependent on simple observation, without experiments," which made their findings imprecise (Meinhof, 1913). However, thanks to experimental phonetics, a science that emerged in the late nineteenth century and was crucial in the laboratory, linguists had the opportunity to conduct research with more sophisticated methods.

Panconcelli-Calzia defined experimental phonetics as the practice of "determining, dissecting, classifying, and researching the conditions of change in phonetic processes occurring in the present, independent of geographical location." This experimentation was, "the intentional, arbitrary creation of a phenomenon under any simplification or change of factors." Untrained observers would "wait patiently" for the appearance of such phenomena, but the experimental phonetician would take the matter into his own hands, using either organic or mechanical methods to produce the desired effects in his subjects (Panconcelli-Calzia, 1921, pp. 11–18).

"Organic" methods were conducted simply, using hearing, sight, or touch. Researchers would watch the faces and mouths of their test subjects to see what sorts of movements they made when certain sounds were produced, or place their hands on the subjects' heads, noses, chests, or larynxes to see how they vibrated during speech. Mechanical or "non-organic" methods included the use of various kinds of machinery. Some of these were designed to "fix"

African language studies in the 19th and early 20th centuries

the movement of speech pictorially, in graphs, and others produced more transitory results. This machinery supplemented the five senses and helped determine how language functioned. X-rays "supported the eye" by displaying "the movements of the diaphragm, if only momentarily and, alas, through the shadow of the liver" (Panconcelli-Calzia, 1921, p. 22). X-rays could further show movement of the larynx, as could a laryngoscope, a tool for peering down the throat. Neither of these, however, produced fixed images that could be analyzed after the fact. Therefore, they were further augmented by machines that captured the rise and fall of sound graphically, as exhibited by airflow. The most important of these was the kymograph, a motorized, rotating drum upon which a stylus charted sound vibrations in sinusoidal curves as the test subject spoke into a tube. Sarah Barrows, an American who visited the Phonetics Laboratory around 1914, enthused that the kymograph represented what was "really a new and indirect way of writing, in which instead of words being transcribed by the hand in the conventional spelling, they are recorded by the instrument as they are formed by the organs of speech" (Barrows, 1913–1914, pp. 66–67). These experiments had to be conducted with living beings. Panconcelli-Calzia disparaged nineteenth-century efforts to study phonetic processes with dead material. The experiments also had to be "harmless." Any invasive procedures, such as tracheotomy, were not acceptable (Panconcelli-Calzia, 1921).

Since colonialism required further investigation of African languages, Meinhof considered Africans indispensable to experimental phonetics and the results coming from his laboratory. Barrows even referred to the African subjects as the laboratory's *Experimentierkaninchen* – its guinea pigs – evoking a particularly chilling image (Barrows, 1913–1914). Africans were seen as useful for the sounds they made, and the items that decorated Meinhof's *Seminar für Kolonialsprachen* at the Colonial Institute constantly recalled the importance of physicality to its purpose. In 1912 the Seminar held an exhibition in which the "tools" of African studies were displayed. The exhibit emphasized the importance of bodies, as opposed to texts, for African linguistics. Shown were "anatomical preparations, models of speech organs, x-ray pictures and plaques."[9] Everywhere the significance of biology and anatomy predominated, reminding visitors that African linguistics and phonetics were physical sciences.

None of this is to suggest that the Africans who worked in Meinhof's laboratory were quiescent, or that they had no role in determining how language was taught and investigated. As I have discussed in greater detail elsewhere, they were key to the success of Meinhof and his colleagues (Pugach, 2007, 2012). In addition to their participation in phonetic experiments, the Africans in Hamburg taught a variety of languages, including Swahili, Hausa, Duala, and Ewe (Pugach, 2012). They had greater control over the dissemination of knowledge in the classroom than in the laboratory. Africans continued to take the lead in linguistic research, conducting it in tandem with Meinhof and his colleagues to produce volumes such as a publication of Ewondo texts (Heepe, 1919). The ostensible author of the book was Meinhof's colleague and fellow Africanist linguist Martin Heepe, but the several Ewondo native speakers with whom he worked – including the chief Karl Atangana – were co-authors, even if they were not listed as such, since they supplied all of the texts in the book (Heepe, 1919).

One of the problems with Meinhof's laboratory practice, however, remained its demotion of Africans in terms of their role as linguists. Where they had once discussed their languages, the vocabulary and grammar, with their German colleagues, they now stood silent if they were not being called on to demonstrate sounds. While there is no record of how the Africans felt about being test subjects, we can speculate that they probably did not like having their throats and mouths touched by German students in the service of experimental phonetics. As *Afrikanistik* shifted from a humanistic discipline to a natural science, Africans had increasingly less input on the study of their own languages.

Conclusion

Hamburg's Phonetics Laboratory made the physical process of language production central to the study of African languages. Meinhof and his colleagues believed that African languages were primitive, and that their primitivity made them ideal for phonetic research. They were deemed similar to the languages that Europeans and others had probably spoken in prehistory (Meinhof, 1936), and to research them was to discover how the earliest speech must have sounded.

The laboratory was also what I call a "hypermetropolitan space," ideal for examining the colonial other and identifying his or her "traits." Students were offered the chance to observe Africans in a controlled environment that would allow their languages to be dissected better than they could be in the colonies. This was a far cry from the research conducted in the nineteenth century, which was largely undertaken in Africa itself, and which included close collaboration between missionaries and Africans to transcribe, translate, and transliterate languages that were, in many cases, being reduced to writing for the first time. With the emergence of experimental phonetics and advanced technology, it became easier to extract linguistic and phonetic information. Languages could be recorded by phonograph in the laboratory and then played back repeatedly until a student was able to mimic the sounds it produced.

The enterprise of research into African languages began in the context of missionization and colonization. Early scholars, many of whom were missionaries, focused on language because they were interested in biblical translation and exegesis, cultural knowledge, and practical communication. They were philologists, whose work was under the influence of scholars such as Herder and Humboldt. Meinhof and Panconcelli-Calzia shifted the terms of the debate when they founded the Phonetics Laboratory. Africanists were now physical scientists, seeking answers to how vocal organs made the sounds that they did. This transition from humanistic to biological pursuit was not a complete one. The interest in biblical translation into newly encountered African languages did not end, and neither did the transcription of folktales and other oral texts. But effort was increasingly funneled into examining African languages from a physical perspective, one that excised them from their cultural context and excluded Africans from collaboration with Europeans.

Notes

1 Some of this chapter is adapted from my book, Sara Pugach, *Africa in Translation: A History of Colonial Linguistics in Germany and Beyond, 1814–1945* (Ann Arbor, MI: University of Michigan Press, 2012).

2 J.S. Vater, who published the first known description of Shilluk, is an example of an early nineteenth-century German scholar who was not a missionary. See J.C. Adelung and J.S. Vater, *Mithridates oder allgemeine Sprachenkunde; Mit dem Vater Unser als Sprachprobe in beynahe fünfhundert Sprachen und Mundarten* (Berlin: Voss, 1812), and Oswin Köhler, "The Early Study of the Nilotic Languages of the Sudan, 1812–1900 – I", *Sudan Notes and Records*, Vol. 51 (1970): 85–94.

3 Ironically, this seems to have been the case despite the profusion of German dialects, some of which are mutually unintelligible.

4 Indeed, Carl Meinhof once even called linguistics and anthropology "auxiliaries" to each other, as evidence collected in one would also benefit research in the other. See Pugach, *Africa in Translation*, 97.

5 The category "Bantu" has of course since been subsumed into the much larger Niger-Congo group. Bernd Heine, Derek Nurse et al., *African Languages: An Introduction* (Cambridge: Cambridge University Press, 2000), Chapter 2.

6 Germany first became a colonial power in the 1880s; indeed, it was German Chancellor Otto von Bismarck who hosted the infamous Berlin Conference that divvied up Africa amongst the European powers in 1884–5.
7 Section on Büttner adapted from Sara Pugach, "Lost in Translation: Carl Büttner's Contribution to the Development of African Language Studies in Germany," in *The Politics of Language Study*, ed. David Hoyt and Karen Oslund (Rowman & Littlefield, 2006), 151–184.
8 With the exception of the deep water port at Walvis Bay, which they did incorporate into the Cape Colony. See Lynn Berat, *Walvis Bay: Decolonization and International Law* (New Haven, CT: Yale, 1990).
9 "Ausstellung des Seminars für Kolonialsprachen," *Deutsche Kolonialzeitung, Organn der Deutschen Kolonialgesellschaft*, Nr. 25, Berlin, 22/6/12, 29. Jg. 1912.

References

Anderson, G.H. (1999) *Biographical Dictionary of Christian Missions*. Grand Rapids, MI: Eerdmans.
"Ausstellung des Seminars für Kolonialsprachen" (1912) *Deutsche Kolonialzeitung, Organn der Deutschen Kolonialgesellschaft*, Nr. 25, Berlin, 22/6/12, 29.
Bank, A. (2006) *Bushmen in a Victorian World: The Remarkable Story of the Bleek-Lloyd Collection of Bushman Folklore*. Cape Town: Juta & Company.
Barrows, S. (1913–1914) *Experimental Phonetics as an Aid to the Study of Language*. Columbus, OH: Ohio State University.
Bearth, T. (2000) "J.G. Christaller. A Holistic View of Language and Culture – and C.C. Reindorf's History." In Paul Jenkins, ed., *The Recovery of the West African Past. African Pastors and African History in the Nineteenth Century: C.C. Reindorf and Samuel Johnson*, 83–101. Basel: Basler Afrika Bibliographien.
Benes, T. (2008). *In Babel's Shadow: Language, Philology, and the Nation in Nineteenth-Century Germany*. Detroit, MI: Wayne State.
_____ (2003) "The 'Living Word': Hamann, Herder, and the Historicization of Linguistic Community." Unpublished conference paper, German Studies Association, 27th Annual Meeting, New Orleans.
Berat, L. (1990) *Walvis Bay: Decolonization and International Law*. New Haven, CT: Yale.
Bersselaar, D. van den (1997) "Creating 'Union Ibo': Missionaries and the Igbo Language." *Africa*, 67(2): 273–295.
Bleek, W.H.I. (1862) *A Comparative Grammar of South African Languages*, Volume I. London: Trübner & co.
Cleve, G.L. (1903) "Die Lippenlaute der Bantu und die Negerlippen, mit besonderer Berücksichtigung der Lippenverstümmelungen." *Zeitschrift für Ethnologie*, 35: 681–701.
Comaroff, J. and J. (1991) *Of Revelation and Revolution*. Chicago, IL: University of Chicago.
Cust, R.N. (2002) *A Sketch of the Modern Languages of Africa*. New York, NY: Routledge.
_____ (1889) "Dr. Schön." *The Church Missionary Gleaner*, 16–17: 36.
Dibone, N. and E. Meinhof (1889) *Marchen aus Kamerun*. Strassburg: Heitz & Mündel.
Errington, J. (2001) "Colonial Linguistics." *Annual Review of Anthropology*, 30: 19–39, www.jstor.org/stable/3069207.
Fabri, F. (1884) *Bedarf Deutschland die Colonien? Eine politische-ökonomische Betrachtung*. Gotha: Perthes.
Frankl, P.J.L. (1999) "W.E. Taylor (1856–1927): England's Greatest Swahili Scholar." *AAP*, 60: 161–174.
Gairdner, W.H.T. (1912) "Missionary Training Methods on the Continent (Series QK-4, Box 1)." Missionsgesellschaften C. England, III Teil, Konf. Brit. Miss. Gesellsch., J.M.C., C. Zirkulare 1. Archiv der evangelischen Missionswerk, Basel Missionary Society, Basel.
Ginio, R. (2002) "French Colonial Reading of Ethnographic Research: The Case of the 'Desertion' of the Abron King and Its Aftermath." *Cahiers d'Études Africaines*, 42(166): 337–357.
Göpfert, J. (1920) "Die Übungsbehandlung von Stotterern in einem Neurotiker Lazarett." *Vox*, 30: 129–140.
Griefenow-Mewis, C. (1996) "J.L. Krapf and His Role in Researching and Describing East African Languages." *AAP*, 47: 161–171.

Grimm, J., W. Grimm and L. Richter (1812) *Fünfzig Kinder – und Hausmärchen*. Leipzig: Reclam.

Hair, P.E.H. (1967) *The Early Study of Nigerian Languages: Essays and Bibliographies*. Cambridge: Cambridge University Press.

‗‗‗‗‗‗‗‗ (1969) "Samuel Ajayi Crowther: A Biographical Note." *African Language Review*, No 8: 81–106.

‗‗‗‗‗‗‗‗ (1987) "Colonial Freetown and the Study of African Languages." *Africa*, 57(4): 560–565.

‗‗‗‗‗‗‗‗ (2014) "Susu Studies and Literature, 1799–1900." In David Dalby, ed., *Sierra Leone Language Review: The African Language Journal of Fourah Bay College*, 2nd Ed. New York, NY: Routledge.

Harries, P. (1988) "The Roots of Ethnicity: Discourse and the Politics of Language Construction in South-East Africa." *African Affairs*, 87(346): 25–52, www.jstor.org/stable/722808.

Hastings, A. (1996) *The Church in Africa, 1450–1950*. Oxford: Oxford University Press.

Heepe, M. (1919) *Jaunde Texte von Karl Atangana und Paul Messi, nebst experimentalphonetischen Untersuchungen über die Tonhöhen im Jaunde und einer Einführung in die Jaundesprachen*. Hamburg: L. Friedrichsen.

Heine, B. and D. Nurse, eds (2000) *African Languages: An Introduction*. Cambridge: Cambridge University Press.

Herder, J.G. (1997) *On World History: An Anthology*, eds H. Adler and E.A. Menze. Armonk, NY: M.E. Sharpe.

Hole, C. (1896) *The Early History of the Church Missionary Society for Africa and the East, to the End of A.D. 1814*. London: Church Missionary Society.

Irvine, J. (1993) "Mastering African Languages: The Politics of Linguistics in Nineteenth Century Senegal." *Social Analysis*, 33: 27–46, www.jstor.org/stable/23163038.

Kirchberger, U. (2007) "Fellow Laborers in the Same Vineyard: Germans in British Missionary Societies in the First Half of the Nineteenth Century." In S. Manz, M. Schulte Beerbühl and J.R. Davis, eds, *Migration and Transfer from Germany to Great Britain*, 81–106. Leiden: Walter de Gruyter.

Koelle, S.W. (1854) *Polyglotta Africana; Or, a Comparative Vocabulary of Nearly Three Hundred Words and Phrases, in more than 100 Distinct African Languages*. London: Church Mission House.

‗‗‗‗‗‗‗‗ (1851) *Outlines of a Grammar of the Vei Language, Together with a Vei-English Vocabulary and an Account of the Discovery and Nature of the Vei Mode of Syllabic Writing*. London: Keegan, Paul.

Köpke, W. (2009) "Herder's Views on the Germans and their Future Literature." In H. Adler and W. Köpke, eds, *A Companion to the Works of Johann Gottfried Herder*, 215–232. Rochester: Camden House.

Langham Brown, R. (1967) *Wilhelm von Humboldt's Conception of Linguistic Relativity*. Berlin: Walter de Gruyter.

Lawrance, B.N., E.L. Osborn and R. Roberts, eds (2006) *Intermediaries, Interpreters, and Clerks: African Employees in the Making of Colonial Africa*. Madison, WI: University of Wisconsin.

Leopold, J. (1999) *The Prix Volney*. New York, NY: Springer.

Lepsius, R. (1863) *Standard Alphabet for Reducing Unwritten Languages and Foreign Graphic Systems to a Uniform Orthography in European Letters*. London: Williams and Norgate.

Marchand, S. (1996) *Down from Olympus: Archeology and Philhellenism in Germany, 1750–1970*. Princeton, NJ: Princeton University Press.

McGetchin, D. (2009) *Indology, Indomania, and Orientalism: Ancient India's Rebirth in Modern Germany*. Madison, NJ: Fairleigh Dickinson.

Meinhof, C.F.M. (1936) *Die Entstehung flektierender Sprachen*. Berlin: Reimer.

‗‗‗‗‗‗‗‗ (1910a) *Die Moderne Sprachforschung in Afrika*. Berlin: Buchhandlung der Berliner ev. Missionsgesellschaft.

‗‗‗‗‗‗‗‗ (1910b) "The Training of Missionaries in Regard to Language." *World Missionary Conference*. Edinburgh.

‗‗‗‗‗‗‗‗ (1912) *Die Sprachen der Hamiten*. Hamburg: L. Friedrichsen.

‗‗‗‗‗‗‗‗ (1913) "Die Bedeutung der experimentellen Phonetik für die Erforschung der Afrikanischen Sprachen." *Vox*, 23/1: 22–26.

‗‗‗‗‗‗‗‗ (1918) "Der Wert der Phonetik für die Allgemeine Sprachwissenschaft." *Vox*, 28: 1–62.

‗‗‗‗‗‗‗‗ (1899) *Grundriss einer Lautlehre der Bantusprachen nebst Anleitung zur Aufnahme von Bantusprachen*. Berlin: Reimer.

Menzel, G. (1978) *Die Rheinische-Mission: Aus 150 Jahre Missionsgeschichte*. Wuppertal: Verlag der Vereinigten Evang, Mission.

Miehe, G. (1996) "Vom Verhältnis zwischen Afrikanistik und Allgemeiner Sprachwissenschaft." *Paideuma: Mitteilungen zur Kulturkunde*, Bd. 42, Zur Geschichte der Afrika Forschung: 267–284, www.jstor.org/stable/40341724.

Mosse, G. (1964) *The Crisis of German Ideology: Intellectual Origins of the Third Reich*. New York, NY: Grosset and Dunlap.

Müller, F. (1879) *Grundriss der Sprachwissenschaft, Bd. II: Die Sprachen der Schlichthaarigen Rassen*. Vienna: Hölder.

Müller, F. (1884) *Grundriss der Sprachwissenschaft, Bd. III: Die Sprachen der Lockenhaarigen Rassen*. Vienna: Hölder.

Nyländer, G.R. (1814) *Grammar and Vocabulary of the Bullom Language*. London: Church Missionary Society.

Oliver, R. (1957) *Sir Harry Johnston and the Scramble for Africa*. London: Chatto & Windus.

Panconcelli-Calzia, G. (1931) "Experimentelle Phonetik und Menschliche Erblehre." *Vox* 17: 107.

Panconcelli Calzia, G. and E.F.K Körner (1994) '*Geschichtszahlen der Phonetik (1941)*' together with '*Quellenatlas der Phonetik (1940)*'. Amsterdam: John Benjamins.

————— (1921) *Experimentelle Phonetik*. Berlin: Walter de Gruyter.

Pawlikova-Vilhanová, V. (2007) "Christian Missions in Africa and Their Role in the Transformation of African Societies." *Asian and African Studies*, 16(2): 249–260.

Pirouet, M.L. (1999) "The Legacy of Johann Ludwig Krapf." *International Bulletin of Missionary Research*, 23/2: 69–75.

Poliakov, L. (1996) *The Aryan Myth: A History of Racist and Nationalist Ideas in Europe*. New York, NY: Barnes and Noble.

Pratt, M.L. (1992) *Imperial Eyes: Travel Writing and Transculturation*. New York, NY: Routledge.

Pugach, S. (2012) *Africa in Translation: A History of Colonial Linguistics in Germany and Beyond*. Ann Arbor, MI: University of Michigan.

————— (2007) "Of Conjunctions, Comportment, and Clothing: The Place of African Teaching Assistants at Hamburg's Colonial Institute, 1909–1919." In R. Gordon and H. Tilley, eds, *Ordering Africa: Anthropology, European Imperialism, and the Politics of Knowledge*, 153–189. Manchester: Manchester University Press.

————— (2006) "Lost in Translation: Carl Büttner's Contribution to the Development of African Language Studies in Germany." In D. Hoyt and K. Oslund, eds, *The Politics of Language Study*, 151–184. Lanham, MD: Rowman & Littlefield.

Ricard, A. (2007) "Charles Sacleux (1856–1943), Fondateur des études Swahili en France." *Histoires et Missions Chrétiennes*, 105–114.

Roberts, L.M. (2010) *Literary Nationalism in German and Japanese Germanistik*. Bern: Peter Lang.

Schilling, R. (1950). "Über die Stimme erbgleicher Zwillinge." *Folia Phoniatrica et Logopaedica*, 2, 98–119.

Schlenker, C.F. (1864) *Grammar of the Temne Language*. London: Church Missionary Society.

Schön, J.F. (1862) *Grammar of the Hausa Language*. London: Church Missionary House.

Schubert, M. (2003) *Der Schwarze Fremde: Das Bild des Schwarzafrikaners in der parlamentarischen und publizistischen Kolonialdiskussion in Deutschland von den 1870er bis in der 1930er Jahre*. Berlin: Franz Steiner.

Schumaker, L. (2001) *Africanizing Anthropology: Fieldwork, Networks, and the Making of Cultural Knowledge in Central Africa*. Durham, NC: Duke University Press.

Sheehan, J. (2005) *The Enlightenment Bible: Translation, Scholarship, Culture*. Princeton, NJ: Princeton University Press.

Spohr, O.H. (1965) "Biographical Introduction." In *The Natal Diaries of Dr. W.H.I. Bleek*. Cape Town: A.A. Balkema.

Steere, E. (1872) "On East African Tribes and Languages." *The Journal of the Anthropological Institute of Great Britain and Ireland*: cxliii–cliv.

Stoecker, H. ed. (1986) *German Imperialism in Africa: From the Beginnings until the Second World War*, 2nd Edn. London: C. Hurst.

Stoecker, H. (2008) *Afrikawissenschaften in Berlin von 1919 bis 1945. Zur Geschichte und Topographie eines wissenschaftlichen Netwerkes*. Stuttgart: Franz Steiner.

Thornton, J. (2017) "Roboredo, Kikongo Sermon," www.bu.edu/afam/faculty/john-thornton/roboredo-kikongo-sermon/. Accessed January 27, 2017.

Uhlig, S. (1986) *Hiob Ludolfs 'Theologica Aethiopica'*. Wiesbaden: Franz Steiner.

Walker, S.A. (1847) *The Church of England Mission in Sierra Leone, including an Introductory Account of that Colony and a Comprehensive Sketch of the Niger Expedition in the Year 1841*. London: Seeley, Burnside and Seeley.

Wallmann, J. (1995) "Was ist Pietismus?" In Andreas Lindt, ed., *Pietismus und Neuzeit XX/1994: Ein Jahrbuch zur Geschichte des neueren Protestantismus*, 11–27. Göttingen: Vandenhoeck und Ruprecht.

Walls, A.F. (2001) "The Eighteenth-Century Protestant Missionary Awakening in Its European Context." In Brian Stanley, ed., *Christian Missions and the Enlightenment*, 22–45. Grand Rapids, MI: Eerdmans.

Wangemann, H.T. (1872) *Geschichte der Berliner Missionsgesellschaft und ihrer Arbeiten in Südafrika*. Berlin: Im. Selbstverlag des Ev. Missionshauses.

Williamson, G. (2004) *The Longing for Myth in Germany: Religion and Aesthetic Culture from Romanticism to Nietzsche*. Chicago, IL: University of Chicago.

2

HISTORICAL LINGUISTICS IN AN AFRICAN CONTEXT

A brief state of the art

Gerrit J. Dimmendaal

Introduction

This chapter presents a brief survey of methods used in order to arrive at a genetic classification of African languages, and more specifically of multilateral or mass comparisons (the second section), as well as the comparative method (the third section). The study of dialect variation is another approach that has led to new insights into genetic diversification and the spreading of linguistic innovations (the fourth section). Language change involves not only divergence but also convergence between languages and other types of contact-induced change, depending on the social conditions involved (the fifth section). As with biological systems, phylogenetic relationships between languages have been represented metaphorically by means of family trees in historical-comparative linguistics. Parallel to more recent developments in biological sciences, rhizotic representations are now favored by some comparative linguists, as these latter models represent not only historical divergence but also convergence between genetically related languages (the sixth section). The present contribution also addresses language ecology, and more specifically the degree of genetic diversity in different parts of the continent, as well as the issue of accretion and spread zones in Africa (the seventh section). The chapter concludes with some suggestions for future comparative studies of African language families (the eighth section).

Multilateral comparisons and the genetic classification of African languages

When the British explorer, Captain James Cook, and his crews sailed across the Pacific Ocean between 1768 and 1779, their three voyages of exploration resulted in an expansion of anthropological, botanical and geographical knowledge, but also of languages spoken in the area. "During the second of these voyages (1772–1775) vocabularies were collected on a number of Polynesian islands, on the large southerly Melanesian island of New Caledonia, and at several locations in the New Hebrides chain (modern Vanuatu)" (Blust 2013: 21), which resulted in the establishment of genetic relationships between languages in the Pacific. During the 18th century, different scholars had started collecting wordlists in languages across the world for comparative purposes; this also involved African languages, as in

Simon Pallas' *Linguarum totius Orbis Vocabularia Comparativa*, published in two volumes in Moscow in 1787 and 1789, and sponsored by the Russian empress Catherine the Great. As a matter of fact, during the Middle Ages Arabic and Jewish scholars had already become aware that lexical and grammatical similarities between two or more languages are at times so abundant that only a common historical origin can explain them. Historical linguistics thus certainly did not start in the West. As early as the 10th century, a physician by the name of Judah ben Quraysh had already identified structural similarities between a group of languages now referred to as Berber and Semitic (Becker 1984, quoted in Frajzyngier and Shay 2012: 4). However, knowledge acquired by scholars in the Middle East did not reach Western scholars until the 12th century, and the latter probably did not become aware of linguistic contributions by the former until the 16th century.

During the 19th century, it was primarily colonial officers and missionaries who made the most important contributions to our understanding of African languages. The details of these various contributions cannot be discussed here for reasons of space. It is important to realize, however, that the early colonial encounter had far-reaching consequences for the conceptualization of linguistic boundaries and ethnolinguistic groupings in the 20th century, and even today, as shown by Irvine (2008).

One of the most prominent contributors to our knowledge of the language map of Africa from this early period was Sigismund Wilhelm Koelle, a German missionary working in the (then) British colony of Sierra Leone, which, like the neighboring country Liberia, had become a home for liberated slaves originating from all over West Africa and the hinterland of the Congo empire. Koelle applied a large-scale comparison of basic vocabulary (which is less likely to be borrowed between languages) and grammatical features of more than 150 African languages, a method that has come to be known as multilateral or mass comparison, the results of which were published in Koelle (1854). This method usually allows accidental similarities in a few words between a small number of languages, which are of no significance historically, to be identified.

Much of the subsequent historical-comparative work on African languages during the 19th century and the early 20th century became marred with racist connotations, also mixing up (from a modern perspective) genetic and typological classifications. The name "Hamito-Semitic," for example, had come to be used for a language family comprising Ancient Egyptian, Berber, Cushitic and Semitic, but the term "Hamite" was also used as a racial term for a type viewed primarily as Caucasoid. Lepsius (1880) distinguished between Hamitic and Semitic languages, as languages of the so-called Northern Zone, with suffixes and gender distinctions, and Bantu, constituting a so-called Southern Zone, using prefixes. Bantu languages were assumed to represent an original stage, whereas languages of the so-called Middle Zone were assumed to be a mixture of Bantu and Hamitic languages, so-called "Mixed-Negro languages." This Middle Zone contained "proto-African" languages and infiltrating Asian languages, but also "Bushman" and "Hottentot," according to Lepsius.

One of the most eminent linguists and anthropologists of the 20th century, the late Joseph H. Greenberg (1915–2001), who had written a doctoral dissertation on the pre-Islamic religion of the Hausa at Northwestern University (USA), took their language, whose genetic classification had played a prominent role in the debate on African languages and their genetic affiliations, as a basis for a fundamental reorientation of the field as it had developed during the roughly 70 years before his innovative contributions. Greenberg presented an initial critical assessment of earlier classifications of African languages in a set of articles between 1949 and 1954, which were published as a monograph in 1955. Based primarily on mass comparison as a method, Greenberg (1955: 101) hypothesized the following sixteen distinct genetic groups:

1   Niger-Congo
2   Songhay
3   Central Sudanic
4   Central Saharan
5   Eastern Sudanic
6   Afroasiatic
7   Click
8   Maban
9   Mimi (of Nachtigal)
10 Fur
11 Temainian
12 Kordofanian
13 Koman
14 Berta
15 Kunama
16 Nyangiya

The label "Afroasiatic" in Greenberg's (1955) classification replaced "Hamito-Semitic," which should be abandoned, according to him, because of its racist connotations and also because the Semitic languages do not occupy any special place in the larger "Hamito-Semitic" complex. In his follow-up study (Greenberg 1963), these sixteen families were grouped into four macro-families or phyla (also referred to as stocks), Afroasiatic, Khoisan, Niger-Kordofanian, and Nilo-Saharan, not in a desire to lump together formerly independent families, as some of his critics have argued, but instead based on the judicious evaluation of the available morphological and lexical evidence.

As may be expected, research by a range of scholars over the past decades has led to the identification of further languages and a reclassification of some of the groups. Table 2.1 summarizes these reactions to Greenberg (1963); for further details, the interested reader is referred to Dimmendaal (2011: 1–8, 75–81, 307–331).

In more recent historical-comparative work on the genetic classification of African languages, as summarized in Table 2.1, it is assumed by different scholars that the genetic picture of languages on the African continent is more diverse than hypothesized by Greenberg (1963). As pointed out by Schadeberg (1989: 72), for example, the noun-class system of Mba (classified as "Eastern" and forming a sub-branch with "Adamawa" within Greenberg's Niger-Kordofanian phylum) manifests formal similarities with noun classes in Niger-Congo subgroups such as Benue-Congo, Kordofanian and Oti-Volta. But other subgroups of Greenberg's Eastern group (renamed Ubangian in later studies) do not match well grammatically or lexically with the core of Niger-Congo, and are better treated as independent groups (Dimmendaal 2011: 319–320).

Some scholars also prefer to treat some of the languages listed in Greenberg (1963) as members of the four major African language families as linguistic isolates. For example, Gumuz and the more recently discovered language Daats'iin, spoken in Ethiopia, may be the last representatives of an African language family that has otherwise become extinct, rather than being members of the Koman group within Nilo-Saharan, as Greenberg (1963: 130) hypothesized.

Gerrit J. Dimmendaal

Table 2.1 Current views on genetic diversity in Africa

Greenberg (1963)	Disputed affiliations

Afroasiatic
    Ancient Egyptian
    Berber
    Chadic
    Cushitic
    Semitic
	• The Western Cushitic branch of Cushitic is now called Omotic, and widely held to be an independent branch of Afroasiatic.
	• Some authors have disputed the genetic affiliation of the so-called Eastern Branch within Omotic to this Afroasiatic branch.

Khoisan
    Northern Khoisan
    Central Khoisan
    Southern Khoisan
    Hadza
    Sandawe
	• Northern Khoisan, Central Khoisan and Southern Khoisan constitute three independent families whose possible historical relationship can no longer be proven, according to Khoisan specialists.
	• Central Khoisan probably forms a genetic unit with Kwadi (a virtually extinct language in Angola) and Sandawe (spoken in Tanzania).
	• Hadza is widely held to be a linguistic isolate.

Niger-Kordofanian
    Niger-Congo
    West Atlantic
    Mande
    Gur
    Kwa
    Benue-Congo
    Adamawa-Eastern
    Kordofanian
	• The name Niger-Kordofanian has been replaced by Niger-Congo (a name first used by Greenberg in 1955, who hypothesized in his 1963 classification that Niger-Congo forms a genetic unit with Kordofanian).
	• Part of Greenberg's Kwa ("Eastern Kwa" languages) has been regrouped as Benue-Congo.
	• Atlantic (Greenberg's West Atlantic) may be an areal grouping consisting of distantly related Niger-Congo branches; this applies in particular to the Bidjogo group.
	• Kordofanian probably consists of two distantly related Niger-Congo families (Katloid-Rashad and Talodi-Heiban); the genetic position of the fifth group, Lafofa, is not clear.
	• Kadu is an independent family rather than a subgroup within Kordofanian.
	• Dogon is an independent family.
	• Ijaw plus Defaka are an independent language family rather than a subgroup within Benue-Congo.
	• Mande is an independent language family.
	• Ubangian (= Eastern) is an independent language family (with the exception of the Mba group, which is probably part of Niger-Congo).

Nilo-Saharan
    Songhai
    Saharan
    Maban
    Fur
    Chari-Nile
    Coman
	• Songhay (Greenberg's Songhai) is an independent language family.
	• Mimi of Decorse is a linguistic isolate (instead of a language belonging to the Maban branch).
	• Mimi of Nachtigal is a linguistic isolate (instead of a language belonging to the Maban branch).
	• Koman (Greenberg's Coman) is an independent language family.
	• Kadu (a subgroup of Greenberg's Kordofanian) may be a Nilo-Saharan subgroup or an independent family.

This also applies to Hadza and other linguistic isolates, several of which were not known to the scientific community at the time Greenberg (1963) published his classification; they are listed in Table 2.2. It should be kept in mind that the status of these languages in terms of their genetic classification is not the same in all cases. Whereas a language such as Laal (in Chad)

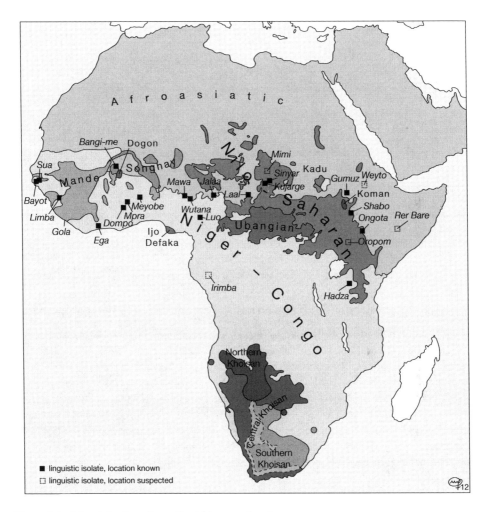

Figure 2.1 Linguistic diversity on the African continent

still has speakers and is relatively well studied, Oropom is known only from a short wordlist published by Wilson (1970), when there were still a few older people who remembered words from this language, which has since become extinct.

Linguists working on languages of the Americas or Asia have wondered why Africa manifests little genetic diversity compared with these other regions. In view of the fact that Africa is the continent from which modern human beings originated and spread successfully over the world – presumably as a result of their ingenious communication system, language – this apparent lack of diversity would seem to be somewhat surprising. However, with probably over twenty isolates and (at least) twelve distinct families (phyla), the total number of families exceeds thirty. Consequently, the linguistic map of Africa is not all that different in terms of genetic diversity (and corresponding typological disparity) from what can be observed elsewhere in the world, at least according to the present author.

While mass comparison results in initial hypotheses about genetic relationships, languages assumed to be related may be compared in order to investigate systematic changes between them by applying the comparative method.

Table 2.2 Linguistic isolates

Bangi Me (Mali)	Limba (Sierra Leone, Guinea)
Bayot (Senegal)	Mawa (Nigeria)
Dompo (Ghana)	Meyobe (Benin, Togo)
Ega (Ivory Coast)	Mimi of Decorse (Chad)
Gola (Liberia, Sierra Leone)	Mimi of Nachtigal (Chad)
Gomba (Ethiopia)	Ongota (Ethiopia)
Gumuz (Ethiopia, Sudan)	Mpra (Ghana)
Hadza (Tanzania)	Oropom (Kenya, Uganda)
Irimba (Gabon)	Rer Bare (Ethiopia)
Jalaa (Nigeria)	Shabo (Ethiopia)
Kujarge (Chad)	Sinyar (Chad)
Laal (Chad)	Sua (Guinea Bissau)
Luo (Nigeria)	Weyto (Ethiopia)
	Wutana (Nigeria)

The comparative method and structural properties of language change

Towards the middle of the 19th century, missionaries had started their work in various parts of East Africa. But the first full-scale descriptions of languages belonging to what is called the Nilotic language family today did not appear until the second half of the 19th century, when missionaries began to study the languages spoken in (what is now) South Sudan and neighbouring countries in an attempt to replace Nilotic spirits and gods by the Roman Catholic Trinity. Nilotic formed a subgroup within Eastern Sudanic in Greenberg (1955: 89–94), which in turn formed a genetic unit with Central Sudanic, Berta and Kunama, called the Chari-Nile branch within Nilo-Saharan, in Greenberg (1963). The history of Nilotic studies again shows how, during the 19th and 20th centuries, the genetic classification of African languages became marred by racist connotations.

Greenberg (1955: 62) hypothesized an Eastern Sudanic family as one of sixteen African language families, as described above. Eastern Sudanic in turn comprised nine groups, among them "Nilotic" and "Great Lakes." The name "Great Lakes" was used by Greenberg in order to avoid a label that had come to be used by other scholars, and also in anthropological studies, namely "Nilo-Hamitic." The term "Hamitic" in the name was reminiscent of Meinhof (1912), *Die Sprachen der Hamiten* (*The Languages of the Hamites*), in which the "Great Lakes" language Maasai was taken as an example illustrating language mixing. According to Meinhof (1912: 211–225), Maasai as a language with gender distinctions (masculine versus feminine nouns) was an ancient "pre-Hamitic" language influenced by "Sudanic" languages (the latter corresponding to Lepsius' Middle Belt). Greenberg (1955) was probably unaware of an unpublished dissertation by Köhler (1948), written under the direction of an influential Africanist in his days, Dietrich Westermann, in which the languages resumed under "Nilotic" and "Great Lakes" were all referred to as "Nilotic." Köhler (1948) divided Nilotic into a Western branch (Greenberg's "Nilotic"), and Eastern and Southern branches (corresponding to Greenberg's "Great Lakes"), a tripartite division still adhered to by modern specialists on this family. Data from these languages are used below to illustrate some basics of the comparative method (Table 2.3). The following cognates from four languages belonging to the Eastern Nilotic branch are examples of lexical roots reconstructed with an initial voiceless velar stop for Proto-Eastern Nilotic, using the comparative method, by Vossen (1982: 450–453).[1]

Historical linguistics in an African context

Table 2.3 Lexical cognates in Eastern Nilotic

Proto-Eastern Sudanic (Vossen 1982)	Bari	Lotuxo	Maasai	Turkana
*-kɔkɔ- 'steal'	-kɔkɔ-	-xoxo-	-	-kɔkɔ-
*-kʊt 'blow'	kʊt	-xʊt	-kʊt	-kʊt
*-kʊdɪ 'armpit'	kʊ-kʊdɪ	-kʊdɪ-	-kitikit-	-kɪrdɪdɪ
*ko-ri 'giraffe'	kuri-	-kori	-	-kori
*kʊɛɲ 'bird'	kwɛn	-xɛɲ	-kwen-	-kɛɲ(ɪ)
*-kɔr 'chicken'	-kor-	-xɔxɔr	-	-kɔkɔr-
*kɛ-wardʸ-e, *kuardʸ-e 'night'	k-waj-	-	-kɛ-wari-	-kwaar(ɪ)
*k	k-	k-, x-	k-	k

The investigation of correspondences between lexical roots belonging to open classes allows one to investigate the question of how regular these correspondences are. The root-initial velar stop in the cognate forms above, for example, can be reconstructed in more than seventy nominal and verbal roots going back to the earliest stages of Eastern Nilotic, as shown by Vossen (1982). The root for 'blow' in these Eastern Nilotic languages is cognate with roots attested in Southern Nilotic (for example -*kʊʊt* in Päkoot) and Western Nilotic (for example -*kʊʊt*in Anywa), and can be reconstructed for their common ancestor, Proto-Nilotic (Dimmendaal 1988: 33). Lexical roots like the one for 'armpit' even predate Nilotic. A cognate form occurs in Surmic (which, like Nilotic, belongs to the Eastern Sudanic branch of Nilo-Saharan in Greenberg's 1963 classification), e.g., Murle *kidikidik*. In fact, this root is widespread across Nilo-Saharan, and found in distantly related languages like the Saharan language Dazaga (Tubu) in Chad, *kilikili* (Dimmendaal 1988: 31).

The comparative method involves not only the identification of lexical and grammatical morphemes that are similar in form and corresponding in meaning, as with mass comparison, but also the identification of regular correspondences between the consonants, vowels (and tones, if present) of cognate morphemes, as in the lexical roots above. (The case of Lotuxo is not further discussed here; the interested reader is referred to Vossen 1982 for further details.)

Such regularities between cognate morphemes in genetically related languages were first established for Indo-European languages by the so-called Neogrammarians in the 19th century, when the concept of the phoneme was not yet in use. They are therefore traditionally referred to as "sound correspondences," but from a modern perspective we are looking at "phoneme correspondences." Nevertheless, information about the phonetic realization of these phonemes is important from a historical-comparative point of view as well. The phoneme /k/ in the Eastern Nilotic language Turkana, for example, is pronounced as a uvular stop (or uvular fricative in fast speech) when adjacent to the vowels /a/ or /ɔ/, and is the result of a merger with a historically distinct phoneme, *q (Dimmendaal 1988: 20), which shifted to and merged with */k/ in Turkana.

Why do these so-called Eastern Nilotic languages form a genetic unit in contrast to other Nilotic languages to begin with? Subgrouping is based on the notion of shared innovations, which may be lexical, phonological or morphological in nature. Thus, Vossen (1982), in his comparative study of Eastern Nilotic languages, arrives at the following subgrouping:

Gerrit J. Dimmendaal

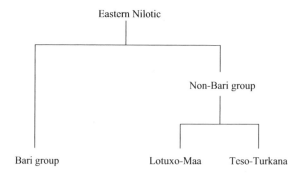

Figure 2.2 The subclassification of Eastern Nilotic languages (Vossen 1982)

The more numerous and the more idiosyncratic identical changes in two or more related languages are, the less likely it is that these occurred independently in these languages. For example, cognate roots for the verb 'steal' in Eastern Nilotic (reconstructed as *-kɔkɔ- by Vossen 1982: 428, i.e., with a partially reduplicated stem) elsewhere in Nilotic show a final lateral, for example *kwal-* in Western Nilotic Acholi. In other cognate roots, final *l* in Eastern Nilotic corresponds to final *l* in Western Nilotic, for example in the common Nilotic root 'compensate, reimburse' *ɪ-col*, which has a reflex *cool* in Western Nilotic Anywa, and *-ɪcol* in Eastern Nilotic Turkana (see Dimmendaal 1988 for further details on common Nilotic roots). In other words, an irregular (and thereby idiosyncratic) change occurred in the verbal root for 'steal' in Eastern Nilotic, which makes it particularly significant for subgrouping. (The final *l* is still found in corresponding nominalized forms, as in Turkana ɛ-*kɔkɔl-an(ɪ)* 'thief'.) The claim that so-called Eastern Nilotic languages form a genetic unit is supported by other shared innovations, such as the formal distinction between masculine and feminine gender as an inflectional property of nouns (which does not occur in Western or Southern Nilotic languages), as well as the use of a causative prefix *-ɪta* with main verbs. Vossen (1982: 224–322) presents a range of additional phonological, lexical and grammatical innovations all pointing towards subgrouping of Eastern Nilotic languages as represented in Figure 2.2.

The application of the historical-comparative method to language families in different parts of the world over the past century has resulted in an inventory of common ("natural") sound changes, such as the intervocalic fricativization of stops, as in the examples from the Eastern Nilotic language Lotuxo in Table 2.3 above, which has parallels in Germanic languages; compare English *eat* or *let* with German *essen* or *lassen*. The cyclical nature of sound change and the role played by both the speaker and the hearer in the reinterpretation of phonological systems is discussed in more detail in Dimmendaal (2011: 23–58).

Vossen (1997) applies the comparative method to Central Khoisan languages and shows that regular sound correspondences and regular sound changes in cognate lexical roots also apply to sounds that are universally rare, such as clicks.[2] For example, the palatal click *ǂ in Proto-Central Khoisan lost its palatal influx in the East-Khoe sub-branch (for example in Deti) and became *c*, as the following three basic vocabulary words (from a set of seventeen cognate lexical roots) illustrate, while the original click *ǂ was retained elsewhere in Central Khoisan, for example in !Ora.

(1) *≠ao 'heart' >≠áó (!Ora)
 > càó (Deti)

  *≠ui 'nose' ≠úí (!Kora)
 > cúí (Deti)

  *≠ã 'enter, insert' >≠ã̀ (!Ora)
 > cã̌ (Deti)

While Greenberg (1963) hypothesized, on the basis of mass comparison, that Central Khoisan, together with Northern and Southern Khoisan, is part of a larger family (or phylum) labelled Khoisan (which replaced the earlier name "Click"), specialists on these languages never accepted his hypothesis. As pointed out by Traill and Nakagawa (2000), for example, extensive borrowing rather than shared inheritance from a common ancestor can explain lexical similarities between Northern and Southern Khoisan languages. Grammatical (function) morphemes tend to be less subject to borrowing (although basically any element may be borrowed from another language), but there is little bound morphology to go by for historical comparisons and the search for cognates in the case of Khoisan languages (as an areal rather than a genetic grouping).

Güldemann and Elderkin (2010) established regular correspondences between Central Khoisan and Kwadi, a language that was assumed to be extinct for several decades, but which is apparently still spoken by a few elderly women in Angola. Their lexical and grammatical reconstructions show interesting formal similarities to the person-number-gender markers, demonstrative system and verbal morphology of Sandawe (a language spoken in Tanzania and also classified as a Khoisan member by Greenberg 1963), thus pointing towards a common genetic origin.

Readers might think that by combining "bottom-up" approaches (by applying the comparative method to well-defined families) and "top-down" approaches (mass comparison), the two may eventually converge, thereby resulting in a clear-cut picture of the genetic classification of African languages. But this is not very likely to happen in the near future, as scholars disagree on what counts as sufficient evidence for the establishment of genetic relationships between languages; see the discussions in Campbell and Poser (2008) for further details.

Language-internal alternation for one and the same morpheme in different morphosyntactic environments may also be used for the reconstruction of earlier forms in a particular language. This so-called internal reconstruction is often used as a complementary method to the comparative method. For example, the idiosyncratic loss of root-final *l in the verb root 'steal', *-kɔkɔ-, in Eastern Nilotic (mentioned above as a shared innovation) may be compared with corresponding nominalized forms where the original *l was retained (as in the Turkana example above). This enables one to reconstruct an original (partially reduplicated) form *-kɔkɔl.

Internal reconstruction may also be applied in order to reconstruct older grammatical features of languages, for example on the basis of inflectional or derivational processes that are no longer productive in a particular language, as these tend to reflect formerly productive alternations; see Dimmendaal (2011: 141–151) for additional discussion and examples.

Languages may differ dramatically in terms of their morphological complexity, as variation within the Nilotic family shows. Much of what is expressed by means of internal morphology in the Dinka-Nuer-Atuot cluster within Western Nilotic, for example, is expressed by means of suffixation elsewhere in Nilotic. While it is common in African languages to transfer the tone of bound grammatical morphemes – particularly suffixes – onto lexical stems, Dinka and the closely related languages Atuot and Nuer also transferred vocalic and consonantal features of suffixes, with subsequent loss of the suffixes, thereby giving rise to a rather complex system of internal (vertical) morphology. While areal contact with typologically different languages is the most common cause for dramatic restructuring processes in languages, the historical source in the case of the Dinka-Nuer-Atuot cluster remains a mystery.

Andersen (2014) gives the following cognate roots and number suffixes for Dinka and Surkum (which belongs to another subgroup within Western Nilotic, the Burun cluster) for nouns referring to paired items, groups, or mass nouns. Such nouns commonly take a singulative suffix in Surkum and numerous other Nilotic and Nilo-Saharan languages, but are marked through internal (vertical) morphology in Dinka.

	Dinka		**Surkum**		
	singulative	plural	singulative	plural	
(2)	wâ̰ar	wä̰r	wár-á̱t	wár	'shoe'
	rjɛ̰́ɛm	rǐm	rím-á̱t	rím	'blood'
	lḛ̂ec	lḛ̀c	lèg-ì̱t	lɛ́k	'tooth'

As these examples show, the singulative suffix -a̱t and -i̱t (which are both attested as singulative markers in Eastern and Southern Nilotic languages and elsewhere in Nilo-Saharan), as members of closed grammatical sets (number-marking suffixes), were absorbed by the root, thereby causing vowel lengthening and diphthongization in Dinka. It is common in a wide range of Niger-Congo, Nilo-Saharan as well as in neighbouring Afroasiatic languages to use the tongue root and pharynx width in order to produce a phonological distinction between advanced and unadvanced tongue root (ATR) vowels, as in Surkum. Andersen (1990) shows that in Dinka the original Western Nilotic system, with five [-ATR] and five [+ATR] vowels, developed into fourteen breathy and creaky voice vowels ([-ATR] *ɪ, *ɛ, *a, *ɔ, *ʊ > (creaky voice) ḭ, ḛ, ɛ̰, a̰, ɔ̰, o̰, ṵ; [+ATR] *i, *e, *ʌ, *o, *u > (breathy voice) i̤, e̤, ɛ̤, a̤, ɔ̤, o̤, ṳ). Whenever creakiness or breathiness occurred with suffix vowels, these features were transferred as a feature onto the inflected root, as in the examples above.

Along similar lines, erstwhile Nilotic derivational and inflectional suffixes on the verb are expressed through internal morphology in Dinka. Prefixes, on the other hand, are more stable (as is also the case cross-linguistically), as with the Dinka tense-aspect prefix *a-*, which is widespread across Nilotic. Alternatively, increment (incorporation of prefixes and suffixes into the original root) occurs as a morphological innovation in languages, as in English *child-r-en*, whereby the *-r-* represents an old plural suffix, still found as such in Germanic languages like German, e.g., *Kind-er*. The most common morphological changes, however, involve analogy, either an extension by analogy with other forms, or a reduction of variation within paradigms (i.e., analogical levelling), as in English *help* and the corresponding past participle *help-ed* from Old English *helpe/holpen*, which was remodeled as an irregular alternation by analogy with the more frequently used regular and productive alternations for verbs involving suffixation, like *walk/walk-ed*, etc.[3] The interested reader is referred to Dimmendaal (2011: 57–58, 101–109) for a more extensive discussion of morphological restructuring.

Dialectological studies and the areal spreading of innovations

Subclassifications of languages and the corresponding family tree are defined on the basis of (presumed) shared innovations unique to two or more languages, or to dialects of one and the same language before these diverged as separate variants. At the same time, one may observe areal spreading of linguistic innovations between dialects or genetically related languages (as well as unrelated languages, as further discussed in the fifth section below) after they split up. Areal diffusion is also attested in Eastern Nilotic languages, for example. While the Lotuxo group shares several unique innovations with Maa, going back to their common ancestor Proto-Lotuxo-Maa (see Figure 2.1 above), there are also a number of innovations not found in Lotuxo, but attested in Maa and another Eastern Nilotic subgroup, Teso-Turkana, including the loss of geminate consonants and consonant alternation accompanying inflection and derivation, which suggests an areal spreading like a kind of wave across the Teso-Turkana and Maa area through language contact. Lotuxo is geographically closer to the Bari languages in South Sudan, and geminate consonants and consonant alternation are common in this Eastern Nilotic branch.

Areal contact through patterns of multilingualism is an important factor in the spreading of phonological and grammatical innovations, but it may also result in the stabilization of features in language areas (as shown by the spreading of clicks in Southern Africa). Innovations start with individuals and spread across networks defined by social boundaries, giving rise to sociolects, or geographical boundaries, and resulting in dialects, whose boundaries are marked by means of isoglosses.

In the case of the Bantu language Swahili, for example, there is a primary division between northern and southern coastal dialects in Kenya and Tanzania (in line with its historical spreading as a coastal language over the past millennium). This contact language also spread into the African interior from the 19th century onwards. Recent research on these western varieties in the Democratic Republic of the Congo revealed that the dialectal variation coincides with major urban centers in the area, including Lubumbashi, Bukavu, Goma, Kisangani and Bunia. According to Nassenstein and Bose (2016), innovations did not spread like waves over these areas, but started in major cities and then spread from there (suggesting a "gravity model," as suggested for English dialects by Trudgill 1983).

The most dramatic restructuring occurred in Bunia Swahili, where different varieties of Swahili are used by speakers as emblematic features expressing different social identities (Nassenstein and Dimmendaal, to appear).

The variety closest to Standard Swahili as spoken in Kenya and Tanzania may be referred to as the acrolectal variety, and the variety at the other end of the continuum, which deviates most strongly from Standard Swahili, may be called the basilectal variety, the label mesolect referring to intermediate forms in the continuum. The basilectal variety of Bunia Swahili is structurally similar to neighbouring Central Sudanic languages, in that it has nine vowels with ATR-harmony instead of five, and tone as a prosodic feature instead of stress, as in Standard Swahili. Like in neighbouring Central Sudanic languages, shortened forms of the independent pronouns are used in Bunia Swahili as proclitic subject markers on the verb (Nassenstein and Dimmendaal, to appear), hence *mi-* (from *mimi* 'I, me') instead of the Standard Swahili prefix *ni-*. Moreover, number marking (expressed by means of noun-class alternations) only occurs for animate nouns in the basilect.

(3) mi=li-uza   ki-tu   mingi
     1SG-PAST-buy   thing(s)   many
     'I bought many things'

Compare the acrolectal variety of Bunia Swahili (which is identical with Standard Swahili):

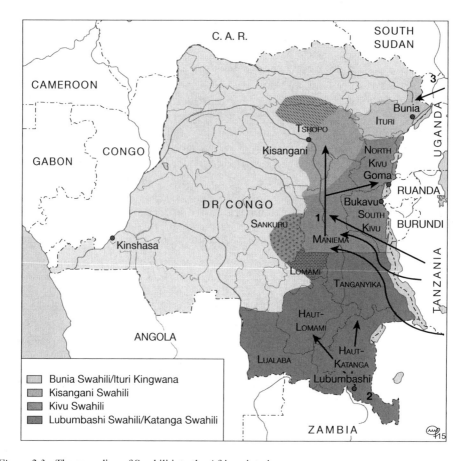

Figure 2.3 The spreading of Swahili into the African interior

(4) ni-li-uza   vi-tu   vy-ingi
    1SG-PAST-buy   CL8-thing   CL8-many
    'I bought many things'

In this respect, basilectal Bunia Swahili resembles northern Bantu languages in the Democratic Republic of Congo, such as Bila, which also borders on Central Sudanic languages. Kutsch Lojenga (2003) shows how the seven-vowel system of Proto-Bantu changed into a nine-vowel system with ATR-based vowel harmony in Bila. For example, the common final vowel -*a* of verb infinitives in Bantu now harmonizes with the root vowel (data from Kutsch Lojenga 2003):

(5) mɪɗ-á   'to swallow'   més-ó   'to put upright'

The "classical" noun-class system (with class prefixes that are common in Bantu, and which probably go back to the earlier stages of Niger-Congo, the family to which Bantu belongs) has also been reduced to a system whereby only animate nouns have separate singular and plural forms in Bila. Other nouns contain a non-alternating prefix *a-*, *amá-* (with variants), *àpà-* (with variants), a homorganic nasal or other petrified prefixes.

Historical linguistics in an African context

(6) N-kpá   ɓa-kpá   'man, person/men, persons'
      kondó   kondó   'tail(s)'

This restructuring in Bila probably resulted from shift-induced interference when speakers of Central Sudanic were incorporated into the Bila speech community and transferred features from their former primary languages into the new dominant (Bantu) language. As the cases of Bila and the pidginized (basilectal) variety of Bunia Swahili show, two distinct social processes gave rise to the same kind of historical restructuring of these languages. However, whereas the use of the basilectal (as against the mesolectal or acrolectal) variety of Swahili functions as an emblematic feature in the negotiation of social identities, there is no such indexed meaning involved in the daily use of northern Bantu languages with an impoverished morphology like Bila.

Other language contact phenomena

When linguists started investigating variation between dialects of different Indo-European languages at the end of the 19th century, it became clear that language change can be rather complex, and that innovations sometimes spread like waves from prestigious, focal areas towards other so-called transitional zones, without necessarily affecting relic or marginal areas. In addition, research on contact phenomena between Romance and Germanic languages in Europe, as well as the restructured varieties of these Indo-European languages as spoken in the Caribbean, showed that most languages are influenced by other languages in their historical development. One of the first scholars to point towards the importance of language contact for our understanding of language change was Hugo Schuchardt (1842–1927), who claimed that all languages are "mixed."

Today, we know that borrowing involves not only the transfer of lexicon (including basic vocabulary and thereby often new phonemes) and grammatical morphemes, but also structural borrowing, i.e., the borrowing of semantic concepts (including idioms) or constructions without borrowing the actual morpheme(s). For example, the Western Nilotic language Luo (spoken in western Kenya and neighbouring regions in Tanzania and Uganda) has borrowed extensively from neighbouring Bantu languages, sometimes referred to by the common ethnonym "Suba" (examples from Tucker 1994: 133):

(7) mɪ-hɪa   wa-hɪa   'child/children'
      mɪ-soŋgʊ   wa-suŋge   'European/Europeans'

In addition, Luo speakers have reinterpreted the first member of (former) lexical compounds as a noun-class prefix by analogy with the structure of borrowed Bantu nouns (Dimmendaal 2011: 193–196).

(8) dho-lúô   'the Luo language (< dhok- 'mouth')'
      ja-lúô   'Luo person (< jal 'guest, stranger')'

Structural borrowing from Bantu in the Nilotic language Luo can also be observed in the verb system. Unlike other Western Nilotic languages, Luo expresses a tense distinction on the verb between events happening earlier today, yesterday, a few days ago, and long ago (as also found in neighbouring Bantu languages like Gusii). The actual morphemes (which procliticize onto the verb) are derived from adverbs of time in Luo (Tucker 1994: 276):

(9)	né `nde	> ne-	'earlier today, recently'
	nyó `ro	> nyo-	'yesterday'
	yá `nde	> yand(e)-	'a few days ago'
	néné	> ne-	'long ago'

These structural changes in Luo are most likely due to shift-induced interference, i.e., the interference from the primary language of people speaking a Bantu language while shifting towards a new first language. The shift itself was motivated by the fact that Luo "became a prestige language, being a medium of upward social mobility, synonymous with modernization, also under the influence of colonial rule" (Dimmendaal 2011: 194).

Alternatively, such dramatic restructuring may come about in a situation where speakers maintain their first language (as an emblematic feature of their distinct social identity). However, due to the frequent use of another (intra)language, in a process referred to as metatypy, the first language is gradually restructured as a result of lexical and grammatical borrowing, and also of "calquing" or structural borrowing. Dimmendaal (2011: 197–199, 359–365) describes a case of metatypy in the Surmic (Nilo-Saharan) language Baale in southwestern Ethiopia, whose speakers consider themselves to be ethnically "Suri" or "Surma," like the neighbouring Tirma and Chai, whose language the Baale speak as a second language. This strong influence has resulted in the borrowing of basic vocabulary from Tirma and Chai into Baale (Yigezu 2005).

From a methodological point of view, it is useful to distinguish between borrowing with maintenance of the primary language, and shift-induced interference involving language shift, even if this is not always easy, especially at deeper historical levels. For example, Ethiopian Semitic languages strongly converged towards distantly related Cushitic and Omotic languages in the area in terms of their sound structures (e.g., the loss of pharyngeals and the innovation of ejectives) and grammar (involving a shift from a verb-initial towards a verb-final structure, from prepositional to predominantly postpositional, and including idioms or metaphors). Only in-depth studies of the nature of social interactions in the area, and more specifically of marriage patterns and language ideologies, can help to clarify the nature of convergence patterns in such cases.

In social contexts where speakers of a range of different languages meet and feel the need to develop an emergency language in order to be able to communicate with each other, a pidginized (simplified) variety of a language may emerge as a contact medium, as with varieties of Dutch, English, French or Spanish in the Caribbean, which are typically associated with Western expansion and colonialism from the 15th century onwards. But this is not the only social historical context where such emergency languages have evolved. Juba Arabic, for example, developed from pidginized Arabic as a contact medium after 1820 (alongside Nubi and Turku Arabic), when soldiers of the Khediv of Egypt, Muhammed Ali, were recruited for the army from (what is now) Sudan and South Sudan. Today, Juba Arabic is the main lingua franca of South Sudan. As Manfredi and Petrollino (2013) point out, in actual fact Juba Arabic forms a socio-linguistic continuum with Standard Sudanese Arabic, and there are no discrete boundaries between acrolectal and basilectal varieties, since Juba Arabic speakers are involved in a socio-linguistic continuum with a high degree of morphophonological variation.

The basilectal variety of Juba Arabic, i.e., the lect deviating most extensively from Standard Sudanese Arabic, has lost the Arabic pharyngeal consonants and gender marking on nouns, and no pronominal subject marking by way of suffixes on the verb occurs, contrary to Standard Sudanese Arabic.

(10) ana   kasuru bab
      1SG   break door

'I broke the door down'

Apart from the passive, there are no valency-increasing or decreasing devices in Juba Arabic, speakers using periphrastic constructions instead. But unlike Standard Sudanese Arabic, stress displacement from the first to the second syllable of a verb is an exponent of passive marking in Juba Arabic (Manfredi and Petrollino 2013: 61).

(11) john   kutú   geni   fi   sijin   (ma   jes)
      John   put:PASS   stay   in   prison   with   army

'John was imprisoned (by the army)'

Strongly reduced morphological structures are one manifestation of pidginization, but whether "pidgins" and "creoles" indeed form a unique brand of languages with their own grammatical properties, as claimed for example by Bakker et al. (2011), or whether they are genetic "orphans", as claimed by Thomason and Kaufman (1988), is a matter of dispute.[4] Like other authors (e.g., DeGraf 2005 and Mufwene 2001), the present author has argued against "exceptionalism" for this type of language contact (Dimmendaal 2011: 230–236), claiming instead that such classifications result from "the colonial gaze" on the spreading of Indo-European languages in colonial times. Pidginization and creolization come by degrees (depending on the sociolinguistic contexts in which they emerge), and whether such changes are gradual or occur in a saltatory manner is irrelevant for genetic classification.

A third type of language emerging in contact situations involves what some authors like to call "mixed languages." As most languages are mixed (i.e., influenced by other languages through contact), the present author prefers to refer to these as syncretic (or intertwined) languages. These tend to develop in newly created communities of practice among formerly distinct communities with rather different cultural backgrounds, such as Mednyj Aleut, as spoken by the offspring of Russian seal hunters in the Aleut region between Siberia and Alaska, where they married Aleut women during the 19th century. Patrick McConvell's in-depth investigation of another syncretic language, Gurindji Kriol in Australia, over several decades, shows that codeswitching (or codemixing) plays an important role in the "making" of such languages; see McConvell and Meakins (2005) for a description.

Within an African context, Songhay lects, strongly influenced by Berber languages such as Tadaqsahek (spoken in Mali and Algeria), probably constitute cases of language syncretism. Souag (2015) describes the sociohistorical context in which this language developed, and shows the strong influence from Berber languages, for example in its voice system, where the causative and passive forms of a range of verbs are virtually identical to the Tamasheq or Tamajeq Berber forms (Table 2.4 examples from Souag 2015: 127):

Table 2.4 Causative and passive forms in Tadaqsahek and Berber

Verb	*Causative in Tadaqsahek*	*Causative in Tamasheq (preterite, aorist)*	*Causative in Tamajeq (aorist)*
enlarge bér	š-ámɣar	-əss -əmɣar-, s-əmɣər	s-əmɣər
be placed keení	š-inšá	-əss-ənsa-, s-ans	s-ansu

Just as creolized languages may decreolize (i.e., converge to the matrix language from which they derived historically), syncretic languages may converge towards the matrix language providing their structural framework, as the cases of the Indo-Aryan language Romani and an African parallel, Ma'a in Tanzania, show. Romani spread across Europe over the past thousand years as the language of people who are popularly stereotyped as "gypsies." During this migration, its speakers, who call themselves Roma (or sometimes Sinti), also switched to Basque, English, Norwegian, Spanish, or other languages for their daily communication. However, as stigmatized groups, they also felt the need to incorporate lexicon and grammar from Romani in order to exclude non-Roma. As a result, syncretic languages like Anglo-Romani in Great Britain were created. Matras et al. (2009) describe this gradual shift from the former primary language Romani to an English-inflected Romani, with English-based predications with a Romani-derived lexicon gradually prevailing.

A parallel process appears to have taken place in the Bantu language Mbugu (also known as Ma'a) in Tanzania. Mous (2003) shows that there is "Normal Mbugu" (similar to neighbouring Bantu languages) and "Inner Mbugu," which manifests strong influence from Cushitic (and, to a lesser extent, Nilotic) in its register. Sources from the beginning of the 20th century show that "Inner Mbugu" contained more features from Cushitic, not only lexically but also grammatically. Today, Mbugu (like modern Anglo-Romani) is characterized by paralexification, or the co-existence of two lexicons, as Mous (2003) calls this phenomenon.

	Inner Mbugu	Normal Mbugu	
(12)	húti	zuja	'to fill'
	hláti	jughua	'to open'

The metaphorical representation of genetic relationships

A language family may be interpreted as a kind of biological organism, whereby the descendants of the ancestral language (or proto-language) constitute daughter languages, as illustrated for Eastern Nilotic above. Higher level genetic units are sometimes referred to as macro-families, phyla or stocks. All three terms have been used in order to refer to larger genetic groupings like Afroasiatic, Niger-Congo or Nilo-Saharan.

Phylogenetic relationships were first represented metaphorically by means of family trees by Indo-Europeanists, in analogy with classificatory techniques used in evolutionary biology. Such family tree representations constitute abstractions, to some extent, because the family tree expresses divergence (as a result of innovations) between genetically related languages. But, as illustrated above, there may also be convergence due to the areal spreading of innovations between genetically related (and unrelated) languages. More recently, such cladistic models have therefore been abandoned by some historical linguists in favour of diagrammatic models expressing reticulation, i.e., the joining of separate lineages on a phylogenetic tree as a result of language contact. A family tree as presented for Eastern Nilotic in Figure 2.2 above may consequently look like Figure 2.4, which is derived from a cladistic representation of Eastern Sudanic (the sub-branch of Nilo-Saharan to which (Eastern) Nilotic belongs), by Schnoebelen (2009).

As a phylogenetic method, the creation of NeighbourNet representations of genetic relationships derives from numerical approximations, themselves based on the counting of cognates (and also taking into account contact phenomena); see McMahon and McMahon (2005) for a detailed and critical discussion.[5] NeighbourNet representations may be useful as complementary metaphorical visualizations of the processes contributing to the present structure

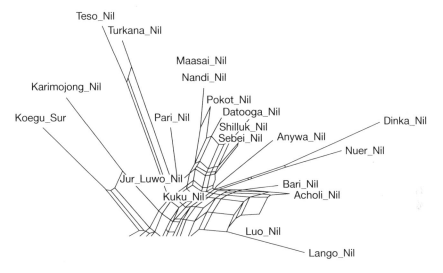

Figure 2.4 NeighbourNet representation of Nilotic based on Schnoebelen (2009)

of a language. But placing an Eastern Nilotic language like Maasai, for example, in a "cloud" with Southern Nilotic languages like Nandi or Pokot (as in Figure 2.4 above), is simply wrong, as careful historical-comparative work shows a clear-cut "family tree" division between the two Nilotic branches, with Maasai sharing a range of unique innovations with Eastern Nilotic languages like Bari, Lotuxo or Turkana, which are not found in Nandi or Päkoot. In a critical assessment of rhizotic models in historical linguistics, Dimmendaal (2011: 276–280) discusses similar problems with respect to the classification of Germanic (i.e., Indo-European) languages like Frisian, which is closely related to English historically (as evidenced by a range of shared innovations), but which is now typologically similar to Dutch as a result of more recent areal contact.

Accretion and spread zones

There is a strikingly uneven geographic distribution of language families across the African continent, as Figure 2.1 illustrates. The three major phyla, Afroasiatic, Niger-Congo and Nilo-Saharan, cover vast areas on the continent, i.e., they constitute expansion zones in the sense of Nichols (1992). These contrast with so-called accretion (or residual) zones, i.e., areas characterized by tremendous genetic and typological diversity, such as the Khoisan area in Southern Africa, the Nigerian "fragmentation belt," the Nuba Mountains in Sudan, and Southwestern Ethiopia. Such uneven distributions raise the question of what the historical dynamics behind language ecology are.

The vast expansion of the Bantu subgroup within Niger-Congo has found a natural explanation in climate change over a first phase of relatively slow and narrow expansion from Cameroon, and a second phase of rapid expansion linked to technological innovations like iron working, as well as changes in the social organization of communities, which allowed agricultural communities to expand rapidly from their original homeland in the Cameroon-Nigeria borderland, according to Bostoen et al. (2015). The same contribution also shows how knowledge from historical linguistics may be integrated with findings from archaeology, botany and genetics in order to reconstruct the cultural history of a specific area.

The vast area covered by pastoralists in Eastern Africa speaking Surmic and Nilotic (i.e., Nilosaharan) languages strongly suggests that the introduction of pastoralism also resulted in the expansion of these two groups, probably also at the expense of other languages or language families, since along the edges and also in the middle of these expansion zones one finds linguistic isolates, such as Ong'ota or Shabo in southern Ethiopia, the last representatives of language families that have otherwise disappeared.

The Nuba Mountains in Sudan, as an accretion zone, involves an area roughly the size of Scotland, with over forty languages belonging to three families, Niger-Congo, Nilo-Saharan and Kadu (assumed by the present author to constitute an independent family). The typological disparity even between genetically related languages in the Nuba Mountains is huge at times. Nilo-Saharan languages in the area belong to the Nubian, Temeinian and Daju groups, which in turn are part of the Eastern Sudanic branch within this phylum. But whereas Nubian languages in the Nuba Mountains are highly tonal with a predominantly verb-final constituent order and extensive case marking, the Daju languages in the same area have a SVO constituent order, no case marking, and at least one member, Daju of Lagowa, has a pitch accent system. Dimmendaal (2015: 25–63) describes this variation in more detail and claims that it is due to the fact that the Nuba Mountains served as a natural refugium for thousands of years, and that its inhabitants tend to be monolingual (Arabic as a lingua franca being a relatively recent phenomenon) while adhering to a "localist" strategy, whereby speaking a distinct language plays a key role.

Nevertheless, there are a few (probably old) typological features that spread between different languages in the Nuba Mountains. Whereas Niger-Congo languages in general tend to be head marking at the clause level (marking the presence of Agent, Patient and other, more peripheral semantic roles on the verb), there is at least one Niger-Congo language in the Nuba Mountains, Moro, with Accusative case (i.e., dependent) marking (as in neighbouring Nubian, i.e., Nilo-Saharan, languages). The following is a Moro example from Ackerman and Moore (2013: 88):

(13) í-g-ʌ-rr-ət̪-ú   káka-ŋ   ŋóreðá
      1SG.SM.CLg-MAIN-pound-APPL$_{BEN}$-PFV   CLg.Kaka-ACC   CLŋ.sesame
      'I pounded sesame for Kaka'

In another Niger-Congo language in the Nuba Mountains, Tima, one finds split ergativity, i.e., a system in which the subject (A-role) of a transitive predication is marked morphologically under specific discourse conditions, but the subject (S-role) of an intransitive predication and the object (P-role) are not. Even more enigmatic is the fact that Tima is radically different from surrounding languages in the Nuba Mountains but typologically similar to Nilo-Saharan languages spoken east and south of the Nuba Mountains, and to Koman (Dimmendaal 2015). Speakers may have followed a localist strategy in their language ideologies (as Tima speakers still like to do), or possibly a distributed strategy. In the latter case, language does not function as an emblematic feature of a distinct social identity; instead, speakers prefer to speak the language of their dominant neighbours (or a close variety thereof) as an adaptive strategy, as is characteristic of pygmoid groups in the forested regions of Central Africa, who speak a Bantu, Central Sudanic or Ubangian language, depending on who their neighbours are.

Some prospects for future research

Tone and vowel harmony in African languages played an important role in the development of phonological theories in the 1980s and 1990s, and continue to play a key role in this respect.

One other area where African languages have played a prolific role within the field of historical linguistics concerns grammaticalization theories, which became a popular topic after the publication of *Grammaticalization: A Conceptual Framework* by Heine, Claudi and Hünnemeyer (1991). The historical development of grammatical morphemes from lexical morphemes, for example of motion verbs like 'go' and 'come' into tense markers, or the functional extension of grammatical morphemes marking space into domains marking time, have been well-known properties of languages for some time now. But the authors of the abovementioned volume claim that grammatical morphemes in general originate from specific grammatical sources and develop into fixed targets. They consequently claim unidirectionality for grammaticalization chains. According to Heine, Claudi and Hünnemeyer (1991: 50), the human body provides a common, convenient vehicle for conceptualizing spatial orientation and, subsequently, temporal orientation, as with the Swahili word *mbele* 'frontside, front part', which is a reflex of Proto-Bantu **m-béede* 'breast, teat'. Its function extended into that of a locative marker ('the front, in front [of]') and temporal marker ('before'), and in this way developed more abstract meanings too.

It is important to keep in mind, as a general principle, that claims about grammaticalization chains have to be supported by empirical evidence, and specifically by applying the comparative method; they cannot simply be assumed on the basis of evidence from the few better-studied language families in the world, not least because more recent research in this domain strongly suggests that there are areal patterns of grammaticalization. (See Dimmendaal 2011: 122–132 for additional critical observations.)

One of the stereotypes of languages on the African continent in the scientific literature is the claim that they constitute "hotbeds" of noun classification or verb extensions. Without denying the inherent interest and importance of these topics, there is so much more to be investigated, including from a historical-comparative point of view. These understudied phenomena (several of which have sometimes been claimed to be absent in African languages) include the historical development of converbs, ergativity, numeral classifiers and object incorporation, to mention but a few topics. More generally, the historical-comparative study of African languages could also make significant contributions to our understanding of language typology and vice versa, as shown, for example, by Ameka and Essegbey (2013) in their innovative survey of verb serialization in West African languages.

Dynamic comparison, involving the integration of historical linguistics and language typology into the study of well-defined language families, would indeed be one desideratum in future studies, as the following example should help to illustrate. Hawkins (2014: 136–183), continuing earlier research along similar lines, argues that there is a cross-linguistic tendency for languages to be consistently head-final or head-initial at the phrasal and clausal level. This presumed "efficiency principle" in terms of processing implies a historical pressure for cross-categorical harmony between phrases (nominal, adpositional, verbal). But when surveying Nilo-Saharan languages with verb-final syntax, one finds no evidence for such a tendency. While distantly related sub-branches like Kunama, Maban, Saharan and Fur are verb-final, noun phrase modifiers tend to follow the head noun in language after language, without any indication that such "mismatches" between head-initial noun phrases and head-final verb phrases are unstable. It is hoped, therefore, that the historical-comparative investigation of morphosyntactic structures in African languages will play an equally important role in our future understanding of language, as their phonetic and phonological structures already do.

There is one further area where future research on African languages will most likely provide interesting new perspectives on language as a dynamic construct co-evolving with culture, including from a historical-comparative point of view, namely multilingualism. In the brief discussion in the fifth section above, some common language contact scenarios were introduced. But, as a result of urbanization, new contact situations are now emerging in multilingual metropoles where "translanguaging" and "codemeshing" are leading to new types of restructuring in languages.

The sheer magnitude in terms of numbers of languages and their complex genetic and typological relations seems to have triggered a widespread scientific desire over the past decades to classify African languages into a few macro families and macro areas. It may now be time to swing the pendulum away from large-scale comparisons and back to the study of lower-level units, as several of these are still awaiting both in-depth genetic and typological comparisons.

Acknowledgements

I would like to express my gratitude to the editors, the anonymous reviewer, as well as Mary Chambers for their questions and critical comments. The help provided by Monika Feinen with the production of the map and the improved quality of the NeighbourNet Graphic is also gratefully acknowledged here.

Abbreviations

APPL	applicative
CL	noun class
BEN	benefactive
MAIN	main clause verb
PASS	passive
PVF	perfective
SG	singular
SM	subject marker

Notes

1 Names like "Turkana" refer primarily to ethnic groups. In actual fact, northern Turkana is different from southern Turkana but almost identical to Toposa, whose speakers claim a separate ethnic identity for themselves (as Turkana people do). Ethnonyms are often taken as bases for linguistic classifications (for example in *Ethnologue*), thereby reflecting 19th-century European (and thereby ethnocentric) conceptualizations of language and social identity.

2 Clicks are an areal feature of three language families treated as a genetic unit, Khoisan, by Greenberg (1963), but as three unrelated families by specialists for these languages: Northern Khoisan, Central Khoisan and Southern Khoisan. In addition, they are found in Hadza and Sandawe (both in Tanzania), as well as in southern Bantu languages and the Cushitic language Dahalo in Kenya.

3 Analogical levelling (or extension) may thus lead to irregular sound changes; other reasons for irregular sound changes involve sporadic change (in words with a high frequency), taboos on the pronunciation of specific words (precluding the extension of otherwise regular sound changes to such words), or the expressive (ideophonic) character of words, which may also result in them being exempted from specific sound changes.

4 Note that this is also the position defended in *Ethnologue* (Lewis et al. 2015), which classifies "pidgins" and "creoles" as languages that are not genetically related to their source languages. For a recent discussion of different types of language contact, the reader is referred to Velupillai (2015).

5 Though based on complex stochastic algorithms, the calculations are similar to lexicostatistics, a method that has become disfavoured because there are numerous counterexamples to its basic premise, that language change tends to be gradual and similar regardless of the social conditions (Dimmendaal 2011: 71–74).

References

Ackerman, Farrell and John Moore 2013. Objects in Moro. In Thilo C. Schadeberg and Roger Blench (eds), *Nuba Mountain Language Studies*, pp. 83–104. Cologne: Rüdiger Köppe.

Ameka, Felix K. and James Essegbey 2013. Serialising languages: satellite-framed, verb-framed or neither. *Ghana Journal of Linguistics* 2(1): 19–38.

Andersen, Torben 1990. Vowel length in Western Nilotic. *Acta Linguistica Hafniensia* 22: 5–26.

Andersen, Torben 2014. Number in Dinka. In Anne Storch and Gerrit J. Dimmendaal (eds), *Number: Constructions and Semantics. Case studies from Africa, Amazonia, India and Oceania*, pp. 221–263. Amsterdam and Philadelphia: John Benjamins.

Bakker, Peter, Aymeric Daval-Markussen, Mikael Parkvall and Ingo Plag 2011. Creoles are typologically distinct from noncreoles. *Journal of Pidgin and Creole Languages* 26(1): 5–42.

Becker, D. 1984. *The Risäla of Judah ben Quraysh: A Critical Edition*. Tel-Aviv University, C'haim Rosenberg School for Jewish Studies.

Blust, Robert A. 2013. *The Austronesian Languages*. Revised edition. Canberra: Research School for Pacific and Asian Studies, Australian National University.

Bostoen, Koen, Bernard List, Charles Doumenge, Rebecca Grollemund, Jean-Marie Hombert, Joseph Koni Muluwa, and Jean Maley 2015. Middle to late holocene paleoclimatic change and the early Bantu expansion in the rain forests of Western Central Africa. *Current Anthropology* 56(3): 354–384.

Campbell, Lyle and William J. Poser 2008. *Language Classification: History and Method*. Cambridge: Cambridge University Press.

DeGraf, Michel F. 2005. Linguists' most dangerous myth: The fallacy of Creole Exceptionalism. *Language in Society* 34(4): 533–591.

Dimmendaal, Gerrit J. 1988. The lexical reconstruction of Proto-Nilotic: A first reconnaissance. *Afrikanistische Arbeitspapiere* 16: 5–67.

Dimmendaal, Gerrit J. 2011. *Historical Linguistics and the Comparative Study of African Languages*. Amsterdam and Philadelphia: John Benjamins.

Dimmendaal, Gerrit J. 2015. *The Leopard's Spots: Essays on Language, Cognition, and Culture*. Leiden: Brill.

Frajzyngier, Zygmunt and Erin Shay (eds) 2012. *The Afroasiatic Languages*. Cambridge: Cambridge University Press.

Greenberg, Joseph Harold 1955. *Studies in African Linguistic Classification*. New Haven, CT: Compass Publishing Co.

Greenberg, Joseph H. 1963. *The Languages of Africa*. Bloomington, IN and The Hague: Indiana University Press, Research Center in Anthropology, Folklore and Linguistics, and Mouton & Co.

Güldemann, Tom and Edward D. Elderkin 2010. On external genealogical relationships of the Khoe family. In Matthias Brenzinger and Christa König (eds), *Khoisan Languages and Linguistics: Proceedings of the 1st International Symposium, January 4–8, 2003, Riezlern/Kleinwalsertal*, pp. 15–52. Cologne: Rüdiger Köppe.

Hawkins, John A. 2014. *Cross-Linguistic Variation and Efficiency*. Oxford: Oxford University Press.

Heine, Bernd, Ulrike Claudi and Friederike Hünnemeyer 1991. *Grammaticalization: A Conceptual Framework*. Chicago, IL: University of Chicago Press.

Irvine, Judith T. 2008. Subjected words: African linguistics and the colonial encounter. *Language & Communication* 28(4): 323–343.

Koelle, Sigismund Wilhelm 1854. *Polyglotta Africana or A Comparative Vocabulary of Nearly Three Hundred Words and Phrases in More than One Hundred Distinct African Languages*. London: Church Missionary House.

Köhler, Oswin 1948. Die südnilotischen Sprachen. Darstellung ihres Lautsystems, nebst einer Einleitung über die Geschichte ihrer Erforschung, ihre Verbreitung und Gliederung. PhD dissertation, University of Berlin.

Kutsch Lojenga, Constance 2003. Bila. In Derek Nurse and Gérard Philippson (eds), *The Bantu Languages*, pp. 450–474. London and New York, NY: Routledge.

Lepsius, Karl Richard 1880. *Nubische Grammatik: Mit einer Einleitung über die Völker und Sprachen Afrikas*. Berlin: Hertz.

Lewis, M. Paul, Gary F. Simons and Charles D. Fennig (eds) 2015. *Ethnologue: Languages of Africa and Europe*. Eighteenth Edition. Dallas, TX: SIL.

Manfredi, Stefano and Sara Petrollino 2013. Juba Arabic. In Susanne Michaelis, Philippe Maurer, Martin Haspelmath and Martin Huber (eds), *The Survey of Pidgin and Creole Languages Vol. III. Contact Languages Based on Languages from Africa, Australia, and the Americas*, pp. 54–65. Oxford: Oxford University Press.

Matras, Yaron, Hazel Gardner, Charlotte Jones and Veronica Schulman 2009. Angloromani: A different kind of language? *Anthropological Linguistics* 49(2): 142–184.

McConvell, Patrick and Felicity Meakins 2005. Gurindji Kriol: A mixed language emerges from code-switching. *Australian Journal of Linguistics* 25: 9–30.

McMahon, April and Robert McMahon 2005. *Language Classification by Numbers*. Oxford: Oxford University Press.

Meinhof, Carl 1912. *Die Sprachen der Hamiten*. Hamburg: Friedrichsen.

Mous, Maarten 2003. *The Making of a Mixed Language: The Case of Ma'a/Mbugu*. Amsterdam: John Benjamins.

Mufwene, Salikoko S. 2001. *The Ecology of Language Evolution*. Cambridge: Cambridge University Press.

Nassenstein, Nico and Paulin Baraka Bose 2016. *Kivu Swahili Texts and Grammar Notes*. Munich: Lincom.

Nassenstein, Nico and Gerrit J. Dimmendaal [To appear]. Bunia Swahili and emblematic language use. Submitted.

Nichols, Johanna 1992. *Linguistic Diversity in Space and Time*. Chicago, IL: University of Chicago Press.

Schadeberg, Thilo C. 1989. Kordofanian. In John Bendor-Samuel (ed.), *The Niger-Congo Languages*, pp. 67–80. Lanham, MD: University Press of America.

Schnoebelen, Tyler 2009. (Un)classifying Shabo: phylogenetic methods and results. In Peter K. Austin, Oliver Bond, Monik Charette, David Nathan and Peter Sells (eds), *Proceedings of Conference on Language Documentation and Linguistic Theory 2*, pp. 275–284. London: SOAS.

Souag, Lameen 2015. Non-Tuareg Berber and the genesis of nomadic Northern Songhay. *Journal of African Languages and Linguistics* 36(1): 121–143.

Thomason, Sarah G. and Terrence Kaufman 1988. *Language Contact, Creolization, and Genetic Linguistics*. Berkeley, CA: University of California Press.

Traill, Anthony and Hirosi Nakagawa 2000. A historical !Xóõ-G|ui contact zone: linguistics and other relations. In H.M. Batibo and J. Tsonope (eds), *The State of Khoesan Languages in Botswana*, pp. 1–17. Mogoditshane and Gaborone: Tasalls Publishing & Books.

Trudgill, Peter 1983. *On Dialect: Social and Geographical Perspectives*. New York, NY: New York University Press.

Tucker, A.N. 1994. *A Grammar of Kenya Luo (Dholuo)*, 2 Volumes. Cologne: Rüdiger Köppe.

Velupillai, Viveka 2015. *Pidgins, Creoles and Mixed Languages: An Introduction*. Amsterdam and Philadelphia: John Benjamins.

Vossen, Rainer 1982. *The Eastern Nilotes: Linguistic and Historical Reconstructions*. Berlin: Dietrich Reimer.

Vossen, Rainer 1997. *Die Khoe-Sprachen: Ein Beitrag zur Erforschung der Sprachgeschichte Afrikas*. Cologne: Rüdiger Köppe.

Wilson, J.G. 1970. Preliminary observations on the Oropom People of Karamoja, their ethnic status, culture, and postulated relation to the peoples of the Late Stone Age. *The Uganda Journal* 34(2): 125–145.

Yigezu, Moges 2005. Convergence of Baale, a Southwest Surmic language, to the Southeast Surmic group: Lexical evidence. *Annual Publications in African Linguistics* 3: 49–66.

3

LINGUISTIC RESEARCH IN THE AFRICAN FIELD

Bruce Connell

Introduction

The inclusion of a chapter on fieldwork in the *Routledge Handbook of African Linguistics* might suggest to some readers a uniqueness in African languages and their multifarious settings that requires adopting a fundamentally different approach to doing linguistic fieldwork than is used in other parts of the world. I don't find this necessarily to be the case; the concerns addressed in numerous textbooks, manuals and anthologies on linguistic fieldwork (e.g., Bowern 2008; Crowley 2007; Newman & Ratliffe 2001; Samarin 1967; Thieberger 2016; Vaux & Cooper 1999; as well as articles too numerous to mention in journals such as *Language Documentation and Conservation*) are, for the most part, equally applicable to the practice of fieldwork on African languages, though with a few notable exceptions their authors are neither Africanists nor have they worked in Africa. (The exceptions include a number of the contributors to Newman & Ratliffe.) It is not my aim in this chapter therefore to recapitulate the content of these sources or that of others referred to below. There are, however, certain aspects of a linguistic situation found often in Africa that, in my view, suggest a particular focus or focusses may be useful or desirable when doing fieldwork in Africa. That is to say, in general and with few exceptions, languages in Africa are underdescribed or, in far too many cases, simply (totally) undescribed. Linguists may know of their existence, or may not. It is still not unusual for a language hitherto unknown to linguists to be 'discovered'. Nigeria, as a case in point, has seen its count of known languages rise from approximately 250 in the 1970s (Hansford et al. 1976), to over 400 in the 1990s (Crozier & Blench 1992), to a recent count of 550 (Blench 2014). Of these 550, Blench reports that for 231 (42 percent) there is *no* available data. This suggests the basic importance of not just collecting wordlists, grammatical paradigms and texts as a starting point in describing a language, but of also discovering exactly what the language is: where it is spoken, who speaks it, when they speak it (and what other languages they speak), what languages it is related to, etc. In other words, whenever such information is not known, a sociolinguistic survey that leads to an understanding of the ecology of the language in question should be part and parcel of fieldwork on the language. Such surveys help to ascertain the basic parameters of a language and its ecology; this is the subject of the second section. Other topics covered that may be somewhat particular to the African context, and their associated research methods, include: aspects of phonetic fieldwork (the third section), especially with respect to tone (the fourth section); consideration of nominal classification (the fifth section); investigation of ideophones (the sixth section); and questions of work on extremely endangered languages (the final section). Overall the approach advocated is largely informed by recent developments in the field of documentary linguistics and a concern for language endangerment. There are no doubt topics that readers may feel should have been discussed; the topics included and the space devoted to each is inevitably to some extent a personal choice. Issues such as how to prepare for fieldwork (e.g., health-related concerns) and appropriate ethical behavior that are well covered in numerous publications, including many of those already mentioned, are not discussed here.

Surveying language knowledge and use

Background

Knowledge and training

The first question that may come to mind is whether one needs specific training in sociolinguistics in order to do survey work. It would seem obvious that a sociolinguist, by dint of his or her training, may be better equipped to prepare and carry out a survey, and afterwards analyze its results. However, anyone who has prepared themselves adequately for their fieldwork in the first place – i.e., taken the time to learn about what they are doing (including having read reports of other survey work), the setting in which they are working (e.g., the cultural background), and especially the people with whom they are working, will be able to design and carry out a survey – though not necessarily on their own – and get useful information from the results. That said, a sociolinguist, or at least a sociolinguist of a certain ilk, may get much more out of survey than others.

The utility of surveys of language knowledge and use

The utility of a survey depends on several factors, among them the questions included, the systematicity with which it is carried out, and the range and number of participants in the survey. Some possible practical uses include the following: first and foremost, valuable information is gained about the linguistic, social and ethnic make up of a community. To the extent that such information is available, it allows for better procedures and better interpretation of data in the more 'strictly linguistic' phases of the fieldwork. Information on how the possible various groups that comprise a community interact is also gained, which, apart from being of interest in its own right, again provides insights that may allow subsequent aspects of the fieldwork to be better conducted. Information concerning language innovation and change, and language shift can also be gleaned; this is of obvious importance when doing fieldwork on a threatened language. More generally, survey results can also be of use to local language committees, government, and non-government agencies, to inform language planning policies, education policy, etc.

Questionnaires

Questionnaires designed to access and ascertain aspects of language knowledge and use are of three general sorts: those that assess the linguistic and general characteristics of a community; those that essentially constitute a language census; and those that look for more detailed information about individuals and their linguistic habits.

The community profile questionnaire

As the name suggests, the community profile questionnaire is intended to give an overall assessment of the linguistic and social setting of the community (see Vossen 1988, 'Village Profile Survey'). It should be conducted prior to individual interviews as information gleaned from it may help to fine-tune the questions included on a survey of individuals. It would normally be conducted with the village head or others knowledgeable of all aspects of the community life, and would seek to answer questions ranging from what ethnicities comprise the village population and what language(s) are in general use or known by the population (are used for education, as a lingua franca, etc.), to questions the answers to which are descriptive of the village; its location, patterns of residence, available amenities, typical occupations of inhabitants, relations with other villages, a brief description of village history, etc.

The household survey

The household survey is like a language census, done door-to-door in the village (or in a representative sample of households). One person responds for the entire household, providing answers to questions pertaining to ethnicity/clan membership (and going back at least one, if not more, generations); village of birth; age of household members; languages spoken (by the respondent, these listed in order of preference and frequency of use); similarly for languages understood but not spoken; languages spoken/known by family members; and a set of questions pertaining to language use, in the home, in the community and in different social settings (Vossen 1988 again provides a sample questionnaire).

The individual survey

The individual survey is similar to the household survey described in the preceding paragraph, though typically more detailed than either the household or village survey and, as its name suggests, its focus is on individuals reporting on their own behavior. It can be done door-to-door or elsewhere that individuals can be interviewed on a systematically sampled basis, for example as a school-based survey (see, e.g., Connell 2015; Schaefer & Egbokhare 1999). It uses a range of age groups or focusses on selected groups. Questions included will aim to solicit personal information (age, sex, religion, occupation, clan, ethnicity); active and passive knowledge of languages; questions pertaining to language use (at home, with parents, siblings, outside the home, in various functional domains); and questions pertaining to attitude. For the latter, answers to specific direct questions can be unreliable, so to get at attitudes toward a language, indirect questions are typically used (e.g., answers to questions such as 'would you like your language to be used for education?', or '. . . to be written?' give an indication as to the respondents' attitudes towards their language); Adegbija (1994) provides discussion of research into language attitudes in sub-Saharan Africa.

Administering a survey

The practice of administering a survey differs somewhat for the different types of survey, first in choosing or selecting participants or respondents. The village profile survey, as mentioned, will usually involve interviewing the village head and/or other knowledgeable members of the community; selection of participants is thus straightforward. For the door-to-door survey (language census), a decision first needs to be made as to how many households to survey; in a small village visiting every household may be feasible, while in larger villages or towns, or where this is for other reasons not possible, either a random sample of households or a targeted section of the population may be used. For school-based surveys, again, one must decide whether to use all the students, or selected classes or age groups. Surveys done in the classroom can be done on paper, with the teacher being available to assist in carrying out the survey.

Pitfalls and problems

Reticence

Reticence or lack of cooperation on the part of the community are possible important problems. People tend naturally to be suspicious of outsiders coming and asking questions, particularly questions of a personal nature. Two strategies can alleviate or ameliorate this; one is to give straightforward and honest reasons as to the rationale behind the survey, recognizing that the rationale may seem distant from the concerns and interests of the community, and to present questions in such a manner that respondents recognize they are under no obligation and are free to decline to answer any particular question. The second is to employ a member of the community itself, ideally someone who is known and respected in the community (and who, by the same token, is well familiar with the community) to assist in carrying out the survey. This not only has the advantage of serving to alleviate suspicions or reticence on the part of community members, but to the extent the assistant is familiar with the people responding, she or he will be able to serve as a check on their answers.

Self-reporting

Questionnaire-based surveys of language knowledge and use involve self-reporting: a method, as discussed, in which participants are asked about, and report, their behavior and/or attitudes concerning the object of research. There are a number of factors that can influence a participant's responses, ranging from their own attitudes to the subject, to forgetfulness, to their mood or being distracted at the time of the investigation. There are various ways (discussed in a substantial literature, e.g., in the disciplines of sociology and psychology) in which the potential negative effects of self-reporting can be mitigated. I mentioned above the desirability of engaging a member of the community itself to conduct or assist in conducting the survey. This may not only have, as mentioned, the benefit of alleviating any suspicions or reticence held by respondents (and at the same time encourage more honest or accurate responses), but a local investigator, in knowing the respondents and their behavior, may also be able to 'challenge' answers he or she thinks may somehow be biased.

A more common way of providing a check on participant responses is use of a follow-up investigation, involving actual observation. Connell (2009) provides one instance, in which data from a survey of the sort described above indicated an age-related difference as to the use of French in a market in rural Cameroon; younger respondents reported greater use of French and older respondents greater use of Fulfulde (as compared with the language of the village). This finding seemed plausible, however a follow-up study, which involved observation of actual language choice/use in the market, revealed no difference between age groups and in fact French was but little used (Fulfulde was used in 42 percent compared with French in 7 percent of transactions). Younger speakers, presumably viewing French as having greater prestige, saw themselves as using it more than they in fact did.

Language in the market

Investigation of language use in market settings, such as that referred to in the previous paragraph, is an interesting means of obtaining information bearing on the multilingual nature of a community, language attitudes, and language shift. Many investigations, such as those conducted in the markets of major urban centers of eight African countries: Mali, Côte d'Ivoire, Togo, Benin, Cameroon, Gabon, Congo, and Zaire (now Democratic Republic of Congo), reported in Calvet (1992), have been questionnaire-based and involve self-reporting. Others have used a form of participant or non-participant observation, in this instance termed 'transaction analysis' in Connell (2009). To my knowledge, the first study of this nature in Africa is that of Cooper and Carpenter (1969, 1976), which involved the observation of language use in interactions between traders and their customers, and reported results of a survey of 23 markets in eight towns, which was conducted as part of the larger language survey of Ethiopia. The eight towns surveyed were chosen as representative of the various geographical regions of Ethiopia. The method involved using 'enumerators', who observed transactions in the market on a single day and recorded details of language use during the transaction. The main finding reported in Cooper and Carpenter showed that use of a particular language was predictable based on the percentage of the population of a town who claimed that language as their home language. Deviations and discrepancies in the data were attributed to the fact that markets are not only visited by townspeople themselves, but also by people from the surrounding countryside, where the home language may have been different from that of the town.

To date, virtually all surveys of language use in a market setting have been conducted in urban markets, presumably in part because of the assumed multilingual nature of urban African markets. There is of course no reason why research of this nature would not be of interest in rural markets, which are very often similarly multilingual. A variation of Cooper and Carpenter's method was used in the study reported in Connell (2009), in a market in a relatively remote, rural region of Cameroon. The study was intended in part as a follow up to a questionnaire-based survey of the sort discussed above, one question in which pertained to language use in the market. It was also, however, designed as a stand-alone study of language choice in the market in its own right. In this study, five commodities were selected as representative of the market as a whole, for the particular season. Local assistants, young men who were born and raised in the village, were engaged as enumerators. They were asked to record the language used, the sex of the customer, and to estimate the age of the customer. In addition, the first language of the trader and any assistants he or she had were noted. The enumerators were asked to note the use of any languages they did not recognize, and to describe any bilingual exchanges, i.e., situations where the trader and client switched language part way through the exchange. They situated themselves relative to the trader in such a way that they would be able to accurately observe and record their observations but remain unobtrusive (having obtained the permission of the trader to monitor their business for the day), so as not to impinge on the trader's business; no questions were to be asked of either traders or customers by the enumerators. In the subsequent analysis, the age estimates as recorded by the enumerators were organized into groups: younger than 18, 18–34; 35–50; older than 50. This allowed for several comparisons: differences according to sex or age, as well as, e.g., according to commodity. Detailed results and discussion are presented in Connell (2009).

It should be pointed out that the different types of survey discussed in this section are not mutually exclusive but can be combined in different ways. While the illustration presented may suggest observation as a follow up to a questionnaire-based survey, as a check on self-reporting, observation studies are most often used in their own right.

Phonetics in fieldwork

The importance of training

There are two aspects of fieldwork to be considered in relation to phonetics; one will be brought to mind by the heading of this section, 'phonetics in fieldwork': what kind of phonetic data need to be considered and collected, especially if one has in mind to document the phonetics of a language. The other is more fundamental, if perhaps more prosaic, in the minds of many: the kind or degree of training in phonetics one should have before undertaking fieldwork.

Many, if not most, current fieldwork manuals or textbooks offer little in the way of guidance or encouragement with respect to practical phonetics – ear training and transcription practice. Bowern (2008) for example, whose chapter entitled 'Fieldwork on Phonetics and Phonology' offers basic information as to the use of different levels of transcription, and steps involved in designing phonetic experiments, appears not to recognize the importance of appropriate training in practical phonetics before leaving for the field. Crowley (2007) offers even less discussion. These may be compared with the treatments found in Samarin (1967) or Kelly and Local (1989), as different as these two are in themselves from each other. Samarin was writing at a time in which fieldwork (and training in practical phonetics) was still relatively common. Kelly and Local post-date that period, but simply take an uncompromising view on the importance of phonetic accuracy and detail. Both Bowern and Crowley, on the other hand, presumably write in recognition of the relatively low priority placed on ear-training and practical phonetics in most linguistics programs today, itself at least in part a result of the diminishment of the importance of field linguistics in the generative era, and at the same time the increasing use of instrumental techniques in phonetics. Bowern at one point goes so far as to recommend using, 'a spectrogram program to check the accuracy of your transcription for voicing etc.' (2008: 37), and I have known colleagues not to trust their ears but to check via spectrogram whether a vowel was nasalized or not. Vaux and Cooper (1999: 89) offer a similar dispirited view regarding tone: 'people's judgements of pitch contours are wrong as often as they are right. It is much better to rely on either the intuitions of native speakers, or instrumental measurements'. It used to be said that a phonetician's (and a field linguist's!) most important tool was his (or her) ears. This is nonetheless true in the 21st century and for the field linguist there is still no substitute for solid training in practical phonetics. There is no technological fix; if deprived of such training in their undergraduate or graduate programs, prospective field linguists should take it upon themselves to find it. The accuracy of one's transcriptions in the field establishes the foundation for all further analyses. The ability to hear voicing distinctions and nasality, and distinguish pitch contours and height is innate, though it takes practice to develop these abilities to overcome the 'phonological filter' of one's own language (and what may amount to the habits of a lifetime).

Phonetics in language documentation

Many, if not most, fieldwork manuals or textbooks similarly include precious little information about phonetic investigation in the field; why documenting the phonetics of a language is important, what aspects of phonetics are important to document, or what kind of data to collect in order to arrive at a satisfactory documentation remains debatable. Ladefoged (2003), a book-length treatment of phonetic fieldwork, and Maddieson (2001), are notable and noteworthy exceptions to this, though in neither case is their discussion oriented toward documentation; i.e., what constitutes a satisfactory 'phonetics component' of a language documentation is not addressed.

When one thinks of language documentation, one tends to think of endangered languages, and when one thinks of endangered languages, especially in the African context, one thinks of languages that are hitherto essentially undescribed. This of course is by no means the only situation we find, but it is certainly a common one, to the extent we may consider it the default expectation. Field research being undertaken towards such a documentation therefore starts from the beginning, or pretty close to it. In order to do a creditable job of collecting the data that will comprise the documentation, clearly the linguist needs to be able to transcribe spoken language accurately and unambiguously. One needs at least to be able to hear and identify new and unfamiliar sounds, and to have the ability to overcome, as mentioned, the phonological filter imposed by one's own language.

Programmatic statements as to what should be included in a language documentation and how a documentation should be presented, such as those found in Himmelmann (1998), Lehmann (2002), or the various contributions in Gippert et al. (2006) among others, devote little attention, if indeed any, to how the sound system of a language, both its phonetics and phonology, is to be presented. If, however, as Himmelmann says, the aim of a language documentation, 'is to provide a comprehensive record of the linguistic practices characteristic of a given speech community . . . [which includes] . . . the observable *linguistic behavior*, manifest in everyday interaction between members of the speech community' (Himmelmann 1998: 166), information on the sounds and sound system of the language must indeed be included. (The emphasis is in the original; I might add that in many respects current recommended practices in documentary linguistics go well beyond a strict definition of 'linguistic behavior'.)

With respect to the types of phonetic structures to include in a documentation, the following list (partially following Ladefoged 2003) can be suggested:

- airstream mechanisms
- phonation types and voicing
- places of articulation
- manners of articulation
- differences in consonant length
- differences in vowel quality
- differences in vowel length
- orality and nasality in vowels
- pitch variation at different levels of utterance
    - syllable, word, phrase
- presence of resonances, prosodies, secondary articulations
    - e.g., palatality, velarity, etc.

In considering the documentation of the phonetics of a language, there is interplay between phonetics and phonology: before knowing what phonetic structures (as per the preceding list) to document, Ladefoged (2003) reminds us that a minimal description of the phonology of the language in question is useful, e.g., its phonemic inventory, as a guide as to what is most important/relevant to the language. This information is not always available: most languages in Africa remain undescribed (recall Blench's 2014 finding of some 230 languages in Nigeria alone for which there is no descriptive material available); for many of those that do have some description available, it is minimal, consisting only of a basic wordlist, perhaps presentation of the phonemic inventory and description of other basic features. Such work may be inaccurate, based on few speakers (often one, the author and his/her intuitions) and should always be verified (cf. Ladefoged 2003: 2). Fieldwork aimed at producing or including a documentation of the phonetics of a language begins at the same place fieldwork has always begun: with accurate transcriptions that can lead to reliable analyses, first to establish the phonemic inventory of the language.

At this point one might ask, 'why such a focus on the phonetics?' Transcription from recordings, even a broad transcription, is a hugely difficult task, especially when there is no recourse to native speakers (documentation should proceed from the expectation of a permanent absence of native speakers; cf. Lehmann's characterization of the primary purpose of documentation: 'to represent the language for those who do not have direct access to the language itself', Lehmann 2001: 5); a representative sample of narrowly transcribed texts provides a substantial guide for further work.

Presenting the phonetic structures of a language

Having arrived at the types of phonetic structures found in a language, and that one might want to include in a documentation, the question arises as to how best to present these structures. While much of the work involved in organizing the documentation may be done after the actual fieldwork period, without knowing beforehand what will or might be included, one will be ill-prepared to achieve the desired goals during fieldwork. In addition to a description in traditional articulatory phonetic terms, a consonant chart (i.e., including allophonic variants, not just phonemes), a vowel chart and/or formant plot, the following, at least, should be considered for inclusion.

Audio representations

Audio recordings in standard, uncompressed (typically WAV) format are a key component of any spoken language documentation; these may be in the form of recorded wordlists, grammatical paradigms, monologues, conversations, stories and other texts, as well as the more obvious recordings intended to be illustrative of the structures in question and, for example, of phonemic contrasts, etc.

Acoustic representations

A selection of recordings representative of the phonetic structures and features of the language should be chosen to form part of the phonetic documentation. These should show the following: a speech waveform; spectrogram; pitch track; and intensity track, and annotated to give a (relatively) narrow transcription in IPA. These can be presented, for example, as annotated Praat files (Boersma & Weenick 2017), with different levels of transcription on different tiers.

Palatograms, linguograms

The techniques of palatography and linguography are not new but remain the most effective way of determining place of articulation and illustrating active and passive articulators. The method has been described a number of times over the years, in publications such Firth (1948), Ladefoged (2003), Anderson (2008), and most recently in a series of YouTube videos (Salffner & Tzika 2012). Details of the technique can be found in any of these publications.

The basic technique involves painting the tongue with a dark substance (typically a paste made of charcoal and olive oil) and having the speaker pronounce a word containing only the consonant under investigation, e.g., 'tea' [tʰi]; the paste will wipe off where contact is made, leaving evidence of the place of articulation. This can then be photographed, using a mirror and taking appropriate care to position both it and the camera for best results. The reverse procedure, coating the upper surface of the vocal tract, will leave a trace on the part of the tongue that makes contact. Of the sources mentioned Ladefoged (2003) provides perhaps the most comprehensive discussion of the method and how to derive maximum information from it. An example palatogram and linguogram are shown in Figure 3.1a and b.

Lip positions associated with different consonants and vowels can similarly be documented photographically; a mirror held against the face at a 45° angle will allow both profile and frontal views to be captured simultaneously (Ladefoged 1964, 2003). Examples are given in Figure 3.2 a and b. A simple and interesting method of tracking lip movements using video, by placing a small paper circle at each of the corners of the mouth and in the center of each lip is suggested in Maddieson (2001).

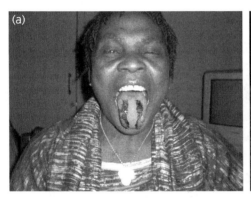 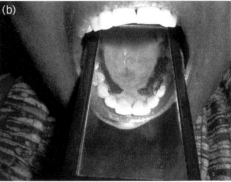

Figure 3.1a and b   Palatogram (left) and linguogram (right) [s]. (Palatogram from sáà̰ 'urinate' and linguogram from àsì 'blood'; the language is Defaka ([afn], Ijoid, Nigeria; speaker AA)

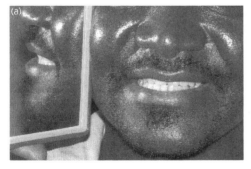 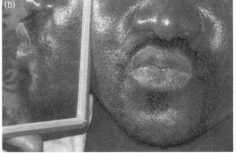

Figure 3.2a and b   Photographs of lip postures for Kpokoro ([btg], Kru, Côte d'Ivoire) [i] (left) and [u] (right). Speaker C

Bruce Connell

Fieldwork on tone

Basic considerations

Linguistic fieldwork in Africa will almost certainly involve investigating tone, all but a handful of languages in sub-Saharan Africa being tone languages, and with a relatively large range of types of tone system and tone inventories being found. Virtually all may be categorized as having register tone (i.e., contrasting pitch height) as opposed to contour tone (contrasting direction and movement; Pike 1948), though this should not be taken for granted. Inventories may range from just one (i.e., a tone contrasting with its absence) or two (High contrasting with Low) tones to as many as four (e.g., Mambila, Connell 2017) or five, as reported in certain varieties of Dan ([dnj] Mande, Côte d'Ivoire; Flik 1977). Tones may combine to form contour or compound tones, so that combinations of the four level tones of Ba Mambila, for example, allow up to 11 surface tone contrasts lexically, with yet others when grammatical tone is taken into consideration. The functions and functional load of tone too varies across languages. Typically, both lexical and grammatical tone may be found in a language, though what grammatical roles are signalled by tone varies widely, as does the extent of lexical contrasts signalled by tone. The degree of mutability of tones, either through phonetic or phonological and morphological processes is similarly variable. And, finally, the domain of tone in a given language needs to be considered, whether the syllable, the morpheme, or some larger unit. All of which suggests one should not approach an unfamiliar language with preconceived notions as to what to expect to find beyond the very basic working hypotheses that tone will be present and that it is likely to function both lexically and grammatically.

Tone is rarely discussed in standard works on field methods (Bouquiaux & Thomas 1992 is an exception), however recent articles by Hyman (2007, 2014) and Snider (2014), and a forthcoming monograph-length treatment by Snider (in prep) fill this lacuna; Himmelmann and Ladd (2008) extend the discussion to prosodic aspects of language more generally. The fieldworker new to tone should become familiar with the recommendations in these sources. Discovery procedures for tone are in many respects the same as those for working on the segmental inventory of a language, with a few important qualifications; the most important difference is the relative nature of tone, e.g., a tone is High only because there is another tone that is lower. In languages with contrasting High and Low tones, it is not uncommon to find a High tone late in an utterance may be lower than a Low early in that same utterance, due to the phenomena known as declination and downstep (see Connell 2011).

Hyman (2014: 526) suggests that, '[l]ogically, there are three separate tasks that one must take up in studying a tone system from scratch . . . [these are] necessarily ordered, with each one feeding into the next':

(i)   determine the surface tonal contrasts and their approximate phonetic allotones. This is first done by considering words in isolation;

(ii)   discover any tonal alternations present in the language, by putting words together to make short phrases or by eliciting paradigms;

(iii) the tonal analysis itself; the interpretation of what has been found in (i) and (ii), which is typically based on a particular set of theoretical considerations.

It is the first of these that is most clearly tied to fieldwork proper, and the second as well comes into play where such alternations are present. Given the relative nature of tone, standard practice (Bouquiaux & Thomas 1992; Pike 1948) is to work with a frame; to find a word or morpheme of known, non-alternating tone (via step ii) which can be collocated with nouns (or other words of other classes); a possessive marker or plural marker, for example. To illustrate, in Ba Mambila the plural marker bɔ consistently bears a Low tone, as does the 1Sg Poss marker, mò; the former precedes the noun while the latter follows. Combining nouns separately with each allows for a confident decision as to the tone found on a particular noun. (While bɔ is a general plural marker across most Mambila and Mambiloid varieties, it appears not to be the case that its tone is consistently the same, as is found in Ba; in other varieties, it is suffixed to the noun and its tone may be conditioned by the tone of the root.) A word of caution may be offered about generalizing the nature of tone across even varieties of the same language. The minimal sets in (1) reveal the four contrastive tone levels in Ba Mambila, following IPA marking conventions.

1 baŋ mo [˥˩]   'my trench'   ba mo [˥˩]   'my bag'
   baŋ mo [˥˩]   'my civet'   ba mo [˦˩]   'my palm (of hand)'
   baŋ mo [˩˩]   'my wound'   ba mo [˩˩]   'my wing'

The illustration in (1) is simple, testing for tone in monosyllables. For longer words the frame will need to be modified appropriately; for example, to test for the tone of the first syllable of a bisyllabic word, the frame should precede the test word, and in any case the technique works only where the tone of the test word doesn't change. For longer stretches of speech, and where grammatical tone is involved (and in the cases just mentioned), being able to reproduce the melody of the tone pattern to the satisfaction of your speaker is important, or having your speaker reproduce the tones on their own, is often useful. Whistling the melody is the technique most often recommended; I have found humming to be more effective.

The phonetic investigation of tone

Phonetic studies of tone have traditionally involved recording speakers in a laboratory setting, whether for investigation of production or tone perception. Such experiments on African languages are much less common than, say, on Asian languages, though this is beginning to change, at least with respect to experiments on production. Current signal processing programs greatly facilitate doing such work in the field. Yet with very few exceptions experimental work on the perception of tone with African languages is an area that remains unexplored.

Tone perception experiments in the field

There are several possible reasons for the relative lack of research on tone perception. One important set of factors is the very nature of tone, that its manifestation is primarily in continuous variations in fundamental frequency, with height and movement of F0 both of potential importance. That tone realization is relative, as discussed above, or, even more obviously, that speakers differ in their overall pitch range, is another compounding factor. Added to these considerations, it is not entirely clear that speakers apportion their tonal space similarly for different tones. This last consideration is especially relevant in multi-level systems – languages with three, four or even five level tones – such as are found in parts of West Africa, with (potentially) the highest and lowest tones of a system having greater leeway, both acoustically and perceptually. Also, while pitch may be assumed to be the primary perceptual correlate of tone, loudness, duration and voice quality may all potentially contribute to tone perception. When these factors are considered together, one concludes that the experimental procedure used for investigating the phonetics of tone must be carefully thought through.

Another important set of factors contributing to the relative lack of research on tone perception, though one of a different nature, is the practical question of access. Of the small amount of perceptual experimentation that has been done on tone, most has therefore been on those few languages with urban populations or with sizable immigrant populations in Western academic centers, for example Yoruba (Bakare 1995; Hombert 1976). Our understanding of tone would benefit greatly from more work on a wider range of languages.

There has, as mentioned, been somewhat more research done on tone perception in Asian languages, particularly on varieties of Chinese. Given the differing characteristics of tone in these two geographical regions, Africa vs Asia, register tone vs contour tone, different methods may serve one type better than the other.

One concern in my own fieldwork has been to contribute to the development of a methodology for the investigation of tone perception that does not rely on sophisticated laboratory facilities, but can be used in the field. My own efforts have been inspired by and are an attempt to build on pioneering work by J.-M. Hombert (Hombert 1988). Here I describe an extension of the method, used for work on tone perception in Mambila. The experimental questions asked were whether the four tones of Mambila, which are reasonably well defined in terms of production, map neatly into four perceptual categories on the basis of pitch height alone, and, to what extent linguistic experience plays a role in shaping the perceptual characteristics of the tonal system.

Mambila, like many languages in Africa, has no written tradition; it is spoken in an area that is relatively remote and where the general level of education is not high. As a result, the kinds of tests or tasks frequently used in phonetic experimentation, common enough in a Western setting, are unfamiliar. The method used to investigate tone perception in Mambila takes these factors into account and includes an appropriate training session for participants.

The stimuli used were based on the range of F0 values found for natural productions by a male speaker of four target words, near minimal set for tone, pronounced in a carrier phrase. All the words used were common everyday words: breast, bag, palm, wing; the carrier phrase consisted of two T4 words, bɔ́ ___ mò, giving meaningful phrases 'my breasts', 'my bags', 'my palms', and 'my wings'. The carrier phrase was intended in part to establish a reference level for the identification of the tones of the target words. A second purpose of the carrier phrase was to help ensure that perception of the stimuli proceeded in a linguistic rather than nonlinguistic mode. The stimuli themselves consisted of a sawtooth waveform for a range of frequencies (ten level frequencies in steps of 5 Hz) with fixed duration and amplitude, such as can be generated by any of a number of commonly used signal processing packages. (A sawtooth waveform was chosen on the basis that, of the options available in the software used, it most closely resembled a glottal waveform.) The resulting stimuli sounded similar to a naturally produced bilabial hum.

Since Mambila is an unwritten language, listeners were given line drawings of objects representing the words containing the target tones ('breasts', 'bags', 'palms', and 'wings'), and were asked to indicate which picture could be associated with each stimuli. A fifth, blank, option was also provided, to be used for stimuli participants found could not be associated with any Mambila tone. Only one participant made use of this option and only on a small number of occasions. The set of five randomizations was played 10 times for each listener, giving a total of 50 repetitions of each stimulus for each person. Responses were recorded on an answer sheet by the experimenter. Participants were run separately. The experiment took approximately one hour to run, with a break of about two minutes given at the halfway point.

Participants were given training before proceeding with the experiment. The length of training needed varied for each, but, for all, consisted of three phases: listening to and identifying naturally produced utterances of the target phrases, to ascertain that listeners could accurately identify words by tone alone (the target words constituted a near minimal set); second, having participants repeat the phrases they heard, but hum rather than articulate the target word, to ensure that participants were able to dissociate the tonal content of words from the segmental material. This also helped to reinforce the notion of hummed tones, as would be heard in the experiment. The third step in the training consisted of having the participant listen to the first set of randomized stimuli, to familiarize them with the actual experimental stimuli. Full details, including discussion of the results of this work, appear in Connell (2000).

Nominal classification

Noun classification is often considered (though perhaps inaccurately) a feature particular to African languages, and so bears some mention here. Noun classification systems (or their vestiges/remnants) are common in Niger-Congo languages and the Bantu languages present paradigm examples of functioning systems. In brief, these are characterized by sets of alternating prefixes marking singular and plural nominal forms; marking is extended to other elements of the noun phrase, in some languages featuring prefixes identical to those on the head noun, in others different prefixes. Nouns are grouped into classes based on the prefixes found; whether class membership should be considered determined by the prefixes of the head noun or its modifiers is debated, but essentially a matter of analysis. Indeed much of the work to be done with respect to nominal classification has more to do with morphological analysis than field practice properly speaking. Class membership is often assumed to be based on some degree of semantic coherence, though field workers should remember that the semantic features often assumed (i.e., that might apply in their own culture and to their own language) may not be applicable to the culture and language in which they are working. Because nominal classification in African languages typically deals with singular/plural marking, including the modifying elements in the noun phrase, the basic advice to be given is to collect the appropriate forms – singular, plural, modifying elements – for all nouns, rather than to assume a single plural marker in the language. Other aspects of nominal classification field workers may need to be aware of are the possibility, as is probably the case in the majority of Niger-Congo languages, that a fully functioning system such as those found in Bantu languages probably does not exist, but rather a vestigial or remnant system, and that the affixes used to mark nouns may be the suffixes rather than prefixes. Good (2012) reviewed the possibilities, from fully functioning to remnant, and discusses the importance of considering the overall shape of a system and its components.

Ideophones

Ideophones have long been recognized as an important characteristic of a great many African languages, and only more recently as relatively widespread elsewhere in the world (Doke 1935; Samarin 1965; Childs 1994; Dingemanse 2012). They are, as Dingemanse (2012: 654) points out, 'easy to identify but difficult to define'. Childs (2003: 118ff) offers a list of (mostly) phonetic/phonological characteristics that allow for their identification, such as use of sounds not part of the regular phonemic inventory, phonation types not otherwise in use in the language, that they are set off by a pause, etc. These tend to focus on the phonologically 'aberrant' or marked nature of ideophones. 'Marked' of course is a relative term, and will vary from language to language.

Definitions have been attempted from various perspectives, and much of the by now fairly substantial literature on ideophones has some emphasis on their definition; with none entirely successful. Dingemanse (2012: 655) suggests that ideophones are 'marked words that depict sensory imagery', a definition that attempts to be broad enough to be cross-linguistically valid while at the same time permissive of language-specific features. Other aspects of the literature focus on their description, classification and analysis in individual languages. Little attention has been devoted to fieldwork practice: how to discover or elicit ideophones (if they can indeed be elicited in the usual sense). Samarin (1967) gives some guidance, though it is mostly devoted to how to organize and classify them once they have been collected.

Given their 'aberrant' nature, discovering ideophones through traditional elicitation techniques is difficult. Dingemanse (2011), however, describes an innovative set of tasks developed as part of the Language of Perception project at the Max Planck Institute, Nijmegen, which proved effective. The tasks included, '(1) a texture booklet with ten different textures; (2) a taste kit with the five basic tastes (sweet, sour, bitter, salt, umami); (3) a color booklet consisting of eighty Munsell-validated color chips; (4) a booklet with twenty shapes; (5) a scratch-and-sniff booklet for twelve smells; and (6) a set of ten sound pairs varying in tempo, loudness, and amplitude' (2011: 80). Speakers of the language under investigation (Siwu [akp], Kwa, Ghana) were presented with the stimuli and asked to name each. Responses were grouped into four categories, one of which was 'ideophone'. (Being able to categorize words as ideophones depended on having previously determined their characteristic shape in Siwu; in this case they are typically longer than nouns and verbs, and feature otherwise deviant structure.)

Ideophones can also be found through recording of spontaneous natural conversation, again, a method employed in Dingamanse's work (reported in Dingamanse 2011 and elsewhere), where several hours of conversation covering multiple interactions (a total of 3,000 utterances) revealed roughly one in 12 utterances to contain an ideophone. Video-recorded natural conversations provide not only information as to what ideophones are present and how frequently they are used, but also insights as to their structure and semantics and how and when they are used. Other information, such as whether they are accompanied by gestures, has occasionally been reported, though this is quite possibly more common than the occasional report would suggest. As both Childs (2003) and Dingamanse (2011), among others, note, ideophones are often accompanied by a sense of playfulness or delight.

Salvage linguistics

A topic which is but rarely discussed in works on field methods (Crowley 2007 is perhaps the sole exception) is how one approaches a situation of doing fieldwork on a moribund language; this absence or scant treatment is noticeable even in works that are focussed on fieldwork on endangered languages. By 'moribund', I mean a situation in which the language in question has few remaining speakers, is not being passed on to younger generations, and in which those who do still speak the language may no longer have complete mastery (if they ever did) or total recall of the language. That is, they may be semi-speakers or even rememberers. Grinvald and Bert (2011) provide discussion on the importance of recognizing different types of speakers in endangerment situations.

Guidance for fieldwork on endangered languages tends to proceed with an assumed or implicit goal of language revitalization; the expectation may be that one will be working with at least reasonably fluent speakers, and that intergenerational transmission still exists or its reestablishment is possible. Reports of cases of 'the last speaker' are of course not uncommon in the literature, and cases can indeed be encountered in Africa. But little to no discussion is found as to actually conducting fieldwork on languages with only very small

Linguistic research in the African field

numbers of speakers, or how the fieldwork situation of such languages differs from other, more stable, languages. So, the question arises as to how to deal with a situation of extreme language moribundity. Perhaps the biggest differences, and certainly what Crowley focusses on, are with the speakers, and with structural differences that may exist between moribund languages and those with greater numbers of speakers which are more stable. Speakers may be old and lack the stamina and/or patience to participate in detailed fieldwork, especially elicitation sessions. Much of the language may have been forgotten or, as is not unusual, only ever incompletely learned, making it difficult, if not impossible, to produce anything approaching a complete or detailed grammatical description. The language may therefore hold little interest for some researchers, for whom producing a descriptive grammar is the goal. Nevertheless, such languages still merit attention for what they can contribute, for example, to our knowledge and understanding of African history, for which language is one of the most important sources of evidence. So, in such cases, one must be prepared to work with speakers who can only give what amounts to partial data on a language, elicited data or narratives that are freely mixed with material from the dominant language, and gather what material one can. Indeed, the loss of a severely endangered language, without having attempted to get as much of it documented as possible, may represent an irretrievable loss of information, both linguistic and cultural, with an attendant gap in our understanding of African languages, cultures, and history.

References

Adegbija, Efurusibina (1994). *Language Attitudes in Sub-Saharan Africa: A Sociolinguistic Overview.* Clevedon: Multilingual Matters.

Anderson, Victoria (2008). Static palatography for language fieldwork. *Language Documentation & Conservation* 2.1: 1–27.

Bakare, C. (1995). Discrimination and identification of Yoruba tones: perception experiments and acoustic analysis. In K. Owolabi (Ed.) *Language in Nigeria: Essays in Honour of Ayo Bamgbose.* Ibadan: Group Publishers, pp. 32–67.

Blench, Roger M. (2014). *An Atlas of Nigerian Languages*, 3rd Ed. Available online at: www.roger blench.info/Language/Africa/Nigeria/Atlas%20of%20Nigerian%20Languages-%20ed%20III.pdf (accessed April 1, 2017).

Boersma, Paul & David Weenick (2017). *Praat: Doing Phonetics by Computer* [Computer program]. V. 6.0.24 (accessed February 2, 2017).

Bouquiaux, Luc & Jacqueline M.C. Thomas (1992). *Studying and Describing Unwritten Languages.* Dallas, TX: SIL.

Bowern, Claire (2008). *Linguistic Fieldwork: A Practical Guide.* New York, NY: Palgrave Macmillan.

Calvet, Louis-Jean (Ed.) (1992). *Les Langues des Marchés en Afrique.* Aix-en-Provence: Institut d'Études Créoles et Francophones (Diffusion: Didier Érudition).

Childs, G. Tucker (1994). African ideophones. In L. Hinton & J. Ohala (Eds) *Studies in Sound Symbolism.* Cambridge: Cambridge University Press, pp. 247–279.

Childs, G. Tucker (2003). *An Introduction to African Languages.* Amsterdam: John Benjamins.

Connell, Bruce (2000). The perception of lexical tone in Mambila. *Language and Speech* 43: 163–182.

Connell, Bruce (2009). Language diversity and language choice: a view from a Cameroon market. *Anthropological Linguistics* 51.2: 130–150.

Connell, Bruce (2011). Downstep. In M. van Oorstendorp et al. (Eds). *Companion to Phonology.* Oxford: Blackwell Publishing, pp. 824–847.

Connell, Bruce (2015). The role of colonialism in language endangerment in Africa. In J. Essegbey, B. Henderson, & F. Mc Laughlin (Eds) *Language Documentation and Endangerment in Africa.* Amsterdam: John Benjamins, pp. 107–129.

Connell, Bruce (2017). Tone and intonation in Mambila. In L.J. Downing & A. Rialland (Eds) *Intonation in African Tone Languages.* Berlin: De Gruyter Mouton, pp. 131–166.

Cooper, R.L. & S. Carpenter (1969). Linguistic diversity in the Ethiopian market. *Journal of African Linguistics* 8: 160–168.

Cooper, R.L. & S. Carpenter (1976). Language in the market. In M.L. Bendor, J.D. Bowen, R.L. Cooper, & C.A. Ferguson (Eds) *Language in Ethiopia*. London: Oxford University Press.

Crowley, Terry (2007). *Field Linguistics: A Beginner's Guide*. Oxford: Oxford University Press.

Crozier, David H. & Roger M. Blench (Eds) (1992). *An Index of Nigerian Languages*. Dallas, TX: Summer Institute of Linguistics.

Dingemanse, Mark (2011). Ideophones and the aesthetics of everyday language in a West African society. *Senses & Society* 6.1: 77–86.

Dingemanse, Mark (2012). Advances in the cross-linguistic study of ideophones. *Language and Linguistics Compass* 6/10: 654–672.

Doke, Clement (1935). *Bantu Linguistic Terminology*. London: Longmans, Green.

Firth, J.R. (1948). Word palatograms and articulation. *Bulletin of the School of Oriental and African Studies* XII.3–4: 857–864.

Flik, Eva (1977). Tone glides and registers in five Dan dialects. *Linguistics* 201: 5–59.

Gippert, Jost, Nikolaus P. Himmelmann, & Ulrike Mosel (Eds) (2006). *Essentials of Language Documentation*. Berlin: Mouton De Gruyter.

Good, Jeff (2012). How to become a 'Kwa' noun. *Morphology* 22: 293–335.

Good, Jeff [to appear]. Eastern Benue-Congo noun classes, with a focus on their morphological behavior.

Grinevald, Collette & Michel Bert (2011). Speakers and communities. In P. Austin & J. Sallabank (Eds) *Cambridge Handbook of Endangered Languages*. Cambridge: Cambridge University Press, pp. 45–65.

Hansford, K., J. Bendor-Samuel, & R. Stanford (1976). *An Index of Nigerian Languages*. Ghana: Summer Institute of Linguistics.

Himmelmann, Nikolaus P. (1998). Documentary and descriptive linguistics. *Linguistics* 36: 161–195.

Himmelmann, Nikolaus P. & D. Robert Ladd (2008). Prosodic description: an introduction for fieldworkers. *Language Documentation and Conservation* 2.2: 244–274.

Hombert, Jean-Marie (1976). Perception of tones of bisyllabic nouns in Yoruba. *Studies in African Linguistics* Supplement 6: 109–121.

Hombert, Jean-Marie (1988). Tonper, un test de perception pour langues toneless: application au bulu. *Pholia* 3: 169–182.

Hyman, Larry M. (2007). Elicitation as experimental phonology: Thlantlang Lai tonology. In M-J Solé, P. Beddor, & M. Ohala (Eds) *Experimental Approaches to Phonology in Honor of John J. Ohala*. Oxford: Oxford University Press, pp. 7–24.

Hyman, Larry M. (2014). How to study a tone language, with exemplification from Oku (Grassfields Bantu, Cameroon). *Language Documentation & Conservation* 8: 525–562.

Kelly, John & John Local (1989). *Doing Phonology*. Manchester: Manchester University Press.

Ladefoged, Peter (1964). *A Phonetic Study of West African Languages: An Auditory-Instrumental Survey*. Cambridge: Cambridge University Press.

Ladefoged, Peter (2003). *Phonetic Data Analysis: An Introduction to Fieldwork and Instrumental Techniques*. Oxford: Blackwell.

Lehmann, Christian (2001). Language documentation: a program. In W. Bislang (Ed.) *Aspects of Typology and Universals*. Berlin: Akademie Verlag, pp. 1–16.

Lehmann, Christian (2002). Structure of a comprehensive presentation of a language. In T. Tsunoda (Ed.) *Basic Materials in Minority Languages. ELRP Publication Series B003*. Osaka: Osaka Gakuin University, pp. 5–33.

Maddieson, Ian (2001). Phonetic fieldwork. In P. Newman & M. Ratcliffe (Eds) *Linguistic Fieldwork*. Cambridge: Cambridge University Press, pp. 211–229.

Newman, Paul & Martha Ratliff (Eds) (2001). *Linguistic Fieldwork*. Cambridge: Cambridge University Press.

Pike, Kenneth L. (1948). *Tone Languages*. Ann Arbor, MI: University of Michigan Press.

Salffner, Sophie & M. Tzika (2012). Palatography Lessons 1–6. Available online at: www.youtube.com/watch?v=wCDuh6dfw6g, (accessed January 2017).

Samarin, William (1965). Perspective on African ideophones. *African Studies* 24.2: 117–121.

Samarin, William (1967). *Field Linguistics: A Guide to Linguistic Fieldwork*. New York, NY: Holt, Rinehart & Winston.

Schaefer, Ron P. & Francis O. Egbokhare (1999). English and the pace of endangerment in Nigeria. *World Englishes* 18, 381–391.

Snider, Keith (2014). On establishing underlying tonal contrast. *Language Documentation & Conservation* 8: 707–737.

Snider, Keith (forthcoming). *Tone Analysis for Fieldworkers*. Dallas, TX: SIL International.

Thieberger, Nicholas (Ed.) (2016). *The Oxford Handbook of Linguistic Fieldwork*. Oxford: Oxford University Press.

Vaux, Bert & Justin Cooper (1999). *Introduction to Linguistic Field Methods*. München: Lincom Europa.

Vossen, Rainer (1988). *Patterns of Language Knowledge and Language Use in Ngamiland in Botswana*. Bayreuth: Bayreuth University.

4

TONE AND TONOLOGY IN AFRICAN LANGUAGES*

Constance Kutsch Lojenga

Introduction

In light of the present-day emphasis on language documentation and description, this chapter on tone and tonology in African languages focusses on a much neglected but very necessary aspect of the topic, namely grassroots fieldwork on tone. Such basic fieldwork is an obvious necessity in order to analyze the tonal system of a language. Before doing fieldwork on tone, the researcher needs to acquire an amount of background knowledge in the domain, which will help him to interpret and analyze his data. This chapter contains both general information about tone languages, particularly regarding typological insights, as well as a practical methodology for doing fieldwork. Listening, mimicking, and learning to hear tone are helpful skills. Various ways of transcribing tone are discussed. The distinction between surface and underlying tones is very important, and floating tones as well as toneless morphemes are discussed. A practical methodology for data gathering is imperative before attempting to analyze the tone system of a language, and a typological background will help in making hypotheses when doing tone analysis. The contrastive function of tone in the lexicon and in the grammar will most likely emerge automatically. Then, there are topics like depressor consonants as well as various frequently occurring tone rules and register phenomena that may operate in a language under study. Finally, a brief chronological overview is given of the development of theoretical approaches to the analysis of the tone system of a language.

Tone languages in the world and in Africa

Tone languages are not a rare phenomenon among the languages of the world. Among the roughly 7,000 languages spoken worldwide, probably more than half are so-called tone languages (Yip 2002: 1). One finds the use of distinctive tone concentrated in three language areas (Voorhoeve 1968: 99):

- a group of American Indian languages;
- many African languages;
- nearly all Sino-Tibetan languages.

With respect to Africa, the great majority of African languages spoken south of the Saharan desert must be considered tone languages. Of the four language phyla, all Nilo-Saharan and all Khoisan languages are tonal. The largest language family of Africa, Niger-Kordofanian, covering about three quarters of Africa's 2,000 languages, contains some non-tonal languages, particularly in the West-Atlantic subgroup; Wolof, spoken primarily in Senegal, being one of them. Some Bantu languages of east and southeast Africa no longer have the full distribution of lexical tone patterns or no longer display any tonal contrasts on words in isolation. However, tonally contrastive patterns may persist in the grammar of these languages. Finally, certain subgroups of Afroasiatic also contain a number of tone languages. Ehret (1995: 67) states that "Phonemic tone is a widespread feature of Afroasiatic, appearing regularly in the languages of the Omotic, Chadic, and Southern and Eastern Cushitic division of the family." As for languages of wider communication on the continent, Hausa (northern Nigeria and surrounding areas), Lingala (Democratic Republic of the Congo), Sango (Central-African Republic), and Dyula (Burkina Faso and Côte d'Ivoire) are all tonal languages. Fulani (West-Atlantic) and Swahili (Bantu) are not.

What is a tone language?

Many people's first response to this question would be that a language is a tone language when it has tonal minimal pairs. Along those lines, Yip (2002: 1) calls a language tonal "if the pitch of the word can change the meaning of the word." Even if tonal minimal pairs may prove that a language is indeed a tone language, the question is if a language can be a tone language even in the absence of tonal minimal pairs. The following are some definitions or statements about what a 'tone language' is. I am quoting several authors from works written long ago, whereby it is clear that each one was influenced by their own experience. Over time, a progression can be noticed in understanding of what a tone language is.

One of the pioneers in the field of tone studies, Kenneth Pike (1948: 3), defined a tone language as "a language having lexically significant, contrastive, but relative pitch on each syllable." William Welmers (1959: 2; 1973: 80) defined a tone language as "a language in which both pitch phonemes and segmental phonemes enter into the composition of at least some morphemes." The following three authors have defined what a tone language is in the context of a language description. Ida C. Ward (1936: 10), who wrote on Ibo (Nigeria), concluded that "A tone language, therefore, is one in which every word in the language has its own individual tone or tone pattern." J.P. Crazzolara (1938: 13) wrote in *A Study of the Acooli Language* (a Nilotic language spoken in Uganda) that the language "makes use of tone or pitch as an essential element or part of its words, verbal forms, and grammar in general." Finally, in *The Phonetics of the Hottentot Language*, Beach (1938) says: "By a tone is meant the relative pitch of any significant speech-element chosen as a unit." He then states that Hottentot has both monosyllabic and disyllabic roots, and that "the number of inherent tones of both monosyllabic and disyllabic roots is identical. A tone, in Hottentot, may therefore be defined as the relative pitch of a root." The authors of these works already had profound insights in the tone systems of the languages they studied. Since then, many articles and books have appeared with studies on tone in a variety of languages. These have greatly increased our understanding of the nature and function of tone. The conclusion is that tone should not primarily be seen as a series of individual pitches realized on subsequent syllables, but rather that the lexical morpheme – most often a monosyllabic or disyllabic noun or verb root – should be seen as the central element that has an inherent tonal melody. Such a tonal melody may consist underlyingly of one or more tones, which are realized on the lexical morpheme to which they inherently belong, or, according to language-specific rules, are realized over a string of tone-bearing units, including some preceding and/or following the lexical root to which they inherently belong. In addition, grammatical morphemes, many of which are monosyllabic, may have their own underlying tone.

Pitch, tone, stress, and intonation

Pitch, tone, and stress are word-prosodic features; intonation is a prosodic feature that is realized on a larger unit: phrase, clause, or sentence.

Pitch is a phonetic term, which is measured in Herz or F0. In a tone language, every tone-bearing unit (TBU) is pronounced on a particular pitch. It is generally called 'tone' once the surface structure has been systematized and/or the underlying system has been analyzed.

In non-tonal languages, polysyllabic words generally consist of at least one syllable that is more prominent than the surrounding syllables, generally called a stressed syllable. The acoustic correlates and auditory features related to this prominence called 'stress' are generally higher pitch, amplitude (loudness), and in some languages also duration (length). The placement of stress may or may not be predictable. In Swahili, which is non-tonal, stress is realized on the penultimate syllable (with just a few exceptions). In Malagasy, which is an Austronesian language spoken on Madagascar, stress placement is not predictable; in fact, minimal pairs for stress can be found.

Intonation is a melody that stretches out over units larger than the word: a phrase, clause, complex sentence, and which has semantic or pragmatic significance. Intonation, therefore, is in principle not incompatible with tone in a tone language, and present studies reveal certain realities of this interaction (Downing and Rialland 2016).

Listening, mimicking, and transcribing tone

Listening and mimicking

Linguists who have a non-tonal language as their mother tongue may wonder how they can hear and mimic the different tones of a tone language. Native speakers of a tone language are often unaware of the different tones and the contrastive function of tone in their language; they 'just speak' their language. However, a good approach to listening to tone and exercises to mimic tone can lead to very satisfactory results. In the same way, for native speakers of a tone language, the awareness of tone can quite easily be raised. It can be observed that children acquire the tones often before they master all the segments of their mother tongue. These 'supra-segmentals' of tone are so basic that they can be used by themselves to communicate meaning. Many ethnic groups in the rainforest of Africa make use of so-called 'talking drums', which produce different pitches representing the tones of the utterances, but without the segmentals. Traditionally, such talking drums were used to communicate messages over a distance much farther than a human voice could reach.

A speaker of a non-tonal language can learn to mimic the tones of words by asking the native speakers to pronounce the word, and then whistle it. The learner should then attempt to mimic the whistling first, and subsequently pronounce the word on the same pitches as the whistle, i.e., he should repeat the performance of the native speaker in the reverse order, and practice first on isolated words (preferable more than one syllable), and subsequently on slightly longer utterances. Most speakers of African languages are or can learn to be good whistlers. In general, it is not culturally appropriate for women to whistle, though some may find the linguistic exercise so interesting that they overcome their embarrassment and can turn into good whistlers. When an outside linguist manages to pronounce words and ultimately read texts on the correct tones of a language, he will get great respect from the native speakers.

Transcribing tone

Before deciding what system of transcription one wants to choose, it is good to consider the various possibilities and their usages.

A rough transcription in a first contact with a language, when one doesn't know yet how many surface-contrastive level and contour tones there are, can be done by drawing pitch traces, placing them in phonetic brackets. These will represent what the linguist thinks he hears, and give an approximation of the relative distance of level pitches and the direction of contours, all to be established with more precision at a later stage.

Accents on top of TBUs (mostly vowels) can conveniently be used to represent the contrastive surface pitches once they have been clearly identified. Three levels can easily be handled within this system. If needed, an extra-high tone can be represented by a double acute accent, and an extra-low tone by a double grave accent.

All possible contour tones can be made as well (though some may need special adaptation on computers).

Table 4.1 Possible level tones

ȁ	extra low
à	low
ā	mid
á	high
a̋	extra high

Table 4.2 Possible contour tones

ǎ	rising contour in general, or low-high rising contour
â	falling contour in general, or high-low falling contour
ã	low-high-low contour
a̋	low-mid rising contour
ā́	mid-high rising contour
ā̀	mid-low falling contour
á̄	high-mid falling contour

Yet another way of transcribing the tones of a language is by using capital letters: L, M, H for Low, Mid, and High respectively, or B, M, H for Bas, Moyen, Haut in French. Such a system can be most helpful for representing the underlying tones. I normally suggest using a dot between the letters to mark the syllable boundaries of the word, and using a sequence of two (or three) letters without dots for contour tones: L.H would be two level tones on two subsequent syllables, whereas LH would be a contour tone on one syllable. If needed, M_1 and M_2 can be used for two contrastive Mid tones, whereas extra-high and extra-low tones can be marked by xH and xL. Features like downstep and upstep are generally represented by a raised downward or upward pointing arrow ($H^{\downarrow}H$, and $H^{\uparrow}H$). A system using capital letters has practical value in that one can write strings of tones in a more abstract way, namely separately from the segmentals. It is therefore useful for marking underlying tones.

Surface and underlying structure

Introduction

In tone analysis, one needs to differentiate between *surface* and *underlying* structure. The surface structure consists of the distinct level and contour pitches we can detect with our ears. However, those surface pitches and pitch patterns on nouns, verbs, and other utterances need to be analyzed. A hypothesis needs to be made of an underlying structure. In some languages, the underlying and the surface structure are closely similar. Those languages often have monosyllabic roots and the tones remain stable, except by possible tone replacement for grammatical purposes. In other languages, a set of rules may have to be posited in order to derive the surface structure from the underlying structure. Such languages generally have longer words, and tones may change influenced by their tonal environment.

The surface structure of a tone language may contain both level and contour tones. Contour tones, consisting of a combination of two unlike tones, can be rising or falling; there are also languages with contours consisting of three tones: L+H+L is a regularly occurring rise-fall. The opposite, H+L+H, is extremely rare, probably because the L tone between two H tones is often set afloat, which results in a $H^{\downarrow}H$ (H downstep-H) realization. When they occur, contours consisting of a sequence of three tones are generally found in a polymorphemic environment.

The underlying structure can often be analyzed into sequences of level tones only. Through historical development, however, syllables may have got lost and two unlike tones may have merged into a contour tone, which has thus phonologized, and can synchronically be considered as a phonological 'prime', i.e., an indivisible unit of what were historically two separate level tones on two syllables or TBUs.

It is important for the analysis to establish the tone-bearing unit: the syllable or the mora. Syllable weight plays a role here (Hubbard 1995; McCawley 1978: 114). If a language consists exclusively of short open, so-called 'light' syllables, all syllables are monomoraic, and the syllable is automatically the unit of tone placement. However, if a language also has closed syllables and/or long vowels, so-called 'heavy' syllables, there are two possibilities: light syllables, consisting of CV only, contain one mora, whereas heavy syllables, CVC or CVV, may consist of two morae, or else they may behave in exactly the same way as the light CV syllables. The distribution of tonal melodies and the behavior of tone rules is the decisive factor in this decision. In most languages with light and heavy syllables, the mora is the tone-bearing unit. In Jita (Bantu JE.25, Tanzania), however, the (short or long) syllable must be considered the tone-bearing unit (Downing 1996).

Tone and tonology in African languages

The actual tone assignment is also a language-specific issue, separate from the decision of whether the language is syllable or mora counting. It may be the case that each mora is assigned one surface tone, i.e., bimoraic syllables may then carry a maximum of two tones. In other languages, a short monomoraic syllable may carry up to two surface tones, whereas a bimoraic syllable may carry up to three surface tones. Contour tones are produced when a syllable or TBU has more than one tone associated to it. In Fur (Kutsch Lojenga and Waag 2004: 19) short, monomoraic syllables can carry a maximum of two tones, whereas long, bimoraic syllables can carry up to three tones on the surface.

Tone-bearing segments

Surface pitch is easily perceptible on the most sonorous sounds (vowels), and increasingly less so on the less sonorous sounds. Vowels, which form the nucleus of the syllable, have an audible pitch realized on them. The most sonorous consonants are the nasal and oral sonorants. They can form the coda of a syllable, and, as such, sometimes have a tonal realization.

KABA (Nilo-Saharan, Central-Sudanic; Central-African Republic)

(1) màñ ~ mãn   'water'
     tòŕ ~ tŏr   'pipe'

Many languages, though, have syllabic nasals, for example as self-standing pronouns or as prefixes to nouns or verbs. Such syllabic nasals form the syllable nucleus in themselves, and, as such, they are a TBU.

LYÉLÉ (Niger-Congo, Gur; Burkina Faso)

(2) ǹ   '2sg   'you, your'   ǹ yē ǹ yálá yáà ? 'Have you sold your millet?'
     ń   '3sg   'he/she, his/her'   ń yē ń yálá yáà ? 'Has she sold her millet?'

ÉBRIÉ (Niger-Congo, Kwa; Côte d'Ivoire) has homorganic syllabic nasals that carry a tone that may or may not be identical to the tone of the following syllable. These syllabic nasals are (mostly frozen) noun-class prefixes or pronouns.

(3) *singular*   *plural*
     áɓá   ḿmá   'palmnut'
     áɓú   ḿmú   'stone'
     m̀pá   -   'foutou' (local dish)
     ádɛ̀   ńdɛ̀   'oilpalm'

Other tone-bearing consonants are rare, but they do exist, e.g, Adioukrou (Niger-Congo, Kwa; Côte d'Ivoire) has, in addition to syllabic m, n, ŋ, at the end of words, also syllabic oral resonants /l, r/ (Hérault 1978).

LENDU (Nilo-Saharan, Central-Sudanic; D.R.Congo) is a language that has experienced vowel loss, so that some words no longer have a vowel as syllable nucleus, but rather a continuation of the onset consonant, /r/, /z/, and /s/. These consonants are tone-bearing, except for the /s/, which is voiceless, and can therefore by definition not have a tonal realization. It has therefore acquired voicing in order to carry a tone on its nucleus (cf. also Kutsch Lojenga 1989: 120). The language has three level tones and a rising tone, all marked on the consonantal syllable nucleus in the examples below.

(4a)	rr̀	'bush, shrub'	ndrr̀	'goat'
	rr̄	'Down's syndrome'	-prr̄.prr̀	'lung'
	rŕ	'medicinal herbs'	kprr̀.kprr̄	'broom'
	rř	'fish, sp.'	mbrr̀	'arrow'
(4b)	-zz̀	'stomach'	dzz̄	'earth'
	zz̀.zź	'plant, sp.'	dzz̀	'weep, mourn' (v)
(4c)	sz̄	'louse'	tsz̀	'laziness'
	sź	'shoe'	tsž	'lawn'
	sž	'carefully'	tsz̀.tsz̄	'banana'

Finally, in the section on depressor consonants, it will become evident that voiced obstruents in the syllable onset can attract a L tone, which is not realized on the consonant itself, but rather on the following vowel.

The underlying structure

The two subjects in this section, toneless morphemes and floating tones, both belong to the topic of the underlying structure, since, on the surface, every TBU must have a tonal realization, and tonal realizations without segments are not possible on the surface.

Toneless morphemes

Ideally, one would want to posit one underlying tone or tonal melody for each morpheme of the language, both lexical and grammatical. However, there are also morphemes without an inherent tone. Their tone depends on the tone of an adjacent mora or syllable, preceding or following, and may either be a copy of that tone, or the opposite, i.e., a polar tone (in relation to the tone of the adjacent syllable).

In FUR (Nilo-Saharan; Sudan), plural marking in nouns consists of a suffix –a following a consonant, and –ŋa following a vowel. These plural morphemes are underlyingly toneless and receive their surface tone by copying the last tone from the tonal melody belonging to the root.

(5)	singular	plural		singular	plural	
	àgàs	àgàs-à	'tree, sp.'	mèrà	mèrà-ŋà	'nut, sp.'
	tálál	tálál-á	'vine, sp.'	kátí	kátí-ŋá	'tree, sp.'
	kádìɲ	kádìɲ-à	'tree, sp.'	tígò	tígò-ŋà	'tree, sp.'
	sòón	sòón-á	'millet'	bàrí	bàrí-ŋá	'tamarind tree'

Floating tones

In the underlying structure, floating tones may be found. Floating tones are tones without a segmental support. Many languages have grammatical morphemes consisting only of a tone. It is possible that the grammatical morpheme once consisted of a segment or a syllable with a tone, but that this segment or syllable has eroded through a historical process, and that the tone alone has 'survived'. On the surface, such floating tones must be linked to a tone-bearing unit.

In KABA (Nilo-Saharan, Central-Sudanic; Central-African Republic), the locative morpheme consists of a floating H-tone postposition, which is attached at the end of the noun.

(6)	bòlò	'hole in a tree'	bòló	'in the tree hole'
	dàrā	'sky'	dàrá	'in the sky'
	kù	'forest'	kǔ	'in the forest'
	njɔ̀	'spring, well'	njɔ̌	'at the well'
	ɓē	'village'	ɓē̌	'in the village'
	ndɔ̄	'fields'	ndɔ̌	'in the fields'

Depressor consonants

Many African languages have so-called 'depressor consonants'. In such languages, there is interaction between a specific set of consonants, normally the set of voiced obstruents, and tonal realizations. The set of voiced obstruents may include, language-specifically, /h/ or /ɦ/, breathy-voiced consonants, and voiced clicks. The most well-known is the tone-lowering effect that such depressor consonants may have: a H tone on a syllable beginning with a depressor consonant is not realized as a level H tone, but as a LH rising tone. However, the effect of depressor consonants can be manifested in various ways (Hyman and Mathangwane 1998: 208 for Ikalanga specifically, and Kutsch Lojenga 2000):

- underlying H and M to be realized as LH and LM;
- H-spread or H-shift to be blocked;
- L tones to be realized at an extra-Low (xL) level.

With respect to the first of these, the tone-lowering effect: the first part of a non-L tone is lowered, and the result is a rising contour.

BUDU (Bantu D.332; D.R.Congo)

(7)	ùbǔkà	'sweet potato'
	ɓòkédǎ	'tree, sp'
	ìgyàgyǎ	'joy'
	gbǔkà	'to yawn'
	hǔnà	'to plant'

MAYOGO (Niger-Congo, Ubangi; D.R.Congo)

(8)	*underlying tones*	*non-depressor C surface tones*			*depressor C surface tones*					
	L.M	ὲkpa	L.M	'arm'	èdū	L.LM	'mouse'	ὲgō̃	L.LM	'savannah'
	L.H	ὲkpa	L.H́	'leaf'	èdu	L.LH	'hole'	ὲgǒ	L.LH	'war'

A less well-known effect of depressor consonants is that they block H-spreading. In themselves, syllables with depressor consonants can occur on a H tone, but H-spreading cannot take place across a syllable with a depressor consonant.

ÉBRIÉ (Niger-Congo, Kwa; Côte d'Ivoire) has two tones underlyingly, but three level tones, L, M, and H, as well as three different falling contours: HL, HM, and a L-falling tone on the surface. H-spreading occurs both within words as well as across word boundaries. The language has a set of depressor consonants, namely the regular voiced obstruents /b, d, dʒ, g, gb, v, z/. Syllables with an initial voiced obstruent can easily be pronounced on a level H tone or on a HL contour tone.

(9) *underlying tones*   *surface tones on roots with depressor C*
    L.H   à.dá   'bat, sp.'
    H.H   á.dɔ́   'monkey, sp.'
    L.HL   ǹ.gwê   'shea butter'
    H.HL   ń.grô   'cheek'

However, the depressor consonants manifest themselves in that they block a H-spread rule. H-spread occurs even within words, between a (frozen) prefix á- or Ń- and the root, but the H-tone spreading is blocked when the root begins with a depressor consonant.

The H.HL melody of the words ápɔ̂ 'body' and áɓî 'drum' have the same surface tonal melody, but are a neutralization of underlying H.HL and H.L, the latter turning into surface H.HL through H-spreading. The underlying forms become visible when combined with the possessive pronoun mɛ̀ 'my'.

(10) *underlying tones*   *mɛ̀ 'my'*
    H.HL   á.pɔ̂   'body'   mɛ̀ pɔ̂   'my body'

    H.L   á.ɓî   'drum'   mɛ̀ ɓì   'my drum'

However, when the root begins with a depressor consonant, H-spreading is blocked.

(11) *underlying tones*   *mɛ̀n 'my'*
    H.L   á.grò   *á.grô   mɛ̀n grò   'my in-law'
    H.L   á.bɛ̀   *á.bɛ̂   mɛ̀n bɛ̀   'paddle'

Finally, depressor consonants may play a role in tonogenesis, the development of extra tone levels in an original two-tone system, which thereby may grow to become a three-tone or four-tone system. Beach (1938: 215) already noticed the influence of consonants on tone and tonogenesis in Khoisan. He compared both the tonal systems and the consonant systems of Nama and Korana, two related languages spoken in Namibia. Korana has both voiced and voiceless stops, /b, d, g and /p, t, k/, whereas Nama only has voiced stops. He concluded that in Nama, a merger must have taken place between voiced and voiceless stops and clicks in such a way that originally conditioned tonal realizations had then developed into contrastive tones.

BILA (Bantu D.311, D.R.Congo), has synchronically a three-tone system, which has developed out of a regular two-tone system by a diachronic development that involves the following two phases:

1   depressor consonants causing L tones to be realized at an xL level, and
2   subsequent devoicing of the depressor consonants, by which the lowered L tones became contrastive and thus gained phonological status, resulting in the present-day three-tone system.

Pairs and sets like the following lead to a recognition of a three-tone system (Kutsch Lojenga 2003: 457).

(12) *tonal melody*   *tonal melody*

H.H	só.á	'fish, sp.'	L.L.H	ɛ̀.kà.ní	'thoughts'
H.L	sú.à	'day'	xL.xL.H	ɛ̈.kä.ní	'folktale'
H.xL	só.ä	'arrow'			

The consonant inventory of Bila is lacking the complete set of voiced egressive obstruents, which do, however, exist in the neighboring related languages Bhele and Komo (though depressor consonants do not play a role in these two languages). Comparison of cognates shows that /b, d, j, g, gb/ in these two languages correspond to /p, t, s, k, kp/ in Bila. These voiceless obstruents, which have voiced correspondences in the other languages, do occur on xL tones in Bila, and are the origin of the xL contrastive level of tone, since the conditioning factor of their voicing has disappeared. Some comparative examples of cognates in the three languages, where tones are marked as follows, for comparative purposes: á H tone, à regular L tone, ä xL tone, only in Bila (Kutsch Lojenga 2003: 456).

(13)

Komo	*Bhele*	*Bila*		
ntábè	ntábì	tápì̈	'branch'	
dèmá	dèmá	tìmá	'to deceive'	
jɔ́	jɔ́	sɔ̈	'basket'	
gàbá	gàbá	käppä	'stick'	
gbómá	gbómá	kpömá	'to bark'	

Systems with depressor consonants are frequently found in three of the four major language families of Africa: Niger-Congo (Bantu, and other subfamilies), Afro-Asiatic (particularly Chadic), and Khoisan. So far, there is virtually no documentation on depressor consonants in Nilo-Saharan.

Typology of tone systems

A typology of tone systems in African languages can be viewed from different angles. Pike (1948: 5), Welmers (1959: 3), Voorhoeve (1968: 103) and Wedekind (1985a: 106–107) have all expressed their views on this matter. My view on this topic is that a typology of African tone systems consists of more than one layer. The primary criterion for classifying African tone systems consists of the number of underlyingly contrastive tone levels. Other criteria for sub-classification may be: (1) the presence or absence of downdrift and/or downstep; (2) the presence or absence of surface contour tones, and within that possibly the source of such contour tones: those that consist of combinations of level tones, or those that may historically derive from a sequence of two tones, but which synchronically may be seen as indivisible units; (3) the presence or absence of depressor consonants, and (4) the presence or absence of specific widespread tone rules, as H-spreading, or H-shifting.

Looking at the number of tone levels, we find languages with two, three, four, and five underlyingly contrastive levels in Africa. In his article on universals of tone, Maddieson (1978: 338) posits that "no known language makes a phonological contrast of more than five tone levels." An example of a language with five contrastive level tones (and one contour tone) is Bench', an Omotic language spoken in the southwest of Ethiopia (Wedekind 1983 and 1985b). Two- and three-tone languages are frequently found in Africa; languages with four or five contrastive levels are a fairly rare phenomenon, only found in a few 'pockets' surrounded by three-tone languages. Wedekind (1985a) has drawn a map showing the areas in which languages with these different numbers of tone levels occur. Many two-tone languages and a number of three-tone languages exhibit tone rules, which influence and therefore change the tonal realizations of words in different tonal contexts. In other three-tone languages, and also in those with four and five tones, tone is stable, which means that the tones of lexical items and grammatical morphemes do not normally change in different contexts, except that there may be a system of tone replacement for grammatical purposes (often in the verbal system). There also seems to be a correlation between the length of words and the number of tonal contrasts: languages that are highly monosyllabic often have more contrastive tone levels, e.g., Lendu with three contrastive levels, or Attié with four contrastive levels (Kutsch Lojenga and Hood 1982). Both languages have contour tones as well, which are not exemplified in the data below.

LENDU (Nilo-Saharan, Central-Sudanic; D.R.Congo)

(14) ɓù 'hole'
ɓū 'tribe'
ɓú 'canoe'

ATTIÉ (Niger-Congo, Kwa; Côte d' Ivoire)

(15) nǎ 'fallow field'
ná 'comb'
nā 'male in-law'
nà 'fruit, sp.'

Methodology for tone analysis

The aim

The aim of a tone analysis is to establish the underlying tones and tonal melodies of every morpheme in the language, both lexical and grammatical, and what their surface realizations are. In order to reach that goal, various steps are necessary: data gathering, organizing the data, listening for tonal melodies, interpreting the results, making a hypothesis for the underlying system, establishing tone rules, based on further tone research. This section provides a methodology containing steps towards a practical tone analysis of an African language. Marlo (2013) has described a discovery procedure that is helpful specifically for Bantu languages, many of which have common and comparable structures.

Data gathering

Listening for tone in text can give an impressionistic idea of what level and contour tones may exist, and whether there is downdrift and/or downstep in a language. It will not lead to a discovery of the basics of the tone system: the number of contrastive tonal melodies on lexical morphemes, and the underlying tone system of the language. It is therefore advisable to start a tone analysis on the basis of lexical material, and end up with texts in which one can account for every surface tonal realization in terms of the underlying structure and a rule system that generates the surface structure from the underlying system.

The grammatical categories that one wants to study first are nouns and verbs in their citation forms. Once the basic system has been discovered on the basis of the lexical data, one can gradually extend the analysis to other parts of speech and to the behavior of tone on longer utterances.

It is assumed that, before attempting tone analysis, the segmental units have been analyzed, and all consonants and vowels can be represented systematically in the data. Knowledge about vowel-length contrasts and consonant gemination is particularly important in preparation for tone analysis. One wants to elicit a basic lexicon of at least 1,000 lexical items, using existing wordlists or by semantic-domain research, either with one native speaker, or preferably with a small group of native speakers. The data should be written segmentally only, without any attempt to mark tone, since one doesn't have a reference frame against which to interpret the pitches one hears.

Organizing the data

The data could be written on separate slips or cards of paper, or could be entered into a database. In the latter case, one should make sure that similar-structure nouns or verbs can be filtered out consistently and exhaustively. When written on paper initially, the speakers of the language can more actively participate in sorting the data according to word and syllable structures, and in establishing the various tonal melodies on the nouns and verbs.

Nouns and verbs should be separated, since they may not display the same number of tones or tonal melodies. Since one wants to focus on the roots of the nouns and verbs, any compound or derived nouns or verbs should be laid aside for the time being and await further treatment at a later stage. Words of any other grammatical categories should not be mixed in with the two main categories of lexical items.

In some languages (e.g., Mande languages), the citation form consists of the root of the word, without any further obligatory pre- or suffixes. These are the easiest, since one doesn't have to do any morphological analysis before starting to listen for the tones. There are also many languages in which the citation form consists of a root with an obligatory pre- and/or suffix (Bantu languages, Gur languages). Since one wants to focus on the roots, one should at least identify those pre- or suffixes, so as to be able to establish the root, preferably without there being any morphophonological processes in the vowels. The next step is to sort the words according to the syllable structure of their roots: monosyllabic roots from disyllabic roots; closed syllables from open syllables.

Listening for surface tonal melodies

The next step is to discover how many different tones or tonal melodies are found on each group of words of similar root and syllable structure. In the past, it has been advocated to use frames for listening for the tones of a substitution item. It was assumed that the frame would remain stable. This is not always the case, however. In most languages, therefore, it is better to start with the words in their citation form – which could also be considered a zero frame. Native speakers can participate actively by pronouncing each word and subsequently whistling its tonal melody, then grouping them according to 'same' or 'different' from other words of identical segmental structure. In a second round, the tones of each group of words should be checked through once again to see if they really all carry the same tonal melody. A different one will stand out immediately. This exercise is also an excellent means of raising native speakers' awareness of tonal contrasts. In addition, the final result might be better than if it were done exclusively based on the hearing of an outside linguist only. Often through interaction and input from native speakers, one might become aware of some fine tonal distinction that may ultimately appear to be contrastive, such as a contrast between a HL or a HM falling contour, or the distinction between a level L tone and a falling L tone at the end of the word.

Following that, the surface-contrastive tonal melodies need to be interpreted, which should result in positing a first hypothesis for the underlying system. Further research in other domains of the language will then confirm the hypothesis and/or point to different details within the first basic hypothesis.

Minimal pairs are good material to illustrate tonal contrasts; however, they are not the only proof that a language is tonal, nor do they necessarily present the full tonal system of the language. But more is needed: when the contrastive tonal melodies are found, the surface pitches need to be interpreted into a systematic surface structure and then analyzed into the underlying system.

Further analysis

Once the basic tone system has been established, the way is open for further tonal research, like the discovery of tonal processes. This should also be done in a systematic way, studying tonal behavior in noun phrases, in verbal conjugations and other morphological structures and subsequently in syntactic constructions. Each morphological structure should be studied separately and exhaustively, so as to investigate all possible variables. In a language with locative suffixes, for example, several nouns of all different tonal melodies should be combined with the locative suffix. The result should reveal whether or not the tones of the noun remain stable, and, if not, what the changes are, and, in addition, to see if one can posit an underlying tone belonging to the locative suffix. If any changes occur, one should try to capture these in rules: H spreading rightward, leftward, or the existence of floating tones, or a polar tone, etc. In the area of syntactic constructions, each and every different tonal pattern in nouns should be combined systematically with adjectives, demonstratives, numerals, possessives and any other free-standing modifier. The aim is, once again, to see if there are tonal changes in the nouns, and, second, to find out what the underlying tone of the modifier is, and if it changes under influence of the tonal melody of the noun. If there are changes, these are expected to be systematic, and one should be able to posit rules to account for the changes. Similarly, with respect to verbs, whether tense/aspect distinctions are expressed morphologically or syntactically, these should be studied with verbs of all different underlying tone melodies, and the tones belonging to the grammatical morphemes should be established as a result. Gradually, a picture will emerge, not only of the basic tone system and the tonal melodies belonging to nouns and verbs, but also of tonal behavior in longer utterances. One may have to revise earlier hypotheses to a certain degree, but, in the end, a clear picture should emerge of the underlying system and a set of rules by which the surface tonal melodies are derived from the underlying system.

Neutralization

At any time it is possible that the tonal melodies found on nouns or verbs in isolation or in a specific morphological or syntactic construction do not give the full range of underlying contrasts that exist in the language. Some underlying contrastive melodies may be neutralized on the surface. This can happen in isolation (zero frame) or in any other frame. When nouns or verbs are investigated in a larger morphological or syntactic context, neutralization may be discovered in that words that seemed to have the same tonal melody in isolation may split up into two or more groups with different tonal melodies in a specific tonal environment (cf. the Ébrié example 10).

Lendu (Nilo-Saharan, Central-Sudanic, R.D.Congo) has verb infinitives on two of the three level tones only: L and M. When studying different inflectional paradigms, it appears that the M-tone infinitives all behave in the same way; L-tone infinitives, however, separate out into three groups with different tones on the verb in their various inflected forms. This means that there are underlyingly four different tone classes in the verbal system of Lendu, three of which are neutralized in having a L-tone infinitive.

Acoustic analysis

When using computer programs like Speech Analyzer or Praat, it is possible to analyze recordings of speech on the computer, a topic treated in detail by Baart (2009). This includes pitch, represented by speech graphs, which show the fundamental frequency (F_0) or Hertz (Hz) of the pitch or pitch patterns of an utterance, including minute details of influence by voiced or voiceless consonants, vowel height, amplitude, etc. Such programs are good for analyzing pitch in a phonetic sense, but they will not directly lead to a phonological analysis in terms of the system of contrastive tones of a language. Sometimes, however, doing instrumental analysis can be helpful for proving a certain unusual or fine tone distinction after having established contrastivity, but which may be hard to detect when listening to whistles only.

The function of tone

In most African languages, a tone or tonal melody forms an integral part of any lexical item, together with the consonants and vowels. However, languages differ widely in how and how much they use tone to signal contrastive meaning. Tone may function contrastively in the lexicon and/or the grammar. The functional load may be defined as "the extent to which a language makes use of tone to signal contrasts, in the domain of the lexicon and/or the grammar" (Katamba 1989: 187). According to the amount of use languages make to signal contrastive meaning, tone has a heavier or lighter functional load in that language.

Languages with predominantly monosyllabic roots generally have a very heavy functional load of tone in the lexicon in that there are numerous noun and verb roots differentiated by tone alone. Languages with disyllabic roots and obligatory class prefixes or suffixes generally have fewer tonal minimal pairs at the lexical level.

More significant, in some sense, are the grammatical distinctions marked by tone alone. Tone may differentiate between two or more TAM forms in the verbal system; tone may be the sole means of differentiating between singular and plural forms of a set of nouns or pronouns; tone may mark the difference between gender, or between subject and object case; locative expressions may be marked by tone alone, or relative clauses may be differentiated from their matrix clauses by tone alone.

The following are some examples of tonal contrasts in the lexicon between nouns or verbs.

NGITI (Nilo-Saharan, Central-Sudanic; D.R.Congo) (Kutsch Lojenga 1994: 95).

(16) ōnzī 'luck'
      ōnzí 'begging'
      ònzì 'wealth'
      ònzǐ 'flea'

Constance Kutsch Lojenga

YAKA (Bantu C.10; Central-African Republic)

(17)	mbókà	'village'
	mbòká	'fields'
	mbóká	'civet cat'

LINGALA (Bantu C.40; D.R.Congo)

| (18) | kò-kómà | 'to arrive' |
| | kò-kòmà | 'to write' |

The following are some examples of tonal contrasts in various domains of the grammar.

Singular-plural marking in the pronominal system

NGITI (Nilo-Saharan, Central-Sudanic; D.R.Congo)

(19)	*person*	*singular*	*plural*
	1	īmā	ìmă
	2	īɲī	ìɲĭ
	3	àbādî	ābádî

Gender marked by tone, followed by case distinctions marked by tone

RENDILLE (Afro-Asiatic, East-Cushitic; Kenya)

(20)	*feminine gender*		*masculine gender*	
	ínám	'girl'	ínàm	'boy'
	ɲìráx	'female baby camel'	ɲíràx	'male baby camel'

(21)	*citation form*		*object*	*subject*
	ínàm	'boy'	ínàm	ìnàm
	mín	'house'	mín	mìn

Locative expressions marked by tone

FUR (Nilo-Saharan; Sudan) (Kutsch Lojenga and Waag 2004)

(22)	*noun*		*locative*	
	kɔ̀rɔ̀	'water'	kɔ̀rɔ́	'in the water'
	dúló	'hole'	dúlò	'in the hole'
	yɔ̀rrá	'hill'	yɔ̌rrà	'on the hill'

Relative clauses differentiated by tone from matrix clauses

ZIMBA (Bantu D.26; D.R.Congo)

| (23a) | mwǎnà ókátʃéè | 'the child played' |
| | mwǎnà òkátʃéè | 'the child who played . . .' |

(23b) mwámòkátʃi ótòémbà   'the woman is singing'
       mwámòkátʃi o̱tòémbà   'the woman who is singing . . .'

Tone marking contrast between TAM paradigms

ATTIÉ (Niger-Congo, Kwa; Côte d'Ivoire)

(24) hã̀ zè   'we have gone'
      hã̀ zē   'we are going'
      hã́ zē   'we ought to go'
      hã́ zè   'let us go'
      hã̀ ze̋   'we didn't go'

Tonal processes and register phenomena

In tone analysis, the easy case is when the surface realization on the TBUs matches the underlying tones on a one-to-one basis. However, tones do not always remain constant or stable in every environment. Many languages exhibit tonal processes in order to derive the surface realization from the underlying structure. This may be due to the presence of toneless morphemes, the insertion of floating tones, boundary tones, and a variety of general and/or language-specific tone rules. Such tonal processes are found in many two-tone languages and a number of three-tone languages. In other three-tone languages and virtually all four- and five-tone languages, tones are quite stable. Tonal changes that do occur in such languages are often related to the verbal inflectional system and are not analyzable in terms of rules, but must synchronically be seen as tonal replacement. It is possible that, diachronically, such languages had fewer tones and a transparent rule system, but, because of erosion of segments or entire syllables, they have developed more contrastive tone levels by which the transparency of a rule system has got lost, and the only explanation of the changes in a non-transparent system is by tonal replacement.

Tonal processes may take place within words, both within roots and between affixes and roots, as well as between words in a sentence.

Frequently occurring tone rules are tone spreading, tone shifting, tonal polarity, Meeussen's rule – the latter two being cases of dissimilation. In addition to such rules, there are register phenomena: downdrift, downstep, and upstep.

Spreading may occur in various forms: *partial* (only covering part of the following syllable, resulting in a contour tone together with the inherent tone of that syllable) or *complete*, in which case it can be *bounded* (only once: to the closest TBU or mora), or *unbounded* (iterative, covering a longer stretch). There is both *H-spreading* and *L-spreading*, and the spreading can be *rightward* or *leftward*. Rightward H-spreading seems to be most frequent, often in conjunction with downstep.

DYAN (Niger-Congo, Gur; Burkina Faso) exhibits both rightward and leftward spreading, as is shown in the following examples of H-tone spreading from left to right. The full domain of the spreading has not yet been established.

(25) fɛ̀rɔ̀   '(to) jump'   má fɛ́rɔ̀   'I am jumping'

H-tone spreading from right to left:

(26)　gbòm　　　　'baboon'　　　　gbóm kú　　　'baboon it-is'

　　　|　　　　　　　　　　　　　　　　

　　　L　　　　　　　　　　　　L　H

H-shifting rules are found quite frequently in Bantu languages in Eastern Africa. A H tone is not realized on the TBU to which it belongs, but rather one or more TBUs further to the right, or even towards the end of the tonal domain.

In DIGO (Bantu E.73; Kenya) H-tone verb infinitives, the H tone belonging to the root is not realized on the root, but, instead, on the following syllable:

(27)　ku-komá　　　'to plant'　　　*ku-kóma
　　　ku-seká　　　'to laugh'　　　*ku-séka

Similar examples can be found in Maganga and Schadeberg (1992: 42), and, without a doubt, in many other Bantu languages in the area. Kisseberth (1984), in his chapter "Digo Tonology," has elaborated this system of H-shifting much more extensively, particularly focusing on verbal derivations and on inflected verbs. Beyond the level of the word, H-shifting may also occur across word boundaries in coastal Bantu languages, e.g., with nouns followed by a possessive pronoun, which are considered as one tonal domain.

Tonal polarity refers to a rule that causes a tone to become the opposite of an adjacent tone, as the example from locative marking in Fur shows (see ex. 22 above).

Meeussen's rule is, in fact, also a rule of tonal polarity: when there are two underlying H tones next to each other, the second H tone becomes L, as shown in the following distant past paradigm from Zimba (Bantu, D.26, R.D. Congo): following a L-tone subject prefix (1sg/pl, 2sg/pl), the verb stem -béká 'cut' has a H melody in this paradigm; however, following a H-tone subject prefix (3sg/pl), the H melody of the verb stem is changed to L following Meeussen's rule.

(28)	*person*	*distant past, sg.*		*distant past, pl.*	
	1	nà-béká	'I cut (e.g., meat)'	twà-béká	'we cut'
	2	wà-béká	'you cut'	mwà-béká	'you cut'
	3	wá-bèkà	'he cut'	bá-bèkà	'they cut'

Downdrift and *downstep* are closely related phenomena, also called automatic and non-automatic downstep respectively. Downdrift is caused by surface L tones; downstep is caused by a floating L tone, which is not realized on the surface. Many languages with downdrift also exhibit downstep, though the reverse is not necessarily true. Downdrift is an automatic or pre-dictable phenomenon, since a H tone following a L tone (or a series of L tones) on the surface is realized lower than the H tone preceding the L tone(s). In downstep, to the contrary, a H tone is followed immediately by a lowered H tone, which is the result of an underlying L tone that is 'trapped' between two H tones and without there being a TBU on which it can be realized on the surface. The L tone may have been set afloat because of H spreading, or it may have been inserted for syntactic purposes. In the latter case, the language may exhibit downstep without downdrift. In both these cases, downstep not only occurs across word boundaries, but may also occur within words, often triggered by H spreading word-internally, as in the following example from KOKO WACHI (Niger-Congo, Benue-Congo, Plateau; Nigeria).

(29)   Ĭ- kpá⁺rá   'kilns'

Both in downdrift and in downstep, lowered H tones set a new 'ceiling' in that, following a H tone, no higher tone can be found any more within the tonal domain. This also means that, following a H tone, there are three possible scenarios: a following H, a downstepped ⁺H, or a L tone, whereas, following a L tone, there are only two possibilities: another L tone or a H tone.

When downstep is found in two-tone languages, the downstepped H tone is realized at a level intermediate between H and L, and is therefore relatively easy to hear and interpret. However, downstep in a three-tone language may or may not be realized at the same level as a mid tone, and therefore is much harder to detect.

In older literature, downstep was indicated by a raised exclamation mark ˈH. At its revision in 1989, the IPA symbol adopted for downstep was changed to a raised downward arrow: ⁺H, marked before the onset of the syllable.

Upstep is in a certain sense the opposite of downstep. However, the phenomenon of upstep has been much less studied, since it went probably unnoticed in many languages. Contrary to downstep, which is often cumulative in African languages, I know of no documentation of an African language that has cumulative upstep. Rather, the type of upstep in African languages found so far is local, one instance at a time, and it generally co-occurs with downstep, which means that there is not much of a downward trend over a phrase, clause or sentence in languages with this phenomenon.

Like downstep, (local) upstep is also a function of a floating L tone: a H tone is raised preceding a realized (surface) or a floating (underlying) L tone. The following H tone is then downdrifted or downstepped because of that same L or floating L tone.

Tone theories

This brief section gives a chronological overview of the most significant theoretical developments in the domain of tone analysis. Pike, in his book *Tone Analysis* (1948), has laid a basis for systematic tone analysis. However, he looked at tone per syllable, rather than, according to our present insights, considering tone as a melody belonging to a morpheme, even if that morpheme consists of more than one syllable. He also worked from surface pitch realizations, and did not attempt to unearth a deeper, underlying level in his approach to tone analysis. If L, M, and H tones are audibly distinctive on the surface and there are some minimal pairs, there are automatically three tonemes. Contour tones are generally considered tonemes as a whole. These were the pre-generative days. His views were a necessary step in the gradual development of further theoretical approaches.

Generative phonology introduced a completely new approach by introducing an underlying level from which the surface realizations are derived by a set of rules. Its origin is the famous work by Chomsky and Halle (1968) *The Sound Pattern of English* (SPE). In generative phonology, speech is considered linear in nature, a sequence of sounds, which can be sliced up into consonants and vowels. Segments were further analyzed into (unordered) bundles of features, represented in feature matrices. Tone belonged to and was super-imposed on the segments, and therefore needed to be defined by features also. Establishing features for tone appeared to be much more difficult than for consonants or vowels, and has been a long-lasting discussion, among others by Wang (1967), Yip (2002), and Hyman (2010). It had to deal with questions such as:

- What kind of and how many features need to be posited for tonal contrasts? The features [high] and [low] can handle no more than three level tones.
- Should there be separate features for contour tones? Contour tones cannot be handled by combinations of features for level tones, since the bundles of features were considered to be unordered.
- Tone is not normally a feature of consonants, therefore, tone rules (which modify the feature specifications) must skip over intervening consonants.

As a consequence, in the 1970s, a number of studies focused on the relationship between segmental and suprasegmental representations, particularly in relation to tone. This led to the theory of autosegmental phonology, a theory of non-linear phonological representations. The main reference here is Goldsmith's (1976) *Autosegmental Phonology*, which was motivated primarily by trying to handle tonal problems in African languages. Suprasegmental research on tone was also done by Leben (1973, 1978). In this theory, tone is no longer a feature belonging to segments, but it is considered to be on an independent level (or tier) of autosegments, for which there is not necessarily a one-to-one relationship between the number of tones and the number of segments. Tones can change, move around and behave independently from segments. Autosegmental theory deals with a number of issues that had remained unsolved previously, such as:

- it allows for looking at tonal melodies independently of the number of syllables and segments in a word;
- contour tones can now be seen as multiple tones linked to one vowel;
- underlying tones can now easily spread or shift to another syllable;
- toneless morphemes can receive a tone by spreading or copying from an adjacent TBU;
- floating tones can be attached to an adjacent TBU.

Some basic principles in autosegmental theory are the association conventions, by which tones are associated to vowels: all vowels need to be associated with at least one tone, all tones are associated with at least one vowel, and association lines may not cross. According to rules, association lines can be added, or deleted. They can spread (in which case one tone is associated to two or more TBUs), with the result that a L tone may be set afloat, which, if found between two H tones, causes downstep on the surface. Another issue that has become clear in separating the tonal tier from the segmental tier is that of the obligatory contour principle (OCP): two identical tones next to each other in the underlying level are generally not allowed, and 'repair' strategies are applied, such as:

- merger: L L -> L and H H -> H;
- dissimilation of the second tone, H H -> H L (Meeussen's rule);
- insertion of a floating L tone causing downstep.

Autosegmental representations, with surface tones marked by accents on the tone-bearing units, and an underlying level with the underlying tone letters linked to the tone-bearing units, including tone-spreading or other rules, are very clear, transparent, and easy to follow, including for native speakers of a tone language who have no formal linguistic background.

Lexical phonology (Mohanan 1986; Pulleyblank 1986) is an approach that helps to differentiate between lexical or word-internal morphophonological processes and postlexical processes, which are either allophonic, or (often gradient) processes across word boundaries. This is relevant for both segmental as well as supra-segmental phenomena.

Further theoretical developments led to a new theoretical approach, Optimality Theory (Prince and Smolensky 1993), a constraint-based theory, which deals with tone as well as all other aspects of phonology. It has its own conventions, which are somewhat less self-explanatory or transparent in the way the constraints are represented, especially in the domain of tone.

Register Tier Theory (Snider 1999) grew out of attempts to account for downstep or upstep, i.e., phenomena in which there is a change of tonal register. It is integrated in lexical phonology, autosegmental phonology, and optimality theory. It is a model for phonological representation of tone in which a multi-tiered approach replaces the single-tier representations for tone.

Conclusion

This chapter focussed on a practical methodology for doing grassroots fieldwork on tone in African languages. Such fieldwork is most important as a basis for language documentation and description. It is clear that a certain background is needed before one can launch into such fieldwork. This background is found in a knowledge of basic concepts of tone and a typology of existing tone systems in African languages, so the researcher can interpret the data and make hypotheses for the analysis of the tonal system. Basic concepts treated in this chapter are: the distinction between surface and underlying tone, depressor consonants, the concepts of function and functional load of tone, frequently occurring tonal processes and register phenomena, with a brief overview of some tonal theories developed in the course of time. All these topics together will lay a solid basis for the methodology and the practical fieldwork of the researcher.

Note

* This chapter is excerpted from a forthcoming and more extensive *Practical Manual for Tone Analysis in African Languages* by the same author.

References

Baart, J. (2009). *Acoustic Phonetics*. Dallas TX: SIL International.

Beach, D.M. (1938). *The Phonetics of the Hottentot Language*. Cambridge: Heffer.

Chomsky, N. and M. Halle (1968). *The Sound Pattern of English*. New York, NY: Harper and Row.

Crazzolara, J.P. (1938). *A Study of the Acooli Language. Grammar and Vocabulary*. London: Oxford University Press.

Downing, L.J. (1996). *The Tonal Phonology of Jita*. Lincom Studies in African Linguistics 05. München: Lincom Europa.

Downing, L.J. and A. Rialland (2016). *Intonation in African Tone Languages*. Phonology and Phonetics [PP] 24. Berlin: De Gruyter Mouton.

Ehret, C. (1995). *Reconstructing Proto-Afroasiatic (Proto-Afrasian): Vowels, Tone, Consonants and Vocabulary*. Berkeley, CA: University of California Press.

Fromkin, V.A. (1978). *Tone: A Linguistic Survey*. New York, NY: Academic Press.

Goldsmith, J. (1976). *Autosegmental Phonology*. PhD Diessertation, MIT.

Hérault, G. (1978). *Eléments de Grammaire Adioukrou*. Abidjan: Institut de Linguistique Appliquée.

Hubbard, K. (1995). Morification and Syllabification in Bantu Languages. *Journal of African Languages and Linguistics* 16: 137–155.

Hyman, L.M. (2010). *Do Tones Have Features?* Paper Presented at Tones and Features: A Symposium in Honor of G. Nick Clements, Paris, June 18–19, 2009. UC Berkeley Phonology Lab Annual Report.

Hyman, L.M. and J.T. Mathangwane (1998). Tonal Domains and Depressor Consonants in Ikalanga. In Larry M. Hyman and Charles W. Kisseberth (eds), *Theoretical Aspects of Bantu Tone*. Stanford, CA: CSLI, pp. 195–229.

Katamba, F. (1989). *An Introduction to Phonology*. London: Longman Group UK.

Kisseberth, C. (1984). Digo Tonology. In G.N. Clements and J. Goldsmith (eds), *Autosegmental Studies in Bantu Tone*. Dordrecht: Foris Publications, pp. 105–182.

Kutsch Lojenga, C. (1989). The Secret behind Vowelless Syllables in Lendu. *Journal of African Languages and Linguistics* 11: 115–126.

Kutsch Lojenga, C. (1994). KiBudu: A Bantu Language with Nine Vowels. In *Africana Linguistica XI*, Tervuren, pp. 127–133.

Kutsch Lojenga, C. (2000). *Depressor Consonants in African Languages.* Paper presented at the Tone Symposium. Tromsö, Norway, June 5–7.

Kutsch Lojenga, C. (2003). Bila (D32). In D. Nurse and G. Philippson (eds), *The Bantu Languages.* London: Routledge, pp. 450–474.

Kutsch Lojenga, C. (2013). Orthography and Tone: A Tone-System Typology and Its Implications for Orthography Development. In Michael Cahill and Keren Rice (eds), *Developing Orthographies for Unwritten Languages*. Dallas, TX: SIL International, pp. 49–72.

Kutsch Lojenga, C. (2013). *'Exotic' Consonants in Congolese Languages.* Paper presented at the Conference on Phonetics and Phonology of Sub-Saharan Languages. Johannesburg, University of the Witwatersrand, July 7–10.

Kutsch Lojenga, C. and M.E. Hood (1982). L'Attié. In G. Hérault (ed.), *Atlas des Langues kwa de Côte d'Ivoire. Tome 1.* Monographies. Abidjan, Côte d'Ivoire: Institut de Linguistique Appliquée et Agence de Coopération Culturelle et Technique, pp. 227–253.

Kutsch Lojenga, C. and C. Waag (2004). The Sounds and Tones of Fur. In Gilley, L.G. (ed.), *Occasional Papers in the Study of Sudanese Languages*. Nairobi: SIL, pp. 1–25.

Leben, W.R. (1973). *Suprasegmental Phonology*. PhD Dissertation. Cambridge, MA: MIT.

Leben, W.R. (1978). The Representation of Tone. In V.A. Fromkin (ed.), *Tone: A Linguistic Survey*. New York, NY: Academic Press, pp. 177–220.

Maddieson, I. (1978). Universals of Tone. In Joseph H. Greenberg (ed.), *Universals of Human Language. Vol. 2. Phonology*. Stanford, CA: Stanford University Press, pp. 335–365.

Maganga, C. M. and Th. C. Schadeberg (1992). *Kinyamwezi: Grammar, Texts, Vocabulary*. Köln: Köppe.

Marlo, M.R. (2013). Verb Tone in Bantu Languages: Micro-Typological Patterns and Research Methods. *Africana Linguistica* 19: 137–234.

McCawley, J.D. (1978). What Is a Tone Language? In V.A. Fromkin (ed.), *Tone: A Linguistic Survey*. New York, NY: Academic Press, pp. 113–131.

Mohanan, K.P. (1986). *The Theory of Lexical Phonology*. Dordrecht: D. Reidel.

Odden, D. (1995). Tone: African Languages. In J.A. Goldsmith (ed.), *The Handbook of Phonological Theory*. Oxford: Blackwell, pp. 444–494.

Pike, K.L. (1948). *Tone Languages: A Technique for Determining the Number and Type of Pitch Contrasts in a Language, with Studies in Tonemic Substitution and Fusion.* Ann Arbor, MI: University of Michigan Press.

Prince, A. and P. Smolensky (1993). *Optimality Theory: Constraint Interaction in Generative Grammar.* New Brunswick, NJ: Rutgers University Center for Cognitive Science Technical Report 2.

Pulleyblank, D. (1986). *Tone in Lexical Phonology*. Dordrecht: D. Reidel.

Snider, K. (1999). *The Geometry and Features of Tone* (Publications in Linguistics 133). Dallas, TX: SIL and University of Texas at Arlington.

Voorhoeve, J. (1968). Towards a Typology of Tone Systems. *Linguistics* 46: 99–114.

Wang, W. (1967). Phonological Features of Tone. *International Journal of American Linguistics* 33.2: 93–105.

Ward, I.C. (1936). *An Introduction to the Ibo Language*. Cambridge: W. Heffer & Sons.

Wedekind, K. (1983). A Six-Tone language in Ethiopia: Tonal Analysis of Benchnon (Gimira). *Journal of Ethiopian Studies* 16: 129–156.

Wedekind, K. (1985a). Thoughts when Drawing a Map of Tone Languages. *Afrikanistische Arbeitspapiere* 1: 105–124.

Wedekind, K. (1985b). Why Bench' (Ethiopia) Has Five Level Tones Today. In U. Pieper and G. Stiekel (eds), *Studia Linguistica Diachronica et Synchronica. Werner Winter sexagenario anno MCMLXXXIII.* Berlin: Mouton de Gruyter, pp. 881–901.

Welmers, W.E. (1959). Tonemics, Morphotonemics, and Tonal Morphemes. *General Linguistics* 4: 1–9.

Welmers, W.E. (1973). *African Language Structures.* Berkeley, CA: University of California Press.

Yip, M. (2002). *Tone.* Cambridge: Cambridge University Press.

5

A SYSTEM-BASED TYPOLOGY OF MOOD IN NIGER-CONGO LANGUAGES*

*Isaac N. Mwinlaaru, Christian M.I.M. Matthiessen, and
Ernest S. Akerejola*

Introduction

This chapter examines the MOOD systems of Niger-Congo languages. MOOD systems have been studied in language typology for the past four decades (e.g., Ultan, 1978; Chisholm et al., 1984; Sadock & Zwicky, 1985; Bybee et al., 1994: Ch. 6; Palmer, 2001; König & Siemund, 2007), with certain properties of imperative and interrogative moods being included in the *World Atlas of Language Structures* (*WALS*) (Dryer & Haspelmath, 2013; see also the contributions in Nuyts & van der Auwera, 2016). In addition, systemic functional linguists have investigated the systemic organization of options in MOOD and of their modes of realization in grammar and phonology (e.g., Matthiessen, 2004; Teruya et al., 2007; Teruya & Matthiessen, 2015; Matthiessen, 2015). In our exploration of the typology of MOOD systems in Niger-Congo languages, we will draw on findings in systemic functional typology as a guide; these findings shed light on variation in MOOD systems in terms of three views (cf. Halliday, 1996; Matthiessen, 2007):

1. Viewed "from above," from the vantage point of the semantics of speech functions (speech acts): the organization of MOOD systems according to the nature of the exchange of meanings in dialogue.
2. Viewed "from below," from the vantage point of the grammatical and phonological resources used in realizing options in MOOD: the strong tendency for MOOD options to be realized either by phonological prosodies or by modal particles placed as juncture prosodies finally or initially in the clause, indicating its status as a dialogic move. Segments may also occur at a lower rank as modal affixes of the verb or particles within the verbal group.
3. Viewed "from roundabout," from the vantage point of the system of MOOD itself—what speech-functional distinctions are grammaticalized, but also from the vantage point of its systemic environment—other interpersonal systems (in particular, POLARITY), textual systems (e.g., whether the interrogative element of an elemental interrogative is given the status of Theme or of Focus) and experiential systems (e.g., which transitivity roles may be interrogated in an elemental interrogative clause).[1]

Of these three views, it is the view "from below" that has been adopted for the largest number of languages in language typology in general, and this view is reflected in the database of languages in *WALS*. But to understand typological variation in the MOOD systems of African languages—and of languages in general—we need to combine the three views; and it is the views "from above" and "from roundabout" that will enable us to explain the realizational patterns that have been identified "from below." Thus, we define MOOD as the grammar of speech functions, that is, in principle, the grammatical reflexes of statement, question, command and offer (cf. König & Siemund, 2007). We say 'in principle' because, across languages, there is no typical or specialized grammatical form realizing offers (cf. Halliday, 1984: 20). It is realized by mood types typical of the other three speech functions.

The study is based on a range of data sources: discourse data from languages we have analysed closely, namely, Akan (Kwa: Tano), Dagaare (Gur: Mabia),[2] Kulango (Gur: Kulango-Lorom) and Ọkọ (Benue-Congo: Nupe-Oko-Idoma), elicited and constructed sentences and descriptive material on a wide range of languages in the Niger-Congo phylum.[3] Our unit of analysis is free (or 'independent') clauses as opposed to bound clauses (e.g., relative, adverbial and nominal clauses), since it is free clauses that serve as the domain of MOOD as defined in this study. Regarding glossing of examples from secondary sources, we use the original glosses by the various authors but, where possible, we make a few modifications for uniformity with our own rules, which is largely based on the Leipzig glossing rules. We begin our analysis by sketching a typological overview of the interpersonal structure of the clause in Niger-Congo languages (the second section) and then discuss the different types of mood and their realizations (the third section).

Interpersonal structure of the clause in Niger-Congo languages

Niger-Congo languages typically have the following interpersonal clause structure: (Subject •) Predicator (• Complement) (• Adjunct) (• Negotiator) (cf. Figure 5.1).[4] The brackets show elements that are optional and the dot indicates that the element does not necessarily appear in the order in which it is presented, although this order is typical across the Niger-Congo phylum (see Akerejola, 2005 and Mwinlaaru, 2017: Ch. 3; forthcoming on Ọkọ and Dagaare respectively; see also Watters, 2000: 197–200). Bantu languages notably display a radical flexibility in the order of elements (Aboh, 2007a). It should also be noted that Complement, Adjunct and Negotiator can occur more than once in the clause.

Languages vary in relation to the degree to which the Subject is treated as a distinct element of the clause (cf. Comrie, 1989: 66–70, 104–123). While it is prominent in many languages of the Gur, Kru and Adamawa-Ubangi families, Kwa and many Benue-Congo languages often

'You will weed the farm well, right?

$F\upsilon$	na	kɔ	=n	a	wɪɛ	vla	wɛ?
2SG	POS.IND.FUT	weed.PFV	FOC	DEF	farm	good	INT
Subject	Predicator			Complement		Adjunct	Negotiator

Figure 5.1 Illustration of the interpersonal structure of the clause in Dagaare

indicate modal responsibility in the clause with pronominal subject affixes in the Predicator. A notable exception within the Gur family is the Kulango cluster, which is typologically like Kwa languages in this regard. The Predicator itself is realized by the verbal group, consisting of the verb, auxiliary verbs and accompanying particles (in languages that have particles). One difference between verbal affixes and particles across Niger-Congo is that while affixes normally agree with the root verb in terms of vowel harmony and other harmony systems, particles maintain their phonological quality irrespective of that of the co-occurring verb, except when they are cliticized.

The possible positions of Adjunct, realized by adverbial units, are clause initial, pre-verb and post-verb positions and this is normally determined by the kinds and sub-classes of adverbs. The Negotiator element, on the other hand, is realized by modal particles that occur as juncture prosodies in clause initial or clause final position (cf. Matthiessen, 2004: 619–621), and, in a few languages such as Gbadi (Kru: Eastern), in clause medial position (cf. Koopman, 1984: 87). It enacts the clause as a negotiable unit in exchange. There are two types of modal particles: those that show delicate mood distinctions in the clause and those that are only attitudinal markers. The Negotiator is another element of typological variation across languages in the sense that it is more prominent in some languages (e.g., Dagaare and Buli, Gur: Mabia; Ọ̀kọ́, Benue-Congo: NOI) than in other languages (e.g., Akan, Kwa: Tano; Kulango, Gur: Kulango-Lorom).

Let's consider the following dialogue between a vendor (B) and a customer (A) to illustrate how some of the elements of the clause are deployed in enacting it as a move in exchange:

(1) Ọ̀kọ́, Benue-Congo: NOI

A:	*A-ma-wa*	*egin*	*owowo*	*ro.*
	3SG.NHM-NEG-be	guinea:corn	new	AGREE
	Predicator	Complement		Negotiator
	'It is not the new guinea corn, right?'			

B:	*Aye*	*ya*	*go.*	
	3SG.NHM.EMP	be	ASSR	
	Subject	Pred.	Negotiator	
	'It is.'			

A:	*I-me-roro*	*ka*	*aye*	*ya*	*ro.*
	1SG-NEG-think	that	3SG.NHM.EMP	be	AGREE
	Predicator		Subject	Pred.	Negotiator
	'I don't think that it is.'				

B:	*Ena*	*e-mi-wa*	*a?*	
	what	3SG.NHM-PFV-be	INT	
	Wh/Complement	Predicator	Negotiator	
	'What is it then?'			

A:	*I-me-din*	[[*onene*	*a*	*wa*	*na*]].
	1SG-NEG-know	DEF.one	REL	be	COMPL
	Predicator	Complement			

'I don't know which one it is.'

B:	*Egin*	*owowo*	*ya*	*o.*
	guinea:corn	new	be	okay
	Subject		Pred.	Negotiator

'It is the new guinea corn, okay.'

This dialogue is rich in negotiation. Almost all clauses end with a Negotiator, mostly indicating the speaker's attitude towards the proposition. The Predicator indicates the process and, in most part, includes pronominal prefixes, polarity and aspect markers. It carries the burden of the argument enacted by the clause. Ọ̀kọ́ accords little importance to Subject. However, the emphatic pronoun *aye* in the second clause and the nominal group *egin owowo* ('new guinea corn') in the last clause are elevated to the status of Subject.

Languages vary with regards to the elements that are essential in showing mood contrasts. In some Niger-Congo languages (typically Gur languages) the Subject, Predicator and Negotiator stand out as the essential elements for enacting the clause as a move in exchange and in showing mood contrasts, either by their presence, absence or their morphological realization. In languages where both the Subject and Negotiator have little importance (e.g., typically Kwa languages), however, the morphology of the verb realizing the Predicator is the key item in determining the mood of the clause. This gives a typology of languages where more interpersonal work is done at clause rank and those where it is done at word rank respectively. These typological differences are, however, a matter of degree and tendencies across languages, with some languages (e.g., Ọ̀kọ́) occupying a mid-region.

Typology of MOOD systems in Niger-Congo languages

The MOOD systems in Niger-Congo show a clear primary distinction between indicative and imperative clauses. There is often some grammatical signal that distinguishes these two primary mood types. Two motifs can be identified here. One is the use of special particles in the Predicator to show differences between indicative and imperative clauses (example (2)) and the other is the difference in verbal morphology (example (3)). While the Predicator in indicative clauses normally include markers of grammatical categories of (primary) tense and modality (including the option of zero-realization in the case of tense), these are absent in the imperative clause. A common realization is also the presence of distinct polarity markers in indicative and imperative clauses. An illustration is given below from Gurene:

(2) Gurene, Gur: Mabia

(a)	*N*	**kan**	*kinyɛ.*
	1SG	NEG.IND.FUT	go.PFV

'I will not go.'

A system-based typology of MOOD *in Niger-Congo*

(b)   *N*   ***ka***   *kini.*

         1SG   NEG.IND.NFUT   go.IPFV

         'I am not going.'

(c)   *Kinyɛ!*

         go.PFV

         'Go!'

(d)   ***Da***   *kinyɛ!*

         NEG.IMP   go.PFV

         'Don't go!'

Examples (2a) and (2b) are indicative clauses while (2c) and (2d) are imperative clauses. It can be observed that each indicative clause has tense marking, future or non-future. The system of tense is, however, absent in the imperative clause. In addition, the polarity markers in the clauses also show mood contrast. The particles *kan* (negative future) and *ka* (negative non-future) do not only realize polarity but also show that the clauses in which they occur are indicative (2a, 2b). This systemic contrast is established by using a different particle *da* to realize negative polarity in the imperative clause (2d).

The second motif is common among Kwa and in many Benue-Congo languages but also in Kulango, which systematically display idiosyncratic characteristics within the Gur family (cf. Bendor-Samuel, 1971: 149). Here, instead of particles, affixes that are normally present in the verb in indicative clauses are absent in the imperative verb form. These are also typically tense markers. The result is that there is a distinction between indicative verb forms and imperative verb forms in these languages. An illustration is given below from Ga:

(3) Ga, Kwa: Nyo

     (a)   ***Mi-i-ya***   *jaanɔ.*

             1SG-PROG-go   market

            'I am going to the market.'

     (b)   ***M-a-ya***   *jaanɔ.*

             1SG-FUT-go   market

            'I will go to the market.'

     (c)   ***Yaa***   *jaanɔ!*

             go   market

            'Go to the market!'

     (d)   ***Nyɛ-yaa***   *jaanɔ!*

             2PL-go   market

            'You go to the market!'

Table 5.1 Primary mood distinctions and their possible sub-types in Niger-Congo

MOOD		Possible subtypes
indicative: declarative		Affirmative/non-affirmative [e.g., Dagaare, Kulango and other Gur languages].
indicative: interrogative	polar	Biased/non-biased 'yes/no' interrogative (marked by different particles) [e.g., Dagaare and other Mabia languages; Ọ̀kọ́], negative 'yes/no' interrogative often indicates bias towards a positive response; alternative interrogative (realized by alternative conjunction and, normally, the diachronic source of non-biased 'yes/no' interrogative particles).
	elemental	Number and kinds of Q-words – participants: human/non-human, singular/plural, quantity and value and, in some languages, noun class [e.g., Wolof, Zulu]; circumstances; process [e.g., Dagaare, Kpelle, Kulango, Yoruba].
imperative		Non-prohibitive/prohibitive (different negative marker from indicative) [e.g., Dagaare, Dagbani, Gurene, Kulango, Yakoma, Zulu]; subjunctive [e.g., Bantu – Sotho, Swahili, Xhosa, Zulu]; immediate/non-immediate [e.g., Mabia languages, Zulu].

Examples (3a) and (3b) are indicative clauses while (3c) and (3d) are imperative clauses. They display different verb forms. For one thing, while the Predicator in the indicative clauses carries tense affixes in addition to person affixes, the Predicator in the imperative clauses does not occur with tense markers (3b, 3c) and can occur without a person marker (3c) (see page 112–113 for details on MOOD in relation to PERSON). In addition, the form of the root verb, *yaa*, in the imperative clause is different from that of the indicative clauses, *-ya*.

Table 5.1 summarizes the delicate distinctions within the indicative and imperative MOODS across the Niger-Congo phylum (see Matthiessen, 2004: 613; Teruya et al., 2007: 874 for a universal account). The rest of the chapter will proceed to discuss them in detail.

Indicative: declarative

The declarative clause is the default realization of statements, the act of giving information. Within the declarative mood, a further distinction is often made between affirmative and non-affirmative in Niger-Congo languages. An affirmative clause asserts and negotiates the positive value of the clause while a non-affirmative clause asserts and negotiates the negative value of the clause. This distinction is exemplified by (4) and (5) below:

(4) Dagaare (Lobr), Gur: Mabia[5]

    (a)   *Bɛ*   *na*   *wa*   ***na.***
             3PL   POS.IND.FUT   come.PFV   AFFR
          'They will come.'

    (b)   *Bɛ*   *kṽ*   *wa*   ***ɪ.***
             3PL   NEG.IND.FUT   come.PFV   NAFFR
          'They will not come.'

(c) *Bɛ na wa nɪ nɪ libir.*
3PL POS.IND.FUT come.PFV CAUS FOC money.SG
'They will bring money.'

(5) Dagaare (Central), Gur: Mabia[6]

  (a) *Ba **na** wa **la**.*
    3PL POS.IND.FUT come.PFV AFFR
    'They will come.'

  (b) *Ba kong wa.*
    3PL NEG.IND.FUT come.PFV
    'They will not come.'

(6) Linda, Adamawa-Ubangi: Banda (Watters, 2000: 208)

  (a) *Àndà ʒú.*
    house COMPL.burn
    'A house burned.'

  (b) *Àndà ʒúʒú **nē**.*
    house COMPL.NEG.burn NAFFR
    'A house did not burn.'

The non-affirmative marker has often been described by many studies on African languages as a double negative marker. It is, however, important to distinguish between POLARITY as a system and the mood contrast established by affirmative and non-affirmative markers in clause final position to emphasize the semantic (or pragmatic) role of these final particles as prosodic cues or stance markers. In the clauses above, for instance, POLARITY is realized by particles (examples (4) and (5)) or the morphology (example (6)) of the verbal group realizing the Predicator. At the end of the clause, the speaker however resonates the polarity value of the clause as an interpersonal 'punch', that is, to establish the negotiatory value of the proposition, as s/he is potentially about to hand over the turn to the listener (see examples (4a, b), (5a), and (6b)). Again, while the modal particles or affixes normally placed within the verbal group also realize primary mood contrast such as indicative and imperative, the final modal particles indicate specific sub-types of the mood such as affirmative (4a) versus non-affirmative (4b) (also see example (2) on indicative-imperative distinction by modal particles in the verbal group). It is interesting that out of the various meanings realized in the Predicator, it is the polarity that is picked up for negotiation at the end of the clause. This prosodic resonance between polarity and mood reflects a general characteristic of interpersonal systems (cf. Halliday, 2008).

Among languages with this affirmative/non-affirmative distinction, there is variation as to which of the mood types is overtly marked. In some languages, such as the Lobr dialect of Dagaare, both are overtly marked as in (4a) and (4b), unless there is end (or completive) focus in the affirmative clause, in which case it is not overtly marked (4c). In other languages, such as Linda and also Kulango, only the non-affirmative is overtly marked (6b), and, in Central Dagaare, only the affirmative is overtly marked (5a). From a cross-linguistic point of view, the non-affirmative is more often overtly marked than the affirmative. One possible explanation for this is that the negative clause is a marked choice in the system of POLARITY and requires more grammatical energy. That is, it puts pressure on the speaker to do more negotiation work. In a corpus of 18 million words, Halliday and James (1993) found that the probability of the occurrence of positive to negative clauses in English discourse is a ratio of 09:01 respectively. The figure we encounter in Dagaare (Lobr), for instance, is not much different. Out of 375 clauses across different registers, positive is 362 (96.5 per cent) and negative is 13 (3.5 per cent), i.e., an average ratio of 9.7:0.3 per text analysed (Mwinlaaru, 2017: §5.4.3). Given this probabilistic tendency, it is understandable that the negative is often favoured for a special mood marking at clause final position, where it serves the need to remind listeners of the negative value of the clause. Further research is, however, required for a detailed investigation of this tendency across languages.

It is also worth noting the absence of one declarative sub-type in Niger-Congo, namely, the exclamative clause. In many languages, there is no specific grammatical marker for exclamation and, where one exists (e.g., in Dagaare and Ọ̀kọ́), it is interpreted as an attitude marker, occurring across declarative and imperative clauses rather than being a specialized term in the system of mood (cf. Moutaouakil, 1999; Mwinlaaru, forthcoming).[7]

Indicative: interrogative

Two main types of interrogative clauses are identified in the languages around the world, namely polar interrogative and elemental interrogative. This section discusses their realization across Niger-Congo.

Polar interrogative

The polar interrogative clause, as the name suggests, enacts a question about polarity, offering an option to the listener to affirm or deny a proposition. Two main types are identified: (1) 'yes/no' interrogative clause and (2) alternative interrogative clause.

(1) Yes/no: 'Yes/no' interrogatives have the following realization possibilities in Niger-Congo:

1   they are either realized by phonological prosody, or
2   they are realized segmentally by juncture prosodies—clause final or initial particles serving as Negotiator.

Phonologically, 'yes/no' interrogative can be realized by a high-low tone on the final syllable in the clause, a rise-falling intonation, final vowel lengthening (or vowel insertion in clauses ending with a closed syllable). Languages that deploy only phonological prosody mostly belong to the Kwa and Benue-Congo families. In the examples from Ga in (7) below, for instance, the interrogative has the same grammatical form as the declarative, with the only contrast being the use of a high tone on the last syllable of the interrogative clause (7b) as opposed to the use of the low tone in the corresponding declarative clause (7a):

(7)   Ga, Kwa: Nyo

    (a)   *O-yè*   *òmɔ̀*   *Jùfɔ̀*.
             2SG-eat.PST   rice   Tuesday
             'You ate rice on Tuesday.'

(b) *O-yè*   *òmɔ̀*   ***Jùfɔ́?***
     2SG-eat.PST   rice   Tuesday
     'Did you eat rice on Tuesday?'

In some languages such as Nkore-Kiga (Benue-Congo: Bantoid), the 'yes/no' interrogative is distinguished from the declarative clause with a voiced vowel in the final syllable in the interrogative clause and by whispering the vowel in the final syllable of the corresponding declarative clause (Taylor, 1985: 6; Dryer, 2013a).

On the other hand, segmental realization of 'yes/no' interrogative is prominent among Gur languages. In languages that are oriented towards this mode of realization, however, there is normally a complementary option of realization through phonological prosody. In the Dagaare examples, for instance, while 'yes-no' interrogative is indicated by the clause final particle *bɪ* in (8a), it is alternatively realized by vowel lengthening in the final syllable of the sentence and a simultaneous high tone, resulting in a Low + High tone combination on *yà(á)*. (In Dagaare orthography or written language, the vowel lengthening is not indicated):

(8) Dagaare (Gur: Mabia)

     (a) *Fʋ*   *tèr =ɪ*   *lìbìr*   *na*   *yà*   ***bɪ?***
          2SG   POSSESS.PFV=FOC money.SG   POS.IND.FUT   pay.pfv   INT
          'Do you have money to pay?'

     (b) *Fʋ*   *tèr =ɪ*   *lìbìr*   *na*   ***yàá?***
          2SG   POSSESS.PFV=FOC money.SG   POS.IND.FUT   pay.PFV
          'Do you have money to pay?'

Languages with segmental marking vary, based on the textual status of the Negotiator in the clause (cf. Matthiessen, 2004: 648–649; Teruya et al., 2007; Dryer, 2013b). It may be assigned (1) thematic status (cf. endnote 1 on 'Theme'), where it orients the clause interpersonally in the initial position (e.g., Ewondo, Benue-Congo: Bantoid; cf. Redden, 1979: 153; Obolo, Benue-Congo: Cross-River; cf. Faraclas, 1984: 96–97; Wolof, West Atlantic: Senegambian; cf. Njie, 1982: 260, 264); (2) clause final position, where it has no special textual status but serves as an interpersonal punch to the clause (e.g., Akan, Dagaare and Ewe); and (3) some languages, such as Dagbani (Gur: Mabia) and Hunde (Benue-Congo: Bantoid), are flexible, allowing either positions. An example is given in (9) from Dagbani:

(9) Dagbani, Gur: Mabia (Issah, 2015: 48)

     (a) ***Bee***   *doo*   *maa*   *di-ri*   *nyuli?*
          INT   man   DEF   eat-IPFV   yam
          'Does the man eat yam?'

     (b) *Doo*   *maa*   *di-ri*   *nyuli*   ***bee?***
          man   DEF   eat-IPFV   yam   INT
          'Does the man eat yam?'

Both clause (9a) and (9b) realize the same proposition, the only difference being the position of the Negotiator. In both cases, it serves as a juncture prosody. In (9a) it enacts the negotiatory value of the proposition at its point of departure while, in (9b), this negotiatory value punctuates the clause. In some languages, such as Hunde, the clause initial particle (i.e., *mbéni*) and clause final particle (i.e., *hé*) are morphologically distinct (cf. Kahombo, 1992: 171; Dryer, 2013b).

Some languages also have a range of particles for adding attitude to the 'yes/no' interrogative, extending its delicacy into a contrast between (1) neutral (10a), and (2) biased (10b, c) sub-types:

(10) Ọ̀kọ́, Benue-Congo: NOI

    (a)   *Y-ŏsúdá*   *gó*   *tu*   *uba*   ***họn***
               3SG-elder:sibling   assist   1PL.ACC   hand   INT
               'Did his/her brother help us?' – neutral question

    (b)   *Y-ŏsúdá*   *gó*   *tu*   *uba*   ***sǒ***
               3SG-elder:sibling   assist   1PL.ACC   hand   INT
               'Did his/her brother help us (I believe he didn't)?'

    (c)   ***Ámá***   *y-ŏsúdá*   *gó*   *tu*   *ubâ?*
               INT   3SG-elder:sibling   assist   1PL.ACC   hand
               'Did his/her brother help us (I believe he did)?'

In these Ọ̀kọ́ examples, clause (10a) is a neutral 'yes/no' interrogative and this is signalled by the Negotiator *họn*. Clause (10b) is a biased 'yes/no' interrogative, where the speaker expects an opposite pole answer to the question (i.e., negative bias interrogative). This is realized by the Negotiator *sǒ*. Example (10c) is similarly a biased 'yes/no' interrogative. However, the Negotiator *ámá*, at the beginning of the clause, indicates an expectation of a same pole answer by the speaker (i.e., positive bias interrogative). These interrogative particles are functionally like intonation and question tags in Indo-European languages (cf. Halliday & Greaves, 2008: 109–125 on intonation and MOOD in English).

(2) Alternative interrogative: The alternative interrogative is a special kind of polar interrogative clause. Instead of anticipating 'yes/no' for an answer, it poses two conjoined propositions as alternative responses to the listener. It is related to the 'yes/no' interrogative diachronically as it is the typical source of 'yes/no' interrogative particles across languages. Particles that serve as Negotiator in the 'yes/no' interrogative normally have the same form as the conjunction *or*, used in the alternative interrogative. This phenomenon is very widespread in Niger-Congo and has been reported for many other African and non-African languages (cf. Heine & Kuteva, 2002: 226–227). Let's consider the following example from Dagbani:

(11) Dagbani, Gur: Mabia (Issah, 2015: 56)

       Bɛ   *nyu-ri*   *kom*   ***bee***   *bɛ*   *bi*   *nyu-ra?*
       3PL.NOM   drink-IPFV   water   CONJ   3PL.NOM   NEG   drink-IPFV
       'Do they drink water or they do not drink?'

If we compare (11) to (9a) and (9b) above, it becomes clear that the 'yes/no' interrogative results from a split of the alternative interrogative clause, where the erstwhile conjunction (11) has grammaticalized to become a juncture prosody, either occurring clause initially (9a) or clause finally (9b) to negotiate the clause as a dialogic move. In the alternative interrogative clause itself, there is no explicit question marker (11). The interrogation is realized by using the alternative conjunction.

Elemental interrogative

Elemental (or 'wh-') interrogative is the most widely studied mood type in Niger-Congo. Cross-linguistically, a distinctive characteristic of this mood type is the presence of a question word ('Q-word') in the clause that queries missing information that the listener is expected to supply. Every language has a special class of Q-words for querying different elements of the clause. Examples of elemental interrogative are given below from Akan (taken from the Kumawood movie *Agya Koo Ahuoyaa*):

(12) Akan, Kwa: Tano

Ɛdeɛn	*na*	*wo-re-yɛ*	*yi*	*a?*	**Ɛdeɛn**		*na*	*wo-hu*
what	FOC	2SG-PROG-do	this	PRT	what		FOC	2SG.see
aduane	*a*	*wo-kɔm*	*sei*	*yi?*	*Wo-kɔm*			
food	PRT	2SG-be:restless	like	this	2SG-be:restless			
saa,	**adɛn?**							
like:this	why							

'What is this that you are doing? Why is it that when you see food you become so restless? You are so restless, why?'

In this text, the speaker uses the Q-words *ɛdeɛn* ('what') and *adɛn* ('why') to enact the clauses as a move in exchange, a demand for information from the listener. Q-words in Niger-Congo languages are typically not similar in their morphological form as they are in Indo-European languages. One language that comes close to morphological similarity is Ọ̀kọ́, which has the following forms: *èra* (who, singular), *èrána* (who, plural) (who), *èna* (what, singular), *ọ́ọ́na* (which, singular, which), *ẹ̀ẹ́na* (which (one), plural), *étẹka* (where), *èmọ̀óna* (when), *ènaǎ* and *gàna* (how). Wolof also has two sets of Q-words, one of which is composed of the morpheme *–u* and a class marker, and the other composed of *-na* and a class maker (cf. example (20)). These are characterised as *u*-forms and *na*-forms respectively (Torrence, 2003).

In addition, Q-words in Niger-Congo are versatile in two ways. First, different Q-words may query the same or similar kinds of information and, second, the same Q-word can query different kinds of information. The first is illustrated by the Akan example in (12), where *ɛdeɛn* ('what') in the second clause and *adɛn* ('why') in the third clause both query reason. As the gloss for *ɛdeɛn* suggests, although it is always possible to assign one meaning to such semantically versatile Q-words in isolation, they do take on different meanings in discourse. The second motif is still illustrated by the Akan Q-word *sɛn* below (from our conversational data):

(13)	*Nti*	*wo,*	*wo-re-kɔ*	*a*		*ɔmo*	*gye*	*wo*	**sɛn?**
	so	2SG	2SG-PROG-go	PRT		3PL	take	3SG	how:much

'So you, when you are going, how much do they charge you?'

(14) *Na*   *wei*   *nso*   *wo-haw*   *ne*   **sɛn?**
CONT   this   too   3SG-problem   be   how
'This one too, how does it concern you?'

(15) *Wo-din*   *di*   **sɛn?**
2SG-name   call   what
'What is your name?'

(16) *Auntie*   *se*   **sɛn?**
Auntie   say   what
'What did Auntie say?'

Sɛn is used here to query value (13), manner (14), attribute (15) and locution (16). Although native speakers will render its default meaning in isolation as 'how much' or 'how many', in discourse, its meaning shifts, querying different kinds of information based on context.

Finally, elemental interrogatives may also take Negotiators (17). This has been reported as a characteristic of Eastern Kru languages such as Gbadi, Guébie and Vata (Koopman, 1984: 87; Sande, 2014).

(17) Vata, Kru: Eastern (Sande, 2014: 6)

Alɔ   *ɔ*   *le*   *saka*   **la?**
who   3SG   eat   rice   INT
'Who eats rice?'

Although we are not able to verify the essence of the Negotiator in the Vata example in (17), in Ọ̀kọ́ (Benue-Congo: NOI) and in languages where such particles occur optionally, the Negotiator adds attitudinal meaning to the clause. In Dagaare, for instance, the particle *ya* can be added to any 'wh-' interrogative clause to show surprise or realize an echo question, as in (18). (The three dots in square brackets indicate suspension points; the dialogue is from *St. Maria* play).

(18) Dagaare (Gur: Mabia)

Son: *Mãa*   *lɪɛbɛ*   *nɪ*   *faara*   *o!* [. . .]
          1SG.   turn.   FOC   priest   PRT
          EMP   IPFV
          'I am becoming a priest!'

Father: *Bʋnʋ* **ya?**   *A*   *sukuul*   *ĩ*   *na*   *γaw*   *fʋ,*   *fʋ*   *bɛ*   *zawrɪ*   *ɛ?* [. . .]
          what   INT   DEF   school   1SG   REL   put.PFV   2SG   2SG   NEG.   refuse.   NAFFR
                                                                               IND.   PFV
                                                                            NFUT
          'What? The school I put you in, didn't you stop?'

The next sub-section will proceed to discuss the characteristics of Q-words in Niger-Congo in detail in relation to the range of transitivity roles they query and their textual statuses in the clause.

Q-WORDS IN RELATION TO EXPERIENTIAL ROLES IN THE CLAUSE

Languages differ with regard to the range of transitivity roles that can be queried by Q-words and the nature and kinds of these Q-words. The relevant variables here are (1) participants,

A system-based typology of MOOD in Niger-Congo

Table 5.2 Illustration of number contrast in Q-words

Dagaare		Ọ̀kọ́		Akan		gloss
singular	*plural*	*singular*	*plural*	*singular*	*plural*	
ãã / ãnʊ	ãmɪnɛ	ɛ̀ra	ɛ̀rána	hwan	hawnom	who
bʊnʊ / bʊʊ	bʊnʊ / bʊʊ	ɛ̀na	ɛ̀na	Ɛdeɛn	Ɛdeɛn	what
buor	bobe	ọ̀ọ́na	ɛ̀ɛ́na	deɛ ɛwo hen	deɛ ɛwo hen	which (one)

(2) circumstance, and (3) process (cf. Matthiessen, 2004: 616; Teruya et al., 2007: 877–879). While perhaps every language has Q-words for querying participants and circumstances, only a few languages have Q-words corresponding to processes.

(1) Participants: Regarding participants, Niger-Congo languages have Q-words for querying human participants ('who'), non-human participants ('what') and participant identification ('which'). While these characteristics are largely universal across languages, in Niger-Congo Q-words also normally take on the typological characteristics of nouns in the language concerned. Thus, depending on the language and the Q-word, they can show number distinction, noun class marking, and may take definite articles. Table 5.2 illustrates the range of possibilities across languages in relation to the system of NUMBER, using data from Dagaare, Ọ̀kọ́ and Akan. As the table shows, human participants ('who') and, to a lesser extent, identifying Q-words ('which'), tend to show number distinctions. Akan queries participant identification with a fossilized construction (*deɛ ɛwo he*) best translated as 'which of them'. Non-human participants ('what') normally do not show number distinction.

In the Mabia family of Gur languages, the definite particle can be used with Q-words to show definiteness where the speaker presupposes that the item to be supplied as an answer will be definite. In such contexts, the interrogative realizes a confirmation-seeking question. The interrogative clause in (19), for example, is a suitable question where both speaker and listener are deciding to divide labour among themselves, with one of them, for instance, going to the farm and the other to the market. Here, the definite article is used to indicate this presupposed meaning and the answer to the question is expected to be definite:

(19) Dagaare

    (a) *A **nyɪnɛ** na fʊ cere?*
         DEF where IDENT.PL 2SG go.IPFV
        'Where is it (that) you are going?' (to the market or the farm?)

    (b) *A wɪɛ pʊɔ na.*
         DEF farm inside IDENT.PL
        'To the farm.'
        Lit. 'In the farm it is.'

This situation reflects a general exotic use of the definite marker in Gur languages, especially those of the Mabia sub-family, where the definite marker even occurs with personal names and other proper nouns. Wolof (West Atlantic: Senegambian) presents an interesting scenario of special Q-words with class marking (cf. Torrence, 2003).[8] As mentioned earlier, the Q-word consists of either the morpheme *-u* or *-na* and a class marker that agrees with the class of the queried item. This resonates with the robustness of class agreement in Wolof (Torrence, 2003). We illustrate this phenomenon below:

(20) Wolof, West Atlantic (Torrence, 2003: 3, 6)

(a) **K-u**   *sàcc*   *gato*   *bi*?
     CL-u   steal   cake   the
     'Who stole the cake?'

(b) **L-u**   *Isaa*   *sàcc*?
     CL-u   Isaa   steal
     'What did Isaa steal?'

Another interesting generalization is the existence of single Q-words across Niger-Congo languages for querying quantity and value ('how many', 'how much', 'how long', 'how far', etc.). Examples are given below:

(21) Denya, Benue-Congo: Bantoid (Abangma, 2002: 56)

(a) *Bɔɔ́*   **á-níí**   *a-cwɔɔ-ɔ́*?
     person   SP.HM-how:many   SP.HM-come-PFV
     'How many people came?'

(b) *Upú*   *ú-kwé*   **ú-níí**?
     houses   SP.NHM-fall   SP.NHM-how:many
     'How many houses collapsed?'

(22) Ga, Kwa: Nyo

(a) **Ehiɛ**   *ohɔ̃ɔ̃*   *oyɔɔ*?
     how:much   2SG.sell.PROG   2SG.beans
     'How much are you selling your beans?'

(b) (*Maŋo*)   **ehiɛ**   *ohe*?
     mango   how:many   2SG.buy.PST
     'How many (mangoes) did you buy?'

Related to the point raised earlier on the overlapping sense of Q-words, it is common in Niger-Congo languages to find Q-words that query specific kinds of participants. For example, while Dagaare has a general Q-word that translates as 'what', *bʋnʋ/bʋʋ*, it has specific words, *ŋmɪn* ('what') and *bo* ('what'), for querying events (23) and idea/locution (24) respectively:

(23) Dagaare, Gur: Mabia (*St. Maria* play)

Ĩ   *pãa*   *ɪ*   **ŋmɪn**?
1SG   ADV   do.PFV   what
'**What** can I do now?'

(24) Dagaare, Gur: Mabia (*Sɛb-Sow Yɛr-bie*, 1996)

A   *Sɛb-sow*   *yel*   *a*   *kɛ*   **bo**?
DEF   scripture-holy   say.PFV   AFFR   PROJ   what
'**What** does the holy scripture say?'

A system-based typology of MOOD in Niger-Congo

These Q-words lie on the borderline between processes and participants. Although they are by themselves participants in the clause, compared with *bʋnʋ/bʋʋ*, they are abstract and query processes rather than entities. It should be noted that while the more general Q-word *bʋnʋ* can substitute both *ŋmɪn* and *bo* in these examples, the two can only be used for the specialized participants they query. *Ŋmɪn* can also query 'whereabout' and can combine with the definite article (*a ŋmɪn*) to query quantity ('how many') or value ('how much').

(2) Circumstances: Circumstantial roles that are queried in the clause consist of time ('when'), place ('where'), manner ('how'), and reason ('why'). Time is typically queried by units that translate as 'which time' (e.g., *debor* or *dabor* in Dagaare; *saha dini* in Dagbani and *ɛmɛrɛ bɛn* in Akan), 'which day' (e.g., *dabɛn* in Akan and *bondali* in Dagbani) and 'what day' (e.g., *nigbà wo* in Yoruba). Although manner can be queried by single morpheme Q-words as in (25), it is often queried metaphorically by the interrogative noun group 'what path' or 'what thing' (26):

(25) Kulango, Gur: Kulango-Lorom[9]

> **Zɪ** *bɔɔ-hɛ* *ɛ* *kuu* *ye* *daagɛ*?
> how 3PL-DO 3SG.ACC born.PFV 3SG.ACC again
> '**How** will they give birth to him again?'

(26) Kulango, Gur: Kulango-Lorom

> **Bɛɛ** *bɔɔgɔ* *bʋ-tʋ* *ti* *lɛ* *nyɪ* *Yowomolia*
> what path 3PL-PASS on CONJ get God
> *bɔ* *hohom* *gʋʋ* *bɔɔ-dʋm*?
> 3SG spirit matter 3PL-talk
> '**How** can we get this spirit of God they are talking about?'
> Lit. 'On **what path** can we pass and get this spirit of God they are talking about?'

Among circumstantial Q-words, it is only 'where' that is consistently realized by single morpheme Q-words across languages.

Reason ('why'), in particular, stands out in some special way in relation to the other circumstances. First, it is the role that is most unlikely to be queried by a single morpheme Q-word. Examples are *ɛdeen enti*, *èná-wore-ka*, and *nítorí kí* ('what reason') respectively in Akan, Ọ̀kọ́ and Yoruba and, on the other hand, *bɔ-zuɣu* and *bʋʋ so* ('what owns') in Dagbani (Issah, 2015: 58) and Dagaare respectively. We illustrate this further below with data from Kulango (27) and Ga (28):

(27) Kulango, Gur: Kulango-Lorom

> **Bɛ-zɪngɛ** *tii* *daa* *ho-goi* *yaa* *bɔ* *perikɛn*?
> what-thing owns always 3SG-return go 3SG mud
> '**Why** does it [pig] always go back to its mud?'
> Lit. '**What thing owns** (that) it always goes back to its mud?'

(28) Ga, Kwa: Nyo

> **Mɛni** *hewɔ* *o-ye* *omo* *Jufɔ*?
> What reason 2SG-eat.PFV rice Tuesday
> '**Why** did you eat rice on Tuesday?'

107

This phenomenon can be interpreted in relation to other Q-words. The general situation is that the more abstract the transitivity role queried by the Q-element is, the more likely that it will be realized metaphorically by more than a single morpheme. Based on this variable, we posit the following scale of abstractness among circumstantial Q-words, starting from the least to the most abstract: 'where > when > how > why'. In other words, across languages, the rightmost item in the scale is more likely to be realized metaphorically than items to the left.

Another characteristic of the amorphous nature of reason is that it is most likely to be realized by a wide range of Q-words. Torrence and Kandybowicz (2015: 257), for instance, list three Q-words for 'why' in Krachi (Kwa: Tano): *nanı, nɛ kumuso, nɛ so*. This phenomenon is best illustrated by the following clauses from Dagaare, where different Q-words are used in querying reason:

(29) *St. Maria* play

Bʋʋ	**so**	*fʋ*	*yele*	*a*	*lɛ*?
what	own	2SG	say.IPFV	DEF	DEM

'Why are you saying that?'
Lit. '**What owns** you saying that?'

(30) *St. Maria* play

Bʋʋ	*fʋ*	*mì*	*lɛ*	*yɛ́rɛ*	*lɛ*?
what	2SG	too	also	say.IPFV	DEM

'Why are you too speaking like that?'

(31) Sɛb-Sow Yɛr-bie (1996)

Bʋnʋ	**yâw**	*na*	*nyı*	*bɔbr*	*mɛ*?
what	sake	IDENT.PL	2PL	look.PFV	1SG.ACC

'For the sake of what are you looking for me?'

(32) Sɛb-Sow Yɛr-bie (1996)

Dmınŋmın	**yâw**	*na*	*fʋ*	*bɔbr*	*kɛ*	*fʋ*
how	sake	IDENT.PL	2SG	speak.PFV	PROJ	2SG
zɛbr =ı	*a*	*Naaŋmin*?				
quarrel=FOC	DEF	God				

'It is for what sake that you want to quarrel with God?'

As the examples show, Q-words that are typically associated with participants (29, 30, 31) and manner (32) combine with other words to query reason in incongruent ways. It is even possible to express (29) in a cleft construction: *Bʋʋ nʋ so fʋ yele a lɛ*? (literally, 'What is it that owns your saying that?').

(3) Process: As mentioned earlier, only a few languages use interrogative verbs (or 'wh-' verbs) (cf. Table 5.1). They are notably restricted to circumstantial processes, especially location, as the following examples from Kulango (33) and Kpelle (34) illustrate:

(33) Kulango, Gur: Kulango-Lorom

Ʋ	*nyına*	**waı**?
2SG	mother	be:where

'Where is your mother?'

108

(34) Kpelle, Mande: Western (Welmers, 1973: 419)
 Sumo   ***kɔɔ*?**
 Sumo   be:where
 'Where is Sumo?'

In these clauses, the Predicator, *wai* (33) and *kɔɔ* (34), is the element that queries the location of the Subject. Yoruba has two interrogative verbs, one of which queries Attribute (35b) and Matter (35c) in addition to Place (cf. Bamgbose, 1966: 54; Akanbi, n.d.). These are *dà* ('be where') and *nkọ́* ('how be', 'what about', 'be where'):

(35) Yoruba, Benue-Congo: Defoid (Akanbi, n.d.: 14)

  (a) *Baba*   *àgbà*   ***dà*?**
       father   elder   be:where
       'Where is grandfather?'

  (b) *Ilé*   ***nkọ́*,**   *ṣé*   *àlàáfíà*   *nilé*   *wà*?
       house   be:how,   do   peace   in:house   be
       'How is home, hope the home is at peace?'

  (c) *Owó*   ***nkọ́*,**   *ṣé*   *iwọ́*   *náà*   *fẹ́*?
       money   be:what:about   do   you   also   love
       'What about money, do you also want?'

In (35a), the Predicator *dà* interrogates the whereabouts of the Subject. On the other hand, in (35b), *nkọ́* interrogates the attribute of Subject, *Ilé* ('house'), while, in (35c), it queries matter, the aboutness of the Subject, 'money', in relation to the listener's desire towards it.

Q-WORDS IN RELATION TO TEXTUAL SYSTEMS

One important typological variable of Q-words across languages is their interaction with textual systems of the clause, notably THEME and INFORMATION (cf. Aboh, 2007b; Heath, 2008: 464). The placement of the Q-element varies with respect to the default textual status they are assigned across languages. Three motifs have been identified across the languages of the world (cf. Matthiessen, 2004: 616–617; Teruya et al., 2007: 877–879):

1   The Q-element is not given any distinct textual treatment in the clause; it occurs *in situ*, where it would appear in a corresponding declarative clause (cf. example (36)).
2   The Q-element is assigned the status of unmarked (i.e., default) Theme in the clause (cf. example (37)).
3   The Q-element is by default assigned information focus (i.e., unmarked focus) in the clause (cf. examples (38) and (39)).

The first is by far the most common in African languages in general, and Niger-Congo in particular (cf. Watters, 2000: 204). An equally prominent corollary to this is that the Q-element can be placed clause initially in a thematic equative (or cleft-construction) as a marked (or contrastive) focused element. In the following example from Kinyarwanda, the default choice is (36a), where the Q-word *nde* ('who') occurs in Complement position, that is, where the queried participant would occur in a corresponding declarative clause. Example (36b), however, illustrates the marked instance, where the Q-element is thematized for marked focus, indicated by the focus marker *ni*:

(36) Kinyarwanda, Benue-Congo: Bantoid (Maxwell, 1981: 167, 168)

(a) *Umogore*   *jiše*   **nde**?
    woman   kill.PST   **who**
    'The woman killed whom?'

(b) *Ni-* **nde**   *umugore*   *jiše*?
    FOC-who   woman   kill.PST
    '**Who** is it that the woman killed?'

Languages where the Q-element is elevated to the status of unmarked Theme are illustrated by Ahan (Benue-Congo: Defoid; cf. Akanbi, 2015), Wolof (West Atlantic: Senegambian; cf. Torrence, 2003) and Ga (Kwa: Nyo). As illustrated in (20), Wolof Q-words are composed of either the morpheme *–u* or *–an* and the class marker of the item queried. By default, they are placed clause initially as unmarked Themes (see page 106). However, the *an*-forms, but not the *u*-forms, can also occur *in situ*, where they take on marked meaning as echo questions (Torrence, 2003). Ga, which also treats the Q-element as default Theme (37a), presents a more flexible scenario, where it is normally possible to also place the Q-element *in situ* (37b) for echo questions (33b) (but see further below on 'why'):

(37) Ga, Kwa: Nyo

(a) A: **Mɛni**   *O-ye*?
        what   2SG.PST-eat.
        '**What** did you eat?'
    B: *Mi-ye*   *omɔ*.
        1SG.PFV-eat   rice
        'I ate rice.'

(b) A: *Mi-ye*   *omɔ*.
        1SG.PFV-eat   rice
        'I ate rice.'
    B: *O-ye*   **mɛni**?
        2SG-eat.PFV   what
        'You ate **what**?'

In summary, as a comparison of the glosses in (37a) and (37b) indicates, one characteristic of languages with the Q-element as unmarked (i.e., default) Theme is that, where it occurs *in situ*, it normally has a marked reading as an echo question.

The third motif, where the Q-element receives default information focus, is exemplified by Yoruba and Aghem below:

(38) Yoruba, Benue-Congo: Defoid (Akanbi, n.d.: 6)

(a) **Ta**   *ni*   *ó*   *kú*?
    who   FOC   3SG   die
    '**Who** died?'

(b) **Kí**   *ni*   *o*   *rí*?
    what   FOC   2SG   see
    '**What** did you see?'

(39) Aghem, Benue-Congo: Bantoid (Hyman, 2005: 1)

(a) *Fil*   *a-mɔ́*   *zì*   ***zín***   *bɛ́-kɔ́?*
friends SP.PST eat when fufu
'**When** did the friends eat fufu?'

(b) *À*   *mɔ̀*   *zì*   ***ndúghɔ́*** *bɛ́-kɔ́?*
EXPL PST eat who fufu
'**Who** ate fufu (today)?'

As example (38) shows, the Yoruba clauses relatively have the same structure as the cleft-constructions discussed for languages with option 1 above. However, in Yoruba, the focused position is the default choice and, even where the Q-element is the Subject of the construction, it is still obligatorily indicated for focus (38a). Unlike in Yoruba, where the information focus position of the clause is initial, in Aghem (Benue-Congo: Bantoid), the default focus position is immediately after the verbal group. Thus, any clausal element can be assigned information focus by placing it immediately after the Predicator, without any special morphological marking (Aboh, 2007b). In (39a), the Q-word *zín* is focused by placing it after the verb *zì* ('eat') and, in (39b), where the queried item is the Agent, the Q-word, *ndúghɔ́* ('who'), is still placed in post-verb position and the Subject of the clause is realized by an expletive pronoun *À*. Readers are referred to Aboh (2007b) for a detailed discussion on the relationship between 'wh-' words and focus in African languages.

It must further be mentioned that there is pressure on languages to place the Q-element in clause initial position and even in languages with option 1, the marked choice is common and sometimes it is the most appropriate choice for particular Q-words. One notable Q-word in this regard is 'why' (cf. pages 107–108). Even in languages where the default placement is *in situ*, 'why' is always thematized (cf. Torrence & Kandybowicz (2015) on Krachi). In Gichuka (Benue-Congo: Bantoid), although it is possible for 'why' to occur *in situ*, it is typically thematized without any focus marking as is required for other *ex situ* Q-elements (Muriungi et al., 2014: 193). In other words, it maintains the same form irrespective of its position in the clause. The implication is that 'why' is treated uniquely as unmarked Theme in Gichuka although, in some languages (e.g., Akan), it is normally given marked (or contrastive) focus.

Further on the imperative

A widespread distinction in the imperative across Niger-Congo is the prohibitive versus non-prohibitive imperative, which resonates with the affirmative/non-affirmative contrast in the indicative mood (cf. pages 98–100). It is common in languages of the Gur (e.g., Dagaare, Dagbani, Kulango), Adamawa-Ubangi (e.g., Yakoma; cf. Boyeldieu, 1995: 131–132) and Bantu (e.g., Zulu; cf. Poulos & Bosch, 1997: 19) families (see also van der Auwera et al., 2013). This distinction is made by the Predicator element in the clause. The typical realization is the presence of a special negative marker in the verbal group. In other words, this negative particle is distinct from the negative particles associated with the indicative clause. In the Dagbani examples below, the non-prohibitive is realized by only the verb as Predicator (40a) while the prohibitive takes negative imperative particles (40b, 40c). The negative marker for a corresponding indicative clause will be *ku* (for future) and *bi* (for non-future).

Isaac N. Mwinlaaru et al.

(40) Dagbani, Gur: Mabia

(a) *Kamna!*
come.PFV
'Come!'

(b) ***Di***   *kana!*
NEG.IMP.IM   come.PFV
'Don't come!'

(c) ***Diti***   *kana!*
NEG.IMP.NIM   come.PFV
'Don't come (when I leave)!'

Alternatively, some languages show this contrast by the presence of both a negative and a person marker on the verb realizing the Predicator in prohibitive clauses (41a) but not on the verb in the non-prohibitive (41b):

(41) Kulango, Gur: Kulango-Lorom

(a) *Mɪ*   *hanawɔ,*   *mɪ*   *veemɔ,*   ***ǐ-a-si***
1SG   elder: siblings   1SG   younger:siblings   2PL-NEG-receive
saa   *gʋʋ*   *hɔɔ*   *lɛ*   *tɪ*   *sa*   *cɛngɛ*   *ɪ!*
this   message   this   CONJ   take   put   aside   NAFFR
'My elder siblings, my younger siblings, don't receive this message and put it aside!'

(b) ||| ***Su***   *ge*   *awaawaatuu*   *lɛ*   *de*   *bɔ-kuu*   *u*   *daagɛ!* |||
accept   3SG.INA   embrace   let   PRT   3PL-born   2SG   again.
'Embrace it and be born again!'

Examples (41a) and (41b) constitute a continuous flow of text (cf. endnote 9). The command here is directed to a plural interactant, signalled by the Vocative element at the beginning of the clause. The Predicator in the first clause requires a person prefix because it is in the prohibitive mood. However, the Predicator in (41b) cannot take a person prefix since it is non-prohibitive. The implication is that the prohibitive clause has the same structural form as a corresponding declarative clause. The difference is indicated by a high-low tone on the pronominal subject prefix in the declarative and a low-high tone on that of the imperative clause.

Another contrast in the imperative mood across languages is that between immediate and non-immediate imperatives, although it seems this is not a common distinction. It has been reported in Zulu (van Rooyen, 1984) and is prominent in Mabia languages (e.g., Dagaare, Dagbani, Gurene, Mampruli), as a sub-distinction within the prohibitive mood. It is exemplified in (40b) and (40c), where respectively the immediate prohibitive is realized by the negative imperative particle *di* and the non-immediate is realized by a distinct negative particle *diti*. In Dagaare, the non-immediate requires an imperfective verb form in addition to the particle.

In addition to these imperative sub-types, a subjunctive mood is predominant in the southern Bantu languages such as Swahili, Zulu and Sotho and it is realized by a distinct verbal morphology (cf. van Rooyen, 1984).[10]

Another important typological variable is the interaction of the imperative with the PERSON system. Three generalizations can be made in relation to this variable:

A system-based typology of MOOD *in Niger-Congo*

1   The imperative occurs with all persons – interactant: speaker/speaker plus; interactant: addressee (singular/plural) and non-interactant.
2   A Subject (for languages where it is always a separate element) or a pronominal subject affix (realized in the Predicator) is required in the imperative mood except where modal responsibility is assigned to a singular addressee.
3   As an alternative to 2, in some languages a pronominal subject affix is required for the prohibitive (i.e., negative imperative) mood but is absent in the non-prohibitive (i.e., positive imperative) mood.

Generalization 1 is found in all the languages where data on the imperative is accessible to us (e.g., Akan, Dagaare, Dagbani, Ga, Gurene, Kulango, Ọ̀kọ́), and perhaps applies to all Niger-Congo languages. Variable 2 is also dominant in Niger-Congo in comparison to 3. Examples can be found in (3c, d) introduced earlier and repeated below as (42a, b):

(42)   Ga (Kwa: Nyo)

(a)   ***Yaa***   *jaanɔ*!
      go   market
      'Go to the market!'

(b)   ***Nyɛ-yaa***   *jaanɔ*!
      2PL-go   market
      'You go to the market!'

Native speakers of Ga will automatically interpret the imperative clause in (42a), where there is no subject marker on the verb, as a command made to a single interactant and (42b), where there is a pronominal subject marker (*Nyɛ-*) on the verb (*yaa*, 'go'), as addressed to more than one interactant (see also example (43) further below for instances of first person plural (43a) and third person (43b) imperatives). We recorded variable 3 in the Kulango dialect cluster only and an illustration is provided in (41), where the Predicator in (41a) carries both a subject and a negative prefix and the Predicator of the clauses in (41b) is realized by the bare form of the verb.

Further, imperative clauses, other than those where modal responsibility is assigned to the addressee, overlap with the semantic region of MODALITY as it is defined for Indo-European languages (for instance), specifically obligation (cf. Palmer, 2001; Halliday & Matthiessen, 2014: 176–192). In this sense, where modal responsibility is assigned to speaker, speaker plus addressee or to a non-interactant, the function of the imperative is to indicate and modulate obligations imposed upon the person concerned (43):

(43)   Ọ̀kọ́, Benue-Congo: NOI

(a)   ***Te***   *ke*   *yo*!
      1PL   PFV   go
      'We should go!' (= 'Let's go!')

(b)   ***Itiye***   *akè*   *n'-ikíba*!
      Itiye   IPFV   collect-money
      'Itiye should be receiving the donations.'

While the English translations here are modalized declarative clauses, the original Ọ̀kọ́ clauses are simply imperative. The 'modality' meaning is, as it were, added to the clauses by the choice of non-addressee as the Subject of the clause. Such imperative clauses enact speech acts ranging from wishes, suggestions through requests to regulations. The specific speech function realized will normally depend on the choice of person, tenor and other contextual variables.

Conclusion

This study examined MOOD systems in Niger-Congo languages. It has shown how various speech functions, specifically statement, question and command, are grammaticalized as mood types across languages. Second, the study discussed the realizations of the mood types by phonological and by lexicogrammatical resources. It also considered the interaction of mood systems with Theme and Focus and the transitivity roles that are queried by Q-elements in elemental interrogative clauses.

Due to space constraints, the study could only present an overview of these issues, and it is practically impossible to exhaust the MOOD systems of the over 1,400 languages of Niger-Congo in a single chapter (cf. Heine & Nurse, 2000: 1). We, however, hope that it will motivate scholars of African languages to undertake an in-depth description of MOOD in individual languages and genetic families. Notably, there is a long tradition of research on MOOD in Southern Bantu, emerging from the work of C.M. Doke (see Gough (1993) for an early review). However, there are many inconsistencies from author to author and MOOD is often confused with tense, mode (in the sense of Whorf (1938[2012]: 146–150)) and other systems of the verbal unit (cf. van der Auwera & Aguilar (2016) for a historical account on the terms 'mood', 'modality' and 'mode'). A system-based approach oriented by the semantics of speech functions can extend our knowledge of the MOOD systems in these languages.

Abbreviations

ACC – accusative; ADV – adverbial particle; AFFR – affirmative; AGREE – agreement (modal) particle; ASSR – assertive; COMPL – completive; CL – class marker; CONJ – conjunction; CONT – continuative; COP – copula; DEF – definite; DEM – demonstrative; EMP – emphatic; EXPL – expletive; FOC – focus; FUT – future; HM – human; IDENT – identifying pronoun; IM – immediate; INA – inanimate; IND – indicative; INT – interrogative; IPFV – imperfective; N- – non; NEG – negative; NOM – nominative; PFV – perfective; PL – plural; POS – positive; PROJ – projection marker; PROG – progressive; PRT – particle; PST – past; REL – relativizer; SG – singular; SP – subject particle; 1 – first person, 2 – second person; 3 – third person.

Notes

* We use small caps (e.g. MOOD) to indicate a grammatical system (which can have different realisations within and across languages) and regular font (e.g. mood) for the same term when it refers to the function of a morpheme or structure or to realisations of the system.
1 Theme in this chapter is used in the sense of the Prague school notion of Functional Sentence Perspective and as it has been defined in systemic functional linguistics (see, e.g., Halliday & Matthiessen, 2014: Ch. 3). It consists of initial elements in the clause that orients it towards its interpretation; a point of departure in the clause. It is thus a pragmatic concept and not a participant role.
2 The Mabia sub-family has also been called Oti-Volta: Western. The name Mabia (which means 'mother's child') was introduced by Bodomo (e.g. Bodomo, 1997, this volume) to appropriately represent

the cultural unity within this group. It is a common address term among speakers in the sub-family for showing solidarity.

3 We thank Comfort Anafo, Elizabeth Agyeiwaa, Mark Nartey, and Raymond Adongo for data on their languages.

4 We write functional labels with initial capitals.

5 Unless otherwise stated, Dagaare examples in this study are from the Lobr dialect, entered in Ethnologue and Glottolog together with the Wule dialect as 'Dagara, Northern' (cf. Mwinlaaru, 2017: Ch. 1).

6 Central Dagaare is known locally among some speakers as 'Ngmere'. It is entered in Ethnologue as 'Dagaare, Southern'. We maintain 'Central Dagaare' because it is the term used by native writers of the dialect (e.g., Bodomo, 1997).

7 In English, although exclamation can be realized by minor clauses and incongruently by interrogative and imperative clauses, it is grammaticalized as a sub-type of the declarative clause (e.g., *What a beautiful girl she is!*) (cf. Halliday & Matthiessen, 2014: 164–165, 195–197).

8 This phenomenon is however not limited to participants (or nominal Q-words), but extends to circumstances since Wolof has classifiers for circumstantial elements in the clause. See an example below (Torrence, 2003: 3):

N-u	*Isaa*	*sàcc-e*	*gato*	*bi?*
CL-u	Isaa	steal-manner	cake	DEF

'How did Isaa steal the cake?'

9 The Kulango examples in this chapter are from *World Language Movies* www.youtube.com/watch?v=vhIUu9JNZmM (except example (33), which is constructed).

10 We found several studies discussing the subjunctive in southern Bantu languages (e.g., Van Rooyen, 1984; du Plessis & Visser, 1993; Taljard & Louwrens, 2003). But we could not find suitable illustrations since the relevant examples are not glossed.

References

Abangma, S.N. (2002). The forms and functions of questions in Denya. *Journal of West African Languages*, XXIX.2, 49–63.

Aboh, E.O. (2007a). Leftward focus versus rightward focus: the Kwa-Bantu conspiracy. *SOAS Working Papers in Linguistics*, 15, 81–104.

Aboh, E.O. (2007b). Focused versus non-focused *wh*-phrases. In E.O. Aboh, K. Hartmann & M. Zimmermann (eds), *Focus Strategies in African Languages: The Interaction of Focus and Grammar in Niger-Congo and Afro-Asiatic*, 287–314. Berlin & New York, NY: Mouton de Gruyter.

Akanbi, T.A. (2015). A descriptive analysis of Àhàn interrogative sentences. *Journal of West African Languages*, XLII.1, 89–105.

Akanbi, T.A. (n.d.). The syntax and semantics of interrogative markers *dà* and *nkọ́* in Yoruba. Available online at: www.academia.edu/11630645/The_Syntax_and_Semantic_of_Interrogative_Markers_Da_and_Nko_in_Yoruba [accessed on July 15, 2016].

Akerejola, E. (2005). A systemic functional grammar of Òkó. Macquarie University: PhD thesis.

Bamgbose, A. (1966). *The Grammar of Yoruba*. Cambridge: Cambridge University Press.

Bendor-Samuel, J.T. (1971). Niger-Congo, Gur. In T.A. Sebeok (ed.), *Current Trends in Linguistics*, Volume 7: Linguistics in Sub-Saharan Africa, 141–178. The Hague & Paris: Mouton.

Bodomo, A. (1997). *The Structure of Dagaare*. Stanford Monographs in African Languages. Stanford, CA: Stanford University, CSLI Publications.

Boyeldieu, P. (1995). Le Yakoma. In R. Boyd (ed.), *Le Système Verbal dans les Langues Oubangiennes*, 113–139. München: Lincom Europa.

Bybee, J., Perkins, R. & Pagliuca, W. (1994). *The Evolution of Grammar: Tense, Aspect and Modality in the Languages of the World*. Chicago, IL: University of Chicago Press.

Chisholm, W.S., Milic, L.T. & Greppin, J.A.A. (eds) (1984). *Interrogativity: A Colloquium on the Grammar, Typology and Pragmatics of Questions in Seven Diverse Languages*. Amsterdam: Benjamins.

Comrie, B. (1989). *Language Universals and Linguistic Typology: Syntax and Morphology, 2nd Edn.* Oxford: Blackwell.

Dryer, M.S. (2013a). Polar questions. In M.S. Dryer & M. Haspelmath (eds). *The World Atlas of Language Structures Online*. Available online at: http://wals.info/chapter/116, [accessed on March 31, 2017].

Dryer, M.S. (2013b). Position of polar question particles. In M.S. Dryer & M. Haspelmath (eds). *The World Atlas of Language Structures Online*. Available online at: http://wals.info/chapter/92, [accessed on April 1, 2017].

Dryer, M.S. & Haspelmath, M. (eds) (2013). *The World Atlas of Language Structures Online*. Leipzig: Max Planck Institute for Evolutionary Anthropology. Available online at: http://wals.info, [accessed on March 31, 2017].

Faraclas, N. (1984). *A Grammar of Obolo*. Bloomington, IN: Indiana University Linguistics Club.

Gough, D.H. (1993). A change of mood. *African Studies*, 52(2), 35–52, DOI: 10.1080/00020189308707777

Halliday, M.A.K. (1984). Language as code and language as behaviour: A systemic-functional interpretation of the nature and ontogenesis of dialogue. In M.A.K. Halliday, R.P. Fawcett, S. Lamb & A. Makkai (eds), *The Semiotics of Language and Culture*, Vol. 1, 3–35. London: Frances Pinter.

Halliday, M.A.K. (1996). On grammar and grammatics. In R. Hasan, C. Cloran & D. Butt (eds), *Functional Descriptions: Theory into Practice*, 1–38. Amsterdam: Benjamins.

Halliday, M.A.K. (2008). *Complementarities in Language*. Beijing: The Commercial Press.

Halliday, M.A.K. & Greaves, W. (2008). *Intonation in the Grammar of English*. London & Oakville: Equinox.

Halliday, M.A.K. & James, Z.L. (1993). A quantitative study of polarity and primary tense in the English finite clause. In J.M. Sinclair, M. Hoey & G. Fox (eds), *Techniques of Description: Spoken and Written Discourse*, 32–66. London & New York, NY: Routledge.

Halliday, M.A.K. & Matthiessen, C.M.I.M. (2014). *Halliday's Introduction to Functional Grammar*, 4th Edn. London & New York, NY: Routledge.

Heath, J. (2008). *A Grammar of Jamsay*. Berlin & New York, NY: Berlin de Gruyter.

Heine, B. & Kuteva, T. (2002). *World Lexicon of Grammaticalization*. Cambridge: Cambridge University Press.

Heine, B. & Nurse, D. (eds) (2000). *African Languages: An Introduction*. Cambridge: Cambridge University Press.

Hyman, L.M. (2005). Focus marking in Aghem: syntax or semantics. Paper presented at the *Conference on Focus in African Languages*, ZAS, Berlin, October.

Issah, S.A. (2015). An analysis of interrogative constructions in Dagbani. *Journal of West African Languages*, XLII.1, 45–63.

Kahombo, M. (1992). *Essai de Grammaire du Kihunde* (Hamburger Beiträge zur Afrikanistik, 1). Münster: LIT Verlag.

Koopman, H. (1984). *The Syntax of Verbs*. Dordrecht, The Netherlands: Foris Publications.

König, E. & Siemund, P. (2007). Speech act distinctions in grammar. In T. Shopen (ed.), *Language Typology and Syntactic Description, Volume I: Clause Structure*, 276–324. Cambridge: Cambridge University Press.

Matthiessen, C.M.I.M. (2004). Descriptive motifs and generalizations. In A. Caffarel, J.R. Martin & C.M.I.M. Matthiessen (eds), *Language Typology: A Functional Perspective*, 537–673. Amsterdam: Benjamins.

Matthiessen, C.M.I.M. (2007). The "architecture" of language according to systemic functional theory: Developments since the 1970s. In R. Hasan, C.M.I.M. Matthiessen & J. Webster (eds), *Continuing Discourse on Language, Volume 2*, 505–561. London: Equinox.

Matthiessen, C.M.I.M. (2015). The notion of a multilingual meaning potential: a systemic exploration, 53 pp. Manuscript.

Maxwell, E.M. (1981). Question strategies and hierarchies of grammatical relations in Kinyarwanda. *Proceedings of the Seventh Annual Meeting of the Berkley Linguistics Society*, 166–177. Available online at: http://journals.linguisticsociety.org/proceedings/index.php/BLS/article/view/2083, [accessed on July 15, 2016].

Moutaouakil, A. (1999). Exclamation in functional grammar: sentence type, illocution or modality? *Working Papers in Functional Grammar 69*. Amsterdam: University of Amsterdam.

Muriungi, P.K., Mutegi, M.K. & Karuri, M. (2014). The syntax of *wh*-questions in Gichuka. *Open Journal of Modern Linguistics*, 4, 182–204.

Mwinlaaru, I.N. (2017). A systemic functional description of the grammar of Dagaare. The Hong Kong Polytechnic University: PhD thesis.

Mwinlaaru, I.N. (2018). Grammaticalizing attitude: Clause juncture particles and NEGOTIATION in Dagaare. In A.S. Baklouti & L. Fontaine (eds), *Perspectives From Systemic Functional Linguistics*, 208–230. London & New York, NY: Routledge.

Njie, C.M. (1982). *Description Syntaxique du Wolof de Gambie*. Dakar: Les Nouvelles Édition Africaines.

Nuyts, J. & van der Auwera, J. (eds) (2016). *Modality and Mood*. Oxford: Oxford University Press.

Palmer, F.R. (2001). *Mood and Modality*, 2nd Edn. Cambridge: Cambridge University Press.

du Plessis, J.A. & Visser, M. (1993). Co-ordination and the subjunctive in Xhosa. *South African Journal of African Languages*, 13.3, 74–81.

Poulos, G. & Bosch, S.E. (1997). *Zulu* (Languages of the World/Materials, 50). München: Lincom Europa.

Redden, J.E. (1979). *A Descriptive Grammar of Ewondo*. Carbondale, IL: Southern Illinois University at Carbondale, Department of Linguistics.

Sadock, J. & Zwicky, A. (1985). Speech Act Distinctions in Syntax. In T. Shopen (ed.), *Language Typology and Syntactic Description, Volume I: Clause Structure*, 155–197. Cambridge: Cambridge University Press.

Sande, H.L. (2014). Classification of Guébie within Kru. Available online at: http://linguistics.berkeley.edu/~hsande/documents/Sande_Classification_ACAL_2014.pdf, [accessed on November 24, 2016].

Taljard, E. & Louwrens, L.J. (2003). On the modal status of Northern Sotho conditionals. *South African Journal of African Languages*, 23.3, 163–174.

Taylor, C. (1985). Nkore-Kiga. (*Croom Helm Descriptive Grammars*). London: Croom Helm.

Teruya, K., Akerejola, E., Andersen, T.H., Caffarel, A., Lavid, J., Matthiessen, C., Petersen, U.H., Patpong, P. & Smedegaard, F. (2007). Typology of MOOD: A Text-based and System-based Functional View. In R. Hasan, C.M.I.M. Matthiessen & J.J. Webster (eds), *Continuing Discourse on Language: A Functional Perspective, Volume 2*, 859–920. London: Equinox.

Teruya, K. & Matthiessen, C.M.I.M. (2015). Halliday in relation to language comparison and typology. In J.J. Webster (ed.), *The Bloomsbury Companion to M.A.K. Halliday*, 27–452. London: Bloomsbury Academic.

Torrence, H. (2003). The syntactic derivation of complex wh-words in Wolof. *GLOW ASIA 2003 Proceedings*. Available online at: http://citeseerx.ist.psu.edu/viewdoc/download?doi=10.1.1.558.2594&rep=rep1&type=pdf, [accessed on August 4, 2016].

Torrence, H. & Kandybowicz, J. (2015). Wh-question formation in Krachi. *Journal of African Languages & Linguistics*, 36.2, 253–285.

Ultan, R. (1978). Some general characteristics of interrogative systems. In J.H. Greenberg (ed.), *Universals of Human Language, Volume 4: Syntax*, 211–248. Stanford, CA: Stanford University Press.

Van der Auwera, J. & Aguilar, A.Z. (2016). The history of modality and mood. In J. Nuyts & J. Van der Auwera (eds), *Modality and Mood*, 9–27. Oxford: Oxford University Press.

Van der Auwera, J., Lejeune, L. with Valentin Goussev (2013). The prohibitive. In M.S. Dryer & M. Haspelmath (eds), *The World Atlas of Language Structures Online*. Leipzig: Max Planck Institute for Evolutionary Anthropology, available online at: http://wals.info/chapter/71, [accessed on April 2, 2017].

Van Rooyen, C.S. (1984). The reassessment of the moods in Zulu. *South African Journal of African Languages*, 4.1, 70–83.

Watters, J.R. (2000). Syntax. In B. Heine & D. Nurse (eds), *African Languages: An Introduction*, 194–230. Cambridge: Cambridge University Press.

Welmers, W.E. (1973). *African Language Structures*. Berkeley, CA: University of California Press.

Whorf, B.L. (1938). Some verbal categories of Hopi. *Language*, 14, 275–286. Reprinted in Carroll, J.B. Levinson, S.C. & Lee, P. (2012). *Language, Thought and Reality: Selected Writings of Benjamin Lee Whorf*, 2nd Edn, 143–158. Cambridge, MA: MIT.

PART II

Sound and syllable system

6
COARTICULATION
Segmental and suprasegmental interactions in Yoruba

Augustine Agwuele

Introduction

Consonant + vowel interactions are as complex as the interaction of tone and segments. Both are complicated and multifaceted. Depending on speakers, vowel context, and speech styles, among many variables, there lacks any isomorphism between phonetic signals and their presumed correlates, and it is thus difficult to cleanly demarcate a consonant from its vowel context. Despite these phonetic variabilities, listeners nevertheless perceive speech signals invariantly. Sussman et al. (1991) described this invariant perception as the non-invariance problem.

The non-invariance issue has been a major preoccupation of linguists, especially phonologists and phoneticians, whose point of departure in their description of human speech sounds is the presumption of the existence of a discrete, static, and context-independent speech segment that corresponds to the serially produced discrete mental category (phoneme) that humans perceive. Successively produced segments are presumed to be qualitatively and temporally distinct (Fowler 1980). In speech, however, there are no discrete, independent or static phonemes. The process of speech articulation forces presumably underlying discrete phonological representations into overlapped continuous and variable outputs that hearers are nevertheless able to understand. For Sweet (1877), speech sounds are points in a stream of incessant change. Perhaps in a bid to maintain the seamlessness of speaking, there is a continuous articulatory movement that causes segments to not only fall short of their articulatory fullness, but, in addition, pushes contiguous segments to exact different influences on neighboring segments as the involved articulators transit from one segment to another. Additionally, contiguous segments are 'run-over' as features overlap, traversing 'boundaries' into one another. Thus "there are no invariant physical cues of segmentalness. There is no extra-human, i.e., on-subjective, way of analyzing the speech continuum into discrete parts corresponding to the notion of segment" (Hammerberg 1976: 335).

The above state of affairs is referred to as coarticulation between segments. This is the phenomenon whereby contiguous elements exert reciprocal influences on one another (Farnetani 1999). Coarticulation affects the very primitives of contrast between phones, i.e., articulatory gestures and their acoustic consequences (Manuel 1990). Coarticulation is a universal and pervasive feature of speech that has been suggested to have perceptual consequences (Fruchter &

Sussman 1997) with adaptive values (Sussman 1999). The major goals of coarticulatory studies, among many, include the quest to (a) resolve the non-invariance problem, (b) understand not only the underlying control mechanisms, but the relation of static, discrete elements of phonology and their realizations during speaking (Kühnert & Nolan 1999), and (c) to understand the factors that affect the extent to which features of a segment interact with those of neighboring segments under varying factors. This chapter presents an acoustic study of coarticulation involving CV segments with mid-tone compared with low-tone in Yoruba, as observed for two speech styles (citation and connected speech). The study applied the tools of Locus Equations (LE) to the interaction of segments across the four stop place categories of Yoruba in order to ascertain whether Yoruba stop + vowel syllables that bear tones exhibit coarticulatory characteristics similar to analogous syllables of languages that exhibit emphatic stress. The result of the study will allow speculations concerning the nature of Yoruba tone either as prosodic or not.

There are several landmark perspectives and approaches to coarticulation. For instance, early European scholars conceptualized speech as involving linear sequencing of articulatory targets that traverse transitional zone because of inertia (Sievers 1876). Transcending this view, Menzerath and de Lacerda (1933), who coined the terms "*Koartikulation* and *Anpassung*," noted that a segment could traverse the zone of transition to impact and influence the production of another segment (coarticulation), or could simply accommodate itself to another within the transitional zone by overlapping. These scholars introduced the idea of anticipatory coarticulation. It was Martin Joos (1948), however, who showed that in a CVC sequence, the influence of each of the two consonants transcend the center of the intervening vowel. He therefore proposed that the contextually induced variation of segments, as could be observed in the acoustic and articulatory dimensions, are due to the "overlapping innervation wave" that waxes (activates) and wanes (deactivates) temporally. Based on articulatory and acoustic studies of VCV sequences in Swedish, English and Russian, Öhman (1966) advanced the co-production view to account for the observation that the formant patterns, including the F2 frequencies at the VC transitions, are both a function of the formant pattern of the upcoming vowel as well as the identity of the preceding vowel. The co-production view suggests that there is a temporal overlap, that is, a diphthongal movement from V_1 to V_2 upon which a consonantal gesture is superimposed.

Since these early classical studies of coarticulation, the non-invariance problem has been the focus of diverse studies involving different theoretical and methodological approaches that could be subsumed into two camps: the gestural and acoustic approaches. The "gestural accounts" group is guided by the view that phonetic category cannot be defined in purely acoustic terms, as such there is no invariant acoustic cue that identifies the stop consonant. Theories that fall within this general framework include: Motor Theory (Liberman & Mattingly 1985, 1989), Direct Realism (Fowler 1986), Articulatory Phonology (Browman and Goldstein 1992), Phonological Development (Studdert-Kennedy 1987, 1989), and Dynamic Specification (Strange 1989).

Opposing the gestural perspective is the notion that properties of speech can be invariantly specified in acoustic signal, this is the "auditory\acoustic perspective." Accounts that fall within this framework include the Acoustic Invariance Hypothesis (Blumstein & Stevens, 1979), Quantal Theory (Stevens 1972), Articulatory Compensation, Auditory Enhancement (Diehl et al. 1991; Diehl & Kluender 1989) and Locus Equations (Lindblom 1963; Krull 1988; Sussman et al. 1991). While scholars generally operate on the assumptions of their chosen paradigm and are thusly influenced, it is nevertheless fair to state that, of all current approaches to coarticulation, the Locus Equations remain perhaps the most successful research phonetic tool that has continued to provide a clean resolution to the conundrum of stop place representation and perception. Locus equation metrics have shown great reliability in quantifying the extent of CV dependencies and in providing orderliness to consonant representations across varied vowel contexts. Because of the success of LEs, the remainder of this chapter will focus on this particular perspective.

Locus equations

Unlike other approaches, especially those that explore F2 transitions (e.g., Delattre et al. 1955; Liberman et al. 1957), the Locus Equations approach, as proposed by Lindblom (1963) and implemented by Sussman and colleagues, does not seek an invariant acoustic cue for each consonant in a syllable that is independent of its vowel context. Instead, the Locus Equations approach captures the lawfulness of (F2 transition) acoustic variability when measured at the categorical level (Sussman et al. 1991) by acoustically representing the entire stop place category. Based on the linear regression form of: F2onset = k × F2vowel + c (where the constants k and c stand for slope of the regression line and its intercept respectively), the Locus Equations are scatterplots that are derived by regressing F2 transitions measured at the CV interface against the F2 from the midpoint of the vowel. The slope parameter is generally interpreted as a phonetic index of place of articulation (Neary & Shammas 1987). It is also presumed to quantify the extent of CV coarticulation as it correlates the extent of F2 at CV with F2 at the nucleus, its putative target (Krull 1987). Essentially, LEs uncovers and gauges the extent to which a particular stop is influenced by lingual activities, most especially the effects of a vowel on the preceding consonant (CV coarticulation). Locus equations that show greater CV coarticulation yield a slope value that is closer to 1. This corresponds to a vocal tract configuration that has a dominant vowel during the release of the consonantal occlusion. For instance, in fast speech, there is a higher dependence of the consonant on the vowel (Agwuele et al. 2008). Where the influence of the upcoming vowel on the preceding consonant is minimal (less coarticulation), the slope value of the Locus Equations tends toward zero. This is the case for stressed segments (Lindblom et al. 2007; Iskarous et al. 2010). Thus, LEs allow inferences about the synergy between articulators when implementing different phonetic contexts (Iskarous et al. 2010; Chennoukh et al. 1997). As a significant tool of analyses in the realm of speech production and perception, especially in characterizing articulatory and perceptual correlates, Locus Equations have been applied to spontaneous and lab speech (Krull 1989; Duez 1992; Ghavami 2016), rate of speech, speaker variation (Whiteside 2016), gender (Sussman et al. 1993), and stress (Agwuele 2015; Lindblom et al. 2009).

African languages and coarticulatory studies

There are two obvious and important reasons for extending the coarticulatory discourse to Yoruba tone-bearing CV segments. As already described, LEs exploit the correlations of F2 onsets with place of articulation (Delattre et al. 1955). Tabain (2000) implemented LEs to measure the degree of F2-variability with respect to its putative target, thus capturing the resistance of the consonant to neighboring vowels. Ghavami's (2002) dissertation examined kinematic discontinuities in anticipatory coarticulation (trough effect), VOT, and voicing distinctions using the Locus Equations parameters. Sussman et al. (2002) further studied input, organizational, and output processing in children with developmental apraxia compared with normal children using Locus Equations. Differences were observed in production and perception among the two groups. Anticipatory coarticulation from two opposing ends of the hyperarticulation-to-hypoarticulation continuum, i.e., emphatic stress and reduced speech induced by fast speaking rates were studied using LEs by Lindblom et al. (2007), Agwuele et al. (2008), and, prior to that, Agwuele (2003, 2005) studied stress in CV syllables using Locus Equations. In all the cited studies, the LEs' parameters, slope and intercept revealed sensitivities to variability induced by context and suprasegmental factors. The parameters consistently and distinctly separate stop place of articulations, affirming their robustness in the coarticulatory studies. Realizing that different perturbations of speech would alter the spectral make up of vowels and their location in space and thereby produce different degrees of coarticulation, and that the existing (i.e., traditional) LEs' parameters do not discriminate nor quantify the contributions of vowel space under emphasis separate from consonant onset contributions (prominence + V contexts), they introduced Modified Locus Equations to capture the pulls and pushes due to contextually and prosodically induced variations. With this new approach, it is possible to clearly understand the source of articulatory movements captured by LE parameters. The modified Locus Equations successfully separated prosodic overlay from contextual vowel variation. Despite its robustness in explicating suprasegmental features, several cross-linguistic applications including fieldwork (Everett 1988), and modification, LEs have only recently been applied to the study of an African language (Agwuele & Sussman 2011; Agwuele 2015 and 2016). A principle of scientific endeavor is that of replication for verification, more so when data that have not been previously explored are employed in that verification process. Thus, it is important to constantly reappraise the effectiveness of LEs' conceptualization of segmental interaction given its perceptual implications.

The study of African languages, especially Bantu, has drawn considerable attention particularly to its pervasive use of lexical tone (e.g., Autosegmental Theory, Clements 1976), but has mostly described tone spreading in tone languages, and vowel and nasal harmony. It attended particularly to the spread of tone across segments as well as the transformation of tone-bearing segments (e.g., assimilation). Data from African languages have not featured much in studies on overlap between segments (i.e., coarticulation), be it overlaps between vowel and consonants or consonants and vowels. Of course, there are token works such as Manuel and Krakow's (1984) study of Shona and Swahili, Manuel's (1990) study that examined lingual coarticulation for five Bantu languages. Hombert (1977) also provided an acoustic study of Yoruba tone as impacted by voiceless and voiced consonants, Maddieson's (1974) study mainly argued for the influence of tone on consonants, focusing on the effects of different tones on VOT of adjacent consonants, and La Velle's (1974) acoustic study of Yoruba speech sounds showed how phonological tone is realized phonetically. Even when the 20th meeting of the African Linguistic Association recognized the need to explore the contribution of African languages to linguistic theory, the absence of phonetics and the heavy presence of phonology and tonology in its proceedings (Bokamba 1990) shows that, in certain regards, African languages still seem to just supply data to exemplify abnormalities or exoticness rather than aiding new theories. Tone and consonant interaction has featured significantly in phonology where implicating features are explored, e.g., Generative phonology (Chomsky & Hale 1968), auto and segmental phonology (Clements 1976; Goldsmith 1976), as well as in cases where constraints permuted to determine co-occurrence, prominence (optimality theory), and where they are studied to understand the development of tone (Hombert et al. 1979; Henderson 1982). Wherever acoustic studies were involved, the greater interest has been in understanding the distribution, sequencing, or spread of features of tone. Scholarship on the coarticulation of tone mostly explores how the 'ideal' tone contours found for isolated syllables are transformed under running speech (see, for instance, Van Nierkerk & Barnard 2012). Not quite explored in segmental coarticulation studies of languages where variation in F0 (tone) is lexical is the role of tone in the interactions of consonant and vowels.

Tone

In part, tone is affined with other suprasegmental factors whose features include fundamental frequency (F0). While stress is defined in terms of duration, intensity and F0, lexical tone is primarily associated with F0. Several of the aforementioned studies have shown that, for languages that use emphatic stress, there is a greater CV bonding under emphasis than without emphatic stress; the role of tone, with properties analogous to stress, in C+V interaction is rarely examined in the same context. Perhaps there is no interaction. Nevertheless, it is worth asking, does lexical tone influence C+V coarticulation?

Since the representation of tone has consequences for coarticulation, the question whether tone is to be represented segmentally, suprasegmentally, or both, was heavily debated at the Congresses of the West African Linguistic Society in the late 1960s and early 1970s (see Fromkin 1974). In the study of tone, the question pertaining to the representation of tone remains important (Leben 1973), and, to the best of my knowledge, remains unresolved. Such a representation implicates whether tone should be viewed as the property of the syllable or of the vowel nucleus itself. The perspective of the generative phonology (Hyman & Schuh 1974; Hyman 1976; Schuh 1978) presumes the existence of tones at an underlying level and their eventual realization at the phonological level. In opposition, Autosegmental Phonology (Goldsmith 1976; Clements 1985) considers tone as separate from other segmental features, that it is realized on a separate tier and whose features could transverse segments. Evidence for this assumed separate tier of tone are the existence of floating tones, and the survival of tone after the deletion of a vowel or segment, or even morphemes that lack tones. The Optimality Theory also accepts two levels of representation. These are the input and output levels. By looking at 'faithfulness' between both, Optimality Theory permutes constraints to explicate phonological processes and interactions.

With respect to the representation of Yoruba tone, Akinlabi (1985), relying on the autosegmental view of phonology, argued that Yoruba tones are stable and that their stability is maintained independent of all other aspects of speech signals, as such they are autonomous segments. Akinlabi further suggested that Yoruba tone and its tone-bearing units (vowels and consonants) occur independently on separate tiers of representation that stand in a relation of formal association with each other, and submitted that this relation/association determines the manner in which they are coarticulated in speech. Thus, for Akinlabi, tone and the segment underlying it are unassociated. This position is in opposition to Courtenay (1969) and Oyelaran (1971), each of whom worked within the SPE paradigm (Chomsky & Halle 1968) and therefore treated tone as a classificatory feature of the vowel. Bamgbose (1965) concluded that "tones behave independently of all other vowel features in Yoruba." What all these studies have in common is the assumption that "tones in Yoruba phonology are autonomous segments whose phonological processes are distinct from those of the syllabic units associated with them" (Akinlabi 1985: 40). The cited works studied assimilation, deletion or association of tone in Yoruba phonological processes.

Several segmental coarticulatory studies have shown that, when segments of a syllable are overlayered with prosody such as emphatic stress or different tempo, the formants (F1 and F2) of stressed or fastly produced segments differ from those without stress or increased tempo. Turner et al. (1995) observed that the F2 onset for stressed tokens move away from the preceding consonant locus rather than moving towards it as predicted. Under emphatic stress, the F1 by F2 vowel acoustic space is expanded relative to their counterpart without stress (Koopman-van Beinum 1980), and Lindblom (1963) reported a centralization effect for unstressed segments and greater assimilation with neighboring consonants. For fastly produced speech, the formant values fall short of values achieved by analogous segments produced under normal speech tempo (Goldman-Eisler 1961; Kohler 1990). Other than formant values, the duration of the vowels that are involved become significantly reduced for segments that are fastly produced relative to those that are produced with emphasis or at a 'normal' tempo. Accompanying the duration reduction, the fundamental frequencies of the segments become flatter. In general, the sentence becomes shorter and its syllables are reduced (Gopal, 1990; Crystal & House 1990). Not all studies have reported the same effects for rate (see Berry & Weismer 2013 for a review). Essentially, depending on the phonology of the language in question and the way the speech tokens are perturbed, there are differential modifications to formants, segmental duration and F0, and these will determine the type of interaction of the segments involved.

Purpose

Given that speech sounds are not produced independently but with the participation of multiple other features of neighboring speech sounds, the goal of the study reported in this chapter was to explore plausible coarticulatory interactions between tone and its CV-bearing syllables. The traditional Locus Equations (as used by Lindblom, Krull and Sussman) and Modified Locus Equations (Lindblom et al. 2007; Agwuele et al. 2008) were applied to Yoruba stops + vowel sequences with Mid and Low lexical tones produced for citation and carrier speech forms. The aims were to (a) provide categorical lawfulness to contextual following vowel variations to Yoruba voiced obstruents, (b) quantify the degree of consonant dependence on vowel for citation and carrier phrase speech styles, and (c) to explore the true nature of Yoruba tone. That is, to determine whether Yoruba tone is endogenous or intrinsic to the vowel that bears it or if it is laid over the vowel prosodically and perturbs the segments on which it is placed in the same manner as emphatic stress in American English.

Method

The Yoruba language has seven vowels [i, e, ɛ, a, ɔ, o, u] and four voiced stop place categories; bilabial \b\, alveolar \d\, velar \g\ and labial-velar \gb\. It has three tones, Low, Mid and High, and it allows both a CV and V syllable types. The data for this study consists of natural, meaningful Yoruba words as this would be expected to show a more routinized and realistic pattern of phonetic implementation relative to when speakers practice and produce nonsense words for immediate research needs. There were two sets of data (citation and carrier sentence/phrase).

The first set of data consisted of V_1CV_2 sequences that were produced in citation form, i.e., lab-speech with two different tonal conditions: (a) V_1CV_2, the V_1 and V_2 of the sequences each are identical and had Mid-tone or, per Akinlabi (1985), were toneless; (b) the same V_1CV_2 words were produced with the two vowels bearing low tone. The intervening consonants were /b, d, g, and gb/. Due to phonological constraints on \u\, only six vowels were studied, these are [i, e, ɛ, a, ɔ, o]. Examples of the tokens are:

([**àbà**]ráméjì vs. [**aba**]raméjì; [**àdà**]bà vs. [**ada**]ha; [**àgà**]dà vs. [**aga**]da)
([**ìbì**]wó vs. [**ibi**]; g[**ìdì**]gìdì vs. g[**idi**]gidi; [**ìgì**]rìpá vs. [**igi**]rere)
(j[**òbò**]jòbò vs. àj[**obo**]; [**òdò**]fin vs. [**odo**]dún; g[**ògò**] vs. g[**ogo**]wú)

Different from /b.d,g/ was labial velar /gb/; the V_1CV_2 consisted of V_1 with a mid-tone and V_2 that was either high or low tone. For instance:

([**agbà**]dà vs. [**agbá**]gbá; [**igbí**] vs. [**igbì**]rí; [**ogbò**]n vs. **ogbó**]n)[1]

Segmental, suprasegmental interaction: Yoruba

The bolded VCVs are the sequences under consideration in this study. Thirteen adult native Yoruba speakers participated in this study. Nine of the subjects were male and four were females. They were all affiliates of the University of Ibadan and none was younger than twenty-two. Each subject produced a total of 144 tokens [$6V_1$ * 4C * 2tones * 3repetitions].

In the second type of data, the same test words were inserted into a carrier phrase of the type: "*Mo pe àbàrámëjì lee meta*" ("I said àbàrámëjì three times"). The subjects were instructed to read the sentence as if they were speaking to their friends. They were to avoid the citation style. For the carrier sentence VCV forms, the intervocalic consonants were /b, d, g/. The four subjects who produced the carrier phrases were also involved in the production of the citation speech. Each of the four subjects was expected to produce a total of 108 tokens [$6V_1$ * 3C *2 tones *3 repetitions] resulting in 432 tokens. Some speakers did not produce the expected tones in the expected places so such tokens were discarded. The study therefore explored interaction of tone with the CV syllable that bears it across stop place categories, two tone conditions, and two speech styles.

Instrumentation

Subjects were recorded in a non-sound treated room of the Phonetics Laboratory at the University of Ibadan in Nigeria, using a uni-directional microphone (RCA RP3503). Subjects were recorded directly without a pre-amp into a Dell Latitude laptop using Praat (Boersma & Weenink 2004). The recorded signals were sampled at 22 kHz, digitized, and filtered using Praat, which was also used for all acoustic display and measurements. Acoustic measurements were made from wide-band spectrograms. The F2 and F1 values were obtained for V_1 and V_2mid, V_1offset, and V_2onset following the procedures established by Sussman and colleagues (1991) and used by others using the Locus Equation as a research rubric.[2] Inaccurately tracked tokens were either manually measured or removed. The F0 and duration values were obtained using Prosody Pro (Xu 2013).

Results and observations

Locus Equations parameters and Yoruba stop place categories by tone

(Traditional) Locus Equations regressions were obtained for each stop place category following Sussman et al. (1991). The F2 transition obtained from the first glottal pulse of the CV interface was regressed against F2 obtained from the midpoint of the post-consonantal vowels. Table 6.1a below provides a summary of the LE's slopes, intercepts, R^2, and standard error of estimate for 13 subjects across the stop place categories /b, d, g/ and /gb/, produced for the Mid-tone and Low-tone conditions.

Similar Locus Equations analyses were performed for the carrier phrase conditions. The resulting Locus Equation's slopes, intercepts, R^2, and F2 standard error of estimate for four subjects are reported in Table 6.1b for the stop place categories /b, d, g/.

The Locus Equations slopes, which have always been interpreted as indexing the degree of coarticulation between V_2 and the preceding consonant (Sussman 2016) or the degree of the consonant's resistance to coarticulation as suggested by Recasens et al. (1997), vary with the stops' place of articulation. In all cases, the steep slopes for /g, gb, and b/ show a higher degree of vowels' influence on the associated consonants. With a slope of 0.60 (citation) and

Table 6.1a LE parameters obtained for 13 subjects (slope, intercept, R² and SE) for Mid-tone and Low-tone conditions of citation speech style (/gb/*: V_1 is Mid tone while V_2 varies between High tone and Low tone)

	Mid-T					Low-T			
Cons.	Slope	y-int.	R²	SE		Slope	y-int.	R²	SE
/b/	0.84	114	0.95	96		0.87	80	0.96	92
/d/	0.60	791	0.83	115		0.60	788	0.84	118
/g/	1.15	119	0.97	89		1.15	117	0.98	109
	Mid to Low tone					Mid to High tone			
/gb/*	1.04	120	0.91	180		1.05	-132	0.9	176

Table 6.1b LE parameters obtained for 4 subjects showing slope, intercept, R² and SE for Mid-tone and Low-tone conditions of carrier phrase style for /b, d, g/

	Mid-TS					Low-T-S			
Cons	Slope	y-int	R²	SE		Slope	y-int	R²	SE
/b/	0.85	150	0.88	128		0.81	162	0.88	132
/d/	0.76	415	0.87	94		0.77	411	0.86	118
/g/	1.05	33	0.92	152		0.98	33	0.93	124

0.76/0.77 (carrier phrase), the slopes for /d/ are shallower relative to the other stops nonetheless closer to 1 than zero. The slopes' steepness for the four stop place categories is patterned as follows /g > gb > b > d/. The same order obtained for the carrier phrase condition absent /gb/.

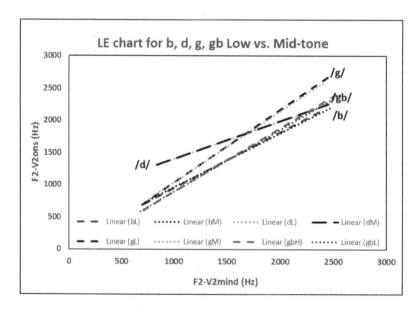

Figure 6.1a Locus Equations showing the trendline for /b, d, g, gb/ comparing Low tone and Mid tone and /gb/ comparing Mid-Low to Mid-High tones for 13 subjects

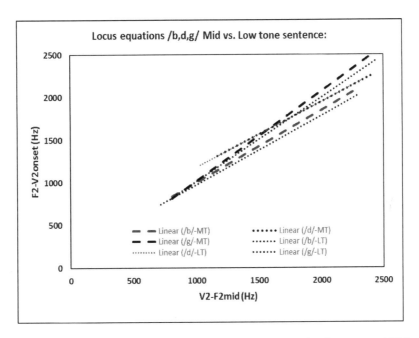

Figure 6.1b   Locus Equations showing the trendline for /b, d, g/ comparing Low tone and Mid-tone for 4 subjects

When the slope values are compared across tone conditions for citation style, the slope for each stop place category remains the same. There was no difference found between Mid- and Low-tone slopes. The R^2, which captures the variance at the onset of the CV interface relative to the vowel nucleus frequencies, are high for both tone conditions (0.8 and above), thus indicating a higher level of linearity between onset and midpoint frequency values. The standard estimate of error (SE) for F2 shows that the data points are equally dispersed around the regression line for both Mid- and Low-tone conditions. Altogether the coefficients revealed no systematic correlation with tone conditions. Although not the focus of interest, comparisons of Locus Equations parameters across speech style (between citation and connected speech) did not reveal any systematic differences except for /d/ and to some extent /g/. The slopes for the sentence conditions are on the average 0.18 higher than the slopes for the citation condition.

The extent of the overlap or similarities across the tone condition of comparisons are further revealed in Figures 6.1a and b. These provide Locus Equations scatterplots for /b, d, g and gb/minus the data points that were removed in order for the trendlines around which they clustered to be more visible to visual inspection. The plots yielded the summary results presented in Tables 6.1a and b.

Observations

1   The stop consonants /b, d, g and gb/ occupied different acoustic space as shown by the Locus Equations slopes and intercepts.
2   The degree of coarticulation for V_1CV_2 (Mid tone) sequences and for V_1CV_2 (Low tone) were similar, actually overlapped. No systematic differences were observed.

Second Order Locus Equations

Following Sussman et al. (1991) and Chennoukh et al. (1997) the plot of slopes values against normalized y-intercept values for the stops /b, d, g, gb/ yielded the second or higher order Locus Equations that provide a simple graphical representation showing the relative separation of the stops within a derived acoustic space. In Figures 6.2a and b, the slope and intercept parameters defined a higher order acoustic space that mainly contrast stop place categories but did not contrast tone conditions. The higher order acoustic display offers insight on the synergy between the articulators across different speech contexts (Iskarous et al. 2010).

Higher Locus Equations for citation form

Were the Yoruba Mid-tone to be considered the neutral tone or the absence of tone, as suggested by Akinlabi (1985) and Pulleyblank (1986), the results would suggest that no articulatory adjustments were made in the production of the Low-tone CV segments.

Higher Locus Equations for sentence form

Different from the citation form, there are systematic observable differences found for the connected speech (sentence condition). The plot revealed an overlap for /d/, but there were clear separations for the labials and velars as a function of tone. These differences were explored using the Modified Locus Equations as introduced by Lindblom et al. (2007). Results are presented below.

Euclidean distance

Another approach that exploits the higher order acoustic space to capture the relative dispersion of stop place categories is the Euclidian distance. To derive the Euclidean distance,

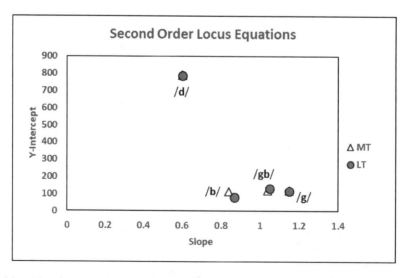

Figure 6.2a Plot of slope by y-intercept (Second Order Locus Equations) derived for 13 subjects from citation style, comparing Mid-tone with Low-tone

Segmental, suprasegmental interaction: Yoruba

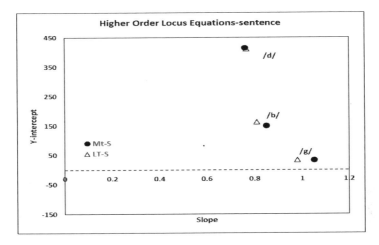

Figure 6.2b Plot of slope by y-intercept (Second Order Locus Equations) derived for 4 subjects from the carrier sentences, comparing Mid-tone /b, d, g/ with Low-tone /b, d, g/ syllables

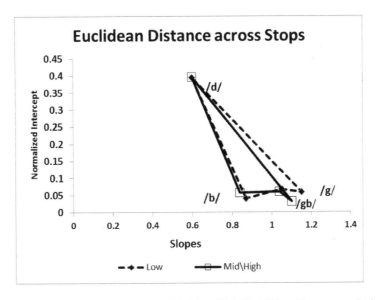

Figure 6.3a Euclidean distances between /b/, /d/, /g/, and /gb/ for Mid and Low tones obtained for 13 subjects from citation condition

mean Locus Equation slopes were plotted against normalized y-intercept for labial, alveolar, velar and labio-velar stops across the different tone conditions. The results are presented in Figures 6.3a and b for the citation and sentence forms.

Euclidean distance for citation form

The perimeter for the Low tone condition is 1.46 relative to 1.43 of the Mid\High tone; the area of the triangle is 0.035 for the Low tone condition and 0.034 for the Mid\High tone conditions.

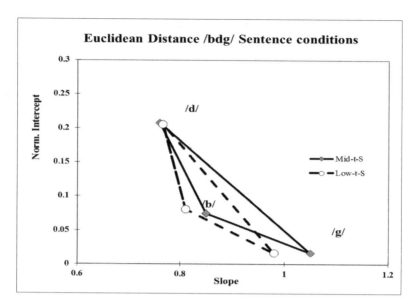

Figure 6.3b   Euclidean distances between /b/, /d/, and /g/ for Mid and Low tones obtained for 4 subjects from connected speech situation

In both instances there are slightly observable differences to the triangles' perimeter due to the y-intercept. It should be noted that the traditional Locus Equations parameters of slope and intercept revealed no differences in the articulation of the CV-segments as a function of tone.

Higher Locus Equations for sentence form

The perimeter for Low tone condition is 0.60 relative to 0.72 of the Mid tone; the area of the triangle is 0.009 for the Low tone condition and 0.011 for the Mid tone condition. The area and perimeter of the triangle were larger for the Mid-tone condition than for the Low tone condition. Unlike the citation form, the sentence condition continues to reveal systematic variations between the collocations as a function of tone especially for /b/ and /g/. These systematic differences would be further explored in order to pinpoint the source of these variations.

Observations

1. In the citation form, Higher Order Locus Equations and Euclidean distance measurements revealed significant overlap between the Mid tone and Low tone CVs.
2. For the sentence condition, both the Higher Order Locus Equations and the Euclidean distances showed systematic differences between the Low tone and the Mid tone CVs.

Locus Equations and tone effects

The preceding sections were obtained by applying the traditional Locus Equations to the four voiced stops of Yoruba. The stability and viability of the Locus Equations paradigm is reaffirmed by its ability to index the degree of coarticulation, to statistically mark stop place category, and to absorb variability, that is provide 'acoustic-based' orderliness for the combination of each consonant with the six different vowels involved in this study. A suitable interpretation for Locus Equations is that "they represent a category-level equivalent class, strongly suggestive of purposeful coding algorithm" (Sussman 2016: 331). What follows is a micro-exploration of the interaction of tone with the segments that bear it.

Vowel space in F2/F1 coordinate: Low vs Mid tone

The six vowels were examined to understand how they occur within the F2 and F1 coordinates under different tonal conditions. The result is shown in Figure 6.4a for the citation form condition and in Figure 6.4b for the carrier phrase condition.

Vowel space for citation condition

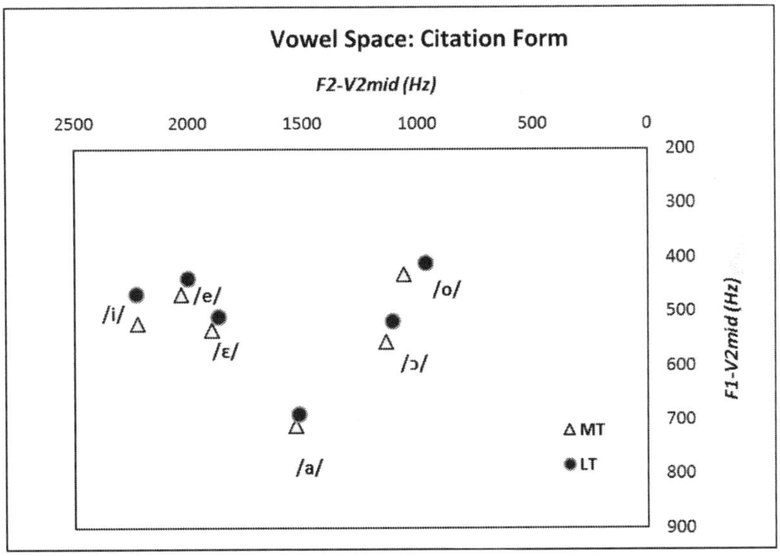

Figure 6.4a   The F1 by F2 acoustic space of the six test vowels as function of Mid and Low tones obtained for 13 subjects, they were produced under citation form. Note a slightly expanded space for the Mid-tone relative to Low tone

Vowel space for sentence condition

Figure 6.4b shows a reduction in the acoustic space. This 'contraction' is similar to the reduction reported for faster speaking rate by Agwuele et al. (2008). Essentially, there appears to be a change in the vowel midpoint as a function of tone for the carrier phrase. Second, the plots of Figures 6.4a and 6.4b were derived from measurements obtained from 13 and 4 participants respectively. Agwuele (2016), which was based on fewer subjects, contradicted Ladefoged and Maddieson (1996: 297), which suggests that Yoruba /e, o/ are closer to /i, u/ than /ɛ, ɔ/. This 2016 finding was not borne out for citation form as shown in Figure 6.4a but affirmed for the carrier phrase condition in 6.4b.

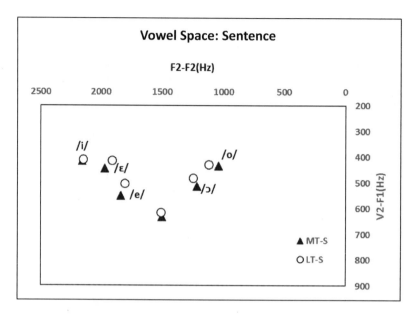

Figure 6.4b The F1 by F2 acoustic space of the six test vowels as function of Mid and Low tones obtained for 4 subjects. Mid-tone vowels occupy slightly larger acoustic space than Low tone vowels

Modified Locus Equations analyses

As reported above, the extent to which tone is involved in the patterning of the segments within the derived acoustic space is not obvious for the citation form context. Systematic differences were noted, however, for the sentence conditions as a function of tone. To further study this noted disparity, Modified Locus Equations (Lindblom et al. 2007) were implemented. This involved two steps. First, multiple regression analyses were performed to explore the role of the F2 transition from V_1-nucleus through the CV_2 interface to V_2-nucleus, as well as the role of the F0 at the nucleus of V_1 and V_2. Multiple regression analyses were performed for each tone condition for /b, d, g/ in order to establish 'neutral tone' baseline equations using the following formula:

(1): $F2onset(V_2) = a + b*F2mid(V_2) + C*F2mid(V_1) + d*F0mid(V_2) + e*F0mid(V_1)$. This first equation is termed the baseline equation.

Step 1: multiple regression analyses

For each tone condition and across /b, d, g/, multiple regression analyses were conducted and the coefficients (a, b, c, d, e), where a is the y intercept, b is the slope due to V_2F2, c is the slope due to V_1F2, d is the slope due to V_2F0, and e is the slope due to V_1F0, were obtained. These are reported in Tables 6.2a and 6.2b for the citation and carrier sentence speech styles respectively. The tables compare the coefficients for each stop place category as a function of tone noting the anticipatory and perseveratory effects of F0 and F2 on the onsets of the CV_2. Resulting P-values display the level of significance of these effects. In all cases, F2-V_2mid was the most significant factor influencing CV coarticulation. V_1-F2mid (c) showed perseveratory influence for /b/ but not for /d/ and /g/. Neither the F0 for V_1 nor V_2 exerted any appreciable influence on the degree of CV-coarticulation.

Multiple regression coefficients for citation form

Table 6.2a Multiple regression coefficients for /b, d, g/ of citation form comparing Mid- and Low-tone conditions. P-value shows the effects of the predicting factors

| | | **coefficients** | | | | | | | | | | | |
| | | **/b/** | | | | **/d/** | | | | **/g/** | | | |
		MT	*P-value*	**LT**	*P-value*	**MT**	*P-value*	**LT**	*P-value*	**MT**	*P-value*	**LT**	*P-value*
intercept	**a**	220	*0.00*	*127*	*0.00*	624	*0.00*	*779*	*0.00*	−101	*0.03*	*23*	*0.00*
anticipatory	**b**	0.75	*0.00*	*0.71*	*0.00*	0.53	*0.00*	*0.51*	*0.00*	1.17	*0.00*	*0.84*	*0.00*
persevatory	**c**	0.11	*0.05*	*0.18*	*0.01*	0.05	*0.48*	*0.07*	*0.38*	−0.06	*0.53*	*0.31*	*0.38*
anticipatory	**d**	−0.62	*0.28*	*−0.51*	*0.19*	0.13	*0.84*	*0.52*	*0.09*	0.63	*0.14*	*0.65*	*0.09*
persevatory	**e**	−0.13	*0.81*	*−0.07*	*0.86*	1.04	*0.12*	*−0.24*	*0.45*	−0.48	*0.30*	*−1.56*	*0.45*

Multiple regression coefficients for connected speech (sentence form)

Table 6.2b Multiple regression coefficients for /b, d, g/ of sentence form comparing Mid- and Low-tone conditions

							coefficients							
		/b/				/d/					/g/			
		MT-s	*P-value*	*LT-s*	*P-value*	**MT-s**	*P-value*	*LT-s*	*P-value*	**MT-s**	*P-value*	**LT-s**	*P-value*
intercept	**a**	233	*0.00*	280	*0.01*	445	*0.00*	371	*0.00*	−81	0.35	2.49	0.97
anticipatory	**b**	0.66	*0.00*	0.81	*0.00*	0.78	*0.00*	0.74	*0.00*	0.47	0.00	0.51	0.00
persevatory	**c**	0.23	*0.01*	0.01	*0.90*	−0.02	*0.88*	0.04	*0.69*	0.63	0.00	0.53	0.00
anticipatory	**d**	−1.54	*0.10*	0.32	*0.74*	0.48	*0.63*	0.88	*0.43*	1.02	0.46	−0.89	0.29
persevatory	**e**	0.57	*0.52*	−1.38	*0.36*	−0.67	*0.44*	−0.66	*0.59*	−1.16	0.42	0.70	0.39

As shown in Table 6.2b, in all cases, the influence of second formant of the post-consonantal vowel remained significant for all the stops, across tone conditions and speech style. The persistent effects of V_1-F2 into CV interface was observed for /b, d, g/ for both tones in the sentence condition. This was not the case for the citation form where V_1-F2 only persisted unto CV_2 for /b/. The F0 exerted no significant impact on the onsets of F2.

Step 2: dissociation of vowel contextual effects

In order to determine whether tone is prosodically overlaid onto the following vowel contextual effects, asset of multiple regression analyses were performed. In the previous secion, the baseline equation was performed for citation form and sentence condition (Low tone, Mid tone). The y-intercepts and coefficients (b, c, d, e) obtained from the baseline equation of the Mid-tone conditions were substituted into the vowel frequencies from the Low-tone conditions and a second regression analysis was performed. These new equations now predict F2 onsets driven by independent variables of the slightly reduced Low tone F2 and F0 midpoints of V_1 and V_2. However, the predictions are modulated by the slope obtained from the Mid tone (neutral) condition. The newly obtained F2-values are now the 'predicted' values. The reasoning behind this method is that a comparison of the predicted F2 onset, the value obtained from Equation (2), with the observed value from Equation (1) would make it possible to determine if an additional factor, different from contextual vowel variations (e.g., tone), is involved.

(2): $F2onset(V_2) = a + b*F2mid (V_2) + C*F2mid (V_1) + d*F0mid (V_2) + e*F0mid (V_1)$.

Mid-tone   Mid-tone   Mid-tone

Before looking at the comparison between the observed and predicted values, the duration of the vowels as a function of tone and speech styles is presented in Table 6.3.

Vowel duration

To further contextualize and make sense of the results of the Modified Locus Equation, it is helpful to verify the duration of V_1 and V_2 measured as a function of tone and as a function of speech style. Table 6.3 provides a summary of the duration of each vowel within each tone condition and style.

Table 6.3 Duration of V_1 and V_2 across Mid and Low tone produced for citation and sentence forms. Values were averaged across subjects and stops

Vs	LT-V1	LT-V1-s	LTV2	LT-V2-s
a	95	77	103	77
ɛ	110	79	116	80
e	105	72	106	75
i	84	51	90	58
ɔ	100	74	110	82
o	93	65	107	68

The values reported in Table 6.3 were derived by averaging duration measurements obtained for each speaker across each stop place consonant within a tone condition. The vowels showed significant differences as a function of style, but not of tone conditions. Thus, there was no difference between the duration of $V_1\backslash V_2$ produced with Mid tone and those produced with Low tone. Paired t-tests were performed to determine if the style of speech was significant. The mean difference between Low tone in citation and sentence form of V_1 was significant [t(35) =11.59, p < 0.000]. There was also a significant difference between the V_2 of sentence forms relative to citation forms [t(35) = 12.26, P < 0.001]. This observation was expected, as faster speech style has been shown to be hyper-articulated and therefore involves some form of reduction as the segments fall short of their putative target (Moon & Lindblom 1989).

Tone effect: citation form

The newly obtained F2 onset values from the implementation of Equation (2) of the Modified Locus Equations were plotted along the observed F2 onsets. The plot in Figure 6.5 shows significant overlap between the observed and the predicted onsets.

The regression coefficients for the plot of Figure 6.5 are presented in Table 6.4 below. For the citation form, the results are consistent with the findings of other analyses previously presented. They show no significant differences despite the tendency for the observed values to have slightly higher slope values.

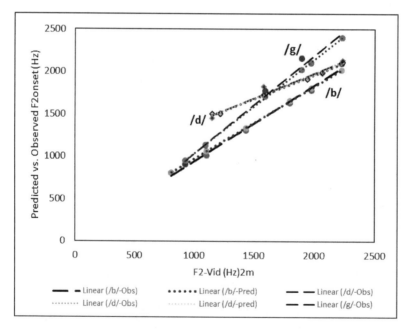

Figure 6.5   Predicted and observed F2 onsets plotted against F2-V$_2$mid. The bolded linear lines fit to the data points represent the predicted F2 onsets, while the dotted linear lines represent the observed data points. Any difference between the slopes of the bolded and dotted lines would represent the degree of coarticulatory effects attributable to the influence of tone

Segmental, suprasegmental interaction: Yoruba

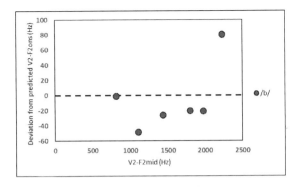

Figure 6.6a

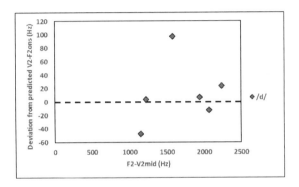

Figure 6.6b

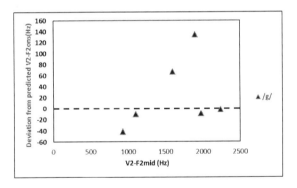

Figure 6.6c

Figures 6.6a, b and c   Deviation of predicted F2 onsets from observed F2 onsets derived for each of the 6 V_2 contexts and averaged across the 13 subjects. The data points below the zero line indicate that the observed onsets were lower than the predicted

A plot of the deviation of the data points from predicted onsets derived for each stop place category averaged across the 13 subjects for each of the 6 vowels yield a parsimonious visual summary of the effects of tone. The plots are presented above in Figures 6.6a for /b/, 6.6b for /d/, and 6.6c for /g/. As suggested by Agwuele et al. (2008), the differences between the 'observed' and 'predicted' represents the degree of coarticulation attributable to

Table 6.4 Summary of the Locus Equations coefficients comparing observed and predicted F2 onsets for citation form

	Predicted		Observed	
	slope	y-inter	slope	y-inter
b	0.85	117	0.90	40
d	0.57	826	0.59	804
g	1.11	76	1.16	−132

tone-induced variation apart from contextual vowel effects. Such differences, based on the presented results, did not obtain for the citation data. The range of the deviation of observed from predicted F2 onsets are less than 50Hz for /b/ and /d/. Except for the one vowel /i/, which showed the observed effect with a higher value of 80Hz. For /g/, the observed value for vowel /e/ is 134Hz higher than the predicted, otherwise the rest are within 60Hz of each other, and likely not perceptible. Figures 6.6a–c are visualizations of the deviation of observed from predicted F2 onsets.

Analogous analyses were performed for the data obtained for the sentence condition for Mid and Low tones. The reason why citation and sentence conditions were not compared is that the goal of the study was to explore the probable influence of tone and thereby determine the status of Yoruba tone, either as endogenous to the vowel or as a suprasegmental factor that is overlaid on the syllable that bears the tone, rather than the exploration of the effects of speech style (tempo) on coarticulation, which would be the reason for a comparison between citation and sentence conditions.

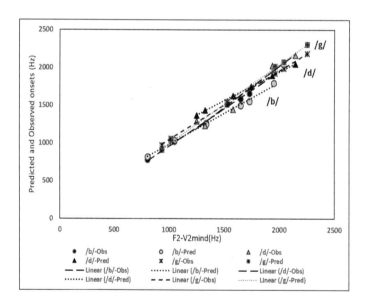

Figure 6.7 Predicted and observed F2 onsets plotted against F2-V_2mid. The bolded linear lines fit to the data points represents the observed F2 onsets, while the dotted linear lines represent the predicted data points. Differences represent the degree of coarticulatory effects attributable to the influence of tone

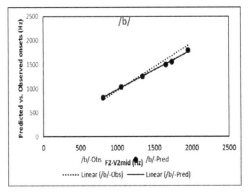 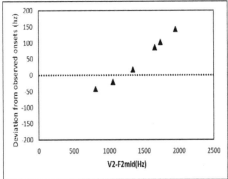

Figure 6.8a

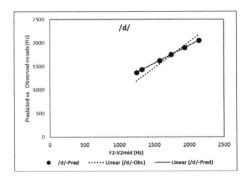 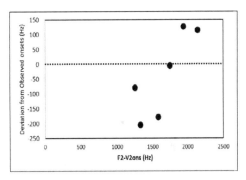

Figure 6.8b

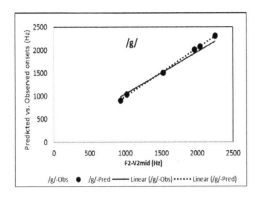 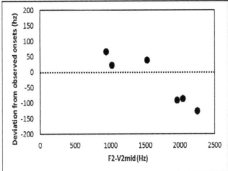

Figure 6.8c

Figures 6.8a, b and c Predicted and observed F2 onsets plotted against F2-V_2mid. The bolded linear lines fit to the data points represents the predicted F2 onsets, while the dotted linear lines represent the observed data points. Any difference between the slopes of the bolded and dotted lines would represent the degree of coarticulatory effects attributable to the influence of tone

Tone effect: connected speech (sentence form)

As visibly shown in the plot of Figure 6.7, the trendlines for the pair of the stops are significantly different. These differences are shown by the Locus Equation coefficients presented in Table 6.5.

As shown in Table 6.5, there are clear differences in the slope and y-intercept values between observed and predicted onsets for the stops. To better understand these differences, paired samples t-tests were conducted to gauge the significance of the reported differences between the observed and predicted F2 onsets. The results, summarily presented in Table 6.6, show that the differences between them were significant for /b, d, g/.

In addition, plots of the deviations between the observed and predicted F2 onsets for each of the six V_2 contexts, averaged across the four speakers, and for each stop place category, reveal how these deviations are related to the higher slopes obtained for the Mid-tone condition. These plots are presented in Figures 6.8a–c. The linear regression lines, fit to the data points

Table 6.5 Summary of the Locus Equation coefficients comparing observed and predicted F2 onsets for sentence form

	Predicted		Observed	
	slope	y-inter	slope	y-inter
b	0.82	159	0.99	−32
d	0.77	417	1.11	191
g	1.05	63	0.92	129

Table 6.6 Summary of the paired-tests coefficients comparing observed and predicted F2 onsets for sentence form, showing the t-statistics and p-value for /b, d, g/

	Obs	Pred	df	t	p-value
b	1379	1330	50	1.72	0.05
d	1659	1695	52	−1.63	0.05
g	1759	1808	43	−2.27	0.01

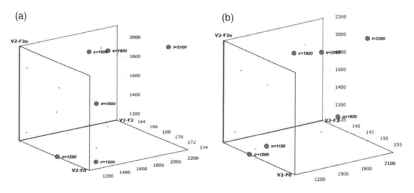

Figure 6.9a Three-dimensional plot of tone and first and second formants of V_2 for Mid tone. The plot shows the dispersion of the six vowels under citation form. Compare the front High and Mid vowels of plot 6.9a to their counterpart of plot 6.9b. Then /a, o, and o/ in their spatial ordering within the dimensional space. Driving the observed differences is F0

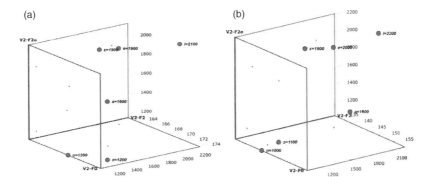

Figure 6.9b Three-dimensional plot of tone and first and second formants of V_2 for Low-tone. The plot shows the dispersion of the six vowels under citation form

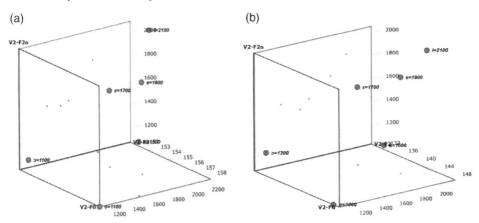

Figure 6.10a Three-dimensional plot of tone and first and second formants of V_2 for Mid-tone. The plot shows the dispersion of the six vowels under sentence form

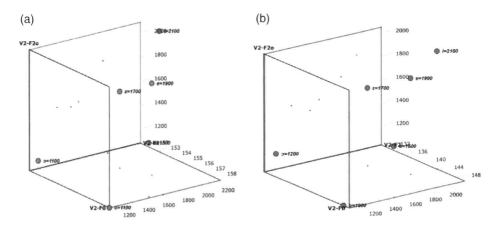

Figure 6.10b Three dimensional plot of F0, first, and second formants of V_2 for Low-tone. The plot shows the dispersion of the six vowels under sentence form. While evincing analogous spatial configurations, the vowels of Low tone relative to Mid tone show differential scaling due to F0

for the observed onsets, deviate significantly from the data points of the predicted onsets. Paired t-tests were performed to determine if the differences in slope as a function of tone were significant. The results as reported in the Table 6.6 above show that the differences were statistically significant.

Three-dimensional diagram of F0, F1 and F2 of V$_2$

A final explication of the role of tone could be derived through a three-dimensional plot involving F0, F1-V$_2$mid, and F2-V$_2$mid. The plots were derived for each of the six vowels averaged across speakers and across stops as a function of tone. Thus, there is one plot for all the vowels in Low tone of citation form relative to the Mid tone of the same citation form. A similar function was also performed for the two tones of the sentence condition. The results are presented in Figures 6.9a and 6.9b for citation form, and Figures 6.10a and 6.10b for sentence form.

Discussion

The methodology employed in the current study derived from the conceptualization offered by Lindblom et al. (2007) and Agwuele et al. (2008). The methodological approach offers a systematic approach to determine and evaluate how the degree of coarticulation, as suggested by the Locus Equation parameters, is influenced by tone, in addition to the expected vowel influence due to contextual variations.

The study investigated the interaction of Mid tone and Low tone with the CV syllable that bears them under citation and sentence speech forms. Two different patterns emerged for each speech condition. For citation speech condition, the traditional and modified Locus Equations reported no significant differences between Mid and Low tone data. However, there were slightly higher, though likely imperceptible slopes differences for the Low tone. Micro-analyses that were performed as part of the Modified Locus Equation process include the multiple regression analyses that used four predictor variables; F0 and F2 from V_1 and V_2. In all the cases, the F2 of the upcoming vowel remains the most significant and singular factor influencing CV coarticulation for both tones. In /b/, Low-tone and Mid tone, F2 of V_1 was found to continue significantly, the perseveratory effect was also observed for /d/ Mid-tone. Neither F0 was found to influence segmental interactions. However, it should be noted that F0 was marginally significant for /d, g/ Low tone (Table 6.2a). Euclidean distance also showed significant overlap between the two tones as provided in Figure 6.2a. Even though the plot of F1/F2 showed close approximation between Mid and Low tone vowels, the tendency for the Mid tone condition to occupy a slightly larger space was noted. Finally, the three-dimensional plot appears to uncover significant F0 effects on Low and back vowels.

The sentence conditions reported both for the traditional and the Modified Locus Equations displayed systematic differences between the Mid and Low tone forms. The slope values differed systematically. The Higher Order Locus Equations were not overlapped, and the Euclidean distances were separate. For both Low and Mid tone, F2 was significant in influencing the extent of CV interactions as shown by the multiple regression analyses. F2-V_1 had a persistent significant effect on /b,/ Mid tone, and for /g/ Mid and Low tone. When observed and predicted data were computed and plotted, significant and convincing differences emerged that were attributed to the effects of tone. Thus, the data from the carrier sentence behaved similarly to stress as reported by Lindblom et al. (2007). However, it is unclear why there is such dissonance between sentence and citation conditions on the effects of tone.

Pertaining to the original questions of the research; the Locus Equations provided categorical lawfulness to contextual vowel variations, artfully quantifying the degree of coarticulation between the interacting CV segments across the stop place categories. The results parallel similar findings reported by the various studies that have implemented the Locus Equations model, e.g., Sussman and Sussman et al. (1989, 1991), Ghavami (2002), Lindblom et al. (2007), Agwuele (2016), among others. Concerning the status of Yoruba tone either as endogamous or intrinsic to the syllable that bears it, the results were inconclusive. At best they differed as a function of speech style. In citation form, the CV segments appeared to be produced with intrinsic tone, while in sentence condition, tone evinced behavior analogous to a suprasegmental factor. Nonetheless, it is probably safe to describe Yoruba vowels as having their inherent pitch/tone.

Notes

1 The bracketing of the VCV sequences in the example for /gb/ is non-committal or is agnostic of the important issue of nasalized vowels in Yoruba (Akinlabi 1985) or nasalization in general. The objective in the selection of test words was that they should be meaningful, they occur in comparable environments and the V_2s should differ in tone.
2 The Praat script, mostly composed by Amanda Miller, was used to obtain formants.

References

Agwuele, A. (2003). "The effect of stress on consonantal loci." In Solé, M.J., Recasens, D. & Romero, J. (eds), *Proceedings of the 15th International Congress of Phonetic Sciences*, Vol. 1, 787–790. Adelaide: Causal Publications.

Agwuele, A. (2005). "Effect of stress on coarticulation." In Slifka, J., Manuel, S. & Matthies, M. (eds), *Sound to Sense: Fifty + Years of Discoveries in Speech Communication*, C109–114. Cambridge, MA: MIT.

Agwuele, A., Sussman, H.M. & Lindblom, B. (2008). "The effect of speaking rate on consonant vowel coarticulation." *Phonetica*, 65(4), 194–209.

Agwuele, A. & Sussman, H.M. (2011). "CV coarticulation in Yoruba: A tonal language." In Sum Lee, W. & Zee, E. (eds), *17th International Congress of Phonetic Sciences*, Hong Kong, 204–207.

Agwuele, A. (2015). "Coarticulation of tone and CV segment in citation and sentence forms." In *Proceedings of the 18th International Congress of Phonetic Sciences*. The Scottish Consortium for ICPhS 2015 (Ed.). Glasgow, UK: The University of Glasgow, paper number 0190, 1–5.

Agwuele, A. (2016). "Interaction of Yoruba tones with VCV segments: Research notes." In Agwuele, A. & Lotto, A. (eds), *Essays in Speech Processes: Language Production and Perception*, 344–365. Sheffield, Equinox Publishing.

Akinlabi, A.M. (1985). "Tonal underspecification and Yoruba tone." PhD Dissertation. Ibadan: University of Ibadan.

Bamgbose, A. (1965). "Assimilation and contraction in Yoruba." *Journal of West African Languages* 2(1), 21–27.

Berry, J. & Weismer, G. (2013). "Speaking rate effects on locus equation slope." *Journal of Phonetics*, 41(6), 468–478.

Blumstein, S.E. & Stevens, K.N. (1979). "Acoustic invariance in speech production: Evidence from measurements of the spectral characteristics of stop consonants." *Journal of the Acoustical Society of America*, 66(4), 1001–1017.

Boersma, P. & Weenink, D. (2004). Praat [Version 4.2]. Doing phonetics by computer. Available online at: www.praat.org.

Bokamba, G.E. (ed.) (1990). "The contribution of African linguistics to linguistic theory". *Proceedings of the 20th Annual Conference on African Linguistics.* Vol.2. No.1. Champaign, IL: Department of Linguistics, University of Illinois.

Browman, C.P. & Goldstein, L. (1992). "Articulatory phonology: An overview." *Phonetic,* 49, 155–180.

Chennoukh, S., Carré, R. & Lindblom, B. (1997). "Locus equations in light of articulatory modeling." *Journal of the Acoustical Society of America*, 102, 2380–2389.

Chomsky, N. & Halle, M. (1968). *The Sound Pattern of English.* New York, NY: Harper and Row.

Clements, G.N. (1976). *Vowel Harmony in Nonlinear Generative Phonology.* Bloomington, IN: Indiana University Linguistics Club.

Clements, G.N. (1985). "The geometry of phonological features," *Phonology Yearbook* 2, 225–252.

Courtenay, K.R. (1969). "A generative phonology of Yorùbá." PhD Dissertation. Los Angeles, CA: UCLA.

Crystal, T.H. & House, A.S. (1990). "Articulation rate and the duration of syllables and stress groups in connected speech." *Journal of the Acoustical Society of America*, 88, 101–112.

Delattre, P.C., Liberman, A.M. & Cooper, F.S. (1955). "Acoustic loci and transitional cues for consonants." *Journal of the Acoustical Society of America*, 27(4), 769–773.

Diehl, R.L., Kluender, K.R., Walsh, M.A. & Parker, E.M. (1991). "Auditory enhancement in speech perception and phonology." In Hoffman, R.R. & Palermo, D.S. (eds), *Cognition and the Symbolic Processes, Vol 3: Applied and Ecological Perspectives*, 59–76. Hillsdale, NJ: Erlbaum.

Diehl, R.L. & Kluender, K.R. (1989). "On the objects of speech perception." *Ecological Psychology*, 1, 121–144.

Duez, D. (1992). "Second formant locus-nucleus patterns: an investigation of spontaneous French speech." *Speech Communication*, 1(11), 417–427.

Everett, C. (1988). "Locus equation analysis as a tool for linguistic fieldwork." *Language Documentation & Conservation*, 2, 185–211.

Farnetani, E. (1999). "Coarticulation and connected speech processes." In Hardcastle, W.J. & Laver, J. (eds), *The Handbook of Phonetic Sciences*, 371–404. Oxford: Blackwell.

Farnetani, E. & Recasens, D. (2000). "Coarticulation models in recent speech production theories." In Hardcastle, W.J. & Hewlett, N. (eds), *Coarticulation, Theory, Data and Techniques*. New York, NY: Cambridge University Press.

Fowler, C.A. (1980). "Coarticulation and theories of extrinsic timing." *Journal of Phonetics*, 8, 113–133.

Fowler, C.A. (1986). "An event approach to the study of speech perception from a direct-realist perspective." *Journal of Phonetics*, 14, 2–28.

Fromkin, V.A. (1974). "On the phonological representation of tone." In Maddieson, I. (ed.), *WPP Studies on Tone from the UCLA Tone Project*, 1–17. Los Angeles, CA: UCLA.

Fruchter, D. & Sussman, H. (1997). "The perceptual relevance of locus equations." *Journal of the Acoustical Society of America*, 102, 2997–3008.

Ghavami, G.M. (2002). "The effects of syllable boundary, stop consonant closure: Duration, and VOT on VCV coarticulation." PhD Dissertation, Austin, TX: University of Texas.

Ghavami, G.M. (2016). "An investigation of locus equations in cited versus spontaneous speech in Persian." In Agwuele, A. & Lotto, A. (eds), *Essays in Speech Processes: Language Production and Perception*, 315–324. Sheffield, Equinox Publishing.

Goldman-Eisler, F. (1961). "The significance of changes in the rate of articulation." *Language and Speech*, 4(4), 171–174.

Goldsmith, J. (1976). *Autosegmental Phonology.* PhD dissertation, MIT. [Published by New York: Garland Press, 1980.]

Goldstein, L. & Browman, C.P. (1986). "Representation of voicing contrasts using articulatory gestures." *Journal of Phonetics*, 14, 339–342.

Gopal, H.S. (1990). "Effects of speaking rate on the behaviour of tense and lax vowel durations." *Journal of Phonetics*, 18, 497–518.

Hammarberg, R. (1976). "The metaphysics of coarticulation." *Journal of Phonetics*, 4, 353–363.

Henderson, E.J.A. (1982). "Tonogenesis: some recent speculations on the development of tone." *Transactions of the Philological Society*, 80(1), 1–24.

Hombert, J.M. (1977). "Consonant types, vowel height and tone in Yoruba." *Studies in African Linguistics*, 8(2), 173–190.

Hombert, J.-M., Ohala, J.J. & Ewan, W.G. (1979). "Phonetic explanations for the development of tones." *Language*, 55(1), 37–58.

Hyman, L.M. & Schuh, R.G. (1974). "Universals of tone rules: evidence from West Africa." *Linguistic Inquiry*, 5, 81–115.

Hyman, L.M. (ed.) (1976). "Studies in Bantu phonology." In *Southern California Occasional Papers in Linguistics*, Vol. 3. Los Angeles, CA: University of Southern California.

Iskarous, K., Fowler, C.A. & Whalen, D.H. (2010). "Locus equations are an expression of articulator synergy." *Journal of the Acoustical Society of America*, 128, 2021–2032.

Joos, M. (1948). "Acoustic phonetics." *Language*, 24(SM23), 1–136.

Kohler, K.J. (1990). "Segmental reduction in connected speech in German: Phonological facts and phonetic explanations." In Hardcastle, W.J. & Marchal, A. (eds), *Speech Production and Speech Modelling*, 69–92. Dordrecht, The Netherlands: Kluwer Academic Publishers.

Koopmans-van Beinum, F.J. (1980). "Vowel contrast reduction: An acoustic and perceptual study of Dutch vowels in various speech conditions." Diss., University of Amsterdam.

Krull, D. (1987). "Second formant locus patterns as a measure of consonant-vowel coarticulation." *Perilus*, Vol. V, 43–61.

Krull, D. (1988). "Acoustic properties as predictors of perceptual responses: A study of Swedish voiced stops." *Phonetic Experimental Research at the Institute of Linguistics*, University of Stockholm, *Perilus*, Vol. VII, 66–70.

Krull, D. (1989) "Second formant locus patterns and consonant-vowel coarticulation in spontaneous speech." *Perilus*, X, 101–105.

Kühnert, B. & Nolan, F. (1999). "The origin of coarticulation." In Hardcastle, W.J. & Hewlett, N. (eds), *Coarticulation: Theory, Data and Techniques in Speech Production*, 7–30. Cambridge: Cambridge University Press.

Ladefoged, P. & Maddieson, I. (1996). *The Sounds of the World's Languages*. Oxford: Blackwell Publishers.

La Velle, C.R. (1974). "An experimental study of Yoruba tone." In I. Maddieson, I. (ed.), *WPP Studies on Tone from the UCLA Tone Project*, 160–170. Los Angeles, CA: UCLA.

Leben, W.R. (1973). Suprasegmental phonology. PhD Dissertation. Cambridge, MA: MIT.

Liberman, A.M., Harris, K.S., Hoffman, H.S. & Griffit, B.C. (1957). "The discrimination of speech sounds within and across phoneme boundaries." *Journal of Experimental Psychology*, 54, 358–368.

Liberman, A.M. & Mattingly, I. (1985). "The motor theory of speech perception revisited." *Cognition*, 21, 1–36.

Liberman, A.M. & Mattingly, I.G. (1989). "A specialization for speech perception." *Science*, 243, 489–494.

Lindblom, B. (1963). "On vowel reduction." Report No. 29, *Speech Transmission Laboratory*, The Royal Institute of Technology, Sweden.

Lindblom, B., Agwuele, A., Sussman, H.M. & Eir Cortes, E. (2007). "The effects of stress on consonant and vowel coarticulation." *Journal of the Acoustical Society of America*, 121(2), 3801–3813.

Lindblom, B., Sussman, H.M. & Agwuele, A. (2009). "A duration-dependent account of coarticulation for hyper-and hypoarticulation." *Phonetica*, 66, 188–195.

Maddieson, I. (1974). "A note on tones and consonants." In Maddieson, I. (ed.), *WPP Studies on Tone from the UCLA Tone Project*, 18–27. Los Angeles, CA: UCLA.

Manuel, S.Y. & Krakow, R.A (1984). "Universal and language particular aspects of vowel-to-vowel coarticulation." *Haskins Laboratories Status Report on Speech Research*, SR-77/78, 69–78.

Manuel, Y.S. (1990). "The role of contrast in limiting vowel-to-vowel coarticulation in different languages." *Haskins Laboratories Status report on Speech Research*. SR-103/104, 1–20.

Mattingly, I.G. & Liberman, A.M. (1988). "Specialized perceiving systems for speech and other biologically significant sounds." In Edelman, G.M.G., Gall, W.E. & Cowan, W.M. (eds), *Auditory Function: Neurological Bases of Hearing*, 775–793. New York, NY: Wiley.

Menzerath, P. and de Lacerda, A. (1933). *Koartikulation, Steuerung und Lautabgrenzung:meine experimentelle Untersuchung*. Berlin, Bonn.

Moon, S.J. & Lindblom, B. (1989). "Formant undershoot in clear and citation-from speech: A second progress report." *STL-QPSY*, 30(1), 121–123.

Neary, T.M. & Shammass, S.E. (1987). "Formant transitions as partly distinctive invariant properties in the identification of voiced stops." *Journal of the Acoustical Society of America*, 15(4), 17–24.

Öhman, S. (1966). "Coarticulation in VCV utterances: Spectrographic measurements." *Journal of the Acoustical Society of America*, 39, 151–168.

Oyelaran, O.O. (1971). "Yoruba phonology." Doctoral dissertation, Stanford, CA: Stanford University.

Pulleyblank, D. (1986). *Tone in Lexical Phonology*. Dordrecht: Eidel.

Recasens, D., Pallares, M.D. & Fontdevila, J. (1997). "A model of lingual coarticulation based on articulatory constraints." *Journal of the Acoustical Society of America*, 102, 544–561.

Schuh, R.G. (1978). "Tone rules." In Fromkin, V. (ed.), *Tone: A Linguistic Survey*, 221–256. New York, NY: Academic Press.

Sievers, E. (1876). *Grundzuge der Phonetik zur Einfuehrung in das Studium der Lautlehre de Indogermanischen Sprachen* [Reprinted 1980]. Hildesheim NY: Olms.

Stevens, K.N. (1972). "The quantal nature of speech: Evidence from articulatory-acoustic data." In Denes, P.B. & David Jr, E.E. (eds), *Human Communication: A Unified View*, 51–66. New York, NY: McGraw-Hill.

Strange, W. (1989). "Dynamic specification of coarticulated vowels spoken in sentence context." *Journal of the Acoustical Society of America*, 85, 2135–2153.

Studdert-Kennedy, M. (1987). "The phoneme as a perceptuomotor structure." In Allport, I.A. Mackay, D., Prinz, W. & Scheerer, E. (eds), *Language Perception and Production*, 67–84. London: Academic Press.

Studdert-Kennedy, M. (1989). "Reading gestures by light and sound." In Young, A.W. & Ellis, H.D. (eds), *Handbook of Research on Face Processing*, 217–222. The Netherlands: Elsevier.

Sussman, H.M. (1989). "Neural coding of relational invariance in speech: Human language analogs to the barn owl." *Psychological Review*, 96(4), 631–642.

Sussman, H.M., McCaffrey, H.A. & Matthews, S.A. (1991). "An investigation of locus equations as a source of relational invariance for stop place categorization." *Journal of the Acoustical Society of America*, 90, 1309–1325.

Sussman, H.M., Hoemeke, K.A. & Ahmed, F.S. (1993). "A cross-linguistic investigation of locus equations as a phonetic descriptor for place of articulation." *Journal of the Acoustical Society of America*, 3(Pt1), 1256–1268.

Sussman, H.M., Fruchter, J.H. & Sirosh, J. (1998). "Linear correlates in speech signal: The orderly output constraint. Target article." *Behavioral and Brain Sciences*, 21, 241–299.

Sussman, H.M., Dalston, E., Duder, C. & Cacciatore, A. (1999). "An acoustic analysis of the development of CV coarticulation: A case study." *Journal of Speech & Hearing Research*, 42, 1080–1096.

Sussman, H.M., Marquardt, T.P., Doyle, J. & Knapp, H. (2002). "Phonemic integrity and contrastiveness in developmental apraxia of speech, investigations." In Windsor, F., Kelly, M.L. & Hewlett, N. (eds), *Themes in Clinical Linguistics and Phonetics*, 311–326. New York, NY: Lawrence Erlbaum.

Sussman H.M. (2016). "A functional role for coarticulation: A locus equation perspective." In Agwuele, A. & Lotto, A. (eds), *Essays in Speech Processes: Language Production and Perception*, 325–343. Sheffield: Equinox Publishing.

Sweet, H. (1877). *A Handbook of Phonetics, Including a Popular Exposition of the Principles of Spelling Reform*. Oxford: Clarendon Press.

Tabain, M. (2000). "Coarticulation in CV syllables: A comparison of EPG and Locus Equation data." *Journal of Phonetics*, 28, 137–159.

Turner, G.S., Kris, T. & Gary, W. (1995). "The influence of speaking rate on vowel space and speech intelligibility for individuals with amyotrophic lateral sclerosis." *Journal of Speech, Language, and Hearing Research*, 38, 1001–1013.

Van Niekerk, D.R. & Barnard, E. (2012). "Tone realisation in a Yoruba speech recognition corpus." In *Proceedings of the 3rd International Workshop on Spoken Languages Technologies for Under-resourced Languages* (SLTU), 54–59. Cape Town, South Africa.

Whiteside, S.P. (2016). "Profiling individual differences in speech production." In Agwuele, A. & Lotto, A. (eds), *Essays in Speech Processes: Language Production and Perception*, 269–314. Sheffield: Equinox Publishing.

Xu, Y. (2013). "ProsodyPro: A tool for large-scale systematic prosody analysis." In *Proceedings of Tools and Resources for the Analysis of Speech Prosody* (TRASP), 7–10. Aix-en-Provence, France.

7

LABIAL-VELARS OF AFRICA

Phonetics, phonology, and historical development

Michael Cahill

Introduction

Labial-velar obstruents (k͡p, g͡b, ŋm, hereafter generalized as KP) are often characterized as "African sounds." Labial-velar consonants occur in at least some languages of all of the 10 main subfamilies of Niger-Congo (Bendor-Samuel, 1989), and many of the languages of Nilo-Saharan as well. They are not unique to Africa, since there are several dozen Pacific languages that have them (especially in Papua New Guinea and Vanuatu), a handful in South America, and a very few elsewhere (Cahill, 2017). However, they are more abundant in this continent than elsewhere, and are widely regarded as an African phenomenon.

In this chapter, the term "labial-velar" will be limited to the stops k͡p and g͡b and the nasal ŋm. The labial-velar glide [w], though related, will not be discussed. There have been claims of labial-velar fricatives in the literature, but, upon closer study, these have not been confirmed. Urhobo and Isoko were reported as having labial-velar fricatives (Ladefoged, 1968; Kelly, 1969), but closer investigation has shown them to actually be the labialized velar fricatives [xw, ɣw]; the friction is all in the velar region, with accompanying lip-rounding (Elugbe, 1986: 32). Similarly, Avatime was reported to have labial-velar fricatives [xφ] and [ɣβ] in Kropp-Dakubu and Ford (1988), but, again, these are more properly [xw, ɣw] (Schuh, 1995; Maddieson, 1998). Ladefoged and Maddieson (1996: 329–332) have an extensive discussion on the phonetic difficulties of producing simultaneous fricatives at two places of articulation, as well as debunking some of the previous claims of multiply-articulated fricatives.

Studies that focus on labial-velars as a major theme are few. Connell (1994) has a detailed study of the phonetic properties of labial-velars in several languages, and Ladefoged and Maddieson (1996) also include a good summary of the phonetics in their chapter on multiple articulatory gestures. Demolin has several phonetic studies of specific languages (e.g., Demolin & Soquet, 1999). In his groundbreaking early work, Ladefoged (1968) deals with the phonetics of labial-velars in several West African languages. Sagey (1990 [1986]) and, with a slightly narrower focus, Ryder (1987) focus on phonological representations. Cahill (1999) also has an overview of many of the same topics covered here, and Connell (1998/1999) also covers several of the issues discussed in this chapter.

Languages vary in their phonological inventories as to which labial-velars are present. In my personal database of languages which have some form of labial-velar, currently with

863 languages, about 715 have complete inventories of their phonemes. Of these, 607 have both /kp, gb/, while 68 have only /kp/ and 47 have only /gb/. The /ŋm/ is present in 167 languages, but there is no language that has only /ŋm/ as a labial-velar, and 131 have a prenasalized /ŋKP/ or /ŋmKP/. These figures will change as more data becomes available, but the current data is extensive enough so the changes will be fairly minimal in terms of percentages.

The KPs are quite restricted phonotactically, occurring most often in word-initial or root-initial position, less commonly morpheme-medially, and almost never word-finally. Adele, a Kwa language of Ghana, is typical; /kp/ and /gb/ are never found morpheme-medially. In all classes of words except nouns, labial-velars are never found word-internally except in redu-plicated forms such as *gbà-gbà* 'really'. Nouns generally have a noun class prefix, and after that the noun stem begins with any consonant, including /kp/ and /gb/, e.g., *è-kpènà* 'ghost', *gè-gbá* 'shirt' (Kleiner, 1989). An example of the unusual word-final labial-velar is found in Adioukrou (Herault, 1983), citing *édʒâgb* 'path' and *sékp* 'fetish'. Also, KPs are most com-monly found in lexical items rather than in function words or affixes.

All the patterns noted in this chapter, whether phonetic, historical, or phonological, are relatively widespread and common, except where noted. Thus the examples are not exhaustive by any means. Rarer phenomena exist, such as the labial-velars with trilled release in Baka and in Efe (Parker, 1985; Demolin & Teston, 1997, respectively). These are shown to be single phonological units by the same criteria as the usual labial-velars. But in this chapter I focus on the more usual and frequent phenomena that labial-velars exhibit.

Since labial-velar sounds are phonologically one unit (cf. the fourth section for rationale), they are properly formally notated with a tie-bar, e.g., k͡p, g͡b, ŋ͡m. However, in the interests of simplicity, I will omit the tie-bar unless I am contrasting a labial-velar unit with a labial-velar sequence. As we will see, the specific phonetics of labial-velars, their historical development, and their phonological characteristics are all intimately connected.

Phonetics

Ladefoged (1968) notes three mechanisms for producing labial-velars.

(1) Mechanisms for producing labial-velars:

  a   Simple pulmonic airstream.
  b   Pulmonic egressive and velaric ingressive airstream. Dorsum slides back, air flows into oral cavity from both directions.
  c   Pulmonic egressive, velaric ingressive, glottalic ingressive airstreams. Partly voiced.

Ladefoged himself notes that these categories are to be treated with caution, in that these are based on few informants from each language, and there is considerable variation in the actual mechanisms. For example, he puts Ibibio in category 2, when later studies put Ibibio firmly in category 3. In spite of this, it is noteworthy that an ingressive airstream, a suction, is present in the majority of languages studied. This has possible implications for the type of sound changes labial-velars undergo, as discussed in the third section.

Besides Ladefoged's data, many others have noted a similar ingressive air mechanism. Connell (1994) assesses this implosion in several different languages by means of acoustic or aerodynamic evidence, or both. Mills (1984) notes that labial-velars in the Tyebaara dialect of Senufo are pronounced "with noticeable suction in the oral cavity, and with a pop upon release."

Dan (Santa) is described as having "bilabial implosion" for /gb/ and "strong bilabial implosion" for /kp/ (Bearth & Zemp, 1967). The Engenni /kp/ and /gb/ are specifically listed as "ingressive," in contrast to the other "egressive" stops (Thomas, 1978). Wilhoit (1999) labels /kp/ and /gb/ as "implosive" in Loma of Guinea and Liberia. Wilson (1961) notes that the Temne /g͡b/ can be implosive. Boadi (2009: 25) notes rather generally that /kp/ and /gb/ are implosive in the speech of some speakers of the Volta-Comoe languages, but there is no contrast with non-implosives, so this is a "redundant" feature. The degree of implosion can of course be quite variable, along with associated effects such as pre-voicing (Connell, 1994).

In contrast, Painter (1970) specifically notes that Gonja is of Ladefoged's first type, with a simple pulmonic airstream. From my own data and fieldwork, Kɔnni also has a simple pulmonic airstream for labial-velars. Welmers (1952) specifically notes that Bariba /kp/ and /gb/ are "produced with neither pressure nor suction in the cavity between the two closures." Though a more thorough study may challenge this, it appears that implosion or the lack of it is a constant phonetic characteristic of an individual language.[1]

Though labial-velars are often characterized as "simultaneous" labial and velar articulations, the reality is slightly more complex. The labial and velar articulations overlap, but with the velar slightly preceding, and the labial slightly lagging. Thus the release is labial, and perceptually more salient than the velar component.

This is seen clearly in the electromagnetic articulography studies of Ewe in Maddieson (1993), in which small metal pellets were glued to the lips and tongue back, and a detector tracked the position of these over time. Figure 7.1 shows the result of the measurements for one Ewe word. The velar closure both leads the labial closure and is released before the labial closure is released. One can also see the high degree of overlap between the two gestures.

More recently, ultrasound measurements have been applied to labial-velars, showing the same pattern as the electromagnetic articulography.

One can predict, therefore, that labial-velar durations would have only slightly longer duration than either a plain labial or a plain velar, and this is in fact borne out. This is one of the pieces of evidence that establishes these as phonological units rather than clusters (see the fourth section). Connell (1994), for example, provides the following data for Igbo:

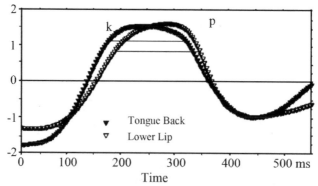

Coordination of lower lip and tongue back movements in the Ewe word **akpa**. Y-axis is vertical displacement; horizontal lines indicate the likely duration of actual contact of the articulator.

Figure 7.1 Electromagnetic articulography measure of Ewe [kp]

Table 7.1 Duration of Igbo stops in ms

	kp	*k*	*p*	*gb*	*g*	*b*
mean duration	143.6	104.3	125.9	129.8	93.3	110.4
standard dev.	16.2	13.3	12.6	21.0	15.6	13.5

Also, a phonetic timing contrast between a [g͡b] unit and a [gb] cluster is found in Kɔnni, with average duration measurements of 166 ms for the cluster [gb] in *kág-bíŋ* 'small roan antelope' and *kɔ́g-bíŋ* 'small cleared area', while the duration of the unit [g͡b] in *kàgbá* 'straw hat' are 73 ms (Cahill, 2007: 130).

One would expect to see spectrographic evidence of a labial release of a word-initial KP, and indeed that is what is often found, for example in spectrograms from Efik, Ibibio, and others cited in Connell (1994) and Ladefoged and Maddieson (1996). However, besides the normal labial release, with the first and second vowel formants (F1 and F2) transitioning into the following vowel, a labial-velar typically has an extremely steep F2 rise into the following vowel, as shown in the Frafra example in Figure 7.2, comparing the words *kpaʔa* and *paka*.

Another result expected in a spectrogram would be that the transitions into the stop would indicate a velar rather than a labial component, perhaps even with the prototypical "velar pinch" in which the loci of F3 and F2 merge in transition into the KP consonant. This can be seen in the Leggbo example *ɛkkpa* in Figure 7.3 (*kkp* indicating a long labial-velar) in which the steep transition of F2 into the following vowel can also be observed.

However, the prototypical velar transition into KP and the extra-steep labial transition out of KP are not always found in actual speech. The velar transition into the KP especially is often unclear; the labial transition is usually more visible. The experienced phonetician can usually hear the contrast between a KP and a P though, even when the spectrographic evidence is less than ideal.

The labial release of a KP has at least three consequences. First, for a person whose first language does not have labial-velars, the KP sounds very much like a labial.[2] In initial exposure to labial-velars, then, they may be mis-identified.

Second, the perception of a KP as a P is largely responsible for the sound change *KP > P being much more common than *KP > K (cf. the third section).

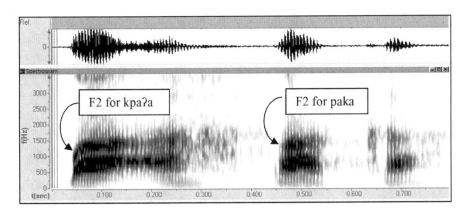

Figure 7.2 Frafra kpaʔa and paka, showing difference of F2 transitions

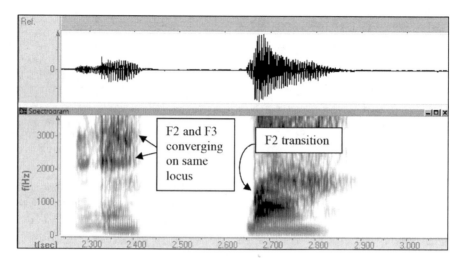

Figure 7.3 Differing formant transitions into and out of Leggbo [kp] in ɛkkpa

Third, the release of KP as a labial is quite probably the root cause of the primacy of [labial] rather than [dorsal] in the phonology of labial-velars (cf. the fourth section).

One might wonder why the onset of a labial-velar is velar and the release is labial ([k͡p]), rather than the other way around ([p͡k]), or even a more simultaneous articulation.[3] Cahill and Hajek (2001) considered three possible answers to this: perceptual salience, articulatory effort, and remnant of the historical processes producing KP (cf. page 156). While these possibilities could all benefit from more investigation, it appears that perceptual salience is probably not a factor in the order of gestures of KP. "Articulatory effort" is notoriously difficult to measure, but several articulatory factors may possibly be relevant: (1) the mechanics of the jaw as a hinge, which upon closing would facilitate the more back articulation to meet earlier, (2) typologically, consonantal metathesis predominantly moves a more back consonant to precede a more front one, (3) the direction of airflow in a pulmonic airstream would naturally open the closure closest to the source of the airstream (velar) first, and (4) with a velaric ingressive airstream, which many labial-velars have, a labial release is required to be after the velar one. Also, as many labial-velars /kp/ historically have *k^w as a source, it is possible that the order of their closures is a reflex of the order of the proto-segment's closure and release. A referee correctly points out that since labial closures are typically longer than velar ones (cf. Table 7.1), if either the velar onset precedes the labial one or if they have simultaneous onsets, one would expect a labial release. All of these are more suggestive than conclusive, and deserve more research. But it appears that the asynchrony of labial and velar gestures in [k͡p] can be attributed to a confluence of several factors, all targeting the same direction of asymmetry.

Several other phonetic aspects of voiceless labial-velars are those generally associated with voiced obstruents rather than voiceless ones, labial-velars having different characteristics than the usual obstruents. First, aspiration in /kp/ is almost always absent or severely reduced compared with other voiceless stops in a given language. Smith (1967) reports aspiration on all voiceless stops in Nupe except labial-velars, which he specifically states are unaspirated. For Konkomba (Steele & Weed, 1966), Kusaal (Spratt & Spratt, 1968), Nafaara (Jordan, 1980), and Sisaala-Pasaale (Toupin, 1995), as well as other languages, /kp/ alone among voiceless stops is specifically noted as not aspirated.[4]

Second, the voiceless /kp/ in some languages often is partially voiced, this pre-voicing being absent in simple voiceless stops (Connell, 1994). Such a /kp/ may still contrast with a fully voiced /gb/, and is correlated with an implosive air mechanism (cf. next paragraph). Innes (1964) notes specifically that in Loko the voiceless counterpart of /gb/ is "initially voiceless, but with slight voicing finally," and even transcribes this as /kb/. Shryock et al. (1996/1997) note that /kp/ in Defaka has the onset of voicing prior to its release.

Finally, recapitulating some of the descriptions of air mechanisms, there is sometimes an implosive air mechanism, even for the voiceless /kp/. For example, Dan (Santa) is described as having "bilabial implosion" for /gb/ and "strong bilabial implosion" for /kp/ (Bearth & Zemp, 1967). The Engenni /kp/ and /gb/ are specifically listed as "ingressive," in contrast to the other "egressive" stops (Thomas, 1978). Again, these three characteristics are generally associated with voiced stops. Consequently, the sound change *kp > gb is not rare; dozens of languages exhibit the results of this merger, possessing only /gb/ but no /kp/, even though other voiceless stops are present (Cahill, 2008). This is discussed more fully in the third section.

Historical development

How labial-velars develop

Regular sound change, borrowing, and genetic inheritance can all be demonstrated as sources of KP, but genetic inheritance is responsible for the majority of occurrences of KP in languages.

In Table 7.2, the language families in **bold** have been specifically reconstructed with KP by various scholars (see Cahill (2017) for specific details). Unbolded families in the list, which have not specifically been reconstructed with *KP, I believe are still likely to have them, based on the existence of KP in many languages in those families. The numbers on the left represent total family members (Lewis et al., 2017); the ones on the right are KP-containing languages from my database. In Kwa, for example, 72 out of 80 daughter languages have KP, and it is likely that the parent language did too. There is a need for systematic reconstruction to confirm this, of course. Note that in some cases I do not have information on all languages in a subfamily, so the number of languages with KP may be higher than listed.

It should be mentioned that even in the proto-languages that have been reconstructed with a *KP, not all daughter languages in these groups have KP. For example, Akan is an unusual Kwa language with no KP (it changed to P historically). Similarly, Supyire is the rare Gur language that lacks KP (again, merging with labials).

Table 7.2 Language families with likely *KP

Central Sudanic	**64**	**(31)**	Defoid	17	(15)
Gur	**97**	**(70)**	**Edoid**	**31**	**(20)**
Kru	**40**	**(39)**	**Ijoid**	**10**	**(10)**
Kwa	80	(72)	**Igboid**	**10**	(9)
Mande	**73**	**(46)**	**Nupoid**	**11**	(5)
Cross River	**68**	**(45)**	Jukunoid	20	(15)
Platoid (Plateau)	54	(52)	Kainji	59	(17)
Adamawa	88	(66)	Ubangi	70	(56)
			TOTAL	**792**	(568)

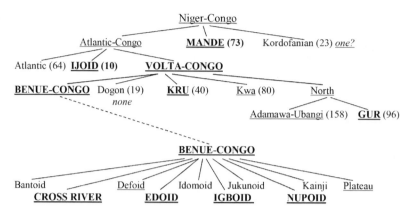

Figure 7.4 Niger-Congo language families with reconstructed labial-velars

The Niger Congo language families are schematized in Figure 7.4. Language families in **BOLD UNDERLINE** have been specifically reconstructed with KP. Language families with unbolded UNDERLINE are those I consider promising for reconstruction with KP.

Borrowing through language contact is the source of KP in dozens of languages, even across major language family boundaries. Bantu languages are a possible case in point. Most lack labial-velars (Grégoire, 2003), though my database includes 76 that do have them. Bostoen and Donzo (2013) show specifically that the origin of labial-velars in the Bantu language Lingombe is the result of borrowing from the neighboring Ubangi languages. Similarly, most Chadic languages do not have labial-velars, but 22 do, and these likely have acquired them through language contact, as Andreas et al. (2009: 25) specifically note for Nyam.

Some languages have been documented to have developed labial-velars by means of regular sound change through history. Of course, this also can happen centuries ago in what we would now refer to as proto-languages. Change in both recent and ancient stages of languages' histories often follow the path *KU > Kw > KP, as Ponelis (1974) discusses with more detail. For example, in the Sawabantu languages (Cameroon), Mutaka and Ebobissé (1996/97) show that a historical prefix *ku- was realized as *kw- before vowels (in a common glide formation process), and then *kw > k͡p in Western Sawabantu.

(2) Evolution of labial-velars

	Eastern Sawabantu	*Western Sawabantu*[5]
'diarrhea'	**kú**ɓwako	**kú**gbako
'sword'	**kw**átá	**kp**átá

There is a glide formation rule in Sawabantu that changes a [u/o] to [w] between a stop and a non-round vowel, thus /kuátá/ [kwátá]. So, above, *kuV changes to kwV, then historically the Western Sawabantu group changed kwV to kpV. Mutaka and Ebobissé (1996/97) propose an account of historical development through a Feature Geometry framework, while Connell (1998/1999), pointing out problems with this analysis, provides an alternative analysis through the gestural viewpoint of Articulatory Phonology.

There are other paths to KP as well, sometimes involving a labialized labial, for example. In the Aghem language of Cameroon, to cite one case, it is likely that labial-velars /kp, gb, ŋm/ developed from labialized labials /pw, bw, mw/ (Hyman, 1979). A relatively unusual change is posited from proto-Nilo-Saharan to proto-Central Sudanic of *gVB > *gbV (Ehret, 2001), affecting the whole group. However, the path through labialized velars is probably the most common one.

How labial-velars change

If *KP has reflexes other than KP itself, they are most likely to be the labial P, as Connell (1991 and other writings) note for Lower Cross languages. As noted, this historical commonality is linked to the perceptually prominent labial release of KP.

The Kwa languages of Cote d'Ivoire and Ghana illustrate the tendency to lose the velar portion, with Abron being a language with /p/ rather than /kp/.

(3) Kwa correspondences I (Mensah, 1983)

Abron	Agni (Anyi)	Baoulé	Nzema	
pám	kpá	kpá	kpá	coudre 'stitch'
àpàràá	kpààlé	kpàlē	--	pangolin
pɔ̀rɔ̀	kpɔ̀lɔ́	kplɔ̀	kpɔ̀lɔ̀	pourrir 'rot'
pùsù	kpùsú	---	kpùsù	secouer 'shake'

Thus far, in my database, 47 languages have /gb/ but lack /kp/, while 68 have /kp/ but lack /gb/. Reasons for this are fully addressed in Cahill (2008). The presence of /gb/ without /kp/ is explained by the historical merger of */kp, gb/ to /gb/. The direction of this change is motivated by the previously mentioned common phonetic characteristics of voiceless labial-velars: the rarity of aspiration in /kp/, often the presence of partial voicing, and sometimes an implosive air mechanism. These are characteristics often associated with voiced stops.

Consequently, the sound change *kp > gb is not rare; dozens of languages exhibit the results of this merger, possessing only /gb/ but no /kp/, even though a full set of other voiceless stops is present. There is a totally different reason for the languages that have only /kp/ but no /gb/, related to the fact that there is *always* another gap in the voiceless stop inventory for these languages. Sometimes all stops are voiceless, and /kp/ is part of this general pattern. In other languages there is most often a lack of /g/. A possibility to be explored in more depth than is possible here relates to the fact that /gb/ historically often has its origin in *gu, that is *gu > gw > /gb/ (along with *ku> kw > /kp/). If *g is lacking, /gb/ will not develop.

Supyire, a Senufo language, shows the end result of both of these developments. Supyire has no labial-velar stops, unlike most other Senufo languages (Carlson, 1994: 8–9). The labial-velar stops in northern Senufo languages first merged voiceless /kp/ and voiced /gb/ into /gb/, then Supyire merged /gb/ with /b/. Sucite and Shenara are examples of the first merger, having no /kp/ but a /gb/, which is quite common, despite the relative uncommonness of other voiced stops relative to voiceless ones (Garber, 1987). Correspondingly, Supyire /b/ has a disproportionately high frequency, the results of combining the frequencies of words with *b, *gb, and *kp.

Table 7.3 Historical development of kp > gb, then gb > b

Cebaara	Shenara, Sucite	Supyire	gloss
kpaʔa	gbaʔa, gbaxa	baga	'house'
gbaʔalagà	gbaʔalaga, ---	bàhàgà	'bedbug'

Note: data from Carlson (1994).

Phonology

Africanists are accustomed to thinking of labial-velars as a single consonantal unit, and it is easy to forget that this may not be a natural assumption for linguists with a non-African background. One of the clearest arguments for the unity of labial-velars rather than an identity as clusters comes from syllable patterns. The most common reason cited in introductory phonologies is that normal syllables of the language in question are CV. No consonant clusters occur word-initially in many of the African languages cited in this chapter, yet KP does occur word-initially.

Another phenomenon showing the unitary nature of KP is that labial-velar consonants reduplicate as undivided units, and are not split in the process. For example, in Ewe, which does have clusters, but only of CL, a reduplicant copies the first consonant of a root. A simple CL sequence is split, but a KP is not, showing KP is a single unit.

(4) Ewe reduplication (Ansre, 1963)

fo	'to beat'	fo-fo	'beating'
bia	'to ask'	ba-biam	'asking'
fle	'to buy'	fe-flee	'bought'
kplo	'to lead'	kpo-kplo	'leading'
gbla	'to exert oneself'	gba-gblam	'exerting oneself'

Left-sided phonology

The onset of KP is velar and the release is labial, so there is an inherent phonetic asymmetry in the consonant, similar to but not involving quite the same issues as affricates. This raises the question as to whether phonological processes of KP are sensitive to edge effects. A few of them are, and these will be examined before turning to more general phonological effects (cf. also Connell, 1998/1999 for further discussion).

The phonological process relating to the left side of a labial-velar is nasal place assimilation, in which a preceding nasal assimilates to the place of the KP. Since there are multiple articulations of KP, one might expect a result of either [ŋmkp], or, if partial assimilation, then [ŋkp] or [mkp]. All of these have been mentioned in the literature.

Relying on published accounts of nasals before KP is a bit delicate, however, for two reasons. One is that, in some sources, there has been an orthographic convention established that does not match phonetic reality. For example, Yoruba uses orthographic <p> to represent /kp/ (Folarin, 1987, inter alia) and orthographic <m> for [ŋm]. Welmers (1973) also notes that *orthographically* for African languages, he prefers to write <ŋ> rather than <m> to represent the labial-velar nasal [ŋm].

The second reason is that, especially for the non-native speaker, the different nasals possible before a labial-velar stop are not always easy to distinguish by ear alone.

Efik illustrates both of these difficulties. Ward (1933: 10) writes that:

> The question as to which nasal consonant is used with **kp** is interesting, since in this plosive, labial and velar articulations occur together. There are some words in which **m** has been written and others in which **ŋ** occurs.

> **mkpa** death;   **ŋkpɔ** thing

It is probable that both articulations are made at the same time, i.e. a labio-velar nasal consonant is used which corresponds to the labio-velar plosive **kp**. . . . I have tested all the words in the Dictionary [Goldie's], beginning with **mkp** and **ŋkp**, and some seem more naturally pronounced with **m** and others with **ŋ**. It is, however, extremely difficult to *hear* which is being said without *seeing* the presence or absence of lip-articulation.

Two points deserve comment here. First is that even though Ward admits the probability of a labial-velar nasal consonant, i.e., **ŋm**, neither she nor Goldie (1862) *ever* write it as such. Welmers (1968: xii) observes that a nasal before /kp/ in Efik is pronounced "with simultaneous closure at the lips and with the back of the tongue," i.e., [ŋm], but Welmers (1973: 47) comments that "For some unknown reason, in the usual orthography of Efik, *mkp* is written in some cases but *ŋkp* in others."

Sagey (1990) cites several languages in which a nasal assimilates to a following labial-velar consonant as [ŋm]. There are also many languages in which a nasal before a labial-velar is reported as [ŋ], as Ryder (1987) pointed out. Both of these are quite common.

The question arises whether there are any true cases of assimilation as [mkp]. There are occasional reports of such in the literature, but there are good reasons to be skeptical as to whether these reflect phonetic reality. A good possibility is that these are all cases of [ŋmkp]. First, from a visual and possibly a perceptual point of view, the labial component of [ŋm] is more salient than the velar component. Noteworthy is Welmers' 1973 comment about preferring to write [ŋm] as orthographic <ŋ> to remind people of the less prominent velar component's presence, for example. Second, almost all of the literature that reports assimilation as [m] does so in a way that indicates the writer has never considered the possibility of [ŋm]. A labial closure is observed, and it is assumed that that is all there is to it. However, there is at least one case where a definitely phonetic [mkp, mgb] exists, in ChiDigo (Steve Nicolle, pc), but here the [m] is the manifestation of the noun class prefix /mu-/ before KP, not the result of assimilation. In other ChiDigo words containing a nasal preceding a KP, the result is [ŋkp] or [ŋgb], e.g., [ŋgbe] 'ground cleared for cultivation'.

Right-sided phonology

A nasal directly following a KP is much less frequent than one preceding it, but several languages exhibit this pattern, either as a syllabic nasal or a nasal release of the KP. Interestingly, these all turn out to be either [kpŋm] or [kpm], with [kpŋ] strikingly absent.

The Gwari nasal /n/ assimilates to a preceding stop in the syllable structure CNV, but only assimilates to a labial, staying coronal after velar stops (Rosendall, 1992). Note the last example in (5)b shows the different assimilation patterns on either side of [gb].

(5)	a.	tnútnúnù	'rubbish'	b.	ɓmà	'break'
		dnásò	'river'		gbmínà	'feather'
		kná	'send'		kpmàmí	'okra'
		ágnáná	'jump'		wʲédʒíŋgbmà	'dark'

Stops in the Tyebaara dialect of Senufo have a phonemic contrast between plain stops and those with a secondary release. The secondary release is generally labialization or palatalization, but the secondary release of KP is nasal before nasal vowels (Mills, 1984):

(6)	kpmɔ̃:	'to beat'	nì-gbmɔ̃:	'herb doctor'

Mada has an unusual syllable type: a stop followed by syllabic nasal (Price, 1989):

(7)   [kpa.kŋ.ki]   'tree stump'
    [kpŋm̀]   'kapok tree'
    [gbŋm̄]   'canoe'

There is some uncertainty as to whether the nasal release after KP is phonetically [ŋm] or [m], but it is definitely not [ŋ] (Price, pc).

From these examples we see the reverse of the pattern of nasal place assimilation that occurs preceding the KP. If preceding, we have either [ŋKP] or [ŋmKP]; if following, we have either [KPŋm] or [KPm]. In either, there is either a full assimilation of the nasal to both places of the KP, or a partial nasal place assimilation that is sensitive to the phonetic edge of the KP to which it is adjacent. When both are considered, the natural conclusion is that partial nasal place assimilation is not relevant to the issue of phonological primacy of one place vs. another (as was asserted in Cahill, 1998, which I now believe mistaken), but is more related to phonetics. Connell (1998/1999) expands in more detail on this basic phonetic notion by invoking the Articulatory Phonology model.

Other phonological patterns

Allophones of KP are not common (KP is often rather inert in a language), but Nzema offers an interesting case, with [tp, db] as allophones of /kp, gb/ before front vowels (Westermann & Bryan, 1952: 90). Similarly, Dagbani has [tp, db] as allophones of /kp, gb/ before front vowels (Wilson & Bendor-Samuel, 1969; Ladefoged, 1968: 11; Cahill, 2007). Westermann and Bryan (1952: 109) also note that Egon (=Eggon) has [tp] before front vowels. These assimilations of KP to the [coronal] place of the following vowel are striking in that they choose the dorsal place to change to coronal, while the labial place remains unchanged. It is also striking that the vowel affects, not the labial place that is phonetically adjacent to the vowel, but the velar place that is released slightly earlier.

(8)   Dagbani (Olawski, 1996)

    [k͡pani]   'spear'   [t͡pi] 'to die'
    [g͡balli]   'grave'   [d͡bi] 'to dig'[6]

In Efik, [kp] appears in syllable-initial position, but [p] does not, and [p] appears in syllable-final position, but [kp] does not. In syllable-final position, the velar component of /kp/ is lost, while the labial component is retained. It appears, then, that [p] and [kp] may be treated as allophones of phonemic /kp/ (Welmers, 1973: 48; Anderson, 1976), though this analysis is not without controversy, since Cook (1969) assigns word-final [p] as an allophone of /b/.

In what appears to be an OCP-type effect, Ngbaka does not permit more than one consonant having the same place of articulation within a simple word (compounds are exempt from this restriction), unless the consonants are completely identical. That is, Ngbaka does not have words like tVdV, pVbV, or gVkV, though it has tVtV, bVbV, or kVkV. In this co-occurrence restriction pattern, the labial-velars group with the labial consonants, so no KP occurs in the same word with another labial (Thomas, 1963; also see Clements, 2000: 129, who says two KPs as in *kpakpo* 'hook' are permissible, but mixing P and KP as in *pakpo* is not).

Likewise, Kukú, a Nilo-Saharan language spoken in Sudan, has a similar restriction. Roots with two alveolar or velar consonants are permissible, but not roots with two labial consonants. Labial-velars pattern with the bilabials; there are no roots with a labial-velar and bilabial consonant (Cohen, 2000).

Kaanse (Showalter, 1997) also has no labial consonants in the same morpheme as other labials, including KP. It is important to note that in all of these languages there is no directionality to the restrictions, that is both *kpVp* and *pVkp* are equally disallowed.

Co-occurrence restrictions with vowels are also present in a number of languages, though far from all. If there are vowels that are disallowed after a KP, it will be either /u/ or /ʊ/ plus other back round vowels. Buli (Kröger, 1992) has almost no cases of KP followed by either /o/ or /u/, though this pattern is not observed at all with either plain labials or plain velars. In Mayogo (McCord, 1989), labial-velars (kp, gb, ŋgb) do not occur before /u/, though they do before all other vowels, and the other labial and velars stops may occur before all vowels. Gwari (Rosendall, 1992) never has /u/ after KP, and only rarely /o/. Igo (Gblem, 1995) has all vowels except /u/ after /kp, gb/. Chidigo (Kelly, 1988) is unusual in having two sources of labial-velars, lexical and derived, and it is only in the lexical ones that there are no round vowels following.

Examples could be easily multiplied. A possible and plausible explanation for this fairly common phenomenon is its connection with the historical origin of labial-velars. Recall that a common historical path of development was *Kua > Kwa > KPa. A KP followed by /u/ would trace back to *Kuu, and this form would not participate in the sound change that produced KP.

On a different note, Silverstein (1973) writes regarding Central Yoruba that "[ɔ̃] occurs only after the labials [b, **gb**, **kp**, m, w]" (my emphasis). Fresco (1970: 124) agrees, citing several other researchers who have found the same thing, and also Fresco (1970: 114–115) notes the Ìfàkì dialect of Yoruba, where [ã] and [ɔ̃] are also in complementary distribution, with [ɔ̃] only after the labial consonants, including labial-velars, and [ã] elsewhere. A similar but not identical pattern is found in the Kétu dialect as well.

Casali (1995) reports that labial-velar stops pattern with other labial consonants in blocking a process of rounding harmony in Nawuri, a Guang language of Ghana. For example, there is a singular noun class prefix /gI-/, in which the vowel becomes rounded if the stem vowel is round. However, if the initial stem consonant is labial, the process is blocked. Interestingly for the purposes of this study, the harmony-blocking consonants include labial-velars:

(9)   a. before [-round] stem vowel:
        [g*i*-ɲi]   'tooth'   [g*i*-ke:li]   'kapok tree'
    b. before [+round] stem vowel:
        [gu-jo]   'yam'   [gu-ku:]   'digging'
    c. before [+round] stem vowel *and* labial stem consonant:
        [g*i*-pula]   'burial'   [g*i*-kpo:]   (type of dance)

Thus in this process in Nawuri, the labial-velars pattern with other labials.

Labial-velars as labials

In this section we make the case that, cross-linguistically, labial-velars have labial as a phonologically primary place of articulation, rather than either dorsal or having the two co-equal places of dorsal + labial.

Sounds with multiple articulations often have one articulation that is obviously more prominent – "primary" – than the other. With a voiceless labialized velar stop [kʷ], for example, the labialization is generally regarded as a secondary modification of the velar stop. However, when both articulations have full closures, as in [kp], then the issue of primacy is not so obvious. Should these doubly-stopped labial-velars be regarded as having one primary place of articulation (either labial or velar), or two coequal places of articulation? Part of past answers to this question depended on the theoretical presuppositions of the writer.

As Anderson (1976) points out, the feature system of Chomsky and Halle (1968) required that a segment was necessarily either [+anterior] or [−anterior]. In this system a labial-velar was either a labial with a secondary velar articulation, or a velar with a secondary labial articulation, and this could be language-specific. Thus Anderson and other researchers looked for evidence in specific languages that would indicate which articulation was primary in that language.

In this era, there were two considerations that pointed to KP as velar. One was partial nasal place assimilation (NKP→ŋKP), which, as we have seen, can be explained on articulatory phonetic terms (the nasal assimilates to the leftmost place of articulation of KP).

Besides this, the other consideration noted by Anderson in favor of velar involved a "filling the gaps" argument. This noted that sounds of languages tend to pattern symmetrically, and so an apparent hole in a phoneme chart in essence should be filled if possible. Applying this to labial-velars, if a language has no /g/ in its inventory, but has /gb/, then that /gb/ fills the gap as a velar, and is considered a velar for phonological purposes in that language. If another language has /kw/ and /kp/, but no /p/, then /kp/ fills the gap as a labial. We have seen in the third section that there are historical reasons for a language having only /gb/ or only /kp/, with more extensive evidence than was available to Anderson. Thus the "filling the gaps" argument loses its force.

Ohala (1979, and Ohala and Lorentz, 1977) also rejected the "filling the gaps" argument, and, based on phonological processes, considered KP to be *both* labial and velar, with both places being equally prominent. However, the only process that pointed toward velar as primary was nasal place assimilation, which we have seen can be explained on phonetic grounds.

In contrast to the scant and inadequate evidence pointing to velar as primary place of KP, there are abundant and varied processes that indicate that labial is the primary phonological place of labial-velars, as discussed in the fourth section on pages 159–161. These include preservation of the labial place in the processes /kp/→[tp] before front vowels and /kp/→[p] word-finally, consonant co-occurrence restrictions, and labial-velars grouping with labials to block vocalic rounding harmony. It is to be noted that most of these do not depend on right-edge effects.

One should note that not every language has processes that would be determinative of primary place of KP. This raises the question of whether all languages have the same phonological representation for KP, or whether there could be language-specific variation. A more constrained theory would indicate the same structure for all languages. That is what I tentatively favor, but a final conclusion will depend on more data from a variety of languages.

Representational models

If [labial] is primary, how is that to be represented in a theory of phonology? Chomsky and Halle (1968) used the feature [anterior] to distinguish [labial] as primary vs. [dorsal] as primary. In this linear phonology model, there was no option for co-equal places. With the advent of autosegmental phonology, and its extension into Feature Geometry (Clements, 1985), the possibilities expanded. Ryder (1987), in the context of Feature Geometry, used a pointer (arrow)

Labial-velars of Africa

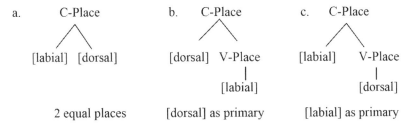

Figure 7.5 Possible labial-velar geometries: extrapolated from Clements and Hume (1995)

to indicate primacy of place. A more fully developed Feature Geometry in Clements and Hume (1995) produced several structural possibilities for labial-velars, depending on whether [labial] and [dorsal] were co-prominent, or one was more primary than the other. These possibilities are seen in Figure 7.5. Note that putting [labial] or [dorsal] under V-Place does not say anything about the stricture of the closure; thus (b) could be the representation of either *kp* or *k^w*.

If [labial] is primary, as suggested by the processes and patterns in the last section, then the geometry in Figure 7.5(c) should be able to account for these patterns, and so it does. In general, it accounts for KP grouping with plain labials as a natural class, since both have [labial] under the C-Place node. It accounts for the neutralizations of KP→P historically and synchronically, via a rule deleting any secondary (V-Place) features in that position. It can also account for the Nzema and Dagbani process KP→TP before front vowels by spreading the [coronal] feature of the front vowel and delinking the [dorsal] feature of V-Place. This is illustrated in Figure 7.6, using /kpi/ for concreteness.

With the widespread adoption of Optimality Theory, Feature Geometry studies declined precipitously; the "hot" questions among phonologists had moved to other areas. Feature Geometry, being a model of representation rather than process, could theoretically be incorporated into Optimality Theory, but there was not much interest in that line of research. A proposal was made to capture the benefits of Feature Geometry within Optimality Theory using Feature Class Theory (FCT, Padgett, 1995, later published as Padgett, 2003), in which classes of features could be referred to by violable constraints. Cahill and Parkinson (1997) asserted that FCT was merely a notational variant of Feature Geometry, and any beneficial results were due not to FCT as such, but to Optimality Theory in which it was embedded. Padgett (1995, 2003) also treated [labial] and [dorsal] as equally prominent in his representation of labial-velars in Feature Geometry and so missed some crucial evidence. No one has tried this to my knowledge, but I assume that the primacy of place could be handled in Optimality Theory by appropriate ranking of constraints.

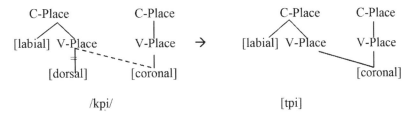

Figure 7.6 Production of [tpi] from /kpi/ by spreading of [coronal] feature

Concluding remarks

The phonetics, historical development, and phonological patterns of labial-velars form an intricate interweaving of dependencies. The labial release of KP especially has far-reaching consequences, with its accompanying perceptual labial prominence. Historically, this is responsible for the very common sound change *KP > P. A labial prominence leads to the labial rather than the dorsal place being phonologically primary, and this means that labial-velars and labials belong to the same natural class in many languages. A multiplicity of phonological patterns are connected with labial-velars having this basic labial identity: consonant co-occurrence restrictions, blocking of [round] spread across labials and labial-velars in Nawuri, Yoruba allowing [ɔ] only after labial and labial-velar consonants, allophonic variation of KP to TP where the labial is retained, and neutralization of labial-velars with labials.

Present-day phonemic inventories and phonotactics have also been influenced by phonetic factors, which have in turn influenced historical developments. The common phonetic implosive characteristics of KP, along with lack of aspiration and often partial voicing, has influenced the historical development of labial-velars, with the merger of *kp and *gb to /gb/. The lack of /u/ after labial-velars in multiple languages can be traced to the historical path of *KuV > *KwV > KPV.

Contrary to some previous investigators, we assert that patterns of nasal place assimilation, especially the common partial nasal place assimilation that yields [ŋkp] and [kpm], are due to the phonetic edge effects of the velar onset and labial release of KP, and not to any primary phonological identity of labial or velar place.

Undoubtedly other sounds of the world's languages also have connections between the phonetics, historical development, and synchronic phonology of those sounds. As usual, more research is called for, but I expect such to strengthen and expand these connections.

Notes

1 Rather unusually, Ega is reported as having a contrast between implosive and non-implosive /gb/, symbolized as /g͡b/ and /ɠ͡ɓ/ (Connell et al., 2002).
2 I have experienced this myself in initial language learning of Ewondo in Cameroon and Kɔnni in Ghana, mis-hearing [kpɔ́m] as [pɔ́m] and [gbɛlɪgɪ] as [bɛlɪgɪ], respectively.
3 Ikalanga (Mathangwane 1999) is specifically asserted to have [p͡kʰ], but sparse data and methodology as well as ambiguous spectrograms make this claim less than well-established. Also, Chomsky and Halle (1968: 322–4), in discussing sounds with multiple closures, incorrectly predict that labial-velars should have either simultaneous release of both closures, or a velar release following the labial release.
4 The only case I am personally aware of with aspirated KP is in Giryama and Duruma (Kutch Lojenga, pc), which have a phonetically aspirated kp. In Giryama, at least, the aspiration is the reflex of a historical nasal, but appears as aspiration on all voiceless stops as a distinctive morpheme.
5 East Sawabantu = Mongo, Pondo, Duala, Mulimba, Batanga, Banɔh, Bapuku. West Sawabantu = Bubia, Kolɛ.
6 Personal recordings of Dagbani words like t͡píní 'guinea fowl' and g͡bíhí 'to sleep' reveal a phonetic detail not previously noted: significant frication in the release of the stop. A more accurate transcription would thus be [t͡pʃíní], [d͡bʒíhí], or more narrowly, [c͡pʃíní], [ɟ͡bʒíhí].

References

Anderson, S.R. (1976). On the Description of Multiply-Articulated Consonants. *Journal of Phonetics*, 4, 17–27.

Andreas, H., Leger, R. & Zoch, U. (2009). The Nyam Language: First Steps Toward a Grammatical Description. In Rothmaler, E. (ed.), *Topics in Chadic Linguistics V* (pp. 23–36). Cologne: Rüdiger Köppe.

Ansre, G. (1963). Reduplication in Ewe. *Journal of African Languages*, 2, 128–132.
Bearth, T. & Zemp, H. (1967). The Phonology of Dan (Santa). *Journal of African Languages*, 6, 9–29.
Bendor-Samuel, J. (ed.). (1989). *The Niger-Congo Languages*. Lanham, MD: University Press of America/SIL.
Boadi, L.A. (2009). A Comparative Phonological Study of Some Verbal Affixes in Seven Volta Comoe Languages of Ghana. Accra, Ghana: Black Mask Ltd.
Bostoen, K. & Donzo, J-P. (2013). Bantu-Ubangi language contact and the origin of labial-velar stops in Lingombe (Bantu, C41, DRC). *Diachronica*, 30(4), 435–468.
Cahill, M. (1998). Nasal Assimilation and Labial-Velar Geometry. In Maddieson, I. & Hinnebusch, T.J. (eds), *Language History and Linguistic Description in Africa. Trends in African Linguistics 2* (pp. 127–136). Trenton, NJ: Africa World Press, Inc.
Cahill, M. (1999). Aspects of the Phonology of Labial-Velar Stops. *Studies in African Languages*, 28(2), 155–184.
Cahill, M. (2007). The Phonetics and Phonology of Dagbani Labial-Velars. Paper presented at Linguistic Society of America Annual meeting, Anaheim, CA, Jan. 4–7, 2007.
Cahill, M. (2008). Why Labial-Velar Stops Merge to g͡b. *Phonology*, 25(3), 379–398.
Cahill, M. (2017). Labial-Velars: A Questionable Diagnostic for a Linguistic Area. In Kaji, Shigeki (ed.) *Proceedings of the 8th World Congress of African Linguistics Kyoto 2015*. Tokyo: ILCAA, Tokyo University of Foreign Studies.
Cahill, M. & Hajek, J. (2001). Why [k͡p]? Paper presented at Linguistic Society of America Annual Meeting, Washington, DC, Jan. 4–7, 2001.
Cahill, M. & Parkinson, F. (1997). Partial Class Behavior and Feature Geometry: Remarks on Feature Class Theory. *Proceedings of NELS 27*, 79–91. Amherst, MA: GLSA (Graduate Linguistic Student Association), Dept. of Linguistics, South College, University of Massachusetts.
Carlson, R. (1994). *A Grammar of Supyire*. New York, NY: Mouton de Gruyter.
Casali, R.F. (1995). Labial Opacity and Roundness Harmony in Nawuri. *Natural Language and Linguistic Theory*, 13, 649–663.
Chomsky, N. & Halle, M. (1968). *The Sound Pattern of English*. New York, NY: Harper & Row.
Clements, G.N. (1985). The Geometry of Phonological Features. *Phonology Yearbook*, 2, 225–252.
Clements, G.N. (2000). Phonology. In Heine, B. and Nurse, D. (eds), *African Languages: An Introduction* (pp. 123–160). Cambridge: Cambridge University Press.
Clements, G.N. & Hume, E.V. (1995). The Internal Organization of Speech Sounds. In Goldsmith, J. (ed.), *A Handbook of Phonological Theory* (pp. 245–306). Oxford: Blackwell.
Cohen, K. (2000). *Aspects of the Grammar of Kukú. LINCOM Studies in African Linguistics 25*. LINCOM EUROPA: Muenchen.
Connell, B. (1991). Accounting for the Reflexes of Labial-Velar Stops. *Actes du XIIème Congrès International des Sciences Phonétiques Vol. 3*, Aix-en-Provence, 19–24 Aug., 110–113.
Connell, B. (1994). The Structure of Labial-Velar Stops. *Journal of Phonetics*, 22, 441–476.
Connell, B. (1998/99). Feature Geometry and the Formation of Labial-Velars: A Reply to Mutaka and Ebobissé. *Journal of West African Languages*, XXVII(1), 17–32.
Connell, B., Ahoua, F. & Gibbon, D. (2002). Ega. *Journal of the International Phonetics Association*, 32(1), 99–104.
Cook, T. (1969). Efik. In Dunstan, E. (ed.), *Twelve Nigerian Languages* (pp. 35–46). London: Longmans.
Demolin, D. & Teston, B. (1997). Phonetic Characteristics of Double Articulations in some Mangbutu-Efe Languages. *Eurospeech (ISCA)* (pp. 803–806). Rhodes, Greece. International Speech Communication Association.
Demolin, D. & Soquet, A. (1999). Double Articulations in some Mangbutu-Efe Languages. *Journal of the International Phonetic Association*, 29(2), 143–154.
Ehret, C. (2001). A Historical-Comparative Reconstruction of Nilo-Saharan. Cologne: Rüdiger Köppe Verlag.
Elugbe, B.O. (1986). Comparative Edoid: Phonology and Lexicon. Delta Series No. 6. University of Port Harcourt Press.
Folarin, A.Y. (1987). *Lexical Phonology of Yoruba Nouns and Verbs*. PhD dissertation, University of Kansas.
Fresco, E.M. (1970). Topics in Yoruba Dialect Phonology. *Studies in African Linguistics*, Vol. 1, Supplement 1.

Garber, A.E. (1987). A Tonal Analysis of Senufo: Sucite Dialect. PhD Dissertation, University of Illinois at Urbana-Champaign.

Gblem, H. (1995). *Description systematique de l'igo*. These de doctorat. Grenoble: Université Stendhals.

Goldie, H. (1862). *Dictionary of the Efik Language (in two parts)*. Edinburgh: United Presbyterian College Buildings.

Grégoire, C. (2003). The Bantu Languages of the Forest. In Nurse, D. & Philippson, G. (eds), *The Bantu Languages* (pp. 349–370). New York, NY: Routledge.

Herault, G. (1983). L'Adioukrou. In Herault, G. (ed.), *Atlas des Langues Kwa de Côte d'Ivoire, Tome 1* (pp. 129–153). Abidjan: Université d'Abidjan, Institut de Linguistique Appliquee.

Hyman, L.M. (1979). Phonology and Noun Structure. In Hyman, L.M. (ed.), *Aghem Grammatical Structure* (pp. 1–72). Southern California Occasional Papers in Linguistics No. 7. University of Southern California.

Innes, G. (1964). An Outline Grammar of Loko with Texts. *African Language Studies V*, 115–173.

Jordan, D. (1980). *The Phonology of Nafaara. Collected Field Notes Series No. 17*. The Institute of African Studies, University of Ghana, Legon.

Kelly, J. (1969). Urhobo. In Dunstan, E. (ed.), *Twelve Nigerian Languages* (pp. 153–162). London: Longmans.

Kelly, J. (1988). The Velar Labials in ChiDigo. In Bradley, D., Henderson, E.J.A. & Mazaudon, M. (eds), *Prosodic Analysis and Asian Linguistics: To Honour R.K Sprigg. Pacific Linguistics*, C–104: 43–50.

Kleiner, R. (1989). Phonology Notes of Gɪdɪrɛ, the Language of the Adele. Unpublished ms., Tamale, Ghana: Ghana Institute of Linguistics, Literacy, and Bible Translation.

Kröger, F. (1992). *Buli-English Dictionary*. Münster: Lit Verlag.

Kropp Dakubu, M.E. & Ford, K.C. (1988). The Central-Togo Languages. In Kropp Dakubu, M.E. (ed.), *The Languages of Ghana* (pp. 119–154). London: Kegan Paul International.

Ladefoged, P. (1968). *A Phonetic Study of West African Languages*, (2nd Edn). Cambridge: Cambridge University Press.

Ladefoged, P. & Maddieson, I. (1996). *The Sounds of the World's Languages*. Cambridge, MA: Blackwell Publishers.

Lewis, M.P., Simons, G.F. & Fennig, C.D. (eds) (2017). *Ethnologue: Languages of the World, Nineteenth Edition*. Dallas, TX: SIL International. Online version: www.ethnologue.com.

Maddieson, I. (1993). Investigating Ewe Articulations with Electromagnetic Articulography. *Forschungsberichte des Instituts für Phonetik und Sprachliche Kommunikation der Universität München*, 31, 181–214.

Maddieson, I. (1998). Collapsing Vowel Harmony and Doubly-Articulated Fricatives: Two Myths about the Avatime Phonological System. In Maddieson, I. & Hinnebusch, T.J. (eds), *Language History and Linguistic Description in Africa. Trends in African Linguistics 2* (pp. 155–166). Trenton, NJ: Africa World Press.

Mathangwane, J.T. (1999). *Ikalanga Phonetics and Phonology*. Stanford, CA: CSLI Publications.

McCord, M.S. (1989). *Acoustical and Autosegmental Analyis of the Mayogo Vowel System*. M.A. thesis, University of Texas at Arlington.

Mensah, E. (1983). Les Systemes Phonologiques des Langues Kwa de Cote d'Ivoire. In Herault, G. (ed.), *Atlas des Langues Kwa de Côte d'Ivoire, Tome 1* (pp. 315–355). Abidjan: Université d'Abidjan, Institut de Linguistique Appliquee.

Mills, E. (1984). *Senoufo Phonology, Discourse to Syllable*. Dallas, TX: Summer Institute of Linguistics.

Mutaka, N.M. & Ebobissé, C. (1996/97). The Formation of Labial-Velars in Sawabantu: Evidence for Feature Geometry. *Journal of West African Languages*, XXVI(1), 3–14.

Ohala, J. (1979). Universals of Labial Velars and de Saussure's Chess Analogy. *Proceedings of Ninth International Congress of Phonetic Sciences, Vol. II* (pp. 41–47). Copenhagen.

Ohala, J. & Lorentz, J. (1977). The Story of [w]: An Exercise in the Phonetic Explanation for Sound Patterns. *Berkeley Linguistic Society*, 3, 577–599.

Olawsky, K. (1996). An Introduction to Dagbani Phonology. Theorie des Lexikons: Arbeiten des Sonderforschungsbereichs 282, Nr. 76. Düsseldorf: Heinrich Heine Universität.

Padgett, J. (1995). Feature Classes. In *Papers in Optimality Theory, University of Massachusetts Occasional Papers in Phonology 18* (pp. 385–421). Amherst, MA: GLSA, University of Massachusetts.

Padgett, J. (2003). Feature Classes in Phonology. *Language*, 78(1), 81–110.

Painter, C. (1970). *Gonja: A Phonological and Grammatical Study*. Bloomington, IN: Indiana University.

Parker, K. (1985). Baka Phonology. *Occasional Papers in the Study of Sudanese Languages*, 4, 63–85. Juba: Summer Institute of Linguistics, Institute of Regional Languages, and the University of Juba.

Ponelis, F. (1974). On the Dynamics of Velarization and Labialization: Some Bantu Evidence. *Studies in African Linguistics*, 5, 27–58.

Price, N. (1989). Notes on Mada Phonology. *Language Data, Africa Series, Publication 23*. Dallas, TX: Summer Institute of Linguistics.

Rosendall, H.J. (1992). *A Phonological Study of the Gwari Lects*. Dallas, TX: Summer Institute of Linguistics.

Ryder, M.E. (1987). An Autosegmental Treatment of Nasal Assimilation to Labial-velars. *Chicago Linguistic Society*, 23(2), 253–265. (*Parasession on Autosegmental and Metrical Phonology*.)

Sagey, E. (1990). *The Representation of Features in Non-Linear Phonology*. New York, NY: Garland Press (revision of 1986 PhD dissertation, MIT).

Schuh, R.G. (1995). Aspects of Avatime Phonology. *Studies in African Linguistics*, 24(1), 31–68.

Showalter, S. (1997). Coup de glotte, nasalité, et schèmes syllabiques en kaansa. Ms, SIL, Burkina-Faso.

Shryock, A., Ladefoged, P. & Williamson, K. (1996/1997). The Phonetic Structures of Defaka. *Journal of West African Languages*, XXVI(2), 3–28.

Silverstein, R.O. (1973). *Igala Historical Phonology*. PhD Dissertation, UCLA.

Smith, N.V. (1967). The Phonology of Nupe. *Journal of African Languages*, 6(2), 153–169.

Spratt, D. & Spratt, N. (1968). *The Phonology of Kusal*. Collected Field Notes Series No. 10. Legon: The Institute of African Studies, University of Ghana.

Steele, M. & Weed, G. (1966). *The Phonology of Konkomba*. Collected Field Notes Series No. 3. Legon: The Institute of African Studies, University of Ghana.

Thomas, E. (1978). *A Grammatical Description of the Engenni Language*. Dallas, TX: SIL.

Thomas, J.M.C. (1963). *Le Parler Ngbaka de Bokanga*. Paris: Mouton & Co.

Toupin, M. (1995). *The Phonology of Sisaale-Pasaale*. Collected Field Notes Series No. 22. Legon: The Institute of African Studies, University of Ghana.

Ward, I.C. (1933). *The Phonetic and Tonal Structure of Efik*. Cambridge: W. Heffer & Sons, Ltd.

Welmers, W.E. (1952). Notes on the Structure of Bariba. *Language*, 28, 82–103.

Welmers. W.E. (1968). Jukun of Wukari and Jukun of Takum. *Occasional Publication No. 16*. Ibadan: Institute of African Studies, University of Ibadan.

Welmers, W.E. (1973). *African Language Structures*. Berkeley and Los Angeles, CA: University of California Press.

Westermann, D. & Bryan, M.A. (1952). The Languages of West Africa. *Handbook of African Languages, Part 2*. London: Oxford University Press for the International African Institute.

Wilhoit, L.K. (1999). *A Principles and Parameters Approach to Loma Grammar*. MA Thesis, University of Texas at Arlington.

Wilson, W.A.A. (1961). *An Outline of the Temne Language*. London: School of Oriental and African Studies, University of London.

Wilson, W.A.A. and Bendor-Samuel, J. (1969). The Phonology of the Nominal in Dagbani. *Linguistics*, 52, 56–82.

8

SYLLABLE STRUCTURE AND VOWEL/ZERO ALTERNATIONS IN MOROCCAN ARABIC AND BERBER

Mohamed Lahrouchi

Introduction

The Modern Arabic dialects of the Maghreb have three phonemic vowels /i, a, u/. These dialects are generally said to have lost the short vowels of Classical Arabic (henceforth, CA) and to have developed a short central vowel [ə], used to break up consonant clusters.[1] A rapid comparison between CA and Moroccan Arabic (henceforth, MA) actually reveals that the latter lost length contrast in the vowels. In a number of items shared by these languages, there is a regular change whereby the long vowels of CA correspond to short vowels in MA, whereas short vowels in CA disappear in MA, resulting in consonant clusters often simplified by means of vowel epenthesis. The following examples illustrate the phenomenon:

(1)   *CA*   *MA*

kataba	ktəb	'he wrote'
kita:b	ktab	'book'
qalb	qəlb	'heart'
sa:hama	sahəm	'he contributed'
kari:m	krim	'generous'

The same situation arises in the Berber languages,[2] except in Tashlhiyt, which allows complex consonant clusters without any vowels (see Dell & Elmedlaoui 2002, and Ridouane 2008). The correspondences in (2) are good examples in this respect:

(2)

    a   *CA*   *Tamazight Berber (Taïfi 1991)*

dˤalama	dˤləm	'accuse wrongly'
ʔalba:b	lbab	'the door'
ɣarraba	ɣərrəb	'go west'
ɣirba:l	aɣərbal	'sieve'

Syllable structure and vowel/zero alternations

b	CA	*Tashlhiyt Berber*	
	saːfara	safr	'travel'
	laːhaqa	lahg	'reach, pursue'
	alkitaːb	lktab	'the book'
	ʔibriːq	lbriq	'tea-pot'

The situation depicted in MA reflects the loss of the ability to associate peripheral vowels to non-branching nuclei, according to Lowenstamm (1991: 959). That is to say, CA short vowels do not surface in MA because they have access to only one skeletal position (see also Kaye 1990).[3] They remain silent as long as the resulting consonant cluster does not violate the language's syllabic requirements. The general observation is that MA, like Berber, prohibits any sequence of more than two consonants. For example, the 3rd masculine singular perfective *ktəb* (1a) has only one epenthetic vowel, whereas the corresponding 2nd singular imperfective *təktəb* 'you write' resorts to a double epenthesis. More interestingly, the position of the vowels can vary depending on the nature of the suffix. The epenthetic vowel that appears between the last two consonants in *ktəb* shifts leftward when a vowel-initial suffix is added (e.g., *kətb-u* 'they wrote', *kətb-at* 'she wrote').

Standard syllable-based analyses generally view the facts just introduced as evidence against complex constituents (see Benhallam 1980, 1989/90; Haddad 1984; Hall 2011; among others), while those couched within the framework of Government Phonology (Kaye *et al.* 1990) make use of empty vocalic nuclei in order to derive the surface clusters. This chapter provides a general overview of these analyses and highlights their implications on the syllable structure of MA and Berber. Moreover, it argues following Guerssel (1990, 1992), Kabbaj (1990) and Kaye (1990) that (1) Tamazight Berber and MA have neither complex onsets nor complex codas, and that (2) the vowel-zero alternations observed therein are better analyzed in terms of lateral relations between nuclei rather than hierarchical syllable structure. In Tashlhiyt Berber, where the epenthetic vowel is found, syllabic consonants arise. The distribution of these consonants will be shown to play a central role in determining the shape of the causative prefix in the same way as plain vowels do in Tamazight Berber.

Syllable-based approaches

A large body of literature has been devoted to vowel-zero alternations. They have been studied in many unrelated languages such as French (Dell 1973; Charette 1990), Polish (Gussmann 1980), Dutch (Booij 1995; Oostendorp 1995), Tangale (Nikiema 1989), Arabic (Benhallam 1980, 1989/90; Haddad 1984; Itô 1989; Kaye 1990; Ali *et al.* 2008 and Hall 2013), and Berber (Bader 1985; Kossmann 1995; Coleman 1996, 2001; Bendjaballah 1999, 2001; Idrissi 2000a, 2000b; Lahrouchi 2001, 2003; Lahrouchi & Ségéral 2010 and Ben Si Said 2014). In many cases, the alternating vowels are analyzed as instances of epenthesis, which allows resyllabifying phonotactically illicit consonant clusters. As a matter of fact, epenthesis occurs in different structural contexts, including the coda position (see Booij 1995 on Dutch, and Awbery 1984 on Welsh), the onset (see Itô 1989 on Temiar), and between identical consonants such as English *meld*[ə]*d* and *tax*[ɪ]*s* (see Frankiewicz 2001 and Bauer 2015).

No complex coda

In the MA dialects it is generally argued that vowel epenthesis occurs into CC clusters to avoid undesirable complex codas, as opposed to complex onsets that may occur in the

Western (Maghrebi) dialects. Evidence for this statement is given in MA (Benhallam 1980, 1989/1990; Kaye 1990 and Boudlal 2001, 2006/2007) and Lebanese Arabic (Haddad 1984, and Hall 2013) below.

		Moroccan Arabic	*Lebanese Arabic*	
(3)	a	rkəb	rikib	'ride'
		ktəf	kitif	'shoulders'
		qfəl	ʔifil	'lock'
		fhəmna	fihimna	'he understood us'
	b	kəbʃ	kibiʃ ~ kibʃ	'ram'
		səbt	sabit ~ sabt	'Saturday'
		qərd	ʔirid ~ʔird	'monkey'
		nəfs	nafis ~ nafs	'self'

In (3a), both languages epenthesize a vowel between the last two consonants, which would otherwise form a complex coda.[4] The forms in (3b) behave the other way around: the last two consonants remain unaffected in MA, while in Lebanese Arabic they can be subject to epenthesis, leading to forms of the same word in free variation. Based on these facts, one can either argue that the coda may be complex in both languages or refer to some category-specific epenthesis to explain why the forms in (3b) behave differently (Echchadli 1986). Another alternative consists in analyzing the final consonant as extrasyllabic (Kaye *et al.* 1986), or adjoined to the coda by a post-lexical rule (Kenstowicz 1986). This amounts to saying that the grammar of the modern dialects has no syllable with a complex coda, and that those of the type in (3b) are marginal syllables, restricted to very specific contexts. Indeed, as noticed by Kaye *et al.* (1986: 62), the CC clusters that would otherwise result in illicit complex codas occur only at the end of the word. In word-internal position, they all behave as heterosyllabic.

The same reasoning holds for initial CC clusters (3a). Modern Arabic tolerates such clusters word-initially, which the standard syllable theory would analyze as complex onsets. In the next section we show that these clusters do not behave as branching onsets.

No complex onsets

One crucial piece of evidence against complex onsets in MA relates to sonority. Word-initial clusters are much less restricted in MA than they are in languages with genuine branching onsets. While most Indo-European languages require that #CC clusters always have a rising sonority profile (e.g., English *blue*, *true*; French *plat* 'dish', *bras* 'arms'), MA imposes no sonority restriction on their distribution. Consider the following examples (O = obstruent, S = sonorant).

(4)	a. OS		b. SO		c. OO		
	ʃra	'he bought'	rʃa	'he corrupted'	ktab	'book'	
	sni	'sign'	nsa	'he forgot'	kdub	'lies'	
	mrˤa	'woman'	rˤma	'he throw'	ʃkun	'who's there?'	
	blaˤ	'swallow'	lbən	'milk'	xbarˤ	'news'	
	gləs	'sit down'	lga	'he found'	dkərˤ	'male'	

MA exhibits sequences of rising sonority (4a), but also their mirror images (4b). The forms in (4c) show clusters with obstruents, some of which have a sonority plateau. The range of word-initial sequences allowed in MA goes well beyond the set defined in (4). Any CC combination is possible, regardless of the relative sonority of the consonants. Apart from geminates and certain NC clusters (see Harrell 1962: 34, and Heath 2002: 356), all other CC clusters can be split by an epenthetic vowel when the phonotactic conditions are met. For instance, the initial cluster in *gləs* 'he sat down' (from CA *ʒalasa*) hosts an epenthetic vowel in the corresponding plural *gəlsu* 'they sat down'. Further evidence for the absence of complex onsets in MA is provided in Shaw *et al.* (2009). The results of their study show a heterosyllabic parsing of initial clusters in words such as *ktab* 'book' and *sbati* 'belt'.

The Berber languages do not diverge from this trend, as no sonority restriction is imposed on their consonant clusters. Word-initial CC may consist of a sequence of stops or obstruent-sonorant, each with their mirror-image. Examples are given in Tashlhiyt Berber.

(5) a. OS   b. SO   c. OO
     kru 'rent'   rku 'be dirty'   kti 'remember'
     bri 'scratch'   rbu 'carry on the back' bsi 'melt'
     gnu 'sew'   ngi 'overflow'   sti 'pick out'
     dlu 'cover'   ldi 'pull'   zdˤarn 'they are able'

In a recent study, Ridouane *et al.* (2014) showed that prevocalic clusters of the type in (5) behave as heterosyllabic, regardless of their sonority profile and their position within the word.

As to word-final position, CC clusters are generally simplified by means of epenthesis in all Berber varieties where no consonant syllabicity is found (e.g., Tamazight Berber *fθəl* 'roll', *dˤləm* 'accuse wrongly'), except for geminates and homorganic clusters, to which we will turn later in the second section. Needless to say that any internal CC that occurs in intervocalic position is syllabified as a coda+onset sequence, according to standard analyses. The reader is referred to Bensoukas and Boudlal (2012a, b) for a comparative study on the phonology of schwa in Tamazight and MA.

The state of affairs in Arabic and Berber, only partially documented here, leads to the view that such languages, which do not impose sequential constraints on clustering and seem to resort to an extensive use of epenthetic vowels, can be analyzed as having only open syllables at the phonological level. This proposal, first made by Guerssel (1990) on Tamazight Berber and Kaye (1990) on MA, has been extended to other Berber varieties (see Bendjaballah 1999, 2005 and Ben Si Said 2014 on Kabyle, and Lahrouchi 2001, 2003 on Tashlhiyt), and to many other languages (see Barillot 2002 and Lampitelli 2011 on Somali, Rucart 2006 on Afar, and Faust 2011 on Hebrew).

The next section will show how the vowel-zero alternations and the surface clusters provide much support for the idea that empty nuclei play a central role in the syllable structure of MA and Berber. The strict CV model (also termed CVCV) will be used as a unifying approach to these phenomena, making the role of standard syllabic constituents unnecessarily redundant.

Strict CV approach to syllable structure and vowel-zero alternations

CVCV model

The CVCV approach to syllable structure (Lowenstamm 1996), which falls within the general framework of Government Phonology (Kaye *et al.* 1990), holds that syllable structure universally boils down to strict alternations of non-branching onsets (i.e., C positions) and non-branching nuclei (i.e., V positions), which interact laterally to derive various syllable types. The familiar closed syllables, complex onsets and nuclei, long vowels and geminates are represented as follows.

(6)

a. closed syllable	b. complex onset	c. long vowel	d. geminate

b   a   r   b   r   a   b   a   b   a

C V C V   C V C V   C V C V   C V C V

[bar]   [bra]   [baː]   [bːa]

As can be seen from these representations, there are no rhymes, no codas and no branching constituents. The differences in the surface syllabic structures lie in the way segments are associated to C and V positions:

a   The postvocalic consonant of the surface closed syllable in (6a) appears in the onset of the second syllable, whose nucleus is empty.

b   The complex onset in (6b) has an empty nucleus between its consonants.

c   The long vowel in (6c) has an empty C between its members, whereas the geminate in (6d) contains an empty V.

Any skeletal position that has no phonetic realization is said to be licensed to remain empty by virtue of the government relation it shares with the neighboring segment. Proper Government (henceforth, PG) is one such relation, which allows a vocalic position to remain empty when followed by a vowel. This proves particularly interesting in explaining the vowel-zero alternations under close scrutiny in this chapter.

Vowel-zero alternations

Proper Government is an asymmetric, local and unidirectional relation contracted by vocalic positions. (7) provides a definition of this relation as currently understood in the relevant literature (see Kaye 1990 and Scheer 2004).

(7) *Proper Government*

        α properly governs ß if

        α and ß are adjacent at the vocalic level

        α is located to the right of ß

        α is not itself properly governed

        no governing domain intervenes between α and ß.

The vowel-zero alternations at issue in MA and Berber are fully handled by this device, which crucially predicts that empty positions cannot be adjacent at the vocalic projection. Any sequence of two adjacent empty positions must realize one, depending on the government relation contracted with the neighboring vowels. The position that escapes PG is generally the one that surfaces at the phonetic level. Let us illustrate this with the MA pair *ktəb / kətbu*:

(8)

a *ktəb* 'he wrote'

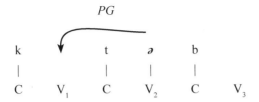

b *kətbu* 'they wrote'

In (8a), V_3 is licensed to remain empty by virtue of being domain-final;[5] therefore it is unable to properly govern the preceding nucleus. This results in the phonetic realization of V_2, which then governs V_1. On the other hand, the inflectional vowel *–u* in (8b) properly governs the preceding V position, which in turn remains inaudible. Then V_1, no more governed, surfaces as [ə]. Almost all cases of vowel/zero alternations in MA comply with this analysis, except for nouns like *qəlb* 'heart' and *ħəbs* 'jail', which exhibit an epenthetic vowel between the first two consonants. Interestingly, these nouns contrast with the verbs *qləb* 'revert' and *ħbəs* 'put in jail'. Following Echchadli (1986), we assume that some category-specific epenthesis is responsible for the distribution of schwa in nouns like *qəlb*. For further details and analysis of the distribution of epenthetic vowels in MA, the reader is referred to Kaye (1990).

The same situation obtains in the Berber varieties that resort to vowel epenthesis. (9) gives the representation of two forms of the verb *xðm* 'to work', which involve three empty nuclei, each of which can surface if it escapes PG.

(9) Tamazight Berber

a *xðəm* 'work!'

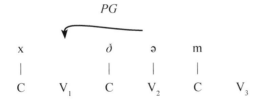

b *xəðməx* 'I worked'

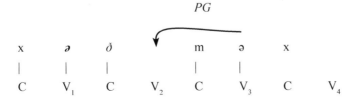

The computation of empty nuclei proceeds in much the same way as it does in MA. Domain-final ones are licensed to remain empty, therefore allowing the preceding nuclei to be realized. In (9a), V_2 surfaces as schwa and then governs V_1, leading to the form *xðəm*, which exhibits an initial CC cluster at the phonetic level.[6] Interestingly, this cluster gets its empty nucleus interpreted in (9b), while V_2 properly governed by V_3 remains silent. In fact, the difference between the two forms in (9) lies in the suffixation of the 1st person marker, which disrupts the distribution of empty vocalic positions. The unidirectional application of PG predicts that any penultimate empty nucleus must surface, except when it is followed by another vowel or when it is a member of a geminate or homorganic cluster. In Tamazight, for instance, neither the final geminate in *ggall* 'swear' nor the final cluster in *θaqbilt* 'tribe' undergoes vowel epenthesis. Their vocalic position remains silent for it is located within a branching structure that prevents it from surfacing. The representations in (10) show how homorganic clusters and geminates, whose integrity is well-documented in the literature (Schein & Steriade 1986 and Hayes 1986), display branching structures within the strict CV approach.

(10)
a.

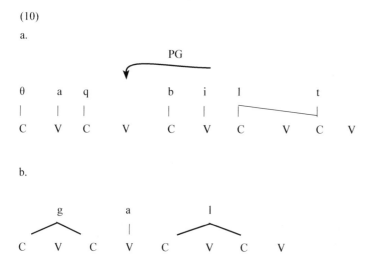

b.

The branching structure of final /lt/ in (10a) not only blocks vowel epenthesis but also prevents the final /t/ from being spirantized, as generally expected for stops in Tamazight (e.g., initial /t/ > [θ] in (10a), /tajdit/ > [θajdiθ] 'she-dog'). According to Ulfsbjorninn and Lahrouchi (2016: 120), this kind of cluster branches by sharing a closure feature (also termed |ʔ| element, cf. Harris 1994 and Backley 2011). The branching structure of the geminates in (10b) allows them to resist epenthesis in a similar fashion.

The facts just discussed clearly show how the strict CV approach captures the distribution of epenthetic vowels and surface clustering under the same operation of Proper Government. There is no need for any specific constraint on syllable margins: the ban of complex coda and onset naturally obtains as the result of the phonological computation of empty vocalic positions. The ones that escape PG are filled with the language-specific default vowel, namely schwa in Berber and MA.

In Tashlhiyt Berber, where no epenthetic schwa is found, syllabic consonants arise. The next section turns to this issue. It is argued that any vocalic position lacking PG systematically hosts one syllabic consonant (see Hammane 2010 on Tashlhiyt; Blaho 2004 and Scheer 2008 on Slavic; Beltzung & Patin 2007 on Coptic).

Syllabic consonants in Tashlhiyt Berber

Words without vowels

One major feature of Tashlhiyt Berber is its extensive use of consonant clusters, which may result in utterances without any vocalic segment (e.g., *tsslkmttnt* 'you made them (fem.) arrive'). Based on this characteristic, Dell and Elmedlaoui (1985, 1988, 2002) argued that in Tashlhiyt any segment, even a voiceless obstruent, can be syllabic (see also Boukous 1987 and Ridouane 2008). The so-called "transitional vocoids," which appear in certain consonant clusters (e.g., *nkər* 'wake up, stand up'; *lkəm* 'arrive'), have no syllabic status according to Dell and Elmedlaoui (2002), while Coleman (1996, 2001) argues that they are epenthetic, filling syllabic nuclei that would otherwise remain empty.

In fact, these schwa-like vowels are found in very specific contexts, that is in the immediate vicinity of sonorants and voiced obstruents. In utterances with voiceless obstruents, no vowels are found (e.g., *kktt* 'go through it (FM)', *ʃʃit* 'eat it (FM)', *tsskʃftstt* 'you fade it (FM)'), contrary to the varieties that resort to scwha epenthesis.

I here adopt the idea that any segment, even a voiceless obstruent, may act as a syllable nucleus. However, I claim that the competition for the nucleus position is not always driven by the relative sonority of segments. Rather, it is the lateral interaction between vocalic positions that determines which consonant can be syllabic.

Syllabic consonants in strict CV

In order to bring out the specificity of Tashlhiyt syllable structure, let us consider the verbs *xðəm* 'work!' and *xəðməx* 'I worked', discussed in Tamazight Berber under (9). In Tashlhiyt, no epenthetic vowel appears in the phonetic form of these verbs. They surface as *xdm̩* and *xd̩mx* (where Ç stands for syllabic consonant).

The strict CV approach along with its government device allows syllabic consonants to attach to vocalic positions. Any position that lacks PG is filled by the consonant immediately to its left. In *xdm̩*, the consonant /m/ fills the V position to its left and then governs the empty V between /x/ and /d/ (11a), whereas in *xd̩mx* it is the consonants /x/ and /d/ that branch into the ungoverned V positions (11b).

(11) *Tashlhiyt Berber*

    a *xdm̩* 'work – imperative 2 sg'

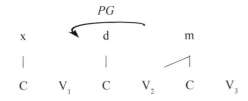

    b *xd̩mx* 'I worked'

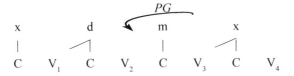

The left-branching representation of syllabic consonants is supported by the distribution of epenthetic vowels in the Berber varieties where only vocalic elements appear in the nucleus position, including the aforementioned Tamazight variety. Indeed, the careful reader will have noticed that the syllabic consonants in Tashlhiyt forms are exactly the ones preceded by an epenthetic schwa in Tamazight. Further evidence is found in languages such as English and German, where many instances of əC are in complementary distribution with syllabic C: In German, for instance, *haːbən* 'to have' and *geːbən* 'to give' alternate with *haːbm̩* and *geːbm̩*, respectively (cf. Clark & Yallop 1995: 68). The reader is referred to Scheer (2004) for similar facts in Czech and Polish.

Further evidence for the proposal put forth in this section is drawn from the length alternation of the causative morpheme. The next section argues that such an alternation derives from the distribution of nuclei, including those hosting syllabic consonants.

Causative formation in Tashlhiyt Berber

In Tashlhiyt, as in many other Berber varieties, the causative verb is built by means of a monoconsonantal prefix attached to a stem. This prefix is realized as single or geminated depending on the properties of the stem. The examples in (12) illustrate the phenomenon.

(12)   *Verb*   *Causative*
 a   mun   'gather'   smun   'pick up'
     brˁbrˁ   'boil'   sbrˁbrˁ   'make boiled'
     gawr   'sit'   sgawr   'make sit'
     bukdˁ   'be blind'   sbukdˁ   'blind'
 b   anf   'move away'   ssanf   'move'
     imlul   'be white'   ssimlul   'whiten'
     knu   'lean'   ssknu   'tilt'
     rˁmi   'be tired'   ssrˁmi   'tire'
     xdm   'work'   ssxdm   'make someone work'
     lkm   'arrive'   sslkm   'make arrive'

The data suggest that verbs beginning with a CV sequence select the simplex variant of the prefix, while those that begin with two consonants take the geminated variant. The verbs that consist entirely of consonants do diverge from this trend. As we will show shortly, the vocalic positions hosting syllabic consonants play the same role as plain vowels.

According to my analysis, the causative prefix is underlyingly simplex (see also Guerssel 1992; Jebbour 1999; Lahrouchi 2001, 2003; Hammane 2010). It geminates by spreading into the following empty onset, which only verbs with an initial vowel or syllabic consonant provide. Otherwise, the prefix remains simplex. The representations in (13) show how the distribution of vowels determines the shape variation of the causative prefix.

(13)

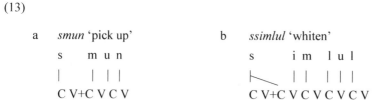

In (13b), /s/ geminates by spreading into the following empty onset. In contrast, in (13a), the prefix remains simplex since the base verb begins with a consonant. The same situation obtains in the verbs that have syllabic consonants: the prefix geminates when it is followed by an onsetless syllable, whose nucleus hosts a syllabic consonant; otherwise it remains simplex. The examples represented in (14) illustrate both situations.

(14)

    a. *Ssx̱dm̩* 'employ'   b. *Sbṛbṛ* 'boil'

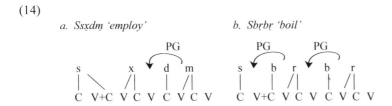

As explained on page 175, PG regulates the distribution of syllabic consonants: any ungoverned V position can host a syllabic consonant, which then governs the preceding V position, just as plain vowels do in the Berber varieties that have no syllabic consonants. As a matter of comparison, the form in (14a) surfaces in Tamazight Berber as *ssəxðəm*, with a geminated causative prefix like in Tashlhiyt, plus schwa epenthesis in the stem-initial position and between the last two consonants. The stem-initial syllable, whose onset is empty, allows the causative prefix to geminate (see 15a). Conversely, a verb *bərgən* takes the simplex variant of the prefix (15b).

(15)

    a. *Ssəxðəm* 'employ'   b. *Sbərgən* 'put on face (scarf)'

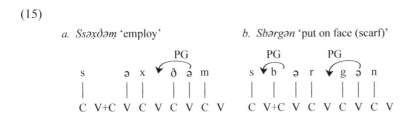

A rapid comparison between these representations and the ones in (14) clearly shows that the shape of the stem-initial syllable, be it headed by a schwa or a syllabic consonant, determines the length variation of the causative prefix. This prefix geminates whenever it is followed by an empty onset position.

The strict CV approach captures clearly the parallel between the distribution of epenthetic vowels and syllabic consonants. Both strategies (epenthesis and consonant syllabicity) lead to the same result: MA and Berber can be analyzed as having only open syllables at the phonological level.

Conclusion

Based on previous work, I have argued that the vowel/zero alternations found in Tamazight Berber and Moroccan Arabic can be explained in terms of lateral relations between empty nuclei, rather than hierarchical structure. Within the strict CV approach, I have shown that consonant clusters result from the computation of empty nuclei, some of which remain silent when they are properly governed by the following vowel. There is no need for any specific constraint on complex constituents, be they codas or onsets.

In Tashlhiyt Berber, where no epenthetic schwa is found, syllabic consonants arise. The distribution of these consonants proceeds in much the same way as the epenthetic vowels in Tamazight Berber and Moroccan Arabic: any empty position that escapes proper government systematically hosts a syllabic consonant. One piece of evidence in favor of this analysis is drawn from the causative formation. I have shown that the distribution of syllabic consonants determines the shape of the causative prefix in the same way plain vowels do: the prefix geminates into the following empty onset, be it adjacent to a vowel or syllabic consonant.

Notes

1 Unlike other Maghrebi dialects, Southeastern Tunisian and Libyan Arabic use [i] as an epenthetic vowel: For instance, CA *xubz* 'bread' and *katabtu* 'I wrote' are realized in Tunisian as *xubiz* and *ktibit* (see Wise 1983: 175). Similar examples are found in Lybian: CA *tˤifl* 'child' and *faʒr* 'dawn' are realized as *tˤifil* and *faʒir* (see Elramli 2012: 67).
2 Berber refers to an Afroasiatic group of languages spoken in large parts of North Africa, mainly in Morocco and Algeria, and to a lesser extent in Mauritania, Mali, Niger, Libya, Egypt, Tunisia and Burkina Faso. Large Berber-speaking communities are also found in Western Europe and Canada. In Morocco, three main varieties are distinguished: Tamazight and Tashlhiyt, the varieties investigated here, are spoken in the Central and Southern Morocco, respectively; Tarifit is spoken in Northern Morocco. Kabyle is the main variety spoken in Algeria. Tamashek or Touareg is found in Niger, Mali and southern Algeria (see Chaker 1992).
3 The proposal has been extended to the Berber languages by Jebbour 1993, Idrissi 2000a, Bendjaballah 2001, Lahrouchi 2001, 2003, and Lahrouchi and Ségéral 2010, among others.
4 The quality of the epenthetic vowel in Lebanese Arabic differs from that in Moroccan Arabic, as can be seen from the data in (3). Generally speaking, the Leventine dialects use the high front [i], while the dialects of the Maghreb generally use [ə].
5 Within the strict CV model, all phonological domains end with a nucleus, which may or may not be licensed to remain empty. This parametric licensing proves necessary in distinguishing languages like English and MA where words can end in a consonant from languages like Italian where they always end in a vowel.
6 *əxðəm* is another pronounciation of the verb (cf. Saïb 1976; Abdelmasih 1971). Forms of this type may exhibit schwa at the beginning, perhaps in order to avoid the initial cluster.

References

Abdelmasih, E.T. (1971). *A Reference Grammar of Tamazight*. Ann Arbor, MI: University of Michigan.
Ali, N.A., Lahrouchi, M. & Ingleby, M. (2008). Vowel Epenthesis, Acoustics and Phonology Patterns in Moroccan Arabic. In *Proceedings of Interspeech*: 1178–1181. Brisbane, Australia.
Awbery, G. (1984). Phonotactic constraints in Welsh. In *Welsh Phonology*, Martin Ball & Glyn E. Jones (eds), 65–104. Cardiff: University of Wales Press.
Backley, P. (2011). *Element Theory: An Introduction*. Edinburgh: Edinburgh University Press.
Bader, Y. (1985). "Schwa in Berber: A non linear analysis." *Lingua* 67: 225–249.
Barillot, X. (2002). Morphophonologie Gabaritique et Information Consonantique Latente en Somali et dans les langues Est-couchitiques. PhD dissertation, University of Paris 7.
Bauer, L. (2015). "English phonotactics." *English Language and Linguistics* 19/3: 437–475.
Beltzung, J. & Patin, C. (2007). Quand le Schwa n'est là. Schwa et Consonnes Syllabiques en Copte. In *Proceedings of JEL '2007*, Olivier Crouzet & Jean-Pierre Angoujard (eds), 15–20. Nantes: University of Nantes.
Bendjaballah, S. (1999). Trois Figures de la Structure Interne des Gabarits: Activité Morphologique du Niveau Squelettal des Représentations Phonologiques en Berbère, Somali et Bedja. PhD dissertation, Université Paris 7.
Bendjaballah, S. (2001). "The negative preterit in Kabyle Berber." *Folia Linguistica* XXXIV/3–4: 185–220.
Bendjaballah, S. (2005). "Longueur phonologique des voyelles en kabyle." *Etudes et Documents Berbères* 22: 47–69.

Benhallam, A. (1980). Syllable Structure and Rule Types in Arabic. PhD dissertation, University of Florida.

Benhallam, A. (1989/1990). "Moroccan Arabic syllable structure." *Langues et Littératures* 8: 177–191.

Ben Si Said, S. (2014). De la Nature de la Variation Diatopique en Kabyle: Étude de la Formation des Singulier et Pluriel Nominaux. PhD dissertation, University of Nice.

Bensoukas, K. & Abdelaziz Boudlal (2012a). " The prosody of Moroccan Amazigh and Moroccan Arabic: Similarities in the phonology of schwa." In *Prosody Matters: Essays in Honor of Lisa Selkirk*, Toni Borowsky, Shigeto Kawahara, Takahito Shinya & Mariko Sugahara (eds), 3–42. Sheffield: Equinox.

Bensoukas, K. & Abdelaziz Boudlal (2012b). "An Amazing substratum in Moroccan Arabic: The prosody of schwa." *Langues et Littératures* 22: 179–221.

Blaho, S. (2004). Interactions of Sonorant and Obstruent Voicing. Master's thesis, Pázmány Péter Catholic University.

Booij, G. (1995). *The Phonology of Dutch*. Oxford: Clarendon Press.

Boudlal, A. (2001). Constraint Interaction in the Phonology and Morphology of Casablanca Moroccan Arabic. Doctorat d'Etat thesis, Mohammed V University, Rabat.

Boudlal, Ab. (2006/2007). "Sonority-driven schwa epenthesis in Moroccan Arabic." *Languages and Linguistics* 18/19: 59–81.

Boukous, A. (1987). Phonotactique et Domaines Prosodiques en Berbère. PhD dissertation, University Paris 7.

Chaker, S. (1992). *Une Décennie d'Études Berbères (1980–1990). Bibliographie Critique: Langue, Littérature, Identité*. Algiers: Bouchène.

Charette, M. (1990). "License to govern." *Phonology* 7: 233–253.

Clark, J. & Yallop, C. (1995). *An Introduction to Phonetics and Phonology*. Oxford: Blackwell.

Coleman, J. (1996). "Declarative syllabification in Tashlhiyt Berber." In *Current Trends in Phonology: Models and Methods*. Vol. 1, J. Durand & B. Laks (eds), 177–218. Salford: European Studies Research Institute, University of Salford.

Coleman, J. (2001). "The phonetics and phonology of Tashlhiyt Berber syllabic consonants." *Transactions of the Philological Society* 99: 29–64.

Dell, F. (1973). *Les Règles et les Sons. Introduction à la Phonologie Générative* (2nd édition 1985). Paris, Hermann.

Dell, F. & Mohamed, E. (1985). "Syllabic consonants and syllabification in Imdlawn Tashlhiyt Berber." *Journal of African Languages and Linguistics* 7: 105–130.

Dell, F. & Elmedlaoui, M. (1988). "Syllabic consonants in Berber: Some new evidence." *Journal of African Languages and Linguistics* 10: 1–17.

Dell, F. & Elmedlaoui, M. (2002). *Syllables in Tashlhiyt Berber and in Moroccan Arabic*. Dordrecht: Kluwer.

Echchadli, M. (1986). Les Processus Morphologiques et Phonologiques des Noms en Arabe Marocain. MA thesis, Montréal, UQAM.

Elramli, Y.M. (2012). Assimilation in the Phonology of a Lybian Arabic Dialect: A Constraint-Based Approach. PhD dissertation, Newcastle University.

Faust, N. (2011). Forme et Fonction dans la Morphologie Nominale de l'Hébreu Moderne: Études en Morpho-syntaxe. PhD dissertation, University of Paris 7.

Frankiewicz, J. (2001). "A syllabic analysis of vowel epenthesis in the suffix *–ed* in English." *Poznan Studies in Contemporary Linguistics* 37: 53–69.

Guerssel, M. (1990). On the Syllabification Pattern of Berber. Montreal: ms, UQAM.

Guerssel, M. (1992). "The phonology of Berber derivational morphology by affixation." *Linguistic Analysis* 22/1–2: 03–60.

Gussmann, E. (1980). *Introduction to Phonological Analysis*. Warszawa: Panstwowe Wydawnictwo Naukowe.

Haddad, G. (1984). "Epenthesis and sonority in Lebanese Arabic." *Studies in the Linguistic Sciences* 14: 57–88.

Hall, N. (2011). "Vowel epenthesis." In *The Blackwell Companion to Phonology*, 5 Vols, Marc van Oostendorp, Colin J. Ewen, Elizabeth Hume & Keren Rice (eds), 1576–1596. Malden, MA & Oxford: Wiley-Blackwell.

Hall, N. (2013). "Acoustic differences between lexical and epenthetic vowels in Lebanese Arabic." *Journal of Phonetics* 41/2: 133–143.

Hammane, K. (2010). La Syllabe en Berbère Tachlhit: Que Peut Apporter la Théorie CVCV? PhD dissertation, University Paris 8.

Harrel, R. (1962). *A Short Reference Grammar of Moroccan Arabic*. Washington, DC: Georgetown University Press.

Harris, J. (1994). *English Sound Structure*. Oxford: Blackwell.

Hayes, B. (1986). "Inalterability in CV phonology." *Language* 62: 321–351.

Heath, J. (2002). *Jewish and Muslim Dialects of Moroccan Arabic*. London: Curzon.

Idrissi, A. (2000a). "On Berber plurals." In *Research in Afroasiatic Grammar*, Jacqueline Lecarme, Jean Lowenstamm & Ur Shlonsky (eds), 101–124. Amsterdam: John Benjamins.

Idrissi, A. (2000b). Towards a Root-and-Template Approach to Shape-Invariant Morphology. PhD dissertation, UQAM.

Itô, J. (1989). "A prosodic theory of epenthesis." *Natural Language and Linguistic Theory* 7: 217–259.

Jebbour, A. (1993). "A note on blind roots in Berber." *Linguistica Communicatio* III: 211–224.

Jebbour, A. (1999). "Syllable weight and syllable nuclei in Tachelhit Berber of Tiznit." *Cahiers de Grammaire* 24: 95–116.

Kabbaj, O. (1990). "La Structure Syllabique de l'Arabe Marocain. MA thesis, UQAM.

Kaye, J. (1990). "Government in phonology: The case of Moroccan Arabic." *The Linguistic Review* 6: 131–159.

Kaye, J., Echchadli, M. & El Ayachi, S. (1986). "Les formes verbales de l'arabe marocain." *Revue Québecoise de Linguistique* 16/1: 61–98.

Kaye, J., Lowenstamm, J. & Vergnaud, J.-R. (1990). "Constituent structure and government in phonology." *Phonology* 7/2: 193–231.

Kenstowicz, M. (1986). "Notes on syllable structure in three Arabic dialects." *Revue Québecoise de Linguistique* 16/1: 101–127.

Kossmann, M. (1995). "La spirantisation dans les Parlers Zénètes." In *Langues du Maroc: Aspects Linguistiques dans un Contexte Minoritaire*, Petra Bos (ed.), 11–19. Tilburg: Tilburg University Press.

Lahrouchi, M. (2001). Aspects Morpho-phonologiques de la Dérivation Verbale en Berbère Tachelhit. PhD dissertation, University of Paris 7.

Lahrouchi, M. (2003). "Manifestations gabaritiques dans la dérivation verbale en berbère tachelhit." *Recherches Linguistiques de Vincennes* 32: 61–82.

Lahrouchi, M. & Ségéral, P. (2010). "Peripheral vowels in Tashlhiyt Berber are phonologically long: Evidence from Tagnawt." *Brill's Annual of Afroasiatic Languages and Linguistics* 2: 202–212.

Lampitelli, N. (2011). Forme Phonologique, Exposants Morphologiques et Structures Nominales: Études Comparées de l'Italien, du Bosnéen et du Somali. PhD dissertation, University of Paris 7.

Lowenstamm, J. (1991). "Vocalic length and centralization in two branches of Semitic." In *Semitic Studies in Honor of Wolf Leslau on the Occasion of his 85th Birthday*, Vol. 2, Alan S. Kaye (ed.), 949–65. Wiesbaden: Harrasowitz.

Lowenstamm, J. (1996). "CV as the only syllable type." In *Current Trends in Phonology Models and Methods*, Jacques Durand & Bernard Laks (eds), 419–442. University of Salford, European Studies Research Institute.

Nikiema, E. (1989). "Gouvernement propre et licenciement en phonologie: le cas du tangale." *Langues Orientales Anciennes, Philologie et Linguistique* 2: 225–251.

Oostendorp, van, M. (1995). Vowel Quality and Phonological Projection. PhD dissertation, Tilburg University.

Ridouane, R. (2008). "Syllables without vowels: Phonetic and phonological evidence from Tashlhiyt Berber." *Phonology* 25: 321–359.

Ridouane, R., Anne, H. & Pierre, A.H. (2014). "Tashlhiyt's ban of complex syllable onsets: Phonetic and perceptual evidence." *Language Typology and Universals* 67/1: 7–20.

Rucart, P. (2006). Morphologie Gabaritique et Interface Morphosyntaxique. PhD dissertation, University of Paris 7.

Saïb, J. (1976). A Phonological Study of Tamazight Berber: Dialect of Ayt Ndhir. PhD dissertation, Los Angeles: University of California.

Scheer, T. (2004). *A Lateral Theory of Phonology: What Is CVCV, and Why Should It Be?*, Studies in Generative Grammar 68.1. Berlin: Mouton de Gruyter.

Scheer, T. (2008). "Syllabic and trapped consonants in (Western) Slavic: The same but yet different." In *Formal Description of Slavic Languages: The Fifth Conference, Leipzig 2003*, Gerhild Zybatow, Luka Szucsich, Uwe Junghanns & Roland Meyer (eds), 149–167. Frankfurt am Main: Lang.

Schein, B. & Steriade, D. (1986). "On geminates." *Linguistic Inquiry* 17: 691–744.

Shaw, J., Adamantios Gafos, P.H. & Chakir Z. (2009). "Temporal evidence for syllabic structure in Moroccan Arabic: Data and model." *Phonology* 26/1: 187–215.

Taïfi, M. (1991). *Dictionnaire Français-Tamazight*. Paris: L'Harmattan.

Ulfsbjorninn, S. & Lahrouchi M. (2016). "The typology of the distribution of Edge: The propensity for bipositionality." *Papers in Historical Phonology* 1: 109–129, http://journals.ed.ac.uk/pihph/index.

Wise, H. (1983). "Some functionally motivated rules in Tunisian phonology." *Journal of Linguistics* 19/1: 165–181.

9

VOWEL HARMONY (BEYOND ATR) AND ITS IMPACT ON MORPHOLOGICAL PARSING*

John Rennison

Introduction

This chapter will not be a detailed taxonomy of the many vowel harmony (hereafter: VH) processes found in African languages with extensive collections of examples, but rather a typologically oriented and theory-driven overview of possible harmony types, be they common or rare, that bear upon the question: "What is the range of VH systems in African languages?" (For an overview of all harmony processes in all natural languages, see Krämer (2003) and Rose & Walker (2011).)

Why "beyond ATR"? Because ATR-harmony is not only over-studied in comparison with the other harmony types (even though not necessarily better understood), but it also involves a phonological property (ATR) that occurs (a) only in vowels, and (b) never as the sole phonological element of a vowel. For an exhaustive treatment of ATR-harmony, see Casali (2003, 2008).

After delineating the kinds of VH that occur, we then consider the usefulness of the discovered systems for that part of morphological parsing which is performed *in the phonological component*, i.e., for the process of discovering, as effectively and quickly as possible, which morphs are contained in a given stretch of the acoustic signal. In this chapter, the term morphological parsing does *not* extend to the morphological component proper, where syntactic/semantic parsing and disambiguation of word structures take place. It is important to bear in mind that phonology only has access to morphs (i.e., the phonological substance or operations that realize a morpheme), not to the content of morphemes (such as word category or affix type).

A perennial problem in the morphological parsing of an utterance is that it crucially depends on the results of the phonological parsing of that utterance. It is not possible to jump straight from the acoustic signal, or even phonetic transcriptions or from structuralist phonemes to morphemes;[1] on the contrary, phonology exists precisely in order to mediate between the speaker's morpheme lexicon (the mental dictionary mapping phonological substance and processes to morphological feature bundles) and the various possible phonetic realizations of that morph. The only way to discover which morphemes a speaker has encoded in the acoustic signal is to apply phonology backwards. This is true no matter which phonological theory is used. It is illustrated by Maxwell (1994) with a rule that assimilates voicelessness in stops:

[−continuant] → [−voiced] / ___ [−voiced]

Unapplication of this devoicing rule to a noncontinuant voiceless segment presents a dilemma: should the underlying segment be reconstructed as having been [+voiced], or was the segment originally [−voiced] (with the rule having applied vacuously)?

Maxwell, 1994

More generally, any given stretch of the acoustic signal may reflect the lexical form of a morpheme directly; or the morpheme may have been changed by one or more phonological rule(s). In the latter case the hearer has to find out which rule(s) might have been applied and reverse these, thereby uncovering the underlying phonological forms of words and allowing the parsing of their morphological composition.

This chapter is couched in terms of Government Phonology (hereafter: GP),[2] and the appropriateness of this theory of phonology[3] for the description of vowels in African languages should emerge here. In some cases, it will be compared directly to an SPE-type (Chomsky & Halle, 1968) approach.

Our roadmap begins with earlier analyses of VH (the second section), taking as an example the treatment of ATR-harmony in Akan. The theory of GP is introduced and followed by descriptions and analyses of VH in various African languages, including Akan. Then further theoretical aspects of VH are considered, as a preliminary to the treatment of parsing in the third section. That section first summarises the roles of phonological and morphological factors in parsing. The application of these factors to VH is then explored. Finally, in the fourth section, some overall conclusions are drawn.

Vowel harmony

Earlier analyses of vowel harmony in African languages: ATR-harmony in Akan

Up to the 1960s the term "vowel harmony" was applied to various African languages, with an emphasis on the description of this relatively newly discovered phonological phenomenon (Awobuluyi & Bamgbose, 1967; Berry, 1957; Carnochan, 1960; Greenberg, 1951, 1963; Ladefoged, 1964; Stewart, 1967). From about 1968 the theory of SPE dictated the mainstream linguistic treatment of VH. This development was fairly problematic because the SPE formalism is oriented towards contiguous sequences of single sounds (segments). Autosegmental Phonology seemed to be a promising alternative because it allowed a single "feature" (i.e., autosegment) specification to be associated with more than one vowel. In the following subsections we will examine the SPE-based and one early autosegmental analysis of Akan. The GP analysis will follow after that theory has been sufficiently outlined.

Berry (1957)

The short description of Akan ATR-harmony by Berry (1957) contains all the relevant facts and insights. His list of vowels with ATR (=Set A) and without ATR (Set B) is repeated in Table 9.1.

His table of possible vowel sequences within radicals, which is repeated and slightly remodelled as Table 9.2, contains two large areas filled mainly with dashes (shown here, with wavy borders).

Vowel harmony (beyond ATR) and impact on parsing

Table 9.1 Berry's (1957: 127) table of the vowel sets, using IPA symbols. Set A has ATR, Set B does not

Set A	Set B
i	ɪ
e	ɛ
æ	a
o	ɔ
u	ʊ

Table 9.2 Berry's (1957: 126) table of vowel sequences in Akan (transliterated to IPA and rearranged for clarity) with his original notes. Shading and borders added

	i	*e*	*æ*	*o*	*u*	*ɪ*	*ɛ*	*a*	*ɔ*	*ʊ*
i	ii	ie	—	io	—	—	—	ia	—	—
e	ei	ee	—	—	(ɛu)[4]	—	—	—	—	—
æ	æi	—	—	—	æu	—	—	—	—	—
o	oi	—	—	oo	—	—	—	—	—	—
u	ui	ue	—	uo	uu	—	(uɛ̃)	ua	(uɔ̃)[5]	—
ɪ	—	—	—	—	—	ɪɪ	ɪɛ	ɪa	—	—
ɛ	—	—	—	—	—	ɛɪ	ɛɛ	—	—	—
a	—	—	—	—	—	aɪ	—	aa	—	—
ɔ	—	—	—	—	—	ɔɪ	—	—	ɔɔ	—
ʊ	—	—	—	—	—	ʊɪ	ʊɛ	ʊa	ʊɔ	ʊʊ

(i) Any digram sequence entered in the Table may be read as either a vv-sequence (**hyia**), or a vCv-sequence (**hyira**), or both.

(ii) A dash implies only that the particular sequence is not found in monomorphematic stems; it may, however, occur (and some do) at morpheme junctures.

(iii) The sequences in parentheses are found mostly in the Akuapem dialect.

The cells in these two areas would combine a vowel from Set A with one from Set B, which is disallowed (*pace* the boxed shaded cells of Table 9.2, namely [ia] and [ua]). In Berry's words:

The vowels of a radical are all of one or [the] other set, that is,

a;a or b;b

or 'mixed' in the following sequence only, a;b (since **i**. . .**a** is possible but **a**. . .**i** is not).

Berry, 1957: 127

The generalization that the only possible mixed sequence is a;b (i.e., in SPE terms, but not) accounts for the observed exceptions [ia] and [ua] (in the boxed shaded cells of Table 9.2) and holds not only for radicals, but also for Akan VH on the (polymorphemic) word and phrase level. Similarly, the restriction on the occurrence of [æ] to "before [i]" and "before [u]" (in the boxed shaded cells) shows clearly that only (in SPE terms) a vowel to the right can ever produce the phonetic vowel [æ].

Schachter and Fromkin (1968) and Stewart (1983)

Across word boundaries a [–Tense] vowel at the end of one word is made [+Tense] when the following word begins with a <u>root</u> with a [+Tense] vowel, but not when the following word begins with a <u>grammatical morpheme</u> (i.e., a prefix) with a [+Tense] vowel. Thus the final vowel of Ak <u>Amma</u> [amma] 'Amma' is made [+Tense] when it immediately precedes the root <u>yi</u> 'remove' as in Ak Amma yii [ammæ jii] 'Amma removed it'. But this vowel is not made [+Tense] when it immediately precedes the [+Tense] prefix [be], as in Ak <u>Amma beyii</u> [amma bejii] 'Amma came and removed it'. These facts would indicate that the vowel of the prefix realized as [be] in <u>beyii</u> is <u>inherently</u> lax (as are, in our opinion, all vowels grammatical prefixes) [. . .].

Schachter & Fromkin 1968: 56

In other words: /amma/ is realised as [amma],[6] not [ammæ] before [bejii], even though the [e] of [bejii] comes from [ɛ] by ATR-harmony. But surely it is the height of the vowel (high /i/ in *jii* but mid [e] in *bejii*), not its status as a root or prefix, that determines whether its ATR can be associated to the preceding vowel. Incidentally, the observation that all vowels in grammatical prefixes are lax (which must surely be true) did not lead them or Stewart (1983) to realize that ATR-harmony always involves the change from [–Tense] to [+Tense] and never the converse.

Autosegmental analyses of vowel harmony in African languages

Strictly speaking, autosegmental phonology also includes GP. In this subsection we consider early autosegmental phonology; GP is dealt with in the next subsection.

From the inception of autosegmental phonology (Goldsmith, 1976; Williams, 1976) scholars like Nick Clements (1977, 1981) exploited its (then) bi-linear structure to deal quite elegantly with vowel harmony. Thus, instead of cluttering rules with (often multiple occurrences of) C_0, it could simply be stated in the specification of the autosegmental tier that the p-bearing units of vowel harmony are vowels. In the early years of autosegmental theory it was believed that only one SPE-type feature could be removed from the feature matrix and placed on an autosegmental tier. This feature was then an autosegment and could only be expressed phonetically by means of association with one or more segment matrices. Unfortunately, Clements' (1977, 1981) analysis of Akan postulates rightward ATR-harmony, which (*pace* the analysis of one local vowel assimilation) does not exist.

In Clements (1977) there is a discussion with Károly Rédei about which feature could be autosegmentalized, since the theory of those days only allowed for one single autosegment. Rédei's interest was Hungarian VH, where both palatality and lip-rounding harmonize. In the meantime phonologists have come to realize that multiple vowel harmony types are possible in the same language. Thus, for example, Mòoré (Gur) has four vowel harmonies: progressive ATR-harmony and regressive umlaut of non-highness, backness-cum-rounding, and palatality. We will see below that these involve precisely all four of the phonological elements of Government Phonology that are available for vowel quality (*pace* tone and nasality).

Vowel harmony within Government Phonology

Government Phonology has "elements" where other theories have distinctive features, and their number is very small (around 6, compared with around 20 for SPE). Moreover, they are monovalent – in Trubetzkoy's (1939) terms "privative" – i.e., an element can be present or not, but it is not possible to refer to the absence of an element, say, in a phonological rule, and much less to assimilate the absence of an element to a position that has it (i.e., SPE [+f] → [–f]).

In terms of GP, we expect that (maximally) every element that contributes to the melody of vowels could potentially harmonize. This is in fact the case. Government Phonology has four elements that determine vowel quality (I, U, A, ATR); the last of these is slightly elusive because it does not correspond to any easily identifiable single acoustic property of the signal. Rather, ATR is relational and can only sensibly be applied to a vowel that already has some other element(s).

The spreading of the tone elements H and L is traditionally not considered to be VH, even though it uses the same mechanisms in GP to capture assimilations of tone, voicing and nasality.

Basic vowel harmony types

The eight logically possible combinations of single element and direction are shown in tabular form in Table 9.3, along with some names of some languages where each of these basic VH types occurs. Of course there are many languages that display each type of harmony; the named languages are ones with which I am more familiar.

Whether these eight categories are sufficient to generate all and only the VH processes found in natural languages is an empirical question and could be regarded as a test for GP theory. In my opinion they generate precisely the set of VH processes found in the world's languages. Note, incidentally, that the feature system of SPE gives no hint at all what might be a possible VH process. We return to this question after first considering the harmony processes of Mòoré and their formalization in GP.

The vowel harmonies of Mòoré

Some languages have more than one VH process, sometimes even in opposite directions (e.g., Mòoré ATR-harmony works from left-to-right, but I, U and A harmony (umlaut) from right to left). Since only the vowels /ɪ, ʊ, a/ occur in the umlaut-triggering suffixes, the only possible conflict between two harmony processes is between A-umlaut and ATR-harmony, since these two elements share an autosegmental tier. In this case, ATR takes precedence, as in the example [bíigʌ́] 'child (sg.)'; there is never anything like [béegá]. Further examples are given in Table 9.7 below.

Table 9.3 The possible basic types of vowel harmony process in GP

	Harmonising element	*Direction*	*Language(s)*
1.	I	→left-to-right	Nyangumarda,[7] Koromfe
2.	I	←right-to-left	Mòoré, Yukuben, Luganda
3.	U	→left-to-right	Nyangumarda, Koromfe
4.	U	←right-to-left	Mòoré, Yukuben, Luganda
5.	A	→left-to-right	Nyangumarda, Luganda
6.	A	←right-to-left	Mòoré
7.	ATR	→left-to-right	Mòoré, Koromfe, Kpololo
8.	ATR	←right-to-left	Akan, Kpololo

Sources: Akan – Berry (1957); Kpololo – Kaye (1985); Luganda – Katamba (1984); Nyangumarda – O'Grady (1974–75) and Geytenbeek (2008). All other languages from my own research.

Figure 9.1 GP representations of the vowels of Mòoré (adapted from Rennison, 1996)

Note: The tense low vowel corresponding to Akan [æ] is [ʌ] in Mòoré. The vowels [ɛ], [ɔ] and [ʌ] are derived, not lexical.

The vowels that result from the umlaut processes may retain the identity of the trigger (as the second half of a diphthong) or may merge the two vowel melodies (e.g., i+a → ɛ). The behaviour of each vowel pair is always the same, but it is unclear what causes merger in some cases but not in others.

We see that the vowels associated to both A and ATR all have A on the right and ATR on the left. This prevents the rightward spreading of ATR for all such vowels; only the vowels /i/ and /u/, which have no A element, are ever able to transmit ATR to the right. This accounts neatly for the otherwise puzzling fact that ATR never spreads from mid vowels. In this respect Mòoré is the converse of Akan (where the order was A-ATR and spreading was from right to left), but also of the northern dialect of Mòoré (called Yaadre), as demonstrated in Rennison (1996).

The processes of I-umlaut, U-umlaut, A-umlaut and ATR-harmony are exemplified in Table 9.4 to Table 9.7 and formalized in Figure 9.2 to Figure 9.5 respectively.

Table 9.4. Examples of I-umlaut in Mòoré.[8] Parts of vowels affected by A-umlaut are bold and underlined

sg. phonetic	sg. lexical	pl. phonetic	pl. lexical	gloss
bõãŋgá	bõ ́+ga	bõìsí	bõ ́+sɪ	'donkey'
zõãŋgá	zõ ́+ga	zõìsí	zõ ́+sɪ	'blind'

Note: Both of the singular forms given here are subject to A-umlaut.

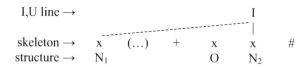

Figure 9.2 GP representation of I-umlaut in Mòoré[9]

Note: N_1 must have a melody (i.e., effectively, must be attached to an I or A element). Any number of ON pairs may intervene between N_1 and O, provided that their N has no melody.

Table 9.5 Examples of Mòoré U-umlaut. Only /i, ɪ, e, a/ can be harmonised; parts of vowels affected by U-umlaut are shown bold and underlined

sg. phonetic	sg. lexical	pl. phonetic	pl. lexical	gloss
kiuugù	kí ́+gʊ	kítù	kí ́+dʊ[10]	'moon'
tíogó	tí ́+gʊ	tíɪdó	tí ́+dʊ	'luggage'
béodgó	bé ́+gʊ	bétó	bé ́+dʊ	'sorrel'
ráoogó	rá ́+gʊ	ráadó	rá ́+dʊ	'male (animal)'

The GP representations presented above contain simple but to-the-point formulations of widely diverging VH process types. (Note that these are the **full** GP representations of the vowels.) Compare this with the massive over-generation of competing theories of phonology. In an SPE approach there is no principled reason why any of the 20 features of Halle

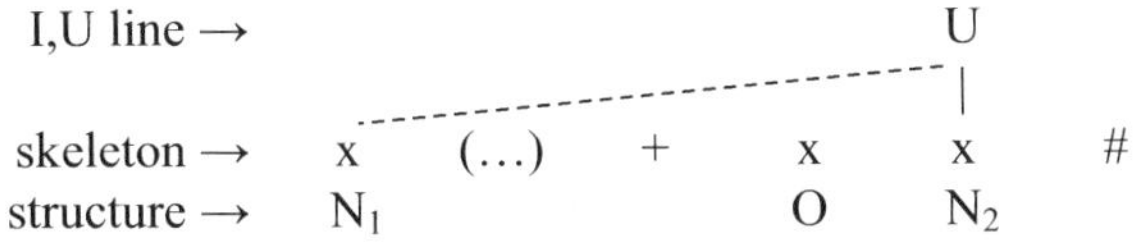

```
I,U line →                           U
                          ┌──────────┤
skeleton →      x   (…)  +    x     x      #
structure →     N₁            O     N₂
```

Figure 9.3 GP representation of U-umlaut in Mòoré

Note: N₁ must have a melody (i.e., effectively, must be attached to an I or Λ element). Any number of ON pairs may intervene between N₁ and O, provided that their N has no melody.

Table 9.6 Examples of Mòoré A-umlaut. Only /ɪ/ and /ʊ/ can be harmonized; the (parts of) vowels affected by A-umlaut are bold and underlined

sg. phonetic	sg. lexical	pl. phonetic	pl. lexical	gloss
bɛndá	bìnd`+a	bìndsí	bìnd`+sɪ	'loincloth'
bíŋgrì	bíŋg`+rɪ	bɛŋga	bíŋg`+a	'bean'
kóaadà	kó+d`+a	koáadbá	kó+d`+bá¹¹	'farmer'
nóbrɪ	nób`+rɪ	nóaba	nób`+a	'nut'

Note: The vowels /i/ and /u/ cannot be affected by A-umlaut; instead, ATR-harmony occurs.

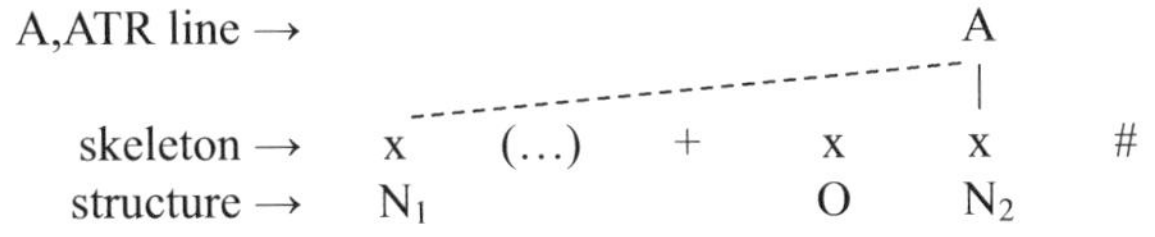

```
A,ATR line →                         A
                          ┌──────────┤
skeleton →      x   (…)  +    x     x      #
structure →     N₁            O     N₂
```

Figure 9.4 GP representation of A-umlaut in Mòoré (adapted from Rennison, 2016)

Note: N₁ must have a melody (i.e., effectively, must be attached to an I or U element). Any number of ON pairs may intervene between N₁ and O, provided that their N has no melody. O may also be empty. ATR-harmony takes precedence over this process.

Table 9.7 Examples of ATR harmony in Mòoré. Only suffix vowels (/ɪ, ʊ, a/) can be harmonized. Vowels above the thick line have ATR, those below it do not

phonetic	lexical	gloss	stem vowel	suffix vowel
túsrí	tús`-rɪ	thousand	/u/	/ɪ/ → [i]
wúlgú	wúl`-gʊ	fog	/u/	/ʊ/ → [u]
bíigʌ	bí`-ga	child/fruit	/i/	/a/ → [ʌ]
wóbgò	wób`-gʊ	elephant	/ʊ/	/ʊ/ remains [ʊ]
jɛ́lá	jíl`-a	problems	/ɪ/	/a/ remains [a]
bòosí	bò`-sɪ	goats	/o/	/ɪ/ remains [ɪ]
bétó	béd`-dʊ	sorrel (pl.)	/e/	/ʊ/ remains [ʊ]
láasí	lá`-sɪ	plates	/a/	/ɪ/ remains [ɪ]

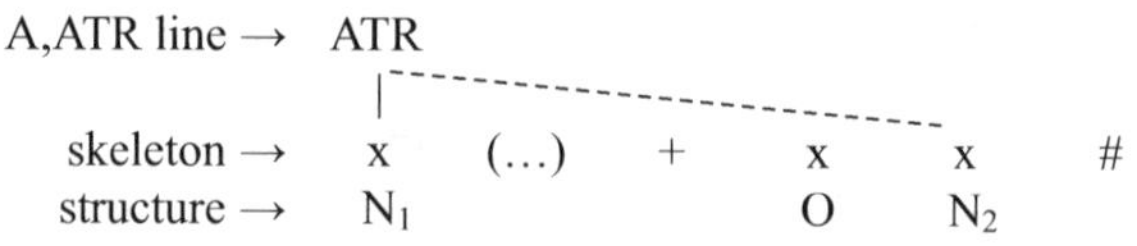

John Rennison

```
A,ATR line →    ATR
                 |‾ ‾ ‾ ‾ ‾ ‾ ‾ ‾ ‾ ‾ ‾ ‾ ‾ ‾ ‾ ‾ ‾ ‾ ‾
  skeleton →    x      (...)    +    x    x      #
  structure →   N₁                   O    N₂
```

Figure 9.5 GP representation of ATR-harmony in Mòoré (adapted from Rennison, 2016)

Note: N₁ can effectively only be /i/ or /u/. Any number of ON pairs may intervene between N₁ and O, provided that their N has no melody. O may also be empty. N₂ may be /ɪ/, /ʊ/ or /a/.

This process takes precedence over A-umlaut. For examples, see Table 9.7.

& Clements (1983) should be disallowed as the active feature of VH.[12] Those phonological features allow for at least 80 VH processes involving a single feature; but many VH processes involve two features (e.g., [+back, +round]) or even more. (In Rennison (1987b) I tried to deal with the vowel harmonies of Koromfe in terms of "backness-roundness-height"-harmony, which involves four SPE features. Recall also that Katamba's (1984) early autosegmental analysis of Luganda VH operated almost exclusively with pairs of the features [±high], [±back] and [±low].) The actual number of VH processes that can be expressed in an SPE framework is huge. To some phonologists this is no problem; to me it is a catastrophe. A good theory of phonology should delineate as precisely and naturally as possible the limits of human phonological systems. The eight basic types of vowel harmony shown in Table 9.3 are enough.

Additional aspects of vowel harmony

Note that up to now we have been concerned only with the VH process *per se*. Clearly, consideration of the triggering, range and blocking of VH will expand the number of logically possible harmony types and produce additional problems for parsing.

A Government Phonology account of ATR-harmony in Akan

The representations of the oral vowels of Akan are given in Figure 9.6.

In Akan, ATR only ever harmonizes to the left. The suffix [i] from /-ɪ/ in words like [o-fiti-i] 'he pierced it' (Stewart, 1983: 116) is not the result of VH, but of a highly restricted and purely local[13] assimilation process that ensures that the disallowed sequence [iɪ] does not arise (cf. Berry's occurring vowel sequences in Table 9.2 above).

In the tense low vowel [æ] the elements on the A,ATR line can only be ordered with A on the left, since ATR-harmony never spreads leftwards from a mid vowel or from [æ]. As in Mòoré, the only vowels that can freely harmonize their ATR element (here: to the left, in

Figure 9.6 GP representations of the vowels of Akan

Note: [æ] is not a lexical vowel; it is always derived.

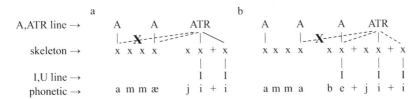

Figure 9.7 GP representations of the vowels in the Akan sentences a) [ammæ yii] 'Amma removed it' and b) [amma bejii] 'Amma came and removed it', based on Schachter and Fromkin (1968: 56)

Note: The attachment of ATR to the right is not a part of VH, but a purely local assimilation between two contiguous vowels.

Mòoré: to the right) are the high tense vowels /i/ and /u/. This neatly accounts for the two vowel sequences beginning with [æ] in the boxed shaded cells of Table 9.2, namely [æi] and [æu].

Now let us consider two crucial examples of ATR-harmony from Schachter and Fromkin (1968), shown in Figure 9.7. In sentence (a) the ATR element can spread one position to the left, producing the vowel [æ], but can spread no farther because the association line of the neighbouring A element blocks it. Associating the ATR element to the first /a/ of the word would produce a line-crossing. (This illicit association is marked with a large X in Figure 9.7a.) In sentence (b), the spreading ATR element is blocked at the vowel [e] and can no longer affect the final vowel of [amma].

Finally, let us not forget that Akan has dialect differences relating to VH. In Stewart's (1983: 121) words: "disharmonic mid vowels [. . .] are admissible in Asante but not in Akuapem." This would suggest that the configuration of tiers is changing from one where ATR and A share a tier to one where they have independent tiers – in which case mid vowels could receive or transmit ATR-harmony.

Why do languages have vowel harmony?

What is VH? What advantage does VH bring? Let us consider two well-known hypotheses proposed by Larry Hyman:

Hypothesis 1:   Root-triggered VH on suffixes derives from post-tonic reduction.

Hypothesis 2:   All VH that does not owe its existence to reduction is anticipatory, i.e., articulatory, perceptual, and/or conceptual "pre-planning".

Hyman 2002: 24

In my opinion, Hypothesis 1 might be correct, but in many languages with VH on suffixes there is no easily recognizable "tonic" syllable, whether by stress or by tonal prominence. So "pre-tonic" and "post-tonic" are difficult concepts to operationalize. Also, Hypothesis 1 is slightly ambiguous: The term "post-tonic" often refers exclusively to the syllable immediately following a stressed syllable. In VH, however, it must refer to **all** harmonizing syllables that follow the stressed syllable – of which there can be many (e.g., the A-harmony of many Bantu languages). Post-tonic reduction typically relates to the first reading (where one syllable is affected), and not to the second (where many syllables are affected). Usually, sequences of unstressed syllables develop secondary stresses (as in the famous English example

ˌhama ˌmeli ˈdanthemum). And finally, the phrase "derives from" may be taken synchronically or diachronically. Diachronically it may be the case, but synchronically the telescoping of the two processes mentioned (post-tonic vowel reduction and VH) would seem to be unlikely. How should a present-day speaker know (or reconstruct) the full forms of the post-tonic vowels if they have all been reduced?

Hypothesis 2, on the other hand, was among my favourites until I analysed Yukuben (see page 197ff below). Note that neither hypothesis includes the notion that increased redundancy aids parsing, irrespective of the direction of the VH. Left-to-right harmony is perseverative whilst right-to-left harmony is anticipatory. Perseveration should allow us to check on the presence of the harmonizing element in the vowels which follow the trigger vowel, and anticipation should allow us to better predict the identity of the trigger vowel (often a root vowel). We will return to this point in the next section.

The effect (and I would assume, the purpose) of all assimilation processes in phonology, including VH, is to increase redundancy (i.e., to multiply-encode phonological information),[14] thereby increasing robustness and aiding parsing. Therefore, from a purely abstract point of view, we ought to find languages with every kind of VH that the human mind is capable of producing. My contention is that we do. Any VH can be used to reconstruct lost information in a noisy channel of transmission.

The harmony domain

It is well known that the term "vowel harmony" is used for two kinds of assimilation that may be fundamentally different in nature. In the first case, which I will term "once only", there is a distant assimilation of vowel quality between precisely two vowels, which are usually in adjacent syllables. This seems to be the general case with umlaut processes, as in Mòoré (on page 185–188 above), but also in Korean and in Germanic languages. However, intervening syllables with silent empty nuclei may be skipped over, and in Koromfe Phrase-Final Filling (to be outlined on page 195 below), even phonetic schwas (of licensed empty nuclei) may intervene between the trigger and the target vowel.

The second case is where the assimilation of vowel quality affects the vowels of a longer sequence of syllables (e.g., ATR-harmony in Akan or Koromfe). This I will term "multiple" VH. In some "once only" harmonies there is no way to discover whether a third vowel would harmonize because none is ever available (e.g., in the Luganda pre-prefix).

Advertising vs. alms

A further distinction seems to be relevant to the typology of VH processes: whether the target vowel would (or would not) be pronounceable without the harmonizing element. When a pronounceable vowel is harmonized, this is "advertising" for the trigger vowel. When an unpronounceable vowel is harmonized, these are "alms" given by the nearest appropriate donor. In effect, the target vowel is not a patient but an agent, seeking melody from any available source. In this second case, the harmonizing properties are not necessarily actively harmonizing, and do not harmonize vowels that are already pronounceable. This is the case in Nyangumarda (non-African) and in the Phrase-Final Filling of Koromfe (see for example Antworth, 1990; Carson-Berndsen, 1998; Cernak et al., 2016; Church, 1987a, b; Fulop et al., 1998; Karttunen, 1983; Koskenniemi, 1983; Maxwell, 1994; Rennison, 1990, 1991; Williams, 1998).

Parsing

Parsing is a complex multi-level and multi-stage operation. It involves the simultaneous analysis of all levels of language structure and the exchange of information between levels. I will assume here that phonological parsing involves at least two stages: the initial recognition of phonological entities and the final recognition of all candidate parses of words and the morphs that they contain. I will term these two stages "initial" and "final" phonological parsing. Whether and how many stages intervene between initial and final phonological parsing must remain a question for future research.

This gives us the following sequence of events:

1   initial phonological parsing (of elements, syllables, feet, words, etc.);
2   initial morphological parsing (of morphs);
3   (possibly intermediate levels of parsing);
4   final phonological parsing (incl. checking of VH);
5   final morphological parsing (of fewer morphs).

It is not the job of the phonological component to assess whether a particular sequence of morph(eme)s makes sense (syntactically or semantically). Rather, it is the job of the morphological component to ensure that the morphs outputted by the phonology can be concatenated to well-formed words (and to reject those that cannot).

Here we will consider phonological and morphological parsing as if they were alone in the universe and had to parse every word exhaustively; but they are not alone, and exhaustive parsing may not always be necessary.

Phonological parsing

Let us first consider some purely phonological aspects of parsing, before moving on to morphological considerations.

The things that phonology can pass on to morphology in speech recognition are:

1   the underlying phonological structure of a word (with candidate morph boundaries);
2   a list of phonological processes that might have been applied; and
3   a list of VH violations for each VH process of the language.

Does right-to-left vowel harmony aid phonological parsing?

A classical view of VH and parsing is that right-to-left harmony makes things easier. The hearer must first accurately perceive the quality of the leftmost vowel of the harmony domain. This vowel quality narrows down the range of possible subsequent vowels, including the trigger (usually the rightmost vowel of the domain). This is good, because it frees up real-time perceptual resources for things other than the precise determination of the quality of every vowel.

Unfortunately, there is no *a priori* way to know whether any parsed vowel is initial, medial or final within its harmony domain. So each subsequent vowel must still be examined with full perceptual resources to determine where the harmony domain is located. In other words, right-to-left VH actually saves no resources at all in the first stage of parsing; and overall it increases the required effort because VH domains must be located and delimited. The cost of parsing varies: To locate the elements I, U or A, a rough estimation of F1 and F2 will suffice. For ATR the precise location of both F1 and F2 are needed (Fulop et al., 1998).

Does left-to-right vowel harmony aid phonological parsing?

At this point, let us dismiss one naïve articulatory view of VH – that of "articulatory perseveration." In this view, the articulators assume a particular pose (e.g., high front tongue body and spread lips in I-harmony) and do not change it until the end of the harmony domain. This might occasionally be the case, but many intervening consonants will require the tongue body and/or lips to move (e.g., a [w]). Also, VH typically does not produce sequences of identical vowels, but rather sequences of vowels that have a particular phonological property.

Left-to-right VH is as unhelpful as right-to-left. In the end, vowel quality must always be fully analysed in order to find out where a harmony domain ends.

Morphological parsing

The morpheme lexicon: the only interface between phonology and morphology

Apologies for stating the obvious in this subsection, but it is important to know what we are and are not dealing with.

Morphological parsing involves splitting a word into its component morphs. Consideration of the ways in which a morpheme can be expressed will be helpful.

There are at least six ways to express a morpheme:

- phonological substance of any kind (including affixes and incomplete structures such as floating tones, and floating vowel or consonant melodies/features/elements);
- changing pre-existing phonological substance;
- by a suppletive process (e.g., *went* as the realization of /go+PAST/); or
- by a regular phonological rule (e.g., ablaut, umlaut);
- deleting pre-existing phonological substance;
- replacement of more than one morph with a portmanteau morph;
- morphophonological readjustments at morpheme boundaries (including floating melodies), as, e.g., in compounds: German "Fugen-s" in *Rettungswagen* 'ambulance', *Schönheitschirurg* 'cosmetic surgeon', or English *–o* in *speedometer, gasometer*;
- any combination of the above.

All of these involve operations on phonological substance, be it addition, subtraction or change. Therefore, it seems clear to me that morphs must be isolated within the phonological component, simply because that is the only part of grammar that can do **anything** with phonological content. Clearly, morphology and phonology work together closely, but their actual interface can only be the morpheme lexicon. Here, phonological substance and phonological operations are mapped to categorial grammatical content. So if we want to know how to express "+NOUN,+HUMAN,+PLURAL" in English, we look this up on the grammatical side of the morpheme lexicon, and on the phonological side we find /piːpəl/ or /pɜːsən+z/. And conversely, if we look up the morph /piːpəl/ on the phonological side of the morpheme lexicon, we find the feature bundle "+NOUN,+HUMAN,+PLURAL". But if we look up the morph /pɜːsən/ we will find only the feature bundle "+NOUN,+HUMAN", and for the morph /z/ we find "+PLURAL" (but also "+GENITIVE" and "3RD PERSON SINGULAR"). The morphological component is responsible for concatenating the feature bundles to make a grammatically well-formed word. The readings "+PLURAL" and "+GENITIVE" cannot be distinguished in the morphology (though they will be in the syntax); but the morphology can eliminate the morpheme "3RD PERSON SINGULAR" from our candidate word because it is not compatible with a word that is "+NOUN".

In speech recognition, then, it is the task of the morphological component to check the grammatical well-formedness of the categorial features of each word (i.e., sequence of morphs) outputted by phonological parsing. Clearly, the phonology is not involved in this checking of grammatical well-formedness; it is only capable of analysing phonetic input into candidate morphs. It is not certain that the phonology will even be able to discover where the word boundaries lie. Some languages mark word boundaries clearly (e.g., the penultimate accent of Swahili), others not so clearly.

The parsing of words into morphs

What morphological parsing does is to take a candidate word and break it down into its component morphs, using the (phonological side of the) morpheme lexicon. The task sounds simple enough, but there can be much complexity in the way morphemes combine to form a phonological word (cf. the morph types listed above). Irrespective of the means used to express each morpheme, in speech production the input to phonology must be strings of phonological content (i.e., well-formed phonological representations, etc.) drawn from the phonological side of the mental morpheme lexicon. These strings can and must be interpreted (licensed) by the available mechanisms of the phonological component (and outputted to the articulatory phonetic module). Conversely, in speech perception the acoustic phonetic module analyses the incoming signal into phonetic units of various sizes (depending on the language and theory involved, a selection of: feature/element, segment, mora, syllable, foot, phonological word, stress group, etc.). These are parsed by the phonological module into (a large number of) well-formed candidate source morphs, which are then looked up in the morpheme lexicon and translated into feature bundles for further processing at higher levels of the grammar.

The most obvious application of vowel harmony to the identification of morphs is to use the domain of VH to demarcate units of a given size. The unit "phonological word" immediately springs to mind because it is the domain of many VH processes, especially ATR-harmony. If, in a language with ATR-harmony that does not allow disharmonic sequences, we have a phonetic sequence that contains only vowels with ATR, followed by a sequence containing non-ATR vowels, it would be a safe bet that there is a word boundary somewhere between the last ATR vowel and the first non-ATR vowel. However, this would only be of limited use, because both the ATR stretch and the non-ATR stretch could contain word boundaries that are undetectable by the "change of ATR status" strategy. This is shown in Figure 9.8, where the bold underlined word boundary $\boxed{3}$ can be detected with the aid of ATR-harmony, but word boundaries $\boxed{2}$ and $\boxed{4}$ cannot.

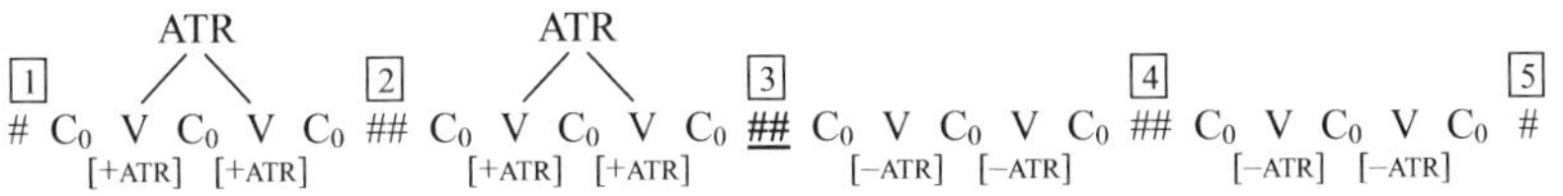

Figure 9.8   A hypothetical utterance in a language with ATR-harmony in the word domain

Vowel harmony as an aid to the identification of word structure?

Given that VH provides no shortcuts for initial phonological parsing, all phonetic and phonological identification of segments and higher-level structures must be carried out (in principle, exhaustively) with no reference to VH. However, it is common that the domain of VH is defined morphologically. A typical domain is the word (with or without clitics), or a well-defined part of a word. Sometimes particular word classes have their own specific type of vowel harmony (e.g., the A-harmony in the verbs of many Bantu languages). Certain local VH processes could be used to locate particular morphological categories. Thus, for example, umlaut in Mòoré (right-to-left I/U/A harmony) takes place between certain (phonetically monosyllabic) noun-class suffixes and a (phonetically monosyllabic) noun stem that meets the minimal length requirement of three CV syllables (cf. the lengthening of CV stems in Table 9.5, endnote 10). In addition, an umlaut domain in Mòoré is almost always also a domain for left-to-right ATR-harmony. So the morphological structure of a noun, i.e., "noun-stem + class suffix", could be checked from right to left for umlaut and from left to right for ATR-harmony.

One might therefore be tempted to refer to categorial morphological information here and claim that once a candidate VH domain and process have been identified, the candidate morpheme types "noun stem" and "noun-class suffix" are also almost automatically identified (*pace* ambiguities of boundary placement). However, categorial morphological information is **not available** to the phonological parsing mechanisms, so unfortunately we cannot utilize it within the phonology.

Vowel harmony as a last-stage checking mechanism

As already discussed, VH processes can be very idiosyncratic. This can be a blessing or a curse for parsing; but in any case it is a problem for linguistic theory, precisely because there is no general pattern. In the remainder of this chapter we will consider various VH processes in the light of their aptness as checking mechanisms. Arbitrarily, we begin with right-to-left processes, then go on to left-to-right.

The Luganda pre-prefix (right-to-left I/U harmony of /a/)

In the augment or pre-prefix of noun-class prefixes in Luganda and many other Bantu languages, lexical /a/ surfaces as phonetic [a] only before an /a/ of the following syllable (i.e., of the noun-class prefix proper); otherwise the augment is raised to [e] before /i/ and [o] before /u/. (The behaviour before mid vowels is usually unknown because only the vowels /i, u, a/ occur in noun prefixes.) Some examples are given in Table 9.8a.

Alongside the languages with the pre-prefix vowels /e, a, o/ there also exist languages like Kinyarwanda, whose pre-prefix is /i, a, u/, i.e., a copy of the vowel of the prefix, which could be accomplished by I/U/A-harmony. Thus, the three examples given in Table 9.8b differ from the Luganda examples only in the quality of the non-low pre-prefix vowels. This difference results from two factors: (1) the nature of the pre-prefix vowel (in Luganda, /a/, but in Kinyarwanda an empty vowel position), and (2) the harmony processes employed: Luganda harmonizes I and U, whilst Kinyarwanda harmonizes I, U and A.

The resulting differences in the representations of the example words are shown in Figure 9.9 for Luganga and Figure 9.10 for Kinyarwanda.

Table 9.8 I/U-harmony in the pre-prefix of Luganda (data from Katamba, 1984) and Kinyarwanda

a) Luganda				b) Kinyarwanda			
o-	mu-	ntu	'person'	u-	mu-	ntu	'person'
a-	ba-	ntu	'people'	a-	ba-	ntu	'people'
e-	ki-	ntu	'thing'	i-	ki-	ntu	'thing'

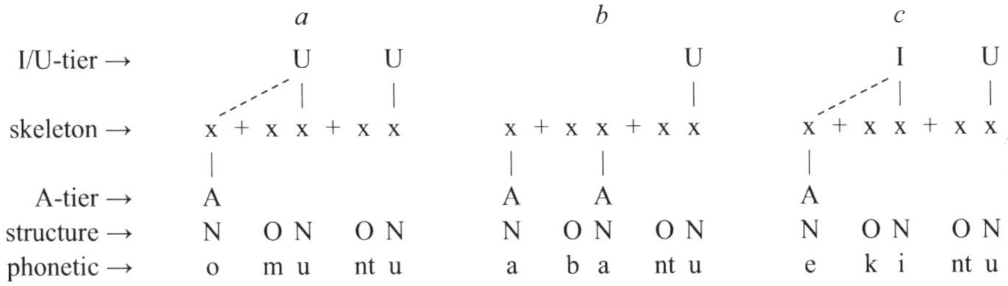

```
                       a                    b                    c
I/U-tier →          U   U                 U                   I   U
                  ╱ |   |                 |                 ╱ |   |
skeleton →     x + x x + x x           x + x x + x x      x + x x + x x
                 |                       |   |              |
A-tier →         A                       A   A              A
structure →    N   O N   O N           N   O N   O N      N   O N   O N
phonetic →     o   m u   nt u          a   b a   nt u     e   k i   nt u
```

Figure 9.9 Right-to-left I/U-harmony in the pre-prefix of Luganda (full GP representations of the vowels). Dashed lines are associations introduced by the harmony process

```
                       a                    b                    c
I/U-tier →          U   U                 U                   I   U
                  ╱ |   |                 |                 ╱ |   |
skeleton →     x + x x + x x           x + x x + x x      x + x x + x x
                                           ╲ |
A-tier →                                     A
structure →    N   O N   O N           N   O N   O N      N   O N   O N
phonetic →     u   m u   nt u          a   b a   nt u     i   k i   nt u
```

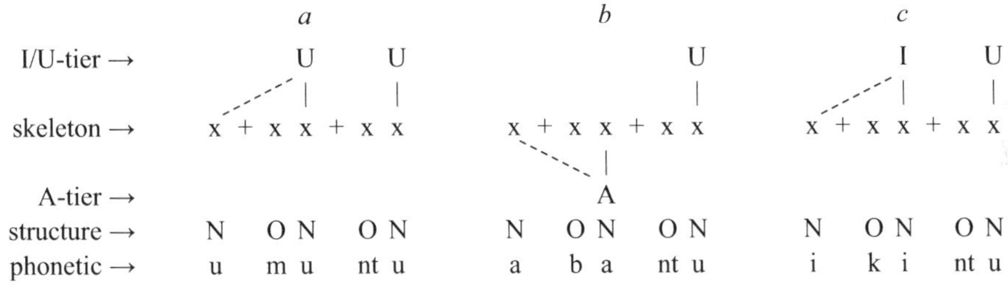

Figure 9.10 I/U-harmony and A-harmony in the pre-prefix of Kinyarwanda – to be revised (full GP representations of the vowels). Dashed lines are associations introduced by the harmony processes

The Kinyarwanda pre-prefix would seem to have the representation in Figure 9.10, i.e., with an additional VH process of right-to-left A-harmony and no underlying A element in the pre-prefix. However, this seems to be a lot of machinery to produce, in the end, a copy of the prefix vowel. Perhaps a copying mechanism (as used, for example, in reduplication processes) might make more sense.

The Koromfe reversive suffix (left-to-right I/U-harmony of epenthetic /a/)

In Koromfe the reversive suffix has six variants, [et, ɛt, ʌt, at, ot, ɔt]. Yet lexically it is /at/, and the mid vowels result from assimilation to the high or mid vowel of the preceding syllable (giving [ɛ] after front vowels and [ɔ] after back vowels). At a more abstract level, and for reasons that would take too long to explicate here (but see Rennison, 1993, 1997a, b, 1999), the reversive suffix is actually /-Vt/, with a lexically empty nucleus that must magically gain an A element, like all other medial epenthetic vowels of Koromfe.

Before going into details, let us note that the ATR-harmony process of Koromfe is quite unspectacular and well behaved. An ATR element in the stem vowel always spreads (multiply) to the suffix vowels.

Koromfe medial harmonized vowels (left-to-right I/U-harmony of epenthetic /a/)

Koromfe has two local VH processes, exemplified in Table 9.9, which affect medial and final vowels respectively. Superficially these processes are similar: both involve the elements I and U, and both operate from left to right (see Figure 9.11). However, the first process (Figure 9.11a) is "advertising harmony" (whereby the I or U element of the first vowel is redundantly repeated in the second vowel) whilst the second (Figure 9.11b) is "alms harmony". This can be seen from two facts about Phrase-Final Filling:

- There is no source for the I element in the final [ɪ] of low-vowel-only words like [gãnatɪ]; it is magic (and, incidentally, the general pattern in Mòoré), but in medial I/U-harmony every I and U element has a lexical source.
- A U element from a consonant is never found as the emergency filler of the final vowel in words that otherwise contain only low vowels, like [gãnatɪ], even if a labial consonant is present (like the [m] in [hãmãndɪ] 'believe, IPFV', which is never *[hãmãndʊ]).

In other contexts the "alms harmony" process of Phrase-Final Filling can use a U element from a consonant – in which case any I element in preceding syllables is ignored. This is shown in Figure 9.12. Moreover, this consonantal U element need not be local, but can be up to three CV-syllables to the left. Three example words from the same stem are given in Table 9.10. At each morpheme boundary a schwa can be realized in slower, more careful speech. Nevertheless, the final epenthetic vowel always successfully finds the consonantal U element of the /b/. Forms like *[hibi], *[hibti] or *[hibtri] are impossible.

Table 9.9 I/U-harmony in Koromfe (Gur). Reversive verb forms with harmonized medial and final vowels (Rennison, 2016)

imperative (phrase-medial)	imperative (phrase-final)	gloss	base verb	gloss
figet	figeti	'dig up'	fig	'bury'
kɛlɛt	kɛlɛtɪ	'open'	kɛl	'close'
gãnat	gãnatɪ	'undo (a bandage)'	gãn	'bandage'
dɔ̃nɔt	dɔ̃nɔtʊ	'take apart, untie'	dɔ̃ɪ̃	'join, tie'
tombot	tombotu	'take off (robe)'	tom	'put on (robe)'
sumbot	sumbotu	'take lid off'	sumb	'put lid on'

Source: Rennison, 2016.

Table 9.10 Koromfe Phrase-Final Filling with a U element from a labial consonant

phonetic pre-pausal	lexical	gloss
hibu	hib	be full (PFV.)
hibtu	hib+t	fill (PFV.)
hibtru	hib+t+d	fill (IPFV.)

Vowel harmony (beyond ATR) and impact on parsing

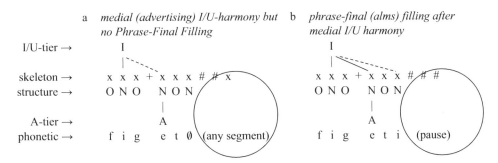

Figure 9.11 GP representations of the first word in Table 9.9, [figet] and [figeti], with medial VH and (in b) Phrase-Final Filling (ATR element omitted for clarity)

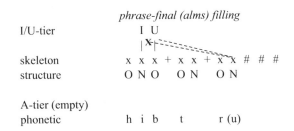

Figure 9.12 GP representation of [hibtru] (ATR element omitted for clarity)

The result of medial harmony is shown in Figure 9.11b with a solid line; only the dashed line is introduced by phrase-final filling.

In Figure 9.12 only the right-hand dashed line is possible; the left-hand dashed line would involve the crossing of association lines.

Suicidal vowel harmony: Yukuben nouns

Some languages have processes that seem to run contrary to VH (e.g., final vowel deletion in Mòoré or stem vowel reduction in Yukuben, which counteract multiple encoding), and some languages have partially self-contradictory VH processes. I term such vowel harmony "suicidal" because it exists even though it can be of no use for parsing. One case of suicidal VH, that of Yukuben nouns, is described here in detail.

The Yukuben nouns shown in Table 9.11 have quite typical phonological shapes: They are disyllabic, the first V or CV being the noun-class prefix. This prefix can be phonetically [V], [kV] or [bV] (where V is any of the five full vowels[15] of the language, [i, e, a, o, u]), except that [bi] is illicit – giving a total of 14 phonetic noun-class prefixes. Yukuben has no vowel length distinction, but the vowels of the noun-class prefixes sound longer because (a) they are in open syllables and (b) second syllables (i.e., stem syllables) are usually reduced to schwa.

As in Luganda, Kinyarwanda, Mòoré and many other Niger-Congo languages, only three vowels occur lexically in noun-class prefixes: /i, u, a/. A phonetic mid vowel in a noun-class prefix is always derived.

There may be more phonetic forms than shown Table 9.11; I have included only those that have been transcribed in our corpus. Note that almost all harmonizing words are also subject to the reduction of the stem vowel to schwa ([ə]) in closed syllables. Yukuben has three register tones that never interact with one another or with the rest of the phonology. The tone of the noun-class prefix is determined by the word stem, i.e., noun-class prefixes are lexically toneless, just like the noun-class suffixes in Mòoré.

The right-to-left I/U-harmony process of Yukuben is formalized in Figure 9.13 (for I) and Figure 9.14 (for U). It should be clear that a noun-class prefix containing lexical /a/ will surface as [e], [o] or [a] depending on the identity of the stem vowel. This is exactly the same VH process that is found in the Luganda pre-prefix, exemplified in Table 9.8 and formalized in Figure 9.9.

However, Yukuben also has a process of A-assimilation, whereby a high prefix vowel is lowered to mid if the stem has an abstract initial floating A element.[16] This means that Yukuben has two classes of stems: lowering and non-lowering. The lowering stems take the noun-class prefix vowels [e, o, a] and the non-lowering stems take [i, u, a].[17] But, quite

Table 9.11 Some disyllabic nouns and adjectives of Yukuben

harmonizing?	stem V reduction	phonetic	lexical	gloss
✓	✓	kēdìŋ / kēdə̀ŋ	ka-⁻dìŋ	good
✓	✓	bètíg / bètə́x	ba-ˋtíg	hills
✓	x	bócùŋ	ba-ˊcùŋ	big
✓	✓	kōwūŋ / kōwə̄ŋ	ka-⁻wūŋ	liver
x	✓	kùtíg / kùtə́x	ku-ˋtíg	hill
x	x	ītə̄b	i-⁻tīb	spears
x	x	ūⁿgāg	u-ⁿgāg	gazelle
x	x	bāⁿgāg	ba-ⁿgāg	gazelles
x	x	kīndàg	ki-⁻ndàg	cow
x	x	íɟú	i-ˊɟú	seeds

Source: Rennison (2014).

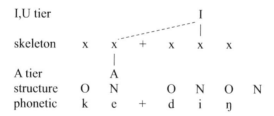

Figure 9.13 Lexical /ka-⁻dìŋ/ 'NCL+good' is harmonized to *[kēdìŋ] / [kēdə̀ŋ]* (with full GP representations of all vowels)

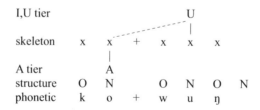

Figure 9.14 Lexical /ka-⁻wūŋ/ 'NCL+liver' is harmonized to [kōwūŋ] / [kōwə̄ŋ] (with full GP representations of all vowels)

Vowel harmony (beyond ATR) and impact on parsing

crucially, the abstract initial floating A element blocks I/U harmony between the stem vowel and the prefix vowel.

Thus a word like [ákūb] 'woman' must be lexically /a-Ákūb/ (with a floating stem-initial A element) and not /a-́kūb/ because the latter form would have to surface as [ókūb], by U-harmony. The floating A of /a-Ákūb/ blocks I/U harmony and allows the noun-class prefix /a/ to surface as [a]. Further examples can be found in Rennison (2014, 2016). For our present purposes, Table 9.12 will suffice to summarize the relevant vowel co-occurrences.

Table 9.12 The sources of the vowels in Yukuben noun-class prefixes. Subscript I, etc. indicate identity

	prefix //	prefix [ ]	stem V //	stem V [ ]	stem-initial floating A?	lowering of prefix V?	I/U-harmony of prefix V?
1	i	i	i, e, u or o	i, u or ə	x	x	x
2	u	u	i, e, u or o	i, u or ə	x	x	x
3	i	e	any$_i$	any$_i$	✓	✓	x
4	u	o	any$_i$	any$_i$	✓	✓	x
5	a	e	e or i	e, i or ə	x	x	✓ (I)
6	a	o	o or u	o, u or ə	x	x	✓ (U)
7	a	a	any$_j$	any$_j$	✓	x	x
8	a	a	a	a (rarely ə)	x	x	x

Table 9.13 Shimizu's (1980: 109–130) "list of Yukuben noun prefixes", quoted from Weitzenauer (2008: 60)

Class		Number of lexemes	Class		Number of lexemes
1	kii	93	22	ai	1
2	kuu	23	23	in	1
3	kVV	32	24	i	8
4	kaa	15	25	u	4
5	koo	9	26	V	16
6	kia	28	27	a	6
7	kwoo	1	28	0	1
8	ken	1	29	buu	27
9	ki	9	30	bVV	125
10	ku	2	31	bee	7
11	kV	6	32	baa	30
12	ke	1	33	boo	2
13	ka	3	34	bia	1
14	ki	1	35	bwaa	1
15	ii	89	36	bwa	1
16	uu	62	37	ben	1
17	VV	138	38	ban	1
18	ee	6	39	bu	1
19	aa	48	40	bV	7
20	oo	27	41	ba	1
21	ia	28			

Note: The notation V indicates that the prefix vowel is identical with the stem vowel that follows it. Recall that in fact Yukuben has no vowel-length distinction and no diphthongs.

In Table 9.12 the phonetic mid vowels are shaded. Their sources can be raising (in 5 and 6) or lowering (in 3 and 4).

Now what does VH get us? As far as I can see, almost nothing. Only cases 5 and 6 harmonize, and it is precisely here that (usually) the source vowel of the harmony is reduced to schwa, thereby also reducing the number of positions where the I or U element is expressed from two back to one. In addition, the generalization that a mid vowel in a noun-class prefix results from I/U harmony of /a/ is now lost. Can we salvage anything for parsing from this mess?

Notice, however, that today we are in a position to ask such questions. Compare the above treatment of the phonology and morphology of Yukuben noun-class prefixes with the earlier taxonomy by Shimizu (1980: 109–130), given in Table 9.13.

Conclusions

One could perhaps question whether consideration of difficult (allegedly marginal) cases can throw light on the relationship between VH and parsing. I think that it can, provided that the data and analysis are sound.

Vowel harmony never aids parsing. . .

We have looked at various aspects of parsing with respect to VH, and only in a few cases has vowel harmony provided unambiguous clues as to morphological structure (e.g., in the pre-prefix vowels of Luganda and Kinyarwanda). It seems clear that the motivation for the development and preservation of VH in phonological systems cannot be to aid phonological or morphological parsing directly. The final nail in the coffin is suicidal vowel harmony, which, if it does anything, actively confuses parsing.

But

As Hyman (2002) implies, VH arises naturally as an assimilatory phonological process. Once VH is established, it can be used secondarily, but with extreme caution, to check some aspects of phonological and morphological structure that correlate with VH **accidentally**. This is perhaps why any type of VH is as useful as any other, therefore there is no natural principle beyond areal convenience whereby languages should develop any particular type of VH. Thus, in Yukuben, either of the two assimilations that produce mid vowels in noun-class prefixes would in itself aid parsing; it is only when they are taken together that they are no help at all.

Notes

* I thank Friedrich Neubarth for comments on this chapter. He bears no responsibility for the remaining shortcomings.

1 For a catastrophic attempt to do the last for Yukuben noun-class prefixes, see the discussion of Shimizu (1980), especially Table 9.13.

2 The elements of GP that are needed for VH are quite simple, few in number and fairly intuitive. Alongside the classic literature (Kaye et al., 1985, 1989, 1990; Lowenstamm, 1996), the reader is encouraged to consult Rennison and Neubarth (2003) and the other articles and bibliography in that volume.

3 Contrary to common beliefs, Optimality Theory is not a theory of phonology and cannot specify what phonology is or does. I am still trying to align a consonant left in a syllable, but nothing in OT tells me what a consonant or a syllable is.

4 The sequence εu seems to be a typo for **eu**. Neither sequence is mentioned anywhere else in the article.

5 Berry states that **uɛ̃** and **uɔ̃** are equated with oral **ue** and **uo** respectively. They can therefore safely be ignored, since **ue** and **uo** are already present in the table.

6 I find it hard to believe that this word contains a geminate [mm], but have preserved the transcriptions of the original.

7 Nyangumarda is an Australian, not an African language. It is included here only because its VH is so spectacular: the language has three vowels (/i,u,a/) and three progressive VH processes (I, U and A-harmony) – cf. Rennison (1987a).

8 The transcriptions of Mòoré used here are close to IPA and do not conform to the official orthography. In particular the vowel qualities and tones differ. However, the convention of doubling the last vowel of a long diphthong is kept. Thus, for example, in Table 9.6 [ʊa] is short and [ʊaa] long.

9 The syllable structure in GP diagrams is represented with the older terms O(nset) and N(ucleus) rather than C(onsonant) and V(owel) or the x and x̲ of Rennison and Neubarth (2003).

10 In Mòoré CV stems gain an extra empty CV before a morpheme boundary (here: the noun-class suffix). Usually it is the vowel of the original CV (here /i/) that associates to the V position of this new empty CV pair; but in this word (and several others with the same suffix) it is the initial consonant of the suffix that spreads to the left, producing a geminate $d+d$ which is realized as phonetic [t]. In this table we have two examples each of vowel lengthening and consonant gemination.

11 Normally, all noun-class suffixes of Mòoré are toneless, and their tone specification is determined (lexically) by the noun stem. In a few rare cases the noun-class suffix /-ba/ seems to have its own H tone; however, such words could be analysed as a 3-tone stem. The singular can only realize two tones, but the plural is long enough to realize three.

12 Admittedly, some seem quite odd, e.g., [±syllabic], [±consonantal], but the point is that the theory does not in principle exclude any feature from any phonological process (as the autosegmental theories, including GP, do). The argument that particular harmonies do not exist is an equally damning criticism of the SPE formalism as the observation that [+high,+low] is impossible because the tongue body cannot be in two places simultaneously. The fault lies with the theory, not with the real world.

13 By "local" I mean processes affecting two vowels with an empty intervening nucleus. On the phonetic level, the two vowels are strictly adjacent.

14 An anonymous reviewer suggests "ease of articulation" as a possible purpose of phonological assimilation. In my view, "ease of articulation" is a phonetic concept that can have far-reaching effects (especially in fast or casual speech). But it cannot be the purpose of phonological assimilation because phonology does not interact with phonetics directly, it simply sends outputs for phonetics to articulate and receives inputs from phonetics which it tries to interpret.

15 The sixth phonetic vowel, schwa ([ə]), is always the result of the reduction of one of the five full vowels in a closed final (i.e., stem) syllable.

16 Alternatively, this stem-initial A element could be regarded as a full vowel /a/ that always merges with the prefix vowel.

17 The underlying prefix vowel /a/ can, of course, be subject to vowel harmony, and therefore has three surface variants: [a], [e] or [o].

References

Anderson, J. M. & Colin J. E. (1980). *Studies in Dependency Phonology* (Ludwigsburg Studies in Language and Linguistics). Ludwigsburg: R. O. U. Strauch.

Anderson, J. M. & Colin J. E. (1987). *Principles of Dependency Phonology* (Cambridge Studies in Linguistics, 47). Cambridge: Cambridge University Press.

Antworth, E. L. (1990). *PC-KIMMO: A Two-level Processor for Morphological Analysis* (Occasional Publications in Computing, 16). Dallas, TX: Summer Institute of Linguistics.

Awobuluyi, A. O. & Bamgbose, A. (1967). "Two views of vowel harmony in Yoruba." *Journal of African Languages* 6: 268–273.

Beckman, J. N. (1997). "Positional faithfulness, positional neutralisation and Shona vowel harmony." *Phonology* 14: 1–46.

Berry, J. (1957). "Vowel harmony in Twi." *Bulletin of the School of Oriental and African Studies* 19: 124–130.

Carnochan, J. (1960). "Vowel harmony in Igbo." *African Language Studies* 1: 155–163.

Carson-Berndsen, J. (1998). *Time Map Phonology. Finite State Models and Event Logics in Speech Recognition* (Text, Speech and Language Technology). Dordrecht: Springer.

Casali, R. F. (2003). "[ATR] value asymmetries and underlying vowel inventory structure in Niger-Congo and Nilo-Saharan." *Linguistic Typology* 7: 307–382.

Casali, R. F. (2008). "ATR harmony in African languages." *Language and Linguistics Compass* 2/3: 496–549.

Cernak, M., Asaei, A. & Bourlard, H. (2016). "On structured sparsity of phonological posteriors for linguistic parsing." *Speech Communication* 84: 36–45.

Chomsky, N. A. & Halle, M. (1968). *The Sound Pattern of English*. New York, NY: Harper & Row.

Church, K. W. (1987a). *Phonological Parsing in Speech Recognition*. Boston: Kluwer.

Church, K. W. (1987b). "Phonological parsing and lexical retrieval." *Cognition* 25: 53–69.

Clements, G. N. (1977). "The autosegmental treatment of vowel harmony." In Wolfgang U. Dressler & Oskar E. Pfeiffer, eds, *Phonologica 1976*. Innsbruck: Innsbrucker Beiträge zur Sprachwissenschaft, 111–119.

Clements, G. N. (1981). "Akan vowel harmony: A nonlinear analysis." In George N. Clements, ed., *Harvard Studies in Phonology 2*. Bloomington, IN: Indiana University Linguistics Club, 108–177.

Fulop, S. A., Kari, E. & Ladefoged, P. (1998). "An acoustic study of the tongue root contrast in Degema vowels." *Phonetica* 55: 80–98.

Geytenbeek, B. (2008). *Nyangumarta. Nyangumarta – English Dictionary English – Nyangumarta Wordlist and Topical Wordlist*. Wangka Maya Pilbara Aboriginal Language Centre, www.wangkamaya.org.au/dictionaries/nyangumarta_ebook/files/nyangumarta%20dictionary%20wordlists%20cover%202008%20print%20ready%20burgman.pdf (accessed June 23, 2013).

Goldsmith, J. A. (1976). Autosegmental Phonology. Doctoral dissertation, MIT. Circulated by Indiana University Linguistics Club. Also available at: dspace.mit.edu/bitstream/handle/1721.1/16388/03188555-MIT.pdf?sequence=2 (accessed April 30, 2016).

Greenberg, J. H. (1951). "Vowel and nasal harmony in Bantu languages." *Revue Congolaise* 8: 813–820.

Greenberg, J. H. (1963). "Vowel harmony in African languages." In *Actes du Second Colloque Internationale de Linguistique Negro-Africaine*. Dakar: West African Languages Survey at the University of Dakar, 33–38.

Halle, M. & Clements, G. N. (1983). *Problem Book in Phonology: A Workbook for Introductory Courses in Linguistics and in Modern Phonology*. Cambridge, MA: MIT Press.

Hyman, L. M. (2002). "Is there a right-to-left bias in vowel harmony?" Ms. Paper presented at the 9th International Phonology Meeting, Vienna, Nov. 1, http://linguistics.berkeley.edu/~hyman/Hyman_Vienna_VH_paper_forma.pdf (accessed November 22, 2016).

Karttunen, L. (1983). KIMMO: A general morphological processor. Ms., *Texas Linguistic Forum*.

Katamba, F. (1984). "A nonlinear analysis of vowel harmony in Luganda." *Journal of Linguistics* 20: 257–275.

Kaye, J. D. (1985). "Kpokolo word list." Ms. File transmitted on BITNET.

Kaye, J. D., Lowenstamm, J. & Vergnaud, J. (1985). "The internal structure of phonological elements: A theory of charm and government." *Phonology Yearbook* 2: 305–328.

Kaye, J. D., Lowenstamm, J. & Vergnaud, J. (1989). "Konstituentenstruktur und Rektion in der Phonologie." In Martin Prinzhorn, ed., *Phonologie*. Opladen: Westdeutscher Verlag (Linguistische Berichte Sonderheft 2/1989), 31–75.

Kaye, J. D., Lowenstamm, J. & Vergnaud, J. (1990). "Constituent structure and government in phonology." *Phonology* 7: 193–231.

Koskenniemi, K. (1983). Two-Level Model for Morphological Analysis. Paper presented at *IJCAI*.

Krämer, M. (2003). *Vowel Harmony and Correspondence Theory*. Berlin: de Gruyter.

Ladefoged, P. (1964). *A Phonetic Study of West African Languages: An Auditory-Instrumental Survey*. Cambridge: Cambridge University Press.

Lowenstamm, J. (1996). "CV as the only syllable type." In Jacques Durand & Bernard Laks, eds, *Current Trends in Phonology: Models and Methods*. Salford: European Studies Research Institute, University of Salford, 419–442.

Maxwell, M. (1994). "Parsing using linearly ordered phonological rules." Ms., www-01.sil.org/computing/lascruces.html (accessed March 18, 2017).

Nevins, A. (2005). "Conditions on (dis)harmony." PhD dissertation, Massachusetts Institute of Technology.

Nevins, A. (2010). *Locality in Vowel Harmony* (Linguistic Inquiry Monograph 55). Cambridge, MA: MIT Press.

O'Grady, G. N. (1974–75). Lecture handouts and notes on Nyangumarda. Ms. Dept. of Linguistics, University of Salzburg.

Pensalfini, R. (2002). "Vowel harmony in Jingulu." *Lingua* 112: 561–586.

Rennison, J. R. (1984). "On tridirectional feature systems for vowels." *Wiener Linguistische Gazette* 33–34: 69–93.

Rennison, J. R. (1987a). "Vowel harmony and tridirectional vowel features." *Folia Linguistica* XXI: 337–354.

Rennison, J. R. (1987b). "On the vowel harmonies of Koromfe (Burkina Faso, West Africa)." In Wolfgang U. Dressler, Hans C. Luschützky, Oskar E. Pfeiffer & John R. Rennison, eds, *Phonologica 1984*. Cambridge: Cambridge University Press, 239–246.

Rennison, J. R. (1990). "Computer models of phonological theories, part 1." *Prague Bulletin of Mathematical Linguistics* 54: 37–56.

Rennison, J. R. (1991). "Computer models of phonological theories, part 2." *Prague Bulletin of Mathematical Linguistics* 55: 5–39.

Rennison, J. R. (1993). "Empty nuclei in Koromfe: a first look." *Linguistique Africaine* 11: 35–65.

Rennison, J. R. (1996). "Mòoré vowels revisited." Paper delivered at the Government Phonology Workshop (November 2, 1996) at the 8th Int. Phonology Meeting, Vienna, www.univie.ac.at/linguis tics/gp/rennison.pdf (accessed May 10, 2015).

Rennison, J, R. (1997a). "Syllables in Koromfe." *Gur Papers/Cahiers Voltaiques* 2: 117–127.

Rennison, J. R. (1997b). *Koromfe* (Routledge Descriptive Grammars). London: Routledge.

Rennison, J. R. (1999). "Syllables in Western Koromfe." In Harry van der Hulst & Nancy A. Ritter, eds, *The Syllable: Views and Facts*. Berlin: de Gruyter.

Rennison, J. R. (2014). "On vowel harmony and vowel reduction: Some observations on canonical shapes of disyllabic nouns in Yukuben, Mòoré and German." In Sabrina Bendjaballah, Noah Faust, Mohamed Lahrouchi & Nicola Lampitelli, eds, *The Form of Structure, the Structure of Form: Essays in Honor of Jean Lowenstamm* (Language Faculty and Beyond, 12). Amsterdam: Benjamins, pp. 37–56.

Rennison, J. R. (2016). "Some vowel harmonies in West Africa: What harmonises, what blocks?" Ms. Paper presented at the 2nd Symposium on West African Languages (SyWAL2016), Dept. of African Studies, University of Vienna, October 27–29.

Rennison, J. R. & Neubarth, F. (2003). "An x-bar theory of Government Phonology." In Stefan Ploch, ed., *Living on the Edge. 28 Papers in Honour of Jonathan Kaye*. Berlin: Mouton, 95–130.

Rose, S. & Walker, R. (2011). "Harmony systems." In John Goldsmith, Jason Riggle & Alan C.L. Yu, eds, *The Handbook of Phonological Theory*. Oxford: Blackwell, 240–290.

Schachter, P. & Fromkin, V. (1968). *A Phonology of Akan: Akuapem, Asante & Fante* (UCLA Working Papers in Phonetics, 9).

Shimizu, K. (1980). *Comparative Jukunoid*, Vol. 1. (Veröffentlichungen der Institute für Afrikanistik und Ägyptologie der Universität Wien, Beiträge zur Afrikanistik 5). Wien: Afro-Pub.

Stewart, J. M. (1967). "Tongue root position in Akan vowel harmony." *Phonetica* 16: 185–204.

Stewart, J. M. (1983). "Akan vowel harmony: The word structure conditions and the floating vowels." *Studies in African Linguistics* 14: 111–139.

Trubetskoy, N. S. (1939). *Grundzüge der Phonologie* (Travaux du Cercle Linguistique de Prague, 7).

Weitzenauer, S. M. (2008). "Numerus in Nominalklassen in Niger-Congo Sprachen am Beispiel des Yukuben." MA thesis, Dept. of Linguistics, University of Vienna.

Williams, E. (1976). "Underlying tone in Margi and Igbo." *Linguistic Inquiry* 7: 463–484.

Williams, G. (1998). "The Phonological Basis of Speech Recognition." PhD dissertation, Dept. of Linguistics, SOAS, University of London, http://web.onetel.net.uk/~geoff_williams/thesis/pdf/00intro. pdf (accessed March 18, 2017).

PART III

Phrase and sentence system

10

WEST AFRICAN SERIAL VERB CONSTRUCTIONS

The case of Akan and Ga

Dorothee Beermann and Lars Hellan

Introduction

Serial Verb Constructions (SVCs) are a construction type that consists of more than one verbal predicate, with none of the verbs taking the other as a complement. They are distinct from auxiliary constructions and, as opposed to Complex Predicate constructions,[1] their predicate components are not nouns or adjectives, but only verbs. The phenomenon was first described by Christaller (1875, p. 141) for Twi, and Westermann (1907/1930) for Ewe. The notion 'Serial Verb Construction' was first used by Balmer and Grant (1929), taken up in Stewart (1963), and is by now a recognized name of the construction. The growing availability of detailed descriptions of serialization across languages has led to a better understanding of the differences between particular forms of serialization,[2] but has also led to growing doubts in the usefulness of the term as it might not refer to a sufficiently coherent phenomenon (most recently Bisang 2009).

Next to the construction itself, the languages that feature it have been scrutinized for possible commonalities. Figure 10.1 represents a list of properties proposed on one such approach (Schiller 1990).

Among the West African language families that have developed SVCs are the Niger-Congo languages of the South and North Volta branch, as well as the Kordofan, Mande and Atlantic languages, and the Ijoid languages. In addition, West African Creoles can be serializing languages (Winford, 1993; Veenstra, 1996).

| little productive morphology |
| no agreement |
| no 'movement' phenomena other than topicalization |
| no passive with marked agent |
| aspect rather than tense system |
| a high degree of syntactic polysemy |
| preference for SVO word order |

Figure 10.1   Typological properties of SVC languages according to Schiller (1990)

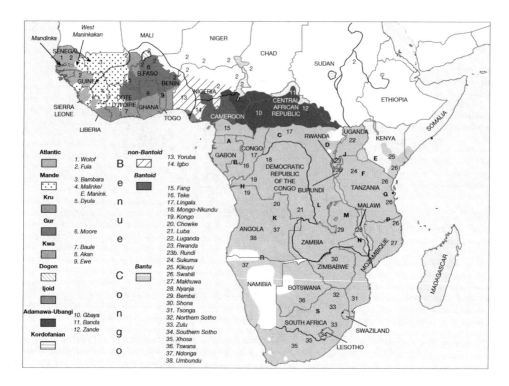

Figure 10.2 Map of African languages

The properties that one expects of a serialization language according to Figure 10.1 may, on the whole, apply to the West African languages mentioned, yet, this set of properties provides neither necessary nor sufficient conditions for a language to become an SVC language. Moreover, being phrased in terms of degree such as 'little morphology' or 'high degree of polysemy', these properties accommodate variation, which is quite realistic since West African languages with a fairly rich verb morphology, such as the languages of the Mountain-Togo region, less inflecting languages such as Akan or Ga, and finally the West African Creole Krio with no inflection, are all serializing languages.

The following section is an exposition of the properties of SVC constructions using Aikhenvald's categories, followed by a discussion of some theoretical issues that have figured prominently in the discussion of SVCs. The third section addresses the general role of verbal valency relative to SVCs. The fourth section discusses possible methodologies for the further study of SVCs. Examples used for illustration are taken mainly from our corpus of Akan and Ga, but our discussion is aimed at the phenomenon in general.

Properties of SVCs

Aikhenvald (2006)

Aikhenvald (2006) suggests that SVCs can be described according to the following four parameters: Composition, Contiguity, Wordhood and Marking. They are characterized as follows (Aikhenvald, op. cit., p. 3):

Composition: symmetrical serial verb constructions consist of two or more verbs each chosen from a semantically and grammatically unrestricted class. Asymmetrical serial verb constructions include a verb from a grammatically or semantically restricted class (e.g. a motion, or a posture verb).

Contiguity versus non-contiguity of components: verbs which form a serial verb construction may have to be next to each other, or another constituent may be allowed to intervene between them.

Wordhood of components: components of a serial verb construction may or may not form independent grammatical or phonological words.

Marking of grammatical categories in a serial verb construction: verbal categories—such as, for instance, person of the subject and object(s); tense, aspect, modality; negation; or valency changes—may be marked just once per construction ('single marking'); or can be marked on every component ('con-cordant marking').

We will comment on these parameters in turn.

Composition: types of sentence schemata

The distinction symmetric vs. asymmetric coincides roughly with Christaller's (1875, p. 141) distinction between 'accidental' and 'essential' combinations, and with the dichotomy later proposed in Osam (1994) between 'Chaining SVC' and 'Integrated SVC (ISVC)', terms that were taken up by Hellan et al. (2003), and which we will employ here. A Chaining SVC is exemplified in (1) and an ISVC in (2):

(1) Ama tuu bayerɛ twitwa noa dii   Language: Akan

"*Ama uprooted (tuber of) yam, cut it in pieces, boiled them (and) ate*"

ama	tu	u	bayerɛ	twitwa	noa	di	i
Ama	uproot		yam	cut	cook	eat	
Ama.SBJ.AGT	*uproot*	PAST	*yam*.DO	*cut*	*cook*	*eat*	PAST
Np	Vtr		N	Vtr	Vtr	Vtr	

(2) Papa no yɛ adwuma de kyɛ aban   Language: Akan

"*The man works for the government for free*"

papa	no	yɛ	adwuma	de	kyɛ	aban
man.SBJ		*do*	*work*.OBJ	*use*	*give_free*	OBJ
N	DET	V1	N	V2	V3	N
Generated in TypeCraft.						*government*

In (2) the ISVC consists of the second and third verb (marked as 'V2' and 'V3'), specifying the beneficiary of the work event.

In general, ISVC verbs may form tight clusters, and one of the verbs may take on a meaning which, although related to its lexical specification, is specialized in the context of the SVC;

such meanings include aspect/tense, polarity, as well as directionality or manner. We may call such verbs the *support* verbs of the construction, or the *satellite* verbs. It is mostly undisputed that chaining as well as Integrated SVCs are mono-clausal and that their verbs share a subject and may share an object. From an analytic perspective the sharing of objects has been more controversial. According to one view they can be shared in chaining constructions across juxtaposed verb phrases, given that the object is semantically licensed by each of the verbs. In ISVCs, on the other hand, where verbs are tightly integrated and objects may play different syntactic and semantic roles, it is less clear whether the sharing of arguments is a structural process or purely semantic in nature (see Hellan et al. (2003) for a suggestion of how to handle argument sharing in different types of SVCs).

For either type of SVC, in all cases the serializing verbs inflect on a par with single finite verbs, that is, in the formally standard way for the language, and each verb can take an object situated in the standard way of a governed NP relative to the verb (that is, notwithstanding the fact that 'support' verbs may have a reduced inflectional pattern and that in SVCs the serialized verbs need to express the same value for TAM as well as polarity).

Contiguity: parameters of wordhood

Contiguity or tightness of verbal elements is observed in West African languages including the creoles that maintain a system of verbal satellites that serve in the expression of TAM and polarity. Contiguity is observed for free verbal satellites in Krio (Jones 1971; Michaelis et al. 2013 (feature 45–46) and Beermann forthcoming). Ga, on the other hand, maintains a system of *preverbs*, that is verbal satellites that are more integrated into the verb such that they form an extended verbal complex with the main predicate (Dakubu 2004a, 2008; Dakubu et al. 2007), and are closer to being verbal clitics than independent verbs. Also here we observe a fixed order, a loss of their ability to inflect, and a tonal contour specific to the cluster. Examples from Ga illustrate this point. In (3) and (4),[3] *kɛ* is transitive, in (3) with a meaning like 'take', in (4) it marks the onset of the event serving as an integral part of a cluster of three verbal clitics and a main verb.

(3) Alɔnte lɛ kɛ adidɔ lɛ ewo Simon daaŋ.[4] **Language: Ga**

"*The cat has put the fly into Simon's mouth.*"

alɔnte	lɛ	kɛ	adidɔ	lɛ	e	wo	simon	daaŋ
cat	FOC	*take*	*fly*	FOC	PRF			*mouth*
N	PRT	V1	N	PRT	V2		Np	N

(4) Ekɛɛ akɛ okɛkabaha. Language: Ga

"*He said that you should not come give (it).*"

e	kɛɛ	akɛ	ò	ˋkɛ́	ká	bà	hã́
3SG	*AOR.say*	*that*	2SG	SBJV	PROHIB.SBJV	INGR	*give*
V		COMP	V				

210

Wordhood of components

Example (4) above illustrates not only contiguity but also (the onset) of wordhood. The string *okɛkabaha* is not only an orthographic word but also has the phonological properties of a word. Different also from serialized verbs in Ga, verbs in an extended verbal complex express tense, aspect, modality, and polarity only once and not iteratively.

Marking

'Concordant marking' is well known, for instance, in Akan, which assigns a single TAM and polarity value in SVCs repeating it on each verb in the chain. Interesting is the case of consecutive marking, where a V1 in the progressive or in the future needs to be followed by verbs that carry an a- prefix.[5] The question is still open on whether the consecutive a-marking is aspectual (Osam 1994) or infinitival in nature (cf. Boadi 2005).

While contiguity, wordhood and marking are parameters central especially for the expression of TAM and polarity in serializing languages, the composition parameter addresses different types of sentence schemata associated with serialization. Figure 10.3 represents Chaining SVCs and Integrated SVCs as 'pure' cases, while Type C represents Chaining SVCs with ISVCs as component parts, thus a possible sentential construct composed from the 'pure' combination types as components. Type C is thus a case where an ISVC constitutes a 'VP slot' in a Chaining SVC. For example in (5), the overall structure is a Chaining SVC. It expresses consecutive non-overlapping events, with the carrying of the fly and locating it in the man's mouth. Internally, however, these two events are expressed as ISVCs. V1 and V2 describe the first event as a TAKE-HAVE event, and the second event is introduced by *de* marking the onset of the PLACEMENT event.

(5) Nti watam nwansena no ahyɛ ne ano mu de akɔto papa no so   Language: Akan

"So, it carried the housefly in its mouth and put it in the man's mouth."

nti	w	a	tam	nwansena	no	a	hyɛ	ne	ano	mu
so	3SG	PRF	take	*house_fly*	DEF	PRF	*wear*	3SG.	*mouth.*	*inside*
								POSS	INSTR	
PRT	V1			N	DEM	V2		PN	N	Nrel

de	a	kɔ	to	papa	no	so
	PRF	*go*	*put*	*man*	DEF	*on.*LOC
V3	V4				DET	PREP

Generated in TypeCraft.

Type A	Chaining SVC	$VP_1 + VP_2 \ldots + VP_n$
Type B	Integrated SVC	$(v^*_{satellite})V_1 \cdots (v^*_{satellite})V_n$
Type C	Complex Chaining SVC	$[\,V_1\,V_2\,]_{VP1} \cdots + [(v^*_{satellite})V]_{VPn}$

Figure 10.3   Main sentence schemata of West African SVCs

Example (6), in a similar vein, describes a series of three events; the first event is described by a single verb while the following events are described by complex constructs, the first being the ICSV *kɔ waree* 'go marry' and the second being the ISVC *de ne yere baa Norway*, which can be interpreted either in a commutative sense as in 'He came with his wife to Norway', or as the theme of a bringing event, as in the free translation in (6).

(6) Ernest kɔɔ Ghana kɔ waree de ne yere baa Norway   Language: Akan

"*Ernest went to Ghana to marry and brought his wife to Norway.*"

ernest	kɔ	ɔ	ghana	kɔ	waree	de	ne	yere	ba	a	norway
SBJ		PAST		*go*	marry	*take*	3SG	*wife*	come	PAST	
Np	V		N	V1	V2	V3	PNposs	N	V4		Np

This SVC sentence pattern, of Type C – the *Complex Chaining SVC*, seems on the whole quite widespread, and can be counted as a *clause type*, while Chaining SVC and ISVC per se represent *combination* types.

Having thus addressed aspects of contiguity, wordhood, marking, and types of sentence schemata associated with serialization, we next turn to central issues in the formalization of SVCs.

Syntactic and semantic 'unity' of SVCs

We now turn to two central themes in the investigation of serialization, namely the structuralist concept of SVCs representing 'one verb', and the cognitive linguistics assumption that an SVC expresses a 'single event'. Originating from different analytic traditions, these two central constructs have influenced theoretical and descriptive linguists alike.

Durie (1997) defines an 'archetypal SVC' as follows: "The archetypal serial verb construction consists of a sequence of two or more verbs which in various (rather strong) senses, together act like a single verb" (Durie 1997: 289–90). Durie's definition perhaps recalls the 'Contiguity' and 'Wordhood' parameter discussed above, but uses the putative one-word nature of SVCs as an encompassing term. The assumption may seem to go naturally together with the assumption that an SVC construction can represent a single event, given a further assumption to the effect that *a single verb expresses a single event*. But is this true? And, more basically, what does it mean to 'express a single event'? We consider the latter question in the next subsection, here we focus on the proposition that an SVC be conceived as a single verb.

SVCs as 'one verb'

Two related circumstances may suggest that the verb sequence in an SVC acts like one verb:

1   The array of overt arguments of serialized VPs in Chaining SVCs and in Integrated SVC schemata of the type '$(v*_{satellite})$ V_1... $(v*_{satellite})$ V_n' is often the same as what one finds in mono-verbal clauses.
2   There is essentially just one exponent of the subject argument either realized as nominal unit or as a pronominal clitic/affix mostly associated with the V1 and rarely resumed in subsequent verbs. Also for objects, V1 is typically the host while all the other occurrences are anaphoric, and morphologically either identical or reduced replicas if not implied.

To illustrate, Example (7), from Akan, is an ISVC that instantiates what can be seen as an extended ditransitive frame. Relative to the overall frame of the construction, the second VP *yii sika* provides the Theme argument, while the third VP *maa yarifɔɔ* expresses the goal. The first VP specifies, with intention and willingness, the modality of the event, and thus does not add to the argument structure of the construction. Thus, although there are three verbs, the number of role-bearing arguments expressed is the same as we would find with a single ditransitive verb.

(7) **Ama de adwenepa yii sika maa yarifoɔ no   Language: Akan**

"*Ama gave money to the sick with good intentions.*"

ama	de	adwene	pa	yi	i	sika	ma	a
Ama.SBJ	*take*	*thought.*	*good*	*take*	PAST	*money.OBJ*	*give*	PAST
Np	V1tr	N		V2tr		N	V3dtr	

yari	foɔ	no
sick.OBJ	NMLZ.AGT	DEF
N		DET

Relative to valency the following examples from Ga make the same point as just made for Akan.

(8) **Hólé-mɔ́**   **bɛntsi-i lɛ**   **ó-hã̌**   **mi**   **Language: Ga**
   raise-IMPER   bench-PL   DEF   2S.SBJV-give 1S PRO   Examples from
   V   N   V   PN   Dakubu (2013)
   "bring me the benches"

(9) **Mi-wo**   **gbekɛ lɛ**   **kɛ-tee**   **skul**
   1S-collect   child DEF   TAKE-go   school
   V   N   V   N
   "I took the child to school."

Comparing the Ga sentences in (8) and (9) with their English translation, Ga lexicalizes a 'Sachverhalt' that is implied in the English event identification, naming the *coming into possession* between the agent and the theme of the following event. That I need to lift a bench before I can bring it, or 'be' accompanied by the child (for example, by first collecting it) is in the English framing of the bringing/taking to a location events *implied*, but not so in Ga. In this sense serialized events arise not only from 'decomposition' in the grammatical articulation of a single event frame, but also through re-framing the event leading to differences in event identification. Thus, for English, we may think of ditransitive frames as expressing X CAUSE Y TO HAVE Z leading to a double-object frame. We can think of the same event in Ga as a HAVE CAUSE HAVE situation, where also syntactically the subject argument does not compose directly with the second HAVE event – the causer of the second event is first the subject argument of a predicate that sets him in a HAVE relation to the theme. The serialization frame thus serves to relate the subject argument of the first predicate, the V1, to the CAUSE HAVE segment of the overall event.

Event				
TAM LOC	Method	Core	Orientation	Rational
Tense	Instrument	Actants	Directionality	Cause
Aspect	Manner		Source	Reason
Modality				Purpose
Location				Result

Figure 10.4 Expanded Event Model (Schiller 2001)

It appears that while event identification, in the sense just outlined, is specific to SVCs and thus part of their semantic signature, this does not entail that it is accompanied by a change in the basic valency specification for the predicates involved. Reconsidering (7) in this light, we see that *de* is transitive and does not share its object and neither does *ma* share its indirect object. What is shared is the object of *yi* thus allowing both of the verbs *yi* and *ma* to fulfil their valency requirements. We will pursue this issue in the next section.

SVCs as 'single complex events'

It is considered a hallmark of Integrated SVCs that they express a single event (cf., notably, Ameka and Essegbey 2013). Using the notion of a *maximally expanded event* (Schiller 2001), we would like to refine this position.

A maximally expanded event, according to Schiller (2001), is specified along the semantic parameters specified in Figure 10.4.

Classificatory studies of SVCs seem to suggest that all of these event attributes can be expressed as components of an Integrated SVC giving rise to different well-known types of SVCs, as there are 'Locative SVC', 'Instrumental SVC', 'Manner SVC', 'Purpose SVC', 'Causal SVC' and so forth (Stewart 2001; Ogie 2009). Conceptually we can conceive of complex events as structures where the construction is compatible with any of the parameters indicated in Figure 10.4. This is compatible with the view that verbs in an ISVC are, on the lexical level, well-behaved verbs of the grammar of the language. As part of a SVC they contribute with their lexical specification to serve in any of the slots of an extended event as suggested in Figure 10.4. The semantic unifiability of its sub-frames constitutes the acceptability of an ISVC and in this sense constitutes a single event.

The idea of single eventhood has been applied also to Chaining SVCs. Defina (2016) reports research investigating the correspondences between *gestures* on the one hand and SVCs and overt event-coordination on the other in Avatime (a Togo Mountain language). Building on evidence from gesture studies, Defina observes that certain one-movement gestures systematically accompany mono-verbal clauses and SVCs, whereas explicit coordination of clauses is systematically accompanied by multi-movement gestures. The gesture studies show no difference between ISVCs and Chaining SVCs (although tests with the latter were relatively few compared with those with ISVCs). Thus, even if there is a correlation between gestures and event structuring, it does not seem to match the event structure differences we associate with Chaining SVCs vs. ISVCs. Therefore, it might be suggested that the one- vs. many-movement gestures reflect not so much single eventhood as, perhaps, narrative packaging.

We know already that chaining and coordination may realize the same state of affairs. Consider then the examples below from Akan (Baah 2015). In both examples Afia, the subject, is topicalized, a subject clitic appears on the V1, and in the (a) cases the V2 shares the subject with V1. The (b) cases are coordinations with *ne* as conjunction, and both verbs express their subjects independently. In both cases the event pattern is that of parallel events – that is, SVCs and coordination express the same event structure.

(10) a Afia ɔ-ɔ-to ndwom sa.
Afia 3SG-PROG-sing song dance
"Afia is singing and dancing."

b Afia ɔ-ɔ-to ndwom ne ɔ-ɔ-sa
Afia 3SG-PROG-sing song and 3SG-PROG-dance
"Afia is singing and dancing."

(11) a Afia ɔ-ɔ-nante kasa
Afia 3SG-PGOG-walk talk
"Afia is walking and talking."

b Afia ɔ-ɔ-nante ne ɔ-ɔ-kasa.
Afia 3SG-PROG-walk and 3SG-PROG-talk
"Afia is walking and (she) talking."

Chaining SVC are, in general, instances of temporal consecutive or overlapping events strung together, and, as each of the consecutive events might take place at different locations, they fail to fulfil what will be normally seen as a logical condition on single events, namely a single (possibly particularized) specification of the spatio-temporal anchoring of the event. From this viewpoint it is thus as expected that ISVCs and Chaining SVCs come out as contrasting in their event status – ISVCs expressing single events in the way explained above, and Chaining SVCs in general not.

Valency of verbs in SVCs

In the preceding sections, we suggested that the array of argument types that can be found within an ISVC will be approximately the same as is found with verbs standing on their own expressing the same type of event. In connection with Figure 10.4, we also suggested that verbs in an ISVC contribute with their lexical specification to serve in any of the slots of an extended event. A looming factor in such consideration is to what extent a serializing language on the whole has valency frames in its verbal system corresponding to what is found in a non-serializing language. From the valency lexicon for Ga created by Dakubu (2013), reported in Dakubu and Hellan (2016), it seems that verb valency is, for Ga, as much of a lexico-grammatical factor as in any non-serializing language.[6] Taking this as indicative of the situation in the Kwa languages, it follows that there must be lexico-grammatical principles by which valency requirements of individual verbs are accommodated relative to the SVC. Since many verbs take more than one frame, it remains to be investigated, for any verb, which of these frames can be used in SVCs. There may also be variation in the position in the verb sequence in which the various valency frames can be used. Satellite verbs often being polysemous, or at least occurring in multiple frames, such investigations will be especially pertinent for ISVCs.

The Ga valency lexicon in question represents about 800 verbs, and many verbs have up to 10–15 frames. It appears that by far the most common configuration is transitive, relatively few verbs occur only in intransitive constructions, and most verbs that occur ditransitively can also occur with only one object. In this vein, the tables below show distributions relative

Table 10.1 The number of verbs that can occur in various valency frames

Class of	Number of verbs
Verbs that occur in intransitive frame only	51
Verbs that occur in transitive frame only	144
Verbs that occur in ditransitive frame only	4
Verbs that occur in intransitive and transitive frame	44
Verbs that occur in transitive and ditransitive frame	9
Verbs that occur in intransitive, transitive and ditransitive frame	6
Verbs that occur in SVC only	20
Verbs that occur in transitive and SVC frame	15
Verbs that occur in intransitive, transitive and SVC frame	14
Verbs that occur in intransitive, transitive, ditransitive and SVC frame	3

Table 10.2 For each type of valency/construction frame how many verbs it can be used with

Type of frame	Number of entries
Intransitive frame	245
Transitive frame	1027
Ditransitive frame	133
SVC	166
Intransitive with a clausal complement	23
Transitive with a clausal complement	42

to 470 of the verbs.[7] Table 10.1 shows the number of verbs that can occur in various valency frames, where also occurrence in an ISVC is included, some in only one type of frame, others in more than one.[8]

Table 10.2 shows for each type of valency/construction frame how many verbs it can be used with (it is possible for one and the same verb to have more than one usage within a given valency/construction type).

Without illustrating these figures further, it seems reasonable to assume that while ISVCs draw their meaning from a limited inventory of semantic parameters, for instance those portrayed in Figure 10.4, the verbs in an ISVC (and obviously also in a Chaining SVC) partake in the construction on the basis of the meanings and valency frames they carry as sole verbs of a sentence.

Methodologies and further research

Ideas relating to prototyping have had a strong influence on the investigation of SVCs, not surprisingly so since it is a way to deal with variation in how languages realize serialization. Prototyping allows for categorizing constructions according to how close they are to the assumed prototypes, which typically reflect theoretical constructs, typological, universal or other. Kroeger (2004), summarizing the literature at the time, presents what he calls characteristic and diagnostic features of SVCs. In addition, he discusses diagnostic tests that serve to "determine whether a particular construction is in fact a 'true' SVC" (Kroeger 2004: 229), that is to say, which come close to representing the prototype. Kroeger's list has been influential and is therefore reproduced here in full.

Table 10.3 Prototypical features of SVCs as suggested by Kroeger (2004: 229–230)

Prototypical features of SVCs
1 Two or more morphologically independent verbs[9] none of which is an AUX.
2 No conjunctions or other overt markers of subordination or coordination.
3 A single intonation contour.
4 Representing a single (possibly complex) event.
5 One tense, aspect, modality and polarity specification, although these features might be specified redundantly in patterns of morphological agreement.
6 Verbs sharing at least one argument.
7 One grammatical subject.
8 No two overt NPs which refer to the same argument.

Given such a set of attributes, a particular serialization can be classified in terms of its deviation from the prototype.

Prototype approaches have been criticized by Bickel (2010) and others before him by pointing out the unavoidable arbitrariness that lies in establishing the prototype. Moreover, linguistic prototypes reflect theoretical assumptions, and this means that to be a non-prototypical serialization simply means that this serialization is less expected than another given standard assumptions.

A good question then is how we can deal with linguistic variation not understood as deviation from a standard but as linguistic diversity. Bickel suggests a multivariate typological approach that aims to integrate quantitative methods and traditional linguistic theory. Different from earlier approaches where a certain construction has to satisfy all criteria reflecting priori assumptions, a multivariate typological analysis measures the distribution of complex structures (constructions) in a space delimited by a given set of typological parameters.

This is interesting in two respects: Multivariate analysis breaks with the perception of linguistic variation as deviation, and, second, it explicitly introduces diversity as an object of theoretical studies. Methodologically, such an approach is demanding, as it requires a suitable dataset and a research design that transforms known linguistic attributes of serialization into measurable scalar parameters. Concerning West African serialization languages, very little linguistic data is public: in our sample we have mainly Akan and Ga, as well as Krio, and thus not the coverage we would need. What is needed is therefore a methodology that not only gives us the resources we need but that is suitable for the work with African languages. Such a methodology needs to proceed incrementally and cyclically. Technically we need to be able to add new parameters as they are discovered, with the possibility of adjusting previous data with the relevant specifications. Pursuing linguistic research that is equally as much resource building as it is analytic must also allow us to redefine the domain of investigation. For example, SVCs are one form of *multiverb constructions* (MVCs); MVCs have in common that the predicate-bearing categories are verbs, and that these are not connected via conjunctions; otherwise, the notion does not require the presence of any of the other SVC properties we have discussed (cf., e.g., Ameka 2003); thus, MVCs are a 'super-set' of whatever constructions may qualify as SVCs. The category of MVCs will include preverb clusters as illustrated in (3) and (4), whose components by assumption are not words and thus not SVCs; the notion will also include 'verbid' constructions in the sense of Dakubu (2004b), which are VPs juxtaposed to VPs but without subject sharing or TAM sharing – these VPs behave as adverbials of time and place. Essential to future research on SVCs might be to extend its scope to MVCs, of which the SVCs might only be a special case. For a data-intensive approach to linguistics, like the one we

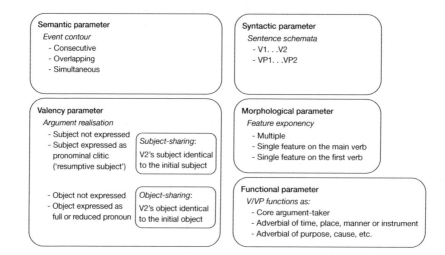

Figure 10.5 Parameters for specification of multi-verb constructions

advocate here, this means that our research data need to be structured flexibly enough to easily adopt to demands of the field.

A parametrized approach to capturing variation for SVC is work-intensive and not without challenges, as it combines resource building with formal linguistic approaches, processes that must be incremental and cyclic. This is not the place for trying to define concise annotation and data storage procedures. However, in this chapter we have named some of the features that need to be considered when capturing SVCs. To conclude this chapter we have brought together in a chart some of the most important aspects.

Conclusion

The chapter has discussed serial verb constructions (SVCs) as found in West African languages, illustrated especially with examples from the Kwa languages Akan and Ga. Starting with an overview over properties of SVCs at large, we especially considered SVC sentence schemata, wordhood issues and agreement patterns. We discussed the 'being one word' approach and the notion of single event. It was important to us to set the notion of single eventhood in relation to valency requirements of the individual verbs that form an SVC. Moreover, we were fortunate since we could work with a Ga valency lexicon of about 800 words created by Dakubu (2013), which allowed us to relate SVC schema to the total inventory of valency frames for Ga. This allows us to see that, at least with Ga, we have a language that is not so unlike in valency to other languages that do not feature SVCs. Overall our study is data-intensive, and also for the future we suggest a corpus-based approach for handling diversity for multi-verb constructions. Our concluding remark is that such an approach may well proceed without any recourse to descriptive, or theoretical or typological prototypes, but rather be based on what one might call a grounded parametrised approach. The diversity of multi-verb constructions is still not descriptively covered or analytically comprehended, and the best strategy for further research is to keep analytic parameters open. With respect to the development of linguistic theory, maybe we can round off with the title of a well-known book: *The Beautiful Ones Are Not Yet Borne.*[10]

Notes

1 See Butt (1997), Andrews and Manning (1999).
2 Among works that may be mentioned: Schachter (1974), Foley and Olson (1985), Payne (1985), Baker (1989), Bodomo (1997).
3 From TypeCraft (typecraft.org).
4 The verb is specified as in the perfect tense, yet since we do not have tonal annotations this might well be a simple PAST. Kropp Dakubu distinguishes between the *e* in aorist and the *e* of perfect with this verb in the context of a 3SG marker (cf. Dakubu 2009, 2013).
5 First described in Dolphyne 1987.
6 This, notwithstanding the circumstance that the types of formally distinguished valency frames obtaining across languages can vary significantly – for instance, preliminary comparisons of valency frame types for Ga and English suggest that they have less than 20 percent of their valency frames in common (see, e.g., Dakubu and Hellan, 2017). For comparative valency studies of other West African languages, see, e.g., Ameka (2013), Creissels (2015), and Schaefer and Egbokhare (2015).
7 Files with entries under each combination are accessible at https://typecraft.org/tc2wiki/Ga_Valence_ Profile in a zipped version, with meaning and examples obtained at the link Ga_verb_dictionary_for_ digital_processing.
8 Quoting from its introduction (Dakubu 2013, p. 2):

> This dictionary focuses on constructions that can be regarded as single clauses, where the criterion for a single clause is that there is only one subject with just one semantic role, and although there may be more than one verb, each with one or more objects, no two objects perform the same semantic role. Verb predicates may therefore be either simple (one (expanded) verb) or complex.
>
> A predicate may be headed by two (in this language, rarely three) verbs (including expanded verbs), which unify both semantically and grammatically to form a *serial verb construction*. What this means in Ga is that there is a single referential subject, which is expressed before the first verb and may or may not be cliticized on the second as a resumptive pronoun. The subject has the same role in respect of both verbs. Each verb may have one or more objects, but each object has a different role, so that the argument roles for the event are distributed across the construction.
>
> All of these multi-verb constructions are to be distinguished from series of otherwise independent verb expressions that relate to different events but for which the subject is not repeated.

9 Kroeger's term 'morphologically independent verbs' seems to have been taken up in Haspelmath (2016), who talks about SVCs as monoclausal constructions "consisting of multiple independent verbs . . . with no predicate–argument relation between the verbs." Both authors thereby seem to refer to the paratactic nature of SVCs.
10 By Ayi Kwei Armah. Published in 1968 by Houghton Mifflin.

References

Aikhenvald, A. Y. (2006). "Serial verb constructions in typological perspective". In A. Y. Aikhenvald & R. M. W. Dixon (eds) *Serial Verb Constructions: A Cross-Linguistic Typology*, 1–68. Oxford: Oxford University Press.
Alsina, A., J. Bresnan & P. Sells (eds) (1997). *Complex Predicates*. Stanford, CA: CSLI Publications.
Ameka, F. K. (2003). "Multiverb constructions in a West African areal typological perspective". In Beermann, D. and L. Hellan (eds) *Proceedings of the Workshop on Multi-Verb Constructions*, Trondheim Summer School.
Ameka, F. K. (2013). "Three place predicates in West African serializing languages". *Studies in African Linguistics* 42(1): 1–32.
Ameka F. K. & J. Essegbey (2013). "Serialising languages: Verb-framed, satellite-framed or neither?" *Ghana Journal of Linguistics* 2(1): 19–38.
Andrews, A. & C. Manning (1999). *Complex Predicates and Information Spreading in LFG*. Stanford, CA: Stanford Monographs, CSLI Publications.

Baah, J. (2015). Iconicity in Verb Serialisation: Re-analyzing Akan SVCs. MA thesis, University of Bergen, Norway.

Baker, M. C. (1989). "Object sharing and projection in serial verb constructions". *Linguistic Inquiry* 20: 513–553.

Balmer, W. T. & F. C. F. Grant (1929). *A Grammar of the Fante-Akan Language*. London: Atlantis Press.

Beermann, D. (forthcoming). "Tense, modality and aspect in Krio: A corpus-based study". In J. Essegbey, D. Kallulli & A. Bodomo (eds) *The Grammar of Verbs and Their Arguments: A Cross-Linguistic Perspective*. Contemporary African Linguistics series of the Language Science Press.

Bickel, B. (2010). "Capturing particulars and universals in clause linkage: A multivariate analysis". In Bril, I. *Clause Linking and Clause Hierarchy: Syntax and Pragmatics*, 51–102. Amsterdam: John Benjamins Publishing Company.

Bisang, W. (2009). "Serial verb constructions". *Language and Linguistics Compass* 3/3: 792–814.

Boadi, L. (1968). "Some aspects of Akan deep syntax". *Journal of West African Languages*, 5.1.

Boadi, L. (2005). *Three Major Syntactic Structures in Akan: Interrogatives, Complementation, and Relativisation*. Accra: Black Mask Limited.

Bodomo, A. (1997). Paths and Pathfinders: Exploring the Syntax and Semantics of Complex Verbal Predicates in Dagaare and Other Languages. Doctoral dissertation, NTNU, Trondheim.

Butt, M. (1997). "Complex Predicates in Urdu". In A. Alsina, J. Bresnan & P. Sells (eds) *Complex Predicates*, 107–149. Stanford, CA: CSLI.

Creissels, D. (2015). "Valency properties of Mandinka verbs". In A. Makchukov & B. Comrie (eds) *Valency Classes in the World's Languages*, 221–260. Berlin: De Gruyter Mouton.

Christaller, J. G. (1875). *A Grammar of the Asante and Fante Language Called Tshi*. Upper Saddle River, NJ: Gregg Press.

Dakubu, M. E. K. (2004a). "The Ga preverb *kɛ* revisited". In M. E. K. Dakubu and E. K. Osam (eds) *Studies in the Languages of the Volta Basin 2*, 113–134. Legon: Linguistics Dept.

Dakubu, M. E. K. (2004b). "Ga clauses without syntactic subjects". *Journal of African Languages and Linguistics* 25.1: 1–40.

Dakubu, M. E. K. (2008). "Ga verb features". In Ameka and Dakubu (eds) *Aspect and Modality in Kwa Languages*, 91–134. Amsterdam & Philadelphia: John Benjamins Publishing Co.

Dakubu, M. E. K. (2009). *Ga-English Dictionary with English-Ga Index*. Accra: Black Mask Publishers.

Dakubu, M. E. K. (2013). Ga verb dictionary with construction templates. Ms.

Dakubu, M. E. K., & H. D. Beermann (2007). "Verb sequencing constraints in Ga: Serial verb constructions and the extended verb complex". In S. Müller (ed) *Proceedings of the 14th International Conference on Head-Driven Phrase Structure Grammar*. Stanford, CA: CSLI Publications, http://csli-publications.stanford.edu.

Dakubu, M. E. K. and L. Hellan (2016). "Ga Verb classes and Valency classes". Paper presented at SyWAL 2, Vienna.

Dakubu, M. E. K. and L. Hellan (2017). "A labeling system for valency: Linguistic coverage and applications". In L. Hellan, A. Malchukov & M. Cennamo (eds) *Contrastive Studies in Verbal Valency*. Amsterdam & Philadelphia: John Benjamins Publishing Co.

Defina, R. (2016). Serial verb constructions and conceptual events in Avatime. PhD thesis, University of Leiden, The Netherlands.

Dolphyne, F. (1987). "On negating the consecutive verb in Akan". *Journal of West African Languages*, 17.2: 70–81.

Durie. M. (1997). "Grammatical structures in verb serialization". In Alsina A., J. Bresnan & P. Sells (eds) *Complex Predicates*. Stanford, CA: CSLI Publications.

Essegbey, J., D. Kallulli and A. Bodomo (eds) (Forthcoming) The grammar of verbs and their arguments: A cross-linguistic perspective-Papers in honor of Lars Hellan. Contemporary African Linguistics series of the Language Science Press.

Foley. J. and S. Olson (1985). "Clausehood and verb serialization". In J. Nichols & A. Woodbury (eds) *Grammar Inside and Outside the Clause*. Cambridge: Cambridge University Press.

Haspelmath, M. (2016). "The serial verb construction: Comparative concept and cross-linguistic generalizations". *Language and Linguistics*, 17(3): 291–319.

Hellan, L., D. Beermann and E. Sætherø (2003). "Towards a typology of serial verb constructions in Akan". In M. E. K. Dakubu and E. K. Osam (eds) *Studies in the Languages of the Volta Basin 1: Proceedings of the Annual Colloquium of the Legon-Trondheim Linguistics Project*, 4–6 December 2002, 61–86. Legon: Linguistics Dept., University of Ghana.

Hellan, L. (forthcoming). "Modeling situation types in grammar". In J. Essegbey, D. Kallulli & A. Bodomo (eds) *The Grammar of Verbs and Their Arguments: A Cross-Linguistic Perspective*. Contemporary African Linguistics series of the Language Science Press.

Jones, E. (1971). "Krio: An English-base language of Sierra Leone". In Spencer, J. (ed.) *The English Language in West Africa*, 66–94. London: Longman Group Ltd.

Kroeger, P. (2004). *Analyzing Syntax: A Lexical Functional Approach*. Cambridge: Cambridge University Press.

Malchukov, A. L. & Comrie, B. (eds) (2015). *Valency Classes in the World's Languages*. Berlin: De Gruyter Mouton.

Michaelis, S. M., P. Maurer, M. Haspelmath & M. Huber (2013). *The Atlas of Pidgin and Creole Language Structures*. Oxford: Oxford University Press.

Ogie, O. (2009). Multi-verb constructions in Edo. PhD dissertation. NTNU. Trondheim. Norway.

Osam, E. K. (1994). Aspects of Akan Grammar. A Functional Perspective. PhD thesis, University of Oregon.

Osam, K. (2003). "An introduction to the verbal and multi-verbal system of Akan". In D. Beermann & L. Hellan (eds) *Proceedings of the Workshop on Multi-Verb Constructions*, Trondheim Summer School. Trondheim: Norwegian University of Science and Technology.

Payne, J. P. (1985). "Complex phrases and complex sentences". In T. Shopen (ed) *Language Typology and Syntactic Description: Volume II Complex Constructions*. Cambridge: Cambridge University Press.

Schachter, P. (1974). "A non-transformational account of serial verb constructions". *Studies in African Linguistics*, Supplement 5: 153–271.

Schaefer, R. B. & F. O. Egbokhare (2015). "Emai valency classes and their alternations". In A. Malchukov & B. Comrie (eds) *Valency Classes in the World's Languages*, 261–298. Berlin: De Gruyter Mouton.

Schiller, E. (1990). "On the definition and distribution of serial constructions". In B. Joseph & A. Zwicky (eds) *"When Verbs Collide": Papers from the Ohio State Mini-conference on Serial Verbs*, 34–64. Columbus, OH: Ohio State University.

Schiller, E. (2001). SVC's Greatest Hits. Hand-out. Stanford University.

Stewart, J. (1963). "Some restrictions on objects in Twi". *Journal of African Languages*, 2.2: 145–149.

Stewart, O. T. (2001). *The Serial Verb Construction Parameter*. New York & London: Garland.

Veenstra, T. (1996). *Serial Verbs in Saramaccan; Predication and Creole Genesis*. Dordrecht: Holland Institute of Generative Linguistics.

Westermann, D. H. (1907). *Grammatik der Ewe-Sprache*. Berlin: Diedrich Reimer.

Westermann, D. H. (1930). *A Study of the Ewe Language*. Oxford: Oxford University Press.

Winford, D. (1993). *Predication in Caribbean English Creoles* (Creole Language Library 10). Amsterdam: John Benjamins.

11

LOGOPHORICITY, LONG DISTANCE REFLEXIVES, AND THE YORUBA ANAPHOR *ÒUN*

Nike Lawal

Introduction

This chapter is concerned with accounting for the behavior of long distance reflexives (LDRs), a type of pronoun that has received considerable attention because of its ability to be bound outside its binding domain contrary to the stipulation of the binding theory. Long distance reflexives are found in unrelated languages across the world, in European languages such as Icelandic, Italian, Norwegian, Russian, in African languages such as Yoruba, Ewe, Mupan, and Abe, and in Asiatic languages such as Chinese, Japanese, and Korean and also in Austronesian languages such as Malay and in several varieties of Indonesian; hence its importance to linguistic theory.

The literature on LDRs has focused on two main issues, namely, their categorical status and their derivation. Regarding the first issue, linguists are not sure whether long distance anaphors are reflexive pronouns or bound anaphors, or if they are simply logophoric pronouns "masquerading" as long distance reflexives (Koopman and Sportiche 1989; Cole and Hermon 1998; Cole et al. 1990, 2006; Thrainsson 1976; Reuland 2016; Reinhart and Reuland 1991, etc.). The difficulty in determining their true status is due to the variability in their behavior: some long distance reflexives appear to be governed by syntactic rules, others by discourse rules, and yet others by both discourse and syntactic rules. Cole and Hermon (1998, 2015) attempt to provide a typology of LDRs meant to cover all the different types of LDRs. As Cole and Hermon (2015) have pointed out, LDRs do not fall neatly into one type or another. Some exhibit the characteristics of pronouns, others of bound anaphors, yet others behave like logophoric pronouns, and there are also others that exhibit the characteristics of all three types in various degrees. The problem is that most of the detailed descriptions of LDRs have focused on just a few languages, mainly Asian languages, and there have been very few detailed descriptions of other language groups, especially the less-known languages such as the languages of Africa. Recently, LDRs from other languages that do not fit the Chinese type have been discovered and this is causing a rethinking of the nature and status of LDRs. Thus, until there are fuller descriptions of LDRs from a wider range of more diverse languages, determining the true status of LDRs will remain a challenge to linguists. This chapter sets out to do exactly that, that is, to provide some new facts on LDRs based on a description of the behavior of the Yoruba LDR *òun* with the goal of helping to add new data to help account for the phenomenon.

The second issue is that of derivation, namely, how to account for LDRs' ability to be bound outside its binding domain. This issue also poses a challenge to linguists that is yet to be resolved. An LDR is generally believed to be derived by covert movement through Infl to [Spec IP] where it gets adjoined to the subject of the matrix or complement clause. There are several versions of the movement approach such as: Koster and Reuland (1991); Huang and Tang (1991); Progovac (1993); Cole and Sung (1994); Reinhart and Reuland (1991, 1993); Reuland (2016); Cole, Hermon, and Huang (2001, 2006); Reuland (1994, 1997); and many others. The movement approach is the most influential but still has problems, its main weakness being its inability to explain why the movement permits island violations, a core principle of linguistic theory. We examine this issue also in this chapter and conclude that the ability of LDRs to violate island constraints may be attributable to the semantic feature ([+logophor]) that occurs on the matrix verb of the matrix clause of LDR sentences. This semantic feature, we suggest, operates at LF to remove the island barrier so that the LDR can move out of syntactic islands. Evidence for this position comes from facts about the behavior of the Yoruba LDR *òun*. Our conclusion is that logophoricity is inherent in all LDRs to varying degrees and the degree of logophoricity permitted in a language plays an important role in determining whether a language with LDR may violate island constraints or not. Another question not examined or discussed in the literature, if we assume that LDRs are derived by LF movement through Infl to the SPEC position of IP, is, why do some languages have LDRs and some do not since all languages have Infl? The Yoruba facts also provide an answer to this question, which is that LDRs are licensed by Infl and hence the type of Infl a language has will determine whether that language will have LDR or not. Three types of Infl are examined, namely case Infl, lexical Infl and functional Infl. We conclude, based on the facts of Yoruba data, that LDRs may be licensed by a case and a lexical Infl but not by a functional Infl. It is further noted that a lexical Infl system may license both local and non-local LDR whereas a case Infl may license only non-local LDR.

The chapter is structured as follows: the first section presents the introduction while the second section discusses the binding theory and its application to English pronouns and reflexives. The third section discusses Yoruba pronouns and the binding theory. The section begins with a comparison of the behavior of the pronoun *òun* with that of the other pronouns in the language viz-a-viz the application of the binding theory and ends with the conclusion that *òun* is a bound pronominal anaphor. The fourth section examines previous analysis of the pronoun *òun* by Pulleyblank and concludes that the Avoid Pronoun Principle does not provide a satisfactory explanation for the behavior of *òun*. The fifth section looks at the concept of logophoricity and compares the behavior of logophoric pronouns with that of *òun*, concluding that *òun* is a logophoric pronoun but that it differs from the classic or core logophoric pronoun that occurs mainly with verbs of saying as *òun* can occur with a wide variety of verbs not found in typical logophoric pronouns. The sixth section compares *òun* with genuine LDRs using Cole and Hermon's typology of LDRs and other criteria applied to LDRs, and concludes that *òun* is a genuine LDR. The seventh section looks at the issue of logophoricity as an aspect of LDRs and classifies LDRs into local and non-local. The eighth section discusses the derivation of LDRs and examines the issue of island constraint violations and concludes that logophoricity is responsible for the LDRs' ability to violate island constraints. The ninth section examines the role of Infl in the licensing of LDRs and argues that lexical and Case Infl may license LDR but not a functional Infl, thereby accounting for why English does not have LDR. The chapter ends with a summary of the main points.

The binding theory

The binding theory, one of the principles of universal grammar (UG), specifies the syntactic environments in which pronouns and reflexives may occur. Although the binding theory in its standard form is no longer regarded as adequate for accounting for the distribution of all pronouns, nevertheless, it is still the main point of reference in discussions of the syntactic distribution of pronouns and pronominal elements. We will therefore base our description of the syntactic constraints anaphors and pronouns are subject to on the standard version. The standard binding theory, henceforth referred to as SBT, in its simplest form may be stated as follows:

(1)　　Binding theory (Chomsky 1981, 1986)
　　　　Principle A: An anaphor is bound in its local domain.
　　　　Principle B: A pronoun is free in its local domain.

Local domain means the minimal or local clause that contains the pronoun or the reflexive.

Pronouns, reflexives and the binding theory

Pronouns (e.g., he, she) and reflexives (e.g., herself, himself) are items that have no independent meaning; they depend on other items that have inherent meaning in the real world (e.g., *John, London, Mrs Jones, the Prime Minister*, etc.) for their meaning; hence they are referred to as bound items, meaning that they are bound to other items that have reference or refer to individuals or entities in the real world. The person or entity that a pronoun is bound to for its meaning is referred to as the antecedent. We illustrate this in example (2):

(2)　　Jane^i loves herself.^{i}

In (2), the reflexive *herself* is bound to the noun phrase (NP) *Jane* who gives it its meaning. On its own, the reflexive has no meaning; we cannot understand who the term *herself* refers to without reference to *Jane*. The device of co-indexing is used to indicate which items refer to the same person. Two items bearing the same index (letter or number) means they refer to the same entity or individual.

According to the SBT a reflexive must be bound in its local domain while a pronoun must be free in its local domain. This is illustrated with the English sentences (3a) and (3b) below:

(3a)　　Mary^i loves herself.^{i}
(3b)　　*Mary^i loves herself. ^{j}

(4a)　　Jane thinks that Mary^j loves herself.^{j}
(4b)　　*Jane^i thinks that Mary loves herself.^{i}

(5a)　　Mary^i loves her.^{j}
(5b)　　*Mary^i loves her.^{i}

(6a)　　*Jane thinks that Mary^i loves her.^{i}
(6b)　　Jane^i thinks that Mary loves her.^{i}

In the example (3a) the reflexive *herself* is correctly bound in its local domain by *Mary* with which it is co-indexed. In (3b), on the other hand, the reflexive is unbound as there is no noun phrase

Logophoricity, reflexives, Yoruba anaphor òun

(NP) in the sentence with which it is co-indexed, hence the ungrammaticality of the sentence (remember reflexives have no independent meaning so they must be bound to an item or entity in the sentence). Example (4a) is grammatical because the reflexive *herself* is bound by *Mary* which is within its local domain. This is consistent with binding principle A (Example (1)), but (4b) is ungrammatical because the reflexive, *herself*, is bound outside its local domain by *Jane*, which is a principle A violation, hence the ungrammaticality of the sentence. Example (5a) is grammatical because the pronoun *her* is not bound to any item in its local domain, that is, it is not co-indexed with *Mary* or any noun phrase in the sentence, so it is free in its binding domain in accordance with the SBT's stipulation that a pronoun must be free in its local domain; (5b) is ungrammatical because the pronoun is bound in its local domain, contrary to the SBT. Example (6a) is ungrammatical because the pronoun *her* is bound by *Mary* with which it is co-indexed, a principle B violation; (6b), on the other hand, is grammatical because the pronoun is free in its binding domain.

Yoruba pronouns and the binding theory

In this section we look at the distribution and behavior of Yoruba pronouns and reflexives viz-a-viz the SBT. Yoruba, like other languages, has the whole range of pronouns, including personal pronouns *ó* (he, she), reflexives pronouns *araàrẹ* (himself, herself), reciprocals *araàwọn* (each other), and others. The focus of this chapter is on the third person singular subject and object pronouns as they are the relevant items in this discussion; we will therefore confine our discussion to these pronouns only. They are presented below:

(7) Yoruba Third Person Singular Pronouns
Subject   *ó*
Object   *rẹ* (him/her)
Reflexives
araàrẹ
òun   self (her self/ him self)

Reflexives and pronouns in Yoruba behave like their counterparts in English in the sense that they obey the SBT as examples (8) and (9) show below.

(8a)   Bọ́lá [i] fẹ́ràn araarẹ.[i]
      Bola loves herself.
(8b)   *Bọ́lá[i] fẹ́ràn araarẹ.[j]
      Bola loves her.
(8c)   *Bọ́lá[i] fẹ́ràn re.[i]
      Bola loves self.
(8d)   Bọ́lá[i] fẹ́ràn rẹ.[j]
      Bola loves her/him.

Example (8a) is grammatical because the reflexive *araarẹ* is bound in its local domain by *Bola* with which it is co-indexed; (8b) is ungrammatical because the reflexive *araarẹ* is unbound, that is, it is not co-indexed with any item within its local domain. Example (8c) is ungrammatical because the pronoun *re* is bound within its local domain by *Bola*, a violation of binding principle B that states that a pronoun must be free in its local domain. In (8d) the pronoun is free in its local domain, i.e., it is not bound in its local domain so the sentence is grammatical. These examples show that Yoruba pronouns and reflexives obey the SBT.

The pronoun *òun*

Òun *(self/him/her) compared with the equivalent English pronoun him/her*

Now let's consider examples with the pronoun *òun* (self).

(9a) *Taiwo sọ pé Bọ́láⁱ fẹ́ràn *òun*.ⁱ
      Taiwo said that Bola like self.
      Taiwo said that Bola likes him. (Bola likes Bola)

(9b) Taiwoⁱ sọ pé Bọ́lá fẹ́ràn *òun*.ⁱ
      Taiwo said that Bola like self.
      Taiwo said that Bola like him. (Bola likes Taiwo)

(9c) *Taiwo sọ pé Bọ́lá fẹ́ràn *òun*ⁱ /*k
      Taiwo said that Bola like self.
      Taiwo said Bola likes him.   (i.e., Bola likes somebody not mentioned in the sentence)

The grammatical contrasts in (9a) and (9b) show that the pronoun *òun* may be co-indexed with the matrix clause subject Taiwo but not with the subject of the embedded clause *Bola* or with an NP outside the sentence (9c). Hence the ungrammaticality of (9a) and (9c). Contrast the Yoruba sentences above with an equivalent English sentence (10) below:

(10) John said that Bill likes him.

The pronoun '*him*' in the English sentence (10) has two possible readings: it may refer to the NP John or to an NP completely outside the sentence. Thus, the sentence could mean Bill likes John or that Bill likes someone else. The equivalent Yoruba sentence (9) has only one interpretation, namely one in which the pronoun is co-referential with the subject NP Taiwo. The sentence cannot mean that Bola likes someone other than Taiwo, that is, the pronoun cannot refer to somebody outside the sentence.

It is clear from the examples (9) above that the Yoruba third person singular pronoun *òun* (self) is an anaphor and not a pronoun since the antecedent or referent of an anaphor must be within the sentence in which the anaphor occurs and this is exactly what we see in the grammatical contrasts in (9a), (9b) and (9c). Further evidence for this comes from the contrast between *òun* and its English equivalent, 'him', in examples (11) and 12) below:

(11) John and Mary spoke to George; John believes that Mary likes him.

(12) Ayọ̀ⁱ ati Taiwoᵏ sọ̀rọ̀ pẹ̀lú Adéʲ ; Ayọ̀ gbàgbọ́ pé Taiwo fẹ́ràn *òun*.ᵐ/*ʲ/*ᵏ
      Ayo and Taiwo spoke with Ade; Ayo believes that Taiwo likes self.
      Ayo and Taiwo spoke to Ade; Ayo believes that Taiwo likes him.

In both (11) and (12) the NPs John and Ayo occur in the same sentence with the pronouns *him* and *òun* respectively. Since anaphors must take their antecedents from within the sentence in which they occur, we should expect that if the pronoun *him* in (11) and *òun* in (12) are anaphors, they should be bound by the NP *John* and *Ayo* respectively, but not by the NP *George* or the NP *Ade* because the pronouns *him* and *òun* do not occur in the same sentence with *George* and *Ade*. We find that, in the English example (10), the pronoun *him* could refer either to *John* or to *George* but, in the Yoruba example, the pronoun *òun* can refer only to the NP *Ayo*; it may not refer to *Ade*. The contrasts show that the English 'him' behaves like a pronoun as it may refer to either of the two NPs *John* or *George* while Yoruba *òun* behaves like an anaphor in that it may only refer to the subject *Ayo*. It cannot refer to an NP outside the sentence. This example further supports the conclusion that *òun* is an anaphor while English 'him' is a pronoun.

Òun and the 3rd person singular pronoun *ó*

Further evidence that shows that *òun* is an anaphor can be seen when we contrast the behavior of *òun* with that of the third person singular object pronoun *ó* (he/she) in the sentences below:

(13a) Taiwo[i] rò pé *òun*[i/* k] sanra.
       Taiwo thinks that self fat.
(13b) *Taiwo rò pé *òun*[i] sanra.
       Taiwo thinks that self fat.

(14a) Ayọ̀[i] mọ̀ pé *òun*[i/*k] le na Bọ́lá.
       Ayo knows that self can beat Bola.
       Ayo knows that he/she can beat Bola.
(14b) *Ayọ̀ mọ̀ pé *òun*[i] le na Bọ́lá.
       Ayo knows that self can beat Bola.

(15a) Ayọ̀[i] sọ pé *òun*[i/*k] fẹ̀ràn Bólá.
       Ayo said that self likes Bola.
       Ayo said that he likes Bola.
(15b) *Ayọ̀ sọ pé *òun*[i] fẹ̀ràn Bọ́lá.
       Ayo said that self likes Bola.
       Ayo said that he likes Bola.

Again, the grammatical contrasts seen from the co-indexing facts in examples (13–15) show that *òun* has no independent meaning. It must be bound to an NP within the sentence in order to have a meaning and this NP must be the subject. Thus, only the subject NP Ayo is a possible antecedent for *òun* in the sentences. *Òun* cannot take an antecedent outside the sentence, nor can it be free (13b, 14b, and 15b). We compare this behavior of *òun* with that of the third person singular object pronoun *ó* in (16), (17), and (18) below:

(16) Taiwo[i] rò pé ó[i/k]   sanra.
     Taiwo thinks that CL   fat.
     Taiwo thinks that self /he/she fat.

(17) Ayo[i] sọ pé ó[i/k]   féron Bọ́lá.
     Ayo said that CL   likes Bola.
     Ayo said that self /he/she   likes Bola.

(18) Ayo mọ̀ pé ó[i/k]   le na Bọ́lá.
     Ayo knows that CL   can beat Bola.
     Ayo knows that self/he/she   can beat Bola.

When we contrast the co-referential possibilities in (13–15) where we have *óun*, with those of (16–18) where we have the third person singular pronoun *ó*, we can see that with the pronoun *ó*

227

we have two possible readings: the first interpretation is where *ó* is co-referential with the matrix subject, and the second is where *ó* refers to someone else outside the sentence. In the examples where we have *òun*, on the other hand, as we saw earlier, there is only one interpretation, namely, one where the pronoun is co-referential with the matrix subject only. Unlike the pronoun *òun*, *ó* may refer to another NP outside the sentence. The grammatical contrasts in (16 and 17) and (18) above support the claim that *òun* is an anaphor while the third person pronoun *ó* is a pronoun.

Òun and the reflexive *araàrẹ* (herself/himself)

Now let's compare the behavior of *òun* with the reflexive *araàrẹ*, which is also an anaphor. As stated earlier, a reflexive is considered an anaphor because it has no meaning on its own; like *òun* it depends on another item in the sentence for its meaning. Contrast the behavior of *òun* with that of the reflexive pronoun *araàrẹ* in examples (19–22).

(19) Taiwo^i féràn *araàrẹ* ^{i} /*òun^i
     Taiwo like self.

(20) Taiwo^i wo   *araàrẹ* ^{i} / *òun^i ninu díngí.
     Taiwo   looked   self   in   mirror.
     Taiwo looked at self in the mirror.

(21) Ayo^i léro pé * *araàrẹ* ^{i} / *òun* ^{i} le na Bọ́lá.
     Ayo thought that self can beat Bola.
     Ayo thought that he can beat Bola.

(22) Ayo^i gbàgbé péki * *araàrẹ* ^{i} / òun^i ti ìlèkùn
     Ayo forgot   that *self/   he shut door.
     Ayo forgot to shut the door.

From examples (19–22) we see that Yoruba reflexive pronoun *araàrẹ* obeys the binding condition for anaphors in the sense that it is bound within its local domain as stipulated in the SBT. The contrary is the case with the pronoun *òun*. *Òun* may, in fact, be bound across several intervening clauses. This is illustrated below:

(23) [Ayo^i fẹ́ [kí Taiwo$_j$ rò [pé Bọ́lá$_k$ féràn *òun*$_{i/ j/ *k}$]]].
     Ayo want that Taiwo think that Bola likes self.
     Ayo wants Taiwo to think that Bola likes him.

(24) [Ayo^i mọ̀ [pé Taiwo^j so [pé Bọ́lá^k fé [ki Adé^m toju *òun* $^{i/j/ k/*m/}$)]]]].
     Bola knows that Ayo said that Taiwo want that Ade take care of self.

As we can see in (23) and (24), the antecedent of *òun* is not restricted to the adjacent embedded clause; any of the subject NPs outside its local domain in (23) *Ayo* or *Taiwo* and (24) *Ayo*, *Taiwo* or *Bola* may be selected as the antecedent of *òun*. In other words, several interpretations can be given to the sentence, depending on which NP is interpreted as being the antecedent. If *òun* is an anaphor as we have shown it to be, then its behavior in (13–15), (16–18), (19–22), as well as (23–24), violates the binding condition for anaphors. *Òun* behaves rather more like a pronoun than an anaphor as it must be free within its local domain. But, unlike a pronoun that can be free within the sentence, *òun* must be bound within the sentence. This makes *òun* a bound pronominal, or a pronominal anaphor, an item not accounted for by the SBT.

The Avoid Pronoun Principle

Pulleyblank's Avoid Pronoun analysis

The only study that attempts to account for the distribution of *òun* that we know of is Pulleyblank (1986). Pulleyblank argues that the co-referential properties of *òun* are due to the Avoid Pronoun Principle (Chomsky 1981). The Avoid Pronoun Principle simply states that a lexical pronoun should be avoided whenever possible in favor of pro or PRO.

(25)   Avoid Pronoun Principle:
       Avoid Pronoun

Pulleyblank argues that in Yoruba, a clitic subject pronoun of an embedded clause always has to be interpreted as disjoint in reference from all c-commanding NPs because it is co-indexed with a variable subject to Condition C. Therefore, by the Avoid Pronoun Principle, *òun* is chosen only when the disjoint interpretation is not required. Thus, according to Pulleyblank, the choice of *òun* over a clitic pronoun is dictated not by the binding principle but by the Avoid Pronoun Principle. This hypothesis is based on the assumption that a null operator appears in the Comp of the matrix clause and, since the subject NP is in the domain of the operator that binds the embedded clitic-NPe sequence, it cannot be co-indexed with the clitic. The configuration (26) illustrates this (Pulleyblank 1986):

(26) OP_j [Taiwo$_i$ rò pé [NPe]$_j$ ó$_j$ sanra]].
       Taiwo thinks that CL fat.

If Pulleyblank's hypothesis is correct, a reading in which the clitic NPe sequence is co-referential with the matrix subject should be impossible, but the following examples (27) through (32) show that this is not the case:

(27)   Taiwo$_i$ rò pé ó$_{i/j}$ sanra.
       Taiwo thinks that CL is fat.
       Taiwo thinks that he is fat.

(28)   Ayo$_i$ so pé ó$_{i/j}$ feron Dupe.
       Ayo said that CL likes Dupe.
       Ayo said that he likes Dupe.

(29)   Ayo$_i$ lérò pé ó$_{i/j}$ le na Femi.
       Ayo thought that CL can beat Femi.
       Ayo thought that he can beat Femi.

Contrast (28–29) above with (30–32) below:

(30)   Taiwo$_i$ rò pé *òun*$_{i/*j}$ sanra.
       Taiwo thinks that he is fat.

(31)   Ayó$_i$ so pé *òun*$_{i/*j}$ fẹ̀ràn Dúpẹ́.
       Ayo said that he likes Dupe.

(32)   Ayó$_i$ lérò pé *òun*$_{i/*j}$ le na Fẹ́mi.
       Ayo thought that he can beat Femi.

When we contrast the co-referential possibilities in (27–29) and (30–32) we can see that the clitic pronoun *ó* may occur in the same environment as *òun*. All the examples in which the clitic appears have two possible readings: the first is where the higher subject is co-referential with the clitic, and the second is where the higher subject is disjoint in interpretation with the clitic. The examples show that the clitic like *òun* can also have a co-referential reading in the same context. In other words, in examples (27–29) and (30–32) both the clitic *ó* and *òun* may refer to the same NP, that is, the higher NP Ayo. Pulleyblank's account rests crucially on the hypothesized null operator appearing in the matrix comp, within the domain of the matrix subject. However, the fact that the sentences in which the clitic appears have two readings implies that the operator need not take maximal scope contrary to what is assumed in Pulleyblank (1986). The null operator can have scope over the embedded clause only in the case where the subject is free in the scope of its operator. This is illustrated in (33):

(33) NP_1. . . . [OP. . . NPe cl]. . .

In (33) the subject NP_1 is free in the scope of the operator so co-reference with the NPe clitic sequence is possible. This configuration accounts for the reading in which the clitic is bound by the matrix subject. The examples here show clearly that the Avoid Pronoun Principle does not account for the distribution of *òun*.

Is *òun* a logophoric pronoun?

Definition of logophoricity

Pronouns that behave like *òun* have been found in some West African languages such as Ewe, Igbo, and Abe. They are referred to in the literature as logophoric pronouns. One of the first formal descriptions of logophoric pronouns is that of Clements in his study of the Ewe pronoun *ye*, which he describes in the following terms:

(34)   The pronoun *ye* is used exclusively to designate the individual (other than the speaker) whose speech, thoughts, feelings, and general state of consciousness are reported or reflected in the linguistic context in which the pronoun occurs.

Clements 1975

A similar definition of logophoric pronouns is given by Sells (1987):

(35)   In contexts embedded under a logophoric verb, and only in these contexts, a special pronominal form called the logophoric pronoun must be used to indicate reference to the person whose speech, thoughts, or perceptions are reported.

The term logophoric pronoun is now widely used to refer to these and other pronouns whose distribution appear to be determined by pragmatic or discourse factors. These pronouns have the ability to be bound outside their binding domains in contradiction of the binding theory. Because of this, it is claimed that logophoric pronouns do not obey c-command, as such they must be governed by discourse rules and therefore fall outside the scope of the binding theory.

We examine this claim below but first we examine the status of the pronoun *òun* to see if it is a logophoric pronoun or not. We begin first by identifying the matrix verbs that are commonly used in logophoric contexts to see whether *òun* may co-occur with them. The most typical of these are verbs of saying or reporting. Examples in Yoruba are *sọ, wí, ní* (say), *kéde* (announce), *sọ fún* (tell). These verbs are inherently logophoric as they present events from the perspective of the subject and *òun* occurs with them as the sentences below illustrate:

(36) Ayọ̀$_i$ sọ pé *òun* $_{i/*j}$ ti borí
      Ayo said that he has won.

(37) Ayọ̀$_i$ kéde pé *òun* $_{i/*k}$ borí
      Ayo announced that he won.

(38) Ayọ̀$_i$ sọ fún Kọ́la$_j$ pé Bọ́la$_k$ mò olópa ti ó fọ́ *òun* $_{i/*j/*k}$ leti.
      Ayo told Kola that Bola knows policeman that he slapped him ear.
      Ayo told Kola that Bola knows the policeman who slapped him.

The examples show that *òun* occurs with typical logophoric verbs such as those in (36–38).

However, *òun* may also occur with a wide range of other complement-taking verbs that are not inherently logophoric. They range from verbs of perception and cognition to verbs denoting emotion, desire, request, etc. Examples of these are *jé* (cause/let), *lérí* (boast), *mò* (know), *gbàgbé* (forget), *ránti* (remember), *fé* (want), *féròn* (like), *bè* (beg), *rò* (think), *puró* (lie), and *tàn* (deceive). These are not typical logophoric verbs:

(39) Ayọ̀$_i$ lérí pé *òun* $_{i/*j}$ maa borí.
      Ayo boasted that he will win.

(40) Ayọ̀$_i$ bè wa péki a je kí *òun* $_{i/*j}$ lo.
      Ayo begged us that we allow him go.
      Ayo begged us to allow him leave.

(41) Ayọ̀$_i$ gbàgbó pé *òun* $_{i/*j}$ ti borí.
      Ayo believes that he has won.

(42) Ayọ̀$_i$ fẹ́ pékí Kola jé kí *òun.*$_{i/*j}$ lo.
      Ayo want that Kola allow him go.
      Ayo wants that Kola to allow him leave.

The examples above show that, although *òun* occurs with typical logophoric verbs, it also occurs with non-logophoric verbs. Thus *òun* exhibits some characteristics that are not characteristic of logophoric pronouns, such as its ability to occur with non-logophoric verbs such as those in (39) to (42) above.

Variable binding and co-reference

Two types of binding relationships are recognized between an antecedent and its bindee; they are variable binding relationship and co-reference relationship. A pronoun receives variable binding interpretation if it must be bound intra-sententially, that is, if it is bound within the sentence in which it occurs, while it receives a co-reference interpretation if it may be bound outside the sentence. It is generally accepted in linguistic theory that pronouns that receive a variable binding interpretation fall under the scope of the SBT, whereas those that receive a co-reference interpretation fall outside the scope of the SBT and are thus logophoric pronouns because they are subject to non-syntactic rules, specifically, discourse rules.

All the examples we have presented above in which *òun* occurs show that the antecedent of *òun* must be within the sentence in which *òun* occurs, that is, it is intra-sententially bound. If *òun* is intra-sententially bound, and we have shown that this is the case, then the binding relationship between *òun* and its antecedent must be that of variable binding and not that of co-reference. *Òun* therefore satisfies the syntactic criteria of variable binding to which pronouns that fall under the SBT are subject. It also means that *òun* is a true anaphor and not a pronoun since pronouns that are bound intra-sententially are regarded as anaphors not as pronouns.

C-command

C-command is another syntactic criteria used to determine whether a pronoun is subject to syntactic constraints or discourse constraints. C-command describes a structural representation of a sentence based on the notion of hierarchical dominance. In the standard definition, a constituent c-commands its sister constituents and any constituents that these dominate. It is generally agreed that pronouns that fall under the binding theory obey c-command and those that do not obey c-command fall under discourse rules. Logophoric pronouns, it is claimed, do not obey the c-command and are thus subject to discourse not syntactic rules and therefore fall outside the binding theory. In all the examples where *òun* occurs, the antecedent of *òun* is the matrix clause subject and this NP is in the specifier position of IP; it therefore c-commands *òun*. We repeat some of the examples below for ease of reference:

(43) Ayọ̀$_i$ sọ fún Bọ́la$_j$ pé Fẹ́mi$_k$ fá ori *òun* $_{i/*j/*k}$
      Ayo told to Bola that Femi shaved head self
      Ayo told Bola that Femi shaved head his head.

(44) Ayọ̀$_i$ tan Bọ́la$_j$ pé *òun* $_{i/*j}$ bori.
      Ayo deceived Bola that self won.
      Ayo deceived Bola that he won.

As (43) and (44) above show, the antecedent of the pronoun is the matrix clause subject and it is in the specifier position of IP so it c-commands the reflexive.

(45) [Spec Ayo [IP   [VP tan Bola [CP [pe IP *òun* bori]

To test that *òun* obeys c-command, let's consider examples with possessive NPs where the antecedent is typically in a non-c-command position. If *òun* obeys c-command, then binding of *òun* by the antecedent should be ungrammatical if the antecedent is in a non c-command position. We illustrate this below in (46) and (47).

(46) [Bàbá^i Ayọ̀]^j so pé Bọ́lá^k sọ iwé òun$^{i *i/j/*k}$ nù.
       Ayo's father said that Bola lost his book.

(47) [Ọ̀re^i Ayọ̀]^j sọ pé Bola^k kọ iwé nípa òun$^{i * i/j/*k}$
      Ayo's friend said that Bola wrote a book about him.

The antecedent of *òun* in (46) is the NP *Baba* while in (47) it is the NP *òre* but these NPs do not c-command *òun* because they are specifiers of the NP Ayo hence are not in a c-command position. We see in (46) and (47) that when *òun* is co-indexed with *Baba* and *ore* the sentence is ungrammatical. However, if the whole NP *Baba Ayo* and *Òre Ayo* is taken as the antecedent of *òun* then the sentence becomes grammatical as the larger NP c-commands *òun* and can therefore serve as its antecedent. The above examples show that *òun* observes c-command.

We have shown in this section that *òun* is a logophoric pronoun but that it is not like most logophoric pronouns as it observes the syntactic constraint (c-command) and also has variable binding interpretation not co-reference interpretation, the two conditions that pronouns that fall under the binding theory must observe. But we have also shown that *òun* violates the SBT condition for both pronouns and anaphors. What then is the true status of *òun*? Below we compare *òun*'s behavior with that of pronouns known in the literature as long distance reflexives (LDR) to see whether *òun* may be categorized as one.

Òun as a long distance bound anaphor

The behavior of *òun* seems to parallel the behavior of pronouns referred to in the literature as long distance reflexives (LDR). Just like *òun*, the uniqueness of long distance reflexives lies in their ability to be bound outside their binding domain. Several studies have been carried out on these pronouns, including Cole Hermon and Sung (1990), Cole and Sung (1994), Sung and Cole (1997), Progovac (1993), and Huang and Tang (1991), among others. Long distance reflexives have been found in several European languages such as Dutch, Italian, Icelandic, Norwegian, and Russian, and in Asian languages such as Chinese and Japanese, and Korean, in African languages such as Ewe, Igbo and Abe, and in Austronesian languages such as Malay. Long distance reflexives are known to exhibit other unique characteristic features that set them apart from ordinary pronouns, which Cole, Hermon and Huang (2006) and Cole, Hermon and Yanti (2010) present as a typology of LDRs that may be used to identify LDRs. We compare the behavior of *òun* with that of the Chinese LDR *siji*, one of the most studied LDRs, using the characteristic features identified by Cole et al.

Mono-morphemic

One characteristic feature that is usually used to identify an LDR is its structure. LDRs are said to have a very simple structure, which is that they tend to be mono-morphemic. *Òun* passes this test as it is mono-morphemic in structure. Unlike the reflexive *araàre*, which is bi-morphemic consisting of two words, *ara* (body) and *re* (your), *òun* consists of a single morpheme. So structure-wise, *òun* is an LDR.

Subject oriented

The second characteristic of LDRs is that they are subject oriented, meaning that only a subject NP may be the antecedent of an LDR. We have shown this to be the case with *òun* as will be illustrated in (48) and (49):

(48) Ayo$_i$ so fún Bóla$_j$ pé Fémi$_k$ bú *òun*$_{i/*j/*k}$.
       Ayo told to Bola that Femi insulted self.
       Ayo told Bola that Femi insulted him.

(49) Ayo$_i$ tan Bóla$_j$ pé òun$_{i/*j}$ bori.
Ayo deceived Bola that self won.
Ayo deceived Bola that he won.

In (48) and (49) it should be possible for the pronoun òun to refer to the NP Bola as well as to the NP Ayo since both NPs c-command the pronoun òun, but this is not the case. Òun may only refer to the NP Ayo and to no other NP. Since the only difference between the NP Ayo and the NP Bola is that the former is a subject while the latter is an object, it is clear that the anaphor òun can only be bound by a subject. It cannot be bound by an object NP. This shows that òun satisfies the subject orientation criteria. In all the examples presented in this chapter we see that the antecedent of òun must always be a subject and no other NP.

Blocking effect

Another well-attested characteristic of LDRs is what is called the blocking effect. It has been observed that some LDRs in some languages, notably Chinese, experience what is called the blocking effect. In these languages binding of the LDR is only possible if all intervening NPs share the same number and person features. When the subject of the subordinate clause does not share the same features with the matrix clause subject, the subordinate clause subject blocks the matrix subject and any higher subject, regardless of person, from being the antecedent of the reflexive. The reflexive *siji* cannot refer to either the matrix subject or the intermediate subject as illustrated in (50a) and (50b) below.

(50a) Zhangsan$_i$ shuo wo$_j$ zhidao Lisi$_k$ chang piping ziji.$_{*i//*j/k}$
Zhangsan say I   know Lisi often criticize self
(50b) Zhangsan$_i$ shuo Wangwu$_j$ zhidao Lisi$_k$ chang piping ziji$_{i/j/k}$
Zhangsan say Wangwu know Lisi often criticize self.

In (50a) binding of *ziji* by the matrix NP *Zhangsan* is blocked, but not in (50b) because the intervening NP *wo* in (50a) has different number and person features. As we can see, the main difference between (50a) and (50b) is that in (50a) the intervening NP has a different number and person features from the antecedent, while in (50b) the antecedent and the intervening NP share the same features, i.e., both are third person.

Yoruba does not observe the blocking effect as the examples below show:

(51) Ade$_i$ rò pé *mo* sọ pé Bọ́la bú òun$_i$
Ade thinks that I said that Bola insulted self.

(52) Ade$_i$ fé kí <u>won</u> rò pé Bọ́la féràn òun$_i$
Ade want that they think that Bola likes self.

In (51) the first person singular pronoun *mo* (I) intervenes between òun and the antecedent Ayo, while in (52) the intervening NP is the third person plural pronoun *wọn* (they). The sentences however remain grammatical. This indicates that the blocking effect is not operative in Yoruba. As stated above, not all LDRs exhibit this feature. It has been noted in the literature that no similar restriction exists in European languages with LDRs. Even in Chinese, which obey the blocking effect, there are certain contexts where the blocking effect does not apply.

Contrast the Chinese examples (53) with (54) below where the blocking effect does not apply (taken from Tang 1989):

(53)   Zhangsan$_i$ gaosu wo$_j$ ziji $_{i/*j}$ de fenshu.
        Zhangsan tell me self DE grade.
        Zhangsan told me about his own grade.

(54)   Zhangsan$_i$ gaosu wo$_j$ ziji $_{i/*j}$ mei bei dahui xuanshang.
        Zhangsan tell me self haven/t by conference select.
        Zhangsan told me that *I/he was not selected by the conference.

It has been suggested (Cole, Hermon and Huang 2006) that blocking could be due to some language internal property since it does not seem to be a cross linguistic phenomenon.

Variable binding interpretation

One of the features that is said to distinguish LDRs from logophoric pronouns is the type of binding relationship that they exhibit. It is argued in the literature that LDRs receive a variable binding interpretation, not co-reference interpretation. We have shown above that *òun* satisfies this criterion as it must be bound intrasententially, which means it is subject to variable binding interpretation not co-reference interpretation.

We have shown above that the reflexive *òun* exhibits all the characteristic features of LDRs listed in Cole et al.'s typology, namely, mono-morphemicity, subject orientation, c-command, and variable binding. *Òun* is therefore a true LDR.

LDRs and logophoricity

We have seen that although *òun* is a LDR, it also behaves like a logophoric pronoun in the sense that it occurs with logophoric verbs of saying, *so, wi, ni* (say) and *so fún* (tell). It is now generally acknowledged that most LDRs exhibit some logophoric tendencies (Huang and Liu 2001). One of these logophoric tendencies that LDRs are said to exhibit is that they are frequently limited to taking antecedents that are prominent in the discourse that is usually the subject of the sentence or clause. Based on this observation, three types of logophoricity have been recognized. The first is SOURCE, the second is SELF, and the third is PIVOT.

(55)
        a SOURCE is used to describe the classic logophoric pronoun that is restricted to verbs of saying. The SOURCE is the source of speech, i.e., the subject of the higher verb of saying.
        b SELF, the individual whose mental states or thoughts the sentence describes (subject of verbs of mental activity).
        c PIVOT, is the perspective of the sentence.

Languages are said to differ with regards to the type of logophoricity they have. Some languages are said to have only SOURCE, others may have both SOURCE and SELF. It has been suggested all three types of logophoricity may license LDRs (Huang and Liu 2001). According to Huang and Liu (2001), LDRs may be licensed by only SOURCE; it may also be licensed by SELF or by both SOURCE and SELF; and in yet other languages it may be licensed by PIVOT.

Types of LDRs

As noted at the beginning of this section and throughout the chapter, the main distinguishing feature of all LDRs is their ability to be bound outside their local domain. However, there are LDRs that may also be bound locally and non-locally. An example is the Chinese LDR *siji*. Compare the behavior of the Chinese long-distance anaphor *ziji* in (56) with *òun* in (57) below:

(56)   Zhangsan^i renwei Lisi^j zhidao Wangwuk^k xihuan ziji.$^{i/j/k}$
       Zhangsan thinks that Lisi knows that Wangwu likes self.

(57)   Bóla$_i$ rò pé Ayò$_j$ mò pé Fémi$_k$ féràn òun$_{i/j/*k}$).
       Bola thinks that Ayo knows that Femi likes self.

As the example shows, the Chinese LDR *ziji* may be co-indexed with the subject *Wangwu* within its local domain or with the subject of the matrix clause Zhangsan. *Òun*, on the other hand, cannot be co-indexed with the subject *Femi* in its local domain as co-indexing of the antecedent Femi with *òun* results in ungrammaticality. The behavior of Chinese LDR *siji* thus differs significantly from that of the Yoruba LDR *òun* in terms of their binding domains. The majority of LDRs discussed in the literature seem to fall into the first category, namely that they may be both locally and non-locally bound, while very few LDRs are in the latter category. Two classes of LDRs have been established based on the above distinction: true reflexives and long distance bound anaphors (Cole et al. 2010). True reflexives are LDRs that may be both locally and non-locally bound, while long distance bound anaphors are those that may only be non-locally bound. The implication of this classification is that *òun* may now be classified as a long distance bound anaphor. The numerous evidence presented in this chapter support the classification of *òun* as a long distance bound anaphor. First, we have shown that *òun* is an anaphor; second we have shown that *òun* has all the characteristic features and behavior of LDRs, namely, it obeys c-command, is subject oriented, is monomorphemic, is long-distance bound, and has variable binding interpretation.

Derivation of LDRs

Movement analysis

Several proposals have been put forward for the derivation of LDRs. The most influential of these is the movement analysis first proposed by Cole, Hermon and Sung (1990) and Cole and Sung (1994). There have been several variants of the movement analysis since these two publications, among which are Progovac (1992, 1993), Reuland (2001), Reinhart and Reuland (1991, 1993), Reuland (2009, 2016), Kornfit (2000), Huang and Liu (2001), Huang and Tang (1991), and others. The movement analysis simply states that LDRs are derived by covert movement through Infl into [Spec IP] position where it gets adjoined to the subject. We illustrate this with the Yoruba example below:
   The sentence

(58)   Ayò mò pe Bólá féràn òun.
       Ayo knows that Bola likes self.
       Ayo knows that Bola likes him.
       Ayò^i [òun^i] mò [CP pé [IP Bólá féràn *t*]]

Although the movement approach is generally accepted it has not been without problems, the most serious challenge being its inability to account for island violations resulting from the movement. It is argued that an LF movement of LDR should not be possible across an island (e.g., a relative clause or an adjunct clause) which in linguistic theory is a barrier to movement (Ross 1967). Such violations have been reported in Chinese LDRs (Progovac 1993; Reinhart and Reuland 1993; Reuland 2001, 2016; Huang and Tang 1991; Cole, Hermon and Huang 2006). We illustrate with the Chinese examples below (taken from Cole, Hermon and Huang 2006):

(59) Zhangsan[i]   renwei [Wangwu kanjian   [CP neige taoyan ziji de ren [k]]] [i/j/k]
Zhangsan   think   Wangwu see   that   dislike self REL person
Zhangsan thinks Wangwu saw the person who dislikes him/himself.
(Zhangsan, Wangwu or the person)

(60) Zhangsan[i]   renwei [Wangwu shuo [CP rugoo Lisi piping ziji],
Zhangsan think Wangwu say   if Lisi criticize self
ta jiu bu qu.
he then not go.
Zhangsan thinks that Wangwu said that if Lisi criticized him/himself,
then he (Wangwu, Lisi, or the person) won't go.

Island violations like the ones reported above for Chinese LDR also occur with the Yoruba LDR *òun* as can be seen in the sentences (61) and (62):

òun in a relative clause

(61) Ayò[i] fẹ́ [ki Bọ́lá[j] rí ọkùnrin   [CP **tí ó fún *òun*** ni aago.][i]
Ayo said that Bola see the man   who he gave self watch.
Ayo wants Bola to see the man who gave himself a watch.
(gave Ayo a watch)

(62) Kẹ́mi[i] rántí pé obìnrin [CP **tí** Bọ́lá[j] **ta ile *òun*[i] fún**] ti lọ si Ibadan]][i/*j]
Kemi remember that the woman that Bola sold house self to has gone to Ibadan.
Kemi remembers that the woman who Bola sold herself/her house to has gone to Ibadan.
(Kemi's house)

òun in an adjunct clause

(63) Màmá[i] ọ̀ mọ̀   [CP **bí Ayọ̀[j] bá rí *òun***]][i]
Mother not know   if Ayo COND saw self.
Mother doesn't know if Ayo saw herself. (saw mother)

(64) Kẹ́mi[i] mọ̀ pé Bọ́la[j] ọ̀ nìí wá [CP **bí Ayọ̀ ò bá pe ọ̀un**]]. [i/j]
Kemi heard that Bola not will come if Ayo not COND invite self.
(invite Kemi)

In (61) and (62) *òun* is within a relative clause while in (63) and (64) *oun* is in an adjunct clause. Movement of the reflexive in LF out of these two clauses that are islands should not be possible but it is. The sentences are perfectly grammatical.

Nike Lawal

Logophoric account

According to Kuno (1987), LDR sentences in many languages have logophoric interpretations, namely that they present an empathetic point of view or perspective towards the speaker. The notion of empathy is defined by Kuno (1987) as:

(65) Degree of empathy
 The degree of the speakers' empathy with x, E (x), ranges from 0 to 1,
 with E (x) = 1 signifying his total identification with X, and E (x) = 0
 a total lack of identification.

Kuno explains that the difference between the Icelandic LDR *sig* and the Japanese LDR *zibun* is due to the fact that the Icelandic *sig* lacks the empathetic use while Japanese *zibun* doesn't. In other words, Icelandic *sig* has low empathy therefore it may not violate island constraints, whereas Japanese *zibun* is able to move out of syntactic islands, thus violating island constraints, because it has high empathy. This, according to Kuno, accounts for why *zibun* is able to move out of islands while Icelandic *sig* is not able to do so, as illustrated in the grammatical contrasts in (68) and (69):

Icelandic

(66) *Jon¹ yrði glaður ef Sigga byði sig¹.
 John would-be (subj) glad if Sigga invited (subj) self.

Japanese

(67) Taro¹-wa mosi Hanako –ga   zibun¹ –o syootai- site –kure-tara ooyorokobi-suru-
 Taro Top   if Hanako Nom self 1 –Acc invite –Ben-Cond be delighted - will
 daroo

The empathy relation (the ranking based on the speaker's empathy) among participants, according to Kuno, correlates with various factors such as person, topicality, animacy, social situation) as well as logophoricity. In other words, the speakers' identification may vary in degree depending on the person or thing that participates in the event or state that the speaker describes in the sentence. When we apply this to the pronoun *òun*, we see that Kuno's observation appears to be correct. We illustrate this with examples (68) and (69) below:

(68a) *Bọ́la¹ ó bínú [CP tí Ayọ̀ ò bá pe òun¹ fún ìpàdé ọla.]
 Bola will be angry if Ayo does not invite self for meeting tomorrow.
 Bola will not be angry if Ayo does not invite self for tomorrow's meeting.
(68b) Kẹ́mi¹ sọ pé Bọ́lá¹ ó bínú [CP ti Ayọ̀ ọ̀ bá pé òun*i /ʲ* fún ìpàdé ọla.]
 Kemi said that Bola will be angry if Ayo does not invite self to meeting tomorrow.
 Kemi said that Bola will be angry if Ayo does not invite her to tomorrow's meeting.
(69a) *Ayọ̀¹ mọ ẹni [CP ti ó mú ìwé òun.¹]
 Ayo knows person who took book self.
(69b) Kọ́la¹ ní Ayọ̀ʲ mọ ẹni[CP tí ó mú ìwé òun*i /ʲ*]
 Kola said Ayo know person who bought house self.
 Kola said Ayo knows the person who took his book.

We should expect both (68a) and (68b) and (69a) and (69b) to be either grammatical or ungrammatical as both have *òun* moving out of an island: *òun* is in an adjunct clause in (68a and b) and in a relative clause in (69a and b). Instead what we find is that the (b) sentences are grammatical while the (a) sentences are not. The grammatical contrasts in the above examples show that *òun* seems to obey island constraints in some sentences but not in others. These contrasts support Kuno's assertion that the degree of empathy shown by the speaker for the subject is higher in the grammatical (b) sentences than in the ungrammatical (a) sentences.

While the Yoruba facts agree with Kuno's statement that the degree of empathy of the speaker has a role to play in allowing LDRs to violate island constraints, it does not agree with Kuno's conclusion that the LDR itself is responsible for determining the degree of empathy of the speaker towards the subject due to the fact that the same LDR *òun* occurs in both the grammatical sentences (which violates island constraints) and the ungrammatical sentences (which do not permit island constraints violations); so it cannot be the LDR per se that allows or does not allow island violations in LDRs, at least not in Yoruba. If two different LDRs were involved in (68a and 68b) and (69a and 69b) Kuno's conclusion that the nature or type of the LDR is what is responsible for island violations would have been correct but, since it is the same LDR in both sentences, his conclusion could not be supported.

So, what is responsible for island violations in (68b) and (69b)? When we look closely at the two sentences (68) and (69), we see that what is different between the grammatical and the ungrammatical sentences is that different types of logophoric verbs occur in their matrix clauses. The matrix verbs in the grammatical sentences are the typical or core logophoric verbs, a verb of saying, whereas the matrix verbs in the ungrammatical (a) sentences are non-core logophoric verbs. This is the only difference between the grammatical and the ungrammatical sentences and the most logical conclusion must therefore be that it is the matrix verb that is responsible for the island violations. The logophoric verb is what determines the degree of empathy of the speaker and subsequently permits the reflexive to violate island constraints. We therefore propose that there be a semantic feature [+ logophoric] on the matrix verbs of LDR sentences and the presence or absence of this feature will determine whether the LDR may violate island constraints or not. We also assume that logophoricity may be a matter of degree: Some verbs may be more logophoric than others; the degree of logophoricity of some verbs may also differ from language to language. Some verbs in one language may be highly logophoric while the same or an equivalent verb in another language may not be. This would explain why LDRs in some languages observe island constraints (e.g., Icelandic *sig*) while some in other languages do not (e.g., Japanese *zibun*).

LDRs and the Infl parameter

Infl and LDR

The question now is why do some languages like Yoruba and Chinese and Icelandic have long distance anaphors while others like English do not? What licenses LDRs and logophoric pronouns? The answer to this question we believe is tied to the Infl parameter. Standard analyses of LDRs, including that of Cole, Hermon and Sung (1990), Cole and Sung (1994), and Cole and Hermon (1997), among others, show that Infl plays a crucial role in determining the presence or absence of LDRs in a language. Cole et al. (1990) state that only languages with a lexical Infl or where Infl has the feature [+M] may license LDRs. If LDRs are licensed by Infl as Cole et al. (1990) suggest, then it is valid to conclude that anti-local LDRs like *òun* must also be licensed by Infl. However, since Chinese Infl may licence LDRs that obey locality constraints, and Yoruba Infl only licences non-local LDRs, we must assume that the two types of LDRs are licensed by two different types of Infls. We give evidence below in support of this hypothesis.

Types of Infl

Rizzi (1986) distinguishes between two types of Infls, a Case Infl and non-Case Infl. According to Rizzi, a Case assigning Infl may license pro but it may not qualify as a proper governor. Rizzi also states that where the head of IP absorbs the nominative case and is specified as [+ Pronoun] having clitic-like pronominal properties, a Case assigning Infl can function as a proper governor. Yoruba seems to provide the evidence in support of Rizzi's hypothesis. In Yoruba, when a subject is extracted, a clitic pronoun must appear in the subject position otherwise the sentence will be ungrammatical. Carstens (1987) argues that the clitic pronoun is inserted in IP to allow the Infl to function as a proper governor for the trace of the subject. This is exactly what Rizzi predicted for a Case Infl. According to Rizzi, a Case Infl may function as a proper governor only when it absorbs the nominative case of the clitic. The fact that subject extraction in Yoruba requires that a clitic pronoun be inserted in the subject position suggests that Yoruba has a Case-Infl.

The second feature of a Case Infl is the ability to license pro (Rizzi 1986). This criterion is also satisfied by Yoruba. As we stated earlier, Yoruba personal pronouns behave like clitics; they do not behave like true NPs or pronominals. For instance, they cannot be conjoined or topicalized. They are therefore regarded as clitics (see also Pulleyblank 1986). Since these pronouns are clitics, they have the status of [pro]. The sentences below illustrate this:

(70a) Ó rí Bólá.
       CL saw Bóla.
       He/she saw Bola.
(70b) Bólá rí i.
       Bola saw CL.
       Bola saw him/her.

Assuming Rizzi's hypothesis about Case Infl is correct, the fact that Yoruba has clitic pronouns that regularly occur as subjects and objects of verbs in sentences suggests that Yoruba has a Case Infl. The example (63) above shows that Yoruba satisfies the two criteria for a Case assigning Infl. From the above evidence, therefore, we may classify Infl into three types and languages may be grouped according to which of the three types of Infl systems they possess.

(71) Infl types

    a Functional Infl /AGR
    b Lexical /Anaphoric Infl /AGR
    c Case Infl /AGR

Rizzi (1986) classifies English as a functional Infl language based on the fact that the Infl in English does not properly govern or license pro; Cole and Hermon also, based on their work on Chinese LDRs, claim that Chinese is a lexical Infl language since Infl functions as a proper governor and also licenses pro (Cole and Hermon 1990, 1994). Based on Rizzi (1986), Yoruba may be classified as a Case Infl language since it licenses pro but does not function as a proper governor. Since both Yoruba and Chinese have LDRs but English does not, we may conclude then that only Lexical and Case Infl languages may license LDRs. We may also conclude that, since Yoruba licenses anti-local LDRs but Chinese does not, only Case Infl languages may license anti-local LDR. The above accounts for why Yoruba and Chinese have LDRs and English does not.

Conclusion

In this chapter we have examined the behavior of the Yoruba LDR *òun* and have concluded, first, that LDRs such as *òun* cannot be accounted for in purely syntactic or semantic terms as their behavior is influenced by both syntactic as well as semantic factors. Second, accounts of LDRs should be extended to include the concept of logophoricity because almost every LDR is to some degree logophoric. Third, based on the evidence presented, we classify *òun* as a genuine long distance bound anaphor (LDBA). Also, based on the evidence from Yoruba, we agree with Thrainsson (1997), Cole, Hermon and Huang (2006), Cole, Hermon and Yanti (2010), and Reuland (2016), and others, that there exists two types of LDRs, the first type that is exemplified in languages like Chinese and Icelandic observes locality constraints while the second type exhibited in languages like Yoruba does not obey locality constraints. The Yoruba data also support Cole et al.'s hypothesis that LDRs are licensed by Infl. The evidence however suggests that two different Infl systems may be responsible for licensing LDRs, a case Infl, which is responsible for licensing the anti-local LDRs and a lexical Infl, which is responsible for LDRs that obey locality. The chapter also suggests that island violations in LDRs may be due to the type of verb that occurs in the matrix clause under which the LDR is embedded. Core logophoric verbs tend to permit island violations while non-core logophoric verbs do not.

References

Carstens, V. (1987). "Adjunct ECP effects in Yoruba." In *Proceedings of the Fifteenth Annual Meeting of the North Eastern Linguistic Society*, 49–62. Amherst: University of Massachusetts Press.

Chomsky, N. (1980). "On binding." *Linguistic Inquiry*, 11, 1–46.

Chomsky, N. (1981). *Lectures on Government and Binding*. Foris, Dordrecht.

Chomsky, N. (1986). *Barriers*. Cambridge, MA: MIT Press.

Chomsky, N. (1995). *The Minimalist Program*. Cambridge, MA: MIT Press.

Clements, G.N. (1975). "The logophoric pronoun in Ewe: Its role in discourse." *Journal of West African Languages*, 10, 141–177.

Cole, P. and Hermon, G. (1998). "Long-distance reflexives in Singapore Malay: An apparent anomaly." *Linguistic Typology*, 2(1), 57–98.

Cole, P. and Hermon, G. (2005). "The typology of Malay reflexives." *Lingua*, 115, 627–644.

Cole, P. and Hermon, G. (2015). "Grammar of binding in the languages of the world: Innate or learned?" *Cognition* 141, 138–160.

Cole, P., Hermon, G. and Huang, C.-T.J. (2006). "Long distance binding in Asian languages." In M. Everaert and H.V. Reimsdijk (eds), *The Blackwell Companion to Syntax* (Vol. 3). Oxford: Blackwell.

Cole, P., Hermon, G. and Lee, C. L. (2001). "Grammatical and discourse conditions on long distance reflexives in two Chinese dialects." In P. Cole, G. Hermon and C.-T. J. Huang (eds), *Syntax and Semantics 33: Long Distance Reflexives*, 1–46. Leiden: Brill.

Cole, P., Hermon, G. and Sung, L. (1990). "Principles and parameters of long-distance reflexives." *Linguistic Inquiry*, 21, 1–22.

Cole, P., Hermon, G. and Yanti (2010). "Anaphora in traditional Jaambi Malay." In R. Mercado, E. Postsdam and L. Travis (eds), *Austronesian and Theoretical Linguistics*, 327–343. Amsterdam/ Philadelphia: John Benjamins.

Cole, P. and Sung, L. (1994). "Head movement and long-distance reflexives." *Linguistic Inquiry*, 25, 355–406.

Comrie, B. and Hyman, L. (1981). "Logophoric reference in Gokana." *Journal of African Languages and Linguistics*, 3, 19–37.

Cunnings, I., Patterson, C. and Fesler, C. (2014). "Variable binding and coreference in sentence comprehension: Evidence from eye movements." *Journal of Memory and Language*, 71, 39–56.

Harris, T. and Wexler, K. (2000)."An ERP investigation of binding and coreference." *Brain and Language*, 75, 313–346.

Huang, Y. (1995). *The Syntax and Pragmatics of Anaphora: A Study with Special Reference to Chinese*. Cambridge: Cambridge University Press.

Huang, C.-T. J. and Liu, C. S. L. (2001). "Logophoricity, attitudes, and ziji at the interface." In P. Cole, G. Hermon and C.-T. J. Huang (eds), *Syntax and Semantics 33: Long Distance Reflexives*, 141–195. Leiden: Brill.

Huang, C.-T. and Tang, C.-C. (1991). "The local nature of the long-distance reflexives in Chinese." In J. Koster and E. Reuland (eds), *Long Distance Anaphora*. Cambridge: Cambridge University Press.

Koopman, H. and Sportiche, D. (1989). "Pronouns, logical variables, and logophoricity in Abe." *Linguistic Inquiry*, 20, 555–588.

Koster, J. and Reuland, E. (eds) (1991). *Long Distance Anaphora*. Cambridge: Cambridge University Press.

Kuno, S. (1972). "Pronominalization, reflexivization, and discourse." *Linguistic Inquiry*, 3(2), 161–196.

Kuno, S. (1987). *Functional Syntax: Anaphora, Discourse, and Empathy*. Chicago: Chicago University Press.

Lasnik, H. and Saito, M. (1984). "On the nature of proper government." *Linguistic Inquiry*, 15, 235–289.

Lawal, N. (2006). "Yoruba pronominal anaphor Oun and the Binding Theory." In J. Mugane, J. Hutchinson, and D. Worman (eds), *Selected proceedings of the 35th Conference on African Linguistics: African Languages and Linguistics in Broad Perspectives* (245–257). Cambridge, MA.

Lawal, N. (1993). "Logophoric pronouns in Yoruba and the movement to Infl versus relativized subject hypothesis." Paper presented at the long-distance reflexives workshop, LSA Linguistic Institute, Cornell, July 5.

Lawal, N. (1993). "Serial verbs in Yoruba as adjunct phrases." *Lingua*, 91, 185–200.

Lawal, N. (1983). On defining complex sentences in Yoruba. PhD Thesis. University of Essex, UK.

Lidz, J. (1996). Dimensions of reflexivity. PhD Dissertation, University of Delaware.

Pica, P. (1987). "On the nature of reflexivization cycle." *North East Linguistic Society*, 17, 483–499.

Pollard, C. and Sag, I. (1992). "Anaphors in English and the scope of the binding theory." *Linguistic Inquiry*, 23, 261–305.

Pulleyblank, D. (1986). "Clitics in Yoruba." In H. Borer (ed.), *Syntax and Semantics: The Syntax of Pronominal Clitics*, 43–64. New York, NY: Academic Press.

Progovac, L. (1993). "Long distance reflexives: movement-to-Infl versus relativized SUBJECT." *Linguistic Inquiry*, 24(4), 755–772.

Progovac, L. (1992). "Relativized SUBJECT: long distance reflexives without movement." *Linguistic Inquiry*, 23, 671–680.

Reinhart, T. and Reuland, E. (1991) "Anaphors and logophors: an argument structure perspective." In J. Koster and E. Reuland (eds), *Long Distance Anaphora*, 283–321. Cambridge: Cambridge University Press.

Reinhart, T. and Reuland, E. (1993). "Reflexivity." *Linguistic Inquiry*, 24(4), 657–720.

Reuland, E. (1994). Commentary: The non-homogeneity of condition B and related issues. In B. Lust, G. Hermon and J. Kornfilt (eds), *Syntactic Theory and First Language Acquisition: Cross Linguistic Perspectives*, 227–246. Hillsdale, NJ: Lawrence Erlbaum Associates.

Reuland, E. (2001). "Primitives of binding." *Linguistic Inquiry*, 32(3), 439–492.

Reuland (2009). "Binding without identity: Towards a unified semantics for bound and exempt anaphors." In S. Lalitha Devi, A. Braneu and R. Mitkov (eds), *Anaphora Processing and Applications*. DAARC 2009. Lecture Notes in Computer Science, vol 5847, 69–79. Springer, Berlin, Heidelberg.

Reuland, E. (2016). "Grammar of binding in the languages of the world: Unity versus diversity." *Cognition*, Feb. 10, http://dx.doi.org.1016/j.cognition.2016.01.020.

Reuland, E. and Sigurjónsdóttir, H. A. (1997). "Long distance binding in Icelandic: Syntax or discourse." In H. Bennis, P. Pica and J. Rooryck (eds), *Atomism in Binding*, 323–34. Dordrecht: Foris.

Rizzi, L. (1986). "Null objects in Italian and the theory of pro." *Linguistic Inquiry*, 17(3): 501–557.

Rizzi, L. (1990) *Relativized Minimality*. Cambridge, MA: MIT Press.

Ross, J. R. (1967). *Constraints on Variables in Syntax*. Cambridge, MA: Massachusetts Institute of Technology.

Sells, P. (1987). "Aspects of logophoricity." *Linguistic Inquiry*, 18, 445–481.

Sigurdisson, H.A. (1990). "Long-distance reflexives and moods in Icelandic." In J. Maling and A. Zaenen (eds), *Modern Icelandic Syntax*, 309–346. New York, NY: Academic Press.

Sung, L. and Cole, P. (1997). "Long distance reflexives and islandhood in Chinese: Head movement versus adjunction to IP." *Journal of Chinese Linguistics*, 25(2), 177–192.

Tang, J.C-C. (1989). "Chinese reflexives." *Natural Language and Linguistic Theory*, 7, 93–121.

Thrainsson, H. (1976). "Reflexives and subjunctives in Icelandic." In papers from the Sixth Meeting of the North Eastern Linguistic Society 6, 225–239.

Thrainsson, H. (1997). "Icelandic long-distance (and other) reflexives: Morphology, syntax and semantics." Paper presented at the long-distance reflexives workshop, LSA Linguistic Institute, Cornell, July 5–6.

Zribi-Herz, A. (1989). "Anaphor binding and narrative point of view: English reflexive pronouns in sentence and discourse." *Language*, 65, 695–727.

12

THE ENCODING OF INFORMATION STRUCTURE IN AFRICAN LANGUAGES*

Nana Aba Appiah Amfo

Introduction

This chapter aims to provide an overview of how two eminent notions of information structure – focus and topic – are encoded in a number of African languages. The notion of information structure has for several decades been of interest to a number of linguists (see, for example, Halliday 1967, Chafe 1976, Jackendoff 1972, Vallduvi 1990, Lambrecht 1994, Bearth 1999, Gundel and Fretheim 2002, Breul 2004, Molnar and Winkler 2006, Amfo 2010, Fiedler and Schwarz 2010, Van der Wal 2015, Güldemann et al. 2015, Féry and Ishihara 2016). Generally speaking, information structure is preoccupied with the manner in which the propositional content of an utterance is organized such that it allows the speaker to highlight new and/or significant information, bearing in mind assumptions about the addressee's mental representations of the issues and entities at stake (Amfo 2010).

The study of information structure allows an interrogation of both formal and communicative aspects of language. The information structure of a sentence therefore provides formal expression to pragmatic reorganization of an intended proposition. For Lambrecht (1994) information structure consists of three important categories, which are (1) presupposition and assertion; (2) identifiability and activation; and (3) topic and focus.

This chapter focuses on the notions of focus and topic and how they find linguistic expression in a number of African languages. It explores the prosodic, syntactic, morphological and lexical strategies that speakers of these languages explore in their attempt to highlight significant and or new information in the communicative process. The chapter examines the identification of topic in these languages, against the background that topic (unlike focus) is not always linguistically marked (Fiedler 2007, Amfo 2010). As a result, the conditions for the linguistic marking of topic are explored as well as the linguistic strategies used in doing so. Finally, this chapter explores the relationship and the phonological identity between focus markers and clausal connectives observed in a number of (particularly Kwa) languages (Fieldler and Schwarz 2005, Fiedler 2007).

Focus and topic

In the discussion on information structure, focus has always remained an essential notion. It has been characterized variously by different authors. Following from Chafe's (1976) characterization, focus is sometimes viewed as the complement of topic, and specifically new information that is communicated about a topic (Jakendoff 1972, Chomsky [1972] 1970). Heine and Reh (1983) consider focus as new asserted information in opposition to given presupposed information. For Dik (1978, p. 19), focus "represents relatively the most important or salient information in the given setting." According to Lambrecht (1994, p. 207), focus is part of the asserted information in an utterance. It is "that portion of the proposition that cannot be taken for granted at the time of speech." It can neither be predicted nor recovered pragmatically. A similar view is shared by Halliday (1967).

Some writers consider focus in a broader perspective. Jacobs' (1983, 1988) and Rooth's definitions as cited in König (1991) consider focus as a means of establishing a relation between the value of the focused expression and a number of alternatives. Dakubu's (2005, p. 2) view is that focus involves "a contrast, a specification of what is salient in contrast to other possibilities . . . newness of information must not necessarily be interpreted as contrasting information as focus can also mean the assertion of a choice among conflicting possibilities." Generally speaking, therefore, "focus may be considered as the highlighting of salient non-derivable information linked to ongoing discourse" (Amfo 2010, p. 198).

Another conception of information structure, which often gets mentioned alongside focus, is topic. The notion of "aboutness" is considered crucial in the characterization of topic by several linguists including Kuno (1972), Gundel (1976), Dik (1978), Reinhart (1982) and Lambrecht (1994). This idea is captured in Strawson's ([1974] 1964) "Principle of Relevance," quoted in Lambrecht (1994), which says that a topic is "what is a matter of standing current interest or concern." For Lambrecht, "[t]he topic of a sentence is the thing which the proposition expressed by the sentence is ABOUT" (1994, p. 118). Therefore, a referent is construed as the topic of a proposition if, within context, the proposition is about this referent and it increases our knowledge of it. Topic is a pragmatic notion; as a result, it goes beyond noun phrases occupying specific argument positions such as subject or object positions. What is significant about the notion of topic is "the pragmatic relation of aboutness and relevance which exists between a specified referent and the proposition in question" (Amfo 2010, p. 216).

The following brief section provides information on the data sources for this chapter. The fourth section examines the linguistic strategies for encoding focus across a number of African languages, and I discuss the linguistic marking of topic in the fifth section. In the sixth section the relationship between identical focus markers and clausal connectives in some Kwa languages is explored. The seventh section is the conclusion.

Data sources

Africa is considered to be linguistically very diverse. While Maho (2004) suggests that there are 1,441 languages present on the continent, Simons and Fennig (2017) provide a much higher figure of 2,144. Greenberg's (1963) original classification of the languages of Africa into four language phyla (Afro-Asiatic, Niger-Korfordian, Nilo-Saharan and Khoisan) has been contested as inadequately representative of the continent's linguistic diversity. More recent classifications estimate a minimum of nineteen language families and isolates (cf. Dimmendaal 2008, Sands 2009). Even though Sands suggests at least twenty language families and isolates, she provides a pragmatic grouping (rather than a genetic classification) of seven language groupings for the purposes of her discussion. These are sign languages, Afroasiatic, Niger-Congo, Nilo-Saharan, Khoisan, Isolates and other African languages.

The examples cited in this chapter include languages from Afroasiatic, Niger-Congo, Nilo-Saharan, Khoisan and Isolates, even though there is a preponderance of examples from languages in the Niger-Congo family, by virtue of its sheer dominance on the continent, and the associated scholarly works available to me. The examples are mostly taken from published articles and conference presentations, as well as reference grammars. Without attempting to comprehensively cover each language group, I exemplify as appropriate, providing an overview of information structural encoding strategies across varied languages in Africa. The chapter takes a descriptive approach in examining the information structural encoding strategies.

Linguistic strategies for encoding focus

As Lambrecht (1994, p. 209) asserts, focus is a "relational pragmatic category." It is therefore a pragmatic notion that finds expression in different languages by various linguistic means. Fiedler and Schwarz (2010) suggest that African languages exploit a variety of means when signaling information structure.

Focus can be signaled phonologically by means of prosodic prominence. It could also be signaled by the use of specific lexical items known as focus markers/particles. Alternatively, a language could signal focus in its grammar by manipulating its unmarked word order. Other languages rely on the use of certain morphemes to highlight new and/or prominent aspects of their utterances. In sum, the linguistic expression of focus could be by phonological, lexical, syntactic or morphological means in specific languages. Sometimes a language makes use of more than one linguistic strategy in the expression of this pragmatic notion. The following sub-sections explore the various linguistic means that African languages use in indicating focus.

Phonological/prosodic strategies

The existence of lexical tone does not preclude the exploitation of pitch/tone for information structural purposes (see, for example, Downing et al. 2004, Downing 2006, 2008, Gordon 2004). Therefore, prosody is exploited, often in combination with other strategies, for the expression of focus in some African languages. For instance, Van de Velde and Idiatov (2016) report that stem initial consonants (SIC) of words in a number of North West Bantu languages that express new information focus or words that are contrastively focused are lengthened. Also, new information focus on final V is realized with stem-initial C-emphasis, and corrective focus on prefix V is realized with prefix C-emphasis.

Downing (2008) shows that some Bantu languages, such as Chichewa, Durban Zulu and Chitumbuka, use phonological re-phrasing (rather than prominence) as the main prosodic feature associated with focus. Downing et al. (2004) suggest that in Chichewa, in situ focus of a VP element is signaled by "only a change in the phonological phrasing of the VP" (p. 169). This involves a phonological phrase boundary after the focused element, while the remaining constituent of the VP forms a separate phonological phrase. In the example below, (1b) is illustrative of object NP focus, while it is V which is focused in (1c).[1]

(1) a *a-na-góná   m-nyumbá   yá Mávúuto.*
       They slept   in-house   of Mavuto.
       'They slept in Mavuto's house.'

    b Where did they sleep? (Object NP focus)
       (a-na-góná m-nyumbá yá Mávúuto)

c   What did they do in Mavuto's house (V focus)
(a-na-góona) (m-nyumbá yá Mávúuto)

[Chichewa; Niger-Congo; Benue-Congo: Malawi.]
Kanerva 1990, p. 170

In addition to phonological rephrasing, Downing et al. (2004) suggest that downdrift is exploited at phonological phrase boundaries as an added prosodic signal of focus.

Syntactic strategies

African languages have a number of syntactic strategies for indicating which part of the sentence is non-derivable and salient (see Bearth 2009, Aboh et al. 2007, Güldemann et al. 2015). Focus could be marked by the use of cleft constructions, movement of the focused element or simply in situ, where the default word order is maintained. Zeller (2015) suggests that the use of a cleft construction may be the most common strategy in indicating focus in African languages. It is possible for the focused element, which is introduced by a copula, to be modified by a relative clause as in (2) and (3).[2]

(2) *nəḥna   ina   nə-ʔabrəhat   zə-rəʔena.*
    we   COP   OM-Abrahat   REL-saw:1PL
    'It is WE who saw Abrahat.'

[Tigrinya; Semitic; Afro-Asiatic: Eritrea, Ethiopia.]
Gragg 1974, p. 75, cf. Zeller 2015

(3) *à   ní n-dórə   mə   m-ʃɔ w-á   à   ká   dórə.*
    It is NMLZ-playing COMP I-chief I-the SBJ FUT   play
    'It is PLAYING that the chief will play.'

[Bafut; Ngemba; Benue-Congo; Niger-Congo, Cameroun.]
Tamanji 2009, p. 185

In some instances, focus could be signaled by placing the focused constituent clause-initially, as illustrated in example (4) below.

(4) *aob   ge   tarasa   ra   mu.*
    man+3M.SG   IND   woman+3F.SG+OBL   PROG see
    'THE/A MAN is seeing the/a woman.'

[Khoekhoe; Central Khoisan; Khoisan: Namibia.]
Haacke 2006, p. 114

According to Watters (2000), focused constituents in some African languages occur in clause-final position, as exemplified in the Rundi example in (5).

(5) *Yohani   a-á-oógeje   néezá   imiduga.*
    John:NC1   SM:NC1-PAST-wash:PERF   well   cars:NC4
    'John washed CARS well (not trucks).'

[Rundi; Bantu; Niger-Congo: Rwanda and Burundi.]
Ndayiragije 1999, p. 411

The encoding of information structure

Another recognized focus position in some Bantu languages is the 'immediately after verb' (IAV) position (Watters 1979, Buell 2009, Van der Wal 2014). As a result an SVO language could express focus by a VSO word order (when the subject is in focus), while a VSO language will result in a VOS word order when the object is focused. In Aghem, the unmarked word order is SVO, however the VSO order presented in (6) indicates that the subject noun 'friends' is in focus.

(6) *à mɔ   zi   á-fín   bé-'kɔ́.*
    EXPL PAST eat   friends fufu
    'The FRIENDS ate the fufu.'

[Aghem; Bantu; Niger-Congo, Cameroun.]
Watters 1979, p. 146

Similarly, in Mambila (Atlantic-Congo), the focused noun phrase occurs after the verb. Any noun phrase occurring before the verb is therefore out of focus. In (7a) and (7b) the nouns occurring word-finally, 'cloth' and 'yesterday', are in focus.

(7) a *Mè   léílé   ŋgeé   naa   cɔgɔ.*
       1SG   yesterday buy   PST   cloth.
       'It was CLOTH that I bought yesterday.'

    b *Mè   cɔgɔ   ŋgeé   naa   léílé.*
       1SG   cloth buy   PST   yesterday.
       'It was YESTERDAY that I bought cloth.'

[Mambila; Atlantic-Congo; Niger-Congo: Chad.]
Perrin 1994, pp. 233–236

Morphological strategies

Some languages resort to certain morphological strategies to indicate focus. It may come in the form of the use of verbal affixes or clitics as well as the use of specific morphemes in marking focus. According to Kalinowski (2015a), this involves the exploitation of verbal morphology. Morphemes may be added, absent, or they may be different from what might be anticipated. Hartmann and Zimmerman (2006) cite Gùrùntùm (Chadic, Afro-Asiatic) as one language in which focus is morphologically marked. This is done by preceding the focused constituent with the morpheme *a*, which is usually realized with a high tone. The focused constituent often remains in situ, but it is possible for it to occur ex situ. What is significant is that it should be preceded by the marker *á*. This is exemplified in (8) and (9).

(8) Q: Á   *kãã   mài   tí   bà   wúmi?*
       FOC what   REL   3SG   PROG chew
       'WHAT is he chewing?'
    A: *Tí   bà   wúm-á   kwálingálá.*
       3SG   PROG chew-FOC   colanut.
       'He is chewing COLANUT.'

[Gùrùntùm; Chadic; Afro-Asiatic: Nigeria.]
Hartmann and Zimmerman 2006, p. 6

(9) Q: *Á   kwá bà   pán   má-ì?*
     FOC who PROG carry water-DEF
     'WHO is carry the water?'
   A: *Á   Hàfsá bà   pàn   má-ì.*
     FOC Hafsa PROG carry water-DEF
     'HAFSA is carrying the water.'

[Gùrùntùm; Chadic; Afro-Asiatic: Nigeria.]
Hartmann and Zimmerman 2006, p. 6

Hartmann and Zimmerman (2006) suggest that the focus morpheme *á* interacts closely with its preceding content word. In (8), it is cliticized to the preceding verb, and takes the tone of the elided final vowel of that verb. Morphologically and phonologically, the focus marker integrates into the preceding content word.

Kalinowski (2015a) reports that in Noon (Niger-Congo, Northern Atlantic), the absence of an expected verbal morpheme provides an indication of the focus structure of the phrase. When the subject is in focus, the verb lacks all tense-aspect-mood (TAM) marking (10a). This can be contrasted with the example in (10b) where the verb is encoded for tense as an indication of non-subject focus.

(10) a *Yëri   dëk Kaan-faa   fúunee.*
        EMPH   live hourse-DEF   DEM.
        'HE lives in the house over there.'

    b *Mi   hot-ee   Demba ga was-aa-ma.*
       I   see-PST   Demba on road-DEF-ANAPH.
       'I saw Demba ON THE ROAD THERE.'

[Noon; Niger-Congo; Northern-Atlantic: Senegal.]
Soukka 2000. pp. 302, 304, cited in Kalinowski 2015a, p. 81

Zeller (2015) reports that focus (and topic) in a number of African languages are marked by special verbal affixes. For instance, in !Xun (Northern Khoisan), focus is indicated by attaching a suffix to the focused constituent. In addition, the out-of-focus part of the sentence is marked by a topic marker. Hausa (Chadic, Afro-Asiatic) makes use of special verbal morphology in addition to an optional focus-marking copula (Newman 2000, Jaggar 2001).

Kalinowski and Good (2014) indicate another morphological focus-encoding strategy. This involves the use of different morphological forms of the verb as a means of signaling focus properties of certain constituents in the sentence. Citing examples from Makhuwa (Bantu, Niger-Congo), they show that this language has two verbal paradigms in certain tenses that are used to indicate the information-structural status of the following constituent. This strategy is similar to valency-changing morphology, such as the use of passive morphemes. However, the determining factor in this case is information structure rather than thematic role assignment. As illustrated in (11), the information structural difference between (11a) and (11b) is evident through the different verbal morphology exhibited by the two verbs.

(11) a *nthiyáná o-hoó-cá   nráma.*
        woman   1SBJ-PERF.DJ-eat rice.
        'The woman ate rice.'

The encoding of information structure

> b   *nthiyáná*   *o-c-aalé*   *nramá.*
>   woman   1SBJ-PERF.CJ-eat   rice.
>   'The woman ate RICE.'
>
>   [Makhuwa; Bantu; Niger-Congo: Mozambique.]
>   *Van der Wal 2011, p. 1735*

Morphological marking of focus is also evident in Likpe, as seen in (12b) when compared with (12a). When the subject of a sentence is in focus, the usual subject agreement marker does not occur on the verb.

(12)   a   *o-sani*   *ə̂-mə̂*   *ə-təkə.n.ko*   *u-sió*   *ə̂-mə̂.*
             NC-man   NC-DET   SBJ-follow   NC-woman   NC-DET.
             'The man followed the woman.'

       b   *o-saní*   *ə̂-mə̂*   *li-təkə.n.ko*   *u-sió*   *ə̂-mə.*
             NC-man   NC-DET   DEP:PST-follow   NC-woman   NC-DET.
             'THE MAN followed the woman.'

                                     [Likpe; Kwa; Niger-Congo: Ghana.]
                                             Ameka 2010, p. 151

In Wolof, a focused verb is presented in the perfective, as illustrated in (13).

(13)   *Peer*   *tekk*   *na.*
      Pierre   eat   PERF.3SG
      'Pierre ATE (And that's that).'

                              [Wolof; Niger-Congo; Northern-Atlantic: Senegal.]
                                       Robert 2000, p. 234

In some languages, like Fula (Niger-Congo, Atlantic-Congo), tense morphemes also encode focus. As a result, the tense morphemes in the language has two forms depending on which constituent of the sentence is in focus.

(14)   a   *cukalel*   *ngel*   *ayn-u*   *puccu ngu,*   *ngel*   *lootaani*   *ngu.*
             Child   the   tend-PFV.FOC   horse   the   he   wash.PFV.NEG   the.
             'The child TENDED the horse, he didn't wash it.'

       b   cukalel   negel   ayn-ata   puccu   ngu.
             Child   the   tend-IPFV4.FOC   horse   the.
             'It is THE CHILD who will tend the horse.'

                              [Fula; Niger-Congo; Northern Atlantic: Senegal.]
                                       Robert 2010, p. 238

Sometimes, it is the nominal morphology that is exploited for the indication of focus. When a subject is focused in Oromo (Cushitic, Afro-Asiatic), the nominative affix is absent, as reflected in the pair of examples in (15a) and (15b) (Kalinowski 2015a).

(15)   a   *Túlluu-n*   *hin-duf-a.*
             T-NOM   FOC-come-3M.SG.IPFV
             'Tulluu will COME.'

Nana Aba Appiah Amfo

b *Túlluu   duf-e.*
T   come-3M.SG-PFV
'TULLUU came.'

[Oromo; Cushitic; Afro-Asiatic: Ethiopia and Kenya.]
Yimam 1988, pp. 368–369

In the Sandawe example in (16) the focused constituent, the object of the construction, is indicated by the suffixation of an inflectional morpheme encoding person, gender and number (PGN).

(16) *ʔàʔá   hĕÛ ⁿlèmésé: nèmà-à   wák'wâ:*
No   this man   African civet cat-3m.sg.PGN   kill
'No, this man has killed AN AFRICAN CIVET CAT.'

[Sandawe; Khoisan: Tanzania.]
Eaton 2005, pp. 21–22

Lexical strategies

A number of African languages make use of free morphemes in indicating focus in utterances. Some authors (Amfo 2010, Akortia 2014, Broohm 2014) have labeled this as a lexical strategy to distinguish it from the kind of focus marking that involves morphological strategies such as affixation, cliticization and the manipulation of verbal and nominal morphology. This strategy basically involves the use of specific (free) morphemes that have been labeled variously in the literature as focus markers, particles or morphemes. Examples of such lexical items that are used to mark focus in a number of African languages include *nà* (Akan, Kwa; Boadi 1974, Amfo 2010), *ní* (Kisi, Southern Atlantic; Childs 1995, 2003, Zeller 2015), *yéyé* (Esahie, Kwa; Broohm 2014), *nɛ* (Dangme, Kwa; Ofoe 2007, Akortia 2014), *lá, lé*, (Konkomba, Gur, Schwarz 2007), *nɪ* (Foodo, Guan; Fiedler 2007), *ka, n, la, mi* (Dagbani, Gur; Hudu 2012, Issah 2012), *ya* (Soninke, Mande; Kalinowski 2015a), *ni* (Ma'di, Nilo-Saharan; Blackings and Fabb 2003), *nẽ* (Kresh, Nilo-Saharan; Brown 1989). The presence of *nẽ* in the Kresh example in (17) is the indication that the verb is in focus.

(17) *ũjũ   ĕté   nẽ.*
He-greeted   him   FOC
'He GREETED him.'

[Kresh, Nilo-Saharan: Sudan.]
Brown 1989, pp. 334–335

It is, however, worth noting that the lexical marking of focus in African languages hardly happens in isolation, an issue to which I return on page 251 ff.

Another lexical strategy used in signaling focus is the use of proforms. According to Kalinowski (2015a), this may come in the form of pronouns or verbal copies depending on whether it is a noun or a verb which is being focused. Edo (Edoid, Niger-Congo) makes use of such a strategy. In (18), focus is indicated by the use of the pronoun *ó*, while in (19), a nominalized copy of the verb is the focus indicating element.

(18) *Òsàró ó   bó   òwá.*
Osaro PRO   build   house.
'It is OSARO who built the house.'

(19) *Òtué   è ré   òzó   tuè   mwè.*
Greeting it be Ozo   greet 1SG.
'It is GREETING that Ozo greeted me.'

[Edo; Edoid; Niger-Congo: Nigeria.]
Omoruyi 1989, pp. 281, 288

In the Nupe (Nupiod, Niger-Congo) example in (20), the verb *gí* 'eat' is copied as is to final position as a means of indicating that it is in focus.

(20) *Musa è   gí   bise gí.*
Musa PRES eat   hen eat.
'Musa is in fact EATING a hen.'

[Nupe; Nupoid; Niger-Congo: Nigeria.]
Kandybowicz 2008, p. 47

Contrary to the Nupe example in (20), in Vata (Kru, Niger-Congo), the verb copy is placed sentence initially as illustrated in (21).

(21) *Lē   à   lē   sàka.*
Eat   we   eat   rice
We are really EATING rice

[Vata; Kru; Niger-Congo: Côte d'Ivoire.]
Koopman 1983, pp. 38

In most African languages where focus particles are used in the encoding of focus, they are often used in combination with other linguistic strategies. This issue of using mixed strategies to signal focus is the subject of the next subsection.

Mixed strategies

In indicating information structure in general and focus in particular, African languages often employ a mixture of strategies. The most common of these mixed strategies are lexico-syntactic and morpho-syntactic.

Lexico-syntactic strategies involve the use of a free morpheme (lexical item), often labeled as a focus marker or particle, and some other syntactic strategy such as the manipulation of the unmarked word order in the language or the use of a cleft or pseudo-cleft construction. In a number of languages, the marked word order involves fronting of the focused constituent to sentence initial position. In the Esahie (Kwa, Niger-Congo) example in (22), a cleft construction is used to present the focused constituent, which in itself is a marked syntactic construction. In addition, the focused constituent 'Yaa' is immediately followed by an obligatory focus particle *yéyé*.

(22) *ɔ-te Yaa yéyé   ye-wo   yɛ nyemene.*
It-be Yaa FOC   3SG-REFL   be beautiful.
'It is YAA who is beautiful.'

[Esahie; Kwa; Niger-Congo: Ghana.]
Broohm 2014, p. 52

In Somali (Afro-Asiatic, Eastern Cushitic), the focused constituent is placed in initial position, and is immediately followed by the focus marker *baa*. As a result, we find both the subject (23a) and the object (23b) in initial positions, an indication that these constituents are in focus in their respective sentences. The information structural status of these constituents is reinforced by the following focus marker *baa*.

(23) a *Habartii baa hadashay oo tiri* . . .
Old woman FOC spoke and said . . .
'The OLD WOMAN spoke and said . . .'

[Somali; Afro-Asiatic; Eastern Cushitic: Somalia.]
Saeed 1999, p. 234

b *Maryan baa Cali dilay.*
Maryan FOC Cal.subj beat.RST.SM
'It was MARYAN whom Cal beat.'

[Somali; Afro-Asiatic; Eastern Cushitic: Somalia.]
Tosco 2002, p. 35

A similar situation is found in Nǁng (Tuu, Taa–!Kwi), where the focus marker *ke* is used in addition to initial placement of the focused constituent (24).

(24) *ǂxanisi ke Katarina aa ǀoba.*
Book FOC Katarina give child.
'Katarina gives the child a BOOK.'

[Nǁng; Tuu; Taa–!Kwi: South Africa.]
Güldemann and Witzlack-Makarevich 2013, p. 6

In (25), the Dangme (Kwa, Niger-Congo) focused constituent is placed in initial position followed by a focus particle, and an optional recapitulating pronoun may be found in the out-of-focus part of the sentence.

(25) *Tòkòtá nɔ nɛ (è) klè pè mò.*
Shoe DEM FM (3SG.SUBJ) big exceed 2SG.OBJ
'THIS SHOE is bigger than you.'

[Dangme; Kwa; Niger-Congo: Ghana.]
Ofoe 2007, p. 89

Both the content question word *mìnɛ* 'what' and the *àcɛɛ* 'beans' in the Foodo example in (26) are placed in the focus pre-sentential position, followed by the focus particle *nɪ*.

(26) Q: *mìnɛ nì ɔcʋm wɪ?*
What FM woman eat.
'What did the woman eat?'
A: *àcɛɛ nɪ ɔ wɪ.*
Beans FM 3sg eat.
'She ate BEANS.'

[Foodo; Kwa; Niger-Congo: Benin.]
Fiedler 2007, p. 100

Focusing of content question words is not uncommon in Kwa languages. In Akan (Kwa, Niger-Congo), for example, question words can be pre-posed in focus position and followed by the focus particle *nà*, even though it is possible to have the question word in situ.

The encoding of information structure

Compare (27) and (28). Focusing of the content question word performs the pragmatic function of highlighting and placing emphasis on the constituent being questioned.

(27) Q: *Kofi kɔ he?*
       Kofi go where?
       'Where has Kofi gone to?'
       A: *Kofi kɔ Kumase.*
       Kofi go Kumasi.
       'Kofi has gone to Kumasi.'

(28) Q: *ɛhe   na Kofi kɔ?*
       where   FM Kofi go?
       'WHERE has Kofi gone to?'
       A: *Kumase na   Kofi kɔ.*
       Kumasi FM   Kofi go.
       'Kofi is gone to KUMASI.'

It is not always the case that the focused constituent is adjacent to the focused particle. In Kisi (Southern Atlantic, Niger Congo), the focused constituent takes initial position while the focus particle is in final position as seen in (29).

(29) *Mààlóŋ ó   có   cùùcúúwó ní.*
       Rice   he   AUX   sow   FOC
       'It is RICE that he is sowing.'

[Kisi; Southern Atlantic; Niger Congo: Guinea and Sierra Leone.]
Childs 2003, p. 134

Similar to the lexico-syntactic strategies, morpho-syntactic strategies involve exploiting word order in addition to the use of certain morphological markers to indicate focus. In Khoekhoe (Central Khoisan), the focused constituent may be placed in initial position in addition to some other morphological marking. According to Haacke (2006), the focused constituent *tarasa* 'woman' in (30) is followed by a subject clitic *b*, while the subject of the sentence follows the declarative particle *ge*.

(30) *Tara-s-a   b   ge   ao-b-a   ra   mu.*
       Woman-3F.SG-OBL he   DECL man-3M.SG-OBL   ASP   see
       'THE WOMAN, he – the man – is seeing.'

[Khoekhoe; Central Khoisan; Khoisan: Namibia.]
Haacke 2006, p. 117

Inflection, combined with word order, is one of the means that Sandawe (Central Khoisan) exploits to indicate focus. In (31), in addition to the presence of a PGN morpheme present on the focused adverb, it is placed in the immediate preverbal position.

(31) *Nâm sómbá ʔútê-sà   ↓tʰímé.*
       Nam fish   yesterday-3F.SG.PGN   cook.
       'Nam cooked the fish YESTERDAY.'

[Sandawe; Central Khoisan; Khoisan: Tanzania.]
Eaton 2005, p. 22

253

Topic marking

Topic marking has not received as much attention in the linguistic literature as focus marking. This does not come as a surprise since, unlike focus, topic in most languages of the world "is not consistently overtly marked (whether prosodically, morphologically or lexically)" (Amfo 2010, p. 215). Overt linguistic marking of topic seems not to be mandatory in many languages. However, according to Andersen (2015), topic marking appears to be widespread in some Western Nilotic languages. For instance, in Dinka (Western Nilotic, Nilo-Saharan), topic is marked by an initial noun phrase in addition to a proclitic on the verb that agrees for number. Andersen suggests that this topic marking strategy of exploiting constituent word order in addition to the use of verbal morphology is attested in Kurmuk (Northern Burun, Western Nilotic) as well. In the Kurmuk example in (32), the topic phrase (in bold) is placed initially in addition to a specific verbal morphology.

(32) a *ṯáarák* ↓*bóor-ú*   *dɛ̀ɛl kʌ*   *ŋìr.*
person skin-PST   goat PREP   knife.
'**The man** skinned a goat with a knife.'

  b *dɛ̀ɛl bóor-út-ì*   *ŋʌ*   *ṯáarák kʌ*   *ŋìr.*
goat skin-PST-NST   NOM   person PREP   knife.
'The man skinned **the goat** with a knife.'

  c *ŋìr*   *bóor-út-↓í*   *dɛ̀ɛl ŋʌ*   *áarák.*
Knife   skin-PST-NST.ADJ   goat NOM   person.
'The man skinned a goat **with a knife**.'

[Kurmuk; Northern Burun; Western Nilotic: Sudan.]
Andersen 2015, p. 510

Wondimu (2013) proposes that topic in Gamo (Northern Ometo, Omotic) may be indicated by morphological, lexical or syntactic means. The use of the different strategies provide an indication of the different topic functions being signaled. The use of the –*ka* morpheme in (33) signals a topic shift.

(33) *Etti-ka*   *"hess-adey   haʔi   awa-n*   *dizee?" gida*   *izi-ka*
They-TOP   this.M-man   now   where-LOC   exist-Q say-3P-PERF-3P   3S-TOP
"ta ʔerikke"   *g-i-d-ees.*
1S know-NEG-1S   say-3MS-PERF-3MS
'[They]$_{Top}$ [said "where is this man now?"]$_{comment}$ and [he]$_{Top}$ [said "I don't know".]$_{comment}$
[Gamo; Northern Ometo; Omotic: Ethiopia.]
Wondimu 2013, pp. 3–4

When the topic of an utterance is overtly indicated by some linguistic means, it often implies a contrast with a different entity that may be expressed overtly within the linguistic context, or that entity can be recovered contextually. According to Zeller (2015), topic is standardly marked by means of left or right dislocation. Additionally, a resumptive pronoun or a pronominal clitic may be present in the accompanying comment clause. In the Akan (Kwa, Niger-Congo) example (34) below, Kodwo is marked as the topic by the particle *dze* because he is being contrasted with another person. At the same time, it signals a change in the topic of discussion. This piece of information is derived from the linguistic context. He is being implicitly compared and

The encoding of information structure

contrasted with another person who prefers to continue with her education, and who had been the topic of the immediately preceding utterances (Amfo 2010).

(34) *Kodwo dze   ɔ-mm-pɛ   dɛ   ɔ-kɔ-sɔw   n'adzesua   do.*
Kodwo CTM   he-NEG-like   COMP   he-MP-continue   his'education   continue.
'As for Kodwo, he doesn't want to continue his education.'

[Akan; Kwa; Niger-Congo: Ghana.]
Amfo 2010, p. 219

Again, in (35), Dangme (Kwa, Niger-Congo) *imi* 'me' is marked as the topic, by means of the topic marker *lɛɛ*, because the speaker's intention is to contrast the referent of *imi* 'me' with another person who is perceived as being younger than him. Indeed, Akortia (2014) suggests that *lɛɛ* is used to create the effect of comparison and contrast.

(35) *Imi   lɛɛ   I wa pe   Afi.*
Me   PRT   I old than   Afi.
'For me, I am older than Afi.'

[Dangme; Kwa; Niger-Congo: Ghana.]
Akortia 2014, p. 72

Notice that in both examples (34) and (35) above, the comment clause contains a resumptive or recapitulating pronoun that picks up the fronted topic. Evidently, when the topic of an utterance is linguistically marked there is either a topic shift or an implied contrast, or both.

Komo (Koman, Nilo-Saharan) has two proclitics, *à=* and *go=*, which superficially mark gender and number. However, according to Otero (2015), a careful analysis of these proclitics indicate that they mark topic – precisely, they indicate identifiability and activation.

(36) *à=ɔ   ʃi hà-ʊ-n.*
ID-rain   ʃi come-AD2-3N.
'The rain came.'

(37) *da   kwì-í-r=gì   yɛlà,   go=giɛrɛn ʃi, i-ʊ-n   yàkà   lí ɓika?*
SUB.1   fall-AD1-3SG.M=gì   then   go=others ʃi, go.PL-AD2-3PL   again   this way.
'When he fell then, the others however, they came this way again.'

[Komo; Koman. Nilo-Saharan, Ethiopia, Sudan, South Sudan.]
Otero 2015, p. 10

Ameka (2010) identifies another group of topic constructions that may be linguistically marked as such in Kwa languages. These he labels as 'topic and comment only constructions'. Even for such constructions, he suggests, as has been observed earlier, the topic phrase "need not be overtly marked" (Ameka 2010, p. 166). Note the optionality of the topic marker *lá* in the Ewe example in (38).

(38) *Núnyá   (lá)   adidó-é   así   mé-tu-nɛ   o.*
Knowledge   TOP   baobab-aFOC   hand   NEG-reach-HAB:3SG   NEG.
'Knowledge (is like) a baobab tree, it cannot be embraced.'

[Ewe; Kwa; Niger-Congo: Ghana.]
Ameka 2010, p. 166

Example (39) illustrates this kind of topic marking in Ga. The clause that follows the topic constituent provides a comment on the marked topic.

(39) *Kòolòó !ɛ,   òkpɔŋɔ !ní.*
Animal TOP,   horse   FOC.
'The animal, it's a horse.'

[Ga; Kwa; Niger-Congo: Ghana.]
Ameka 2010, p. 166

In addition to the topic-comment function signaled by overt topic markers in African languages, overt linguistic marking of topic may be used to perform a 'scene-setting' function (cf. Lambrecht 1994, Amfo 2010, Broohm 2014). This function is evident when whole clauses rather than noun phrases exhibit overt linguistic topic marking. In such instances, the assertion in the topic clause provides background information and serves as a basis for presenting the information in the utterance that immediately follows. The Akan and Esahie examples in (40) and (41) are illustrative of the above.

(40) *Árábá nyé   àwófó nó   tsé   dzé,   nàásó   né   dzín   á.*
Araba COM   parents DEF   stay   CTM,   CONTM   POSS   name   FM.
'Indeed Araba stays with the parents, but it is just in name.'

[Akan; Kwa; Niger-Congo: Ghana.]
Amfo 2010, p. 220

(41) *Me   nnya sika   dé   a,   n-gɔ   hɔ.*
1SG   get   money CTM   CM   1SG-will   go.
'If I get money, I will go.'

[Esahie; Kwa; Niger-Congo: Ghana.]
Broohm 2014, p. 120

Clausal connectives and focus markers

Kalinowski (2015b) suggests that focus particles in African languages derive from copulas, demonstratives, deictics and relative clauses. In this section I discuss the possible clausal connective source for focus particles in some Kwa languages, namely Akan, Dangme, and Ga, all spoken in Ghana, and Foodo, spoken in Benin.

The first thing that is striking is the phonological identity of the focus particles in these languages, and clausal connectives that perform coordinating functions.

The consistency of the observed phonological identity should not be dismissed as coincidental as a result of an immediate apparent lack of logical explanation for that. In their examination of the focus constructions in five Gur and Kwa languages, Fiedler and Schwarz (2005) propose that many of these focus constructions can be analyzed as bi-clausal constructions comparable

Table 12.1 Focus and clausal connectives in some Kwa languages

Language	Focus particle	Clausal connective
Akan	nà	nà
Dangme	nɛ	nɛ
Foodo	nɩ	nɩ
Ga	nì	nì

The encoding of information structure

to clause sequencing in narration. They contend that grammaticalization may obscure such narrative structures. Their assertions are largely based on observed similarities between the out-of-focus part of the focus constructions and narrative clauses. This continues to be a matter for further research in individual languages and language groups. Indeed, the phenomenon described above, where there is phonological identity between the focus marker and clausal connective is not restricted to Kwa languages. Güldemann and Witzlack-Makarevich (2013), in discussing the *ke*-constructions in Khoekhoe (Central Khoisan, Khoisan), suggest that the marker plays the role of a discourse linker as well as a focus marker.[3]

All the Kwa languages mentioned above, for which there is phonological identity between focus particles and clausal connectives, tend to mark focus by the use of mixed strategies. As a result, it is not the mere presence of the focus particle that suggests a focused constituent. The particle, when used, is done in combination with other syntactic strategies. In Akan, the obligatory focus particle *nà* combines with either fronting or clefting to indicate focus as seen in (42) and (43):

(42)　*ɛ-yɛ*　　*Amo*　*nà*　　*ɔ-di-i*　　　　*aduane no*　　*nyinaa.*
　　　　it-COP　Amo　FM　　he-eat-COMPL　food　DEF　　all.
　　　　'It is Amo who ate all the food.'

(43)　*Amo nà*　　*ɔ-di-i*　　　　*aduane no*　　*nyinaa.*
　　　　Amo FM　　he-eat-COMPL　food　DEF　　all.
　　　　'AMO ate all the food.'

In essence, then, especially when a cleft construction is used, there is no structural difference between a focus construction and a coordinating (narrative) construction as in (44):

(44)　*Ama di-i*　　　　*aduane no*　　*nyinaa nà*　　　*ɔ-da-e.*
　　　　Ama eat-COMPL　food　DEF　　all　　CONJ　she-sleep.
　　　　'Ama ate all the food and she slept.'

It can be argued that the constructions in both (42) and (44) are bi-clausal, with *nà* serving as a clause linker. Note that in (42) the structure of the second clause, the out-of-focus clause, is preserved, due to the presence of a recapitulating pronoun represented as *ɔ*. One can thus infer that *nà* is a general marker of clause connectedness. The specific role it plays in a particular construction is contingent on the semantics and pragmatics of the individual units that it links.

In Dangme, like Akan, the use of the focus particle in focus constructions is obligatory. Again, in Akan, it is not used in isolation; its use combines with the placing of the focused constituent in initial position. Clefting may be used to indicate focus, however it does not combine with the use of the focus particle *nɛ*. The absence of the focus particle in constructions that involve clefts, in addition to the absence of a pronoun trace in the out-of-focus part of the focus construction, provides indication of further gramaticalization in Dangme of a bi-clausal construction into a single one. In spite of this, the linking role of the particle *nɛ* is still evident as it links the focused constituent with the main clause or the predicate, as the case may be.

There is the clearest indication in Ga that the taunted focus particle may after all not be the primary focus indicating element. In this language, the placing of the focused constituent in initial pre-subject position is the primary means of indicating focus. The focus particle is required in addition to this strategy only when the focused constituent is the grammatical subject of the construction. Clearly, the role of *nì* as a focus particle in Ga is minimized. It continues to play its role as a linker though, connecting the focused constituent to the rest of the construction, where required. It stands to reason then that the primary role of these particles is to provide linkage between units of complex clauses. At the extreme end of the continuum, the linkage is between two (or more) clauses. As we move along the continuum, we observe variations in the kinds of constituents that are linked by these particles, such as a phrase and a clause. Subject to further research in individual languages, one may speculate that the original coordinating linking role of these particles may be evolving to take on a more general clause linkage role.

Conclusion

This chapter has presented strategies for the encoding of information structure in a cross section of African languages. It has been noted that African languages resort to the use of phonological, syntactic, morphological and lexical strategies in indicating focus. Often, more than one of these strategies are exploited for the purposes of marking focus. Thus, a language may resort to lexico-syntactic or morpho-syntactic means of signaling focus.

Topic marking is not obligatory in African languages; a situation that pertains in other languages of the world. When African languages tend to mark topic, it is by the use of topic markers in the form of free or bound morphemes or the exploitation of word order. It was observed that when topic is marked what is communicated is a topic shift or a contrast or both. This is also done for the purposes of identifiability and activation. Additionally, a topic-comment construction can linguistically be marked as such. As a result, the clause that follows the topic constituent provides a comment (often additional information) on the topic of the clause. Finally, when a whole clause is marked as the topic of an utterance, it serves as a scene-setting clause for the following clause.

The phonological identity between some focus markers and clausal connectives in some Kwa languages provides the basis for an exploration of the relationship between these two groups of markers and, by extension, focus constructions and clausal conjunctions. Subject to further investigations in specific languages, the tentative conclusion is that these markers may be viewed as general markers of linkage. The semantics and pragmatics of the constructions and constituents they link provide input for a more specific characterization of the markers in context.

I conclude that the linguistic encoding of focus and topic in African languages is varied and sometimes complex. Specific languages and language groups explore various linguistic resources available through the phonology, morphology, syntax and lexicon of the languages, for the communication of salient discourse information. More significantly, the study of the linguistic expression of information structure in these languages provides an avenue for the interaction of interface studies within linguistics.

Notes

* I acknowledge the support of my research assistant, Mary Edward, in the collation of data for this chapter.
1 Note that bracketing is used to indicate phonological phrase boundaries.
2 The examples used in this chapter are mostly from published tests/articles, conference presentations and reference grammars. I have kept the (interlinear) glosses as they are in the original, except that, for consistency, I use small caps in indicating the focused constituents.
3 There is the need for further study to ascertain the extent of this phenomenon in this language group and possibly others.

References

Aboh, E. O., Hartmann, K. & Zimmermann, M. (2007). *Focus strategies in African languages: The interaction of focus and grammar*. Berlin: Mouton de Gruyter.

Akortia, P. T. (2014). *Lexical marking of information structure in Dangme* (MPhil thesis, Norwegian University of Science and Technology, Trondheim, Norway). Retrieved from https://brage.bibsys.no/xmlui//bitstream/handle/11250/244332/743791_FULLTEXT01.pdf?sequence=1.

Ameka, F. (2010). Information packaging constructions in Kwa: Micro-variation and typology. In E. O. Aboh and J. Esegbey (Eds), *Topics in Kwa syntax* (pp. 141–176). Dordrecht: Springer.

Amfo, N. A. A. (2010). Lexical signaling of information structure. *Linguistics* 48(1), 195–225.

Andersen, T. (2015). Syntacticized topics in Kurmuk: A ternary voice-like system in Nilotic. *Studies in Language* 39(3), 508–554.

Bearth, T. (1999). The contribution of African linguistics towards a general theory of focus: Update and critical review. *Journal of African Languages and Linguistics* 20(2), 121–156.

Bearth, T. (2009). Operator second and its variations in Mande Languages. In P. Zina (Ed.), *The verb and related areal features in West Africa: Continuity and discontinuity within & across*. Sprachbünd frontiers. München: LINCOM.

Blackings, M. and Fabb, N. (2003). *A grammar of Ma'di*. Berlin: Mouton de Gruyter.

Boadi, L. A. (1974). Focus-marking in Akan. *Linguistics* 140, 5–57.

Breul, C. (2004). *Focus structure in generative grammar: An integrated syntactic, semantic and intonational approach*. Amsterdam: John Benjamins Publishing Company.

Broohm, O. N. (2014). Information structure in Esahie. MPhil thesis, University of Ghana.

Brown, D. R. (1989). Information focus in Kresh. In M. Lionel Bender (Ed.), *Proceedings of the fourth Nilo-Saharan conference* (pp. 325–346). Hamburg: Helmut Buske Verlag.

Buell, L. (2009). Evaluating the immediate postverbal position as a focus position in Zulu. In M. Matondo, F. McLaughlin and E. Postdam (Eds), *Selected proceedings of the 38th Annual Conference on African Linguistics* (pp. 166–172). Sommerville, MA: Cascadilla Proceedings Project.

Chafe, W. (1976). Givennes: Contrastiveness, definiteness, subjects, topics and point of view. In C. N. Li (Ed.), *Subject and topic* (pp. 25–56). New York, NY: Academic Press.

Childs, T. (1995). *A grammar of Kisi*. Berlin: Mouton de Gruyter.

Childs, T. (2003). *It's everywhere! More on the S-Aux-O-V-Other Atlantic*. Paper presented at CALL 33. University of Leiden.

Chomsky, N. (1972 [1970]). Deep structure, surface structure, and semantic representation. In N. Chomsky (Ed.), *Studies on semantics in generative grammar* (pp. 62–119). The Hague: Mouton.

Dakubu, M. E. K. (2005). *The syntax of focus in Ga and Akan, and the significance of related constructions*. Paper presented at the conference on focus on African languages. Humboldt University, Berlin, 6–8 October.

Dik, S. C. (1978). *Functional grammar*. Amsterdam: North-Holland.

Dimmendaal, G. J. (2008). Language ecology and linguistic diversity on the African continent. *Language and Linguistics Compass* 2(5), 840–858.

Downing, L. J. (2006). The prosody and syntax of focus in Chitumbuka. *ZAS Papers in Linguistics* 43, 55–79.

Downing, L. J. (2008). Focus and prominence in Chichewa, Chitumbuka, and Durban Zulu. *ZAS Papers in Linguistics* 49, 47–65.

Downing, L. J., Mtenje, A. & Pompino-Marschall, B. (2004). Prosody and information structure in Chichewa. *ZAS Papers in Linguistics* 37, 167–186.

Eaton, H. (2005). Focus as a key to the grammar of Sandawe. *Occasional Papers in Linguistics (OPiL)* 1, 9–37. Languages of Tanzania [LOT] Project, University of Dar es Salaam.

Féry, C. and Ishihara, S. (Eds) (2016). *The Oxford handbook of information structure*. Oxford: Oxford University Press.

Fiedler, I. (2007). Focus expressions in Foodo. In I. Shinichiro, S. Jannedy and A. Schwarz (Eds), *Interdisciplinary studies on information structure* (pp. 897–1114). Potsdam: Potsdam University.

Fiedler, I. & Schwarz, A. (2005). Out-of-focus encoding in Gur and Kwa. In I. Shinichiro, M. Schmitz and A. Schwarz (Eds), *Interdisciplinary studies on information structure 3* (pp. 111–142). Potsdam: Potsdam University.

Fielder, I. and Schwarz, A. (2010). *The expression of information structure: A documentation of its diversity across Africa*. Amsterdam, Netherlands: John Benjamins Publishing Company.

Frajzyngier, Z. (2001). *A grammar of Lele*. Stanford: CSLI Publications.

Givón, T. (1975). Serial verbs and syntactic change: Niger-Congo. In C. N. Li (Ed.), *Word order and word order change* (pp. 47–112). Austin: University of Texas Press.

Gordon, M. (2004). A phonological and phonetic study of word-level stress in Chickasaw. *International Journal of American Linguistics* 70, 1–32.

Gragg, G. B. (1974). Cleft sentences in Tigrinya. *Journal of African Languages* 11(3), 74–89.

Greenberg, J. H. (Ed.) (1963). *Universals of language*. London: MIT Press.

Güldemann, T. and Witzlack-Makarevich, A. (2013). *The risks of analysis without spoken language copora: clause-second ke in Richtersveld Nama and Nǀng. Information structure in spoken language corpora*. University of Bielefeld.

Güldemann, T., Zerbian, S. and Zimmermann, M. (2015). Variation in information structure with special reference to Africa. *Annual Review of Linguistics* 1, 155–178.

Gundel, J. (1976). *The role of topic and comment in linguistic theory*. Indiana University Linguistics Club. Bloomington, IN: Indiana.

Gundell, J. K. and Fretheim, T. (2002). Information structure. In J. Vershueren, J.-O. Ostman and C. Bulcaen (Eds), *Handbook of pragmatics* (pp. 1–17). Amsterdam and Philadelphia, PA: John Benjamins Publishing Company.

Haacke, W. H. G. (2006). Syntactic focus marking in Khoekhoe (Nama/Damara). *ZAS Papers in Linguistics* 46, 105–127.

Halliday, M. A. K. (1967). Notes on transitivity and theme in English: Part II. *Journal of Linguistics* 3, 199–244.

Hartmann, K. and Zimmermann, M. (2006). Focus marking in Guruntum. Ms, Humboldt University, Berlin.

Heine, B. and Reh, M. (1983). Diachronic observations on completive focus marking in some African languages. *Sprache und Geschichte in Afrika* 5, 7–44.

Hudu, F. (2012). Dagbani focus particles, a descriptive study. *Journal of West African Languages* XXXIX.I, 97–129.

Issah, S. A. (2012). Phrasal identificational and contrastive focus in Dagbani. *Journal of West African Languages* XXXIX.I, 76–96.

Jacobs, J. (1983). *Fokus und skalen: zur syntax und semantik der gradpartikeln im Deutschen*. Tubingen: Niemeyer.

Jacobs, J. (1988). Fokus-hintergrund-gliederung und grammatik. In H. Altmann (Ed.), *Intonationsforschungen* (pp. 89–134). Tubingen: Niemeyer.

Jaggar, P. J. (2001). *Hausa*. Amsterdam: John Benjamins Publishing Company.

Jakendoff, R. (1972). *Semantic interpretation in generative grammar*. Cambridge, MA: MIT Press.

Kalinowski, C. (2015a). *A typology of morphosyntactic encoding of focus in African languages*. PhD thesis, State University of New York at Buffalo.

Kalinowski, C. (2015b). A typology of focus encoding in African languages. Presented at the 2015 meeting of the Association of Linguistic Typology Albuquerque, New Mexico.

Kalinowski, C. and Good, J. (2014). Non-canonical head-marking of information structure in African languages. Paper presented at the workshop on information structure in head-marking languages. Max Planck Institute Nijmegen, 28–29 March.

Kandybowicz, J. (2008). *The grammar of repetition: Nupe grammar at the syntax–phonology interface*. Amsterdam: John Benjamins Publishing Company.

Kanerva, J. M. (1990). *Focus and phrasing in Chicheŵa phonology*. New York: Garland.

Koopman, H. (1983). *The syntax of verbs: From verb movement rules in the Kru languages to Universal Grammar*. Dordrecht: Foris.

König, E. (1991). *The meaning of focus particles: A comparative perspective*. London & New York, NY: Routledge.

König, C. (2008). Khoisan languages. *Language and Linguistics Compass* 2/5, 996–1012.

Kuno, S. (1972). Functional sentence perspective: A case study from Japanese and English. *Linguistic Inquiry* 3, 269–320.

Lambrecht, K. (1994). *Information structure and sentence form: Topic, focus, and the mental representation of discourse referents*. Cambridge: Cambridge University Press.

Maho, J. (2004). How many languages are there in Africa, really? In K. Kromber and B. Smieja (Eds), *Globalisation and African languages: Risks and benefits* (pp. 279–296). Berlin: Mouton de Gruyter.

Molnar, V. and Winkler, S. (2006). *The architecture of focus*. Berlin: Mouton de Gruyter.

Ndayiragije, J. (1999). Checking economy. *Linguistic Inquiry* 30(3), 399–444.

Newman, P. (2000). *The Hausa language: An encyclopedic reference grammar*. New Haven, CT: Yale University Press.

Ofoe, L. C. (2007). Focus constructions in Dangme. MPhil thesis, University of Ghana.

Omoruyi, T. O. (1989). Focus and question formation in Edo studies in African linguistics. *Studies in African Linguistics* 20(3), 279–300.

Otero, M. A. (2015). Nominal morphology and 'topic' in Ethiopian Komo. Information structure and Nilotic languages. In O. Hieda (Ed.), *Studies in Nilotic linguistics 10* (pp. 19–35). Tokyo: ILCAA.

Perrin, M. (1994). Rheme and focus in Mambila. In S. H. Levinsohn (Ed.), *Discourse features in ten languages of West-Central Africa* (pp. 231–241). Dallas, TX: Summer Institute of Linguistics and the University of Texas Arlington.

Reinhart, T. (1982). *Pragmatics and linguistics: An analysis of sentence topics.* Indiana University Linguistics Club. Bloomington, IN: Indiana.

Robert, S. (2000). Le verbe wolof ou la grammaticalisation du focus. In B. Caron (Ed.), *Topicalisation et focalisation dans les langues africaines* (pp. 229–267). Leuven: Peeters.

Robert, S. (2010). Focus in Atlantic languages. In Ines Fiedler and Anne Schwarz (Eds), *The expression of information structure: A documentation of its diversity across Africa* (pp. 233–260). Amsterdam: John Benjamins.

Saeed, J. (1999). *Somali.* Amsterdam: John Benjamins Publishing Company.

Sands, B. (2009). Africa's linguistic diversity. *Language and Linguistic Compass* 3(2), 559–590.

Schwarz, A. (2007). The particles lé and lá in the grammar of Konkomba. In S. Ishihara, S. Jannedy and A. Schwarz (Eds), *Interdisciplinary studies on information structure*, Vol 18 (pp. 115–139). Potsdam: Potsdam University.

Simons, G. F. and Fennig, C. D. (Eds) (2017). *Ethnologue: languages of the world, Twentieth edition.* Dallas, TX: SIL International. Online version: www.ethnologue.com.

Shinichiro, I., Schmitz, M. and Schwarz, A. (Eds) (2005). *Interdisciplinary studies on information structure 3.* Potsdam: Potsdam University.

Soukka, M. (2000). *A descriptive grammar of Noon.* Munich: Lincom Europa.

Strawson, P. F. (1974 [1964]). Identifying reference and truth values. In D. D. Steinberg and L. A. Jakobovits (Eds), *Semantics: An interdisciplinary reader in philosophy, linguistics and psychology* (pp. 86–99). Cambridge: Cambridge University Press.

Tamanji, P. N. (2009). *A descriptive grammar of Bafut.* Köln: Rüdiger Köppe Verlag.

Tosco, M. (2001). *The Dhaasanac language.* Köln: Rüdiger Köppe Verlag.

Tosco, M. (2002). A whole lotta focusin' goin' on: Information packaging in Somali texts. *Studies in African Linguistics* 31(1/2): 27–53.

Vallduvi, E. (1990). *The informational component. Philadelphia.* PhD thesis, University of Pennsylvania.

Van de Velde, M. and Idiatov, D. (2016). *Stem-initial accent and C-emphasis prosody in north-western Bantu.* Special workshop on areal features and linguistic reconstruction, ACAL 47, 23–26 March, Berkeley, California.

Van der Wal, J. (2011). Focus excluding alternatives: Conjoint/disjoint marking in Makhuwa. *Lingua* 121(11), 1734–1750.

Van der Wal, J. (2014). *Morphological marking of term focus.* Paper presented at the workshop on information structure in head-marking languages. Max Planck Institute, Nijmegen, 28–29 March.

Van der Wal, J. (2015). Information structure, (inter)subjectivity and objectification. *Journal of Linguistics* 51(2), 425–464.

Watters, J. R. (1979). Focus in Aghem: A study of its formal correlates and typology. Masters thesis, University of Los Angeles.

Watters, J. R. (2000). Syntax. In B. Heine and D. Nurse (Eds) *African languages: An introduction* (pp. 194–230). Cambridge: Cambridge University Press.

Willianson, K. & Blench, R. (2000). Niger Congo. In B. Heine and D. Nurse (Eds), *African languages: An introduction.* Cambridge: Cambridge University Press.

Wondimu, H. (2013). *Topic in Gamo.* Colloquium on Linguistics, Humboldt Universität zu Berlin.

Yimam, B. (1988). Focus in Oromo. *Studies in African Linguistics* 19(3), 365–384.

Zeller, J. (2015). The syntax of African languages. Ms, University of KwaZulu-Natal.

13

BANTU APPLICATIVES AND CHIMIINI INSTRUMENTALS[1]

Brent Henderson

Introduction

Applicative structures in Bantu have received an enormous amount of attention in the generative syntactic literature, going back to the early days of 'principles and parameters' thinking. The core of the great interest in these constructions is that although applicatives share a common function – that of adding an extra object to the argument structure of the verb – their syntactic and semantic properties vary substantially.[2] What looks (morphologically) like similar applicative structures may therefore have different syntactic properties across different Bantu languages; furthermore, different semantically defined sorts of applicative structures may have different syntactic properties within the same language. Sometimes these differences are reflected morphologically, but often they are not.

Given this, research on Bantu applicatives has tended to focus on two aspects: (1) nailing down the descriptive, typological possibilities of Bantu applicatives and their corresponding syntactic properties, and (2) offering explanations for the typological variation. Over the past 25 years, such research has yielded an impressive example of how scientific understanding progresses as explanatory proposals have been repeatedly met with new data that counters them, the latter typically followed up by more insightful proposals. Ultimately this has led to greater descriptive and explanatory progress on this topic. In the next section, I review this progress, starting with the work of Marantz (1984) and Baker (1988) and ending with the insights of Jeong (2007). I argue that Jeong (2007) represents a general breakthrough on the topic due to the fact that she locates the source of the syntactic typology of applicatives in the syntactic structure itself and not in some secondary system (such as case or phase features) as others have argued. Jeong's core insight is that interpretation need not be isomorphic with syntactic structure. Rather, there may be a variety of syntactic structures compatible with the same general interpretation at the interfaces. I argue this represents an interesting approach to syntactic typology worth pursuing: the set of syntactic structures that can receive a particular interpretation defines the expected syntactic typology for structures expressing that interpretation. I argue this is correct and further flesh out Jeong's insight by offering two possible syntactic structures she does not consider in her set of possible applicative structures. These structures must be possible as they are allowed by general principles of the grammar. They are therefore expected to be realized. I show that they are, presenting my own work on instrumental applicatives in Chimiini as well as data from so-called 'high locative' applicatives in Zulu as discussed by Buell (2005).

Applicatives in Bantu: a brief history

It was noticed early on that not all Bantu applicatives allow for the same behavior of their objects. Two of the first systematic studies of this variation are found in Baker (1988) and Bresnan and Moshi (1990), both of which characterize the variation as being properties of applicatives in particular languages. They label these 'symmetric' and 'asymmetric' languages based upon whether the two objects in an applicative double object construction behave the same way (symmetrically) or differently (asymmetrically) with regard to a cluster of morphosyntactic properties. For example, Bresnan and Moshi (1990) identify several points of parametric variation between Kichaga, which they take to be typical of symmetric languages, and Chichewa, which they take to be typical of asymmetric languages. Three that have been especially salient in the literature are listed below:

(1)   In an applied double object structure:

   a   Symmetric languages allow either object to passivize; asymmetric languages allow only the applied object to passivize.
   b   Symmetric languages allow either object to be expressed as an object marker on the verb; asymmetric languages allow only the applied object to be expressed as an object marker.
   c   Symmetric languages allow the theme/patient direct object to be unexpressed while the benefactive is expressed; asymmetric languages require both objects to be expressed.

Bresnan and Moshi (1990) make the case that these differences (and interactions between them) result from the fact that in asymmetric languages only the applied object has the properties of a 'true' object of the verb, while, in symmetric languages, both arguments have true object properties. This is essentially the approach of other earlier authors looking at this same variation, though the details of analysis contain important differences. For Bresnan and Moshi, for instance, the difference follows from a constraint – present in asymmetric languages, but absent in symmetric ones – that only one object may be intrinsically classified as semantically unrestricted (and therefore unrestricted with regard to various syntactic operations). Thus, in symmetric languages, more than one object can be classified unrestricted and therefore much freer syntactically.

In similar veins, Keenan and Comrie (1977) argue that, in some languages (symmetric languages, to use Bresnan and Moshi's terms), the grammatical roles of Object and Indirect Object are collapsed, allowing more than one argument with the Object role. Marantz (1984) locates the variation in the theta grid, arguing that transitive verbs in symmetric languages can assign two theta roles while those in asymmetric languages can only assign one (leaving the second object a non-theta marked phrase, inaccessible for various syntactic processes). Baker (1988) builds on this, but locating the variation in the system of case assignment. Taking applicative heads to be independent in the syntax (as incorporated adpositional elements), Baker argues that symmetric languages like Kichaga have applicative heads that assign structural case while applicative heads in asymmetric languages like Chichewa do not. Since Baker takes syntactic processes such as passivization and object marking to depend upon the presence of structural case, this explains why symmetric languages allow these processes for both objects while asymmetric languages allow it only for the applied object.

Though differing in details, all of these approaches have in common the assumption that differences between symmetric and asymmetric applicatives should be located in differences in various systems that affect the properties of arguments (theta role system, case system, functional feature system) and not in the syntactic structure itself. That is, in these approaches symmetric and asymmetric applicatives do not differ in their basic syntactic structure. This assumption was challenged by Pylkkänen (2002) who picked up on an insight brought forward by Marantz (1993). In comparing Bantu applicatives with English double object structures, Marantz noted that, while indirect objects in English are always internal to the event described by the VP, this is not always the case with applied objects in Bantu. Some of the latter are external to the event, the most obvious being locative or instrumental applicatives in which the applied object names an instrument the event was carried out with or a location where the event took place.

(2)   Mavuto   a-na-umb-ir-a   mpeni   mtsuko   *Chichewa*
       Mavuto   3SG-PST-mold-APPL-FV   knife   waterpot
       'Mavuto molded the waterpot with a knife.'

Baker 1988: 354

Pylkkänen (2002) builds on this insight, arguing that the difference between internal and external applied arguments should be reflected syntactically. She thus argues for two basic kinds of applicatives, *low applicatives* in which an applicative operator (implemented as a head in the syntax) establishes a relationship between two individuals, and *high applicatives* in which the applicative operator relates an individual and an event. The two structures offered for these applicative types are spelled out in (3):

(3)   a. High Applicatives   b. Low Applicatives

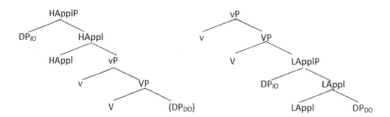

As Pylkkänen notes, at least one of the points of parametric variation noted by Bresnan and Moshi is immediately captured by the structural differences above, namely unspecified object deletion (1c). Recall that symmetric languages like Kichaga allow a theme to be unspecified in the presence of an applied object while this is not possible in asymmetric languages like Chichewa. In the latter, both arguments must be expressed. The structures in (3) capture this: since the applied object is external to the VP in (3a), the VP can be intransitive, as in Kichaga. In (3b), on the other hand, the applicative head (LAppl) directly relates the theme object to the applied object. That is the function of the head itself. Therefore, both individuals must be present and neither can be left unspecified, as in Chichewa. To put the generalization another way, this explains why unergatives can be applicativized in Kichaga, but not in Chichewa:

Bantu applicatives and Chimiini instrumentals

(4)   a N-ǎ- ǐ-lyí-í-à   m-kà   *Kichaga*

FOC-3SG-PRES-eat-APP-FV   1-wife

'He/She is eating for/on the wife.'

Bresnan and Moshi 1990: 151

    b   M-lenje   a-ku-lemb-er-a   mfruimu   *(chimangirizo).   Chichewa

       1-hunter   3SG-PRES-write-APPL-FV 9- chief   7-essay

       'The hunter is writing for the chief.'

Alsina and Mchombo 1989: 500

Likewise, the fact that low applicative structures relate two individuals entails that a relationship must hold between those individuals, typically one of possessing or receiving. This explains another asymmetry: why double object constructions in languages like English require a semantic possessive relationship between the two objects while applied constructions in Kichaga have no such requirement. Thus, *Terrence baked Alicia a cake* means that the cake was baked so that Alicia could have it. The equivalent sentence in Kichaga, however, need not have this meaning (though it is one possible interpretation). Rather, the cake might be being baked on behalf of the person mentioned, so that they would not have to do it, but the cake may be intended for someone else entirely.

Pylkkänen's work opens the door to the possibility that syntactic differences between applicative types might arise from the syntactic structures themselves, which in turn is based on semantic compositional reasoning (namely whether an applicative head relates an individual to an event or another individual).[3] McGinnis (2001, 2005) takes this notion further as a potential explanation for variation in applicatives, asking whether all of the systematic differences between symmetric and asymmetric applicatives can be derived from the high/low distinction in applicative structures. Previous work had already attempted to make symmetric/asymmetric differences follow from the descriptive notion that in symmetric applicatives an 'escape hatch' was available for the lower object to raise over the applied object, while in asymmetric applicatives this was not possible and the lower object was 'frozen' in place (see Anagnostopoulou 2003; Ura 1996; McGinnis 1998). McGinnis (2001) improves on these analyses by suggesting an explanation based in phase-theory (Chomsky 2001). In particular, she argues that HApplP is a phase while LApplP is not. As a phase, HApplP therefore has the possibility of Edge features that allows the edge of the phase to act as an escape hatch for lower arguments. It is possible, then, for the lower object to move to the edge of this phase, making it accessible to higher syntactic operations, such as passivization and object pronoun incorporation (or object agreement). This explains why the lower object can be agreed with or passivized in symmetric applicatives. Since LApplP is not a phase, there is no possibility for the lower object to 'leapfrog' over the higher applied object. Therefore, any operation that targets a lower object will only have access to the applied object since it will be a closer goal for such operations under minimality.

While explaining some of the core differences between symmetric and asymmetric applicatives, note that McGinnis' account predicts a strong correlation between symmetric/asymmetric syntactic and semantic properties. Thus, applicatives that behave symmetrically should have high applicative semantics (the applied object should be external to the event) while applicatives that behave asymmetrically should have low applicative semantics with a possessive relationship between the applied object and the theme. As Bissell-Doggett (2004) points out, however, this is not always the case. Some (semantically) high applicatives display asymmetric syntactic behavior while some (semantically) low applicatives display asymmetric syntactic behavior.

For example, locative applicatives in Kinyarwanda are used when there is no possession relationship between the two objects, a high applicative in Pylkkänen's terms. Yet the direct object cannot passivize, making it 'asymmetric' in Bresnan and Moshi's terms.

(5) a Ishuûrii   ry-oohere-j-w-é-ho   igitabo n'úúmwáalímu.
      school   AGR-send-ASP-PASS-FV-LOC   book   by teacher
      'The school was sent the book by the teacher.'

    b *Igitaboi   cy-oohere-j-w-é-ho   ishuûri n'úúmwáalímu.
      book   AGR-send-ASP-PASS-FV-LOC   school by teacher
      'The book was sent to school by the teacher.'

Kimenyi 1980: 96

To account for this variation, Bissell-Doggett (2004) as well as McGinnis (2001, 2005) adopt the assumption that phases may differ cross-linguistically. In some languages, for example, the vP phase might have an extra EPP-feature, allowing both lower objects to move to its specifier. This would allow symmetric passivization in low applicatives, given Pylkkänen's structures. Similarly, McGinnis argues that the high applicative head, a phase, might lack an extra EPP feature in some cases, making movement of the lower theme object to its specifier impossible, thereby explaining cases of high applicatives with asymmetric behavior.

The problem with this approach, as Jeong (2007) points out, is that in at least one understanding of phases, having an EPP/Edge feature is what makes a phase a phase. Claiming there are phases without EPP features or that EPP features of phases may vary cross-linguistically, considerably weakens the entire phase-theoretic framework on which McGinnis' initial analysis depends. Encountering more problems, McGinnis and Gerdts (2004) note that constituency conflicts in multiple applicatives in Kinyarwanda seem to require that some phases be merged acyclically. They argue that a high applicative structure might be late-merged below a low applicative structure, violating the Extension Condition. Though this allows them to account for the facts, it does seem that weakening phase theory and allowing acyclic merge are two very high prices to pay for the empirical coverage.

Jeong argues, however, that these costly moves are unnecessary. Her key insight is that the problems encountered in McGinnis' accounts follow from the assumption that semantic composition dictates syntactic structure in a one-to-one mapping. This leave McGinnis restricted to Pylkkänen's structures in (3) above. Jeong argues that this assumption is unnecessary. Rather, it might be the case that several different syntactic structures are compatible with the same semantic interpretation. After all, Pylkkänen's original insights were semantic, not syntactic in nature. High applicatives, for example, are not applicatives with a particular syntactic structure; rather they are defined as applicatives in which an individual is related to an event. The syntax might have several different ways of accomplishing this. An applicative head such as the one Pylkkänen and McGinnis assume is one, but another might be a preposition, which also serves to relate individuals to events.

Along these lines, Jeong proposes three possible structures for high applicatives. In all of them some head (HAppl or P) relates an individual to an event. Their relevant semantics is therefore consistent across structures. However, the syntactic structures themselves are quite different and might result in different syntactic behaviors. For example, Jeong argues that high applicatives with asymmetric behavior have a structure like that in (6c) while those with symmetric properties have a structure like that (6a).[4]

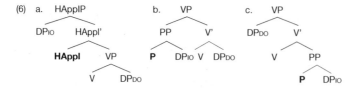

As Jeong notes, the structure in (6b) and (6c) are compositionally equivalent to the structure in (6a) due to the assumption of bare phrase structure (Chomsky 1995), which dictates that the superficial labels of X, X' and XP are actually equivalent copies of the same label. The only difference in the structures is that in (6c) the PP is initially merged with an event with an unsaturated predicate (since the DO has not yet been merged) while in (6a) and (6b) it is merged with an event with a saturated predicate. Examples (6a) and (6b) differ in whether the head introducing the applicative individual selects for the VP (6a) or is a part of the VP (6b).

A good candidate for (6b) is locative applicatives in Kinyarwanda. Locatives in Kinyarwanda can be expressed either as prepositional adjuncts or as arguments of an applied verb. In the latter case, a marker resembling the preposition appears at the end of the verb. As others have noted, this marker is unlike the derivational applied morpheme used in benefactives and instrumentals in the language, looking more like a prepositional or pronominal element. Evidence for its status as the latter comes from its similarity to corresponding prepositions, its use of the '-o of reference' common in forming pronominal clitics in the language, and the fact that it appears outside all other inflection on the verb, even the inflectional final vowel suffix. Note also (in the (c) examples below) that the applicative clitic and the preposition may not co-occur.

(7) a Umufuundi   y-oome-tse   amatafaari **ku** rukuta
        builder   AGR-PST.stick-ASP   bricks   **on** wall
        'The builder stuck bricks on the wall.'

Kimenyi 1980: 32

     b Umufuundi y-oome-tse-**ho**   urukuta amatafaari
        builder   AGR-PST.stick-ASP-**LOC** wall   bricks
        'The builder stuck bricks on the wall.'

Ngoboka 2005: 46

     c *Umufuundi y-oome-tse-**ho**   amatafaari **ku** rukuta
        builder   AGR-PST.stick-ASP-LOC bricks   on wall

(8) a Umwaana   y-a-taa-ye   igitabo **mu** maazi
        child   AGR-PST-throw-ASP   book   **in** water
        'The child has thrown the book into the water.'

     b Umwaana   y-a-taa-ye-**mo**   amaazi igitabo
        child   AGR-PST-throw-ASP-**LOC** water book
        'The child has thrown the book into the water.'

Kimenyi 1980: 91

     c *Umwaana   y-a-taa-ye-**mo**   igitabo **mu** maazi
        child   AGR-PST-throw-ASP-LOC book   in water

Note the (a) examples above are straightforwardly cases of Jeong's structure in (6c) while the (b) examples are arguably instantiations of her structure in (6b) with the preposition left-cliticized onto the end of the verb.

In contrast to the locative applicative, instrumentals in Kinyarwanda employ a different applicative marker, *ish*, which appears suffixed to the verb stem and inside of any inflectional suffixes. These applicatives arguably have the structure in (6a), employing a high applicative head.

(9) Úmwáalímu   y-a-andik-iish-ije imibáre íngwa ku   kibaho.
     teacher   3SG-PST-wrote-INST-ASP math   chalk on   board
     'The teacher wrote math with chalk on the board.'

Kimenyi 1980: 109

267

Note that all of these applicatives are High Applicatives in Pylkkänen's sense since all relate an individual to an event, locatives through a P head and benefactives and instrumentals through an Appl head. However, they each use different syntactic structures and display morphological differences. Interestingly, they also have different syntactic properties. Benefactive and instrumental applicatives are symmetric in Bresnan and Moshi's sense: either of the applied or theme objects may passivize or be expressed as an object marker. Word order between the two objects is also relatively free in these applicatives. On the other hand, locative applicatives such as those in the (b) examples above are asymmetric: only the applied (locative) object may passivize or be incorporated. This follows from the fact that the structure in (6b) is similar to a low applicative structure in the sense that the applied PP is in the specifier of the same projection that has the theme as its complement. It is possible, then, that whatever principles restrict syntactic behavior in low applicative structures similarly restrict high applicatives that have this structure.[5]

Expanding the landscape of applicatives

The implications of Jeong's work go beyond understanding applicatives. They suggest a general approach to syntactic analysis that might be summarized something like this: given the semantic structure of a particular construction, what are the possible syntactic structures compatible with it? Given enough linguistic variation, one would expect all such compatible structures to be realized in one language or another.

Using this logic, this chapter proposes to two additional possible structures for high applicatives that would be equivalent to Jeong's structures semantically. One would be to merge HAppl above a fully saturated vP; that is, above the initial position of the subject. In such a structure, the applied head relates an individual to a fully saturated event. On page 277 below, I show that this structure is employed in certain Zulu locative applicatives, as discussed by Buell (2005).

(10)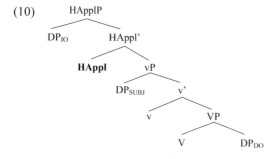

A second structure possible under these assumptions is merging of the applied head to the completely unsaturated predicate head:

(11)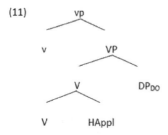

I refer to this possibility as 'Direct Merge' following Embick's (2004) analysis of English verbs that incorporate an instrumental manner component such as in *John hammered the metal flat*. Embick argues that the root HAMMER is directly adjoined to a light verb and does not head a larger projection. A cursory examination suggests that Chimiini (and possibly all Bantu languages) do not have such verbs, instead expressing the concept of instrumental manner with instrumental applicatives or prepositional phrases (an interesting typological generalization that should be further explored). The important point in the present analysis, however, is the fact that the applicative head in (11), being direct merged, does not head its own projection and therefore cannot syntactically license an applied argument. I assume, however, that it has the semantics typical of high applicatives, namely relating an individual to an event. I argue this is the structure employed by Chimiini instrumental applicatives. I explore this analysis in the following section.

Instrumental applicatives in Chimiini

Instrumental vs. benefactive/recipient applicatives

With regard to benefactive and recipient applicatives, Chimiini is an 'asymmetric' language, allowing only the indirect object to passivize.[6]

(12) a Maana/   Ø-m-pik-il-ile   maalimu /   chaakuja
         1child   3SG-3SG.OBJ-cook-APP-PST   1teacher   7food
         'The child cooked teacher food.'

      b Maalimu/   Ø-pik-il-il-a   chaakuja/   na maana
         1teacher   3SG-cook-APP-PST-PASS.FV   7food   by 1child
         'The teacher was cooked food for by the child.'

      c *Chaakuja/   sh- pik-il-il-a   maalimu/   na maana
         7food   7AGR-cook-APP-PST-PASS.FV   1teacher   by 1child
         'The food was cooked for the teacher by the child.'

Looking at object agreement, the verb may only agree with the applied argument in these constructions, not with the direct object (cf. 12a):

(13) *Maana/   Ø-sh-pik-il-ile   maalimu/ chaakuja
       1child   3SG-7OBJ-cook-APP-PST   1teacher 7food
       'The child cooked food for the teacher.'

Interestingly, post-verbal word order of the benefactive and direct object is variable; however, the unmarked order is that in (12a) above. When the direct object is closest to the verb, this effects a contrastive focus reading on the object (a so-called Immediately After the Verb effect). Note, however, that this does not affect object agreement facts. The verb in (14) may still only agree with the applied object:

(14) Maana/   Ø-m-pik-il-ile   chaakuja/   maalimu
      1child   3SG-3SG.OBJ-cook-APP-PST   7food   1teacher
      'The child cooked FOOD for the teacher.'

Benefactives applicatives are also symmetric with regard to topicalization and relativization: either the direct object or the benefactive may be topicalized or relativized.

(15) a Chaakuja/ maana/ Ø-m-pik-il-ile maalimu
      7food 1child 3SG-3SG.OBJ-cook-APP-PST 1teacher
      'The food, the child cooked it for the teacher.'

    b Maalimu/ maana/ Ø-m-pik-il-ile chakuja
      1teacher 1child 3SG-3SG.OBJ-cook-APP-PST 7food
      'The teacher, the child cooked the food for him.'

(16) a chaakuja ch-a maana/ Ø-m-pik-il-ile maalimu
      7food 7-REL 1child 3SG-3SG.OBJ-cook-APP-PST 1teacher
      'The food that the child cooked for the teacher.'

    b maalimu w-a maana/ Ø-m-pik-il-ile chaakuja
      1teacher 1-rel 1child 3SG-3SG.OBJ-cook-APP-PST 7food
      'The teacher that the child cooked food for.'

Finally, the benefactive object in such an applicative can be freely questioned:

(17) maana/ Ø-m-pik-il-ile naani/ chaakuja?
                                 who 7food
     1child 3SG-3SG.OBJ-cook-APP-PST
     'Who did the child cook food for?'

In striking contrast, instrumental applicatives display opposite behavior for nearly all of these properties, though they employ the same applicative morphology. First, they do not allow variable word order after the verb. Rather, the instrument argument must come after the direct object if it appears post-verbally.

(18) a Nuuru/ Ø-tilang-il-ilee nama/ chisu
      Nuru 3SG-cut-APP-PST 9meat 7knife
      'Nuru cut the meat with a knife.'

    b *Nuuru/ Ø-tilangililee chisu/ nama

Moreover, object agreement is not possible with the instrumental applied object while it is possible with the direct object (though only if the latter is animate).

(19) a *(chisu)/ Nuuru/ Ø-sh-tilang-il-ilee nama
      7knife Nuuru 3SG-7OBJ-cut-APP-PST 9meat
      'The knife, Nuuru cut the meat with it.'

    b luti/ Haliima/ Ø-m-big-il-ile miizi
      11stick Haliima 3SG-3SG.OBJ-hit-APP-PST 1thief
      'The stick, Haliima beat the thief with it.'

    c *Chisu / Nuuru/ Ø-i-tilang-il-ilee nama
      7knife Nuuru 3SG-9OBJ-cut-APP-PST 9meat
      'The knife, Nuuru cut the meat with it.'

Though generally Chimiini (like most Bantu languages) allows a pro-dropped argument to trigger agreement on the verb, agreement with the instrument is impossible even if the latter is absent from the clause, or if the clause lacks a direct object:

(20) a Ø-na-k-ihṯaja   miiwaani/   x-(*ya)-soomela
       3SG-PRES-INF-need   4.glasses   INF-4OBJ-read
       'He needs glasses to read with.'

    b maaḻimu/   Ø-na-kh-(*chi-)-som-esh-elez-a   chibuuku
       1.teacher   3SG-PRES-INF-7OBJ-read-CAUS-APP-FV   7.book
       'The teacher is teaching with a book.'

With regard to passivization, instrumental applicatives appear to be symmetric (but see below). Either the instrument or the patient may passivize. Contrast this with (12) above:

(21) a ḻuti/   ḻ-big-iḻ-iḻ-a   miizi/   na Haliima
       11stick 11AGR-hit-APP-PST-PASS.FV   1thief   by Haliima
       'The stick was used to hit the thief by Haliima.'

    b ḻuti/   miizi/ Ø- big-iḻ-iḻ-a   na Haliima
       11stick 1thief 3SG- hit-APP-PST-PASS.FV   by Haliima
       'The stick, the thief was hit with it by Haliima.'

In addition, topicalization and relativization are actually asymmetric with instrumental applicatives: only the instrument may appear as a left-dislocated topic or the head of a relative clause:

(22) a *Miizi/ Haliima/ Ø-m-big-iḻ-iḻe   ḻuti   (cf. 15b)
       1thief   Haliima 3SG-3SG.OBJ-hit-APP-PST   11stick
       'The thief, Haliima hit him with a stick.'

    b ḻuti   ḻ-a   Haliima/ Ø-m-big-iḻ-iḻe   miizi
       11stick 11-rel   Haliima 3SG-3SG.OBJ-hit-APP-PST   1thief
       'The stick that Haliima beat the thief with.'

    c *Miizi w-a Haliima/ Ø-m-big-iḻ-iḻe   ḻuti
       1thief 1-rel Haliima 3SG-3SG.OBJ-hit-APP-PST   11stick
       'The thief that Haliima beat with the stick.'

Finally, an instrumental object in an instrumental applicative cannot be questioned:

(23) *Nuuru/   Ø-ṯilang-iḻ-iḻee=ni /   nama
     Nuru   3SG-cut-APP-PST=what   9meat
     'What did Nuru cut the meat with?'[7]

The differences between benefactive/recipient applicatives and instrumental applicatives is summarized in Table 13.1.

As the table shows, instrumental applicatives have the opposite syntactic typological properties from benefactive applicatives in Chimiini, even though they share the same morphology. In the follow section, I attempt to explain this variation in syntactic terms.

Table 13.1 Differences between benefactive/recipient and instrumental applicatives in Chimiini

Property	Ben/recip. applicative	Instrument applicative
Variable order of IO and DO	YES	NO
Object agreement with either object	NO (applied only)	NO (animate PAT only)
Passivization of either object	NO (applied only)	YES
Relativization/topicalization of either object	YES	NO (applied only)
Questioning applied object	YES	NO

Explaining instrumental applicatives

In this section I make the case that the variation observed in the previous sub-section follows from differences between the syntactic structure associated with benefactive/recipient applicatives in Chimiini and that associated with instrumentals. The former seem to have a structure like that in (24), basically Jeong's structure in (6c) above:

(24)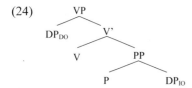

Instrumentals, however, have the structure in (25) in which an applicative head undergoes direct merge with the bare predicate head:

(25)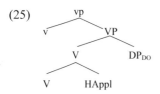

Note the HAppl head in (25) does not project syntactically and therefore cannot introduce an overt argument. Nevertheless, following Jeong (2007), I assume the head still works as a semantic operator on the predicate, introducing a new argument variable. When the INSTR individual is merged later on (as a topic), it will bind this variable.

(26)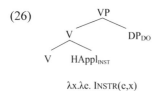

$\lambda x.\lambda e.$ INSTR(e,x)

Syntactically, the difference between the structure in (24) and that in (25) is that in (25) the applicative head, being direct merged, cannot project a specifier in order to introduce a DP that can be identified with the instrumental argument. Rather, this argument must be introduced later, as a peripheral topic or by discourse.

Below I argue that all of the differences between instrumental applicatives and benefactive/ reciprocal applicatives discussed above follow from the syntactic differences in (24) and (25), and in particular from the fact that in instrumental applicatives the instrumental DP, when present, is always a topic outside the vP.

Word order

Recall the generalization that BEN/RECIP applicatives have the post-verbal order IO DO (as well as the marked order DO IO) while INSTR only allow DO INSTR. Our claim is that in the latter case the INSTR is outside the verb phrase. Evidence for this comes from Chimiini's phrasal phonological properties, which have been extensively studied (Kisseberth and Abasheikh 1974, 2011). I focus here on properties of accent. In most cases, the right edge of a phonological phrase in Chimiini is defined by the right boundary of a maximal syntactic phrase. In most contexts, each phonological phrase receives a penultimate pitch-accent. In some grammatically defined contexts, however, final accent appears instead of penultimate, such as in clauses with first and second person verbs. Crucially, final accent carries through to subsequent phrases. Thus, a phrase containing a second person verb, as in the benefactive applicative in (27b), will have final accent, but so will the phrase immediately after it:

(27) a Ø-m-pik-il-ile   maalímu/   chaakúja
         3SG-3SG.OBJ-cook-APP-PST   1teacher   7food
         'She/he cooked food for the teacher.'

      b Ø-m-pik-il-ile   maalimú/ chaakujá
         2SG-3SG.OBJ-cook-APP-PST   1teacher   7food
         'You (sg) cooked food for the teacher.'

This is not the case in Instrumentals, however. Rather than appearing with final accent, the applied argument has penultimate accent.

(28) n-tind-il-ilee   namá/   chísu
      1SG-cut-APP-PST   9meat   7knife
      'I cut the meat with a knife.'

One way to interpret this data is to suggest that the carryover of accent to subsequent phrases is based upon depth of embedding: a final accent on a phrase will carry over to other phrases that are more deeply embedded. I have argued, however, that the instrumental DP in (28) is not in the vP, but higher in the structure. It is therefore not more deeply embedded than the verb phrase in (27) and so does not get the final accent.

The idea that instrumental DP is a peripheral topic and not within the vP also explains the restriction on the word order *V INSTR PAT observed above (despite the fact that benefactive applicatives allow flexible post-verbal order). As a peripheral topic, INSTR cannot appear between the V and its complement PAT since both are in the vP and the INSTR argument is not.

Object agreement

I assume that since the INSTR is not merged within vP, it is not a possible goal for object agreement. Therefore, the verb may never agree with the instrument, as seen in the facts in (19) above. Even when the instrument is absent from the clause, a null *pro* argument cannot be licensed by agreement within the vP.

Given that the instrument is not within the vP, it also cannot be an intervener for agreement with the direct object. Agreement with direct objects is therefore possible as in (18b) above, unlike in other types of applicatives. A bit more mysterious, however, is the fact that agreement with direct objects is only possible with animate direct objects. Inanimate direct objects do not allow it, even if they are absent from the sentence:

(29) *Chisu/ Nuuru/ Ø-i-ṯilang-iḻ-iḻee   (ṉama)
      7knife Nuuru 3SG-9OBJ-cut-APP-PST   9meat
      'Nuuru cut the meat/it with the knife.'

I posit that this asymmetry follows from the way object agreement works in Chimiini, as well as from a general constraint that I posit for the language, given in (30), which I assume operates at the level of information structure:

(30) SINGLE TOPIC CONSTRAINT: Sentences may have only one topic.

Note that if I am correct that instruments in instrumental applicatives are always topics, the constraint in (30) rules out the possibility of anything else in instrumental applicatives being a topic. This observation sheds light on the facts above. In general, Chimiini allows optional agreement with inanimate objects, but with the effect that agreed-with inanimates take on a topic-like quality. This is a common property of Bantu languages where object agreement with inanimates is often linked to definiteness or D-linking effects (see, e.g., Hyman and Duranti 1982; Kisseberth and Abasheikh 1976 for Chimiini; Reidel 2009). In the sentence in (31), for example, *chakuja* cannot be interpreted as 'some food,' but must refer to particular food whose identity will be known to the hearer (whether the overt NP is present or not).

(31) Fatiima/ Ø-sh-pish-iile   (chaakuja)   *Chimiini*
      Fatima 3SG-7OBJ-cook-pst   7food
      'Fatima cooked the food/it.'

Object agreement with animate objects, however, does not have this character. Though it is not strictly obligatory in Chimiini, it is very common and does not affect the interpretation of the object NP. Thus, *muntu* in (32) can be interpreted as a person known to the hearer or as 'anyone'.

(32) Juma   ha-ku-m-ona   muntu
      Juma   3SG-PST.NEG-3SG.OBJ-see   1person
      'Juma didn't see the person/Juma didn't see anyone.'

These facts, together with the constraint in (30) that allows only one topic per clause, explain the restrictions on object agreement in Instrumentals. Instrumental NPs are always topics, and so are agreed-with inanimate object NPs. Therefore, object agreement with inanimates is impossible in instrumental applicatives. Agreement with animate objects, however, is fine as these needn't receive a topic interpretation.

Passivization

If the instrumental applied object is never in the VP, then it follows that the object of the verb should be able to passivize, unlike in benefactives. No intervention effects are expected.[8]

Bantu applicatives and Chimiini instrumentals

(33) luti/   miizi/   Ø-big-i̱l-i̱l-a   na Haliima
     11stick 1thief   3SG- hit-APP-PST-PASS.FV   by Haliima
     'The stick, the thief was hit with it by Haliima.'

It is less expected that that the INSTR should be able to passivize since it is never inside the vP to begin with. Yet this construction is possible:

(34) luti/   l-big-i̱l-i̱l-a   miizi/   na Haliima
     11stick 11AGR-hit-APP-PST-PASS.FV   1thief   by Haliima
     'The stick was used to hit the thief by Haliima.'

The full facts of passivization are complicated and I cannot fully deal with them here. For now, I simply appeal to the long-standing observation that, in some constructions in certain Bantu languages, subjects have the properties of topics (Schneider-Zioga 2007, among many others). I have just argued that instrumental arguments are always topics in Chimiini when they are overt. With that in mind, I propose that in passives like those in (34), the instrumental argument does not undergo typical passive movement from an internal theta-marked position in the vP, but is rather merged directly into the topic/subject position.[9]

Topicalization/relativization

Recall from (22) above that in instrumental applicatives only the applied object may be topicalized or relativized. As I stated in (30), only one topic is allowed per clause in Chimiini. Therefore, no other argument may be topicalized in an instrumental applicative. As for relative clauses, it is in general not possible for a relative clause to contain a topicalized phrase:

(35) *Maana   w-a   chakuuja/   Ø-pish-iile
     1child   1-REL   7food   3SG-cook-PST
     'The child that, the food, he cooked it.'

Since the INSTR in instrumental applicatives are topics, the only way for an instrumental applicative clause to avoid having an internal topic is for the instrumental argument itself to be relativized. Therefore, only the INSTR may be relativized in these constructions, explaining the asymmetry.

Questioning the applied object

If indeed the INSTR in instrumental applicatives are always topics, it follows that they should not be able to be focused or replaced by inherently focused elements such as interrogative pronouns. This explains why the INSTR cannot be questioned in an instrumental applicative. In order to question an instrumental element, rather, the prepositional structure (rather than the applied) must be employed:

(36) Muke/   Ø-tilanz-ile   kaa ni/   nama
     1woman   3SG-cut-PST   with what   9meat
     'What did the woman cut the meat with?'

Multiple applicatives: BEN + INSTR

A single clause may be both a benefactive as well as an instrumental applicative. However, 'stacking' of applicative morphology is disallowed. Only one applicative morpheme is present.[10] Such applicatives behave exactly as single INSTR applicatives with regard to topicalization/relativization: BEN or PAT may not topicalize/be relativized (I illustrate with topicalization here):

(37) a ḷkoombe/ muke/ Ø-m-pakuḷ-iḷ-e   maana/ zijo
         11spoon   1wife 3SG-dish.out-APP-PST   1child 8food
         'The spoon, the woman dished out food with it for the child.'

      b *Zijo/   muke/ Ø-m-pakuḷ-iḷ-e maana/ ḷkoombe

      c *Maana/   muke/ Ø-m-pakuḷ-iḷ-e zijo/   ḷkoombe

In these multiple applicatives, a post-verbal INSTR is impossible (compare with plain instrumental applicatives). The INSTR must be the subject of a passive, a topic, head a relative, or be absent from the sentence altogether.

(38) a *muke/   Ø-m-pakuḷiḷe   maana/   zijo/   ḷkoombe
         1.woman   3SG-dish.out-APP-PST   1.child 8food   11spoon
         'The woman dished out food for the child with a spoon.'

      b ḷkoombe/ Ø-m-pakuḷ-iḷ-a   maana/ zijo
         11spoon   3SG-dish.out-APP-PST.PASS.FV 1child 8food
         'The spoon was used to dish out the food for the child.'

      c ḷkoombe   ḷ-aa   muke/ Ø-m-pakuḷ-iḷ-o   maana/   zijo
         11spoon   11-REL 1wife 3SG-dish.out-APP-PST.REL 1child 8food
         'The spoon that the woman dished out food with it for the child.'

      d ḷkoombe/ muke/ Ø-m-pakuḷ-iḷ-e   maana/   zijo
         11spoon 1wife 3SG-dish.out-APP-PST   1child   8food
         'The spoon, the woman dished out food with it for the child.'

      e Hamadi/ Ø-uz-ile   ḷkoombe/ kh-pakuḷ-iḷ-a   maana/   zijo.
         Hamadi 3SG-use-PST   11spoon   INF-dish.out-APP-FV 1child   8food
         'Hamadi used a spoon to dish out food for the child.'

As long as the INSTR is not post-verbal, the clause otherwise behaves as a benefactive: the BEN may be passivized or object-marked and the PAT may not be.

(39) a ḷkoombe ḷ-aa   maana / Ø-m-pakuḷ-iḷ-a   zijó
         11spoon 11-REL 1child 3SG-dish.out-APP-PASS.PST.FV 8food
         'The spoon that the child was dished out food to with.'

      b *ḷkoombe ḷ-aa zijo / zi-m-pakuḷ-iḷ-a   maaná
         11spoon 11-REL 8food   8AGR-dish.out-APP-PASS.PST.FV 1child
         'The spoon that the food was dished out with to the child.'

These facts are consistent with our analysis that the topic status of the INSTR as well as the one-topic-per-clause restriction in Chimiini limits syntactic variation. Furthermore, if the INSTR and BEN applied argument are introduced in fundamentally different ways, it is expected they would be combinable in a single clause.

To conclude this section, all evidence points to the idea that the INSTR argument in Chimiini instrumental applicatives is always introduced as a peripheral topic to the clause. This is expected in light of the proposal that the applicative head undergoes direct merge with the verb. Not heading its own phrase, it is unable to introduce the INSTR argument inside the vP, but does introduce the individual variable that can be bound by an instrumental DP later introduced and base-generated as a topic or via discourse.

Locative applicatives in Zulu (Buell 2005, 2007)

The other structure logically predicted by Jeong's (2007) approach to the typology of applicatives is a high applicative head selecting for a full vP, complete with external argument. I argue here that certain locative applicatives discussed by Buell (2005, 2007) make use of this structure.

(40)

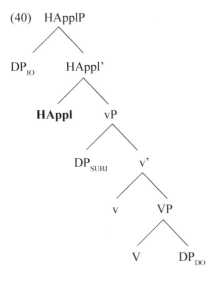

Buell (2005, 2007) discusses two kinds of locative applicative constructions in Zulu. One is fairly typical of Bantu locatives: a locative argument appears with locative morphology.[11] In Zulu, the argument may appear with a verb with or without applicative morphology.

(41) A-bantwana   ba-fund-(el)-a   e-sikole-ni   *Zulu*
     2-2.child   2.AGR-study-APP-FV 7-7.school-LOC
     'The children study at the school.'

Buell 2005: 181

A second kind of locative applicative is termed by Buell (2007) as a 'semantic locative'. In these constructions the locative argument has no locative morphology, but appears as a DP. Moreover, the applicative morphology on the verb is required and the locative appears in subject position.

(42) a Lesi   sikole   si-fund-el-a   izingane   ezikhubazekile
        7.this 7.school   7AGR-study-APP-FV   10.children   10.handicapped
        'Handicapped children study at this school.'

b Lesi   sikole   si-ya-fund-el-a
   7.this 7.school 7AGR-DJ-study-APP-FV
   'This school is studied at (it hasn't been closed down).'

Note that the verb displays subject-verb agreement with the locative subject and not with the post-verbal agent. Note also that the verb is not passive, but active. Buell also shows that the locative DP in (42) can be relativized and clefted as well. Topics cannot generally be relativized or clefted in Zulu. The facts thus suggest that the locative in (42) is a true subject of the clause, in SpecTP.

(43) a Ngi-bon-e   i-sikole   e-si-fund-el-a   a-bantwana ba-kho
        1SG-see-PERF 7-7.school   REL-7.AGR-study-APP-FV 2-2.child   2.of-you
        'I saw the school that your children studies at.'
     b Y-i-sikole   esinye   e-sifund-el-a   a-bantwana ba-mi
        COP-7-7.school 7.other   rel-7.AGR-study-APP-FV 2-2.child   2.of.me
        'It's another school that my children study at.'

Given the conclusion that the locative is the subject of the clause, Buell (2005) argues that this requires a structure in which the locative is merged above the position where the agent is merged, providing a structure nearly identical to the one proposed here. Buell terms the head introducing this locative *Loc1P* to contrast it with other locatives in Zulu that are introduced lower in the structure.

Locative DP merged above the agent

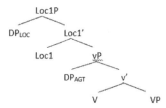

Buell's 'semantic locatives' in Zulu, then, seem to fill another logical possibility for high applicatives, predicted by Jeong's approach: an applicative head that relates an individual to an already full-saturated event.

Conclusions

By giving up the assumption of a one-to-one mapping between syntax and semantic composition, Jeong (2007) allows for high applicatives to have a variety of syntactic structures, discussing three such structures and their syntactic properties. In this chapter I've argued that Jeong's approach logically predicts two additional syntactic structural types for high applicatives, one in which the applied head directly merges with a completely unsaturated event, and one in which the head selects for a fully saturated event that already includes an external argument. The former, I've argued, is instantiated by Chimiini instrumental applicatives, which I have argued never merge the applied argument as an argument within the VP but always as a peripheral topic when present. The latter, I have suggested, has been independently argued to exist in Zulu by Buell (2005, 2007). This chapter thus puts Buell's findings in their typological context.

Notes

1 Chimiini is also known as Chimwiini or Chimi:ni in the literature. It is a Bantu language of the southern Somali coast, now highly endangered due to most of its speakers fleeing Somalis in the early 1990s. Many of the empirical generalizations discussed for Chimiini instrumental applicatives here were first discovered by Charles Kisseberth and Mohamed Imam Abasheikh in their joint work on the language in the late 1970s and 1980s. I am deeply grateful to Dr Kisseberth for sharing his unpublished notes on Chimiini with me and to Dr Abasheikh for his insightful work on his native language. The Chimiini data presented here has been confirmed and/or collected by working with Chimiini speakers in Atlanta, Ohio and Kenya. This work was funded by the NSF/NEH Documenting Endangered Language program (PD50009-09).

2 Bantu languages use applicatives for other functions that do not add an argument to the valency of the verb, such as emphatic and reflexive uses. I do not address these here. See Maarten and Mous (2016) for a recent discussion.

3 Note that locating the source of variation in the syntax of applicatives themselves also destroys the notion that the symmetric/asymmetric distinction is due to some sort of language-wide parameter such as the theta properties of verbs or differences in a relational or thematic hierarchy between languages. Pylkkänen's solution thus allows for the possibility that the same language may have more than one type of applicative, an empirical fact widely recognized as a problem for previous analyses.

4 The structure in (6c) also solves McGinnis and Gerdts (2004) constituency puzzle, allowing a DO to c-command an IO while still having the semantics of a high applicative.

5 Jeong (2007) invokes Abels' (2003) version of anti-locality to explain why low applicative structures as well as the structure in (6b) tend to result in asymmetric behaviors. Briefly, anti-locality dictates that an XP may not move to the specifier of the head that selects it. Therefore, Spec,VP cannot be an escape hatch for the lower theme in (6b) while Spec,HApplP in (6a) can.

6 The forward slashes in the data represent phonological phrase boundaries that are important for understanding certain phonological processes in Chimiini. See Kisseberth and Abasheikh (2011) for a detailed introduction to the basic facts.

7 The interrogative pronoun 'what' is realized as a verbal enclitic in Chimiini. Fronting the pronoun as a focus fronted or cleft construction is also ungrammatical.

8 Note that the instrument in (32) is also fronted. The construction is more marginal with the instrument following the verb.

9 A reviewer points out that if subjects are topics, then any sentence with an overt subject and an overt instrumental argument in an instrumental applicative has two topics, violating my proposal in (29). However, Schneider-Zioga (2007) argues in detail that subjects in Kinande are topics *unless* something else has been topicalized/focused in the clause. In such cases, subjects are not topics but are in fact in Spec,TP. She presents a variety of arguments for this, a subset of which can be replicated for Chimiini. My explanation is the same: exactly in those cases where something else is in the left periphery, subjects are not topics, but are in Spec,TP. Unfortunately, space limitations here prevent me from fully making the case for this conclusion.

10 We assume this to be a morphological quirk of the language. In many cases sequences of homophonous or identical morphemes are reduced to one instance of expression. For example, the verb in (37) should be *pakulilile* if all morphemes were spelled out. Also, *zijo* refers to particular kinds of food, not food generally, but the word has no direct concise translation in English.

11 Buell (2005) refers to this as a PP. However, it is not clear this is the right characterization. As he points out, it behaves like a DP argument in many ways, though is distinguished in its ability to appear as an adjunct and in its locative morphology.

References

Abels, K. (2003). Successive-cyclicity, anti-locality, and adposition stranding. PhD dissertation, University of Connecticut.

Alsina, A. and S. Mchombo (1989). "Object asymmetries and Chichewa applicative construction." In *Theoretical aspects of Bantu grammar*, S. Mchombo (ed.), 17–45. Stanford, CA: CSLI.

Anagnosotpoulou, A. (2003). *The syntax of ditransitives*. Berlin: Mouton/de Gruyter.

Baker, M. (1988). *Incorporation*. Chicago, IL: Chicago University Press.

Baker, M. (1997). "Thematic roles and syntactic structure." In *Elements of grammar*, L. Haegeman (ed.), 73–137. Dordrecht: Kluwer.

Bissell-Doggett, T. (2004). All else unequal. PhD dissertation, MIT.

Bresnan, J. and L. Moshi (1990) "Object asymmetries in comparative Bantu syntax." *Linguistic Inquiry* 20: 1–50.

Buell, L. (2005). Issues in Zulu verbal morphosyntax. PhD dissertation, UCLA.

Buell, L. (2007). "Semantic and formal locatives: implications for the Bantu locative inversion typology." *SOAS Working Papers in Linguistics*, 105–120.

Chomsky, N. (1995). "Bare phrase structure." In G. Webelhuth (ed.), *Government and Binding Theory and the Minimalist Program*, 385–439. Oxford: Blackwell.

Chomsky, N. (2001). "Derivation by phase." In *Ken Hale: a life in language*, M. Kenstowicz (ed.), 1–50. Cambridge, MA: MIT Press.

Demuth, K. (1995). "Questions, relatives and minimal projection." *Language Acquisition* 4(1&2): 49–71.

Embick, D. (2004). "On the structure of resultative participles in English." *Linguistic Inquiry* 35(3): 355–392.

Henderson, B. (2006). The syntax and typology of Bantu relative clauses. PhD dissertation, MIT.

Hyman, L. and A. Duranti (1982). "On the object relation in Bantu." *Syntax and Semantics* 15: 217–239.

Jeong, Y. (2006). The landscape of applicatives. PhD dissertation, MIT.

Jeong, Y. (2007). *Applicatives: Structure and interpretation from a minimalist perspective*. Amsterdam: John Benjamins.

Keenan, G. and B. Comrie (1977). "Noun phrase accessibility and universal grammar." *Linguistic Inquiry* 8: 62–100.

Kimenyi, A. (1980). *A relational grammar of Kinyarwanda*. Berkeley, CA: University of California Press.

Kisseberth, C. and M. I. Abasheikh (1974). "Vowel length in Chi Mwi:ni: a case study of the role of grammar in phonology." In A. Bruck, A. Fox and M. W. La Galy (eds), *Papers from the parasession on natural phonology*, 193–209. Chicago, IL: Chicago Linguistic Society.

Kisseberth, C. and M. I. Abasheikh (1976). "The 'object' relationship in Chimiini." *Studies in the Linguistic Sciences* 6: 100–129.

Kisseberth, C. and M. I. Abasheikh (2011). "Chimiini phonological phrasing revisited." *Lingua* 121: 1987–2013.

Marten, L. and M. Mous (2016). "Non-valency-changing valency-changing derivations." *Frankfurter Afrikanistische Blätter* (forthcoming).

Marantz, A. (1984). *On the nature of grammatical relations*. Cambridge, MA: MIT Press.

Marantz, A. (1993). "Implications of asymmetries in double object constructions." In *Theoretical aspects of Bantu grammar*, S. Mchombo (ed.), 113–150. Stanford, CA: CSLI.

McGinnis, M. (1998). Locality in A-movement. Doctoral dissertation, MIT.

McGinnis, M. (2001). "Variation in the phase structure of applicatives." *Linguistic Variation Yearbook* 1: 105–146.

McGinnis, M. (2005). "UTAH at Merge: evidence from multiple applicatives." *MIT Working Papers in Linguistics* 49, 183–200.

McGinnis, M. and D. Gerdts (2004). "A phase-theoretic analysis of Kinyarwanda multiple applicatives." In *Proceedings of the 2003 CLA Annual Conference*, Sophie Burelle and Stanca Somesfalean (eds), 154–165.

Ngoboka, J. P. (2005). A syntactic analysis of Kinyarwanda applicatives. Unpublished MA thesis, University of KwaZulu-Natal, Durban, South Africa.

Pylkkänen, L. (2002). Introducing argument. PhD dissertation, MIT.

Riedel, K. (2009). The syntax of object marking in Sambaa. PhD dissertation, University of Leiden.

Schneider-Zioga, P. (2007). "Anti-agreement, anti-locality and minimality: the syntax of dislocated subjects." *Natural Language and Linguistic Theory* 25(2): 403–446.

Ura, H. (1996). Multiple feature-checking. Doctoral dissertation, MIT.

Zeller, J. and J. P. Ngoboka (2005). "Kinyarwanda locative applicatives and the Minimal Link Condition." *Southern African Linguistics and Applied Language Studies* 24(1): 101–124.

14

THE FORM AND FUNCTION OF DAGBANI DEMONSTRATIVES

Samuel Alhassan Issah

Introduction

This chapter examines the properties of demonstratives in Dagbani, a Southwestern Oti-Volta language of the Central Gur (Mabia) family spoken mainly in Northern Ghana. The work focuses on the morphological properties, internal structure, distributional properties, semantics and pragmatics of the Dagbani demonstratives, an area of the language that has remained largely uninvestigated. The study of demonstratives has received some appreciable level of attention in the linguistics literature: Lakoff (1974), Bhat (2013), Diessel (2013a, 2013b) and Rybarczyk (2015), just to mention a few. Within the Gur phylum, a known piece of work that has attempted a systematic formal account of the structure of demonstratives is Sulemana (2012) who gives an analysis of demonstratives in Buli couched within the theoretical tenets of generative syntax.

Dixon (2003: 61–62) defines a demonstrative simply as "any item, other than 1st and 2nd person pronouns, which can have pointing or deictic reference." He proposes that all languages may have at least one demonstrative, even though their types, forms and functions may vary in different languages. This suggests that although the existence of demonstratives in languages may appear a near universal phenomenon, their inventory, morphological composition and function is a language-specific property. Notwithstanding the language internal idiosyncrasies that demonstratives may display, Dryer (2007) proposes that they possess common grammatical properties in most languages.

There are two classes of demonstratives that have been identified in languages: demonstrative pronouns, which occur as NPs, and demonstrative modifiers of nouns (which are traditionally called demonstrative determiners). Dryer (2007: 104–105) further proposes that "demonstrative modifiers of nouns like adjectives, are common either before the noun or after the noun among both OV and VO languages, though in both type of languages, demonstrative-noun order is slightly more common." I shall demonstrate later in this work that, in Dagbani, the demonstrative determiners are post-nominal modifiers yielding the order NOUN>DEM.

Diessel (1999a) gives a more detailed characterization of demonstratives. He groups demonstratives into various types based on three main parameters: syntactic, pragmatic and semantic properties. He further proposes that demonstratives are typologically deictic expressions that have specific functions in natural languages. In the Diesselian approach, demonstratives do not just include adnominals and pronouns, but also locational adverbs such as the English *there* and *here*. Diessel (1999a: 160), who provides a detailed account of demonstratives using a sample of 85 languages, postulates that "the vast majority of grammars that I consulted use semantic labels such as 'proximal' or 'near speaker' in order to characterize meanings of demonstratives. These labels are, however, only rough approximations. The meaning of a demonstrative is often more complex." I discuss the Dagbani demonstratives in the light of the characterization of Diessel (1999a) since his categorization best describes the grouping of this class of words in Dagbani.

According to Diessel (1999a), demonstratives cross-linguistically comprise two different kinds of features: (1) deictic features – responsible for indicating the distance of an entity from the deictic center, and (2) qualitative features – which specify some unique semantic property like animacy, gender and human or non-human status of a referent. I show that the second type of features, which are the qualitative features, are not a feature of the demonstrative class of words in Dagbani. If Dagbani were to display this property, then there would be a difference in the choice of demonstrative determiners based on the grammatical feature of animacy and also for gender or humanness, a fact that does not hold for the distribution of demonstratives in the language. However, the differentiation based on deictic feature is demonstrated to be valid for Dagbani since we make the contrast between the proximal demonstrative **ŋɔ́** 'this', and the distal demonstrative **ŋɔ́ há/sá**[1]. The distal demonstrative is expressed via an addition of the overt distal marker **há/sá** to the proximal demonstrative **ŋɔ́** 'this'. Thus, this semantic distinction in Dagbani tallies with the typological claim of Diessel (1999a: 50) that all languages have at least two types of demonstrative terms: a demonstrative term that codes that the intended referent is nearby the speaker and another demonstrative term expressing that the intended referent is far away from the speaker. Diessel (2013a), however, opines that, although demonstratives are generally distance-contrastive, in a language like German they are deictically non-contrastive, suggesting that these words are probably definite articles rather than demonstratives.

Demonstratives are generally associated with a deictic function in natural languages. Levinson (1983: 54) asserts that: "deixis concerns the ways in which languages encode or grammaticalize features of the context of utterance or speech event, and thus also concerns ways in which the interpretation of utterance depends on the analysis of that context." In the view of Adger (2004: 204) "demonstratives signify that the speaker assumes that the hearer will be able to identify the referent of the phrase as being close or far away, in either spatial or in discourse terms." Rybarczyk (2015: 29), also proposes that demonstratives are "typically distance-oriented and their original function is to facilitate identification of referents by coding their physical distance from the speaker or, less frequently, the hearer." Rybarczyk (2015: 30) further argues that a language like English has two deictically contrastive demonstratives, both of which morphologically inflect for number 'this/these' (proximal) and 'that/those' (distal). From a typological perspective, most languages are argued to have a two-way contrast in the inventory of demonstratives. However, notwithstanding this typological assertion that languages generally have a two-way deictic contrast, language internal idiosyncrasies suggest that there are languages that have more than two-way deictic distinction. For instance, Levinson (1983) posits that Tlingit, a language spoken in North West America, and Samal, spoken in the Philippines, have a four-way distinction, while Malagasy, an Austronesian language, has also been established to have a six-way distinction.

Pragmatically, demonstratives are cross linguistically used to draw an interlocutor's attention to objects or location within a discourse. This has been established in natural languages and it is argued by Boadi (2010: 19), in his discussion of Akan demonstratives, that demonstratives share a pragmatic function/feature similar to determiners, in that demonstratives are also used "to track down referents and to bring them into conversational space". This pragmatic function is the motivation behind the argument that the grammatical words that are used as demonstratives are typologically deictic in nature. They are specifically locational deixis in that they concern themselves with the spatial locations of referents relevant to an utterance in a given discourse.

Lakoff (1974: 345) proposes three main uses of the English demonstratives *this* and *that* ("including their plural forms *these* and *those*" respectively). These functions include their usage as: (1) indicators of spatio-temporal deixis when they function as 'pointing' devices, (2) use in discourse deixis or anaphora, where demonstratives refer back (or forward) to prior (or future) discourse, and (3) their use as emotional deixis markers. Lakoff (1974), however, further points out that while the first function is the 'basic' use of demonstratives, the second and third are extended uses of demonstratives. He further admits that the third function is quite hard to 'pin down' in most languages.[2]

The data are from two different sources. These include data based on the author's native speaker's intuitions that are augmented with text-based data. The author of this chapter is a native speaker and has constructed some of the data based on a native speaker's knowledge. To ensure that the data constructed using native intuitions were not influenced by any agenda, the author employed the use of language consultants who cross-checked the data to ensure their grammaticality and contextual appropriateness. Secondly, these constructed data are augmented by text-based data drawn from Dagbani works such as Abdallah (2015), and Pazzack (2012). When data is taken from written texts, the author indicates the source by indicating against the data the names, year of publication and page numbers of the texts from which the data are taken. All the data from texts are modified by the addition of tonal markings.

Notwithstanding the fact that demonstratives are very crucial in accounting for different aspects of natural languages, a systematic description of this word class has not received the deserved attention in many African languages including Dagbani. In this chapter what the author seeks to do is to provide data and discussions that bring to light the form and functions of demonstratives in Dagbani. Though the chapter might appear to be presenting the similarities and differences of Dagbani demonstratives with both genetically related and unrelated languages, thereby making it typologically relevant, the chapter also is intended to contribute to the theoretical literature on generative grammar in the study of demonstratives. This is because there is also a theoretical gap in the study of this word class in most African languages, of which Dagbani is no exception.

The discussion in this chapter will proceed as follows: The second section introduces some basic grammatical features of Dagbani as this relevant to understanding the later discussion on the syntax of demonstratives. In the third section I discuss the different types of demonstratives in Dagbani and their linguistic features including: morphological, syntactic, and semantic/pragmatic features couched within the theoretical tenets of generative grammar. I also propose a unified internal structure of demonstratives in this section. Conclusions and summary appear in the fourth section.

Some basic grammatical features of Dagbani

In this section I present a brief discussion of some grammatical features of the language, which will be relevant to the discussion in this chapter. Dagbani is a tonal language, and so differences in meaning of two segmentally similar pronounced words can be based on the tone with which they are said. The tonal system of Dagbani is characterized by two level tones, high and low, represented by (´) and (`) respectively. In addition, there is a downstep tone (a lowering effect occurring between sequences of the same phonemic tone). In this work only phonemic tones are marked. The tonal contrast is exemplified in (1).

(1) a **gbállí**   'grave'.
     b **gbállì**   'zana mat'.
     c **báá**   'dog'.
     d **bàà**   'muddy area'.

Tense is marked by independent syntactic particles occurring before the verb. These particles indicate the time depth of the action and have been referred to as time depth particles in the Gur literature as in Bodomo (1997, 2001) and Olawsky (1999), or time reference markers as in Atintono (2013). Aspect is marked by suffixes and there is only overt morphological marking of case on pronominal NPs but never on lexical nouns.

I also discuss the basic sentence structure and give an overview of the word order facts in Dagbani. A discussion of the word order facts is relevant because it lays the foundation of an understanding of later discussions on the distributional properties of demonstratives in the language. In terms of canonical word order, Dagbani, like many Gur languages, has a constituent order that is fixed: the subject generally precedes the verb and the verb is then followed by an object if any. This yields a strict SVO sentence pattern for the canonical sentence structure. Knowledge of the canonicity of the language is important because it has been suggested in the literature, e.g., Greenberg (1963) and Dryer (2007), that the distribution of the three core constituents of a clause in natural languages, which include the Subject (S), Verb (V), Object (O), has implications for the syntactic patterning of some items within the syntactic system of languages. The sentences in (2a) and (2c) exemplify the basic sentence pattern of the language.[3] The ungrammatical sentences in (2b) and (2d) are borne out of the fact that they deviate from the canonical structural pattern of the language.

(2) a **Samata**   **chέhí**   **tákàrá**   **máá.**
        Samata   tear   paper   DEF
        'Samata has torn the paper'.

     b ***Tákàrá**   **máá**   **Samata**   **chέhí.**
        paper   DEF   Samata   tear
        'Samata has torn the paper.'

     c **Abu**   **kú-Ø**   **bú-á.**
        Abu   kill-PERF   goat-SG
        'Abu has killed a goat'.

     d ***Abu**   **bú-á**   **kú-Ø**
        Abu   goat-SG   kill-PERF
        'Abu has killed the goat'.

Structurally, nominal modifiers, such as the definite article (3a), the adjective (3c), the numeral (4a), and the quantifier (4c) generally follow the nouns they modify.[4] When the determiners precede the nouns they modify, the resulting structures become ungrammatical as evident in (3b), (3d) and (4b, 4d).

(3)   a   **Bí-á**   **máá**   **dá-rí**   **lá**   **búkù**   **máá.**
             child-SG   DEF   buy-IMPERF   FOC   book   DEF
             'The child is buying the book.'

      b   ***Máá**   **bí-á**   **dá-rí**   **lá**   **búkù**   **máá.**
             DEF   child-SG   buy-IMPERF   FOC   book   DEF
             'The child is buying the book.'

      c   **Páɣ'[5] víɛ̀ll-í**   **kà**   **shíkúrú**   **máá**   **ní.**
             woman beautiful.SG   be.there.NOT   school   DEF   LOC
             'There is no beautiful lady/woman in the school.'

      d   ***Víɛ̀ll-í**   **páɣ-à**   **kà**   **shíkúrú**   **máá**   **ní.**
             beautiful-SG   woman-SG   be.there.NOT   school   DEF   LOC
             'There is no beautiful lady/woman in the school.'

(4)   a   **Bí-hí**   **ánàhí**   **sá**   **kàná**   **kpè.**
             child-PL   four   TRM   came   here
             'Four children came here yesterday.'

      b   ***Ánàhí**   **bí-hí**   **sá**   **kàná**   **kpè**
             four   child-PL   TRM   came   here
             'Four children came here yesterday.'

      c   **Bú**   **só**   **yòlí**   **kpé**   **nà**   **yí-lí**   **ŋɔ́**   **máá**   **ní.**
             goat   certain   TRM   enter   DM   house-SG   DEM   DEF   LOC
             'A certain goat recently entered this house.'

      d   ***Só**   **bú**   **yòlí**   **kpé**   **nà**   **yílí**   **ŋɔ́**   **máá**   **ní.**
             certain   goat   TRM   enter   DM   house   DEM   DEF   LOC
             'A certain goat recently entered this house.'

However, when it happens that a noun, an adjective, numeral, and demonstrative co-occur with the same noun, they have a strict syntactic ordering, yielding the syntactic order: Noun > Adjective >Numeral >Demonstrative. This syntactic order is argued by Cinque (2005: 320) to be very pervasive in natural languages. This is explicated by the data in (5).

(5)   a   **Dù**   **víɛ̀l-á**   **ánàhí**   **ŋɔ́.**
             room   nice-PL   four   DEM
             'These four nice rooms.'

      b   ***Víɛ̀l-á**   **dù**   **ánàhí**   **ŋɔ́.**
             nice-PL   room   four   DEM
             'These four nice rooms.'

c **Bí**   yó-yá   àtá   ŋɔ́.
   child   naughty-PL   three   DEM
   'These three naughty children.'

d ****Bí**   ŋɔ́   yó-yá   àtá
   child   DEM   naughty-PL   three
   'These three naughty children.'

From this brief discussion of the word order facts of Dagbani, it is clear that the NPs occur to the left of determiners, meaning that the determiners are post nominal structural elements. Based on this empirical evidence that NPs precede the determiner, I account for this structural relation within the theoretical tenets of the DP-hypothesis of Abney (1987). Within the approach, NPs are complements of D. Accounting for the relationship between nouns and determiners in Dagbani, in which the general pattern appears to be that the NP precedes D, I propose that the complement (NP) undergoes overt syntactic movement to the specifier position of DP, accompanied by various intermediate landing sites, for which I refer the reader to Cinque (2005). This proposed structural representation is given as in (6).

(6)
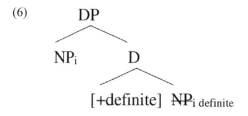

Aboh (2004) makes a similar claim for Gungbe, arguing for NP movement to the specifier of DP over N moving to D. In the discussion that follows, I present one piece of evidence adopted from Aboh (2004) to show that Dagbani behaves similarly, in the sense that there is a movement of NP to spec-DP. The two different types of movement that have often been articulated are: (1) Noun (N) movement to D, as articulated in Davies and Dresser (2005), and (2) NP movement to specifier DP, as articulated in Aboh (2004) and Cinque (2005). Within the proposal that there is movement, the next question that comes to mind is evidence in favor of the particular type of movement that exists in Dagbani.

In his attempt to argue in favor of NP movement to specifier of DP over N moving to D in Gungbe, Aboh (2004) posits that the Gbe languages generally lack inflectional morphology as compared with the Romance languages where N-raising is prevalent. The absence of inflectional morphology on the nouns is analyzed as evidence for the lack of N-raising in these languages. Similarly, in Dagbani the definite features associated with the demonstrative determiners are not affixed to the noun as observed in a language like Japanese, as argued by Davies and Dresser (2005). Just like in the Gbe languages, Dagbani lacks a rich inflectional morphology, which has been used by Aboh (2004) to motivate N to Spec raising. Sulemana (2012) makes similar remarks for Buli, another Gur language spoken in the Upper East Region of Ghana.

In order to account for this movement, I adopt the Minimalist assumption of Chomsky (1995: 262), that "the operation Move is driven by morphological considerations: the requirement that some feature F must be checked." The head of the DP is D which bears the features [+definite, +deictic]. The movement of the NP complement to specifier position of DP therefore creates the needed Spec-Head configuration for the features on D to be checked.[6] By employing the Spec-Head feature checking approach to agreement, it means that the NP must carry a [+definite] feature as well. This required structural relationship, the Spec-Head configuration, the syntactic condition under which the uninterpretable features associated with a head can be checked, is similar to Wh-movement in English, where the Wh-word moves to Spec CP to check the [+Q +WH] features of C as articulated in Chomsky (1995), Sabel (2000) and Carnie (2013).

Types of demonstratives in Dagbani

This section is a systematic discussion of the various forms of demonstratives identified in Dagbani. It focuses on an examination of the morphological, syntatic and semantic/pragmatic features of the demonstratives. I discuss the demonstrative determiner, demonstrative pronoun and demonstrative adverbial. As earlier pointed out, only the basic function of demonstratives as 'pointing device' is discussed in this chapter without consideration of their extended uses.

Demonstrative determiners in Dagbani

Demonstrative determiners occur in nouns and indicate their spatio-temporal relationship with the speaker. Like most other modifiers in Dagbani (as briefly pointed out in the preceding section), the demonstrative determiner follows the noun that it modifies.

With regard to the semantic interpretation of demonstrative determiners, Dagbani makes a distinction between distal and proximal demonstrative determiners, a fact that motivates an argument in favor of two-way deictically contrastive demonstrative determiners. I demonstrate that the semantic notion of proximal demonstrative is marked with **ŋɔ́** 'this', while that of the distal deictic notion is marked with a combination of the proximal demonstrative **ŋɔ́** together with the distal marker **há/sá**. In accounting for the semantics of **ŋɔ́**, I postulate that there are two plausible accounts that one could give for its semantic interpretation. One is to assume that there is a null proximal marker in Dagbani yielding **ŋɔ́** +Ø proximal, and the other is that the default interpretation of **ŋɔ́** on its own is proximal but, combined with **há/sá**, it yields distal. I adopt this latter proposal for the convenience of analysis. In terms of syntactic distribution however, both the proximal and distal demonstrative determiners are post nominal items. The distribution of these demonstrative determiners is explicated in (7) and (8).

(7) a **Búkù**   **ŋɔ́**   **víèlí**   **pám**.
    book   DD   nice.BE   a lot
    'This book is very nice.'

Pazzack 2012: 58

    b **Bí-á**   **ŋɔ́**   **ká**   **ń**   **bɔ́-rá**.
    child-SG   DD   FOC   1SG   want-IMPERF.
    'This child (that) I want.'

Pazzack 2012: 58

    c ***ŋɔ́**   **bí-á**   **ká**   **ń**   **bɔ́-rá**.
    DM   child-SG   FOC   1SG   want-IMPERF.
    'This child (that) I want.'

(8) a **Bɛ́**   **yí**   **páái**   **tíŋà**   **ŋɔ́**   **há**   **bɛ́**   **nì**   **nyá**   **lɔ́ɔrí**.
    2PL   COND   reach   town   DD   DM   2PL   FUT   see   lorry
    'If they get to that village they would get a lorry.'

b **Bú-hí**   **ŋɔ́**   **há**   **ń**   **sáyim-Ø**   **bìndírígú**   **máá.**

goat-PL   DD   DM   FOC   spoil-PERF   food   DEF

'Those goats (and not any other) have spoilt the food.'

c ***ŋɔ́**   **há**   **bú-hí**   **ń**   **sáyim-Ø**   **bìndírígú**   **máá.**

DD   DM   goat-PL   FOC   spoil-PERF   food   DEF

'Those goats (and not any other) have spoilt the food.'

In terms of the contrast between proximal and distal demonstratives, what pertains in Dagbani parallels what is in the English language, as evident in the data below taken from Wolter (2006: 22), which illustrate the distributional contrast between the proximal and distal forms of demonstratives in the English language.

(9)   a   [holding a painting] I like this/*that painting.

b   [pointing at a painting, medium distance away] I like this/that painting.

c   [pointing at a distant painting] I like *this/that painting.

d   The observations suggest this/*that idea: that the climate is changing.

It should be mentioned that when plural nouns occur with the demonstrative determiner, the plural feature is marked on the former but never the latter, as is further explicated in (10) and (11).

(10)   a   **Dú-rí[7]**   **ŋɔ́**   **há**   **nyèlá**   **dú' pàl-á**

Room-PL   DD   DM   COP   room new-PL

'Those rooms are new (rooms).'

b   ***Dú-ú**   **ŋɔ́-nímá/*rí**   **há**   **nyèlá**   **dù' pàl-á**

room-SG   DD-PL   DM   COP   room new-PL

'Those rooms are new (rooms).'

(11)   a   **Bú-hí**   **ŋɔ́**   **sá**   **dɔ́yí-Ø**   **lá**   **sɔ́hìlá**

goat-PL   DD   TRM   deliver-PERF   FOC   yesterday

'These goats littered yesterday.'

b   ***Bú-á**   **ŋɔ́-nímá**   **sá**   **dɔ́yí-Ø**   **lá**   **sɔ́hìlá**

goat-SG   DD-PL   TRM   deliver-PERF   FOC   yesterday

'These goats littered yesterday.'

The ungrammaticality of sentences (10b) and (11b) is borne out of the fact that the plural features are marked on the demonstrative determiner and not the nouns as should be the case. This then forms the basis for the proposal that the demonstrative determiners of Dagbani do not inflect for number features. I have discussed the demonstrative determiners of Dagbani and the following conclusions can be made: (1) in terms of their distribution, they are post nominal in the sense that they follow the nouns they modify; (2) they make a semantic contrast between proximal and distal; and (3) they do not inflect for number since plural features are marked on the nouns they occur with.

Per this current analysis, one fundamental question that arises is how we can account for the fact that when demonstrative determiners occur with nouns, the Num features are marked on the nouns and not the demonstrative determiners. Proposing a unified theoretical internal structure for Dagbani DemP, I assume that in Dem+N constructions, the noun moves to Spec-NumP for N+Num, the whole NumP moves to spec DemP for N+Num +Dem, only that, this time, in contrast to Dem Pronouns, Dem⁰ is overt. Then the whole DemP moves to Spec DistP, yielding the right syntactic order N+Num, Dem+**há/sá**.

Demonstrative pronouns in Dagbani

This sub-section investigates the linguistic properties of demonstrative pronouns. I show that, unlike demonstrative determiners, which occur with nouns, the demonstrative pronouns substitute for NPs. I concentrate on their morphosyntactic, pragmatic/semantic features. Demonstrative pronouns cross linguistically are also used to show or point to an entity or object present in the context, but differ from their demonstrative determiner counterparts in the sense that they substitute for nouns and so, distributionally, do not occur with NPs. Just as we have demonstrated the demonstrative determiners in the preceding section, Dagbani makes only a two-way distinction with respect to the proximity of an object relative to the speaker, with regard to the use of demonstrative pronouns, as in English (e.g., *this is good* vs. *that is my house*). The demonstrative pronouns are homonymous with demonstrative determiners in many other languages such as English. The similarity in form of some of the demonstratives falls in line with the typological claims of Diessel (1999b: 3) that "the majority of languages use the same demonstrative forms as independent pronouns and together with a co-occurring noun." He further showed that, out of a sample of 85 languages gathered, only 24 of them were found to make a formal distinction between pronominal and adnominal demonstratives. Diessel (1999a) refers to the demonstrative pronouns as pronominal demonstratives. Diessel (2013b) contends that, though in most natural languages pronominal and adnominal demonstratives are morphologically identical, there are also languages in which pronominal and adnominal demonstratives are often formally distinguished in the sense that they can have different stems or different inflectional features. Diessel illustrates the claim that there can be morphological differences between pronominal and adnominal demonstratives using the French *celui* and *celle*, which are used pronominally, and *ce* and *cette* accompany a noun (adnominal demonstratives).

(12)   Donne-moi   ce   livre-là   et   garde   celui-ci   pour   toi.
       Give-me   this   book-there   and   keep   this.one-here for   you
       'Give me that book and keep this one for you.'

It is important to point out that, unlike the demonstrative determiners, demonstrative pronouns make a morphological contrast between singular and plural form. To account for this observation, it was earlier proposed that the demonstrative pronoun ŋɔ́ 'this' moves to the specifier position of the functional NumP and, depending on whether Num is plural or singular, then the plural morpheme **-nímá** is realized yielding **ŋɔ́-nímá** or the zero morpheme, in which case we have **ŋɔ́**. The two-way contrast in number in the demonstrative pronoun in shown in Table 14.1.

Table 14.1 The number distinction of demonstrative pronouns

Demonstrative pronoun	Singular	Plural	Gloss
Proximal	ŋɔ́	ŋɔ́nímá	this/these
Distal	ŋɔ́ há	ŋɔ́nímá há	that/those

The sentences in (13) and (14) illustrate the morphological marking for plural in demonstrative pronouns in both proximal and distal demonstrative pronouns.

(13) a ŋɔ́   bé   shíkúrú   máá   ní
         DEMPR   there   school   DEF   LOC
         'This (one) is in the school.'

      b ŋɔ́-nímá   bé   shíkúrú   máá   ní
         DEMPR-PL   be.there   school   DEF   LOC
         'These (ones) are in the school.'

      c Kárímbá   máá   yèlí-yá   ní   ŋɔ́   vièlá
         teacher   DEF   say-PERF   that   DEMPR.   nice
         'The teacher said that this (one) is nice.'

      d Kárímbá   máá   yèlí-yá   ní   ŋɔ́-nímá   vièlá
         teacher   DEF   say-PERF   that   DEMPR-PL   nice
         'The teacher said that these (ones) are nice.'

(14) a ŋɔ́   há   yí   lá   sílìmíìn   tíŋà   ná.
         DPR   DM   come FOC   whiteman   land   DIRM
         'That (one) comes from the white man's land (abroad).'

      b ŋɔ́-nímá   há   yí   lá   sílìmíìn   tíŋà   ná.
         DPR-PL   DM   come FOC   whiteman   land   DIRM
         'Those (ones) come from the white man's land (abroad).'

      c ó   kòhí-rí   lá   ŋɔ́   há
         3SG   sell-IMPERF FOC   DPR   DM
         'S/he is selling that (one).'

      d ó   kòhí-rí   lá   ŋɔ́-nímá   há
         3SG   sell-IMPERF FOC   DPR-PL   DM
         'S/he is selling those (ones).'

A close look at the data in (13) through (14) indicates that though the demonstrative determiners and demonstrative pronouns are homonymous, they differ in terms of their distributional and morphological properties. While it was shown that the demonstrative determiners are modifiers, it is apparently clear that demonstrative pronouns work as heads of NPs, occurring in both subject (13a, 13b) (14a, 14b) and object positions (13c, 13d) (14c, 14d). Morphologically, as pointed out earlier, we observe that, unlike the demonstrative determiner counterparts, demonstrative pronouns make a distinction between singular and plural forms as evident in the data presented in (13) and (14). The fact that Dagbani demonstrative pronouns inflect for number is not typologically unusual. Dalrymple (2012: 2), for instance, argues that "number marking can appear on pronouns or nouns, indicating the number of members in the group referred to, or as agreement marking on determiners, adjectives, verbs, prepositions, and other categories."

Within the pragmatic domain, these demonstrative pronouns, just like the demonstrative determiners, are used to draw the interlocutor's attention to objects within a discourse. They therefore help in tracking or narrowing the scope of discourse by focusing on particular items. The use of the demonstrative ŋɔ́ 'this' or ŋɔ́ há 'that' therefore narrows the domain of the conversation or discourse to some item based on the deictic center. This has cross linguistically been demonstrated to be the pragmatic function of demonstratives.

Considering the fact that there is a specification for number value in the demonstrative pronouns, I propose the presence of a functional head within the Demonstrative Phrase claimed to be the Number Phrase, NumP. The NumP projection is well articulated in Ritter (1991). This functional head is headed by Num which hosts the number markers within the DemP. I further propose the presence of the distal phrase (DisP), a functional projection proposed to be projected above Demonstrative Phrase and headed by the distal markers. The proposed internal (base) structure of the DemP is outlined in (15).

(15)

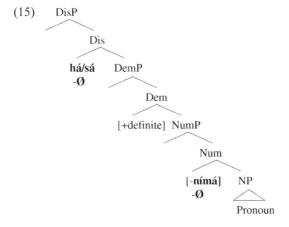

In accounting for the proposed internal structure of the demonstrative phrase, I contend that the demonstrative pronoun ŋɔ́ starts out as complement to NumP, and for that matter as NP, and then moves to the specifier position of the functional NumP. If it happens that Num is plural, then the overt plural morpheme -nímá is realized, yielding the right predictive order ŋɔ́-nímá. On the other hand, if Num is singular, you get ŋɔ́ (Ø - há / sá). Thereafter, the whole NumP moves to the specifier of DisP to get the heads of the DisP to follow, which gives the ordering ŋɔ́-nímá há/ sá. This kind of successive movement is what Cinque (2005: 317) refers to as 'roll-up' movement.

Locational/demonstrative adverbs in Dagbani

The term 'demonstrative adverb' is adopted from Fillmore (1982: 47), who uses this notion for locational deictics such as the English *here* and *there*. A locative/demonstrative adverb is a type of adverb that refers to a location. Generally, this class of demonstratives functions as verb modifiers. They are also referred to as adverbial demonstratives in the linguistic literature. In this chapter I use the terminology adverbial demonstratives to refer to these kinds of demonstratives. Just like the demonstrative determiners and pronouns, the adverbial demonstratives' system consists of a two-way semantic contrastive system; the demonstrative **kpè** 'here' and **ní** 'there'. While the former indicates proximity to the speaker, the latter indicates that the deictic reference is farther away from the speaker. These two locational adverbs can, however, be augmented by the distal marker **há**, which indicates that an object is remote from both the speaker and the hearer. I therefore analyze the adverbial demonstratives as portraying a two-way semantic contrast that can be augmented by the distal marker **há**.

Syntactically, adverbial demonstratives are identified to have three main positions in which they occur, as my data provisionally indicate. It is, for instance, possible for locational adverbs to occur with possessive determiners in a noun phrase, as in (16). It is also possible for adverbial demonstratives to occur as adverbial complements in the object position, as explicated by data in (17). In this adverbial complement position, the adverbial demonstratives can optionally be followed by another adverbial element and, finally, they can also occur in structures in which they function as modifiers of a preceding head noun, as exemplified by data in (18). Amfo (2007: 137) makes similar distributional claims of locational demonstratives in Akan, a Kwa language. The distribution of adverbial demonstratives is exemplified in data in (16) through (18).

(16) a **ó**   **kpè[8]** **ká**   **nɔ́ŋ-á**   **dím-Ø.**
         3SG.POSS   here   FOC   scorpion-SG   sting-PERF
         'This part of his/her body that the scorpion has stung' (lit: his/her here (that) a scorpion has stung).

      b **Bí-á**   **máá** **kpè** **há**   **dééí**   **dáŋ-à**
         child-SG   DEF   here   DM   collect   wound-SG
         'That part of the child is wounded' (lit: the child's there is wounded).

      c **Ǹ**   **ní**   **málí** **yúm**
         1SG.POSS DET   there   has   sore
         'This part of my body has a sore' (lit: my there has a sore).

      d **Bú-á**   **ní**   **bí**   **bɔ́-rí**   **kóm**
         goat-SG   there   NEG   want-IMPERF water
         'That part of a goat does not like water' (lit: a goat's there does not like water).

(17) a **Napari**   **káǹná** **kpè** **sáhá** **kám**
         Napari   come   here   time   every
         'Napari comes here all the time.'

                                                                    Abdallah 2015: 7

      b **Bɛ̀**   **sá**   **cháŋ** **kpè** **há**
         3PL   TRM   go   here   DM
         'They went there yesterday.'

      c **Napari**   **kɔ́-rí**   **ní**
         Napari   till-IMPERF   there
         'Napari tills/farms there.'

      d **Bonnayo**   **kù**   **cháŋ** **ní**   **há**
         Bonnayo   NEG   go   there   DM
         'Bonnayo would not go there.'

(18) a **kpè** **lóórí-nímá** **kà**   **dáà**
         here   lorry-PL   have.NOT   market
         'From here, lorries are not expensive.'

      b **Kpè** **há**   **bí-á**   **kám**   **bɔ́-rí**   **shíǹtání**
         here   DM   child-SG   every   want-IMPERF quarrel
         'From there, every child wants troubles.'

      c **Ní**   **bíǹdírígú** **nyáɣísí** **pám**
         there food   delicious   very
         'Food from there is very delicious.'

The form and function of Dagbani demonstratives

Table 14.2 Summary of the formal features of demonstratives in Dagbani

Demonstrative type	Syntax	Morphology	Semantics	Pragmatics
Demonstrative determiners	• occur as modifiers	do not inflect for number	proximal/ distal dichotomy	focuses interlocutor's attention to objects in a discourse
Demonstrative pronouns	• occur as heads of NPs • cannot occur as modifiers	inflect for singular/ plural contrast	proximal/ distal dichotomy	focuses interlocutor's attention to objects in a discourse
Adverbial demonstratives	• occur as modifiers of NPs • occur as heads of NPs	do not inflect for number contrast	proximal/ distal dichotomy	focuses interlocutor's attention to locations in a discourse

> d **Ní há   páɣì-bá   málí kárímbáání**
> there DM   woman-PL have pride
> 'Women from there are very proud.'

Morphologically, locational/demonstrative adverbs do not make a distinction between singular and plural, leading to the conclusion that they do not inflect for number.

However, there is a context in which these adverbial demonstratives can be marked for plural using the plural morpheme **-nímá**. When this happens there is a slight change in the semantics, in which case they no longer function as locational adverbials but would refer to the people located in a particular domain. This is explicated in (19).

(19) a **Kpè-nímá jé   vúrí   yúŋ.**
        here-PL   like.NOT noise night
        'The people (of here) do not like noise at night' (lit: the people here do not like noise at night).

    b **Ní-nímá chèmí ká   sókám   zórí bá.**
        there-PL make   CONJ everyone fear 2PL.OBJ
        'The people of there have (and not any other) have made everyone fear them' (lit: the people living there have made everyone fear them).

    c **Kpè-nímá há   ká   ǹ   yú-rà.**
        here-PL   DM   FOC   1SG.SUBJ like-IMPERF
        'The people of there (and not any other) that I like' (lit: the people there are the people that I like).

From the aforementioned facts about the demonstratives of Dagbani, Table 14.2 below gives a summary of the linguistic features of the various forms of demonstratives discussed in this chapter.

Summary and conclusion

In this chapter I concentrated on describing and analyzing the syntax, morphology, semantics and pragmatics of demonstratives in Dagbani. I have discussed three distinct forms of demonstratives: the demonstrative determiner, demonstrative pronoun and adverbial demonstratives.

The semantics and pragmatics of the various forms of demonstratives are shown to be the same. Advancing a theoretical contribution to the study of the internal structure of demonstratives, I showed the demonstrative projects a phrase (DemP) that takes a NP as its complement. The observation that the demonstrative occurs as a post nominal structural element is explained by the movement of NP to Spec DemP as a result of the definite feature of Dem that needs to be checked against the definite feature of the NP. Accounting for the fact that the number marking is an essential property of the DemP, where there is a contrast between singular and plural, I argue for the projection of a functional NumP headed by Num. In accounting for the observation that the demonstrative pronoun has the morphological feature contrasting for number, I proposed that the demonstrative pronoun ŋɔ́ starts out as a complement to NumP and moves to the specifier of NumP. When Num is plural, then it yields **ŋɔ́-nímá**, while in cases of singular Num we get **ŋɔ́**. After this, the entire NumP moves to the specifier of DemP, which gives the right ordering **ŋɔ́-nímá há**. Arguing for a unified structure for the demonstratives in Dagbani, I account for the observation that Num is marked on nouns when they occur with demonstrative determiners by proposing that the noun moves to Spec-NumP for N+Num, the whole NumP moves to spec DemP for N+Num+Dem, only that, this time, in contrast to Dem Pronouns, Dem^0 is overt. Then the whole DemP moves to Spec DistP, yielding the right syntactic order N+Num, Dem+**há/sá**. Observing that these distal markers are overt morphological units, I propose for the projection of an additional functional projection within the DemP, aside the NumP which is labelled as DisP. This functional head is headed by Dis and so hosts the overt distal marker. This functional projection is argued to be projected above DemP. This chapter is important because, to the best of my knowledge, there is no known systematic linguistic documentation of Dagbani demonstratives. Thus, demonstratives had hitherto not received any attention from researchers of Dagbani.

Abbreviations

1	1st Person
2	2nd Person
3	3rd Person
CONJ	Conjunction
COP	Copular
DD	Demonstrative Determiner
DEF	Definite Article
DEMPR	Demonstrative Pronoun
DM	Distal Marker
DIRM	Directional Marker
FOC	Focus Marker
FUT	Future Marker
IMPERF	Imperfective Aspect
OBJ	Object
PERF	Perfective Aspect
PL	Plural
POSS DET	Possessive Determiner
SG	Singular
SUBJ	Subject
TRM	Time Reference Marker

Notes

1 The difference between **há** and **sá** is dialectal. The former distal marker is used by the Nayahili (Eastern dialect) while the former is used in the Tomosili (Western dialect).
2 For purposes of space and the fact that discourse deixis in Dagbani is quite a complex domain that needs particular attention, I concentrate mainly on the pragmatic uses of demonstratives without a discussion on their extended uses.
3 While asserting that the strict SVO cannot be altered, it should also be mentioned that for information structural purposes, e.g., in focus marking, constituents can be dislocated within the sentence structure which results in changing this sentence canonicity.
4 For details on the interaction between nominals and determiners see Issah (2013).
5 When nouns occur with certain modifiers in Dagbani, part of the noun, proposed in the literature to be the class marker, is lost. For a discussion on this, readers are referred to Olawsky (1999, 2004) and Issah (2013).
6 I take cognizance of the fact that in current views of Minimalism, Spec-Head configuration is not a requirement for feature checking. This has given rise to the notion of AGREE, Chomsky (2000, 2001) Zeijlstra (2012) among others. Though their view of feature checking also adheres to the theoretical claims of Chomsky (1995) that there is a syntactic correlation between uninterpretable and interpretable features, they opine that features can be checked at a distance unlike Chomsky (1995) who holds that elements must be in Spec-Head relationship for features to be checked. I opt for the proposal of Chomsky (1995) because it addresses the problem at hand conveniently.
7 The suffix **–rí** is an allomorphy of **–nímá**. Readers should recall my earlier assertion that noun class system is a prominent feature of the Dagbani grammar where nouns have predictable singular and plural markers depending on the class to which they belong.
8 This structure is a fronted construction in which there is movement of the NP, **ó kpè** 'his/her here' from the lexical to the functional layer.

References

Aboh, E. O. (2004). *The Morphosyntax of Complement-Head Sequences*. Oxford: Oxford University Press.
Abney, S. (1987). The English Noun Phrase in Its Sentential Aspect. Doctoral Dissertation, MIT.
Adger, D. (2004). *Core Syntax: A Minimalist Approach*. Oxford: Oxford University Press.
Amfo, N. A. A. (2007). Akan Demonstratives. In D. L. Payne and P. Jaime (eds), *Selected Proceedings of the 37th Annual Conference on African Linguistics*. Somerville, MA: Cascadilla Proceedings Project, pp. 134–148.
Atintono A. S. (2013). The Semantics and Grammar of Positional Verbs in Gurenɛ: A Typological Perspective. A thesis submitted to The University of Manchester for the degree of Doctor of Philosophy in the Faculty of Humanities.
Bhat, D. N. S. (2013). Third Person Pronouns and Demonstratives. In M. S. Dryer and M. Haspelmath (eds), *The World Atlas of Language Structures Online*. Leipzig: Max Planck Institute for Evolutionary Anthropology (available online at: http://wals.info/chapter/43).
Boadi, A. L. (2010). *The Akan Noun Phrase: Its Structure and Meaning*. Accra: Black Mask Ltd.
Bodomo, A. B. (1997). *The Structure of Dagaare*. Stanford, CA: CSLI Publications.
Bodomo, A. B. (2001). The Temporal Systems of Dagaare and Dagbane: Re-Appraising the Philosophy of Linguistic Relativity. *Journal of Cultural Studies* 3(1): 43–55.
Carnie, A. (2013). *Syntax: A Generative Introduction: 3rd Edition*. Oxford: Wiley-Blackwell.
Chomsky, N. (1995). *The Minimalist Program*. Cambridge, MA: The MIT Press.
Chomsky, N. (2000). Minimalist Inquiries. In R. Martin, D. Michaels and J. Uriagereka (eds), *Essays on Minimalist Syntax in Honor of Howard Lasnik*. Cambridge, MA: MIT Press, pp. 89–155.
Chomsky, N. (2001) Derivation by Phase. In Michael Kenstowicz (ed.), *Ken Hale: A Life in Language*. Cambridge, MA: MIT Press, pp. 1–52.
Cinque, G. (2005). Deriving Greenberg's Universal 20 and its Exceptions. *Linguistic Inquiry* 36(2): 315–332.
Dalrymple, M. (2012). Number Marking: An LFG Overview. *Proceedings of the LFG12 Conference*. Stanford, CA: CSLI Publications.

Davies, D. W. and Dresser, C. A. (2005). The Structure of Javanese and Madurese Determiner Phrases. In J. Heinz and D. Ntelitheos (eds), *UCLA Working Papers in Linguistics 12, Proceedings of AFLA XII*, 57–72.

Diessel, H. (1999a). *Demonstratives: Form, Function and Grammaticalization*. Amsterdam: John Benjamins.

Diessel, H. (1999b). The Morphosyntax of Demonstratives in Synchrony and Diachrony. *Linguistic Typology* 3: 1–49.

Diessel, H. (2013a). Distance Contrasts in Demonstratives. In M. S. Dryer and M. Haspelmath (eds), *The World Atlas of Language Structures Online*. Leipzig: Max Planck Institute for Evolutionary Anthropology (available online at: http://wals.info/chapter/41, accessed on April 4, 2017).

Diessel, H. (2013b). Pronominal and Adnominal Demonstratives: In M. S. Dryer and M. Haspelmath (eds), *The World Atlas of Language Structures Online*. Leipzig: Max Planck Institute for Evolutionary Anthropology (available online at: http://wals.info/chapter/42, accessed on April 4, 2017).

Dixon, R. M. W. (2003). Demonstratives: A Cross-Linguistic Typology. *Studies in Language* 27(1): 61–112.

Dryer, M. S. (2007). Noun Phrase Structure. In T. Shopen (ed.), *Language Typology and Syntactic Description. Vol. II: Complex Constructions* (2nd Edition). Cambridge: Cambridge University Press, pp. 151–205.

Fillmore, C. J. (1982). Towards a descriptive framework for spatial deixis. In R. J. Jarvella and W. Klein (eds.), *Speech, Place, and Action*. Chichester: Wiley, pp. 31–59.

Greenberg, J. (1963). Some Universals of Grammar with Particular Reference to the Order of Meaningful Elements. In J. Greenberg (ed.), *Universals of Language*. Cambridge, MA: MIT Press, pp. 73–113.

Issah, A. S. (2013). The Structure of the Dagbani Simple Noun Phrase. *South African Journal of African Languages (SAJAL)* 33(2): 203–212.

Lakoff, R. (1974). Remarks on 'this' and 'that'. In *Proceedings of the Tenth Regional Meeting of the Chicago Linguistic Society*. Chicago, IL: Chicago Linguistics Society, pp. 345–356.

Levinson, S. C. (1983). *Pragmatics*. Cambridge: Cambridge University Press.

Olawsky, K. J. (1999). Aspects of Dagbani Grammar, with Special Emphasis on Phonology and Morphology. Unpublished PhD dissertation, Munich: Lincom.

Olawsky, K. (2004). What Is a Noun? What Is an Adjective? Problem of Classification in Dagbani. *Journal of African Languages and Linguistics* 25: 127–148.

Ritter, E. (1991). Two Functional Categories in Noun Phrases: Evidence from Modern Hebrew. In Susan Rothstein (ed.), *Perspectives on Phrase Structure: Heads And Licensing, Syntax and Semantics* 25. San Diego, CA: Academic Press, pp. 37–62.

Rybarczyk, M. (2015). *Demonstratives and Possessives with Attitude: An Intersubjectively-Oriented Empirical Study*. Amsterdam: John Benjamins Publishing Company.

Sabel, J. (2000). Partial Wh-movement and the Typology of Wh-questions. In U. Lutz, G. Muller and A. von Stechow (eds), *Wh-Scope Marking*. Amsterdam: John Benjamins, pp. 409–446.

Sulemana, A. (2012). The Structure of the Determiner Phrase in Buli. An MPhil thesis submitted to the department of linguistics, University of Ghana.

Wolter, K. L. (2006). The Semantics and Pragmatics of Demonstrative Noun Phrases. Doctoral dissertation, University of California Santa Cruz.

Zeijlstra, H. (2012). "There is only one way to agree". *The Linguistic Review* 29: 491–539.

Dagbani texts

Abdallah, I. (2015). Ghanaian language and culture: BECE tilaa zang ti Dagbang shikuru bihi ban be JHS. Unpublished. Tamale.

Pazzack, A. P. (2012). Notes on Dagbani Grammar: Bachituɣa mini yɛltɔɣa biɛhigu. Uew. Unpublished.

15

EXPERIENCER PREDICATIONS IN CHADIC

A study of the semantics-syntax interface

Zygmunt Frajzyngier

Background and the aim of the chapter[1]

The term 'experiencer' within a number of linguistic theories designates a semantic relationship that refers to the participant who experiences a state, e.g., 'I' in 'I felt cold' (Matthews 1997: 122). English, German, Russian, French, and many other Indo-European languages sometimes encode the experiencer as a subject of the clause, as in the example above and others, such as 'I love', 'I enjoy'; French *j'aime*; and Russian *(ya) l'ubl'u* 'I love'. The same languages sometimes code the experiencer not as a subject but as a direct or indirect object, e.g., English 'it pains me that . . .'; French *il me plait* 'I like it' (lit. 'it pleases me'). In some Indo-European languages, such as German and Polish, the experiencer is marked by the same form that marks the indirect object:

(1) **mir**   *ist*   *kalt*
    1SG:DAT be   cold
    'I am cold'.
    mir   *gefällt* *dieses* *Pferd*
    1SG:DAT please   DEM:NOM horse
    'I like this horse'.
    mir   *tut*   *der*   *Zahn*   *weh*
    1SG:DAT do   DEF:NOM tooth   sore
    'I have a toothache'. (German)

In some languages, in addition to marking the experiencer with the dative case, the clause has the point of view of the subject marker ('short reflexive' in Russian, Polish, German, Dutch; 'reflexive' in French, Spanish, Italian), a marker that changes the point of view of the unmarked form of the verb (Frajzyngier 1999). Here is an example in Polish:

(2) *podoba* **mi**   **się**   *twoja*   *praca*
    please   1SG-dat REFL   2SG:NOM work:NOM
    'I like your work'. (Polish)

This is similarly observed in Russian where the point of view marker (glossed REFL) is suffixed to the verb:

(3) *mn'e   nravitsa*
   1SG:DAT   please:REFL
   'I like' (lit. 'to me pleases')

Traditional questions with respect to the experiencer have to do with which subjects are interpreted as experiencers. Dowty (1991: 579), for example, proposed that the experiencer is sentient/perceiving and is distinct from the stimulus, which is not sentient/perceiving. The same or similar predicate can occur with either the experiencer subject or the stimulus subject:

Experiencer subject:	Stimulus subject:
x likes y	y pleases x
x fears y	y frightens x
x supposes (that) S	(it) seems (to) x (that)
x regards y (as)VP	y strikes x (as) VP
x is surprised by y	y surprises x
x is disturbed by y	y disturbs x

The main question addressed in this chapter is why experiencers are sometimes coded as subjects and sometimes as non-subjects in languages that have the category subject. This question is important for a number of reasons: (1) An answer to this question can provide an explanation for the alignment of grammatical relations and hence for the formation of clauses; and (2) it may also serve as a heuristic tool in that it may reveal which semantic relations are actually coded in a given language. One of the ways to answer this question is to conduct a cross-linguistic examination of predications where experiencers are coded as non-subject and languages where experiencers are coded as subjects. Another tool is to examine the same question within a single language.

A brief note on terminology: the terms 'subject' and 'object' in the study of this chapter refer to syntactic relations, without any implication of the semantic relations involved. The terms 'agent', 'patient', 'experiencer' and 'indirect object' refer to semantic relations. The terms 'nominative, 'dative', and 'accusative' refer only to case marking.

The interest of Chadic languages

Chadic languages, the largest and most typologically diverse family within the Afroasiatic phylum, constitute a particularly fertile object of investigation because they display considerable variation with respect to the coding of experiencers. Some languages code experiencers as non-subjects, other languages code experiencers as subjects, and there are languages in which some experiencers are coded as subjects and others as non-subjects. It is important to find out whether the various ways of coding the experiencer are accidental or whether there is some principle behind them. The present study is the first of its kind for any African language family.

In some Chadic languages, the experiencer predication includes states corresponding to 'fear', 'like', 'be tired', 'be hungry', 'be angry', 'be ashamed', 'feel pain', 'have a toothache' or other type of pain, 'feel bitter', 'have bad luck', 'have good luck', 'be cheated', 'prefer', 'have rabies', as well as some predications that in English would be considered non-states, e.g., 'stumble'.

These facts call for a more precise definition of the term 'experiencer', a definition that is not based on an analogy with English or with some other language.

The working definition in the present study is that the experiencer is a semantic relationship whereby a participant in the event is in a state resulting from the event but does not control the event. The experiencer predication is a predication that represents the event from the point of view of the experiencer.

Languages differ as to which predicates require the experiencer to be coded as non-subject and which languages code the experiencer as subject. For example, the predicate 'fear' has the experiencer as non-subject in some languages and as subject in others. This fact indicates that the mere semantic relationship between the verb and its arguments is not the deciding factor that determines the way the experiencer is coded.

Anticipating the analyses to come, I propose that the fundamental factor that determines whether the experiencer is coded as subject or non-subject is the orientation of the predicate with respect to the goal. If the predicate in a given language represents the event from the point of view of the goal, i.e., indicates that the subject does something with respect to some other entity, the experiencer is coded as a non-subject. If the predicate represents the event from the point of view of the subject, i.e., indicates how the subject is affected by the event or how the event concerns the subject, the experiencer is coded as the subject. These two conditions are independent of whether or not there is a second argument, e.g., an object, in the clause.

The importance of the point-of-view category is that it does not depend on the relationship between the verb and the event or state it refers to. In one language, a predication or a verb referring to a given event may represent the point of view of the subject, while, in another language, the verb referring to the same event may represent the point of view of an argument other than the subject. For example, the verb corresponding to 'break' in Wandala represents the point of view of the subject, while in Polish the verb 'break' represents the point of view of the goal. In English, the verb 'break' does not have a default point of view, as the subject may be either the thing broken or the thing/entity that broke something else.

These two hypotheses are examined in Chadic languages from the three branches of the family: East, Central, and West. In some of these languages the default value for all transitive predicates is the point of view of the goal, and in other languages the default point of view of transitive verbs is that of the subject. In some languages, there are predicates that inherently represent the point of view of the subject and predicates that inherently represent the point of view of the goal, while in other languages there are morphological markers that tell the listener whether to view the event from the point of view of the subject or from the point of view of the goal.

The study presented in this chapter is organized as follows: I first describe experiencer predication in several languages, starting with a language that has a dedicated experiencer predication used with a large number of experiencers, then proceed to discuss languages that have fewer experiencer predications. I then analyze similarities and differences in experiencer predications across languages, and finally test whether the hypotheses about the conditions for the coding of the experiencer are supported by the data at hand.

Lele (East Chadic)

The reason the discussion of individual languages starts with Lele is that in this language there exists a specific construction that chiefly encodes the experiencer role. Lele is an SVO language, as illustrated by the following example (all data for Lele are from Frajzyngier 2001 unless another source is given):

(4) *kara   màglí   kanya*
    people   prepare   thing
    'People arrange things . . .'

Unlike in many other Chadic languages, the default point of view of transitive verbs in Lele is the point of view of the goal; i.e., these verbs tell the listener to consider the event as directed at the goal. The evidence for the goal being the default point of view of the verb is provided by the fact that the language has the morphological marker *cà*, identical with the noun 'head', whose grammatical function is to change the point of view from that of the goal to that of the subject, as illustrated by the following examples.

(5) *yàábú-dú   na   ŋ   án   kwání*
    tell DAT-3F   HYP   1SG   leave   outside
    *ba   ŋ   jìb   **cà-nìŋ**   ná   kòyè   ba*
    COM   1SG bump   head-1SG ASSC thief COM
    ŋ   dìgr-ìy
    1SG   kill-3M
    'He told her: "leaving the house I bumped into a thief [lit. I hit my head against a thief] and killed him."'

In the example above, the noun phrase *cà-nìŋ* 'my head' is not merely the object of the transitive verb but also marks the change of point of view from the object to the subject. The evidence for this function is provided by the use of the form *cà* 'head' in intransitive predications:

(6) *cànìgé   dàgè   ná   tamáĺ-y   kìn-gé   **cà***
    Canige   3PL   ASSC   wife-3M return-3PL   head
    ***dí-gè**   dà   Dèbréŋ*
    GEN:PL-3PL PREP   Debreng
'Canige and his wife returned to Debreng' (not 'Canige and his wife returned their head').

Evidence for the grammatical function of the noun *cà* 'head' is provided by its occurrence in idiomatic expressions coding the point of view of the subject:

(7) *haba   bé-ŋ   cà-m*
    find:IMP dat-1SG head-2M
    'be successful!' (lit. 'find me your head').

Compare a similar predication with a noun other than *cà*, where the point of view is that of the goal:

(8) *haba   bé-ŋ   wédré*
    find:IMP DAT-1SG car
    'find me a car'.

The property of experiencers is that they do not control the event in the ordinary sense of the verb control; i.e., the clause in which the experiencer occurs does not indicate that the experiencer triggered the state. An experiencer cannot be the subject of a transitive predication

Experiencer predications in Chadic

in Lele, as this would produce an internal semantic contradiction between the role of the experiencer in the clause and the role of subject in a clause that represents the point of view of the goal. Since the experiencer cannot be the subject of a transitive predication Lele codes the experiencer as the object of the verb *ne* 'make'. The subject of such a predicate is either the trigger or the locus of experience. Here are various types of internal experiences coded by the experiencer predication.

Being tired: The subject is the noun *gílalé* 'tiredness'. The object represents the person or people who are tired:

(9)   *kàw′*   *gé*   *gàg*   *tùwà*   *dùgì-gè*   *gílalé*
     walk   3PL   till   sun   drown-3PL   tiredness
     pínyà   ***nè**-gè*
     also   make-3PL.OBJ
     'They walked till the sun had drowned them and tiredness overwhelmed them' ('lit. tiredness made them').

Being sick: Body is the subject. The person who is sick is the object:

(10) *kus-iy*   ***ne**-y*
     body-3M   make-3M.OBJ
     'he is sick' (lit. 'his body makes him').

The importance of this particular example is that it provides evidence that it is the construction with the verb *ne* and the noun 'body' that ensures the interpretation of the experiencer predication, rather than any individual component of the construction.

Being hungry: Hunger is the subject. The people or animals who are hungry constitute the object.

(11) *time*   ***nè***   *kara*   *sí dé*
     hunger   make   people   a lot
     'People are very hungry' (lit. 'hunger makes people very much').

Being ashamed: Shame is the subject. The person who is ashamed is the object:

(12) *kàsìyà*   ***nè***   *tamá-ŋ*   *néy*
     shame   make   woman-DEF   very much
     'The woman was very ashamed . . .' (lit. 'shame makes woman a lot') (data from Frajzyngier 2001).

Experiencing moral consequences of misbehavior: The noun 'word' is the subject. The experiencer is the object:

(13) *gi*   *deŋli*   *kib-iŋ*   *dé*   *gudá*   ***kolo***   *nè-gì*
     2M   listen   mouth-1SG   NEG   today   word   make-2M
     'You have not listened to what I said and today you are suffering' (lit. 'word makes you').

Suffering the swelling of testicles: The sickness of swelling of testicles is the subject. People who suffer from this affliction are the object:

(14) *hòmnyá*   *dùglò*   *kérgew*
sickness   swelling of testicles
nè   *kara*   *nèy*
make   people   very much
'People suffer a lot from the swelling of testicles'.

Garrigues-Cresswell & Weibegué 1981: 28–29

Having stomach pains: The stomach is the subject and *ne* 'make' is the predicate. The experiencer, viz. the person who suffers, is the object of the verb *nè*. There is also another noun phrase following the verbal piece: *hòmnyá* 'pain, sickness':

(15) *tamá*   *kùlòn-dò*   *nè*   *nè-dù*   *hòmnyá*
woman   belly-3F   COP   make-3F   pain
'The woman's belly ached'.

Garrigues-Cresswell & Weibegué 1981: 2–3

Falling, being in love: The noun *mìsèú* 'love', 'sexual arousal' is the subject, followed by the verb *nè* 'make' and then by a noun or object pronoun representing the person in love:

(16) *mìsèú*   *nè-y*
love   make-3M
'He is in love' (lit. 'love makes him').

(17) *mìsèú*   *nè-dù*
love   make-3F
'She is in love'.

(18) *mìsèú*   *nè*   *cànigé*
love   make   Canige
'Canige is in love'.

It appears that the object of the verb *nè* 'make', i.e., the experiencer, is the topic of the clause. The evidence for this hypothesis is provided by the fact that the unmarked subject of the follow-up clause is interpreted as identical with the experiencer of the preceding clause. Consider the following sentence, where the experiencer in the first clause is the noun *gònì* 'hyena'. The hyena is also the inferred subject of the next clause:

(19) *time*   *nè*   *gònì*   *àlá gùmyá*   *dú*   *dé*
hunger   make   hyena   but large   3F   NEG
'Hyena is very hungry but it [hyena] is not large'.

The importance of this example is that both nouns, *time* 'hunger' and *gònì* 'hyena,' are feminine in Lele, and if *time* 'hunger' were indeed the topic, one would interpret the sentence as meaning 'hyena is hungry but its hunger is not big'. The evidence that the noun *time* 'hunger' is feminine is provided by the fact that the subject pronoun that agrees with the nominal subject is feminine:

(20) *time*   *jogú-ŋ-*   ***dú***
hunger   bother-1SG-**3F**
'Hunger, it bothers me'.

The predicate *ne* is deployed in a few predications other than the experiencer predication. The expression *ne kur*, lit. 'make place/time', is used to encode the state of affairs as represented by the subject rather than an action directed at another participant:

(21) *iyà   nè   kur   nèny´ lay*
     wound   make   place/time   very much also
     'wounds are numerous'.

                                            Garrigues-Cresswell & Weibegué 1981: 30–31

(22) *gìdìrè   gùúgùje   ná   kàlo   nè   kur   dẽl*
     moon   warbling ASSC   cold   make   place   surpass
     gìdìrè   go   kùb   kàlo
     moon   REF   mouth   cold
     'During the month of warbling, the cold is even greater than during the month of the beginning of the cold'.

                                            Garrigues-Cresswell & Weibegué 1981: 30–31

The use of the noun *kur* 'place' as the object of the verb *ne* 'make' is consistent with the way experiencers are coded, in that the object is non-controlling. Additional support for the proposed hypothesis in Lele is provided by examples in which the experiencer is coded as the subject. The notion of fearing something uses the verb *sondri* 'fear':

(23) *tamá-ŋ   sòndrí ná   se   ày   tòrò   è   ìm*
     woman-DEF   fear   ASSC   INCEPT   take   hen   go   bury
     'The woman became scared, took the hen, and buried it'.

The reason that the experiencer of the notion 'fear' is coded as the subject is that the verb *sòndrí* 'fear' is inherently intransitive and, without any additional markers, represents point of view of the subject.

Conclusions about Lele

The default point of view of transitive verbs in Lele is the point of view of the goal. The evidence for this default point of view is provided by two facts: Unlike other Chadic languages, Lele does not have a goal marker, and, second, unlike some other Chadic languages, Lele has an overt marker whose function is to code the point of view of the subject.

Given the fundamental property of transitive predications in Lele, i.e., that they code the default point of view of the goal, it is natural that experiencers do not occur as subjects of transitive verbs, as this would lead them to be interpreted as controllers. The experiencers are therefore marked as syntactic objects of a construction with the verb *ne* 'make' as a predicate, while the trigger of the experience is the subject of the clause. As shown in example (19), the experiencer is also the topic of the clause.

Wandala (Central Chadic)

For nominal arguments, Wandala codes a two-way distinction between subject and non-subject, i.e., an argument that is not marked by a preposition but which may have a variety of semantic relations with the verb. Such relations may correspond to the direct object in English; the indirect object in Russian, marked by the dative case; or the addressee, as marked by the vocative case in some Indo-European languages. Nominal arguments, whether subjects or non-subjects, follow the verb in the pragmatically neutral clause in Wandala. The grammatical roles of nominal arguments are marked by inflectional markers on the verb or on a non-verbal constituent that immediately precedes the noun phrase. In the completive aspect, the grammatical relationship subject is marked by the final vowel *a* on the constituent preceding the noun phrase. The non-subject role of the noun phrase, when it follows a constituent other than the verb, is marked by deletion of the final vowel of the constituent that immediately precedes the noun (Frajzyngier 2016). Wandala has three types of predications, and every verb in the language has inherent properties that correspond to these predications. One type of predication is the goal-oriented predication, which directs the listener to consider what the subject is doing with respect to the goal. Verbs that are lexicalized for this predication, called Class 1 verbs, always have controlling subjects. A predication with a Class 1 verb cannot contain the third-person singular object pronoun. Another type of predication is the non-affected subject, non-goal predication. With verbs that have lexicalized this predication, called Class 2 verbs, neither the subject nor the second argument changes shape or posture; however, the subject may change place. The third type is the affected-subject predication, which directs the listener to consider how the event affects the subject. Verbs in this class, Class 3, include 'break', 'crack', and verbs indicating a change of posture or shape of the subject.

Certain properties for which verbs have been lexicalized can be changed, in that non-goal-oriented verbs can have a goal marker added. There are, however, no devices to change the goal-oriented verb into a non-goal-oriented verb. How the experiencer is coded with a given verb depends on the inherent properties of the verb with respect to goal orientation or subject orientation of the predicate.

When the predicate is selected from the class of goal-oriented verbs, the experiencer is marked as non-subject by deletion of the final vowel of the constituent that immediately precedes the noun. Recall that the subjects of Class 1 verbs are controllers. Coding the experiencer as the subject would constitute a semantic contradiction between the meaning of the construction and the intended properties of the experiencer. Therefore, it is the entity that triggers the experience, not the experiencer, that is marked as the subject. Following are some of the internal experiences for which the experiencer is coded as non-subject.

Fear/be afraid. The subject is the noun *yàwè* 'fear', the predicate is the goal-oriented verb *jà* 'hit', and the object is the person or people who fear. Wandala does not have the verb 'fear':

(24) *jà-tə̀r-jè*   **yàw**   **md**   *nà*   *wá*
hit-3PL-hit:EF   fear:Ø   people:Ø   DEM   COM
'The people there were afraid' (lit. 'the fear hit the people').

Have something stuck in the body: The entity that is stuck is the subject and the person's body part is marked by a prepositional phrase. The verb *ŋàŋà* 'catch' is goal-oriented. The pronominal third-person direct object of a goal-oriented verb is unmarked in Wandala, as is the case in the example below:

(25) *ŋà*   *žžàrà*   *mbàtè*   *ŋàŋà*   *yàlw*   *á-t*   *kwárà*
1EXCL   look:OBJ   and indeed   catch   zucchini   PRED-T   throat
'We looked at it. And indeed he had a zucchini stuck in his throat' (lit. 'It was a zucchini that seized him in the throat').

Being hungry: The noun *wáyà* 'hunger' is the subject, the predicate is *ŋà* 'catch, seize', and the entity that is hungry is the object:

Experiencer predications in Chadic

(26) àa   à   ŋ-yá   bà   wáyà   ì   s   kàtá gdzàr-á-ŋà
      ah,   3SG   catch-1SG:E.F. FOC   hunger 1SG come ask   children-GEN-2
      mà   bù   knì   wá
      HYP   two   C.FOC   COM
      'Ah, I am hungry [lit. hunger seized me], and I came to ask for at least two of your children'.

Placing the noun phrase before the verb, as in the first clause of the above example, codes topicalization in Wandala. The evidence that the verb *ŋà* 'catch' is goal-oriented is provided by the fact that the third-person singular object pronoun cannot occur with this verb:

(27) índàlè   šìgàš   àmb-á-rà   **ŋàŋà**   wàyà
      hyena   leave:Ø outsidecompound-GEN-3SG   catch   hunger
      'Hyena left her house hungry' (lit. 'hyena left its compound, hunger seized it').

Pain: For the expression of pain, the body part that aches is the subject and the entity that suffers the pain is non-subject. For a toothache, 'tooth' is the subject, the predicate is the verb 'bite' (again, a goal-oriented verb), and the entity that has the toothache is the non-subject (the tooth bites the experiencer):

(28) à   bà-n   gdz-á-r   nà   à   và-n   gò ŋàn
      3SG   say-[pause] child-GEN-3SG DEM   3SG   tell   to 3SG:Ø
      àmmá   à   w-ì   łàr   nà   wá
      mother! (voc)   3SG   bite-1SG tooth DEM   COM
      á   zàrà   kùrgùn-á-rà
      what   something   medicine-GE-3SG
      'Her child tells her: Mother, I have a toothache, what is the medicine for it?'

(29) dá-m-dà   dò   mbá-r   wá   áŋkwà   gdzàr pàllè
      go-IN-go   go   home-GEN-3SG COM   exist   child one
      ndz   à   wà-nà   łàrè
      PAST   3SG   bite-3SG   tooth
      'When she returned home [she found out] that one of her children had developed a toothache in the meantime'.

(30) àa,   sèy   bà   kà   tátày   kùmú   łàr   nà   à
      ah,   then   FOC   2SG   search:Ø if not tooth:Ø DEM   3SG
      w-ì-w   mà
      bite-1SG-bite:Ø   mother
      'Ah, you have to look for him, if not, it is not good. I have a toothache, mother' (lit. 'tooth bites me').

Anger: The heart is the subject of the predication, the predicate is the goal-oriented verb 'hit', and the experiencer is the non-subject:

(31) já-jà   órvóŋlè
      hit-hit   heart
      'He became angry' (lit. 'the heart hit him' (the third person singular object is unmarked).

305

Stumble: The equivalent of the English notion 'stumble' has the person who stumbles as the object, and the subject is the thing against which the person stumbles. The predicate *jà* 'hit' represents the point of view of the goal:

(32) bà   klà ùrà ksé   à   j-íyà   ktàpàrà
     FOC   all time   3SG   hit-1SG   obstacle
     á   tɔ̀   bàràmà
     PRED   T   road
     'All the time I stumble on the road' (lit. 'an obstacle hits me all the time on the road').

Having rabies: Rabies is the subject, the predicate is the verb 'bite', and the entity that gets rabies is non-subject, e.g., 'dogs' in the example below:

(33) á   dàbà   nó   vìyà   vàyè   bà   krá-hà
     PRED   reason   PRES   rainy season   often   FOC   dog-PL
     tá   à   wà-trá   vàlà
     3PL [error]   3SG   bite-3PL   rabies
     'Because in the rainy season, dogs get rabies' (lit. 'rabies often bites dogs').

Having good luck: Good luck is the subject, the predicate is the equivalent of 'find', and the person who will have good luck is marked as non-subject:

(34) àyá   únnɔ̀   ŋà   dàbà-dàbà   kwà
     ah well   DEM   1EXCL   follow-follow   H. kò
     mbàné   á   **šà-ŋrà-šà**   **hérè**
     perhaps 3SG   find-1EXCL-find luck (Ar.)
     'Ah well, that thing we are going to follow up on, that perhaps, good luck will find us' (i.e., 'we will become lucky').

An almost identical alignment of subject and object exists in the Polish experiencer predication involving good luck (and bad luck), where 'good luck' is the subject and the person who finds good luck is the object:

(35) spotkało   ich   szczęście
     meet:3SG:N:PAST:PRF   3PL.ACC   good luck:NOM
     'Good luck met them'.

As in Wandala, the Polish verb *spotkać* 'meet' is a goal-oriented verb, as evidenced by the fact that in order to make the predication subject-oriented, the verb must be accompanied by the short reflexive marker *się*:

(36) Gdzieś   już   **się**   spotkał
     somewhere   already   REFL   meet:3SG:M:PAST:PRF
     z   tym   nazwiskiem
     ASSC   DEM:INSTR   last name:INSTR
     'He has seen that name somewhere' (Polish National Corpus).

In some predications in Wandala, the experiencer is coded as the subject because the predicate involved is not goal-oriented, and therefore the predication can be interpreted as coding the point of view of the subject. The predication that describes having bad luck or misfortune in Wandala has a different structure than the predication that describes having good luck. The subject is the entity that has bad luck; the predicate is the verb *màgà* 'make'; and 'bad luck', realized by the term *dòɲírè* 'black head', is the non-subject, as coded by position after the verb. The importance of this example is that it confirms the hypothesis that whether the experiencer is coded as the subject or non-subject depends on the inherent point of view of the verb. The verb *màgà* 'do' belongs to a class of verbs that have a non-affected subject and non-affected second argument; it is not a goal-oriented verb. The verb *màgà* does not mean 'manufacture'.

The evidence that *màgà* is a non-goal oriented, non-affected object verb is provided by the fact that it takes the third-person singular object pronoun *–n*:

(37) *séi   bà   má   yìc-íic   kùmù   má   màgà-   **n ɔ́stà**-rà*
     then,   FOC   1INCL   cut-cut   if not   1INCL   do-3SG   how-Q
     'We have to cross [the river], otherwise, what will we do?'

(38) *áŋkwà   dùksɔ́   kà   màgà-ná   kà*
     exist   thing   2SG   do-3SG   2SG
     'Was there anything you did?'

The fact that *màgà* is not a goal-oriented verb explains why the experiencer of this particular state is coded as subject rather than as non-subject. There is no contradiction between the inherent meaning of the verb and the semantic relationship of the experiencer:

(39) *á   kyà   lvà-á   zzòŋ   kɔ́nì   mà   màgà   dòɲírè*
     PRED   by   business-GEN   donkey   C.FOC   1INCL   make   blackness
     'Because of the business of the donkey, we had bad luck' (lit. 'black head').

Similarly, 'feeling bitter' has the experiencer as the subject, because in Wandala, the predicate *cìnà* 'feel' does not belong to the goal-orientation class:

(40) *ádàbà   ŋán   kìnì   á   cìnà   mtáŋ   k   ìrè*
     because   3SG   also   3SG   feel   good   NEG:Ø   head
     'Because he also, he will feel bitter' (lit. 'he will not feel good with respect to head').

The verb *wàyà* 'like, love' also belongs to the class of non-affected and non-controlling subject, and therefore, the experiencer can be coded as subject:

(41) *áŋkwè   žíl   mtú   wàyà-r   kà   bà   ítàrèe*
     exist   man   or   love-3PL   NEG   FOC   3PL
     'Or else, there is a man, but they [the girls] don't like [him]'.

Conclusions about Wandala

The data from Wandala support the hypothesis in the following way. There are three fundamental predications in Wandala: (1) goal-oriented; (2) affected subject; and (3) non-affected subject and non-affected object. The experiencer is coded as object only when the predicate chosen belongs to the goal-oriented class. With the remaining two classes of verbs the experiencer is coded as subject, because in these two predications the subject does not imply control.

Zygmunt Frajzyngier

Pero (West Chadic)

Pero (West Chadic) is an (S)VO language, i.e., the third-person subject does not have to occur in the clause. Like all other Chadic languages, Pero does not have the category passive, which is one of the indicators that the default point of view for transitive verbs is the point of view of the subject:

(42) *n-páll-tù*   *lò*   *cì-tók-nà*   *dóè n-wát-tù-n*
SEQ-pack-VENT   animals   REL-kill-VENT.COMPL   all SEQ-go-VENT-caus
mínà
home
'They will pack all the animals which they have killed and take them home'.

Even though, on the face of it, as seen from the perspective of languages like English, the example above may indicate that the subject is in control, that does not mean that the clause represents the point of view of the goal. When a transitive verb occurs with one argument only that argument is the one that does not control the event, and is often the semantic patient of the event:

(43) *círíp-ì*   *yù*   *kàr-ánì*
fish-DEF   inside   cut-NOMIN
'The fish is cut'.

(44) *lúttù-i*   *n-kùm-i*
bag-DEF   SEQ-fill-SEQ
'and the bag filled up'.

Compare the verb *kùm* 'fill' with two arguments, with the subject controlling the event:

(45) *cì-kùm-ko-èe-nò*   *kòngóo-nò*
2F.SG-fill-COMPL-PRE.PRO-1SG   stomach-1SG
'You fed me well' (lit. 'you filled my stomach').

Here is an example with the subject of the relative clause as the patient of the matrix clause *mù-káyù* 'should be chased':

(46) *báy*   *mì-ádó-kò*   *lò*   *mù-káyù*
dog   REL.PL-eat-COMPL   meat   OPT-chase
'Dogs which have eaten meat should be chased away'.

The data available for Pero contain only a few expressions involving experiencers. In those few examples, the experiencers are not subjects, are not controllers, and are not coded as subjects.

The experience of 'becoming old' has the experiencer as the subject. The predicate is the verb *yì* 'make', and the object is the property-concept noun *mánjínà* 'old':

(47) *má*   *mù gbúdú-kò*   *yi-kò*   *mánjína*   *tà-cádù kúndùl*
TEMP   grow-COMPL   make-COMPL   old   FUT-take kundul
'When one has grown and become adult one would acquire a kundul (a deity)'.

The coding of experiencer may depend on the aspect and mood. Thus the expression corresponding to 'be ashamed', in the indicative clause marked for completive aspect, has the experiencer coded as object of the verb 'break'. The subject is *cig* 'body':

(48) *cìgú-nò*   *ɓùl-kò*
body-1SG   break-COMPL
'I am ashamed' (lit. 'my body broke').

In the prohibitive mood, the experiencer is the addressee and the body is the object:

(49) *kàt-ɓùlò*   *jig-kò-m*
PROH-break   body-2M-NEG
'Do not be ashamed' (lit. 'do not break your body').

Frajzyngier 1989: 162

Conclusions for Pero

The default point of view for transitive verbs in Pero is the point of view of the subject. As a result, the experiencer is coded as the subject, as in example (42) and (48).

Mina (Central Chadic)

Mina (Central Chadic) has the form SVO in non-sequential clauses and the form S PREP-O V in sequential clauses:

(50) *séy gáw*   *dəɗ*   *ngàz*   *à*   *zá*
so hunter   remove   leg   3SG   COMP
á   *n*   *kwáyàŋ*   *ɓət-ú*
PRED   PREP   squirrel   take-3SG
'Then, the hunter took off a leg [of a game animal], and told the squirrel, "Take it"'.

Mina codes the subject's concern, empathy, or lack of concern through the clause-final particles *kà* 'concern' and *zà* 'lack of concern':

(51) *kə*   *ngə*   *ngàzə-ngən*   *ká*
PRF   break   leg-3SG.POSS   CON
'He broke his leg' (the speaker empathizes with subject; the third-person singular subject is unmarked).

The default point of view for transitive verbs is that of the controlling subject, as evidenced by the existence of two predications, each of which represents the event from the point of view of the non-controlling subject. The common characteristic of these predications, as shown in the examples below, is that they represent the experiencer as defined earlier in this study.

Coding the internal state of the subject

The lexeme *tàlàŋ* 'head' has been grammaticalized to code the state of the subject. The subject is the only participant in the event, even though the clause has the noun *tàlàŋ* as the object:

Imperfective:

(52) à   łék   tàlàŋ
     3SG remember   head
     'He remembers'.

Perfective:

(53) kə̀   łék   tàlàn   zá
     3SG remember head   EE
     'He recalled'.

The verb *wáy* 'forget', with the noun *tàlàn* as object, is the evidence that there is no other participant in the event:

(54) kə̀   wáy   tàlàn   zá
     PRF forget   head   EE
     'He wasted time'.

(55) séy   tàkár-yíì   kə̀   wáy   tàlàŋ   tsáy   zà
     so   turtle-PL   PRF   forget   head   finish   EE
     kə́   dàr
     INF   dance
     'So the turtles are completely preoccupied with the dance'.

Without the marker *tàlàŋ*, the verb *wáy* does not exclude the existence of another argument:

(56) kə̀   wáy   zà
     PRF forget   EE
     'He forgot [something]' (goal-oriented).

The verbs *mbú* 'unite' and *tsúk* 'isolate' must have the object noun *tàlàŋ* to indicate that it is the subject that gets united or isolated:

(57) wà   ángə̀   í   kə̀   káh   tsáy   zə̀   syì   í
     DEM   if   3PL   PRF   bury   finish   EE   COM   3PL
     ndí   **mbú**   **tàlàŋ**   tə̀tə̀   kə́   hàŋ   tús   dàp
     HAB   unite   head   3PL   INF   cry   INTENS   just
     'If they have buried, they get together to weep profoundly'.

(58) tàlàŋ   mə̀   mbùw-yí   zə̀   syì   kó   í
     head   REL   unite-STAT   EE   COM   QUANT   3PL
     ndə̀váy í   ndə̀   **tsúk**   **tàlàŋ**   tə̀tə̀
     go where 3PL   go   isolate   head   3PL
     dáp   skə̀   vù
     just   NEG   Q
     'If they unite, no matter where they go, they isolate themselves'.

Mina also has a verb whose main function appears to be to code the experiencer predication. The experiencer is the object, and the subject is the entity that triggers experience. The verb *màr*, which occurs with expressions of experience, is here glossed as 'do' in analogy with the similar predication in Lele described earlier in this study:

(59) *wáŋ*   *màr-á-k-rà*
     sleep   do-GO-1SG-PROG
     'I am sleepy',
     wáŋ   *már-rà*
     sleep   do-PROG
     'he is sleepy' (third-person singular object is unmarked).

(60) *mítìsh*   *màr-á-k-rà*
     hunger   do-GO-1SG-PROG
     'I am hungry'.

The only other usage of this verb is in the expression corresponding to watching or tending cattle:

(61) *à*   *màr*   *ɮíì*
     3SG   tend   cattle
     'He tends cattle, he is a cowherd'.

For the notion 'to be ashamed', the subject is the noun *hùwà* 'shame' and the predicate is the verb *dzə́* 'kill'. The third-person singular object pronoun is not overtly marked:

(62) *hú*   *kə́*   *dzə́ zà*
     shame   PRF   kill EE
     'He is ashamed' (lit. 'shame killed him').

The stative predication has the marker *mə̀*, glossed as REL, and the suffix *–ì*, glossed as AFF for 'affected':

(63) *hú*   *mə̀-dzə́-wì*
     shame   REL-kill-AFF
     'He is ashamed'.

The predication 'cough' has the noun *kə̀rtsáh* 'cold, cough' as a subject. The predicate is *mə́l* 'catch' and the object is the person who has the cold:

(64) *kə̀rtsáh*   *kə́*   *mə́l*   *dzàláŋ*   *zà*
     cough   PRF   catch   Jalan   EE
     'Jalan is coughing' (lit. 'the cough caught Jalan').

The default point of view for transitive verbs in Mina is that of the goal. Therefore, the experiencer argument, which cannot have a goal, cannot be coded as the subject.

Mupun (West Chadic)

Mupun (West Chadic) marks the category subject by the position preceding the verb and the category object by the position following the verb, in the SVO pattern:

Zygmunt Frajzyngier

(65) *kaddaŋ*   *mo*   *neer*   *lusim*   *nə*   *mo*   *le*   *naar*
when   3PL   surround   leopard   DEF   3PL   put   middle
'When they surround the leopard, they put him in the middle'.

Some verbs in Mupun are inherently goal oriented, and these verbs cannot occur with a non-controlling argument as subject. The verb 'to spread', for example, can occur only with a controlling subject and non-controlling object:

(66) *nəhən*   *nə*   *pwer*   *nlər*   *nə*
mother   DEF   spread   shirt   DEF
'mother spread the shirt'

but:

(67) **nlər*   *nə*   *pwer*
shirt   DEF   spread
for 'the shirt is spread'.

Like many other Chadic languages (cf. Frajzyngier 1984), Mupun does not have intransitivizing means, i.e., devices whose primary function is to indicate a change in the valency of the verb or, in other definitions, to indicate that the subject has a different semantic role than the one expected with the given verb. As a result, for some verbs the same form is used whether the subject is the semantic agent or patient. Compare the following sentences with the verb *den*. In a clause with two arguments it has a transitive meaning corresponding to 'put':

(68) *n-den*   *siwa mbəlu nə*   *n-ɓut*
1SG-put   grain com DEF   PREP-inside
'I put the maize inside'.

(69) *n-den*   *da*   *nə*   *n-ɗuk*   *ɓin*
1SG-put   calabash DEF   PREP-on   bench
'I put the calabash on a bench'.

In a clause with only one argument, the verb *den* has an intransitive meaning corresponding to 'be'. Its subject is the entity that was put, and not the entity that was putting:

(70) *da*   *ka*   *den*   *a*   *ɓin*
calabash   HABIT   put   PREP   bench
'the calabash is on a bench'.

(71) *da*   *ka*   *den*   *ndər*   *ɓin*
calabash   HABIT   put   under   bench
'the calabash is under a bench'.

The fact that the single argument of a transitive verb is the semantic patient rather than agent indicates that the default point of view of the verb is the point of view of the subject, i.e., the listener is directed to consider what happens to the subject rather than what the subject does to some other entity. Given this property, one does not expect the existence of specific experiencer predications in the language, because experiencers are expected to be coded in the same

Experiencer predications in Chadic

way as all other subjects. This is borne out by the data. Thus, the experiencer of the verbs corresponding to 'like' and 'hate' is coded as the subject by position before the verb:

(72) *ba   n-dem   wat brəŋ   fen   də   wu cin kas*
　　 NEG   1SG-like   steal horse   1SG   REL   3M do NEG
　　 'I don't like his stealing of my horse'.

(73) *wat   brəŋ   fen   də   wu cin le   kə   n-an   **kwar** wur   dî*
　　 steal   horse   1SG   REL   3M do make   comp   prep-1SG hate 3M   COMP
　　 'His stealing of my horse made me hate him'.

Although the point of view of the subject is the default point of view for many verbs, and therefore the experiencer is coded most often as subject, there are nevertheless three specific experiencer predications involving the predicates, *dien* 'like', *wal* 'like' 'prefer', and *siwàl* 'pain'. (The glosses are the best approximation of the meanings of these forms.)

With these predicates, the experiencer is coded as indirect object by the preposition *n*. The experiencer predication has a unique structure, with the predicate in clause-initial position and the experiencer marked by the preposition *n*:

[Predicate *n*-NP]

(74) *siwal   n-ha   a   ni*
　　 pain   PREP-2M   PRED   Q
　　 'where does it hurt you (m)?'

(75) *iwal   n-yi   a   ni*
　　 pain   PREP-2F   PRED   Q
　　 'where does it hurt you (f)?'

A clause containing both the experiencer and the trigger of experience has the form [Predicate *n*-NP1 (*a*) *n*-NP2/V], i.e., the predicate is in clause-initial position, and the two arguments—the experiencer and the trigger of the experience, in that order—are both marked by the preposition *n*. The optional marker *a* represents the copula, which in other constructions marks contrastive focus. Here is an example with the predicate *dien* 'prefer' in the experiencer predication:

(76) a *dien   n-an   a   n-mo*
　　　　 like   PREP-1SG COP   PREP-3PL
　　　　 'I like them'.

The second argument of the clause may be a verb phrase rather than a noun phrase:

(76) b *dien   n-an   n-taŋ   takarda*
　　　　 like   PREP-1SG PREP-read book
　　　　 'I like reading books'.

　　 c *dien   n/mbə-war   n-cet   gwom*
　　　　 like   PREP/PREP-3F   PREP-cook food
　　　　 'She likes to cook'.

The predicate *wal* 'like, prefer' can occur in the predication that codes the point of view of the experiencer and in the predication that does not code the point of view of the experiencer.

313

The importance of this fact is that the inherent properties of the verb do not determine the form of the clause; the predications grammaticalized in the language do. Here are examples of the verb *wal* with the experiencer and the trigger of experience, but no subject:

(77) yi   sat   nə   **wal**   **n-yi**   a   n-brəŋ
    2F   say   COMP   like   PREP-2F   COP   PREP-horse
    'You (f) said that you like a horse'.

(78) **wal**   **n-ɣa**   a   n-lua
    prefer   PREP-3SG   COP   PREP-meat
    'He likes meat'.

The structure with the verb in clause-initial position and with both of its arguments marked by the preposition *n* is limited to the few experiencer predications. The use of any other verb in this structure yields an ungrammatical sentence:

(79) *se   n-an   a   n-lua   əɣ
    eat   PREP-1SG   COP   PREP-meat   goat
    for 'I ate goat meat'.

A question about the trigger of an emotion is also marked by the preposition *n*:

(80) **wal**   n-xa   a   **n-mi**
    like   PREP-2M   COP   PREP-what
    'What do you like?'

Here are examples of the same verb, *wal*, occurring in a predication that does not code the point of view of the experiencer, where it is most likely closer to the meaning 'choose':

(81) a   n-**wal**   a   n-brəŋ
       1SG-like   COP   PREP-horse
       'I prefer a horse'.

    b   a/yi   **wal**   a   n-brəŋ-e
       2M/2F   like   COP   PREP-horse-Q
       'So, you prefer a horse?'

Conclusions about Mupun

The default point of view in the Mupun transitive predication is that of the subject, and most experiencers are coded as subjects. The question of why the experiencers of verbs corresponding to 'like' and 'pain, ache', are marked as non-subjects can be explained by the fact that these predicates can never occur with a controlling subject. The predicate *wal*, on the other hand, can be used in predications coding the non-experiencer point of view, where it carries the meaning close to 'choose'.

Hdi (Central Chadic)

Hdi (Central Chadic) is a verb-initial language, with the subject following the verb. The non-subject argument follows the subject. The language has several constructions which, with the appropriate verbs, allow for the inference that the subject is the experiencer. One of these is the stative aspect, marked by the particle *ndà* preceding the verb:

(82)   *kàbgà*   *m̀ndrá*   *tsá*   *m̀ndú-xà*   *yá*   *yà*   **ndá**   **snà**
     because   clan   DEF   man-PL   DEM   DEM   STAT   know
     tá   *tsáf-tá*   *dùvúl*   *yà*   *ngá*   *lmú*   *ndá*   *tsí*
     OBJ   make-REF   metal   DEM   for   war   ASSC   3SG
     'It is because this clan knows how to make metals to go to war with'.

Hdi has grammaticalized morphological markers coding the point of view of the subject and the point of view of the goal. The point of view of the subject (called subject/source orientation in Frajzyngier and Shay 2002) is marked by the vowel *u* added to the verbal root. With some intransitive verbs, the marker *-ú* is the default marker, as is the case with the verb *mt* 'die', *f* 'boil', and *rw* 'dry':

(83)   *kà*   *mt-ú-tá*   *dá-nì*
     SEQ   die-SO-REF   father-3SG
     'and his father died'.

(84)   *fú-fá*   *ìmí*
     heat-heat   water
     'the water boiled'.

(85)   *rwú-rwá*   *xìyá*
     rot-rot   guinea corn
     'the guinea corn dried'.

(86)   *bádz-ú-bádzá*   *lgùt*
     spoil-SO-spoil   cloth
     'the cloth spoiled'.

Such verbs cannot be used with the goal-oriented marker *a* and with an inanimate subject:

(87)   *bádzá-bádzá   *lgùt*
     spoil:GO-spoil   cloth
     for 'the cloth spoiled'.

A marker entailing the existence of a controlling subject must be added to the verb if an agent is to be the subject. With this particular verb, the inclusion of the agent requires 'additional argument' *-ná*:

(88)   *bádz-í-n-bádz-í*   *tá*   *lgùt*
     spoil-AWAY-3-spoil-1SG   OBJ   cloth
     'I spoiled the cloth'.

Representing the event from the point of view of the subject does not preclude the agentive role of the subject and does not preclude the presence of another argument in the clause. The subject/source-oriented marker may imply action for the benefit of the subject:

Zygmunt Frajzyngier

(89) *kà   klá-úgh-tà   kà   f-ù-d-ú-tà*
SEQ   take-D:SO-REF   SEQ   put-SO-ALL-EP-REF
'He took it out [of the pot] and ate it up' (lit. 'put it in himself').

(90) *kà   ks-ú-tá   ùvá   tá   vàzák*
SEQ   touch-SO-REF   cat   OBJ   rooster
'And Cat devoured Rooster'.

Eating one's fill is coded by the point of view of the subject marker *u*:

(91) *z-ú-zà*
eat-SO-eat
'he ate everything' (cf. Spanish: *él se comió*; Russian: *on najelsja*).

Compare the unmarked point of view:

(92) *tà   zá   dàfá   kùl   xàd(ú)   dàlí*
IMPF   eat   food   without   lack   sauce
'He is eating mush without sauce'.

The distinction between the point of view of the subject and the point of view of the goal is illustrated on the verb *dvà* 'like'. The vowel *á* with high tone codes the point of view of the goal:

(93) *fitík   dvá-fà-á-ká   ti-i'í   wù*
since   like-UP-NEG-2SG   OBJ-1SG   NEG
'Since you do not like/choose me . . .' (said by a jilted protagonist).

The vowel *u* codes the point of view of the subject. If the vowel *u* is added directly to the verbal root, the verbal stem means 'to love', a process that does not involve control:

(94) *kà   dv-ú-tá   mákwà   tá   zvàxw*
SEQ   like-SO-REF   girl   OBJ   bat
'The girl loved the bat'.

If the vowel *u* is added to the stem ending in *á* and is realized as *–ugh-*, the meaning of the verb involves control on the part of the subject 'choose, select, prefer':

(95) *kà   dvá-úgh-tá   mákwà   tá   zvàxw*
SEQ   like-SO-REF   girl   OBJ   bat
'The girl chose the bat [for herself]'.

The default point of view for other verbs is the point of view of the subject, and the experiencers with such verbs are marked as subjects. This is the case with the verb *głón* 'fear', *li'ià* 'wake up', and another verb meaning 'like', *kúmá*:

(96) *kà   głón-gá-f-tá   kděri   tá   głəŋəə, kà*
SEQ   fear-INN-UP-REF   Kderi   OBJ   fear   SEQ

316

xàn-tsí	*xàdà*
sleep-3SG	there

'Kderi was afraid and spent the night there'.

(97)
lì'íà-f-tà	*tsá*	*mndù*	*yá*		*tà*	*xánì,*
wake-UP-REF	DEF	man	DEM		PREP	sleep
kə̀'á	*ká-'á*	*ná*	*kdîx-á –ní*	*á*	*wà*	
COMP-3SG	COMP-3SG	COMP	donkey-GEN-SG	NEG	NEG	

'When the man woke up, he realized that it was not his donkey'.

(98)
tà	*kúmá-í*	*tá*	*ná*	*skálú*	*ná*
IMPF	like-1SG	OBJ	DEM	dance	DEM

'I like this dance'.

An interesting exception with respect to the experiencer is the predication involving illness, where 'illness' is the subject, the predicate is the verb *ksà* 'catch', and the person who is ill is marked as the object:

(99)
ksá-f-tà	**dángwà**	*t-íì*		*kày*	*mántsá*	*wà*
catch-UP-REF	illness	OBJ-1SG		then	then	NEG
lá-x-à-dá	*tà*	*lòpitál*	*má*	*xàdú*	*kwóbù*	
go-DOWN-1SG-GO	PREP	hospital (Fr.)	but	lack	money	

'When I became ill, I went to a hospital, but there was no money then' (lit. 'When the illness caught me . . .').

Summary for Hdi

Hdi does not have a specific experiencer predication because the default point of view for many verbs is that of the subject. For verbs that do not have a default point of view, the point of view of the subject can be marked by the marker –*u*. All semantic experiencers corresponding to experiencers of other languages, for instance Lele, are coded as subjects of the clause.

Gidar (Central Chadic)

Gidar (Central Chadic) is an SVO language. There are several classes of verbs, one of which is inherently goal oriented. The other classes of verbs are not inherently goal oriented. With the non-goal oriented verbs, the single argument of a potentially transitive verb is the affected rather than the controlling participant:

(100)
màsə́rgà	*à-ngròf-kò*
pot	3M-break-PRF

'The pot broke'.

With two arguments, the subject of such verbs is controlling and the object is affected:

(101)
à-ngrófu-k	*màsə́rgà*
3M-break- PRF	pot

'He broke a pot'.

With the non-goal oriented classes of verbs, experiencers are coded as subjects:

(102) tà-tá ŋl-úu-nì
  PROG-3F love-TOT-3M
  'She loves him'.

Here is an example with the verb *rg* 'hurt':

(103) nà-rgá-kà
  1SG-hurt-PRF
  'I hurt' [about interior pains only].

To change the orientation of the verb, the goal marker *á* must be added:

(104) nà-rg-á-kà
  1SG-thresh-GO-PRF
  'I threshed it'.

Notice that the mere presence of a syntactic object, i.e., the second argument of the verb, is not the exponent of the presence of the goal:

(105) à-dá-k gàdáf
  3M-cook-PRF belly
  'He became nervous, angry' (lit. 'he cooked belly') (Bidzar dialect).

In order to indicate that a participant other than the subject has become nervous, the goal marker *á* must be added to the verb:

(106) à-dá-k gàdáf dáfá
  3M-cook:GO-PRF belly man
  'He made us nervous' (lit. 'he cooked man's belly'). (As in some other languages, the first-person singular or plural is the default interpretation when no other participant is mentioned with the expression 'make nervous'.)

With some predicates, however, experiencers are coded as objects rather than subjects. This coding appears to be an outcome of the choice of predicates and the nouns necessary for the coding of a given situation. In the predication corresponding to 'have a headache' the subject is the head, the predicate is *ássá* 'ache', and the experiencer is the object of the clause:

(107) kíi-w tà-y ássá-wà
  head-1SG PROG-M ache-1SG
  'I have a headache' (lit. 'my head aches me').

Note that in Russian and Polish, which have distinct experiencer predications, the predication corresponding to having a headache is coded in the same way as other goal-oriented predications in those languages:

Experiencer predications in Chadic

(108) *M'en'a   golova   bolit*
    1SG:ACC   head:NOM   ache:3SG.PRES
    'I have a headache' (Russian).

In the Gidar expression corresponding to 'be cold', the subject is the noun *sàmyà* 'cold', the predicate is the verb *dà* 'cook', and the experiencer is the object:

(109) *dɔ́*   *móm*   *pùmó*   *máli*   *tà-ì*   *dɛ̀wè*
    ASSC   morning   tomorrow   chief   PROG-3M   sit
    sàmyà   *tà-ì*   ***dà-ní***
    cold   PROG-M   cook-3M
    sòmbò   *à-dé-kè*
    Sombo   3M-go:VENT-PRF
    'The next morning, the chief was sitting, he was cold, and Sombo came'.

I have no explanation for why in the expression corresponding to 'feel cold' the experiencer is coded as the object. It is possible that once the verb 'cook', which inherently represents the point of view of the subject, was chosen as the predicate, there was no way to include the noun 'cold' in the clause. In my data on Gidar there is no verb corresponding to 'feel'. On the other hand, this example may well represent a fossilized expression corresponding to 'he is cold' in English, which does not indicate the temperature of the subject either.

Conclusions about Gidar

In Gidar, most experiencers are coded as subject because, for a large number of verbs, the default point of view is that of the subject. In a few expressions, the experiencer is coded as the object. These expressions involve the verb corresponding to 'having a headache' and 'feeling cold'. I have no explanation for these two expressions.

Overall conclusions

The aim of the study was to explain why, in some expressions, semantic experiencers are coded as subjects, and, in other expressions, as non-subjects. This difference in coding may occur both language-internally and cross-linguistically, whereby the same verb in one language has the experiencer as subject and in another language has the experiencer as direct, or sometimes indirect, object. The study proposed that the main factor determining the way the experiencers are coded is the category of point of view of a predication. When the default point of view is that of the subject, the experiencer is coded as the subject. When the point of view is other than the subject, the experiencer is coded as object. Although the study was conducted on several Chadic languages, it answered a general linguistics question, a question that so far has not been asked even for best studied Indo-European language. The study is therefore a contribution of African linguistics to linguistic theory.

Abbreviations

1   first person
2   second person
3   third person

ACC	accusative
ASSC	associative
C.FOC	contrastive focus
CAUS	causative
COM	comment
COMP	complementizer
COMPL	completive
CON	concern
COP	copula
DAT	dative
DEF	definite
DEM	demonstrative
EE	end-of-event
EP	epenthetic
EXCL	exclusive
F	feminine
FOC	focus
FUT	future
GEN	genitive
GO	goal
HABIT	habitual
IMPF	imperfective
INCEPT	inceptive
INCL	inclusive
INF	infinitive
M	masculine
NEG	negative
NOM	nominative
NOMIN	nominalizer
OBJ	object
PAST	past
PL	plural
PRED	predicator
PREP	preposition
PRF	perfective
PROG	progressive
PROH	prohibitive
Q	question
QUANT	quantifier
REF	referential
SEQ	sequential
SING	singular
SO	subject orientation
T	target
TOT	totality
VENT	ventive

Note

1 The study is based on the Chadic languages Lele, Wandala, Hdi, Mina, Gidar, Pero, and Mupun, for which I have first-hand data, as shown in the list of references. The analyses and associated terminologies presented here supersede the analyses and terminologies used in the sources listed.

I am most grateful to numerous language assistants whose names are acknowledged in the sources, without whose original help on individual languages the current comparative work would not have been possible. I am also grateful to the NSF, NEH, the University of Colorado, and the Fulbright Program, which have supported my previous work. I am also most grateful to Erin Shay for the important substantial and editorial comments on several versions of this work. I am grateful to an anonymous reader of this paper and the editors of this volume, Augustine Agwuele and Adams Bodomo, for their comments.

References

Brekke, M. (1988). "The experiencer constraint." *Linguistic Inquiry* 19.2: 169–180.

Dowty, D. (1991). "Thematic proto-roles and argument selection." *Language* 67.3: 547–619.

Frajzyngier, Z. (1984). "On the proto-Chadic syntactic pattern." In *Current Progress in Afro-Asiatic Linguistics: Papers of the International Hamito-Semitic Congress*, John Bynon (ed.). Amsterdam & Philadelphia: Benjamins, 139–160.

Frajzyngier, Z. (1989). *A Grammar of Pero*. Berlin: Reimer.

Frajzyngier, Z. (1993). *A Grammar of Mupun*. Berlin: Reimer.

Frajzyngier, Z. (1999). "Domains of point of view and coreferentiality: System interaction approach to the study of reflexives." In *Reflexives: Forms and Functions*, Frajzyngier and Curl (eds). Amsterdam/ Philadelphia: Benjamins, 125–152.

Frajzyngier, Z. (2001). *A Grammar of Lele*. Stanford Monographs in African Linguistics. Stanford: CSLI.

Frajzyngier, Z. (2008). *A Grammar of Gidar*. Frankfurt: Peter Lang.

Frajzyngier, Z. (2012). *A Grammar of Wandala*. Berlin and New York: Mouton de Gruyter.

Frajzyngier, Z. (2016). "Inflectional markers of sentential parsing." *Lingua*: 1–33.

Frajzyngier, Z. and E. Johnston, with A. Edwards (2005). *A Grammar of Mina*. Berlin/New York: Mouton de Gruyter.

Frajzyngier, Z., Roger P., Paul E. and M. Schwabauer, with E. Shay and H. Tourneux (2015). *Dictionary of Hdi: A Central Chadic Language of Cameroon*. Cologne: Koeppe.

Frajzyngier Z. and E. Shay (2002). *A Grammar of Hdi*. Berlin: Mouton de Gruyter.

Frajzyngier, Z. and E. Shay (2016). *The Role of Functions in Syntax: A Unified Approach to Language Theory, Description, and Typology*. Amsterdam and Philadelphia: Benjamins.

Garrigues-Cresswell, M. and C. Weibegué (1981). *Livre de Lecture Lélé*. Sarh: Centre d'études linguistiques.

Matthews, P.H. (1997). *The Concise Dictionary of Linguistics*. Oxford: Oxford University Press.

Verhoeven, E. (2010). "Agentivity and stativity in experiencer verbs: Implications for a typology of verb classes." *Linguistic Typology* 14: 213–251.

PART IV

Language and society: theory and practice

16

TRANSLATION THEORY AND PRACTICE PAST AND PRESENT

Applying the Target Audience Criterion to some West African languages

Keir Hansford

Introduction

There is an erroneous opinion among some present scholars that translation theories are a modern invention, or at the most going back no further than John Dryden (1631–1700). Apparently, conflicts between so-called *literal* translations, *free* translations, and *paraphrastic* translations go back to Roman times. I am indebted for much of the following brief historical overview to Douglas Robinson (1997) (henceforward cited as WTT) who cited extracts from some 90 authors over more than 2,000 years who were at times engaged in translation, or had strong opinions on how a translation should be done. I am also indebted to Shuttleworth and Cowie (1997) (henceforward cited as DTS) for a comprehensive guide to numerous translation theories.

I offer a summary of some of the more modern theories, and, despite their proliferation in modern times, show that they do not depart very much from what has gone before, but often expand and clarify the basic principles. I will then try to draw common threads together, and seek examples of how some theories, particularly focusing on the *Target Audience*, have been applied in practice to some West Africa dramas written in English, and the Christian scriptures in one West African language.

Early translation theories

The Romans translating from Greek to Latin

When the Romans had overcome the Greeks by their superiority in warfare, they soon discovered in the Greek language a vast array of intellectual writings and literature that they had to acknowledge were superior to the Latin of the Romans. They discovered that the Greeks had already produced world-class poets such as Hesiod, Pindar and Homer, to mention only a few, and playwrights such as Aeschylus, Euripides and Sophocles. Roman intellectuals and orators set about translating these works, and, in particular, speeches of Greek orators and Homer's lyric poems the *Iliad* and the *Odyssey*, whilst readily recognising the difficulty of the task. Marcus Tullius Cicero (103–43 bc) tried his hand at translating some speeches of Aeschines and Demosthenes into Latin, not as an interpreter, but as an orator. He states:

325

keeping the same *style* and *forms*, or as one might say, the figures of thought, but in language which conforms to our usage. And in so doing I did not hold it necessary to render *word for word*, but I preserved the general style and force of the language.

WTT 9, italics mine

From Philo Judaeus (*c.* 15/10 BC–45/50 AD) we get the first technical words describing types of translation, *metaphrasis* i.e., changing single words, and *paraphrasis* i.e., changing whole phrases (WTT 14). These became the mainstay of translation theory from Marcus Fabius Quintilianus (Quintilian) (35–96 AD) in his *Institutio oratori* for the next millennium and a half. By contrast Horace (Quintus Horatius Flaccus) (68–8 BC) recommended that an author *imitate* a known work, and not try to translate it, and so create a *new work* of his own.

These three principles were summarised by John Dryden (1631–1700) in his famous classifications as *metaphrases, paraphrases,* and *imitations* (WTT 19).

Translations of Greek and Latin poetry into English

For translations of poetry one needs a different theory or theories, because poetry has both *form* and *content*, as translators of Homer and Virgil have found over two millennia. In poetry, apart from *metre, rhythm, rhyme,* and *broken lines,* which are common but not obligatory features of *form*, it is the *content* that is the ultimate test, because *metre* and *rhyme* and *rhythm* do not translate well from one language to another, and broken lines can be arbitrary.

Translations of the Bible

As regards translation of the Judeo/Christian Scriptures, another approach or theory was necessary. Before the Christian era a supposed group of 70 scholars were given the task of translating the Hebrew scriptures (i.e., the Old Testament) into Greek. It became known as the *Septuagint*, hereafter referred to as the LXX. The *Target Audience* was Jews who had been scattered about the Roman empire and were brought up speaking Greek, and so they found reading the Hebrew scriptures difficult.

But in the Roman empire of the later centuries, the *Target Audience* would be primarily Christians and Jews whose first language was Latin. So, the LXX and the emerging canon of the Christian scriptures needed to be translated into Latin for them. Many had translated the gospels or other parts of the Bible into Latin during the first three centuries of the Christian era, but it was Eusebius Hieronymous (Jerome) (347–419) who was entrusted with the task of making a definitive version of the whole Bible into Latin. His *source texts* (ST) were earlier Latin versions, the Hebrew Scriptures, and the *Septuagint*. One source was Origen's *Hexapla*, a parallel edition in six columns: the Hebrew text in both Hebrew and Greek characters, and four different Greek translations. Jerome's version of the complete Bible, both the Old Testament and New Testament, is known as the *Vulgate*, completed in the years 391–406 AD. It became the Roman Catholic Church's official version for over one and a half millennia.

In summary, says Robinson, Jerome's method of translation of the Vulgate stressed the *accurate* transmission of the *meaning* of the text. Robinson also notes (WTT 43) that later Christian leaders such as Augustine (354–430), Gregory (540–604) and Thomas Aquinas (1224–1274) all endorsed Jerome's view that translation of Scripture should be *sense-for-sense*, and *not rigidly literal*.

The first complete Bible in English was translated probably by Nicholas of Hereford, who was part of the team supervised by John Wycliffe, and was published in 1387. This was translated direct from the Latin *Vulgate*, a fact that was, centuries later, felt to be inadequate because it was not translated from the Hebrew (OT) and Greek (NT). The first edition proved difficult to read, because it was very literal. So another of the team headed by John Purvey did an extensive sense-for-sense revision, which when published became extremely popular (WTT 54).

The arguments and disputes in Wycliffe's time and in the following two centuries, both in England and on the continent of Europe, were not about literal or free translations, but about who the *Target Audience* should be, i.e., whether the Bible should remain in the Latin, and be interpreted orally into English by priests and ecclesiastically endorsed scholars, or should be translated into the vernacular of the people for anyone to read and interpret without clerical guidance.

Modern theories of translation

Among the many modern theories of what a good translation should be like, and how it should be accomplished, certain words occur again and again. I will later deal with these in their relevant context.

Foundational to all modern translation theories, and before any discussion of *accuracy* and other considerations, the two basic questions to be determined first are:

- What is the *Target Audience* (TA)?
- What should be the *Source Text* (ST)?

After that the questions mainly relate to the *quality* of the translated text. These are:

- Accuracy (fidelity, faithfulness to the ST)
- Clarity (in the TL)
- Naturalness (in the TL)
- Meaningfulness (in the TL).

The handbook par excellence on how to apply these principles, aimed especially at students of translation principles and methods, and the mother-tongue translators whom they will later team up with, is Barnwell (1984: 14–15).

Before discussing different types of translation, it is necessary to note that the old theories mentioned above are these days subsumed in, or incorporated in, other theories with different names.

For whom is a translation meant? The case of Scripture

It may seem obvious, but is sometimes forgotten, that the many theories extant today vary because they may speak for different *Target Audiences* (TA). For example, taking the forty-plus translations of the Bible into English in the last six hundred and more years since the Wycliffe Bible appeared, the TA has not always been the same. The King James' Version (KJV) (otherwise known as the Authorised Version (AV)) was the result of political and religious battles following William Tyndale's translation of the NT and parts of the OT. Tyndale wanted his version to speak to ordinary uneducated people. Several English versions by other translators were published after Tyndale, and the one that gained the most popularity was the Geneva Bible (1560). However, King James hated the footnotes in these Bibles, and especially in the Geneva Bible which criticised Kings as tyrants, and he willingly agreed to a new translation being made if it omitted footnotes and comments (except if they pertained to the meaning of a ST word). The language of the AV (1611) however was partly archaic even when published, but today still has a huge popularity because of long usage and the beauty of its phraseology. Many of the versions in recent years have attempted to use more modern phraseology, and want the average person to be able to understand the *meaning* without a lot of personal study. The most popular version in use today is the New International Version (NIV) (1978 and subsequent minor revisions).

As for translations for a TA of a people who are new to having any literature in their language and are new to Christian teachings, or who hear the Bible read to them in a language that is not their own (e.g., a lingua franca such as Akan in large parts of central Ghana), the type of translation must take account of their lack of understanding. So, for example, *implicit* information readily accessible to the SL speakers and readers, or to a TA who are very familiar with Christian teachings, will need to be made *explicit*. Should this implicit information be *intra text* or by pericope headings and introductions and a glossary, even all of them at once? These are still matters of debate. This and two types of *implicit* information will be discussed later.

For whom is a translation meant? Non-Scripture

As for non-Scriptural translations, the TA may vary widely. Examples of different TA include:

Business interchange of correspondence

Businesses usually rely on known and trusted intermediary professional translators to translate communications across language boundaries, by mail or e-mail, whether they be bilingual speakers of the SL or of the TL, rather than try to interpret the ST themselves. *Accuracy* would be the main criterion for a good translation.

Instructions for users of machines, e.g., computers, printers

The quality of the translation depends very much on the ability of the human translator, whose own language would be the one widely spoken where the machine was manufactured, and it often betrays the mother tongue of the translator interfering with the production of a natural and accurate translation (TT).

Countries affected by European Union legislation

In the European Parliament, for example, there is a group of interpreters who translate orally into the various languages of Europe represented there whilst a speaker has the podium. There is no time to check out the translation. When it comes to writing out what has been said, more checking has to be done for *accuracy*, which is the primary requirement. Likewise, for any legislation, and resultant Directives and derivative Regulations, *accuracy* is the main requirement. But the TA will be legislators, politicians and lawyers who speak the relevant TL. The same would be true for international treaties.

Novels, operas, films, plays

It is here that many of the translation theories and practice differ. For example, should the Target Text (TT) of a novel be totally like a novel originally written in the TL? Or should it retain elements of *foreignness* to make it remind readers of the SL? In subtitles for a film, is there a maximum length of TT to fit in with each frame? Or should the words be repeated in the TL by the same actor and be *dubbed* with synchronisation of the lips? In an opera performed live on stage in another language, e.g., Italian, French, Russian, that is not familiar to the live TA, how accurate should the translation be? Often the restricted physical width of the supratitles board above the stage allow only for two lines that are shortened versions of what is being sung.

As for plays, examples will be given later from some articles concerning plays that are written in English by West African writers whose first language is native to his own area of origin. But the English is heavily influenced by the author's own native language.

Machine translation

This term means that the machine translates using an inbuilt dictionary and grammar. Despite the initial euphoria sixty years ago, and its continuance as a staple of science fiction, machine-made translation still fails to beat the human brain in *accuracy* and *naturalness*, because it is a human brain that created the machine and another human brain that writes the translation program. If a machine is programmed to produce an interlinear word-for-word translation, the result is very likely to be extremely *unnatural* and full of misread synonyms and grammatical versus semantic misread meanings.

Such machine-made translations have sometimes been used by Bible translators in the following situation. A Bible text has been translated from English or French or other colonial language into the TL by a speaker of the TL, and it needs to be checked for *accuracy* to the ST, and *clarity* and *naturalness* in the TL by a consultant who is not one of the translators. An *interlinear literal* back translation into the SL would be inserted under the TT, and additionally a free translation back into the SL will be given as a third line. Such a *back translation*, if done by machine, is liable to have more faults of *accuracy* and *naturalness* than make its use worthwhile.

In the translation of the Bible in Chumburung of Ghana (Abwareseŋ Wǫrẹ-ɔ (God's word Book) (2009)), a handwritten back translation was made by a native speaker of the language who had not been involved in the translation process.[1]

Descriptive translation studies

A few words are necessary at this point under this heading because it was cited by the authors Aziza and Mebitaghan (2014) as a theory that they have used in writing about Urhobo proverbs. It was an influential theory introduced by Holmes (1988), later taken up by Toury (1985 and 1995). More details can be found in DTS: 39. Suffice to say that the theory is *target language oriented*. This is a *sine qua non* of such modern theories of Bible translation as *Dynamic Equivalence* and *Functional Equivalence*.

Pragmatics

Without this being a formal theory, a *pragmatic* element is often to be found in other theories, including *Relevance Theory*. In other words, the *content* of the message is more important than the *form* of the ST.

Relevance Theory

This was a theory proposed by Sperber and Wilson (1986) to summarise and simplify previous theories of speech acts. Gutt (1991) applied the theory to translation, especially translation of the Christian Scriptures. As he has made clear in lectures, it is a theory of how translation works, not a methodology. His focus is on *implicatures* and on *context*.

What should be the source text of the Scriptures?

Original source

As mentioned on page 329, the other major consideration is the Source Language (SL) and Source Text (ST). Disputes about these are now largely confined to the past, when arguments raged as to whether the Bible should be translated from the Latin of the Vulgate, or from the original Hebrew and Greek. As for the Koran, the view strongly held by Moslems since it was written is that it remains in the original Arabic and not be translated, at least not in written form. However, for the Christian Bible it has been accepted from the time of the Septuagint (LXX) that there should be translations into the vernacular of peoples who did not and do not understand the SL. However, there are still disagreements as to which Greek text should be used, e.g., The Textus Receptus of Desiderius Erasmus (1516), with its subsequent revisions by Robert Stephanus (1546–51) and by Theodore Beza (1565–98), or other texts with *apparatus* showing variants from other early manuscripts, or from the Dead Sea Scrolls, or other early sources (Brake 2008: 225–234). This has impeded acceptance by some English-speaking Christian readers who mistrust any translation not based on the Textus Receptus.

Indirect translation

However, all that is a counsel of perfection, especially where translation of the Bible is being done by a team of mother-tongue speakers of a minority language, who should be fluent in the national language or the lingua franca of the area in which they live, but have little or no knowledge of the original Hebrew or Greek. African translators will have to translate from the national language such as English, French, Spanish, Portuguese, or from a lingua franca such as Hausa, Akan or Swahili. Such a translation is known as *indirect translation* (DTS: 76–77). In all cases the translation would have to be guided and approved by a consultant who has knowledge of or access to the Greek and Hebrew STs and to relevant commentaries. The resultant TT (Translated Text) will need significant amounts of *extra-text* explanatory information, in the form of introductions, footnotes, and a glossary. Such a translation is still deemed *faithful*, inasmuch as it *resembles* the original in "relevant respects" (Gutt 1991: 111; DTS: 77). How much *intra-text* explanatory material is to be allowed is still a matter of debate. See especially page 338 below concerning *implicit* information made *explicit*.

Another form of indirect translation is where the ST is a computer version of a Bible or New Testament in a linguistically related language, to which a consistent-changes program is applied. This program is made to write a pseudo-translation into the TL by applying a set of consistent differences between the SL and the TL. The problems with this method, I believe, outweigh the advantages. For example:

- the consistent changes have to be identified by a competent linguist and written by a competent programmer;
- the resultant TT has to be checked thoroughly by speakers of the TL, as well as by a consultant, since similarities between two languages can result in misunderstandings and false results.

The better method, if possible, is to use a translator who is a speaker of the TL and is also fluent in the SL. He/she can then both copy and change at the same time. This method was successfully used in Nigeria for the Odual NT using the Abuan NT as the ST.

Accuracy and fidelity

Literal translation

A literal translation seeks for accuracy, but because of the differences between the *grammar* and *word orders* of the SL and the TL it can rarely be a word-for-word translation, even between two closely related languages (Nida 1964: 156). Such a *word-for-word* rendering would only be appropriate as an *interlinear* translation, of interest only to scholars of the SL and Comparative Linguistics. The term has been used for centuries, and has been refined by theorists, as I will try to make clearer in the following sections.

Word-for-word translation

This term has been used by and since Cicero (see page 326), and is often considered to be the same as literal translation. However, it is better understood as the most extreme form of *literal* translation, in that it substitutes each word of the ST with its nearest equivalent in the TT, without regard for differences in syntactic structure or word order. That makes it only really useful in back translations and linguistic studies (DTS: 198).

Within this framework one can subsume the term *gloss translation*. According to Nida (1964: 159) (DTS: 67) this is when the translator tries to reproduce as *literally* and *meaningfully* as possible the form and content of the ST. Such a translation is only a step away from an *interlinear translation.*

Metaphrase (metaphrasis/metaphrastic translation)

This is the term borrowed by Dryden from ancient writers (see page 326), and criticised by him as a *word-for-word line-by-line translation* that is like a dancer on a tight rope with legs tied.

Linguistic translation (DTS: 19)

This term has been used by some scholars as meaning the same as *close translation*, and by some scholars as a useful approach when translating some sacred texts that are considered as inviolable (DTS: 94). However Nida and Taber (1969/1982), in the context of Bible translation, have defined such translation as one "in which only information which is *linguistically implicit* in the original is made *explicit* and in which all changes of *form* follow the rules of *back transformation* and *componential analysis*" (italics mine). Moreover, they claim that only this kind of translation of the Bible can be considered *faithful*, seemingly to be contradicted by

Gutt (1991: 111). See page 330 above. Likewise, *cultural translations* (page 331) would not be regarded as sufficiently *faithful*).

Direct translation (DTS: 40–42)

In the framework of *Relevance Theory* (Sperber and Wilson 1986), Gutt (1991) defines *direct translation* as one of two possible types of translation, each on opposite ends of a cline. For Gutt *context* is a very important feature to note both in the world of the SA and the *context* familiar to the TA. The TA may not understand the *context* of the ST and what the SA would have understood from the ST, without some form of explanation that is *extra* TT, and so read or hear false *implicatures* by which they will misinterpret the particular passage in the TT. This is why the TA needs to be supplied with explanatory material, but by what means is still to be discussed in later sections.

Thick translation

This is a term coined by Appiah (1993: 817) as a translation "that seeks with its annotations and its accompanying glosses to locate the text in a rich cultural and linguistic context," by introductions, headings, footnotes and glossaries. The purpose of providing such information is to engender in the TA a deeper respect for the *source culture* (SC) and a greater appreciation for the way that people of other backgrounds have thought and expressed themselves (DTS: 171). This would be appropriate especially for a translation from, say, an African language into English, but could equally be appropriate for a translation of Bible texts into an African language.

Formal equivalence translations (DTS: 61)

The term *formal equivalence* sometimes overlaps with or subsumes older ideas of *literal translation*, listed above. It is the term familiar today in the context of Bible translation, explained by Nida (1964: 159) as a translation that "focuses attention on the message itself, in both *form* and *content*" (italics mine), and by Nida and Taber (1969/1982: 201) as "the quality of translation in which the features of the *form* of the source text have been mechanically reproduced in the receptor language." It allows the ST to speak in its own terms rather than attempting to adjust to the circumstances of the receptor audience (TA). This may sometimes distort the grammatical and stylistic patterns of the receptor language (TL), and hence distort the message (Nida and Taber 1969/1982: 201). It has a concern for *accuracy* and, if possible, retention of the original wording of the ST (Nida 1964: 159).

It is to be noted that many modern versions of the English Bible try to outdo others in being *accurate* and *faithful* to the ST, but using more modern English than the KJV (e.g., RSV, NRSV, NKJV, NASV, NIV, to mention just a few).

Free translations

This is a wide-ranging term, which by its nature engenders strong empathy or strong opposition, especially in the field of Bible translation. Within this loose term there are other more precise definitions, such as are next described.

Translation theory and practice past and present

Sense-for-sense translation

In the context of Bible translation, the term *sense for sense translation* gained favour with such persons as Jerome and other Church Fathers (see page 326). This was the general term, used from Cicero's time (see page 326), to describe a translation that emphasises transfer of the *meaning* or *spirit* of the ST over *accurate* reproduction of the original wording (DTS: 151). It is the opposite of *word-for-word* translation. It seeks to conform to the *linguistic* and *textual* norms of the TL, so that it will not sound foreign. The debate about what this really means continues to rage down to the present time.

Paraphrase translation (paraphrasis)

As noted on page 326, this term has been in use since Roman times. It was defined as *changing whole phrases*, in contrast to *metaphrasis*. In modern times the word has a wider, more popular meaning of a *free rendering or amplification* of a passage whilst *keeping the sense*. Examples of such translations of Scripture would include *The Message* (TM) as the most extreme form of this type, and others such as *The Amplified Version* (AmpV), and less obvious examples such as *J. B. Phillips New Testament* (JBP), *The Living Bible* (LB), the *New Living Translation* (NLT), and the *New Century Version* (NCV). Whether a particular version can be classed as a paraphrase is an ongoing matter of debate.

Imitation

Again, this is a term known from Roman times, and Horace was one who approved of it. As stated on page 326, he recommended that an author *imitate* a known work, whether Greek or Latin, and not try to translate it. This then would not be appropriate for Bible translation, or indeed for any secular text in which *accuracy* and *fidelity* are important considerations.

Cultural translations: translations that speak like the target language

In this section I intend to deal with those translations that focus on finding words and phrases that are *natural* and *cultural* equivalents for the ST words and phrases, and which hopefully read as if the TT was the original ST, especially in Bible translations, such that the TA will exclaim that God at last speaks their language.

Idiomatic translation

This was a term introduced by Beekman and Callow (1974), and later used by Larson (1984) in the field of Bible translation, to refer to a strategy that aims for the TT to read as *naturally* as possible. This strategy is similar to *dynamic equivalence*. It is defined as a translation that has the same *meaning* as the SL, but is expressed in the *natural* form of the RL (DTS: 73). Thus, the *meaning* rather than the *form* is retained (Larson 1984: 10). As stated before, it aims to make the TT read like it was the ST. This view of translation can be argued to be the same as *cultural translation* (Nida and Taber (1969/82). It is the opposite to *linguistic translation* (page 331). As defined by Beekman and Callow (1974: 201) it is the use of a *real-world referent* from the *receptor culture* (RC) for an *unknown* (to the TA) *referent* of the original (SC), both the referents having the same *function*. They issue warnings that it should be used sparingly.

However the dominant Bible translation theory today is *functional equivalence*, the more modern term for *dynamic equivalence*. Practical examples are given more fully in Barnwell (1974, 1980 and 1984).

Dynamic equivalence translation

This phrase was introduced by Nida (1964) in the context of Bible translation. If the message of the ST has been transported into the TT, such that it produces in the TA the same *response* as that of the SA, it succeeds in being *dynamically equivalent*. This has to be achieved by *analysis*, *transfer* and *restructuring* (Nida and Taber 1969/1982: 200). This will involve changing ST terms that are obscure into TT terms that are more *culturally appropriate*, also making linguistically ST *implicit* information *explicit* in the TT, and also building in a certain amount of *redundancy*. What is *linguistically implicit* is a matter more difficult to resolve. Other implicit information will more appropriately be given in introductions, headings, footnotes and a glossary.

Functional equivalence translation

This phrase was defined by House (1977: 42) for evaluating the TT, particularly in respect of its *function*. However, the term *functional equivalence* is more widely known today as having replaced the term *dynamic equivalence* of Nida. According to de Waard and Nida (1986: viii), the new term is less open to misinterpretation, and its use serves to highlight the *communicative functions* of translating.

Translation of secular literature: West African examples

The following three subsections deal with cases of some Nigerian languages and Nigerian English influencing the TT. The TT was written in English, and there is no overt ST, even if the author has given a kind of glossary or other explanatory *extra-text* material in English. The author is himself the 'translator'. There is no overt translation theory, but it is arguable that there was one in the author's head, which has heavily influenced his *style* and *form* and *content*. Strictly they are not examples of translation as such, but the authors have each used words and expressions from their native language, which is Yoruba for Rotimi and Osofisan and Esan for Yerima. They have used proverbs, literal renderings of words and structure, loans, transliteration, as well as *code-mixing* and *code-switching*, and *imitation* of ancient Greek tragic heroes.

Yoruba source for English plays and other works

Owoeye (2011) has studied plays by Ola Rotimi: *Kurunmi* (1971) *Ovonramwen Nogbaisi* (1974), *The Gods are Not to Blame* (1971) and by Femi Osofisan: *Tegonni: An African Antigone* (1999), which are in English, but on Yoruba cultural themes and with Yoruba characters. She shows how the Yoruba language has influenced the English used: "What is clearly evident from these plays is that the characters, even though they speak the English language, are Yoruba" (Owoeye 2011: 7). Concerning Osifan she makes similar observations.

Thus, we see that, though the authors have not overtly expressed their use of any theory of translation, they have had regard to:

- who is the intended *Target Audience* i.e. trilingual speakers of Yoruba and Standard English and Nigerian English;
- the *Target Language*, i.e. a Yoruba-influenced Nigerian English;
- *naturalness of style and vocabulary* in the Target Text;
- *an assumed Source Text* being in the author's native language, even if only in the author's head;
- *an ST author* who is also the translator.

Owoeye and Dada (2015) have also studied the works of Wole Soyinka, Rotimi and Osofisan. In their abstract, they seek to prove that "The study reveals that authentic or complete equivalence in translation which seeks to preserve all of the information in the text while preserving it in good form is a mirage" (Owoeye and Dada 2015: 108).

The authors also give examples of how untranslatable words are dealt with by Soyinka in *Death and the King's Horseman* (2010):

(1)   To search for leaves to make **ètùtù**
       Opened wide enough to take a ha'penny **róbó**
       One day he cast his time-smoothed **òpèlè**
       Brother to a **sìgìdì**, bring home my wine . . .

12–13

The playwright has to leave the words **ètùtù**, **róbó**, **òpèlè** and **sìgìdì** in their original Yoruba, and give an *explanation* in a glossary (Owoeye and Dada 2015: 119).

Esan source for English plays

Quite similar to the Yoruba-based plays mentioned in the previous subsection, Ugorji and Osiruemu (2007) have studied the drama *Dry Leaves on Ukan Trees* by Yerima (1997). The authors showed convincing examples of the influence of Esan on the English of the drama, e.g., African variations of English, loans, semantic adjustments, transliteration, figurative expressions, parables and proverbs, metaphors, cultural practices and world view.

Translating Urhobo proverbs into English

In Aziza and Mebitaghan (2014) the authors state that their studies of Urhobo proverbs use Toury's (1995) descriptive translation theory. They say:

> To Toury, texts and modes of behaviour are situated in the appropriate cultural settings and textual components contextualized in their texts. . . . The translator may . . . retain features in the SL and transpose them in the TL. It is the prospective function of the translation, via its textual linguistic make up and the relationship which would tie it to the original, which yields and governs the strategies which are resorted to during the production of the TL (Target Language) text in question, and hence, the translation act as a whole (Toury 2012: 6).
>
> *Aziza and Mebitaghan 2014: 4*

I copy one of these proverbs below (Aziza and Mebitaghan 2014: 11):

(2)	Proverb	Literal meaning	Recommended English translation	Translation principle
	Ă riá kẹ ọmọ́, ĕ rhìvwẹ́ kẹ́ẹ̆	You can chew food for a baby but cannot swallow it for him.	You can force a horse to the stream but you cannot force it to drink.	Idiomising translation

Functional equivalence as applied to Scripture in practice

I now seek to show how *functional equivalence* has been applied in practice to the translation of the Bible into the Chumburung language of Ghana.[2] The English version used is the NIV. The *Target Culture* and *Target Language* were the primary consideration in this translation. The translators were six TL speakers, who were skilled in their own language and English, and were church-going Christians. They were familiar with local church language (Akan: Asante), but were at pains to avoid borrowing from Akan if a Chumburung expression was more *meaningful*. Their draft translations were crossed-checked with one another, with local Chumburung speakers (both Christian and non-Christian) who were not involved in the drafting of the translation), and finally with the consultants who were myself and my wife Gillian (who died in 2011).

Problems of non-equivalence

In the Chumburung (Ghana) TC the word for God is **Wuribwarẹ**, generally understood to be the same as the Creator God known to Jews and Christians and Moslems alike. But it is a personal name, parallel to the word Jehovah ~ Yahweh and Allah, not a general or group word, so 'gods' are not of the same category at all. This produces a restriction on how 'God of gods' is translated.

(3) **Kasẹŋtiŋ si, Wuribwarẹ, nyaŋpe nẹ mọnẹ i suŋ-o,**
Truly   God,   master that you worship,
de kẹyaalẹŋ   ɔ kyɔ   ikisi pɛɛɛ,
has power   he exceeds   local-gods all
nẹ ɔ gyẹ awure pɛɛɛ bamọ nyaŋpẹ
and he is   kings all   their master

Daniel 2.47

What if there is no equivalent in the whole language? It was found that there are no adjectival equivalents of words for emotions and characteristics, such as 'sad, stubborn, discouraged, distressed' and a whole host of others. Not unlike other West African languages, these emotions and characteristics are most often translated by circumlocutions or *body metaphors*, e.g.,

(4)	he is sad	**mọ̀ akatɔ a pee**	his eyes have reddened
	he is stubborn	**mọ̀ ẹsẹbɔ bọ lẹŋ**	his ears possess strength
	he is distressed	**kabɔrẹ-rɔ i duŋwi mọ̀**	his throat pains him

Translation theory and practice past and present

Natural idioms and expressions

Parables

It is generally accepted that the parables of Jesus were fictional and the longer ones tell a story. Such a long story is a **kitee**, which is fictional, and should never be used to mean a true 'story'. Now such stories in Chumburung usually have a traditional rhetorical question *opening*, e.g., translated in Scripture as **N gye owure ko ya dɛɛ kyena aaa?** Mat.18.23 "Is there not a certain king who once lived?" And, if there is a *moral*, then a traditional ending **amo e gye saasebɛɛ** Mat. 18.34 "That is that"? (untranslatable).

Rhetorical questions

In the ST if the *implicit* answer is yes, e.g., "If a man owns a hundred sheep, and one of them wanders away, will he not leave the ninety-nine on the hills and go to look for the one that wandered off?" Mat.18.13, will need a confirmatory grunt from the audience to the rhetorical question. If there is actual audience participation, the reader may say, **Bɛɛɛ mo e ba ayeba nee eee?** "Or am I lying?"

Cultural substitution or adaptation

To take one example, a millstone is not known in Chumburung culture, but a grindstone is known. However, in the ST of Matthew 18.6 the word millstone is used, not as an illustration of grinding, but of a heavy weight. It is a *metaphor*, and so can be replaced by 'a big stone'. This keeps the direct *meaning* of the passage, and avoids distraction from the *function* of the words.

If the problem word is a metaphor, then a more natural comparison or phrase was substituted, as in:

(5) **mò atɔ buŋsɛ a fwiiri   pareparepare**
     his clothes   whitened   IDEO
     'his clothes were white as snow'   Mat. 28.3.

Ideophones

Disagreement was initially met about the use of *ideophones*, of which Chumburung natural texts are full, as if they were not appropriate for Scripture. This objection was overruled by all the translation team, as these expressions were both powerful and *natural* as in:

(6) **Ne bware a su-ro *gburi gburi gburi*, ne elɛɛlɛɛ a gyi *melɛɛ melɛɛ melɛɛ*,**
     And rain cried   IDEO,   and lightning ate IDEO
     ne sweere a leŋkpaŋ *kpuŋ kpuŋ kpuŋ*.
     and earth   shook   IDEO
     "And there came peals of thunder, rumblings, flashes of lightning and an earthquake."

Rev.8.5

Passives

Passives are a problem because Chumburung has none. The general equivalent is '*They* did something'. However, in many cases the *implicit* agent must be made *explicit* to avoid misinterpretation, e.g.:

Keir Hansford

(7) He appeared in a body, · He revealed himself to us as a human being.
was vindicated by the Spirit, · And God's Holy Spirit revealed how he pleased God.
was seen by angels, · And God's messengers saw him.
was preached among the nations, · And the world's people heard the speaking of the good news about him,
was believed on in the world, · and they believed on him.
was taken up in glory. · And finally, he returned to go and sit in his greatness in heaven.
1 Tim. 3.16 · Chumburung back-translation

Calques, transliterations and loans

(8)	English	Chumburung
Transliteration	Melchizedek	**Marikii-Sadukii**
Loan (from Akan)	baptise	**bɔ asuu**
Calque-Semantic extension of TC term	sacrifice (repairing i.e., propitiating a local god)	**lɔŋŋɔ Wuribwarɛ** (repair God)
Translation of original meaning	mannah	**ntetɔ -nɛɛ** (what-is-it?)
Invention of a new phrase	Passover	**Wuribwarɛ-a-kya-anɛ-yɔwɛ a ateese kigyibɛɛ-ɔ** (God-has. helped-us-left-us-safe food eating-time)
Invention of a new phrase (disambiguated)	eternal life	**ŋkpa na kukyure nɛ a mɔŋ de kɛɛ-ɔ** (life *and rest* that have no end)

Implicit information made explicit

Since the Chumburung Bible is for a TA of persons who have little knowledge of the Christian Scriptures, or of the SC, and whose local religion is of a Creator God who has delegated power to local gods and spirits, more *implicit* information needs to be made *explicit*. In keeping with the principles of *functional equivalence* the translators have tried to be *faithful* to the *meaning* of the ST, whilst being *natural* to the TL. There are two types of *implicit* information:

1. Information that is implicit in a particular word, which the SA would readily know, e.g., town names have had added *in-text* information e.g., that they are towns, that rivers are rivers, that lakes are big ponds, that seas are seas. Names of humans however are left unmarked as being the default interpretation.

(9) **nɛ Yeesuu a yɔ Yɛrɔsalɛm maŋ-nɔ.**
and Jesus PAST go.to Jerusalem town-in
"And Jesus went to Jerusalem."

John 2.14

2. Information that will interpret passages that are difficult to understand, even to persons long accustomed to reading or hearing them in church. Scholarly debates continue as to whether inclusion of such information *in-text* is permissible. The Chumburung team have opted for *in-text* explication in many cases, of which this example is simple. In this passage, the information made *explicit* is in italics (italics mine):

(10) Jesus entered the temple area and drove out all who were buying and selling there. He overturned the tables of the money changers and the benches of those selling doves.
Mat. 21.12

After that Jesus entered God's worship place *courtyard. And he saw* merchants *sitting there* selling and buying *things. Some were sitting at their tables* changing *Rome land* money *into Judah land money. Some of them sat on stools* selling doves. *So Jesus found them there* and he pushed over their tables and their stools and drove them away.
Chumburung literal back-translation

Proverbial names

It was found that Chumburung has a very natural and fruitful way of creating *proverbial names*, such that every new-born child is not only given a name indicating the day of the week on which they were born, but also a unique proverbial word or phrase as an additional name. e.g., **abrɛsɛ yii** 'the elders have departed' or **anɛ maa muri** 'we will not die out'. This proved very useful in devising descriptions of God, e.g.:

(11) **Bo̱-e̱le̱ŋ-ɔ-kyɔ-ɔke̱maa-Bware̱**
Possesses-strength-he-exceeds-all-God
"Almighty God."

Translations of poetry

Translation of secular poetry

As mentioned on page 326, translations of poetry need a different set of theories, because where the ST was recognised in the time of its composition as poetry, it can almost never be reproduced in its original poetic *form*, but can only really be recognised by its poetic *content*. Lefevere (1975: 37) however mentions *metrical translation* as one, but flawed, method of translating poetry. This is an attempt to preserve the *metre* of the ST in the TT. Likewise, he mentions *rhymed translation* as another method, which likewise is flawed because it can impose a structure on the TT that was not there in the ST. Examples can be found in the works of authors translating Homer's *Odyssey*, which is not written in rhyme but in Greek metre, which cannot be naturally reproduced in English, and doubtless many other languages (Higham and Bowra 1938: xlvii–lix). Some translators in recent centuries have attempted to translate into English rhymed stanzas, e.g., J.W. Mackail in Higham and Bowra (1938: 77). The other, and I maintain better, method is blank verse, i.e., there is no rhyme, but the *form* is in English irregular metre and broken into lines of roughly equal length (Fagles 1996). Fagles has captured the *spirit* and *fire* of the original without being archaic or too dull and prosaic, and so has made the *content* sound like the great poetry that it was and still is.

Another example of *rhyming* is Dorothy Sayers' translation of Dante's *Divine Comedy* (*Paradise* was completed by Barbara Reynolds after her death) (1962), in which she followed the ST's line-final syllable pattern of *aba bcb cdc* and so on.

Translations of poetry in Scripture

Early translations of the Bible, such as the KJV and Luther's German Bible, made no attempt to distinguish poetic passages from prose. Each verse is numbered and begins at the left margin, irrespective of whether the passage was poetry or prose in the ST. This obscured the parallelism of the Hebrew couplets that form *sense rhymes*, which in the Psalms are readily apparent. The Chumburung Bible TT has imitated this *format* of couplets, but it is not a *literal translation*, rather it conveys the *meaning* in a fully *natural* way.

In fact, there are more passages that can be interpreted as poetry in the ST, such as Job, Proverbs, Ecclesiastes, Song of Songs, and the Prophets, and which are often recognised as such by the NEB and JB in their formatting. In fact, the Chumburung Bible has also formatted 1 Corinthians 13 as poetry, with line breaks patterned as in the Psalms.

Conclusion

Decisions as to what *type* of translation is needed in any situation depend very much on the intended audience (TA, RA). This will determine the degree of necessity for *fidelity* to the ST, *clarity* and *naturalness* to the TA, i.e., how *literal* or *free* it should be. Examples of plays written in English by West African dramatists have been given to show how their SL, i.e., Yoruba and Esan, have greatly affected the choice of words.

As for translating the Christian scriptures, the rules may be stricter than for secular texts. The Bible in Chumburung (Ghana) has been shown to be a *dynamic translation*, attempting to be *faithful* to the *meaning* of the ST, but using *natural* and *clear* TL, with many *culturally equivalent* renderings. It exhibits *functional equivalence*. But it is also aided by some introductions for the OT books, some pericope headings with cross-references to parallel passages, and a glossary to explain the *context* and *meaning* of certain things, persons and customs found in the SC.

Translation of poetry presents many problems because the translation of *form* in the shape of *metre*, *rhythm* and *rhyme* is almost impossible to achieve. The best that many have tried to do is the use of *equivalent forms* known in the TL, thus making the result more like an *imitation*. *Blank verse*, reproducing the *spirit* and *fire* of the ST, seems to me the better option.

Abbreviations

RA = TA	Receptor Audience	ST	Source Text
RC	Receptor Culture	TA = RA	Target Audience
RL = TL	Receptor Language	TC	Target Culture
SA	Source Audience	TL	Target Language
SC	Source Culture	TT	Target Text
SL	Source Language		

Bible versions

AmplV	Amplified Version	NCV	New Century Version
AV	Authorised Version (=KJV)	NEB	New English Bible
JB	Jerusalem Bible	NIV	New International Version
JBP	J. B. Phillips New Testament	NKJV	New King James' Version
KJV	King James Version =AV	NLT	New Living Translation
LB	Living Bible	NRSV	New Revised Standard Version
LXX	Septuagint	RSV	Revised Standard Version
NASV	New American Standard Version	TM	The Message

Notes

1 Two Chumburung men translated the NT, and the same two men and four others translated the OT. The writer of this chapter was the consultant for the NT, and he and his wife Gillian Hansford were consultants for the OT and NT revision. They were both conversant in Chumburung.

2 Chumburung is spoken in Northern and Volta Regions of Ghana by about 65,000 people or more. There is vowel harmony in Chumburung, with the following vowel phonemes in the +ATR set, **i, e, o, u**; and the following in the -ATR set, **ẹ** (= ɪ), ɛ, ɔ, **ọ** (= ʋ). The vowel /**a**/ is in both sets. The letter **ŋ** is used for phonetic [ŋ] and /**ny**/ for the palatal nasal. The digraphs /**ky**/ and /**gy**/ are pronounced like English /**ch**/ and /**j**/ respectively.

References

Abwarẹsẹŋ Wọrẹ-ɔ (God's word Book) (2009). *The Bible in Chumburung of Ghana*. Wycliffe Bible Translators with Bible League and Ghana Institute of Linguistics Literacy and Bible Translation.

Appiah, K. A. (1993). "Thick translation". *Callaloo* 16:4, 808–19.

Aziza, R. O. and Mebitaghan, R. O. (2014). "Issues in transcribing and translating Urhobo proverbs". *Journal of West African Languages* XLI.2, 3–12.

Barnwell, K. (1974, 1980, 1984). *Introduction to Semantics and Translation*. Horsleys Green, Bucks: Summer Institute of Linguistics.

Beekman, J. and Callow, J. (1974). *Translating the Word of God*. Grand Rapids, MI: Zondervan.

Brake, D. L. (2008). *A Visual History of the English Bible*. Grand Rapids, MI: Baker Books.

Fagles, R. (1996). *Translation of Homer's* The Odyssey. London: Penguin Classics.

Gutt, E.-A. (1991). *Translation and Relevance*. Oxford: Basil Blackwell.

Higham, T. F. and Bowra, C. M. (Eds) (1938). *Oxford Book of Greek Verse in Translation*. Oxford: Clarendon Press (OGV).

Holmes, J. S. (1988). *Translated! Papers on Literary Translation and Translation Studies*. Amsterdam: Rodopi.

Holmes, J. S. (1988a). "The name and nature of translation studies". In J. S. Holmes, *Translated! Papers on Literary Translation and Translation Studies*. Amsterdam: Rodopi.

House, J. (1977). *A Model for Translation Quality Assessment*. Tubingen: TBL Verlag Gunter Narr.

Larson, M. L. (1984). *Meaning-Based Translation: A Guide to Cross-Language Equivalence*. Lanham, MD: University Press of America.

Lefevere, A. (1975). *Translating Poetry: Seven Strategies and a Blueprint*. Assen and Amsterdam: Van Gorcum.

Nida, E. A. (1964). *Towards a Science of Translation with Special Reference to Principles and Procedures involved in Bible Translating*. Leiden: E. J. Brill.

Nida, E. A. and Taber, C. R. (1969/1982). *The Theory and Practice of Translation*. Leiden: E. J. Brill.

Osofisan, F. (1999). *Tegonni: An African Antigone*. In Recent Outings. Ibadan: Kenbim Press 12–141.

Owoeye, O. K. (2011). "Yoruba based Nigerian English in the drama of Ola Rotimi and Femi Osofisan". *Journal of West African Languages* XXXVIII.2, 3–19.

Owoeye, K. and Dada, S. A. (2015). "Creativity and translation in Nigerian literature: Yoruba authors in focus". *Journal of West African Languages* XLII, 3–17.

Robinson, D. (Ed.) (1997). *Western Translation Theory from Herodotus to Nietsche*. Manchester, UK: St. Jerome Publishing (cited as WTT).

Rotimi, O. (1971). *The Gods Are Not to Blame*. London: Oxford University Press.

____ (1971). *Kurunmi*. Ibadan: University Press Nigeria.

____ (1974). *Ovonramwen Nogbaisi: An Historical Tragedy*. Benin: Ethiope Publishing Corp. and Ibadan: Oxford University Press Nigeria.

____ (1977). *Our Husband Has Gone Mad Again*. Ibadan: Oxford University Press Nigeria.

Sayers, D. L. and Reynolds, B. (1962). *The Divine Comedy: 3 Paradise*. Harmondsworth: Penguin Classics.

Shuttleworth, M. and Cowie, M. (1997). *Dictionary of Translation Studies*. Manchester, UK: St. Jerome Publishing (cited as DTS).

Soyinka, W. (2010). *Death and the King's Horseman*. Ibadan: Spectrum Books Limited.

Sperber, D. and Wilson, D. (1986). *Relevance: Communication and Cognition*. Oxford: Blackwell.

Toury, G. (1985 and 1995). *Descriptive Translation Studies and Beyond*. Amsterdam and Philadelphia: John Benjamins Publishing Company.

Toury, G. (2012). *Descriptive Translation Studies and Beyond*, Revised Edition. Amsterdam and Philadelphia: John Benjamins Publishing Company.

Ugorji, C. U. C. and Osituemu, E. O. (2007). "Nigerian English in Dry leaves on Ukan Trees". *Journal of West African Languages* XXXIV 1, 3–23.

de Waard, J. and Nida, E. A. (1986). *From One Language to Another: Functional Equivalence in Bible Translating*. Nashville: Thomas Nelson.

Yerima, A. (1997). *Dry Leaves on Ukan Trees*. Ibadan: Kraft Books Ltd.

17

THE REPRESENTATION OF AFRICAN LANGUAGES AND CULTURES ON SOCIAL MEDIA

A case of Ewe in Ghana

Elvis Yevudey

Introduction

Social media has provided an expedient platform for speedy information dissemination with over 1.7 billion users worldwide. With increasing access to social media such as Facebook and Twitter come both opportunities and challenges for the (re)vitalisation of languages, particularly minority languages. The UNESCO figures project that about half of the world's languages may be endangered or die by the end of this century. This global linguistic situation has informed this study in exploring how minority languages such as Ewe (a Gbe language spoken in Ghana) are faring in the language market on platforms such as Facebook. The study involves analyses of posts from eight selected Ewe-focused groups on Facebook. The thematic areas of the study include sociocultural features such as the photographic representation of the dress codes of the Ewe people, food, and cultural ornaments. Linguistic features such as the adaptation of Ewe fonts, and bilingual practices such as codeswitching (CS) and translanguaging on the social media pages are explored.

The inception of the World Wide Web (www), thus the web, re-invented and additionally advanced the medium of communication such that most face-to-face interactions such as meetings, interviews, conferences, just to mention a few, can be carried out via audio-visual mediums (e.g., Skype, Facebook, etc). The arrival of the web is described metaphorically as a transition from Web 1.0 to Web 2.0 (O'Reilly 2012 quoted in Seargeant & Tagg 2014; Androutsopoulos 2010). Web 2.0 refers to interaction technologies associated with computer-mediated communication (CMC) and has contributed to the significant sociolinguistic changes currently being witnessed (Reershemius 2016). The web plays a crucial role in globalisation by providing diverse and multiple means of communication. It can be alluring to equate globalisation to telecommunication, transportation, shipping, and banking, where countries with high-standard achievements in these industries are acclaimed to be globalised countries. Countries with less achievement in these major sectors are considered as either less privileged or underdeveloped. The concept of globalisation has attracted the attention of both the business world and academia, of which linguists and especially sociolinguists have a keen interest (Wright 2016; Blommaert 2010; Pennycook 2007; Coupland 2003; Appadurai 1996).

Globalisation is not a new concept, and 'indeed, "it's nothing new" proves to be one of the least new things to say about globalisation, but it is an important observation' (Coupland 2010: 1). Globalisation offers a great deal for not only economic development, but also linguistic development (Duchêne & Heller 2012). Globalisation, as Blommaert (2010: 4) posits, 'is like every development of the system in which we live, something that produces opportunities as well as constraints, new possibilities as well as new problems, progress as well as regression'.

One of the key components of globalisation is language. English is considered one of the global languages (Saraceni 2015; Mufwene 2010; Guilherme 2007; Crystal 2003; Nunan 2003, 2001), if not the global language, and functions as a lingua franca (House 1999; Seidlhofer 2001, 2005). The prediction that the English language will be a countable noun is phenomenal (Crystal 2000). The widespread use of English across the globe poses a threat to other languages. Languages play instrumental roles in attaining a developmental agenda, particularly in this era when multilingualism and bilingual/multilingual code choices have become the norm (Canagarajah 2013; García 2009). Virtual communication via social media has become a necessity, particularly due to high mobility. On social media, language use is dynamic and rapidly evolving. The World Wide Web is pivotal in creating social domains for language use (Coupland 2003: 466). Speakers have the tendency to use linguistic forms and styles in their posts and, as such, 'language provides a powerful mechanism through which globalized media can become re-localized' (Honeycutt & Cunliffe 2010: 229). However, many languages are not represented in the globalisation agenda (Blommaert 2010). Global majority languages include Chinese, Spanish, English, Arabic and Hindi, just to mention a few (Lewis, Simons, & Fennig 2016). These languages are used predominantly in day-to-day interactions, adopted as languages of business and development, and have substantial social media presence. The list of the 23 most dominant world languages presented by *Ethnologue* does not have much representation of African languages. The majority of the African languages are not used in the global development agenda, but rather the ex-colonial languages are privileged and used as official languages in most African countries (Blommaert 2017; Djité 2008). Colonial languages such as English, French and Portuguese became privileged languages in many African countries after independence. These ex-colonial languages are the preferred languages of business, trade and economics within and across the borders of Africa (Ndhlovu 2017). Countries such as Ghana, Nigeria, Liberia, Kenya, Sierra Leone, Zambia, Tanzania and most Anglo-African countries adopt English as the official language, while the indigenous languages are used for intra-country communications. Equally, in the Francophone-African countries such as Togo, Benin and Ivory Coast, French is used as the official language. The situation in former Portuguese colonies in Africa is the same. Portuguese has official status in Cape Verde, Guinea-Bissau, Angola, Mozambique, Equatorial Guinea, and São Tomé and Príncipe. The dominance of ex-colonial languages in most African countries has relegated the indigenous African languages in their functionality and development.

Social media sites play a significant role in the lives of many people. For instance, Facebook and Twitter create platforms for people to generate and maintain their social capital. They therefore close the social gap when people become physically disconnected from an offline social network (Honeycutt & Cunliffe 2010). Focused groups on social media are often motivated by the desire to create a platform and network for people with similar interests, goals and/or identities. This study is interested in one such type of focused groups, which is the minority language group. The research aim is to explore how minority African languages are faring in the language market on platforms such as Facebook, with a focus on Ewe. Ewe is the Westernmost language of the Gbe language cluster, a subgroup of the Kwa language family (Capo 1991; Duthie 1996). It is spoken in Ghana, Togo, Benin and some parts of Nigeria

(Collins et al. 2017; Ameka 1991) by over two and half million people (Ameka & Essegbey 2006). The ensuing section presents discussions on the use of minority and majority languages on social media and how users of social networking sites mediate between these languages in their online communications.

Minority languages and social media

A language can be described as minority or majority based on factors including, but not limited to, the number of speakers, functionality, learning and teaching materials in the language, and the socio-economic importance of the language. The term minority can be quite equivocal and misleading. A language may have many speakers but may be a minority language due to limited functionality and vice versa. The triglossic model presented by Batibo (2005) throws light on the positionality of a given language in a multilingual context with respect to other languages. In the African context, as exemplified by Batibo, the ex-colonial languages are at the High (H) level of the stratum, followed by the majority African language(s). The majority African languages are Low (L) with respect to the ex-colonial language and H in functionality compared to other minority African languages. The minority African languages are L in the spectrum when compared to the majority African languages and the ex-colonial languages. This stratification demonstrates that a language may be H or L with respect to other languages based on functionality and status. In this study, Ewe spoken in Ghana is considered as a minority language based on its positionality and functionality when compared to English. It is important to draw a distinction between Ewe spoken in Ghana and Togo. The role of Ewe in Togo is different from its role in Ghana. Ewe has an official status in Togo and functions as one of the national languages in addition to Kabiye (cf. Essizewa 2007; Ameka 1991), whereas this is not the case in Ghana. Though Ewe is used as a medium of instruction from pre-school to higher levels, it is not accorded a high functionality in terms of usage in parliament, national trade and commerce, and communication on the global front.

The use of social media can vary based on race, gender, age, and ethnicity. In the American context, social media preferences vary by race and ethnicity where Latinos and Blacks are more likely to use Instagram than Whites, and less likely to use Pinterest (Krogstad 2015). In exploring the use of social media in Nigeria, Fink et al. (2012) state that ethnicity and location of the users are paramount in the description of data from social media. In the European context, studies have explored the use of minority languages such as Welsh on social networking sites such as Facebook (e.g., Cunliffe et al. 2013) and Twitter (Jones et al. 2013; Cunliffe 2009). These studies unravel the opportunities and challenges that new media has for the use of minority languages. Exploring the use of language on social networking sites among young Welsh speakers, Cunliffe et al. (2013) ascertain the language use patterns of the young pupils, the factors that influence their language use, and their attitudes towards the use of minority languages like Welsh on Facebook. Comparing the responses from speakers from the north west of Wales and south east of Wales, the former consider themselves as first-language Welsh speakers whereas the latter consider themselves as first-language English speakers. Though there are differences in the perceived first language of the pupils, there is no significant difference between the oral and online language preference of the pupils. However, pupils who share Welsh and English in their repertoires are highly likely to use English in their online communication (Cunliffe et al. 2013: 345).

Examining how speakers of heritage languages make use of digital media, Reershemius (2016) explores the case of Low German, a minority language spoken mainly in northern Germany. The Facebook groups dedicated to Low German give the speakers the opportunity to contribute Low German words, phrases and other corpus-based inputs toward language maintenance (Reershemius 2016: 6). Contributions on the pages involved bilingual practices and translanguaging between Low German and German. These bilingual code choices exhibit the linguistic backgrounds of the members who are bilingual in both Low German and German. Other studies have demonstrated the use of social media for pedagogic purposes (Omoregie 2014; Bosch 2009). For example, among students in the University of Cape Town, adopting computer-based teaching and learning tends to be appreciated by the young generation often described as 'Net Genres or Digital Natives' (Bosch 2009: 196). However, the challenges lie in the inability of some teachers and students in using Facebook/social media and, in addition, to limited resources, which inhibit widespread computer-based pedagogy.

Within the Ghanaian context, multilingualism is the norm rather than the exception. Speakers maximise their linguistic resources via switching between repertoires when communicating with like bilinguals (Dzameshie 1994). Codeswitching and translanguaging as language contact phenomena are pervasive in Ghana. Studies on language contact are carried out via the concept of codeswitching. Codeswitching studies have focused on switching between the official language, English, and the indigenous languages. Therefore, we can talk about Ewe-English CS (e.g., Amuzu 2012; Dzameshie 1996), Dangme-English CS (e.g., Nartey 1982), Ga-English CS (Vanderpuije 2011), Akan-English CS (e.g., Asare-Nyarko 2012; Forson 1979). Codeswitching occurs on a daily basis at homes, workplaces, marketplaces, radio stations and even classrooms in Ghana. Comparatively, the most studied of these contexts is the classroom, as evidenced by studies such as Agbozo (2015); Owu-Ewie and Eshun (2015); Yevudey (2013); Amekor (2009); Owu-Ewie (2006). These studies present the pedagogic relevance of bilingual and multilingual code choices in the classroom and how such code choices advance pupils' language acquisition, particularly the acquisition of English as a second language, and content comprehension. There are receptions toward CS in Ghana both in formal and informal contexts, and studies have shown that there are generally positive attitudes toward such code choices (Nuworsu 2015; Yevudey 2015; Chachu 2013). The prominence of these bilingual practices has been heightened by the media in Ghana, especially radio station networks. Program managers of various radio stations in Ghana employ codeswitching as a means to reach out to a wider audience (Brobbey 2015; Flamenbaum 2014; Yevudey 2009[2012]).

The use of social media such as Facebook and Twitter has experienced a significant growth in the past half a decade with about 1,243,840 users (social media statistics/Ghana.html). The majority of these users are 18 to 24, and are mainly located in cities and towns where there is relatively good internet connectivity. English is the predominant language used both on individuals' pages and by networking groups, partly due to the function of English as a language of commonality among speakers from different linguistic backgrounds. On the other hand, it can be argued that most social network users in Ghana adopt English as the medium of communication due to incompetence in writing the indigenous languages and for linguistic convenience. Aside from this English dominance, there is a considerable amount of indigenous language usage on social networks like Facebook with some groups particularly dedicated to a specific language and/or ethnic group. Posts and comments on Facebook are characterised by 'truncated words, and from the Ghanaian linguistic perspective, idiophones, and words or phrases from either GhaPE (Ghanaian Pidgin English) or the indigenous languages for example "papa" (so much), "kuraa" (not at all), chaley/chale (appellation to a friend) etc.' (Adika 2012: 162). The use of truncated forms, for instance, is not unique to Ghanaian code choice, but associated with new media communications such as phone texting and social network messaging. Commenting on the dominant use of English on social networking and other communication technologies such as mobile phones, Adika (2012: 164) postulates that 'the new technologies would only increase the spread of English and with it the concomitant but gradual nativisation processes'.

The above studies have presented the use of minority languages on social media, and the linguistic choices and motivation of social networking users. Electronic technology, in this case Facebook, plays an important role in the use of endangered and minority languages, and in their (re)vitalisation of which Ewe is part of the minority group. The aim is to ascertain whether minority languages such as Ewe are present on social media and to explore how the speakers of Ewe use their language on Facebook. Second, the motivations behind the creation of Ewe-focused groups on social media are presented in addition to how the users construct their identities. The research questions explored are:

1   How are speakers of Ewe using their language on social media such as Facebook?
2   What are some socio-cultural and linguistic features in the posts?
3   What are the competence, opportunities and desires of the Ewes when it comes to using Ewe on Facebook?

Language use on social media: the COD model and data

The COD model identifies three crucial elements that condition the position of a language in society. First, people must have the *competence* to use the language, but this is only meaningful if there are actual *opportunities* to do so in daily life. The competence and the opportunities are useful conditions when people *desire* to use the language. Social media sites are therefore crucial as they form an essential part of daily human activities (Moring 2013: 40). The model offers a backdrop to exploring the impact of language use in daily life, in this case the impact of language use on social media (Grin et al. 2003). In some regards, code choices and communication patterns on social media can reflect the linguistic practices among interlocutors in their offline communication. The three elements of the model: *competence*, *opportunities* and *desire* are crucial to understanding the use of minority languages such as Ewe on social media, and how the use of language can promote language maintenance and (re)vitalisation. Based on the model, this study presents how minority languages such as Ewe are faring in the language market on platforms such as Facebook, and further explores the sociocultural and linguistic features exhibited on the pages of the Ewe language groups.

Eight Ewe groups on Facebook were used for this study. These groups were selected based on their focus on creating a platform for sharing Ewe culture and identity. Furthermore, the group sampling is carried out via the 'Related Groups' feature, which is described as 'a list of groups that have the most group members in common with the group that you are viewing' (Honeycutt & Cunliffe 2010: 231). This related group feature of Facebook pages enables the researcher to explore related pages, in this case Ewe groups, on Facebook. Posts and comments, including words, pictures, videos, were extracted from the selected pages between January and April 2016, and qualitative analyses was carried out. Adopting the qualitative approach provides a basis for describing the language use in context, and to interpret the processes in the expression of culture and identity (Silverman 2014). The Ewe language communities on Facebook create a link between Ewes at home and in the diaspora. Such Facebook platforms serve as a bridge. Facebook was particularly chosen for this study due to its commonality among internet users, especially in Ghana. Statistics reports have shown that 77 per cent of Ghanaian adult internet users or smartphone owners use social networking sites (www.pewglobal.org/). Though the above statistic shows that many adults in emerging and developing (middle-income) nations like Ghana use social networks, it is equally important to note that many people are disadvantaged in this technological race due to lack of education and economic factors.

Table 17.1 below presents the name of the Ewe language groups on Facebook, the number of members and their accessibility status (thus whether *open* or *closed* groups). Most of the groups were open and easily accessible. The sampled Ewe groups have a total of 83,832[1] members. As presented under the data analysis section, not all the members of these groups were indigenous Ewes and the groups were not restricted to only Ewes. The pages were inclusive platforms for both Ewes and non-Ewes to share both linguistic and socio-cultural experiences, which elucidate the motivations behind the creation of these groups. The sociolinguistic features demonstrated on these pages are the focus of the ensuing sections.

The use of Ewe on Facebook: socio-cultural and linguistic features

Socio-cultural features

Individual users and groups have at their disposal the ability to construct and present their identities, and they can establish networks of people with similar interests (Boyd & Ellison 2008). Identities on such social platforms can differ from the actual day-to-day identities of the individuals. There is a fluidity in identity construction on social media. Identity is 'a set of resources which people draw upon in presenting and expressing themselves via interaction with others, rather than being a stable, predetermined property of an individual' (Tagg & Seargeant 2016: 339). Social network users may have one or more profiles for varying purposes either for personal usage or for professional purposes, therefore there is no single identity that can be associated with a user or group of users. Ewe-focused groups aim to project and share the identities of the Ewes. This is illustrated by the names of the groups and their aims. Furthermore, the aims and descriptions of the groups are reflected in the posts and comments on the pages. For instance, the aim of the *Ewe & Proud*-focused group is to translate Ewe names into English. Among the Ewes, and equally among other language and ethnic groups in Ghana, names form an integral part of people's identity. The Ewes may name

Table 17.1 Eight selected Ewe groups on Facebook

Group name	Members	Open/closed
Anlo Ewe Community Forum[2]	24,108	Open
Ewe language only	19,673	Closed
I'mEwe	12,549	Open
Ewe culture	12,252	Open
MODERN EWE	10,990	Open
Ewe and proud	3,316	Open
ANLO EWE COMMUNITY FORUM	853	Open
Ewe literary Prize	91	Open
Total members	83,832	

a child based on the circumstances around his or her birth (as in examples (1)–(6)), or name them after an ancestor of the family, based on the day they are born (as in examples (7) and (8)), just to mention but a few. In particular, there are four naming paradigms: (1) the day of the week a person was born; (2) indigenous/local name; (3) English name (also referred to as Christian/baptismal name); (4) Family/surname name. Some of the names presented below have more than one meaning. The meaning variations may be based on synonyms such as 'se', which can be 'god/God or the Lord' and/or the intended meaning ascribed by the family. Some of the names have two orthographies such as example (3). Both orthographies are anglicised in the sense that the Ewe orthography would have been *sewɔdɔ*, and example (6) would be *Akplɔm* (more discussions on font adaption in the next section).

The aim of *Ewe & Proud*:

> Our aim: To educate the public on the meaning of Eʋe names.
>
> The priority being Eʋes who do not know the meaning or significance of their Eʋe names or cannot speak the Eʋe language.

The *Ewe Culture*-focused group aims to showcase the history, marriage, kinship, food, language, music and dance of the Ewe as they believe these are the things that define who the Ewes are. The wallpaper shows one of the cultural dances among the Ewes called *agbadza*. Agbadza is a traditional dance among the Anlos (Aŋlɔ) from Southern Volta of Ghana. It requires specific costumes for both male and female, of which the male costume is presented in the picture. On the Facebook pages there are videos of Ewe cultural dances such as bɔbɔbɔ (also written as borborbor), which originates from Kpando, akpese from Central Volta, and agbadza.

As the name of the page implies, the main linguistic aim of the *Ewe language only* page is to promote the exclusive use of the Ewe language. On the wallpaper of the page, there are bilingual practices through translations in Ewe, English and French. There are also bilingual practices through intrasentential switching (Amuzu 2012; Myers-Scotton 1993) as in in the sentence *facebook EƲE Language Only Habɔbɔ* 'Facebook Eʋe Language Only Group'. The various code choices in this post signify the various linguistic choices among bilingual/multilingual speakers. The description of the *Anlo Ewe Community Forum* group presents itself as providing a platform for people who identify with the Ewe heritage to share and promote common interests through sharing information and experiences.

Table 17.2 Ewe names and their meaning

	Name	Meaning(s)
1	Amewusika[3] Amesushika	Man is worth more than Gold
2	Shika	Precious stone/Gold
3	Sewordor/ Sewodor	God works/ The Lord works
4	Selawoe	The listener has done it/God will do it
5	Sefa	God is calm/God is peaceful
6	Akplorm	He will guide me/He will lead me
7	Kofi	Male of Friday birth
8	Afi	Female of Friday birth

Anlo Ewe Community Forum (part of the group description):

The Ewe forum was created for anyone who identifies with the Ewe heritage including, the Language, People and Culture to come together in harmony and to promote a common interest through the exchange of information and experience by talking about our Geography, History, Education, Development, Health and Social Welfare issues in and for our communities. All friends and well-wishers with this common purpose are welcome and in particular anyone from any of the Gbe language clusters of Èʋè gbè, Gɛn gbe, Aja gbe, Fɔn gbè, and Mina gbe.

Beads are very precious ornaments among the Ewes. In one of the posts, a member shared thoughts on the value of beads among the Ewes using monolingual Ewe. Extract 1 presents comments on a written piece on the history and the importance of beads among the Ewes by member A. Member B commented in Ewe (the word 'yield' is a technical error and it is a suggestive text of *yi ɖe* <u>go ALLATIVE</u> 'go' based on the context). The word *kplɔ* was written as *kplo*. Member D switched intersententially between Ewe and English. Such bilingual code choice is also used in offline communications.

Extract 1: Importance of beads among the Ewes

A: DZONU
    Dzonu enye kesinɔnu gã na nyɔnuwo le Eʋenyigba dzi, eye wobunɛ gɔ̃ abe ga ene. Nyɔnuwo tsɔa dzonu wɔa lekee, wodoa dzonu ɖe kɔ, alɔnu, ali kple klo, eye emea ɖewo donɛ ɖe afɔgɔme hã. Dzonu vovovowo li; suewo li eye gãwo li; gblɔewo li, eye xɔasitɔwo hã li. Esiwo nye yevutɔ wɔwɔawo la mexɔ asi o; tomedzonuwo xɔa asi ŋutɔ eye bubu le wo ŋuti wu; woyɔa wo bena dzonu *fufu*iwo alo agumedzonuwo. Dzonua ɖewo *f*e asi sẽ ŋutɔ ale be nyɔnu hotɔwo koe *f*lea wo.
B: Akpe woe ga kplo mi **yield** afee.
C: Akpe
D: **Marvelous work of art**. Etu Togbuiawo do vavan.

Translation:

A: Bead is a precious ornament for women among the Ewes, and it is considered even as money. Women use beads to accessorise, they wear it on their neck, wrist, waist and knee, and some people wear it on their ankle. There are various types of beads; there are small ones and big ones, cheap ones and expensive ones. Those made abroad are not expensive; beads made from stones are expensive and they are well respected; such beads are referred to as 'dry' beads. Some beads are so expensive such that only rich women can afford them.
B: Thanks for taking us home. (Metaphorically to mean sharing traditions and histories with them.)
C: Thanks
D: **Marvelous work of art**. You have indeed met the grandfathers.

The commonalities in the groups observed are in the promotion of the Ewe language and culture. The Ewe speakers have created the *opportunity* to use their language through the creation of such Ewe-focused groups, and have the *desire* to promote their language and culture.

Linguistic features

Adaptation of Ewe fonts

The posts on the Ewe-focused groups show some linguistic features. In Table 17.3 presented below, Ewe fonts are adapted with English fonts or roman scripts. For example, the open-mid back vowel /ɔ/ is represented as a close-mid back vowel [o] or as [or] (examples (1) and (2)). There are also adaptations of consonant sounds as shown in examples (3) and (4). Tones such as high tone /ˊ/, low tone /ˋ/ and nasal /˜/ are often not marked in the posts. The adaption of Ewe sounds and omission of tone markings may lead to a gradual diminishing of appropriate writing of Ewe words, which may lead to language loss and extinction.

Bilingual practices, codeswitching and translanguaging in the posts

There are bilingual practices such as codeswitching and translanguaging on the Facebook posts. On the Ewe-focused groups observed, there are instances of bilingual practices between Ewe and English. The Extract 2 presents comments on a post. A member shared a picture of a locally made doughnut. Member E, as the translations show, posted that the English call the food 'Doughnut', the Akans call it 'Boflot' and asks members to state how the Ewes call that food. Members F, G, and H stated that Ewes refer to the food as 'Botokoe'. The conversation turn by member I presents a member who is an Ewe, but grew up in a non-Ewe community, therefore does not know the name of the food. Member I adopted a bilingual code choice, switching between Ewe and English intersententially. In response to member I's comment, member J uses a metaphorical expression to mean member I has refused to learn the Ewe language by alluding to that as refusing to marry from his hometown.

The switches to Ewe in the posts, as earlier stated, demonstrate adaptation of Ewe sounds. The voiceless bilabial fricative /ƒ/ is represented as voiceless labiovelar fricative [f] as in **afe** (comment by member J). In the sentence by member J, *ŋutɔ* was written as **nutor** and /srɔ/ was written as **sr)**. The use of bilingual practices on the Facebook posts reflect the linguistic realities of offline code choices of bilingual and multilingual speakers in Ghana. The adaptation of the Ewe fonts can be attributed to the lack of easy access to Ewe keyboards, therefore speakers engaged in online communications in Ewe using the roman/English fonts and other symbols.

Table 17.3 The adaptation of Ewe fonts in online communication

Adapted form	*Original form*	*Sound variations*
1 Ametowoyona	Ametɔwoyɔna	/ɔ/ > [o]
2 Etornam	Etɔnam	/ɔ/ > [or]
Selorm	Selɔm	
Lorné	Lɔné	
Lorlornyo	Lɔlɔ̃nyo	
Sefakor	Sefakɔ	
Tsortsorke	Tsɔtsɔke	
3 Sitsofe	Sitsoƒe	/ƒ/ > [f]
Mawufelorlor	Mawuƒelɔlɔ̃	
Afe	Aƒe	
4 Amenyuiade	Amenyuieɖe	/ɖ/ > [d] [Ð]
5 Sr)	Srɔ̃	/ɔ/ > [ )]

Elvis Yevudey

Extract 2: Ewe-English bilingual practices

E: **Inglisia wo be** 'Doughnut'
     Bluawo be '<u>Boflot</u>'
     Ke Eʋeawo ɖe, aleke mie yɔna nuɖuɖu sia?

F: Botokoe

G: Botokoe

H: Botokoe

I: I especially need to be educated because **nyemetsi de afe oo**.pls
    let the education floooow.

J: Hahaha haa "ekawo nutor . . . de sr) le afe negbe"

Translation:

E: The English say 'Doughnut'
    The Akans say '<u>Boflot</u>'
    So the Ewes, how do we call this food?

F: Doughnut

G: Doughnut

H: Doughnut

I: I especially need to be educated because **I have not grown up in my
    hometown**. pls
    let the education floooow.

J: Hahaha what? "it is up to you . . . marry from your home(town) you refused"

Bilingual practices of codeswitching and translanguaging also occurred in Extract 3. Member K posted a comment asking why Ewes are more respectful than other tribes. Most of the comments were in English with the use of some truncated forms. Some of the forms included *u* 'you', *ur* 'your', *nd* 'and', *tanx* 'thanks', *bn* 'being', and *bcos, cos, bcs* 'because'. The conversation exchange was exclusively in English. However, member K who posted the comment in English acknowledged the comments switching to Ewe.

Extract 3: Ewe-English bilingual practices

K: Why is it that we the Ewe's are more respectful than the other tribes? Top of
    Form.

L: bcos humbleness move people highier

M: Because of the colonial masters under which we were.# the Germans.

N: We are timid, not respectful.

O: I agree

P: Ooh Mr. Kami, are u sure the Ewe a timid nd rather not respectful? Go a little
    bit into the recent history of the Ewes from Nortsie to Ghana. We will give u the
    respect nd if u take that for our timidity, we strike. Nortsie-Agorkoli, in modern
    day Ghana, u can talk of the Koptokas, Rawlingses etc. We detest bn suppressed.

Q: Show how u conducted the survey n show us ur results.

R: Bcs we were made in the real image of the creator thanks

S: Cos of de training given to us from de house tanx

T: That's our nature & inheritance from our parents

K: AKPE NA MI KATA.

K: Thank you all.

The use of Ewe on Facebook: competence, opportunities and desires

Language attitudes and identities are ascertained based on three factors including competence, opportunities and desire. Posts on the observed focused groups on Facebook show that speakers of Ewe demonstrate their competence in the language and have created the opportunity to use their language. In addition, members have shown the desire to use their language by posting in Ewe and are willing to teach non-Ewe speakers the language.

Identity constructions in offline and online communication may exhibit some similarity but more often vast differences. In face-to-face communications, speakers have at their disposal the communicative resources such as gestures, tone and intonation in creating meaning differences; and the physical location of the communicative event may have an impact on the communication pattern. In online communication, however, internet and social network users have 'a wealth of online environments through which the everyday construction of identities are mediated by textual and multimodal tools involving what are arguably new literacies and communicative genres' (Thorne & Black 2011: 258). Identity constructions are dynamic and varied (Beinhoff & Rasinger 2016; Blommaert 2005; Norton 2000). Social network users may present similar or different identities in their offline and online communication. As Tagg and Seargeant (2016) present:

> Performance of identity on Facebook are sociolinguistically interesting for two main reasons: first, because the resources which people have at their disposal differ markedly from those typically associated with identity construction in face-to-face spoken contexts; and second, because the online context of Facebook allows for a high degree of selectivity in how people present themselves. These factors resonate with, and extend, contemporary ideas about the way that identity operates as a set of resources which people draw upon in presenting and expressing themselves via interaction with others, rather than being a stable, predetermined property of an individual.
>
> *p. 339*

In the posts observed on the Ewe-focused groups on Facebook, speakers exhibit various identities in terms of their linguistic competences, cultural values, and general attitudes toward Ewes and non-Ewes in the groups. In their comments, identity and attitudes are intertwined. Some members assumed that a person who identifies as an Ewe should have some competence in the Ewe language. As Extract 4 presents, member U expressed the opinion of being an Ewe but cannot understand or read Ewe. In a response, member V 'wonder' why member U identifies as Ewe, but cannot understand or speak Ewe.

Extract 4: Language attitudes toward Ewes who cannot speak Ewe

U: Am pleading all those who are writing in ewe because some of us are ewe but we dont understand it and also we can not read so pls

V: We will do our best but i wonder how u a ewe wtut hearing ur lang

Attitudes toward non-Ewes who do not speak Ewe are different. As presented in Extract 5, member W expressed being non-Ewe, but is fascinated by the Ewe language and culture. Members expressed a warm welcome by stating the characteristics of Ewes as being 'caring and lovely people, therefore you [the non-Ewe] are safe' (comment by member X). Members such as AA, AB, AC and AD attempted to teach member W some Ewe expressions such as *woezor* '(you are) welcome'. However, member AE questioned, using Ghanaian Pidgin

English, whether the page is for Ewe classes. Member W therefore expressed the passion to learn the Ewe language as 'small'. In general, there are more receptive and positive attitudes toward non-Ewes who cannot speak Ewe than toward Ewes who cannot speak Ewe. Linguistically, there were switches between Ewe, Standard English and Ghanaian pidgin on the pages. In addition, there were instances of the use of truncated forms such as *ur* 'you're, your', *y* 'why', *dis* 'this', *u* 'you', *wtut* 'without', *lang* 'language', etc.

Extract 5: Language attitude toward non-Ewe speakers

W: I'm not an Ewe but the language and your culture practices amaze me always. Hope you all wouldn't mind treating me well as part of you and also teach me your language? Thanks!

X: We are caring and lovely people, therefore you are safe

Y: You are very welcome to our community!

Z: It's a pleasure being in the Ewe world

AA: welcome send ur word and we transilate it in ewe for u to learn

AB: Woezor. Mega tsidzi kroa oo. Norvi mikataa mienye.

AC: Woe zor (**ur welcome**)

AD: Woezor, means welcome. [name] that's my first tot

AE: teach pas, y dis place by #EWE_CLASS.

W: It doesn't matter where this place is. As realistic how I am to learning, small I will

AF: Thanks too

AG: woezor

Translation:

AB: Welcome. Do not worry. We are all one people.

AC: Welcome, means welcome. [name] that's my first tot

AG: welcome

Conclusions

The code choices on these pages represent the linguistic diversity and plurality among the group members. The various code choice patterns involved monolingual Ewe and English, and switching between Ewe and English. In addition to these, there are other languages such as Ghanaian Pidgin English and French, which are adopted in some of the posts. Bilingual practices such as codeswitching and translanguaging have become part of the repertoire of bilingual and multilingual speakers such that it has become unmarked code (Agbozo 2015; Yevudey 2015; Chachu 2013; Amuzu 2012). Linguistically, truncated forms of English words are used. There are instances of adaptation of Ewe fonts and occurrences of bilingual practices such as codeswitching and translanguaging between Ewe and (Ghanaian Pidgin) English. In terms of Ewe, the adaptation of sounds and omission of tone markings may lead to a gradual diminishing of an appropriate writing system of Ewe words, which may lead to language loss and extinction. This study therefore recommends that software providers for smartphones and computer devices should create Ewe keyboards and, for that matter, keyboards for minority languages, to enable speakers to use the appropriate writing forms that will advance language revitalisation and maintenance. It must be acknowledged that there are Ewe keyboards for Android and iPhones, however, they are not often used. More visibility of such useful technological resources is therefore necessary.

Social networking sites have a crucial role in language (re)vitalisation. The use of minority languages and endangered languages via electronic technology will contribute to the development of the language (Crystal 2000). Communication through the internet referred to as Web 2.0 has advanced on social interactions through multimodal content sharing and social networking and, as such, 'the new technologies have made the Internet a far more interactive space, where bottom-up activities prevail' (Reershemius 2016: 2). The Ewe-focused groups observed use multimodal content in their communicative activities on the pages. Texts, audio-visuals and pictures are used in presenting the language and the socio-cultural values of the Ewes. These signify the importance of language in its various forms in preserving personal, cultural and national identities (Dzahene-Quarshie & Moshi 2014). Identity serves as the motive behind the creation of the Ewe-focused groups. The groups aim to share and promote the Ewe heritage including language, culture and history with speakers of Ewe and anyone who identifies with the Ewe heritage.

The third research question aimed to explore the competence, the opportunities and the desires of the Ewes toward their language use. The Ewes and Ewe-focused groups on Facebook project and promote their culture and language through their posts and comments. The analyses of the posts on the pages based on the model show that most members on the page have *competence* in the language and use it when appropriate during their Facebook communication. They have created the *opportunity* to use their language, and share and maintain their culture; and have demonstrated a *desire* to maintain the language and culture through the creation of the groups. The analyses further show that minority languages such as Ewe are represented on social media. Therefore, creating translated interfaces and direct contents from the languages would contribute to language maintenance and development, and increase the accessibility to non-Ewe speakers.

Notes

1 The total number of members on the Ewe focused groups as at 30 April 2016.
2 There are two Anlo Ewe community forums. One with an upper case name, 'ANLO EWE COMMUNITY FORUM', and a second group with the same name but with each word starting with an upper case letter, 'Anlo Ewe Community Forum'. The number of members of the former was 853 members and of the latter was 24,108 as at 21 April 2016. Both groups were sampled for this research.
3 *Amewusika* or *Amewushika* – 'Man/human being is worth more than Gold' – the variation between the two written forms is based on dialectal variations. In the southern variety of Ewe such as the Anlo (Aŋlɔ) the voiceless alveolar fricative is realised as a voiceless post alveolar frication /ʃ/ and it is realised in other varieties such as Wedome (Uedome) as the voiceless alveolar fricative /s/. The form adopted for the standard orthography is the voiceless alveolar fricative.

Further reading

Crystal, D. (2006). *Language and the Internet* (2nd Ed.). Cambridge: Cambridge University Press.
Kelly-Holmes, H. (2012). 'Multilingualism and the media'. In M. Martin-Jones, A. Blackledge & A. Creese (eds), *The Routledge Handbook of Multilingualism*. New York, NY: Routledge, pp. 333–345.
O'Keeffe, A. (2011). 'The media'. In J. Simpson (ed.), *The Routledge Handbook of Applied Linguistics*. New York, NY: Routledge, pp. 67–80.

References

Adika, G. S. K. (2012). 'English in Ghana: growth, tensions, and trends'. *International Journal of Language, Translation and Intercultural Communication*, Vol.1, pp. 151–166.
Agbozo, G. E. (2015). Language choice in Ghanaian classrooms: linguistic realities and perceptions. MPhil. Thesis, Norwegian University of Science and Technology. Trondheim: Norway.

Amekor, K. C. (2009). Codeswitching as a medium of instruction in selected schools in the Volta region. MPhil. Thesis. English Department, University of Ghana.

Ameka, F. K. & Essegbey, J. (2006). 'Elements of the grammar of space in Ewe'. In S. C. Levinson & D. Wilkins (eds), *Grammars of Space*, pp. 359–398. Cambridge: Cambridge University Press.

Ameka, F. (1991). Ewe: its grammatical constructions and illocutionary devices. PhD Dissertation, Australian National University, Canberra: Australia.

Amuzu, E. K. (2012). 'Socio-pragmatics of conversational codeswitching in Ghana'. *Ghana Journal of Linguistics*, Vol.1(2), pp. 1–22.

Androutsopoulos, J. (2010). 'Localizing the global on the participatory web'. In Nikolas Coupland (ed.), *The Handbook of Language and Globalization*, pp. 203–231. Chichester, UK: Wiley-Blackwell.

Appadurai, A. (1996). *Modernity at Large: Cultural Dimensions of Globalization*. Minneapolis, MN: University of Minnesota Press.

Asare-Nyarko, C. (2012). Akan-English code-switching in some selected churches in Accra. MPhil. Thesis, Department of Linguistics, University of Ghana, Legon. Accra: Ghana.

Batibo, H. (2005). *Language Decline and Death in Africa: Causes, Consequences, and Challenges* (Vol. 132). Clevedon: Multilingual Matters.

Beinhoff, B. and Rasinger, S. M. (2016). 'The future of identity research: impact and new developments in sociolinguistics'. In S. Preece (ed.), *The Routledge Handbook of Language and Identity*, pp. 572–585. London: Routledge.

Blommaert, J. (2017). 'Redefining the sociolinguistic "local": examples from Tanzania'. Available online at: https://alternative-democracy-research.org/2017/03/22/redefining-the-sociolinguistic-local-examples-from-tanzania/ [accessed on 22 March 2017].

Blommaert, J. (2010). *The Sociolinguistics of Globalization*. Cambridge: Cambridge University Press.

Blommaert, J. (2005). *Discourse: A Critical Introduction*. Cambridge: Cambridge University Press.

Bosch, T. E. (2009). 'Using online social networking for teaching and learning: Facebook use at the University of Cape Town'. *Communication*, Vol. 35 (2), pp. 185–200.

Boyd, D. and Ellison, N. (2008). 'Social network sites: definition, history, and scholarship'. *Journal of Computer-Mediated Communication*, Vol. 13, pp. 210–230.

Brobbey, S. (2015). Codeswitching on Ghanaian radio talk-shows: bilingualism as an asset. A thesis submitted for the degree of MPhil. The University of Bergen. Bergen: Norway.

Canagarajah, S. (2013). *Translingual Practice: Global Englishes and Cosmopolitan Relations*. London, New York, NY: Routledge.

Capo, H. B. C. (1991). 'A comparative phonology of Gbe'. *Publications in African Languages and Linguistics, 14*. Berlin and Garome: Foris Publications Labo Gbe (Int).

Chachu, S. (2013). 'Ghana television and radio advertisements: codeswitching as a type of language use in the context of unity in diversity'. In H. Lauer, N. A. A. Amfo & J. Boampong (eds), *The One in the Many: Nation Building Through Cultural Diversity*, pp. 80–96. Accra: Sub-Saharan Publishers.

Collins, C., Postal, M. P. and Yevudey, E. (2017). 'Negative polarity items in Ewe'. Ms, NYU and Aston University. Available online at: http://ling.auf.net/lingbuzz/002651, (forthcoming in *Journal of Linguistics*).

Coupland, N. (2010). 'Introduction: sociolinguistics in the Global Era'. In N. Coupland (ed.), *The Handbook of Language and Globalization*, pp. 1–27. Chichester, UK: Wiley-Blackwell.

Coupland, N. (2003). 'Introduction: sociolinguistics and globalisation'. *Journal of Sociolinguistics*, Vol. 7(4), pp. 465–72.

Crystal, D. (2003). 'English as a global language'. In *Encyclopaedia of Language and Education* (2nd ed.). Cambridge: Cambridge University Press.

Crystal, D. (2000). 'Emerging Englishes'. *English Teaching Professionals*, Vol. 14, pp. 3–6.

Cunliffe, D. (2009). 'The Welsh language on the internet: linguistic resistance in the age of the network society'. In G. Goggin & M. McLelland (eds), *Internationalizing Internet Studies: Beyond Anglophone Paradigms*, pp. 96–111. New York, NY: Routledge.

Cunliffe, D., Morris, D. and Prys, C. (2013). 'Young bilinguals' language behaviour in social networking sites: the use of Welsh on Facebook'. *Journal of Computer-Mediated Communication*, Vol.18(3), pp. 339–361.

Djité, P. G. (2008). *The Sociolinguistics of Development in Africa*. Clevedon, Buffalo: Multilingual Matters.

Duchêne, A. and M. Heller (2012). 'Multilingualism and the New Economy'. In M. Martin-Jones, A. Blackledge & A. Creese (eds), *The Routledge Handbook of Multilingualism*, pp. 369–383. London: Routledge.

Duthie, A. S. (1996). *Introducing Ewe Linguistic Patterns*. Accra: Ghana Universities Press.

Dzahene-Quarshie, J. & Moshi, L. (2014). 'The dilemma of language in education policies in Ghana and Tanzania'. *Cross-Cultural Studies*, Vol. 36, pp. 149–173.

Dzameshie, A. (1996). Toward a global explanation of unmarked codeswitching: evidence from Ewe-English bilingual codeswitching. Unpublished monograph.

Dzameshie, A. (1994). Communicative competence and code choice: The case of codeswitching by a bilingual family. Unpublished monograph.

Essizewa, K. E. (2007). *Sociolinguistic aspects of Kabiye-Ewe bilingualism in Togo*. Ann Arbor, MI: ProQuest Dissertations Publishing, 3283359.

Fink, C., Kopecky, J., Bos, N. & Thomas, M. (2012). 'Mapping the Twitterverse in the developing world: an analysis of social media use in Nigeria'. In *International Conference on Social Computing, Behavioral-Cultural Modeling, and Prediction*, pp. 164–171. Berlin and Heidelberg: Springer.

Flamenbaum, R. (2014). 'The pragmatics of codeswitching on Ghanaian talk radio'. *International Journal of Bilingualism*, Vol.18(4), pp. 346–362.

Forson, B. (1979). Codeswitching in Akan-English bilingualism. PhD Thesis. Department of Applied Linguistics, University of California, Los Angeles.

García, O. (2009). *Bilingual Education in the 21st Century*. Oxford: Wiley-Blackwell.

Grin, F. & T. Moring, with D. Gorter, J. Häggman, D. Ó Riagáin & M. Strubell (2003). *Support for Minority Languages in Europe. Final Report on a Project Financed by the European Commission*, Directorate Education and Culture. Available online at: http://europa.eu.int/comm/education/policies/lang/langmin/support.pdf, [accessed on 1 February 2016].

Guilherme, M. (2007). 'English as a global language and education for cosmopolitan citizenship'. *Language and Intercultural Communication*, Vol. 7(1), pp. 72–90.

Honeycutt, C. & Cunliffe, D. (2010). 'The use of the Welsh language on Facebook'. *Information, Communication & Society*, Vol. 13(2), pp. 226–248.

House, J. (1999). Misunderstanding in intercultural communication: interactions in English as a lingua franca and the myth of mutual intelligibility. In C. Gnutzmann (ed.), *Teaching and learning English as a Global Language*. Tüumbingen, Germany: Stauffenburg Verlag. *Studies in Second Language Acquisition*, 24(1), pp. 73–89.

Jones, R. J., Cunliffe, D. & Honeycutt, Z. R. (2013). 'Twitter and the Welsh language'. *Journal of Multilingual and Multicultural Development*, Vol. 34(7), pp. 653–671.

Krogstad, J. M. (2015). *Social Media Preferences Vary by Race and Ethnicity*. Pew Research Center. Available online at: www.pewresearch.org/fact-tank/2015/02/03/social-media-preferences-vary-by-race-and-ethnicity/, [accessed on 9 December 2016].

Lewis, M. P., Simons, G. F. & Fenning, C. D. (eds) (2016). *Ethnologue: Languages of the World, Nineteenth edition*. Dallas, TX: SIL International, online version: www.ethnologue.com.

Moring, T. (2013). 'Media markets and minority languages in the digital age'. *Journal on Ethnopolitics and Minority Issues in Europe*, Vol. 12(4), pp. 34–53.

Mufwene, S. S. (2010). 'Globalization, global English, and world English(es): myths and facts'. In N. Coupland (ed.), *The Handbook of Language and Globalization* (Vol. 64), pp. 31–55. Chichester, UK: John Wiley & Sons.

Myers-Scotton, C. (1993). *Duelling Languages: Grammatical Structure in Codeswitching*. Oxford: Clarendon Press.

Nartey, J. (1982). 'Codeswitching, interference or faddism? Language use among Educated Ghanaians'. *Anthropological Linguistics*, Vol. 24, pp. 183–193.

Ndhlovu, F. (2017). 'Southern development discourse for Southern Africa: linguistic and cultural imperatives'. *Journal of Multicultural Discourses*, Vol. 12(2), pp. 1–21, http://dx.doi.org/10.1080/1744714 3.2016.1277733.

Norton, B. (2000). *Identity and Language Learning: Gender, Ethnicity, and Educational Change*. London: Longman.

Nunan, D. (2003). 'The impact of English as a global language on educational policies and practices in the Asia Pacific region'. *TESOL Quarterly*, Vol. 37(4), pp. 589–613.

Nunan, D. (2001). 'English as a global language'. *TESOL Quarterly*, 35(4), pp. 605–606.

Nuworsu, A. (2015). Language use in interethnic marriage ceremonies in Great Accra. MPhil. Dissertation. Linguistics Department: University of Ghana, Legon. Accra: Ghana.

Omoregie, F. K. (2014). 'The use of Facebook in theatre studies'. In E. A. Arua, T. Abioye & K. Ayoola (eds), *Language, Literature and Style in Africa: A Festschrift for Professor Christopher Olatunji Awonuga*, pp. 85–98. Cambridge: Cambridge University Press.

Owu-Ewie, C. and Eshun, E. S. (2015). 'The use of English as medium of instruction at the Upper Basic Level (Primary four to Junior High School) in Ghana: from theory to practice'. *Journal of Education and Practice*, Vol. 6(3), pp. 72–82.

Owu-Ewie, C. (2006). 'The language policy of education in Ghana: a critical look at the English-only language policy of education'. In J. Mugane et al. (eds), *Selected Proceedings of the 35th Annual Conference on African Linguistics*, pp. 76–85. Somerville, MA: Cascadilla Proceedings Project.

Pennycook, A. (2007). *Global Englishes and Transcultural Flows*. London: Routledge.

Reershemius, G. (2016). 'Autochthonous heritage languages and social media: writing and bilingual practices in Low German on Facebook'. *Journal of Multilingual and Multicultural Development*, pp. 1–15, http://dx.doi.org/10.1080/01434632.2016.1151434.

Saraceni, M. (2015). *World Englishes: A Critical Analysis*. London and New York, NY: Bloomsbury.

Seargeant, P. & Tagg, C. (2014). 'Introduction: the language of social media'. In P. Seargeant & C. Tagg (eds), *The Language of Social Media: Identity and Community on the Internet*, pp. 1–19. Basingstoke: Palgrave Macmillan.

Seidlhofer, B. (2005). 'English as a lingua franca'. *ELT Journal*, Vol. 59(4), pp. 339–341.

Seidlhofer, B. (2001). 'Closing a conceptual gap: the case for a description of English as a lingua franca'. *International Journal of Applied Linguistics*, Vol. 11, pp. 133–58.

Silverman, D. (2014). *Interpreting Qualitative Data*. London: Sage Publications.

Tagg, C. & Seargeant, P. (2016). 'Facebook and the discursive construction of the social network'. In A. Georgakopoulou & T. Spilioti (eds), *The Routledge Handbook of Language and Digital Communication*, pp. 339–353. New York, NY: Routledge.

Thorne, L. S. & Black, R. (2011). 'Identity and interaction in internet-mediated contexts'. In C. Higgins (ed.), *Identity Formation in Globalizing Contexts: Language Learning in the New Millennium*, pp. 257–277. Berlin: Walter de Gruyter.

Vanderpuije, A. J. (2011). Ga-English codeswitching in radio and television advertisement. MPhil. Master's Thesis, Department of Linguistics, University of Ghana, Legon. Accra: Ghana.

Wright, S. (2016). *Language Policy and Language Planning: From Nationalism to Globalisation*. London: Palgrave Macmillan.

Yevudey, E. (2015). 'Translanguaging as a language contact phenomenon in the classroom in Ghana: pedagogic relevance and perceptions'. In Angouri, J., Harrison, T., Schnurr, S. & Wharton, S. (eds), *Learning, Working and Communicating in a Global Context*, pp. 259–270. Proceedings of the 47th Annual Meeting of the British Association for Applied Linguistics, University of Warwick, Coventry. London: Scitsiugnil Press.

Yevudey, E. (2013). 'The pedagogic relevance of codeswitching in the classroom: insights from Ewe-English codeswitching in Ghana'. *Ghana Journal of Linguistics*, Vol. 2(2), pp. 1–22.

Yevudey, E. (2009[2012]). Ewe-English codeswitching on radio. BA Dissertation, Linguistics Department, University of Ghana, Legon. [Published 2012, *Codeswitching on Radio in West Africa: A Case of Ewe-English Codeswitching in Ghana*. Germany: Lambert Academic Publishing.]

18

SUSTAINABLE LANGUAGE TECHNOLOGY FOR AFRICAN LANGUAGES

Arvi Hurskainen

Introduction

Africa has a peculiar history of language development. Before colonial times the area south of the Sahara was speaking exclusively African languages. The colonial period changed the situation so that mainly three European languages, Portuguese, French and English, became the languages of the elite, while the local population continued to use their local languages. Now, after the end of the colonial times, the situation continues to be much the same. One would have expected that the role of imported foreign languages would have diminished and local language policies would have developed communication systems based on local languages. However, this has not taken place. Those three foreign languages continue to dominate in official matters across Africa, although most people are hardly able to communicate using these languages. The elites in each country employ for governmental business a language that the ordinary people do not understand. Therefore, the majority of the population are marginalized and excluded from power politics. Although there is much talk about the importance of local languages, very little concrete action is made to improve the situation (Myers-Scotton 1990; Bamgbose 1991, 2000).

The digital age potentially offers new possibilities for developing the status of local/ indigenous languages, and such development would be in line with the UN resolution on the rights of indigenous people, "that control by indigenous peoples over developments affecting them and their lands, territories and resources will enable them to maintain and strengthen their institutions, cultures and traditions, and to promote their development in accordance with their aspirations and needs."[1] The UN specifically emphasizes the rights to develop, maintain and transfer own language. The enhancement of local languages might aid proper intercultural communications across vastly different language divides. Systems for translating from speech to speech have already been constructed and tested (Nakamura 2009). The subject of debate is still the way in which one language should be translated to the other. For example, Google Translate (GT) has traditionally used English as the interlingua, through which translation is carried out between two languages. Furthermore, GT has used statistical machine translation (SMT) methods (Och 2006), which it recently has enhanced with neural machine translation (NMT) methods (Turovsky 2016). The NMT system creates its own cryptic 'interlingua', through which translation is facilitated between various languages.

Currently, the main trend in translation technology is to develop translation systems based on SMT and NMT. These methods are suitable for closely related languages that, in addition, have large masses of human-translated texts for training the translation system. According to Och (2005), a solid base for developing a usable statistical machine translation system for a new pair of languages from scratch would consist of a bilingual text corpus (or parallel collection) of more than 150–200 million words, and two monolingual corpora each of more than a billion words. Statistical models from these data are then used to translate between those languages. Unfortunately, these requirements are not satisfied with most African languages.

Translation systems

There are two main approaches for developing machine translation. One is a method that makes use of detailed analysis of the source language, and converts the message into the target language by making use of linguistic information and lexicon. The other method makes use of statistical likelihood of correct translation by comparing translation alternatives found in parallel corpus texts.

Statistical Machine Translation (SML)

The increasing calculation power of computers has tempted researchers to test and develop approaches to translation that were totally out of reach during the pre-computer time. An example is machine translation using statistical methods (Koehn 2010). Because statistical methods use calculation in the translation process without human input, these methods have become very popular in translating between major languages. For instance, Google Translate and Microsoft Translator use statistical approaches in their applications. The largest translation consortium, the European Union (EU), also develops translation applications using mostly statistical methods.

Given that statistical machine translation has received wide support and application, it is reasonable to ask if the same methods should be applied to African languages. In order to answer this question, it is necessary to investigate whether African languages have sufficient preconditions for developing successful statistical translation applications.

For statistical translation methods to succeed, two major preconditions must be satisfied, (1) the relative similarity between language pairs, and (2) sufficiently large masses of parallel texts. By parallel texts we mean texts that have been translated from one language to another by humans. The parallel texts form the basis for the translation system to search for translation examples. These texts are used for training the system as well as in the actual translation process of new texts.

Let us consider first the availability of parallel texts for various language pairs. Globally, the translated fiction books form the single largest source of parallel texts. There are millions of books translated by humans into several languages. Only part of this source, if made available, would form a huge source for training SMT systems. Copyright restrictions are an obstacle in using these resources effectively. The European Union's policy is to translate official documents into all EU languages. Also, the United Nations translates its official documents into six official languages. Over the years this work has been done by humans. These carefully translated documents from various domains form a huge database of parallel texts for machine translation. Since all types of new texts have been written using computers for several years, new parallel texts become increasingly available.

If we look at the availability of parallel texts in African languages, the situation is quite different. Apart from Bible translations there are very few parallel texts between African languages. Between former colonial languages and African languages the situation is better, but still far from the amounts needed. In some countries, such as Tanzania and Kenya, some government documents are in the official languages, English and Swahili. These countries use English and Swahili as their official languages. On the part of fiction, there are very few translated books, and even fewer of them are available in computer form. We can conclude that African languages do not have sufficient amounts of parallel texts for statistical machine translation systems to develop.

The second condition for statistical machine translation to succeed is the similarity of source language and target language. Africa has a large number of closely related languages with very similar morphological and syntactic structure. For example, Bantu languages form such a cluster, the joint noun class system and similarity in word order form a fruitful basis for statistical machine translation. However, because parallel texts are not available, the first necessary precondition is not satisfied. Another problem is that the major need for text-based machine translation is between African and European languages and not between two African languages. Therefore, even the second requirement, that is, language similarity, is not satisfied. On the basis of the above one is tempted to draw the conclusion that statistical machine translation is not a viable solution in Africa.

Rule-based machine translation (RBMT)

Fortunately, in addition to statistical approaches, there is also the so-called rule-based, or symbolic, approach to machine translation. This approach in fact was common until the 1990s, and only when large masses of parallel texts became gradually available did statistical approaches start to dominate. The rule-based approach is radically different from the statistical approach. While the latter has nothing to do with linguistics or language theory, the former is entirely based on linguistic knowledge. In the statistical approach, sequences of characters are compared in source text and target text, and the correct translation is selected on the basis of statistical likelihood. Because no language analysis is included in statistical approaches, no generalizations can be made. Therefore, model translations should be found for each surface word sequence. This leads to the requirement for ever-increasing masses of parallel texts.

In rule-based approaches no parallel texts are needed. The basic components are (1) the comprehensive morphological analyzer of the source language, (2) the morphological and semantic disambiguator of the source language, (3) the syntactic analyzer of the source language, (4) a system for isolating multi-word expressions, (5) the bilingual dictionary for transferring the lexical information of the source language into target language, (6) a rule system for converting the lexical forms into surface forms, (7) a rule system for controlling the correct word order in the target language. These are just the basic components, and additional computing for correcting and adjusting the process is needed.

In order to be able to construct the basic components of a rule-based system, one needs (1) a good dictionary of the language, and (2) a thorough knowledge of the grammar of that language. This means that for a non-linguist it is very hard to construct a rule-based system. It is like working out a comprehensive linguistic description of the language. In fact, a comprehensive language analysis system contains more grammatical information and is more accurate than any of the traditional grammar books. The construction process also forces the developer to include in the system such features that are not described in ordinary grammars.

When the language is described on a grammatical level, it is possible to make generalizations. Instead of writing rules for surface phenomena, it is possible to write rules using linguistic tags and thus reduce the need of rule writing drastically. The system will be compact and it can be installed in most environments.

One major weakness of using statistical methods is that it performs poorly in languages with complex morphology. In African languages, especially Bantu, verbs are particularly complex. A verb may have many different forms, at least theoretically. Statistical methods can hardly cover all of the many different forms. In fact, when looking at the output of statistical translation systems, one finds failures especially in their handling of verbs. With rule-based methods it is possible to construct a full-coverage analyzer that never fails to analyze a verb form, or any other form, if it is grammatically correct.

Distrust between SMT and RBMT developers

A research team at Montreal University has suggested a new approach to machine translation (Cho et al. 2014). At the center of the system is a neural network called RNN Encoder-Decoder that consists of two recurrent neural networks (RNN). In this system, one RNN encodes a sequence of symbols (usually words) into a vector representation, and the other RNN decodes the representation into another sequence of symbols. Neural machine translation is in fact an extension of statistical machine translation, and it is not yet known how successful it will be. In any case it requires large masses of parallel corpora and extensive computer power. And, above all, it ignores the explicit linguistic knowledge. The problems encountered in this method include its poor performance with rare words and long sentences, and methods are being sought for solving the problem (Luong et al. 2015).

There is discussion on hybrid approaches, where statistical machine translation is enhanced by introducing linguistic knowledge into the system. What this precisely means is not known. And if the need for linguistic knowledge is acknowledged, why not introduce this knowledge at the start?

Hybrid approach

The research shows that neither SMT nor RBMT produces fully correct text. Both have weaknesses, although of very different kinds. This has led to the idea of hybridization, enhancing the existing system with features of the other. Most often the approach has been to have a statistical approach as a base and the translation result is enhanced with rule-based components (Zbib et al. 2012; Nielssen and Ney 2004). Also, rule-based systems can be enhanced with statistical components (Habash et al. 2009). It is claimed that better translation results can be achieved using a hybrid combination of these approaches (Labaka et al. 2014). Nevertheless, the quality of translation continues to be relatively low and research continues for finding better quality testing methods (Felice and Specia 2013; Birch et al. 2010).

Although SMT is the dominant method in MT, it is not self-evident that it is the best method in most cases. When the source language (SL) and target language (TL) are structurally very different, SML seems to encounter serious problems (Habash et al. 2009). We see the same in examples below.

Comparing Google Translate and SALAMA

In the following section we will make tests with two different systems in translating between structurally very different languages, Swahili and English. Currently the only SML system for

Swahili is Google Translate (GT). And the only fully rule-based system available for translating between Swahili and English is the Swahili Language Manager (SALAMA). Because both systems are 'pure' systems, in that they do not include hybrid components, it is possible to compare the performance of both approaches. The advantage of choosing these languages is that GT will not be put in a disadvantaged position, because English is the core language of the GT system. Therefore, GT does not need to translate via English to a third language, as it normally does. Examples will be given on both translation directions.

Structure of tested translation systems

According to the information available, GT is based on the statistical approach. Apparently, it is to some extent enhanced with morphological analysis, although this component seems elementary. No proper documentation on its structure has been available to us. Documents from the Tanzania government have very likely been used in training the system. This conclusion can be made on the basis of fairly good translation results of these documents on the web.

The SALAMA has a totally different approach. It has no statistical element. It makes heavy use of the grammar and lexicon of the language. In semantic selection, it uses default translation. That is, each lexeme has a default gloss in the target language. This is selected if no rule selects another interpretation. The structure of SALAMA resembles the processing method of OpenLogos (Scott and Barreiro 2009; Barreiro et al. 2011) including a modular pipeline structure.

In the Swahili to English component, the core engine is the morphological analyzer based on finite state technology (Koskenniemi 1983; Hurskainen 1992). In disambiguation and syntactic mapping, as well as in isolating multiword expressions, SALAMA uses Connexor's Constraint Grammar parser (Karlsson 1995; Tapanainen 1996; Hurskainen 1996, 2004).

The English to Swahili translator uses a Dependency Parser for English (Järvinen and Tapanainen 1997) for morphological analysis, disambiguation and syntactic mapping. The result is further modified with several sets of rules written in the Constraint Grammar environment (Tapanainen 1996) and with rewriting rules. The operation of SALAMA is described elsewhere (Hurskainen 2007, 2012).

We demonstrate the differences in performance between Google Translate and SALAMA using example sentences from the news media. There are examples of both translation directions. The purpose of this comparison is to show what the strengths and weaknesses of each approach are in translating between very different languages such as Swahili and English. The aim is not to prove the supremacy of one system over the other.

Examples from Swahili to English translation

(1) *Tunaomba Watanzania wavute subira, tunaelewa kuwa watu wana shauku. Kuhusu jeshi hilo kushindwa kuwakamata watuhumiwa katika matukio ya milipuko ya awali iliyotokea Arusha, Jumapili alisema hata wahalifu na walioko nyuma ya matukio haya ni werevu na wana akili za kukwepa mkono wa dola.*
GT

> We Tanzanians NO patience, we understand that people are interested. About the army fail to arrest suspects in cases of initial explosions occurred Arusha on Sunday said that criminals and those behind these events are smart and do not mind the dodgy hand of dollars.

SALAMA

We ask the Tanzanians to be patient, we understand that the people have desire. Concerning this troop to fail to catch the suspects in the events of the first explosions which happened in Arusha, Jumapili said even the lawbreakers and who are there behind these events are wise and have intelligence of avoiding the hand of the state.

Comments

Google Translate apparently does not have the means for identifying multiword expressions. The string *wavute subira* is a form of the multiword expression *vuta* 'pull' *subira* 'patience'. Put together they mean 'be patient'. SALAMA has isolated it and translates it correctly.

Google Translate does not translate the string *jeshi hilo* correctly as a troop attempting to arrest the suspects. Instead it interprets that soldiers are accused. The proper name *Jumapili* is not recognized as a person name but translated as 'Sunday'. The string *wana akili* is translated as 'intelligent children' instead of 'have intelligence'. GT translated *dola* as 'dollar', although it means here 'state'.

Example (2) demonstrates problems encountered in translating complex verb forms.

(2) *Mwenyekiti wa Bunge, Samuel Sitta alisema tayari amekwishawasiliana na Rais Kikwete kuhusu vikao vya Bunge analoliongoza.*
   GT

   Chairman of the National Assembly, Samuel Sitta said already kwishawasiliana and President Kikwete about the sessions he loliongoza.

SALAMA

   The chairman of Parliament, Samuel Sitta said already he has communicated with President Kikwete concerning the sessions of the Parliament which he leads.

Comments

The sentence has two common verbs that GT fails to translate, obviously because of their complicated structure. It seems that in the current development phase GT tries to figure out the subject prefix and some tenses of the verb only. However, here it fails to identify the extended tense marker *mekwisha*. If the verb has other prefixes, such as relative and object prefix, the system fails. The verbs *wasiliana* and *ongoza* are frequent verbs and they should be recognized by the system. The word *Bunge* disappears mysteriously.

Concordance and word order are important features of Swahili. In translating from Swahili to English, concordance is not a problem, but word order of long noun phrases might be.

(3) *Vitabu vyangu vizuri vile vitatu vilivyowapendeza wanafunzi vimekutwa baada ya kutafutwa.*
   GT

   My books vilivyowapendeza well as three students vimekutwa after searchable.

SALAMA

   Those my three good books which pleased the students have been found after searching.

Comments

Here is a test sentence to see how the two systems translate long noun phrases. All words belong to the core vocabulary. However, the verbs *vilivyowapendeza* and *vimekutwa* are unknown to GT. The words *vitabu vyangu vizuri vile vitatu* belong to the same noun phrase meaning 'those my three good books', but GT recognizes only the first two of them and then messes up the rest. Also the string *baada ya kutafutwa* is interpreted in a strange way. There are two overlapping multiword expression candidates, *baada ya* (after) and *ya kutafutwa* (searchable). Google Translate chooses the latter one and translates it as 'searchable', but by so doing it loses the latter part of *baada ya*. Yet GT translates it happily as 'after', although *baada* without a referent cannot have a sensible meaning.

One of the most difficult problems in machine translation is how to handle multiword expressions (MWE) so that correct translation can be generated. There are several types of multiword expressions. The example in (4) contains perhaps the most difficult case to implement. The MWE has four components, two of its words inflect, and the structure is arbitrarily discontinuous. This means that the head word of the MWE *nyumba* is detached from the rest *za kulala wageni*. Yet the structure has the meaning 'guest house' that inflects in singular and plural.

(4) *nyumba zangu nzuri na ghali hizo tatu za kulala wageni*
    GT

    my beautiful and expensive houses three guest

SALAMA

    these my three good and expensive guest houses

Comments

The example demonstrates the ability of the systems to control word order as well as to isolate discontinuous multiword expressions. *Nymba zangu nzuri na ghali hizo tatu* would be a noun phrase in itself. However, in this case also the words *za kulala wageni* are part of the noun phrase, because the words *nyumba* and *za kulala wageni* together constitute a multiword expression meaning 'guest houses'. Google Translate loses the words *hizo* and *za kulala*. The word 'three' is in the wrong place, and if *wageni* is translated as 'guest', it should be in plural. As a whole, the translation does not make sense. The SALAMA masters even cases of complicated word order. Particularly noteworthy is that it also handles discontinuous multiword expressions correctly, even such ones where parts of structure have an unknown distance from each other.

Examples from English to Swahili translation

In this section we test how Google Translate and SALAMA translate some complex word and sentence structures. We pay attention particularly to word order, concordance, and correct word formation in the target language. The examples below were extracted from Kenyan and Tanzanian English newspapers, and from the Internet.

Arvi Hurskainen

(5) Post-editing, or the editing done to improve machine-translated content to a publishable quality, has long been part of the translation repertoire in one form or another.
  GT

> *Post-editing, au editing kufanyika ili kuboresha mashine-kutafsiriwa maudhui ya publishable ubora, kwa muda mrefu imekuwa sehemu ya tafsiri ya Répertoire katika namna moja au nyingine.*

SALAMA

> *Uhariri wa kufanyika tena, au uhariri kuboresha maudhui iliyotafsiriwa kwa mashine kwa ubora tayari kwa kuchapisha, kwa muda mrefu umekuwa sehemu ya mkusanyiko wa maonyesho wa tafasiri katika umbo moja au jingine.*

Comments

Google Translate does not recognize words 'post-editing' or 'editing'. The word 'done' is translated with the stative infinitive form of the verb *fanya* 'do'. In the word 'machine-translated' the latter part is not recognized. The word 'publishable' is also unknown. In the verb *imekuwa* there is the wrong subject marker. It should be 'u' to refer to the subject *uhariri* of the noun class 11. The word 'repertoire' is strangely translated as *Répertoire*.

(6) This now commonplace tool has brought with it gains in productivity, more efficient resource management, and incredible value in research and development of MT itself – popular data-driven methods like Google Translate are largely reliant on human translations!
  GT

> *Hii chombo sasa ni kawaida umeleta faida katika tija, usimamizi wa rasilimali na ufanisi zaidi, na thamani ya ajabu katika utafiti na maendeleo ya MT yenyewe – mbinu maarufu data inayotokana kama Google Tafsiri kwa kiasi kikubwa ni kujitegemea juu ya tafsiri ya binadamu!*

SALAMA

> *Hii ala ya kawaida sasa imeleta nayo manufaa katika tija, menejimenti fanisi zaidi ya viingizia, na thamani isiyoaminika katika utafiti na maendeleo ya MT yenyewe – mbinu zenye msingi katika data zinazopendwa kama Google Translate ni zenye kutegemea kwa kiasi kikubwa tafsiri za kibinadamu!*

Comments

It is impossible to know where the subject prefix 'u' comes from in *umeleta*, because neither *chombo* nor *kawaida* belong to noun classes that agree with 'u'. Also, the translation of the first part is wrong and the words 'with it' are without translation. The sequence 'more efficient resource management' is translated as *usimamizi wa rasilmali na ufanisi zaidi*, although it should be *menejimenti fanisi zaidi ya viingizia*. The adjective 'data-driven' is translated as *data inayotokana*, although the more correct translation would be *inayotokana na data*.

Also, the adjective 'reliant', translated as *ni kujitegemea*, is not grammatically correct, and the verb should not have the reflexive prefix *–ji-*. The string 'human translations' is plural. Also 'Google Translate' is a named entity and should not be translated.

In the example in (7) we test how the systems handle long noun phrases and concordance.

(7) Those my three good and expensive books that pleased students have been found.
   GT

Wale yangu vitabu vitatu nzuri na gharama kubwa kuwa radhi wanafunzi zimepatikana.

SALAMA

Vitabu vyangu vizuri na ghali vile vitatu ambavyo viliwapendeza wanafunzi vimepatikana.

Comments

This example demonstrates how the systems handle long noun phrases. The words 'those my three good and expensive books' constitute a noun phrase. Google Translate gives a translation for each word, but it is not able to control the word order or concordance. The failure is understandable because GT does not control word order or concordance with grammatical rules. On the other hand, SALAMA has translated the sentence correctly. For a rule-based system, even long noun phrases are not a problem, because the concordance rules as well as word order rules control the translation.

(8) *The Nation* established that the Cord team had received crucial information from Safaricom which lawyers were using to analyse the results released by the IEBC.
   GT

Taifa imara kwamba Cord timu walipokea habari muhimu kutoka Safaricom ambayo wanasheria walikuwa kutumia kuchambua matokeo iliyotolewa na IEBC.

SALAMA

The Nation lilihakikisha kwamba timu ya Cord ilikuwa imepokea taarifa nyeti kutoka Safaricom wanasheria gani wakikuwa wakitumia kuainisha matokeo yaliyotolewa na IEBC.

Comments

The name of the newspaper is *The Nation* and it should not be translated. The verb 'established' is translated with the adjective *imara*. The past perfective form 'had received' is translated with past tense *walipokea*, but with the subject prefix of the wrong class. The correct translation is *ilikuwa imepokea*. Again, 'were using' is translated so that the first verb is inflected correctly, but the second one is in infinitive *kutumia*. It should be *walikuwa wakitumia*. Again, GT does not get the relative structure correct. There is an attempt to form the relative verb structure *iliyotolewa*, but the concordance is wrong. The SALAMA misinterpreted the word 'which' as an interrogative pronoun and translated it as *gani*.

Discussion

The examples above demonstrate the types of problems that a SMT has in translating between languages such as Swahili and English. The same text translated with the RBMT system shows the main differences in performance between these two systems. Below we sum up the findings of the translation tests.

Assessment of Swahili to English translation

Many kinds of problems can be found in translating from Swahili to English. Here we discuss some of them.

Identification of word forms

There occur frequently such word forms in Swahili that GT does not recognize. The reason is probably not the small number of the so-called 'words' included in the system. Many such lexical words that are not recognized are probably listed in the system. Problems come from the vast number of different forms that the word may take. In particular, Swahili verbs are a nightmare for a statistically operating translation system because each Swahili verb may have millions of surface forms, at least in theory. Also, in practice, some commonly occurring verbs were found to have more than 2,000 different forms each in a small corpus of 2 million words.

The SALAMA is based on the analysis of each word form. While it is using finite-state methods, it is possible to describe even very complicated word structures, such as Swahili verbs. Therefore, if SALAMA encounters an unknown word, it is probably a typo or a word of a different language. Such unknown words do not affect the basic translation process.

Handling multiword expressions (MWEs)

Google Translate does not have proper means for handling MWEs. Names of companies, government agencies and titles seem to have been handled to a large extent in GT. However, these are the simplest types of MWEs because they are 'frozen'. They do not inflect and they do not allow other words within the word cluster. The majority of Swahili MWEs inflect and some of them allow other words within the MWE word cluster.

It is also very important to note that a word cluster that is a MWE in one context is not necessarily that in another context. Therefore, MWEs must be defined in an environment where text context can be made use of for concluding whether the word cluster is a MWE or not in that particular context.

Furthermore, there must be a mechanism for identifying the members of the MWE in non-continuous MWEs for producing the correct translation, including the correct word order.

The SALAMA has addressed the problems of treating the MWEs. They are handled in the environment where rules can be written for constraining the application of rules. Therefore, each type of constraint can be handled. Such constraints include the context in sentence, the need to inflect the MWE cluster, the need to allow other words within the MWE, and the need to (re)define the part of speech of the MWE. The correct definition is important in producing correct surface text.

Handling complex noun phrases

The performance of the two translation systems in handling noun phrases was tested in examples (3), (4) and (7) above. The example sentences were constructed according to

Sustainable language technology for African languages

grammatical rules. Google Translate apparently knows that a numeral follows the noun, and that an adjective follows the noun. However, the way the GT system combines word pairs is incomprehensible. How is it possible that from the string *vitatu vilivyowapendeza wanafunzi* one can get a translation 'three students'? This even violates the basic rule that the noun precedes the numeral.

The SALAMA translates long noun phrases according to grammatical rules. This is possible because the system first makes a detailed analysis of each word form and then makes use of the tags in constructing disambiguation and mapping rules. Even complicated grammatical phrases are not a problem for SALAMA.

Handling proper names

Correct treatment of proper names in MT is very problematic. Various types of proper names require different treatment. Some proper names, such as person names, are transferred to TL as such. However, many person names have a form that could also be an ordinary word. If such a word is inside the sentence and begins with a capital initial, it is likely a proper name. Example (1) demonstrates this. Yet GT interprets *Jumapili* as an ordinary word and translates it as 'on Sunday'. The SALAMA identifies it as a person name. If such a word begins the sentence, the problem is even bigger, because all sentence initial words have a capital initial.

The only safe solution for handling ambiguous proper names is to give to such words two interpretations, one for ordinary word and one for proper name. The selection is then made using context-sensitive rules, which sometimes are very complex.

Such proper names that are multiword expressions are easier to handle because they do not get easily mixed with ordinary words. Names of ministries and organizations are examples of easy cases.

Comparison of GT and SALAMA in Swahili to English MT

The methods used by these systems to translate are very different. Because SALAMA is based on language analysis, it does not normally encounter unknown words, except new proper names and words of other languages. The SALAMA analyzes and translates the most complicated verb structures, including verb compounds.

Google Translate produces sometimes excellent translation. This is the case especially when the source text is close to what was used in training the system. Then sometimes it messes up the text completely, leaves out words, changes the part-of-speech category, etc.

SALAMA is weak in producing correct articles in English, because Swahili does not use articles. Only the presence or absence of the definite article is implemented. The indefinite article is not produced in the current system. Due to its approach, GT is sometimes able to produce also a correct indefinite article.

Assessment of English to Swahili translation

Coverage of vocabulary

It could be expected that because the SL English is an isolating language, GT would have equivalents for common words. Example (5) above has four unknown English words. The SALAMA has identified all the words because it has an extensive analysis system of English and a large dictionary for mapping the Swahili equivalents.

Complex verb forms

The correct production of Swahili verb forms is a nightmare for GT. Some common and simple verb forms are produced correctly, but it does not even make an attempt to translate forms with relative and object prefixes. The SALAMA translates even the most complicated verb structures. This is possible because the system first produces the appropriate tags and then converts them to surface form. An example of a compound verb is in (8) above. Google Translate translates the words 'the Cord team had received' as *Cord timu walipokea*. The SALAMA translates it as *timu ya Cord ilikuwa imepokea*. The form in English is past perfective, and it should be translated using the auxiliary verb *kuwa*.

Concordance

Perhaps the worst nightmare for statistical MT is the production of concordance in noun phrases and verb phrases. A revealing example is (7). It has seven words that have to agree with *vitabu* 'books'. It is a noun of class 8. In GT translation, none of the seven words has the correct agreement marker. The last words 'have been found' was translated otherwise correctly, but the subject prefix concordance was wrong. This example suggests that GT has no method for controlling class agreement. In verbs, the default seems to be class 9 for singular and class 10 for plural, if the subject is not animate.

Mapping of words and word order

English and Swahili have very different word orders. It is also common that a word is mapped to a cluster of words, and a cluster of words is mapped to a single word. Furthermore, Swahili uses verb prefixes, such as subject, relative and object prefixes, to mark expressions that are represented by separate words in English. All this complicates translation. The SALAMA has a system for handling these phenomena on the basis of grammar. Google Translate seems to have problems with MWEs, verb prefixes, and with word order in noun and verb phrases.

Problems in detecting translation errors

Developers of SMT systems are well aware that it is often very difficult to know why translation failed. Therefore, research has been done on finding better ways for finding the sources of failure (Wisniewski et al. 2013). The solution often used is to accumulate more parallel texts in the belief that, when there is more material, the likelihood of finding correct matches improves. Larger corpora also produce better statistics of alternative translations.

In working with RBMT systems, especially if the structure of the system is modular, it is always possible to detect the source of translation error. To know what is the best way to correct the error requires deep knowledge of the system and experience in trying various methods. At which point in the processing sequence should the correction be made? How general should the new rule be so that it has a maximum effect without causing wrong translation elsewhere? Such considerations are necessary for optimizing the translation system.

Applications derivable from the rule-based approach

In addition to MT, the rule-based approach makes it possible to develop a number of other high quality applications. Below we discuss some of them.

Spelling checkers and linguistic taggers

A comprehensive and accurate morphological tagger alone, without disambiguation, is an excellent resource for such applications as spelling checkers and dictionary search. Spelling checkers help to identify typing errors and are therefore useful for anybody who types text. The morphological analyzer can be used for helping in the use of electronic dictionaries, because the analyzer finds the base form of inflected words. The dictionary user may type any form of the word and the system leads the user to the dictionary entry of the base form. We will discuss more on dictionaries below in the section 'Dictionary compilation'.

If the morphological analyzer is enhanced with a disambiguating module, this tool can be used for tagging text corpora. The so-called POS-tagged corpora are produced using such tools. In addition to this basic POS-tagging, many kinds of features can be added to the analyzer. These include syntactic mapping, morphological and syntactic features, and even lexical glosses in another language. For example, the Helsinki Corpus of Swahili 2.0 with 25 million words was tagged using such an extensive tagger (http://urn.fi/urn:nbn:fi:lb-2014032624).

Dictionary compilation

If the language analysis system is carefully constructed so that it has high-quality components, it is possible to use the system for converting a corpus into a dictionary (Hurskainen 2008). Not only must the analysis system have high recall and precision scores, but also the disambiguation system must be high quality so that ambiguity can be resolved reliably. This is particularly important for finding the correct examples of use in text, as well as for producing correct frequency counts. The isolation of multiword expressions adds to the value of the result because constructions of more than one word can also be searched.

If we consider languages that have no proper dictionary but which have a sizeable amount of written texts, these texts could be collected as a corpus and made use of for compiling a dictionary.

Advantages of the system include: (1) the word to be searched can be typed in any inflected form; (2) no lexical words are omitted; (3) word frequencies in the corpus will be available; (4) cross-references will be produced; (5) multiword expressions can also be searched; (6) example sentences will be retrieved – together with translation if such an application is provided.

Even a large corpus contains only part of the words used in communication. The dictionary system can be enlarged by also adding such words that do not occur in the corpus. In this case, the system produces only the default lexical information of the word without examples of use.

Perhaps the most fascinating feature in such modern dictionaries is that any form of the word can be entered, and the system finds the base form of the word and all information attached to it. This requires that a morphological analyzer first processes the entered word to find out the base form and possibly other morphological information, which is then used in searching matches.

If the dictionary is initially compiled from a Swahili corpus, the result is a Swahili–English dictionary. Such a dictionary can, with little effort, be converted into an English–Swahili dictionary. When the user enters an English word, the system produces all glosses of that word in Swahili, together with use examples on the basis of Swahili equivalents. In this application, however, the word must be typed in base form. Inflected forms cannot be used because the system does not include an analyzer of English.

Dictionary testing

With the help of a comprehensive morphological analyzer it is possible to test the quality of dictionaries (Hurskainen 2002). The existing master lexicon is first reduced to match the lexical entries of the dictionary to be tested. Then this reduced lexicon is used for analyzing the text corpus. For example, if the dictionary was intended for normal text, such as used in news media, a large corpus of news texts is suitable for testing. The test result shows two things. First, it shows such words that were not recognized. This means that these words used in text were not included in the dictionary. Second, it also shows such words in the dictionary that were never used in text. In other words, the system reveals how well the dictionary covers the language used in news texts.

Intelligent language learning systems

Each language type has some learning areas that are particularly difficult to grasp. Bantu languages use a noun class system that results in complicated agreement patterns across the sentence structure. Learning the use of all noun classes with their class markers, including exceptions, is a nontrivial task. For the learner, it is often difficult to make sure that the structure is correct. Printed grammar books normally have serious gaps in advising the learner. And at the very least it is often very difficult to find the place where the problem is discussed.

With the help of the complete language analysis system it is possible to construct many types of modules for helping the student in learning (Dickinson and Herring 2008; Hurskainen 2009, 2010). The learner can test whether the expression is grammatically correct. The system responds if the string has a mistake, the system informs about the type of error and gives advice on how to proceed. Errors can be in typing the word, in concordance, in word order, etc. The learner is interactively advised until the expression is correct.

In addition to testing the structures, several types of guided lessons can be constructed. Self-tutoring learning courses can be constructed. The learner does not necessarily need a human tutor; the system functions as a tutor. The system does not have limitations in regard to vocabulary or word forms. All of several millions of word forms can be used in learning.

Vocabulary compiler

The language teacher as well as the learner are often in a situation where the translation of a new text is cumbersome. Dictionaries do not always help and their use takes unnecessarily much time. By using a sophisticated language analyzer it is possible to compile vocabularies for any text. The vocabulary list is produced so that first the whole text is analyzed. Then the most frequent words are removed and only less frequent words are retained. The length of the vocabulary list can be tuned according to the level of the learner. A beginner needs longer lists than an advanced learner.

Bootstrapping the rule-based approach to other languages

Because under-resourced languages have a constant shortage of finance for developing language technology, it would be wise to make use of existing technology. The rule-based approach does not require parallel corpora or any other types of massive data sources. The basic requirements include a dictionary and a grammar for modelling the morphological analyzer. More advanced applications require a good environment for writing rules for disambiguation and syntactic mapping, as well as for isolating MWEs.

A technology developed and thoroughly tested for one language can be applied to another language, especially if the languages have similar features. Therefore, a system developed for Swahili can be transferred without major effort to other Bantu languages.

It is often argued that rule-based language technology is expensive to develop compared with statistical approaches. It is true, because rule writing is a human activity and as a task is far from trivial. However, if the grammar is properly integrated into the system, it is done for future generations and other applications can be developed on this basis.

For example, an intelligent language learning system, earlier developed for Swahili, was applied to learning Runyakitara spoken in Uganda (Katushemererwe and Hurskainen 2011). Mapping between disjoining and conjoining writing systems in Bantu languages was also developed for two Bantu languages, Kwanyama and Northern Sotho (Hurskainen and Halme 2001; Hurskainen et al. 2005, 2006).

Conclusion

This chapter demonstrates the strengths and weaknesses of statistical and rule-based machine translation systems. The content of the chapter is somewhat provocative. It reminds us that if statistical methods continue to predominate, most of the world's languages will be marginalized. The gap between dominant and local languages is going to increase. With the help of tests made on the performance of both kinds of translation systems, we hope to have demonstrated that rule-based translation systems are suitable for machine translation of highly inflectional languages. Computers offer huge potential for global human communication, and only a fraction of their possibilities has been used. However, it is dangerous to believe that mathematical calculations and algorithms alone can solve translation problems. Human knowledge of how languages behave is a huge resource. That knowledge should be fed into the translation process, and from the beginning and not only when statistical methods fail.

It is possible to develop high-quality language applications, such as MT, for an under-resourced language, without extensive language resources. This suggests that no technical barrier exists for extending viable language technology to less resourced languages, including languages with complex inflection and derivation. The tests made in this chapter even suggest that SMT between such languages as Bantu languages and English encounters no insurmountable problems. The development of language resources needed for rule-based technology requires a covering dictionary of the language and knowledge of its grammar. Several applications can be developed on the basis of these resources.

Note

1 61/295. United Nations Declaration on the Rights of Indigenous Peoples.

References

Bamgbose, A. (1991). *Language and the Nation. The Language Question in Sub-Saharan Africa*. Edinburgh: Edinburgh University Press for the International African Institute.

Bamgbose, A. (2000). *Language and Exclusion: The Consequences of Language Policies in Africa*. Hamburg: LIT Verlag Munster.

Barreiro, A., Scott, B., Kasper, W. and Kiefer, B. (2011). "OpenLogos machine translation: philosophy, model, resources and customization." *Machine Translation*, 25(2), 107–126.

Birch, A., Osborne, M. and Blunsom, P. (2010). "Metrics for MT evaluation: evaluating reordering." *Machine Translation*, 24(1), 15–26.

Cho, K., van Merrienboer, B., Bahdanau, D. and Bengio, Y. (2014). "On the properties of neural machine translation: encoder–decoder approaches." In *Proceedings of SSST-8, Eighth Workshop on Syntax, Semantics and Structure in Statistical Translation*, D. Wu, M. Carpuat, X. Carreras, E. M. Vecchi (eds). Stroudsburg: ACL.

Dickinson, M. and Herring, J. (2008). "Russian Morphological Processing for ICALL". *The Fifth Midwest Computational Linguistics Colloquium (MCLC-5)*. East Lansing, MI.

Felice, M. and Specia, L. (2013). "Investigating the contribution of linguistic information to quality estimation." *Machine Translation*, 27(3–4), 193–212.

Habash, N., Dorr, B. and Monz, C. (2009). "Symbolic-to-statistical hybridization: extending generation-heavy machine translation." *Machine Translation*, 23(1), 23–63.

Hurskainen, A. (1992). "A two-level computer formalism for the analysis of Bantu morphology: an application to Swahili." *Nordic Journal of African Studies*, 1(1), 87–122.

Hurskainen, A. (1996). "Disambiguation of morphological analysis in Bantu languages." *Proceedings of COLING-96*, Proceedings of the 16th conference on Computational Linguistics, Volume 1, pp. 568–573. Stroudsburg, PA.

Hurskainen, A. (2002). "Tathmini ya kamusi tano ya Kiswahili (Computer evaluation of five Swahili dictionaries)." *Nordic Journal of African Studies*, 11(2), 283–300, ISSN 1235-4481.

Hurskainen, A. (2004). "Optimizing disambiguation in Swahili." In *Proceedings of COLING-04*, The 20th International Conference on Computational Linguistics, Geneva 23–27 August, pp. 254–260.

Hurskainen, A. (2007). "A rule-based environment for Swahili development." *MultiLingual*, 18(8), 53–58, ISSN 1523-0309.

Hurskainen, A. (2008). "SALAMA dictionary compiler: a method for corpus-based dictionary compilation." *Technical Reports in Language Technology*. Report No 2, www.njas.helsinki.fi/salama.

Hurskainen, A. (2009). "Intelligent computer-assisted language learning: implementation to Swahili." *Technical Reports in Language Technology*, Report No 3, www.njas.helsinki.fi/salama.

Hurskainen, A. (2010) "Language learning system using language analysis and disambiguation." *Technical Reports in Language Technology*, Report No 9, www.njas.helsinki.fi/salama.

Hurskainen, A. (2012). "Quality Swahili machine translation." *MultiLingual*, 23(7), 39–42, ISSN 1523-0309.

Hurskainen, A. and Halme, R. (2001) "Mapping between disjoining and conjoining writing systems in Bantu languages: implementation on Kwanyama." *Nordic Journal of African Studies*, 10(3), 399–414, ISSN 1235-4481.

Hurskainen, A., Louwrens, L. and Poulos, G. (2005). "Computational description of verbs in disjoining writing systems." *Nordic Journal of African Studies*, 14(4), 438–451, ISSN 1235-4481.

Hurskainen, A., Louwrens, L. and Poulos, G. (2006) "Describing verbs in disjoining writing systems. In finite-state methods in natural language processing." *Proceedings of the Workshop on Finite State Methods and Natural Language Processing*, held September 1–2 2005 in Helsinki, A. Yli-Jyrä, L. Karttunen and J. Karhumäki (eds), FSMNLP 2005, LNAI 4002, pp. 292–294. Berlin and Heidelberg: Springer Verlag.

Järvinen, T. and Tapanainen, P. (1997). "A dependency parser for English." *Technical Reports*, No. TR-1. Department of General Linguistics, University of Helsinki.

Karlsson, F. (1995). "Designing a parser for unrestricted text." In Karlsson F. et al. (eds), *Constraint Grammar: A Language-Independent System for Parsing Unrestricted Text*, 1–40. Berlin: Mouton de Gryuter.

Katushemererwe, F. and Hurskainen, A. (2011). "Intelligent computer assisted language learning system: implementation on Runyakitara". In M. Kizza (ed.) Vol. VII, *Special Topics in Computing and ICT Research*. Kampala, Uganda: Fountain Publishers.

Koehn, P. (2010). *Statistical Machine Translation*. Cambridge: Cambridge University Press.

Koskenniemi, K. (1983). *Two-Level Morphology: A General Computational Model for Word-Form Recognition and Production*, Publication No. 11. Department of General Linguistics, University of Helsinki.

Labaka, G., España-Bonet, C., Màrquez, L. and Sarasola, K. (2014). "A hybrid machine translation architecture guided by syntax." *Machine Translation*, 28(2), 99–125.

Luong, M., Ilya, S., Quoc, V. L., Oriol, V. and Wojciech, Z. (2015). *Addressing the Rare Word Problem in Neural Machine Translation*, arXiv:1410.8206 [cs.CL].

Myers-Scotton, C. (1990). "Elite closure as boundary maintenance: the case of Africa." *International Journal of the Sociology of Language*, 103, 149–163.

Nielssen, S. and Ney, H. (2004). "Statistical machine translation with scarce resources using morpho-syntactic information." *Computational Linguistics*, 30(2), 181–204.

Nakamura, S. (2009). "Overcoming the Language Barrier with Speech Translation Technology." *Science & Technology Trends – Quarterly Review*, No. 31.

Och, F. (2005). *Statistical Machine Translation: Foundations and Recent Advances*. Google, retrieved December 1, 2016.

Och, F. (2006). *Statistical Machine Translation Live*. Google Research Blog, April 28.

Scott, B. and Barreiro, A. (2009). "OpenLogos MT and the SAL representation language." In *Proceedings of the First International Workshop on Free/Open-Source Rule-Based Machine Translation*, Juan Antonio Pérez-Ortiz, Felipe Sánchez-Martínez and Francis M. Tyers (eds). Alicante, Spain: Universidad de Alicante, Departamento de Lenguajes y Sistemas Informáticos. 2–3 November, pp. 19–26.

Tapanainen, P. (1996). *The Constraint Grammar Parser CG-2*. Publications No. 27. Department of General Linguistics, University of Helsinki.

Turovsky, B. (2016). *Found in Translation: More Accurate, Fluent Sentences in Google Translate*. The Keyword Google Blog. Google, retrieved March 23.

Wisniewski, G., Singh, A. K. and Yvon, F. (2013). "Quality estimation for machine translation: some lessons learned." *Machine Translation*, 27(3–4), 213–238.

Zbib, R., Kayser, M., Matsoukas, S., Makhoul, J., Nader, H., Soliman, H. and Safadi, R. (2012). "Methods for integrating rule-based and statistical systems for Arabic to English machine translation." *Machine Translation*, 26(1–2), 67–83.

19

LANGUAGE PLANNING FOR SUSTAINABLE DEVELOPMENT

Problems and prospects in Ghana

Paul Agbedor

Introduction

Countries all over the world are concerned with development issues, and each year they try to determine the state of their economies. They consider economic markers such as GDP, GNP, per capita income, and other economic indicators. Politicians and economists try to identify the factors that affect the state of their economies. They consider employment rates, provision of energy for industries to thrive, workers' remuneration issues, health-care provision and education as the major issues for consideration in the developmental agenda. Hardly ever do they consider the role of language in the equation. This chapter examines the role of language planning in the development of Ghana and shows that the indigenous languages of Ghana have very important roles to play in sustainable development, which involve two important ingredients – education and development communication. We begin by examining the notion of language planning and a few definitions.

Definitions of language planning

When we talk of 'planning', a majority of people think of economic planning and town and country planning. People hardly ever think of language being planned. The notion of language planning, as an academic discipline, is a young one, but has attracted tons of research. Language Planning (henceforth LP) is an interdisciplinary field that emerged as a branch of sociolinguistics in the 1950s and 1960s. It became a very popular discipline during the period of colonialism across the world, where the colonial masters had to deal with the multiplicity of languages in the various colonies, most of them in Africa. European missionaries who went into these colonies to introduce a new religion – Christianity – could be described as the first language planners. They were engaged in developing grammars, writing systems and dictionaries for the indigenous languages of the colonies. This was followed by the translation of the Bible into those indigenous languages to facilitate the conversion to Christianity, by making it possible for the converts to read the Bible in their own languages. These activities fall under what is referred to as language planning. Among the early language planning scholars are: Haugen (1969); Kloss (1966); Fishman (1968, 1971); Rubin and Jernudd (1971); Weinstein (1980); Cooper (1989); and Tollefson (1991).

The term language planning has been defined in various ways, but I will provide three main definitions here. The first one is by Fishman (1971), who defines it as: "the organized pursuit of solutions to language problems, usually at the national level." Weinstein (1980: 55) defines it as: "government-authorized, long term sustained and conscious effort to alter a language itself or to change a language's function in a society for the purpose of solving communication problems." Cooper (1989: 45) sees language planning as: "deliberate efforts to influence the behavior of others with respect to the acquisition, structure, or functional allocation of their language codes."

Fishman's definition seems quite broad in the sense that it talks of solutions to language problems, which can be varied. But he specifically indicates that it is a national issue, not an individual one. Weinstein's definition is more specific by drawing attention to specific characteristics of language planning, that is, it is long term, sustained and conscious. Like Fishman, he also ascribes language planning to a national authority, but, to him, the aim of language planning is to solve communication problems. Apart from that, Weinstein's definition points at two types of activities that LP performs – it either makes changes in the language itself or changes the functions of the language. The former is what Kloss (1966) terms *corpus planning*, and the latter is termed *status planning*. Perhaps the most elaborate definition is that of Cooper (1989), which captures the two types of LP in Weinstein's definition and adds a third one, which is *acquisition planning*.

These definitions show that there are three main types of language planning, namely *status*, *corpus* and *acquisition* planning. Status planning has to do with the allocation of functions to languages in a nation. Some of these functions include: official language, national language, regional language, language of education, language of the media. Decisions to determine these functions for various languages are status planning decisions. Corpus planning deals with changes in the language system itself. These changes may include: deciding on a writing system and type of script, writing grammars of the languages, vocabulary expansion, standardization, making dictionaries, etc. Corpus planning may take place in response to a status planning decision. For example, if a language has its status raised to a national language, then that language has to undergo corpus planning to put it into writing if it has not yet been written. If it is already written, then vocabulary expansion becomes necessary for it to perform the new functions assigned to it. Acquisition planning has to do with efforts to promote the learning and use of a language. This may also be necessitated by a status planning decision. Using the previous illustration, if a language is raised to the status of national language, then efforts have to be made to spread the learning and use of the language as widely as possible.

In a nutshell, we can describe language planning as any activity that assigns functions to languages, or works on the structures of a language, or promotes the learning and use of a language. All these activities are aimed at solving problems of communication within a community or state.

The notion of development

The goal of development is often assumed to be economic, i.e., to increase national output and wealth, often by industrialization. The traditional indicator of economic development in this view of development is the Gross National Product (GNP). When development studies began as a field of study after the Second World War, it was taken for granted that the main problem was simply how to provide economic growth. Once this was done, it was assumed, the wealth thereby created would sooner or later 'trickle down' to the grassroots and make people better off – although this might not happen right away (Foster-Carter, 1985). This view was never universally accepted, however, and in recent years it has been widely criticized. Current thinking about development is summed up in Bodomo (1996). It asserts that development involves socio-cultural, political and economic transformation. In other words, a high GNP does not necessarily make each individual in a country economically self-sufficient. Real development ensures that every individual can meet his/her needs through his/her own capability. This individual development automatically translates into the development of the entire nation.

Sustainable development

There is currently a global concern about the environment and more and more people and governments are talking about 'sustainable development'. Sustainable development is defined as "development that meets the needs of the present without compromising the ability of future generations to meet their own needs" (WCED, 1987: 43). This definition is well-captured in the English proverb "live and let live." In other words, the present generation should live their lives in such a way that the future generations can also live a full life. We must not destroy the environment for the future generations to suffer the consequences.

Most human activities in pursuit of economic growth do a lot of damage to the environment, as they put pressure on environmental resources. The essential needs of vast numbers of people in the developing world – for food, clothing, shelter – are not being met. Meeting these needs requires not only a new era of economic growth for nations in which the majority are poor, but "an assurance that the poor get their fair share of the resources required to sustain that growth" (WCED, 1987: 8). Such equity would be aided by political systems that secure effective citizen participation in decision making. Sustainable development, therefore, is not a fixed state of harmony, but rather a process of change in which the exploitation of resources, the direction of investments, the orientation of technological development, and institutional change are made consistent with future as well as present needs. Since sustainable development involves full participation of all citizens, the educational system should provide all citizens with the basic education necessary for their participation in sustainable development programs. Since language is a vital tool in human communication (and, therefore, vital in education), it is important that people are instructed, educated or informed in a language they can handle for fuller understanding and participation. This calls for community-based language policies that will take into consideration the specific language situation in each community. The language of education is, therefore, very crucial in multilingual societies like Ghana.

The ingredients of development

Having explored the notion of development, let us discuss and examine some of the factors that can be considered as ingredients to development. In other words, what are the factors that drive positive development of a nation? When we consider the current thinking of development (Bodomo, 1996), what can be called the 'full life' notion of development, then we are not looking at only basic needs like food, clothing, shelter and health, but a total development of the people, that is, we have to consider the economic, social, and political development of each individual, which translates into the development of the entire nation. The economic, social and political indicators of development can be enhanced through the natural resources that a nation has, education, which provides knowledge and skills to exploit the resources, and the capacity to sustain and preserve the positive practices that would help maintain a high standard of living for the future generations. Of all these factors, education (both formal and informal), and communication seem to be the most crucial because a country that has many natural resources but does not have the know-how to exploit these resources, will remain poor. Apart from giving us the knowledge and skills to manage the resources, education can also promote our social and political development. Education helps people to become conscious about the environment and how to preserve it for the future generations. It will also help people to adopt best practices as far as their occupations and health are concerned; education will help people in their political awareness and the exercise of their civic rights and responsibilities. Effective communication of government policies also leads to economic, social and political development. In the following sections we take a closer look at education and communication.

Multilingualism, education and development

We have identified education as a crucial element in development, and that language is the most important tool through which education is carried out. Therefore, the role of language in development cannot be overemphasized. However, education delivery becomes a complex exercise in multilingual situations. The question arises as to which of the several languages in the society should be used in education. Is it possible to involve all the languages in education? What are the limitations?

In colonial times, African countries were slapped with language policies that did not give much attention to the indigenous languages at all. Multilingualism was thought to be a barrier to national integration, and hence to development (Schwartz, 1965 cited in Bamgbose, 1991; Pool, 1971; Alexandre, 1972, cited in Bamgbose, 1991). Schwartz (1965, cited in Bamgbose, 1991) thought that differences between indigenous languages keep the people apart, perpetuate ethnic hostilities, weaken national loyalties and increase the danger of separatist sentiment. For Pool (1971), language diversity slows down economic development by (1) breaking occupational mobility, (2) reducing the number of people available for mobilization into the modern sector of the economy, and (3) preventing the diffusion of innovative techniques. For Alexandre (Bamgbose, 1991), each local language is intimately related to a tribal culture, thus the use of a local language reinforces attachment to a tribe, thereby going against the current of national sentiment. This type of orientation towards language is what is referred to as language-as-problem orientation (Ruiz, 1984). As a solution to the multilingual problem, the colonial languages were thought to be the best means of educating the African because it put all the people at equal disadvantage, since the colonial language was no-one's first language and everyone had to learn it from scratch. The colonial languages were also seen as unifiers, since they would serve as a common means of communication. However, multilingualism today is the norm rather than the exception because most nations are now multilingual due to the massive movement of people across the globe. One can hardly find monolingual states today because of such movements or emigrations. Therefore, there is the need to manage multilingualism in such a way that it can bring development to the people.

But, as noted by Bamgbose (1991), the real causes of divisiveness and underdevelopment in Africa has nothing to do with language. To him, the factors that contribute to divisiveness are (1) the exploitation of ethnicity by the elites in order to gain political and economic advantage, (2) the problem of sharing scarce resources, with the inevitable competition for jobs, positions, facilities, etc., (3) uneven development, and (4) external instigation based on nationalistic, ideological and religious motives.

Communication and development

Communication involves the sharing of information among people on all kinds of subjects. Since we are dealing with development issues here, we will focus on the notion of development communication, or communication for development.

Development communication is defined as "an approach to communication which provides communities with information they can use in bettering their lives, which aims at making public programmes and policies real, meaningful and sustainable" (www.thusong.gov.za/document/artic_pres/dev_comm.htm).

Communication is a key ingredient in development because it ensures the dissemination of information on matters that are relevant for improvement of life. Through communication, we teach new skills and new ways of doing things that will benefit the recipients. Communication creates awareness amongst communities about new developments that will promote their careers and make them more productive. For example, in agriculture, through communication we can disseminate information to farmers on best practices in agriculture, including: access to higher-yielding crops, methods of storage and preservation of their produce, marketing outlets, appropriate use of fertilizers and pesticides, etc. In matters of health, communication can create awareness about disease-preventing measures, personal hygiene, environmental protection activities, etc. Civic education and political awareness can all be enhanced through communication.

Communication, like education, is done largely through language. Just as the language of education becomes a complex issue in education in multilingual communities, so does the language of communication in such communities. The question is: are we able to provide information that will lead to positive development in all the languages in a multilingual community? The more languages there are, the more complex the situation becomes. In other words, it is easier to manage three or four languages than to manage ten to forty languages.

Proposed solutions to multilingual problems in Ghana

As noted earlier, multilingualism poses problems for language planning, that is, the management of many languages in order derive maximum benefit from them is a Herculean task. Various solutions to the multilingual problem in Ghana have been proposed. In this section I examine proposals from two authors that seek to address the problem – Bodomo (1996) and Owu-Ewie (2006).

Bodomo (1996) acknowledges the multilingual problem in Ghana, but thinks that it can be managed. He proposes a trilingual model for education and communication for Ghana. The trilingual model corresponds to the three levels of political administration, that is, national, regional and district. He calls the model localized trilingualism. This model ensures that each person who has gone through Ghana's educational system should be able to speak and write three languages at least. The proposal is represented as follows:

primary/district level   –   mother tongue (MT)

secondary/regional level –   MT + regional African language

tertiary/national level   –   MT + regional African language + world

language

At the primary/district level, the language of education and communication should be the most common mother tongue. As noted by Bodomo, the linguistic profile of most districts in Ghana is monolingual, and therefore this does not pose much of a problem for implementation. While the mother tongue (MT) is being used as the language of instruction at the primary/district level, a regional lingua franca would be taught as a strong school subject, to enable it to take over as the language of instruction at the secondary/regional level. The use of the MT at the primary/district level, according to Bodomo (1996), would enable students to completely grasp the belief and knowledge systems of the society. It would also encourage local initiatives and ensure mass participation in grassroots development. By the end of primary education, the school child would be bilingual in the MT and a regional lingua franca.

At the secondary/regional level, a regional lingua franca is to be used as a language of instruction, and, as Bodomo noted, "one must start teaching the official language as a strong school subject." Again, as he noted, in the African context, we tend to have homogenous administrative regions, in the sense that one main language is used for inter-ethnic communication. Before the student enters a university, he or she is trilingual in the MT, a regional lingua franca and the official language.

At the tertiary/national level the official language, which would have been introduced at the secondary level, becomes the medium of instruction. Bodomo also proposes that one or two indigenous languages should be promoted as national/official languages, while the foreign official language is maintained transitionally and eventually replaced as an official language.

To address the problem of the urban areas where most classrooms are likely to be multilingual, Bodomo (1996) proposes that sociolinguistic surveys should be conducted to identify a common indigenous language for the purpose of instruction.

Bodomo's proposal could be described as a decentralized language planning, where the policy varies from one district or region to another, since the linguistic situation may not be the same in each district or region. It will ensure that the individual who passes through the educational system becomes trilingual, and the languages of communication across the country will be at least three – MT at the district level, a regional lingua franca at the regional level, and the official language at the national level. The model ensures that everybody is involved in the development process.

One thing that is not clear in the proposal has to do with the level at which the teaching of English should be introduced. According to the model, English (the official language) should be introduced at the secondary level. Even though it said that the official language should be taught as 'a strong school subject', it is not certain whether three years of intensive teaching of English would give the students enough grounding for it to be used for instruction at the tertiary level. Even with the current situation where English is introduced right from the primary level, the proficiency level is generally poor. One other problem has to do with the urban multilingual classroom situation. Bodomo proposes a sociolinguistic survey to identify a common indigenous language. A similar proposal is made in Agbedor (1994), who indicates that the sociolinguistic survey might not always yield one common indigenous language, but two or three. In such cases, Agbedor (1994) proposed that the class could be divided into language groups and taught as such. In other words, when two indigenous languages are identified as common languages in the classroom, then the class should be divided into two groups according to the languages identified. Bodomo's (1996) proposal came without a word on how the proposed policy could be implemented and issues that might arise during its implementation.

One other author who addresses the multilingual problem in Ghana's education is Owu-Ewie (2006). Owu-Ewie was reacting to the English-only policy introduced by the President

Kufour administration in 2002. He criticized and debunked the reasons given for the English-only policy that included: (a) the previous policy was being abused, especially in the rural schools, where teachers never spoke English, (b) students were not able to write good English, (c) the urban classroom problem, (d) lack of material in the Ghanaian languages, (e) lack of Ghanaian language teachers, (f) lack of standard written form for Ghanaian languages, (g) English is the lingua franca of Ghana, (h) Rockwell's study that indicates that children transfer from L2 to L1 better.

Owu-Ewie debunked all these reasons and went on to propose a late-exit framework for education in Ghana. He stated that the policy that existed before the English-only policy did not produce the desired results because it was an early-exit policy. He identified two problems with the early-exit policy: (a) the exit was premature, and (b) the transition process was too abrupt. The late-exit proposal was based on a similar proposal by Ramirez and Merino (1990), in which 40 percent use of the mother tongue until 6th grade was proposed. In the case of Ghana, Owu-Ewie suggested that the mother tongue should be used till Primary Four, while English gradually takes over from Primary Five. At Primary Five, Ghanaian Language and Culture, Music, Dance, Integrated Science and Mathematics would continue to be taught in the mother tongue, while Environmental Studies, Physical Education, Religious and Moral Education would be taught in English. At Primary Six, English would be used as medium of instruction for all subjects, except Ghanaian Language, Music and Dance. He also proposed that a second Ghanaian language should be introduced at the Junior High School level. According to him, the late-exit policy he proposed would achieve the following:

a   It would bridge the gap between home and school language.
b   It would make learners literate in two languages.
c   It would give learners enough exposure in the first language (L1) to make them balanced bilinguals and ensure cognitive and academic development.
d   It would enable learners appreciate their culture.

For the planning and implementation of the policy, Owu-Ewie proposed a bottom-up approach, beginning with fact-finding (Bamgbose, 1991) at the community level. The fact-finding would enable the community to determine the language(s) suitable for instruction in the community. The decision-making would involve parents, teachers, learners and language coordinators. He also proposed district, regional and national language coordinators to monitor the implementation of the policy. Regional and National Language Advisory Boards were also proposed to handle language issues in their various jurisdictions. To make implementation more effective, Owu-Ewie proposed the education of the community members and teachers on the policy. He also advocated the training of teachers in the teaching of both the Ghanaian languages and English. Teachers should also be trained to write materials for teaching. He also advocated for capable parents to be engaged as bilingual aides to assist learners whose L1 is not the majority language of the community. He also emphasized change of attitude of the community towards Ghanaian languages, government support and backing for the policy, and the empowerment of the Bureau of Ghana Languages to produce Ghanaian language materials for schools. Posting of teachers, he suggests, must be done based on first and second languages of the teachers.

One criticism of the proposal that we would like to make is the definition of the late-exit policy. The early-exit policy advocates three years of mother tongue instruction, with transition to English from Primary Four. Ouw-Ewie's proposal suggests the transition point to be Primary Five, which, to me, would not make any difference. An extra year of instruction in the mother tongue may not necessarily bring the desired difference. I think a six-year mother tongue education would give the students better grounding in the mother tongue and a good foundation in English for a smooth transition. We support the claim that the transition is too abrupt, and that it should be gradual, but we think the gradual transition should begin at the Junior High School (JHS) level. This author argues that subjects like Integrated Science and Mathematics should continue to be taught in the mother tongue at the transition point in Primary Five because it would facilitate better understanding of the subjects. A similar argument can be made for subjects like Environmental Studies, and Religious and Moral Education. We think a six-year mother tongue instruction would give the students better grounding in all the subjects, and they can then transit to English gradually from JHS 1, which is the beginning of another stage of basic education.

One common thread that runs through Bodomo's (1996) and Owu-Ewie's (2006) proposals is the fact that both authors advocate the use of the indigenous languages and that language planning should start at the community (micro) level. This is important if mass participation in development is to be assured. The two proposals differ in their focus; while Bodomo's (1996) proposals encompass both education and development communication at the three administrative levels, Owu-Ewie (2006) focuses on only education. One other way in which the two proposals differ is that Bodomo advocates the eventual replacement of English as the official language and the development of trilingualism; Owu-Ewie's proposal would result in bilingual or trilingualism, with English remaining the official language.

A few points need to be mentioned in reaction to the proposals. The first is the language of evaluation or assessment. It has been the practice in Ghanaian schools that even though the policy advocates Ghanaian language instruction, assessments are done (with the exception of Ghanaian language tests) in English. In other words, lessons are supposed to be taught in the Ghanaian language, but examinations are conducted in English. So, the language of instruction does not match the language of examination. This does not make for a fair assessment. I think the biggest problem has to do with implementation of policy. The early-exit policy, which has been criticized by Owu-Ewie, could have yielded better results if the policy had been well implemented. That is where monitoring and evaluation of policy becomes crucial. It is a well-known fact that monitoring in public schools in Ghana is extremely weak, compared with what happens in the private schools. The latter are seen to be producing better results because of effective monitoring.

With regard to Bodomo's advocacy for replacement of English as the official language, we would submit that English still has an important role to play in international communication and development communication at the national level. We would submit, following South Africa, that some major Ghanaian languages be developed to take on a joint official language status with English.

Bodomo's proposals would make development communication more effective. Most African nations have agricultural-based economies. It is expected that these countries should at least be self-sufficient in food supply. As noted earlier, self-sufficiency in such basic needs as food, health care and basic education are essential prerequisites for any plunge into industrialization. An educational system in which as much equal opportunity as possible is given to every citizen is more desirable. All children have the right to be educated, and language should not be a barrier to that education. This should be reflected in an economic model in which all citizens have the opportunity to progress as far as their resources can take them. There are several other constraints to further education (e.g., economic), and language should not be added to that.

One other thing that has to be kept in mind is the fact that education is for people, and should make the people who benefit from it wholesome – wholesome in the sense that it would enable every learner to stretch his or her potential for growth to the fullest extent. Education should offer all possible conditions for the realization of the ideal profile envisioned of an educated person. Among the attributes of an educated person are, first, that s/he must be well informed and directed toward continuous self-improvement to maintain excellence. The rapidly developing frontiers of science and technology, coupled with the growing complexity of social structure, give rise to knowledge. This explosion of knowledge requires man to learn more and to know more about people and the world around them. This tendency brings education far beyond the bounds of the school and makes it a lifelong process. Second, an educated person must have a positive self-identity and a sense of competence – competence in dealing with the world. An educated person must also be healthy – mentally and physically. Since providing adequate health care requires an enormous amount of money (and most of the third world countries cannot afford that), the best approach is preventive medicine. The primary health care program should educate the people on how to take good care of themselves and to protect themselves from disease, by observing some very simple rules of hygiene. This form of education should begin right from the classroom and continue throughout life. The following facts about Ghana are taken into consideration.

- The majority of the people do not speak the official language (English). So the question of how effective communication between the rulers and the masses of the people can be promoted arises. Moreover, most school children do not use the colonial language at home. It is the Ghanaian languages that dominate in all domains except the classroom (for school children) and the offices (for the Civil Servants and others). English is as important for international communication as the Ghanaian languages are for intra-national communication. There is no doubt that English opens the door to new knowledge, new skills and new understanding outside the local environment. But it is not all the people that make use of that knowledge, because not all the people reach the level where they can have direct access to information in English. When we talk about the computer age, how many of the world's population actually depend on computers for their survival? Even if they do, how many actually know how the computer works? When we consider all the inventions that have contributed to the civilization of today, what percentage of the world's population was actually involved in the real inventions? Almost negligible. The majority are consumers of what the minority have invented.
- There are a lot of drop-outs in the school system. Apart from economic reasons, these drop-outs could also be related to the inability to cope with the English language. Most of these drop-outs end up not being able to read in either the MT or the colonial language. Statistics show that a majority of Ghanaians do not go to school beyond the basic level (i.e., JHS/Middle), and, at this level, their English proficiency level is very low. According to the 2010 Population and Housing Census (PHC), about 82 percent of Ghanaians have education below Senior High School (SHS).
- Most of the people are engaged in occupations that do not require the colonial language in order to be effective. The 2010 PHC shows that out of 9,657,179 people who are employed in Ghana, about 8,047,510 (over 90 percent) are engaged in agriculture, crafts, service and sales, and elementary occupations. These are occupations that do not require English to perform.

At this juncture, we would like to make the following suggestions for a successful language policy in Ghana.

1   The first point is that language planning does not take place in a vacuum. It affects people. This implies that there must be research into the actual language use in the society. The findings of sociolinguistic research would serve as input to policy formulation (Bamgbose, 1989). Most of the time, policies are formulated without the background fact-finding. Nor are the policies well implemented or even evaluated. The actual language use input could be obtained by either conducting a sociolinguistic survey at the national level, or the elicitation of such information could be included in a national census. This information will give the government a fair idea of the real language situation, which will help identify the major languages for development.

2   We would like to reiterate Bamgbose's (1991) comments that African governments should desist from what he called the "avoidance principle," where most governments fail to make the necessary decisions for fear of political upheavals. Language planning policies that are made with input from the people will attract very little opposition.

3   Policies should be evaluated frequently to see how successful they are, with a view to making revisions. But changing policies any time a new government comes in does not serve any purpose. Ghana was cited as having changed policies several times over a few years, without much research or evaluation (Ansah, 2014).

4   A Language Academy is necessary to work on the major languages of Ghana, with a view to elaborating and modernizing those which are fully standardized, and standardizing those that are not fully standardized. The Bureau of Ghana Languages is responsible for the publication of material in the Ghanaian languages. The Bureau could be changed into a language academy, with membership reviewed to include more linguists and other professionals whose work would be relevant.

5   The Adult Literacy Campaign should be reactivated vigorously, and efforts must be made to provide the new literates with enough reading materials to prevent them from relapsing into illiteracy. The aim of the campaign is to make the majority of the people literate at least in their own Ghanaian languages for easy dissemination of information, which would eventually lead to the welfare and well-being of the majority of the population. The literate parents will also be able to help their children with their school work at home, especially where the home and school language are the same.

6   The training of teachers should be re-examined; all students entering the teacher training college should be made to study at least one of the major Ghanaian languages. If people want to teach in a region other than their own, they should learn the language of the region. In the primary schools, teachers should be as competent as possible in the regional language that is to be used for instruction. Efforts should be made to reduce the number of untrained teachers in the system.

7   One important issue that militates against a successful indigenous language policy is what is referred to as *elite closure* (Scotton, 1990). This refers to the vested interest of the elite in perpetuating the use of 'the language of rule' (Pool, 1993), in this case English, in the higher domains in order to preserve the privileges with which this language is associated. In so doing, the elite isolate themselves with their privileged language, English, from the rest of the population and their languages (Kamwangamalu, 2013). The elite, who constitute the rulers of this nation, only pay lip service to the promotion of Ghanaian languages, while they send their own children to English-only private schools. In that regard, it might

be prudent to make sure that the policy is implemented in all categories of schools in Ghana. I see education as making its beneficiaries positive change agents, and our young people who have the privilege of going to school should be able to help the underprivileged majority with the knowledge they have acquired to promote development, and the Ghanaian languages are the best means to do that (see Bodomo, 1996 for an anecdote).

Conclusion

This chapter aimed to examine the role of language planning in sustainable development. We started by briefly examining the concept of language planning and the types of LP. The concept of development was also examined, and it was observed that the 'full life' notion of development is ideal for anybody. That is, development should not be only economic; it must also be social and political. It is noted that sustainable development requires a massive mobilization of the entire population. This calls for policies at the community level and the indigenous languages have become indispensable. Proposals for language policy by two authors, Bodomo (1996) and Owu-Ewie (2006), were discussed. The two proposals make a strong advocacy for the employment of indigenous Ghanaian languages in education and development communication. Other authors have made similar calls in favor of Ghanaian languages. These include Anyidoho (2004), Ando-Kumi (1994, cited in Owu-Ewie (2006)), Agbedor (1994).

All the observations made above can, if adequately addressed, bring a great deal of improvement in education in Ghana and, as a result, economic, political and social progress. But the question that is always raised when it comes to education is money – and most African countries are not in good financial positions to undertake some of the expansions in education. But that is what economics is all about – the management of scarce resources. That is where priorities have to be made, depending on the available resources. Other things have to be sacrificed for the most important (opportunity cost). The most important things a developing nation needs are food, education, health and shelter – basic things. No country has more resources than they need. The important thing is to derive the maximum benefit from the scarce resources. To address these issues requires a strong political will and commitment to serve the interests of the people.

References

Agbedor, P. (1994). Language planning for national development: the case of Ghana. PhD thesis, University of Victoria, BC, Canada.

Ansah, G. (2104). "Re-examining the fluctuations in language-in-education policies in post-independence Ghana". *Multilingual Education* 4:12, 1–15. Available online at: www.multilingual-education.com/content/4/1/12.

Anyidoho, A. (2004). "English only as medium of instruction in Primary 1–3?" *Legon Journal of Humanities* XV: 81–97.

Baker, C. (1993). *Foundations of Bilingual Education and Bilingualism*. Clevedon, Philadelphia, Adelaide: Multilingual Matters Ltd.

Bamgbose, A. (1989). "Issues for a model of language planning." *Language Problems and Language Planning* 13: 24–44.

Bamgbose, A. (1991). *Language and the Nation*. Edinburgh: Edinburgh University Press.

Bodomo, A.B. (1996). "On language and development in Africa: the case of Ghana". *Nordic Journal of African Studies* 5(2): 31–51.

Cooper, R.L. (1989). *Language Planning and Social Change*. Cambridge: Cambridge University Press.

Fishman, J. (1968). "Nationality-nationalism and nation-nationism". In J.A. Fishman, C.A. Ferguson & J. Das Gupta (eds), *Language Problems of Development Nations* (pp. 39–52). The Hague: Mouton.

Fishman, J.A. (1971). "The sociology of language: an interdisciplinary social science approach to language in society". In J.A. Fishman (ed.), *Advances in the Sociology of Language* (pp. 217–404). The Hague: Mouton.

Foster-Carter, A. (1985). "Sociology and development". In M. Haralambos (ed.) *Sociology: New Directions*. Causeway Books.

Haugen, E. (1969). "Language planning, theory and practice". In A.S. Dil (ed.), *The Ecology of Language: Essays by Einar Haugen*. Stanford, CA: Stanford University Press.

Kamwangamalu, N.M. (2013). "Language-in-education policy and planning in Africa's monolingual kingdoms of Lesotho and Swaziland". In J.W. Tollefson (ed.), *Language Policies in Education: Critical Issues*. Abingdon, UK: Routledge.

Kloss, H. (1966). "Bilingualism and nationalism". *Journal of Social Issues*, 23(2): 39–47.

Kloss, H. (1968). "Notes concerning a language-nation typology". In J.A. Fishman, C.A. Ferguson and J. Das Gupta (eds), *Language Problems of Developing Nations* (pp. 69–86). London, New York, Sydney, Toronto: John Wiley & Sons, Inc.

Menken, K. and Garcia, O. (2010). *Negotiating Language Policies in Schools: Educators as Policymakers*. New York, NY: Routledge.

Owu-Ewie, C. (2006). "The language policy of education in Ghana: a critical look at the English-only language policy of education". In J. Mugane et al. (eds), *Selected Proceedings of the 35th Annual Conference on African Linguistics (ACAL)*. Somerville, MA: Cascadilla Proceedings Project.

Phillipson, R. (1992). *Linguistic Imperialism*. Oxford: Oxford University Press.

Pool, J. (1993). "Linguistic exploitation". *International Journal of the Sociology of Language* 103: 31–55.

Pool, J. (1971). "National development and language diversity". In J. Rubin and B.H. Jernudd (eds.), *Can Language be Planned?* (pp. 213–230). Honolulu: The University Press of Hawaii.

Ramirez. J. and Merino, B.J. (1990). "Classroom talk in English immersion: early-exit and late-exit transitional bilingual education programs". In R. Jacobson and C. Faltis (ed.), *Language Distribution Issues in Bilingual Schooling* (pp. 65–103). Clevedon, UK: Multilingual Matters.

Rubin, J. and Jernudd, B.H. (1971). *Can Language Be Planned?* Honolulu: An East-West Center Book.

Ruiz, R. (1984). "Orientations in language planning". In S. McKay and S. Wong (eds.), *Language Diversity: Problem of Resource?* (pp. 3–26). Cambridge, New York, Philadelphia: Newbury House Publishers.

Scotton, C.M. (1990). "Elite closure as boundary maintenance". In B. Weinstein (ed.), *Language Policy and Political Development* (pp. 25–52). Norwood, NJ: Ablex.

Skutnabb-Kangas, T. (2000). "Multilingualism and the education of minority children". In T. Skutnabb-Kangas and J. Cummins (eds), *Minority Education: From Shame to Struggle* (pp. 9–44). Clevedon, UK, Philadelphia, PA: Multilingual Matters.

Tollefson, J. W. (1991). *Planning Language, Planning Inequality: Language Policy in the Community*. London: Longman.

Tollefson, J. W. (ed.) (2013). *Language Policies in Education: Critical Issues*. Abingdon, UK: Routledge.

UNESCO (1953). *The Use of Vernacular Languages in Education*. Paris: UNESCO.

UNESCO (1988). *Compendium of Statistics on Literacy*. Paris: UNESCO.

Weinstein, B. (1980). "Language planning in Francophone Africa". *Language Problems and Language Planning* 4(1): 55–77.

World Commission on Environment and Development (WCED) (1987). *Our Common Future*. Oxford: Oxford University Press.

PART V

Creative expressions and cultural life

20

THE LANGUAGE OF YOUTH IN AFRICA

A sociocultural linguistic analysis

Heather Brookes and Roland Kouassi

Introduction

Youth in many countries on the African continent have developed distinct ways of speaking with their peers. These ways of speaking often appear to be quite different from the first language varieties of African languages spoken in these communities. As a result, they have attracted a great deal of attention because, in many cases, the way they speak is almost unintelligible to other members of the communities in which they reside. This lack of intelligibility has tempted linguists to call them 'languages' and to analyze and classify them within the framework of autonomous linguistic systems. These ways of speaking have names given to them either by linguists or community members but not by the users themselves.

In this chapter we review and compare research on the language practices of youth in four different sociocultural contexts: *Tsotsitaals* in South Africa, *Sheng* in Kenya, *Nouchi* in the Ivory Coast and *Camfranglais* in Cameroon. We show that these ways of speaking developed in urban areas most likely among certain marginalized groups of male youths. Although these practices were initially associated with delinquent groups, they are also present among the general urban male youth population and more recently among rural male youth. We demonstrate that these practices are performance-based styles that function to create and maintain social divisions among male social networks. As they have become more broadly symbolic of a modern cosmopolitan African identity, rural and female youth and older speakers as well as the media make use of features associated with male youth talk for pragmatic and symbolic purposes. We show that co-option into public spaces and commodification have transformed features of these practices into iconic symbolic resources that speakers draw on in combination with local varieties and other symbolic resources to express a cosmopolitan African identity.

We argue that there is little evidence to suggest a popular view that the language practices of youth in Africa are developing into new first languages. We examine the theoretical and methodological approaches linguists have employed to study these phenomena. We demonstrate that these approaches, the multiplicity of languages speakers employ, and the failure to look at the relationship between these youth practices and existing local first language varieties have led to this misinterpretation. We argue that these phenomena are best understood from an interactionist and functional theoretical perspective.

Language practices among youth in four African countries

South Africa: Tsotsitaals

South African historians were the first to note the emergence of distinct ways of speaking associated with particular groups of black male youth coinciding with rapid urbanization in the context of colonization in the early 20th century in and around Johannesburg (Glaser 2000). These practices were most prominent among delinquent male groupings and appeared to vary from one community and area to another. In some cases, these varieties appear to have been given names although it is not clear whether the speakers themselves, their communities, researchers or others named their ways of talking.

Early studies on these ways of talking noted its rapidly changing slang lexicon that was coined or adapted from different South African languages and its use of either an Afrikaans grammatical base or one of the South African Bantu languages, most often Zulu. However, linguists disagreed on how to categorize these youth varieties with scholars suggesting that they were slangs (Schuring 1983; Mfusi 1992; Mojela 2002), creoles (Makhudu 2002; Mfenyana 1977), code-switching varieties (Slabbert and Myers-Scotton 1996), lingua francas (Mojela 2002; Schuring 1983; Slabbert 1994), low varieties in a diglossic relationship (Rudwick 2005), antilanguages (Makhudu 2002; Stone 2002; Brookes 2004; Kiessling and Mous 2004), registers (Mfusi 1992) and even emerging languages (Ntshangase 1993, 2002). There was also no consensus on the motivation for these practices. Some suggested that it was to ameliorate ethnic divides (Msimang 1987) and to create a common form of communication among speakers of different languages because of language contact in a multilingual context (Mojela 2002; Schuring 1983; Slabbert 1994).

A widely held approach up until 2008 was that one could treat these phenomena as separate varieties and even separate languages as they appeared so distinctly different from the first languages of these communities and were often unintelligible to outsiders. Ntshangase (2002) proposed that linguists classify these phenomena into two varieties: *Tsotsitaal* based on the structure of Afrikaans and *Iscamtho* based on either Zulu or South Sotho. Ntshangase (2002) claimed that these varieties had their origins in specific gang argots spoken in Johannesburg in the early 1900s although there is no evidence for this claim (Brookes and Lekgoro 2014).

Treating these phenomena as fully-fledged linguistic codes underlay the majority of linguists' attempts to describe their semantic and structural characteristics. They tried to find systematic differences in their formal features in relation to existing languages and to fit them within existing language typologies. Despite these attempts, including work by scholars who claimed to be users of these varieties (e.g., Ntshangase 1993), no coherent findings or theoretical framework emerged as to how to understand these phenomena.

These earlier studies based their conclusions on small decontextualized elicited samples and interviews without providing much, if any, information about their informants' use of these practices, level of involvement in these ways of speaking or their position within these speech communities. There was also a widespread implicit assumption that males were representative of all speakers. As a result, findings were not always clear about who the users of this way of speaking were.

Some research suggested older males and women also knew and used these ways of speaking (Ntshangase 1993). From data provided, we also see how informants who were likely peripheral to the main practitioners of these ways of speaking claimed that certain grammatical features were part of these varieties (Kiessling and Mous 2004) when they were in fact present in urban varieties of Bantu languages (Brookes 2014). In interviews, informants also gave examples that mixed the lexicon of different generations and areas. The lexicons from different groups and townships were then lumped together based on outsider informants' receptive knowledge. Informants also sometimes gave examples mixing the syntactic base languages of different generations and different areas within one example that did not reflect what could have been the case on the ground (see Mesthrie and Hurst 2013 for examples).

Up until the late 2000s there were few systematic studies of these phenomena among actual users within a single speech community. Two exceptions were Calteaux (1994) who studied youth in Thembisa, a black township east of Johannesburg, and Hurst (2009) who researched youth in Khayelitsha, a black township in Cape Town. However, their data were based on self report, interviews and elicitation rather than on spontaneous conversations among users. Nevertheless, Hurst's work on young men in one Cape Town township provided evidence that this way of talking was age and gender specific, and that such practices were best understood within the theoretical framework of style and stylistic practices that included not only language but also gesture, music, clothing and particular outlooks. She proposed the term stylect to characterize male youth patterns of talk in which the lect indicated a lexicon that was a distinctive part of the speech style.

Based on Hurst's insights, his own experience and previous studies, Mesthrie (2008) in his article, "I've been speaking Tsotsitaal my whole life without knowing it," observed that there might be different names for these phenomena, different lexicons and different base languages, but they could all be understood as the same practice of inserting a lexicon into the syntactic structure of a preexisting language. He suggested that although the central feature was the lexicon, this way of talking was also marked by particular gestures and intonation. From existing literature he hypothesized that it was likely that there were different levels of male speech that could be understood as a continuum from the styles of ordinary youth to delinquent ones and prison slangs. He proposed that a generic name 'tsotsitaals' be used to label these phenomena. He argued that these phenomena as markers of both age and male identity would be unlikely to metamorphose into a first language as Ntshangase (2002) and others have argued.

In 2014, Brookes (2014) published the first systematic longitudinal ethnographic study of male youth linguistic practices using data from spontaneous interactions among black male youth in Johannesburg. This research, begun in the mid-1990s, shows that young men from their late teens until their late twenties engage in these ways of talking in interactions with their peers mainly in street corner groups (skeems – as they are called) on the township streets. These practices involve using the most common local urban Bantu variety into which speakers insert a slang lexicon. However, what also marks this way of speaking is its performative nature, its use of gestures and intonation. Township male youth did not and do not name this way of talking but describe it with the verb *ukuringa* 'to ring []'. Her recordings of spontaneous interactions revealed different stylistic practices (lexicon, gesture, intonation and performative strategies as well as stance, clothing, musical tastes and activities) among young men with different orientations to local and global trends that differed across and distinguished different social levels. Youth whose orientation was towards mainstream participation and global trends used less slang and had different gestural behavior and intonation from youth whose orientation and status was bound up in antisocial activities and crime. The latter made up the central hardcore of male township youth whose ways of speaking were lexically and metaphorically dense and whose gestural behavior, intonation, prosody and rhetorical features including strategies of linguistic manipulation set them apart from other male youth. Brookes (2014) also demonstrated that these practices were only fully utilized and expressed in performative moments among male youth as part of negotiating and maintaining status and as part of the social process of authenticating a social identity, that of an urban, streetwise, sophisticated township masculinity.

Historical research tracking previous generations of youth from the 1970s back to the 1940s showed that the base language shifted from Afrikaans to local Bantu varieties at the time of forced removals in the 1960s (Brookes and Lekgoro 2014). Before 1948, people of mixed race and black South Africans had lived together in township areas next to white settlements. However, in line with apartheid ideologies, those of mixed race who were mostly Afrikaans speaking and Bantu language speakers were separated into different townships during the 1950s and 60s. Without mother tongue speakers of Afrikaans, male youth in the new townships reserved for Bantu language speakers began to use their own languages as the base language for their slang lexicon. This evidence confirms that these ways of speaking were not separate linguistic varieties with different origins as Ntshangase (2002) claimed, but a practice of inserting a slang into an existing language. The study found that older males no longer engaged in these practices although they would from time to time use a word or phrase to index their urban and/or streetwiseness persona or to express sociability among their peers and with the younger male generation.

Further ethnographic work analyzing spontaneous interactions among female youth also confirms the gendered nature of these practices (Maribe and Brookes 2014). In their study of lesbian youth, they found that some young women would draw on a very small well-known portion of the slang lexicon of male youth to express multiple social meanings including a modern cosmopolitan South African, a butch versus femme identity and to construct their sexual roles in relation to their partners. This work demonstrated that speakers draw on words and phrases indexical of social meanings to express social identities and to create particular social roles. In the case of lesbian women, their limited use of male slang served to index multiple social meanings simultaneously around persona, identity and sexual roles.

With the advent of democracy in 1994, black South Africans began to integrate into mainstream life and to participate more fully in its institutions including business, government and the media. Township youth with mainstream aspirations and global tastes were the first to be involved in mainstream media. Initially, there was a strong tendency for youth representations in the media to imitate American English and hip-hop styles, but this American *wannabe* 'want to be' image did not have widespread appeal. Most township youth, especially antisocial groups, rejected these types of images as inauthentic to their identity as Africans.

However, in 1998, mainstream public television produced the first series that focused on the lives of youth in the township and accurately portrayed both their language practices and the different social levels and identities. The television series was called *Yizo Yizo*, and it became one of the most successful local series ever. *Yizo Yizo* made producers and corporates realize that to have widespread appeal it was essential to represent local youth culture and practices, and the media began to incorporate more of the local linguistic features and local styles into mainstream programming and advertising.

The result was the creation of a new hybrid youth variety representing a cosmopolitan African youth identity drawing on both well-known (old) and recent local youth slangs and global linguistic resources and styles. Local linguistic resources symbolic of the modern streetwise township youth became an important strategy in marketing and advertising to target African youth. One of the effects of representing previously marginalized practices in the public domain was the advent of a meta-commentary about the language of youth and attempts to value it by authenticating it as a language and devalue it by lamenting its use as reflecting a deterioration in the language competence of youth. Talking and writing about youth language in academia and the media resulted in the establishment and spread of specific names drawing mainly on Ntshangase's (1995) proposal to name Bantu-based youth varieties *Iscamtho* and Afrikaans-based varieties *Tsotsitaal*. Naming has encouraged acts of formalization and authentication based on dominant perceptions of languages as distinct and autonomous varieties. Attempts have and continue to be made to consolidate and formalize it with print and online dictionaries as well as translating biblical passages or attempting to use it to write newspaper articles. However, due to its limited semantic domains, most of these written attempts resort to urban varieties of African languages with slang lexicon only able to cover certain semantic domains in these texts.

As online communication has increased, so new words and phrases appear within public spaces and discourses. These words no longer necessarily originate from male youth practices on the township streets but are invented in a different social and linguistic space by new youth elites that have access to public discourses. Some of these innovations may become part of linguistic practices among male and female township youth. With increasing participation in mainstream life since 1994, new features that are the product of interactive street corner practices among marginalized male groups no longer have the same value and symbolic capital they had during apartheid, and they no longer set the linguistic trends on the township streets or in wider society.

The linguistic features of antisociety elements no longer have the symbolic capital because their users no longer have the social capital. The production and reproduction of symbolic resources and the power relations between groups of speakers has shifted (Bourdieu 1977; Zhang 2005). Under apartheid, black youth could not participate in or aspire to success within mainstream life. They turned to making it big outside the mainstream and aspired to be like those who were monetarily successful through thwarting the system. These antisocial elements ruled the township streets and youth networks and were either admired for their wealth and daring or feared because of their violence and crime (Brookes 2014). With the advent of democracy, the balance of power began to shift. Those youth who opted for mainstream opportunities now enjoy a material lifestyle that is far in excess of that of the antisocial elements that remain and that once ruled the streets. Youth no longer aspire to a lifestyle of the antisociety.

Since democracy, the practices of male youth on the township streets have gradually entered a new linguistic market involving both commodification and new forms of identity and prestige. Symbolic capital and the power to create symbols that are valued has shifted. The new elites use township talk including features of Tsotsitaal, as well as new national and global features to express a new cosmopolitan African identity. Being a hip urban South African is the ability to draw on some of the features of the *kasi* 'township [ghetto]' while also able to function in different domains with different languages. The use of some iconic features of youth speech in the public domain is part of symbolizing a modern cosmopolitan urban South African identity rather than the emergence of a new language.

Kenya: Sheng

In Nairobi, young men also developed a particular way of speaking that involved inserting a slang lexicon into the local variety of Swahili (Githiora 2002; Kiessling and Mous 2004). The slang lexicon is coined or drawn from languages such as Swahili, Luo, Gikuiyi, Masai, Luhya, and coastal languages such as Giriama and Taita as well as English (Githiora 2002). There are different variations of the slang in different areas of Nairobi (Githiora 2002). In the more affluent areas of Nairobi, such as Westlands where English is more dominant than Swahili, youth from the late teens to late twenties also have a particular way of speaking that uses English as its base into which slang (adapted mainly from English) is inserted (Abdulaziz and Osinde 1997).

The Swahili-based practice has been labelled Sheng and the English-based one, Engsh. However, it is not clear who named these ways of speaking. Abdulaziz and Osinde (1997) and Kiessling and Mous (2004) suggest that Engsh emerged as a reaction to Sheng by middle-class youth who wished to distinguish themselves from the class of Sheng speakers. However, Barasa (2010) suggests that Engsh is simply a form of Sheng using a different base language. Barasa (2010: 309) points out that Engsh is used to express a posh personae. "It is a symbol of being polished and fashionable." However, upper middle class youth do not distance themselves from Sheng. They claim to use Sheng even when they cannot produce it (Githiora 2016). There seems to be general consensus that these practices called Sheng began in a part of Nairobi called Eastlands, a poor area where the British invaders forced native Kenyan workers to live, and it later spread to other parts of the city (Abdulaziz and Osinde 1997; Githiora 2002; Spyropoulos 1987). A number of scholars believe it emerged in the late 1960s or 1970s (Osinde 1986; Abdulaziz and Osinde 1997; Spyropoulos 1987; Githinji 2005, 2006a, 2006b, 2008). Kiessling and Mous (2004) also suggest that Sheng emerged in the 1970s, but that it has its 'roots' during the colonial era because of increased migration by different ethnic groups to urban areas. Mazrui (1995) claims that it has its origins in a professional slang of the underworld and may go back as far as the 1930s. Kiessling and Mous (2004) also suggest it may have originated from a criminal argot, but, as they point out, there is no evidence to confirm that this is the case. Spyropoulos (1987) claims that Sheng emerged in 1963 among migrants to Nairobi who had limited knowledge of English and Swahili as well as school dropouts. She suggests it spread from Eastlands through the informal sector, e.g., shoeshine boys, curio sellers, hawkers and parking boys. Abdulaziz and Osinde (1997) report that this way of speaking began with "wayward teenagers" to create an ingroup language and an identity marker that then spread out to other youth in the area.

Several scholars argue that Sheng is a form of code-switching that arose to fulfill the function of a lingua franca and evolved as a hybrid form due to inadequate knowledge of either Swahili and English on the part of migrants (Mazrui 1995; Spyropoulos 1987). Others suggest it is primarily a slang and has some features of a pidgin (Abdulaziz and Osinde 1997; Githiora 2002) although, more recently, Githiora (2016: 1) suggests that it is an "age-marked urban variety of Kenyan Swahili." As some features of Sheng are used in social media (Mutonya 2008), in advertising (Kariuki et al. 2015) and heard in schools, police stations, among adults, homesteads, banks, universities and political rallies, Githiora (2016) and others (Karanja 2010) now argue that it has spread to other domains and therefore it is an emerging urban non-standard vernacular or dialect.

Despite the claim of an emerging language/code, scholars point out that it is still primarily urban male youth who use these ways of speaking in their *bazes* 'friendship groups' (Githiora 2002, 2016; Githinji 2008) and speakers generally abandon these practices in their late twenties (Abdulaziz and Osinde 1997).

Sheng is generally associated with youth culture (Mbugua 2003; Samper 2004) and functions as a marker of identity (Githinji 2006a; Samper 2002), although it also was and still is to some extent associated with the underclasses and symbolic of delinquency. Young women report that they may use some slang but generally claim they are not speakers/users of Sheng (Githinji 2008; Githiora 2002). Male youth use Sheng to distinguish themselves from the rest of society, in particular their rural counterparts and the older generation. Githiora (2002) points out that Sheng is part of male sociability in informal settings associated with toughness, masculinity and local solidarity. It is a means of creating an ingroup, indexing local identities and enhancing covert prestige (Githiora 2002; Githinji 2008). However, some studies claim that Sheng is also used more generally on the streets in the informal business section

(Githiora 2002; Spyropoulos 1987). It has also spread to youth in rural areas (Githiora 2002; Ogechi 2002, 2005), to market places, as well as featuring on television and in the media and is spreading across age and class.

The grammatical structure of Sheng appears to be Nairobi Swahili and, for Engsh, it is English (Abdulaziz and Osinde 1997). The major feature of Sheng is its lexicon and it is continuously revitalized as a tool to mark local identities and distinguish one group from another (Githinji 2006a). The lexicon is developed through borrowing, coinage and relexicalization (Ogechi 2005). New words emerge and spread if speakers believe they are popular (Githinji 2006a). However, the vocabulary is limited to certain semantic domains. Githiora (2002) elicited narratives from youth using Sheng. In these narratives, Sheng words only occurred in certain semantic domains such as police, crime, sex, alcohol, drugs and violence where there was considerable overlexicalization of words for violence and illicit or taboo topics (Githiora 2002). Overlexicalization is a common feature and is related to the concerns of youth (Githinji 2006a, 2008). For example, in his study of representations of women in the Sheng lexicon, Githinji (2008) found that there is proliferation of words that are often derogatory for girls and their bodies. The meanings of words are often fluid and the lexicon changes from one generation to the next with speakers identifying certain words as no longer part of the current lexicon (Abdulaziz and Osinde 1997; Githinji 2006a). In informal interviews in Nairobi, the first author also found that older men report that their sons' Sheng has a different lexicon from the one they used in their youth. The lexicon can also be highly localized, varying from one baze to another, and the same word can mean different things (Githinji 2006a). Githinji (2006a) points out that there are subdivisions with youth social networks that are marked by differences in the slang variety that relate to identities and stances within the social networks of youth in Nairobi. Well-known words and phrases in Sheng have spread out into mainstream media and these features are used in advertisements, newspapers, health interventions and political messaging (Githiora 2002; Mutonya 2008). Kariuki et al. (2015) suggest that the incorporation of Sheng into advertising occurred from the 1980s onwards as the result of the expansion of regional trade and a growing market-based economy. The spread of the lexicon into public discourse has led to claims that Nairobians and other Kenyans are undergoing language shift to Sheng. However, Kariuki et al.'s (2015) analysis of advertisements shows that advertisers draw on Sheng lexicon differently to create different linguistic styles depending on the audience. To target youth and low-income earners, companies use more Sheng words within the grammatical framework of Swahili. Adverts targeting university students use English words also within the framework of Swahili. Kariuki et al. (2015) describe the latter as using English to coin Sheng words. What is evident from their analyses is that advertisers draw on what they perceive as different social groups' styles of practice. Speakers engage in creating particular styles of talking that differentially draw on features of different languages to express who they are in relation to others depending on context. The use of Sheng words is still a marked usage rather than a default naturalized code. As Kariuki et al. (2015) describe, it is "loaded." They also show that advertisers coin their phrases, using the same practices of manipulation that Sheng users employ, to appeal to consumers.

The incorporation of some Sheng words into public discourse shows that some aspects of Sheng have shifted from once being stigmatized through association with delinquents and gangsters to being used by churches, corporate business and government to appeal to youth and a cosmopolitan identity (Kariuki et al. 2015). Aspects of Sheng have become part of popular youth culture and increasingly feature in music. They have become symbolic resources in the expression of 'coolness,' and being city slick and city smart. It is used as a marketing tool because it is associated with notions of originality, change, urban sophistication and youthfulness (Mutonya 2008). As Githiora (2002) describes, even upper middle class Nairobi youth who use an English slang (Engsh) claim to know and use Sheng even though they do not know it and cannot produce it.

Features of Sheng circulate as symbolic resources in public discourse to express a modern cosmopolitan Kenyan identity, particularly among youth but also among the general population, and are used in public discourse to appeal to youth. Its indexicality as a marker of 'coolness' and its appeal to youth may also have motivated such practices to spread to youth in rural areas, especially with increasing urbanization and movement between urban and rural areas (Ogechi 2002, 2005).

There have also been many attempts to document Sheng in dictionaries and to promote it as a fully-fledged urban language (Mbaabu and Kazungu 2003; see GoSheng www.gosheng. org; Rudd 2008). GoSheng is active in promoting the use of Sheng. However, their translations into Sheng are in fact Kenyan Swahili with a very small part of the lexicon in Sheng for only certain semantic domains (see Githiora 2016 for an example). A few scholars claim that Sheng is a new language and is becoming the first language of long-term Nairobians (Rudd 2008). However, he compares examples from male and female self-report interview data with Standard Kenyan Swahili instead of comparing it with local versions of Nairobi Swahili. Consequently, the grammatical features that he claims are unique to Sheng are in fact also found in local versions of Nairobi Swahili.

In every-day talk about language, the term 'Sheng' is now used by Nairobians as a general label to cover a vast array of argots and in-group ways of speaking among different groups or 'communities of practice' such as Mathathu 'taxi' drivers, street market sellers, touts, etc. Despite these attempts at authenticating it as a complete linguistic code, like youth languages in other parts of Africa, its features are symbolic resources used in particular contexts and for particular purposes to express social identities, and can be best understood as part of linguistic styles that express stances, personae and identities.

Cote d'Ivoire: Nouchi

Cote d'Ivoire, in West Africa, is a former French colony where France still has significant influence. The first mission of France in the country occurred in 1687 when the missionaries settled in Assinie with the official objective of spreading the Christian gospel. During the Berlin Conference of 1885, France was given colonial rule over the Côte d'Ivoire. Côte d'Ivoire became an official French colony in 1893. Grand Bassam, a previously established French administration fort, became the official capital. The French ruled Cote d'Ivoire from 1893 until 'independence' in 1960 as a constituent of the Federation of French West Africa (Handloff 1991).

During their rule, the French applied a method of assimilation and cooperation. They understood the power of language to frame minds and re-structure cultural systems and practices. So they imposed French as *the* language of education and administrative purposes. No one could speak other languages at school.

After 'independence' on August 7, 1960, the first constitution promoted the French language as the official language. The constitution of 2000 still endorses French as *the language of the nation*, without any systematic status for the other over 60 languages. Even after Côte d'Ivoire gained 'independence', the French continued to have a strong influence on Ivoirian minds, culture and life.

The first published text presenting Nouchi is a newspaper article entitled "Le Nouchi, un langage a la mode" (Nouchi, a fashionable language) written by Alain Coulibaly and Bernard

Ahua and published in *Fraternité Matin* on September 6, 1986. The roots of Nouchi can be traced back to the 1970s (Kouadio 1990, 2006). It emerged on the streets in the ghettoes of Abidjan, among male urban youth communities with very little or no formal education (Kiessling and Mous 2004). However, it may have emerged earlier with rapid urbanization when Abidjan became the capital in 1934. Nouchi was called the *chapali du djassa* 'the language of the ghetto' (Appessika 2003). It was spoken by "bad boys" or "tough guys."

According to Kouadio (2006), Nouchi "*est né dans la rue et parlé par les jeunes en rupture avec la société*" (is born on the street and spoken by the youth that are antisociety) (Kouadio 2006: 188). Nouchi was used as an argot or slang helping to hide and protect their activities from undercover police officers. According to Kouadio (1990), the term Nouchi comes from the Susu language meaning Mustache or nose (nou) hair (chi). The following prayer in Nouchi is an illustration:

E seher! C'est mou su moi deh!
Mais ye ketekete ye eu trois togo!
Ye pee zeguen togo ae de pouess
Viens on ha gbo!
Seher c'est sa ki est la hoo!
(Le Magnific)
E seher! C'est mou su moi deh!
Oh Lord! It is soft on me-FOC
Oh Lord! Life is so difficult for me!
Mais ye ketekete ye eu trois togo!
But I have struggled I have had three hundred francs!
But I have struggled and got three hundred francs.
Ye pee zeguen togo ae de pouess
I have bought attieke hundred francs with two fish
I have bought attieke hundred francs and two fishes.
Viens on a gbo!
Come we will eat
Let's share.
Seher c'est sa ki est la hoo!
Lord, that's it-FOC.

This example demonstrates the way in which speakers coin and resemanticize the lexicon. *Mou* is from French meaning 'soft', 'easy'. But here, *mou* is used to mean 'difficult' or 'tough'. *Deh* is an Ivorian popular term used to emphasize an idea. *Kêtêkêtê* is a lexical creation meaning to struggle little by little. *Togo* is the word for the hundred-franc coin. *Zeguen* is the Nouchi for attieke (a cassava couscous made in Cote d'Ivoire). *Pouess* is the word for fish, from poisson (French). *Gbo* is a lexical creation meaning 'eat'. Nouchi is parasitic on *Francais Populaire Ivorien* 'Ivorian Popular French,' because this variety was the type of French spoken by the early school-drop-outs or the youth with no formal education. However, as the language permeated other speech communities with more 'standard' forms of French, the base varied. Indeed, the French spoken in Ivory Coast displays a 'standard' form called Ivorian French, and a 'sub-standard' form called Ivorian Popular French.

There is also a version of Nouchi based on Dyula. Kouadio (1990, 2006) gives the following reasons that caused the advent and perhaps the spread of Nouchi: the "*ivoricentric*" tendency to *tordre le cou au Français*; the massive drop-outs and other school failures that occurred in the 1970s and 1980s; the high immigration rate and rural exodus; and the advent of Zouglou, a popular music style that uses Nouchi for political and social protests. Nouchi was practiced for three main reasons: as a tool for identity construction in an urban setting, as a tool for peer group activities, and as a tool for intercommunication, since many youth did not share a common language. Some scholars suggest it is a contact 'language' involving dynamic mixing of Ivorian languages, French, English, as well as other European languages (Kouadio 2006; Kube-Barth 2009; Newell 2009). The speakers of Nouchi, the *Noussi* or the *Ziguehi*, founded a tool to reduce or wipe out communication barriers existing between speakers not competent in French and belonging to different linguistic backgrounds. But this communication tool was strongly coupled with a way of resisting mainstream identity ('resistance identity', Castells 1997) – a kind of 'resistant' youth culture (Kiessling and Mous 2004: 17) while constructing and endorsing a new social positioning, through linguistic structural reconstruction and code-mixing along with rich lexical innovation.

Historically, Nouchi seems to have started going mainstream in the first half of 1990 as a consequence of the end of the single party system and the advent of multipartyism, and especially its use by Zouglou singers. Indeed, Zouglou was born in the university student community and was a unifying factor for a whole generation. The use of Nouchi by university students certainly helped redefine its status and its community of practice.

This argotic status and thus the negative perception has been withering away as features of Nouchi penetrate households, schools, colleges and universities (Kube 2005; Boutin 2002). Today, Nouchi is characterized by a complex status, according to the community of practice. In literature it is presented as language on its own (Ayewa 2005; Sande 2015), a variety of French (Aboa 2012, 2011; Kube-Barth 2009); a sociolect (Kouadio 2006); and an urban youth language (Lafage 1998; Kiessling and Mous 2004; Aboa 2011). We could also call it a style or a register.

The different interpretations may be linked to two factors: the representativeness of the sample used for research, and the difficulty in clearly delineating the acrolectal (standard), the basilectal (popular French), and Nouchi. There is a thin line between Ivorian popular French and Nouchi (Kouadio 2006). There is also a general tendency to mix codes. Moreover, although there is a general agreement that the base language is French, data from the field display differences in the base form, not only based on the first language of the speaker, but also the language of the community of practice of which he/she is a member.

The development of Nouchi is showing contemporary widespread acceptance across gender, social status and contexts of interaction. It is used on national TV and radio, in advertising for major global brands, and in political discourse. The 'language' is endorsing a function of Ivorian (urban) (youth) identity construction and maintenance, especially because of its pan-spatial and pan-ethnic status. Scholars have been associating Nouchi – or hinted at such a fact – with a more Ivorian national identity, symbolizing a type of unity that Ivorian languages, standard French or Ivorian popular French cannot build (Kouadio 1990; Aboa 2011; Newell 2009, 2012; Nash 2013).

Cameroon: Camfranglais

The sociolinguistic space of Cameroon created a new sphere for dynamic language contact when Francophone and Anglophone Cameroon reunited in 1961 (Kouega 2003). This reunification occurred in a country of about 275 national languages (Gordon 2005). The contact between some of those languages consequently generated pidgins and other hybrid languages such as Pidgin English, Camfranglais and Franfulfulde (Machetti and Siebetcheu 2013).

The term Camfranglais was coined by Ze Amvela in 1989 (Kouega 2003). It is a hybrid/mixed language (Manga 2000) that was developed by "secondary school pupils who have in common a number of linguistic codes, namely French, English, Pidgin and a few widespread indigenous languages." They use the language to hide their communication from other members of the community when they are in the same interactional environment (Kouega 2003: 23). For Kiessling and Mous (2004), it is a highly hybrid sociolect of the urban youth. Tiayon-Lekobou (1985: 49) defines Camfranglais as "*langue des bandits*" (the language of gangsters).

It is "a mixture of Cameroonian languages, French (fr.: Francais); English (fr.: Anglais), Pidgin English and even other European languages such as Spanish or German, French being clearly the syntactic base" (Stein-Kanjora 2008: 118). According to Kouega (2003):

> Camfranglais sentences are based on the French sentence structure, which generally supplies almost all the function words of an utterance; as for the content words, they come from French, English, Pidgin and the indigenous languages. Most utterances contain at least one English or Pidgin key word like 'wait', 'go', 'back', 'ba-hat' (bad heart: to refuse, reject), 'commot' (come out = go for an outing). Other terms come from the background languages like 'ndolo' (noun: love; verb: to pamper a girl) or are new creations like 1 Camfranglais is a "*parler mixte issu du mélange du français, de l'anglais, des langues nationales et même du pidgin [. . .] et diverses formes de l'argot estudiantin*" 'jo'(guy), 'boc'(wear), and brand names of goods like Kenzo (a type of expensive shoes).
>
> *Kouega 2003: 25*

For Kiessling and Mous (2004), "The genius of Camfranglais is that it integrates non-French lexical items into a French morphosyntactic frame" (Kiessling and Mous 2003: 4). On the politics of Camfranglais, Kisseling and Mous (2004) displays "adolescent speakers as icons of 'resistance identity'" (Castells 1997), i.e., they consciously create and constantly transform this sociolect of theirs by manipulating lexical items from various Cameroonian and European sources, to mark off their identity as a new social group, the modern Cameroonian urban youth, in opposition to established groups such as the older generation, the rural population and the Cameroonian elites who have subscribed to the norms of "la francophonie" (Kiessling and Mous 2004: 1). For Lobe-Ewane (1989), Camfranglais "signals rebellion against authority and societal expectations. It is often associated with opposition to authority figures."

Speakers consciously manipulate the structures of English and French and add units from Ewondo, Douala, Bassa and other Cameroonian languages (Lobe-Ewane 1989). The manipulation is morphophonological (lege for village, rem for mere . . .) and morphosyntactic (see Kiessling and Mous 2004). Camfranglais serves the purposes of peer or horizontal communication, resistance identity (Castells 1997, 2001; Kiessling and Mous 2004), and an identity project (Castells 1997; Kiessling and Mous 2004), which clears ethnic barriers to constitute a Cameroonian youth urban identity that indigenous languages are unable to construct since they are indexicals of the rural world. Quoting Castells (1997), Cameroonian Pidgin English cannot help either in that they connote illiteracy and backwardness (Kiessling and Mous 2004).

Youth language practices compared

The studies done in South Africa, Kenya, Ivory Coast and Cameroon show that the language practices of youth in these four countries are strikingly similar. These practices have all emerged among male youth and seem to have been most prominent, and/or may have started, among antisocial/delinquent or marginalized youth. No one can be sure of the exact origin of these practices, but they all emerged in urban areas among young men as rapid urbanization took place within colonial and oppressive political contexts that involved the enforced placement of different linguistic groups into confined areas without infrastructure, services and amenities, leading to unemployment particularly among youth, poverty and crime.

In overcrowded and volatile social spaces, young men negotiated their place and status within male social networks. Young men had to draw on and create symbolic resources in the presentation and performance of self to align and distinguish themselves from other male groupings and to compete for and maintain their positions within and across hierarchies of male groups. Language and bodily action would therefore have been the key tool in creating different styles to express social distinctions, personae and stance. Distinguishing different groups based on styles would have been particularly important in a socially volatile context. Different lexicons were an important marker of identity and a rapidly changing lexicon a way of including and excluding others.

A distinct and changing lexicon was a way of maintaining secrecy and in-group allegiances among groups, especially those involved in antisocial activities, hence a strong association between an unintelligible lexicon and delinquent groups (tsotsis, gangsters, bad boys), and the suggestion is that it is among these groups where these practices may have originated.

In all four contexts, these practices are grammatically parasitic on existing languages. The base language varies from one community to another and even within the same speech community if more than one language is spoken. There is no evidence for systematic structural variations from local languages, although some forms of grammatical manipulation are possible for pragmatic purposes (see Brookes 2014). Lexical items undergo both semantic changes and morphological adaptation to the base language.

The lexicon is the key indexical feature of this way of speaking. The lexicon is adopted and semantically adapted from a variety of languages. It is limited to particular semantic domains where certain topics related to the activities, experiences and concerns of young men are over-lexicalized. It appears that the lexicon varies among groups and changes with each generation. Where systematic recordings of male social groups have been done, lexical variation also appears to mark different social levels among young men (Brookes 2014). In addition, the lexicon is part of a larger stylistic complex that includes body language, gestures, intonation, clothing, music and different activities and outlooks. We can therefore categorize these practices as linguistic styles that are employed as a tool in the expression of identities and social differentiation. These styles and their features have taken on particular social meanings and become indexical of different types of male youth. Across all four contexts, these practices are indexical of the streetsmart urbanite and a symbol of being part of a modern African identity. Therefore, other speakers may sometimes use a highly iconized and well-known feature or features to show their belonging to the urban milieu, to express a city slick and streetsmart persona and to either align with, or distinguish themselves from those around them.

In all four countries, these linguistic practices are still primarily male and indexical of a streetwise and city slick masculinity. Although it appears that women know and might make use of some of the lexicon, they did not and still do not participate in male sociality where these practices occur. The reason for the strongly gendered nature of these ways of talking is the divide between male and female social spaces and roles, with women restricted to domestic spaces while young men occupy public spaces where they developed a male street culture. However, as traditional gender divides become less rigid, it seems that some of the features of these ways of talking are increasingly indexical of a general urban cosmopolitan identity rather than a male one, and therefore women may, under certain circumstances, produce them.

In all four contexts, political and economic changes (the overthrow or withdrawal of illegal European invaders) at different times created a situation in which Africans took control of mainstream institutions. Previously marginalized cultural and linguistic practices entered mainstream discourse through the media, music and other art forms. Naming these linguistic practices, extracting them from actual contexts of use, and subjecting them to study within a particular theoretical paradigm and framing them within the common sense and dominant ideological view of language, led to their reinvention, creating different representations and interpretations of these phenomena. As artefacts of a vibrant urban male youth street culture, they have become linguistic resources available to a wider social milieu to be used as markers of urban identity and status. They have been co-opted into a different linguistic market where the original users and sources of these creative practices no longer control social spaces and discourses or enjoy the same status. As Africans took over institutional positions the European invaders previously occupied, economic marginalization decreased and the prestige attached to being successful by thwarting the colonial system began to diminish. Consequently, the language of the 'bad boys', the tsotis 'crooks' and 'bandits' is no longer the central source of linguistic prestige and power. As Githiora (2002: 174) points out "Sheng [and its functions] is a reflection of a larger social process and internal social relations, such as class division, age and gender within a highly multilingual context."

Urbanization and colonization created a sudden and rapid process of migration and urbanization at the beginning of the 20th century. This social change led to intense and sustained language contact and the emergence of urban varieties along with the emergence of these youth communicative phenomena. The second major social change has been the ending of illegal occupations by European countries, and, in cases like South Africa, the advent of democracy.

These social changes have meant that Africans gradually begin to take roles in mainstream institutions such as the media, business and government. Consequently, these practices that were largely outside of mainstream life become part of the broader symbolic market and become an object of value for both commodification and legitimization.

The restructuring of social and economic access and commodification of youth subcultures has shifted the social capital of symbolic resources and the way in which they are valued and used in creating new social distinctions (Zhang 2005). Features of these varieties are appropriated as symbolic resources by youth-directed media in the construction of a particular social identity. Youth language has become a talking point in the media and people attempt to name it and use it in written form. It is included in dramas on television about local life and is an important part of local music. Advertisers use it to characterize their products with particular social meanings. It is at this point that it has become an object of study with the main focus on collecting primarily the lexicon as evidence for a single systematic code and the claim of linguistic shift.

Approaches to the study of language among youth

Given the evidence that these so-called 'languages' are not single monolithic codes but multimodal and multilingual performative linguistic practices tied to specific groups of users and domains that result in different styles, why then is there such a strong push to claim these practices as new linguistic codes that are causing speakers to undergo language shift (see McLaughlin 2009 for completely unsubstantiated claims)? We suggest that there are several reasons for these claims. The first is that the majority of studies take a very narrow perspective on language. Researchers working on the language of youth in African societies have treated these practices within the framework of autonomous linguistic codes or varieties that are bounded separate entities. Linguists have then attempted to describe the formal features, mainly the lexicon and syntactic structures, of these assumed systems and to classify them in terms of language typologies as to whether they exhibit features of pidgins, creoles, code-switching varieties, slangs, anti-languages or argots.

In attempting to claim fully-fledged language status, scholars have tried to identify a systematic lexicon and new syntactic structures as evidence of a separate linguistic system. However, performative practices show that the lexicons are inherently variable and they have yet to demonstrate systematic differences in syntactic structure. Where linguists claim to have identified systematic differences, they have been comparing language among youth with standard varieties instead of local first language varieties (see Brookes 2014; Githiora 2002; Kiessling and Mous 2014). Where youth language has been compared with local first language varieties, these same structural features are found in both (Gunnink 2014). A few decontextualized examples of structural deviations are likely to be instances of linguistic manipulation in the moment and not evidence of a systematic shift in grammatical structure.

Second, this view of language as an independent system in the minds of speakers has meant that linguists have largely relied on traditional language documentation approaches that involve eliciting decontextualized examples of the code from one or more speakers in order to describe formal features, mainly the lexicon and the grammatical structure. One speaker's knowledge is considered evidence of a language system. However, if pragmatic purposes shape these practices based on linguistic strategies governed by aesthetic norms, that include the use of features from different languages, how is it possible to categorize these practices as belonging to a single linguistic system? It is precisely the strategy of being able to utilize different existing systems in conjunction with intonation, gesture and the manner of use that makes it a performative practice and style.

Third, not only has the source of data for most of these studies been speakers' latent knowledge that has been reproduced outside of the context in which it is found, but also studies do not interrogate the identity and position of the informants in relation to the users of this practice. Community members may have or have had different levels of engagement in these practices. As Labov (1972) pointed out, linguists' informants are often those peripheral to the core practitioners.

Another source of data for linguists has been the media, including advertising and written texts that have tried to use the lexicon and phrasing of youth languages, dictionaries and, more recently, internet sites that exchange new words and phrases. These sources of data combine features of the practice from different sources, areas, periods and often reflect elites' perceptions and peripheral knowledge of these practices. While advertisements may reflect patterns of speaking, they are not actual patterns of speaking but stereotypical representations that might appeal to different audiences. These sources provide important information, but are not direct evidence of language use or shift among speakers. Linguists have failed to distinguish between new social changes creating new linguistic markets in which new centers of power harness the social meaning of linguistic features to create new project identities and what speakers actually do on the ground.

Fourth, there are very few studies that systematically record spontaneous naturally occurring samples of youth language practices or link these practices to the social contexts in which they are embedded. Not a single study of Sheng, Nouchi or Camfranglais is based on systematic recordings of spontaneous data in situ. Occasionally, researchers provide isolated examples that they have observed. In one case, the claim that speakers are undergoing language shift to Sheng is backed up with one example of the use of a Sheng greeting between a bank teller and a client (Githiora 2016). Isolated examples that contain a word or two of Sheng in an interaction cannot be enough evidence of a language shift. Without spontaneous data that also includes details of who uses it, when, under what circumstances and for what purposes, a partial and somewhat distorted picture of these phenomena has emerged.

The invisibility of women's speech has led us to think that these phenomena are representative of the entire population and to miss the fact that these ways of speaking at the local level are first and foremost an expression of a certain type of masculinity. Githinji (2008) has suggested that there may be a variety of Sheng spoken among women, however, no one has produced any evidence for this claim and, in fact, the evidence suggests the contrary. Samper (2002) points out that women who use features of Sheng are labelled prostitutes and that for women it does not have the same advantages as it does for men. A systematic study of spontaneous conversations among women in South Africa showed that most women do not utilize features of this way of talking (Maribe and Brookes 2014). However, more work on larger samples is needed. Linguists fail to recognize their role in the process of what Bucholtz and Hall (2005) call 'linguistic authentification'. Studying a linguistic phenomenon results in formalizing knowledge about it. Part of this process involves collecting, categorizing and naming. Creating a single lexicon out of different areas and generations to make it into a monolithic language entity distorts the nature of these phenomena. Applying existing linguistic categories to new phenomena without understanding their communicative and social functions in situ has also led to miscategorization. The impact of linguists naming a set of practices as a monolithic linguistic code has created an imagined object of study.

Claiming that these language practices among youth are developing into languages of wider communication would mean that youth linguistic practices are replacing existing languages or merging with them. A number of studies suggest that the spread of the slang vocabulary into other domains is evidence that youth language will become the primary language of communication and replace other urban varieties. However, the data do not support this claim. For such a claim to be true, speakers would be able to use the language of youth across all domains. But, as we can see, the lexicon of these languages is limited to a few semantic domains mainly relating to the concerns and activities of youth. When used to translate documents or in narratives, the slang lexicon only occurs in these semantic domains.

The little in situ data that are provided suggest that linguistic variation can be understood not in terms of the replacement of one code by another but as symbolic resources being used to construct identity. Features of youth language are indexical of a cosmopolitan and 'cool' modern African identity that people incorporate into their speech for pragmatic, relational and identity purposes. The social meaning of these features depends on their distinctiveness in relation to other varieties as part of this cosmopolitan identity. Selecting and combining different semiotic resources gives value to the cosmopolitan style. In such circumstances the idea that youth languages would spread to become first languages is absurd.

It is odd that these claims about languages among youth in Africa becoming people's mother tongues is never made in relation to youth languages elsewhere in the world. One reason for this may be the extent to which youth languages in Africa can draw on so many different languages and this level of multilingualism has made them seem more exotic than they actually are. Another more sinister reason is that linguists are approaching language practices in Africa with an underlying ideological view that exoticises the other within a racist evolutionary framework.

References

Abdulaziz, M. H. and Osinde, K. (1997). "Sheng and Engsh: Development of Mixed Codes among the Urban Youth in Kenya." *International Journal of the Sociology of Language*, 125, 43–63.

Aboa, A. L. (2011). "Le Nouchi a-t-il un avenir?" In *Sudlangues* n°16, 44–54. Dakar, www.sudlangues.sn.

Aboa, A. (2012). *Langue Française et Identité Culturelle Ivoirienne*. Available online at: www.ltml.ci/site/new/index.php/revues-du-ltml/361-revue-n-6-du-ltml-issn-1997-4257.

Ahua, B. and Coulibal, Y. A. (1986). "Nouchi : un langage a la mode." In *Fraternite Matin*, 6 September, 2–3.

Appessika, K. (2003). Understanding Slums: Case Studies for the Global Report on Human Settlements. The case of Abidjan, Ivory Coast, www.ucl.ac.uk/dpu-projects/Global_Report/pdfs/Abidjan.pdf.

Ayewa, N. K. (2005). "Mots et contexts en FPI et en nouchi." *Actes des 7eme Journées scientifiques AUF-LTT*. Bruxelles: Edition Archives Contemporaines/AUF.

Barasa, S. N. (2010). Language, Mobile Phones and Internet: A Study of SMS Texting, Email, IM and SNS Chats in Computer Mediated Communication (CMC) in Kenya. PhD Dissertation: University of Leiden.

Bourdieu, P. (1977). "The Economics of Linguistic Exchanges." *Social Science Information*, 16, 645–668.

Boutin, B. (2002). Description de la Variation: Études Transformationnelles Desphrases du Français de Côte d'Ivoire. Thèse de doctorat, Université de Grenoble.

Brookes, H. J. (2004). "A First Repertoire of South African Quotable Gestures." *Linguistic Anthropology*, 14(2), 186–224.

Brookes, H. J. (2014). "Urban Youth Languages in South Africa: A Case Study of Tsotsitaal in a South African Township". *Anthropological Linguistics*, 56(3–4), 356–388.

Brookes, H. J. and Lekgoro, T. (2014). "A Social History of Urban Male Youth 'Varieties' in Stirtonville and Vosloorus, South Africa." *Southern African Linguistics and Applied Language Studies*, 32(2), 149–159.

Bucholtz, M. and Hall, K. (2005). "Identity and Interaction: A Sociolinguistic Approach." *Discourse Studies*, 7(4–5), 585–614.

Calteaux, K. (1994). A Sociolinguistic Analysis of a Multilingual Community. PhD Dissertation: Rand Afrikaans University, South Africa.

Castells, M. (2001). *The Internet Galaxy, Reflections on the Internet, Business, and Society*. Oxford: Oxford University Press.

Castells, M. (1997). *The Power of Identity, the Information Age: Economy, Society and Culture. Volume 2*. Oxford: Blackwell Publishers.

Githinji, P. (2005). Sheng and Variation: The Construction and Negotiation of Layered Identities. PhD dissertation, Michigan State University.

Githinji, P. (2006a). "Bazes and Their Shibboleths: Lexical Variation and Sheng Speakers' Identity in Nairobi." *Nordic Journal of African Studies*, 15(4), 443–472.

Githinji, P. (2006b). "Insults and Folk Humor: Verbal Transgressions in Sheng's Mchongoana." In Dwyer, D. (ed.), *The Joy of Language. Proceedings of a Symposium Honoring David Dwyer on the Occasion of his Retirement*, 35–45, www.msu.edu/~dwyer/JOLIndex.htm.

Githinji, P. (2008). "Sexism and (Mis)representation of Women in Sheng." *Journal of African Cultural Studies*, 20(1), 15–32.

Githiora, C. (2002). "Sheng: Peer Language, Swahili Dialect or Emerging Creole?" *Journal of African Cultural Studies*, 15(2), 159–181.

Githiora, C. (2016). "Sheng: The Expanding Domains of an Urban Youth Vernacular." *Journal of African Cultural Studies*, DOI: 10.1080/13696815.2015.1117962.

Glaser, C. (2000). *Bo-Tsotsi: The Youth Gangs of Soweto, 1935–1976*. Cape Town: David Phillip.

Gordon, R. G. (2005). *Ethnologue: Languages of the World*, 15th edition. SIL International.

Gunnink, H. (2014). "The Grammatical Structure of Sowetan Tsotstitaal." *Southern African Linguistics and Applied Language Studies*, 32(2), 161–171.

Handloff, R. E. (ed.) (1991). *Ivory Coast: A Country Study*. Washington, DC: Federal Research Division of the Library of Congress.

Hurst, E. (2009). "Tsotsitaal, Global Culture and Local Style: Identity and Recontextualisation in Twenty-First Century South African Townships." *Social Dynamics*, 35(2), 244–257.

Karanja, L. (2010). "'Homeless' at Home: Linguistic, Cultural, and Identity Hybridity and Third Space Positioning of Kenyan Urban Youth." *Education Canadienne et Internationale*, 39(2), 1–11.

Kariuki, A., Kanana, F. and Kebeya, H. (2015). "The Growth and Use of Sheng in Advertisements in Selected Businesses in Kenya." *Journal of African Cultural Studies*, 27(2), 229–246.

Kiessling, R. and Mous, M. (2004). "Urban Youth Languages in Africa." *Anthropological Linguistics*, 46(3), 303–341.

Kouadio, N. J. (1990). "Le Nouchi Abidjanais, Naissance d'un Argot ou Mode Linguistique Passagère?" Actes du Colloque International de Dakar, Décembre. In *Des Langues et des Villes*, 373–383. Coll. Langues et Développement, Paris: Didier Erudition.

Kouadio N'Guessan, J. (2006). "Le Nouchi et les Rapports Dioula / Français." *Des Inventaires Lexicaux du Français en Afrique à la Sociologie Urbaine . . . Hommage à Suzanne Lafage. Le Français en Afrique*, n° 21, 177–191. Nice: ILF – CNRS.

Kouega, J.-P. (2003) "Camfranglais: A Novel Slang in Cameroon Schools." In *English Today*, 19(2), 23–29.

Kube-Barth, S. (2009) "The Multiple Facets of the Urban Language Form, Nouchi." In McLaughlin, F. (ed.), *The Languages of Urban Africa*. London: Continuum, 103–114.

Labov, W. (1972). *Language in the Inner City: Studies in the Black English Vernacular*. Philadelphia: The University of Pennsylvania Press.

Lafage, S. (1991). "L'argot des Jeunes Ivoiriens, Marque D'Appropriation du Francais?" In: Denise Français- Geiger and Jean-Pierre Goudaillier (eds), *Langue Française 90: Parlures Argotiques*. Larousse, 95–105.

Lafage, S. (1998). "Hybridation et Français des Rues à Abidjan." In Queffelec, A. (ed.), *Alternances Codiques et Français Parlé en Afrique*. Actes du colloque (Aix-en- Provence, Septembre 1995). Aix-en-Provence: Universite de Provence, 377: 279–291.

Lobe-Ewane, M. (1989). "Cameroun: Le Camfranglais." *Diagonales*, 10: 33–4.

Machetti, S. and Siebetcheu, R. (2013) "The Use of Camfranglais in the Italian Migration Context." *Tilburg Papers in Cultural Studies*, No 55: 1–15. University of Tilburg.

Makhudu, D. (2002). "An Introduction to Flaaitaal." In Mesthrie, R. (ed.), *Language in South Africa*. Cambridge: Cambridge University Press, 398–406.

Manga, T. (2000). *La Politique Linguistique au Cameroun. Essai D'Aménagement Linguistique*. Paris: Karthala.

Maribe, T. and Brookes, H. J. (2014). "*Vela, re a ringa*: 'Of course, we speak [boys' talk]': The Role of Tsotsitaal in the Performance of Black, Lesbian, Youth Identities." *Southern African Linguistics and Applied Language Studies*, 32(2), 119–214.

Mazrui, A. (1995). "Slang and Code-Switching: The Case of Sheng in Kenya." *Afrikanistische Arbeitspapiere*, 42, 168–179.

Mbaabu, I. and Kazungu, N. (2003). *Sheng-English Dictionary: Deciphering East Africa's Underworld Language*. Dar es Salaam: Taasisi ya Uchunguzu wa Kiswahili, Chuo Kikuu cha Dar es Salaam.

Mbugua wa Mungai (2003). Identity Politics in Nairobi Matatu Folklore. PhD Dissertation. Hebrew University, Jerusalem.

McLaughlin, F. (ed.) (2009). *The Languages of Urban Africa*. London: Continuum.

Mesthrie, R. (2008). "'I've been speaking Tsotsitaal all my life without knowing it': Towards a Unified Account of Tsotsitaals in South Africa." In Meyerhoff, M. and Nagy, N. (eds), *Social Lives in Language: Sociolinguistics and Multilingual Speech Communities*. Amsterdam: John Benjamins, 95–109.

Mesthrie, R. and Hurst, E. (2013). "Slang, Code-Switching and Restructured Urban Varieties in South Africa: An Analytic Overview of Tsotsitaals with Special Reference to the Cape Town Variety." *Journal of Pidgin & Creole Languages*, 28(1), 103–130.

Mfenyana, B. (1977). Isi-khunsha nesitsotsi: The Sociolinguistic of School and Town Sintu in South Africa (1945–1975). MA Dissertation: Boston University.

Mfusi, M. (1992). "Soweto Zulu Slang: A Sociolinguistic Study of an Urban Vernacular in Soweto." *Language Matters*, 23, 39–83.

Mojela, V. M. (2002). "The Cause of Urban Slang and Its Effect on the Development of the Northern Sotho Lexicon: Contemplative Article." *Lexikos*, 12, 201–210.

Msimang, T. (1987). "Impact of Zulu on Tsotsitaal." *South African Journal for Languages*, 7(3), 82–86.

Mutonya, M. (2008). "Swahili Advertising in Nairobi: Innovation and Language Shift." *Journal of African Cultural Studies*, 20(1), 3–14.

Nash (2016). Le Nouchi, le Tchapali du Djassa. http://mahmaison.overblog. com/2016/09/le-nouchi-le-tchapali-du-djassa.html, (retrieved on December 5, 2016).

Newell, S. (2009). "Enregistering Modernity, Bluffing Criminality: How Nouchi Speech (and Fractured) the Nation." *Jola: Journal of Linguistic Anthropology*, 19(2), 157–184.

Newell, A. (2012). *Modernity Bluff: Crime, Consumption and Citizenship in Cote d'Ivoire*. Chicago: The University of Chicago Press.

Ntshangase, D. K. (1993). The Social History of Iscamtho. MA Dissertation, University of the Witwatersrand.

Ntshangase, D. K. (1995). "Indaba yami i-straight: Language and Language Practices in Soweto." In Mesthrie, R. (ed.) *Language and Social History: Studies in South African Sociolinguistics.* Cape Town: David Philip, 291–297.

Ntshangase, D. K. (2002). "Language Practices in Soweto." In Mesthrie, R. (ed.), *Language in South Africa.* Cambridge: Cambridge University Press, 407–418.

Ogechi, N. O. (2002). Trilingual Codeswitching in Kenya: Evidence from Ekegusii, Kiswahili, English and Sheng. PhD Dissertation, Hamburg: University of Hamburg.

Ogechi, N. (2005). "On Lexicalization in Sheng." *Nordic Journal of African Studies*, 14(3), 334–355.

Osinde, K. (1986). An Investigation into the Social and Structural Aspects of an Evolving Language. MA thesis, University of Nairobi, Kenya.

Rudd, R. W. (2008). Sheng: The Mixed Language of Nairobi. PhD Dissertation, Ball State University.

Rudwick, S. (2005). "Township Language Dynamics: siZulu and isiTsotsi in Umlazi." *Southern African Linguistics and Applied Language Studies*, 23(3), 305–317.

Samper, D. (2002). Talking Sheng: The role of a Hybrid Language in the Construction of Identity and Youth Culture in Nairobi, Kenya. PhD Dissertation, University of Pennsylvania.

Samper, D. (2004). "'Africa is still our mama': Kenyan Rappers, Youth Identity and the Revitalization of Traditional Values." *African Identities*, 2(1), 31–51.

Sande, H. (2015). *Selected Proceedings of the 44th Annual Conference on African Linguistics*, Ruth Kramer et al. (eds), 243–253. Somerville, MA: Cascadilla Proceedings Project.

Schuring, G. (1983). "Flaaitaal." In Claassen, G. and van Rensburg, M. C. J. (eds), *Taalverskeidenheid.* Pretoria: Academica, 116–133.

Slabbert, S. (1994). "A Re-evaluation of the Sociology of Tsotsitaal." *South African Journal for Linguistics*, 12(1), 31–41.

Slabbert, S. and Myers-Scotton, C. (1996). "The Structure of Tsotsitaal and Iscamtho: Code Switching and In-Group Identity in South African Townships." *Linguistics*, 34, 317–342.

Spyropoulos, M. (1987). "Sheng: Some Preliminary Investigations into a Recently Emerged Nairobi Street Language." *Journal of the Anthropological Society of Oxford*, 18(1), 125–136.

Stein-Kanjora, G. (2008). "Parler comme ca c'est vachement cool! or How Dynamic Language Loyalty Can Overcome Resistance From Above." *Sociologus*, 58(2), 117–141.

Stone, G. (2002). "The Lexicon and Sociolinguistic Codes of the Working-Class Afrikaans-Speaking Cape Peninsula Coloured Community." In Mesthrie, R. (ed.), *Language in South Africa.* Cambridge: Cambridge University Press, 140–153.

Tiayon Lekobou, C. (1985) Camspeak: A Speech Reality in Cameroon. Maitrise dissertation, University of Yaounde.

Zhang, Q. (2005). "A Chinese Yuppie in Beijing: Phonological Variation and the Construction of a New Professional Identity." *Language in Society*, 34, 431–466.

21

AFRICAN YOUTH LANGUAGES

The past, present and future attention

Sandra Nekesa Barasa

Introduction

Youth languages have always raised curiosity not only among scientists but also in general. This is because of their unique characteristics that differentiate them from mainstream languages. Some of their main characteristics include their reflection of the generational youth phenomenon, modernity and change. In some cases, some youth varieties are enshrouded in secrecy and exclusion, thus making them more extraordinary. A number of these youth languages are in Africa, which is not surprising given that Africa is a highly multilingual continent.

This chapter focuses on several African Youth Languages (AYLs) in the East, West, and South regions of Africa. Unfortunately, I could not cover all the AYLs, and especially none in the horn of Africa, for example Yarada K'wank'wa (Hollington, 2016) in Ethiopia, and Rendók in Sudan, due to limited literature sources, coupled with space constraints. I begin by explaining the concept of African (urban) youth languages, and then present an overview for each of the selected AYLs using seminal and contemporary literature, and scientific studies in the field. Next, I highlight some converging focal insights into AYLS in general. Finally, I propose, with suggestions of effective approaches, a better method to obtain reliable data in order to make credible generalisations.

African urban youth languages (AUYLs) or African youth languages (AYLs)?

The phenomenon of AYLs is evasive in many ways beginning right from its terminology given that the very definition of the youth languages is, up to now, still unresolved. So far, the term 'African urban youth languages (AUYLs)' itself, as used over the years by Abdulaziz and Osinde (1997), Kießling and Mous (2004), Brookes (2014), Wilson (2015) and Nassenstein (2016), is not supported by all scholars in the field. Two points of contention are that, first, these languages are not simply urban youth languages – they have spilled beyond urban boundaries, and, second, they are currently not only used by the youth (Féral, 2012).

This observation has been discussed by various scholars including Beck (2010) who argues that the so-called urban youth languages are also used in non-urban contexts and as registers. Hurst and Mesthrie (2013: 18) claim that existing terminology for these varieties, such as 'urban youth language' (Kießling & Mous, 2004), are inadequate, and even inaccurate now that the range of users extends beyond youth. Mitsch (2016: 67) has also claimed that this tag excludes large portions of African youth, especially those who do not reside in big African metropolises. In line with these arguments, Féral (2012: 25) explains that linguistically it is pertinent to distinguish "youth languages" from other "urban languages" spoken by the youth. In a similar vein, youth languages are not necessarily restricted to urban areas. The general picture is that whereas these languages originated in urban areas, they have now spread to rural regions beyond the cities, thus the term 'urban' should be used distinctively.

In general, I concur with Nortier and Dorleijn's (2013) view that youth languages do not have clear rules regarding their 'packaging' for them to be identified as youth languages. They explain that it might require only a single word, or expression, or a different pronunciation, or even a whole conversation, or perhaps the gestures used (Brookes, 2014), or the region where it is spoken, to characterise them as youth languages. Therefore, my definition of youth languages in this chapter is loosely based on a collation of studies – which accord that youth languages are initiated and actively used by juveniles (adults use it less); are spoken in urban centres (and now spilling over to rural areas); are markers of identity and modernity; and that they symbolise youth in-group membership. In order to capture this notion in this chapter, I will now adopt the term African Youth Languages (AYLs).

Besides the terminology, AYLs have been described inconsistently by different scholars. For example, the languages have been described as urban vernaculars (Beck, 2010; McLaughlin, 2009), underworld languages (Mbaabu & Nzuga, 2003), non-standard or substandard languages (Finlayson & Slabbert, 2003; Mattiello, 2005), and hybrid languages (Bosire, 2006; Samper, 2002). Other studies have postulated that these AYLs are not languages but slangs (Kießling & Mous, 2004; Kouega, 2003; Mazrui, 1995), registers and shibboleths (Githinji, 2006), 'highly stylised slang register' (Mesthrie & Hurst 2013: 125) and even 'non-standard/ youth and urban varieties' (Hurst, 2008; Hurst et al., 2012).

In as much as there is no main agreement on what these languages are, my assessment is that these languages: are not slangs because their structure is far more complex than merely the use of jargon; they are not pidgins because they co-exist with other lingua francae; they are not creoles, because they are not yet stable enough to be established as native languages. The tag of 'non-standardness' is too broad to describe them because this could also refer to informal mainstream varieties such as Swahili in (inland) Kenya. They could be hybrid languages, but there is more to them than mixing languages. Similarly, they could be registers, but this is a narrow compartmentalisation of their use because their usage is broader than the particular contexts for registers. They are also not ethnolects and I tend to agree with Eckert, (2008: 26), Nortier and Dorleijn (2008) and Stroud (2004) that the terms ethnolects, varieties or dialects are somewhat restricted and static. These terms presume 'a fixed set of more or less stable or static linguistic norms' (Nortier, 2008: 4) – a problem shared by all denominations such as varieties, styles or all the types of -*lects*, which tend to represent language as a fixed rather than as a fluid entity (Gadet & Hambye, 2014: 189). The label ethnolect presupposes ethnicity, which is not necessarily the case in AYL. In fact, one of the roles of AYL is to defuse ethnic divisions.

In order to understand the concept of youth languages in general, some references are worth reading. Halliday (1976) is one such, which introduced the idea of 'anti-languages' and has been used by many studies to explain the notion of youth languages in society. Although Halliday did not mention youth languages specifically, his idea of anti-languages fully captures the phenomenon of youth languages. Halliday confirms that anti-languages are complex to define because of the many forms that they take. He states that the 'most clearly defined (anti-languages) . . . have specific reference to alternative social structures, as well as the additional attributes of secret languages and professional jargons; and hence they are full of overt markers of their anti-language status' (583). According to Halliday, anti-languages are based on the same grammar as the variety of the language that is spoken in the local community – their main difference is in the use of vocabulary. These languages use different vocabulary or the same vocabulary with a different meaning, but only when necessary to communicate matters related to the subculture, and in order to distinguish themselves from other languages (Halliday 1976: 571).

Another useful reference is Myers-Scotton (1993) on the Matrix Language Frame (MLF) model. Although this model was initially developed with a focus on code-switching in multilingual contexts, it has been cited numerously in the discussion of the base language used in youth languages. Youth language studies often use it to explain how the grammar of a standardised language is used as a base/matrix by youth languages in order to insert their linguistic innovation. In this chapter I will also adopt the term matrix language loosely to refer to the standard languages' grammar used for each of the youth languages under discussion.

An influential review article that would be termed as one of the earliest seminal overviews of literature on AUYLs is by Kießling and Mous (2004). This was one of the earliest reviews to focus on several AYLs from different regions including South Africa's Tsotsitaal and Iscamtho, Congo's Indoubil and Lingala ya Bayankee, Cameroon's Camfranglais, Tanzania's Bongo flava, and Kenya's Sheng and Engsh. The article linked the development of AYLs to the economically poor and overcrowded city suburbs, in which the youths seek some form of identity by developing a language to defy and exclude other members of the community. I will present some of these languages in detail in the next section of this chapter.

More recent publications that are enlightening on AYLs include a special issue on the dynamics of youth languages in Africa edited by Mensah (2016). This publication consists of articles with the focus ranging from style, language attitudes, discourse markers, and identity construction among youths. The publication however is not particularly geared towards urban areas, but the youth in general – this approach confirms that AYLs are no longer confined to only urban areas.

Another relatively recent publication (in 2015) is a more specific journal issue on urban youth vernaculars in Africa. This issue focuses on youth languages in the eastern and southern region of Africa. Its point of departure is that it highlights the use of the AYLs in new domains such as in the media and corporate advertising. This shows that AYLs have reached their maturity and are now moving on to advanced domains of public communication. In the introduction to this journal issue, Githiora (2016b) comments that AYLs 'have moved away from the margins, by becoming important resources in various media platforms, advocacy, information sharing, politics, and crucially, by facilitating creativity and innovation'. Unlike the former linguistic descriptions, this distinctive focus provides useful insights on the status of AYLs in the general society.

South Africa

The Tsotsitaal phenomenon has been well studied since the early 1990s. However, just as the general AYL phenomenon, the nature of Tsotsitaal has not been agreed upon.

'Tsotsitaal' is a multi-word, i.e., 'tsotsi' that translates to 'criminal' and 'taal' means language. However, the etymology of the term 'tsotsi' is not certain. Deumert (2014: 3) and Molamu (1995) discuss proposals made to account for this hazy etymology in detail, for example by pointing out suggestions that the term tsotsi might be from one of South Africa's vernaculars such as a mispronunciation of the Afrikaans term 'zoot' ('suit' i.e., dress well), or it might have been isiXhosa's 'ukutsolisa' ('to sharpen' i.e., look sharp), or itsolo (dandy), or perhaps Sesotho's '*ho tsotso*' ('to sharpen') – or it could be even linked to '*tutsi*' which is an ethnic group in Rwanda (see more of this discussion in Deumert, 2014).

In addition to the etymological uncertainty, there has also been confusion over the meaning of the term Tsotsitaal in AYLs – does it refer to the general AYL phenomenon in South Africa, or does it specifically refer to the AYL variety that uses Afrikaans as its base language? It has since been proposed that the term should appear as a homonym with a slight distinction in the form of the initial letter '*t*', which would appear as either uppercase or lowercase. The lowercase '*tsotsitaal(s)*' is used as a blanket term referring to the general South African youth language phenomena, while the uppercase Tsotsitaal acts as a proper noun in reference to the Afrikaans-based variety of *tsotsitaal* (Mesthrie, 2008; Slabbert & Myers-Scotton, 1996).

The distinction between Tsotsitaal and tsotsitaal is not always adhered to, especially when the lowercase 't' appears at the beginning of a sentence e.g., in Hurst and Buthelezi's (2014) definition that 'Tsotsitaal is a South African language phenomenon spoken in urban centres around South Africa which involves the use of a range of linguistic and semiotic resources as part of a process of styling an urban identity' (185). Another strategy to distinguish the two meanings involves using the term '*flaaitaal*' to refer to the Afrikaans-based tsotsitaal (Makhudu, 2002). Interestingly though, Brookes (2014: 364) points out that the speakers themselves do not label their languages. These labels are from linguists who channel them to the media, and the media in turn channel them back to the speakers.

The main tsotsitaals are Tsotsitaal and Iscamtho. Their regional varieties include *isiTsotsi*, *Kasitaal, Gamtaal, Ringas*, etc. (Brookes, 2014; Hurst & Buthelezi, 2014). These varieties use similar (tsotsitaal) vocabulary by immersing it in a distinct matrix language such as Afrikaans, English or an African language (Brookes, 2014; Hurst, 2008). For example, the varieties of Iscamtho use an African Bantu language – usually Zulu or Sotho – as the matrix language (Mfusi, 1992; Msimang, 1987; Rudwick, 2005).

Nonetheless, it is important to note that the issue of matrix languages is only a generalisation at face value. As Mesthrie (2008) claims, a variety may use a certain matrix language though a deeper analysis shows that it also exhibits different morphological patterns that are clearly not part of the matrix language (Brookes, 2014, p. 379; Molamu, 2003, p. xxv). Additionally, some varieties are, for example, used in Code Switching (CS) contexts. Mesthrie and Hurst (2013) refer to these as hybrid language varieties – thus it is not always the norm that a given variety only uses a single matrix language.

Many studies, such as Mfusi (1992), Mesthrie and Hurst (2013), Beyer (2014), Hurst and Buthelezi (2014), concur that the Tsotsitaal phenomenon started in the 1930s–1940s in Johannesburg's economically poor and racially mixed townships. The tsotsitaals, Iscamtho and Tsotsitaal, have been relatively well described in terms of the languages involved. In a bid to explain the spread of Iscamtho, most studies have adopted the Ntshangase (1993, 1995) theory that it gained popularity when Afrikaans became less admirable after the apartheid period. However, Brookes and Lekgoro (2014) explain that it was the forced evacuation of 'Afrikaans mother-tongue speakers from Bantu speaking groups . . . from Stirtonville to Vosloorus in 1964 (that) caused the demise of Afrikaans-based Tsotsitaal in black urban townships in Johannesburg and other areas in Gauteng and a major shift to Bantu-based ones' (382).

Nevertheless, the tsotsitaal phenomenon has since spread to the whole country. According to Beyer (2014), the 'contemporary urban youth varieties of South Africa originally developed in young male-dominated networks signalling an urban, streetwise identity, quite often coupled with some kind of gang-related background' (249). Up to now, tsotsitaals are mainly used by young urban black men (Brookes, 2014; Hurst, 2009; Hurst & Mesthrie, 2013), and that it links historically with a 'criminal' identity construct. See Glaser (1992) for a detailed description of the Tsotsi culture from the 1930s.

There have been many studies on tsotsitaals since the 1970s. Early studies focused on categorising tsotsitaals as creoles (Mfenyana, 1977) and urban lingua franca (Msimang, 1987). In the 1990s the majority of the studies concentrated on distinguishing tsotsitaals using the different matrix languages (see Ntshangase, 1993; Slabbert & Myers-Scotton, 1996). Most of the aftermath studies in the 2000s are of a wide range including a narration of tsotsitaal's historical development and a descriptive dictionary by Molamu (2003).

Besides the description of language, other studies have immersed tsotsitaals in a socio-cultural context for ethnographic results. Brookes (2014) explains that most of these studies have concluded that tsotsitaals are used by male youth, i.e., gender- and generation-based categories. Other studies have described tsotsitaal's extra-linguistic features and accounted for its functions, e.g., as urban lingua francae, anti-languages, secret languages, stylects, etc. (see Hurst & Buthelezi, 2014: 104) for a detailed account of the different functions as proposed by different scholars). Hurst (2008) and Brookes (2014: 357) are other studies that have provided a rich background and analysis of style and functions of the Cape Town Tsotsitaal.

As the use of tsotsitaals spreads and becomes widely spread in South Africa, current studies have shifted to scrutinising other linguistic aspects of the language such as figurative speech and gestures; for example Hurst's (2016) study on the use of metaphor in Tsotsitaal and how this use illuminates Tsotsitaal's anti-language aspects. Another example is Brookes' (2014) study on variation in Tsotsitaals by focusing on different styles ranging from those close to urban languages to more metaphorically dense anti-language styles that are reserved for the inner circle. In spite of all these efforts to study and fathom tsotsitaals, there is still more that needs to be done as will be shown in the third section of this chapter.

Kenya

The AYLs associated with Kenya are Sheng and Engsh. With close to 50 publications so far, Sheng is the most studied AUYL in Africa since the 1980s. Similar to other AYLs, the etymology of the name Sheng is not clear. According to Mazrui (1995: 171), Sheng is based on Swahili, and the term Sheng is an acronym for Swahili-English, which are supposedly the languages that make up Sheng. However, it is not clear why the first part is *sh* and not *sw* (for *Sw*ahili). The derivation of the term Engsh is a bit more clear because, as Abdulaziz and Osinde (1997) and Githinji (2006) claim, the term Engsh is derived from inverting the letters in the word Sheng, as a way to reverse the symmetry of languages (i.e., the first letters *Eng* denote the matrix language).

One issue here is that it seems that both Sheng and Engsh only feature English and Swahili, but that is not the case. They have been shown to use other languages such as Kenyan vernacular languages and even Afrikaans (see Ogechi, 2005; Barasa, 2010). An explanation could be that perhaps Swahili and English were the languages that featured in these AYLs at the beginning, but, over time, the AYLs have expanded their scope due to a wider range of language contact.

In terms of origin, it is not entirely clear when Sheng first came into being. Early studies, such as Abdulaziz and Osinde (1997), Kembo-sure (1992), Mazrui (1995), Mkangi (1985), Osinde (1985) and Spyropoulos (1987), posit that Sheng existed as early as the 1950s but only became prominent in the 1970s. They explain further that it originated from socioeconomically poor neighbourhoods in Nairobi as a protest code.

According to most scholars, Sheng is mostly spoken in lower income urban neighbourhoods mainly by male youth. However, as I have already pointed out, Sheng (and other AYLs) has since spread to non-urban areas as well. Engsh, on the other hand, was originally spoken in the posh Westlands neighbourhoods of the city – but has also spread countrywide to middle and upper middle class youth (both male and female) – more so by females (Barasa & Mous, 2017). Both Sheng and Engsh signal an urban streetwise identity – prestige, generational rebellion, linguistic innovation, ethnic neutrality, although Engsh extends this identity to a more *glocal* level, i.e., Engsh speakers are seen as sophisticated, educated, and internationally modern.

In an attempt to understand Sheng, scholars have described it in various ways, e.g., a non-standard variety of Kenyan Swahili (Nassenstein, 2016); extensive code-mixing (Mazrui, 1995); pidgin (Githiora, 2002; Osinde, 1985; Samper, 2002); urban vernacular (Githiora, 2016b); shibboleth (Githinji, 2006); order of discourse mixed language (Meierkord, 2011); sociolect (Samper, 2002); hybrid variety/code (Githinji, 2006); unstable youth variety (Kariuki et al., 2015: 230). Mazrui (1995) and Githinji (2006) sum it up in their claim that 'Sheng defies the classification categories such as pidgin, creole, slang (in spite of the acronym), or jargon. This is because although it exhibits features that characterize all these categories, none can be said to exhaustively capture its various peculiarities' (Githinji, 2006: 446). Similarly, Engsh has been characterised as Nairobi 'slang' (Githiora, 2002), however, as an AYL, it is more elaborate than slangs (Kießling & Mous, 2004).

In terms of varieties, it has been pointed out that Sheng has registers (Githiora, 2016a) and localised dialects for different neighbourhoods or 'bazes' (Githinji, 2006), e.g., Dandora, Calif, Buruburu, Kaloleni, Majengo and Mathare (see Samper, 2002; Ogechi, 2005; Bosire, 2006; Githinji, 2009). According to these studies, the difference between the varieties is mainly in lexicon, and its function is to maintain a tight in-group identity. It is interesting that, having said this, some studies still treat Engsh as a slang or variety of Sheng (Githiora, 2002), yet Engsh does not serve to maintain a tight in-group identity and neither does it only differ from Sheng through lexicon (see Barasa & Mous, 2017).

As I have already mentioned, there are many publications on Sheng. One foundational literature cited numerously is by Mazrui (1995). It serves as a clear introduction and background by determining what Sheng is, and what it is clearly not in terms of its features. Another popular study on youth languages in Kenya is by Abdulaziz and Osinde (1997) who trace the development of both Sheng and Engsh by giving detailed descriptions and examples. Other publications on Sheng include Beck (2010), Bosire (2006), Ferrari (2009), Githinji (2009), Githiora (2002), Kembo-sure (1992), Ogechi (2005), Osinde (1986), Rudd (2008), Samper (2002) and Spyropoulos (1987). A majority of these studies on Sheng have mainly focused on describing its linguistic features, distinguishing it from code-switching, and discussing its manifestation of protest against linguistic norms.

Recent studies have immersed Sheng in to the sociolinguistic context now that Sheng has spread in the whole country. These studies show how it is used, for example, in public transport (matatu) (wa Mungai, 2003, 2013), in schools (Momanyi, 2009), in music and poetry (Vierke, 2015), in advertisements (Kariuki et al., 2015), in media, politics, education and corporate advertising (Githiora, 2016a), in social media (Barasa, 2010), and in gender (Githinji, 2008). A different approach is taken by Barasa and Mous (2017) who study the 'non-use' of Sheng in an attempt to answer the question that, since Sheng is so widespread, why is it not used in all contexts? They proceed by pointing out some contexts in which Sheng does not appear, for example in official documents, and give explanations on possible reasons.

As it may have been noticed from my review above, not many studies have tackled Engsh. Nassenstein (2016: 85) observes that the existence of Engsh has for long not been certified although it was mentioned by Kioko and Muthwii (2003) and Kießling and Mous (2004). In fact, Engsh is mostly only mentioned in passing in studies whose focus is on the development of Sheng (Githinji, 2009; Githiora, 2002). Other studies vaguely juxtapose it with Sheng, e.g., Njogu and Oluoch-Olunya's (2007) statement that '(f)urther to Sheng is another rather dormant youth variety called Engsh' (136). A possible reason for this may be that Engsh is mostly treated as part of Sheng. However, there are some in-depth studies on Engsh such as Barasa and Mous' (2017) comprehensive description of Engsh; Meierkord's (2011) study on Engsh in magazines and newspapers; and Barasa's (2010) account of Engsh in social media. It could thus be said that there should be more studies on Engsh to clearly show its point of departure from Sheng.

Cameroon

Camfranglais is the AUYL in Cameroon's urban centres including Yaounde, Douala, Tiko, Kribi, Nkongsamba, Bafoussam and Bamenda. This AYL has also been referred to as *Franglais*, or *Frananglais*. However, it has been argued that these two terms refer to the codeswitching and mixing French and English – and that these terms better describe the Canadian codeswitching phenomenon rather than Camfranglais.

The name Camfranglais, coined by Ze Amvela (1983), is an acronym that symbolises a mix of Cameroonian languages (*Cam*); French (*fr*), English (*anglais*) (Kouega, 2003). Although this acronym presupposes that Camfranglais is a mix of indigenous Cameroon languages, French and English – with French as the matrix language – there is evidence of the presence of other African and European languages such as Lingala (from Congo), German, Spanish and even Latin. (See Kouega, 2003 and Nchare, 2010 for examples.) These elements might have perhaps been incorporated in the language after the coinage of the term.

Similar to Sheng and tsotsitaals, Camfranglais has been widely studied. Early studies proposing the existence of Camfranglais include Ze Amvela (1983), Tiayon-Lekoubou (1985), Koenig et al. (1983) and Mbah and Mbah (1994). A foundational study that gives an overview of Camfranglais is by Ntsobé et al. (2008). This study discusses the origin of Camfranglais and presents a linguistic analysis by providing sample Camfranglais texts. It also discusses the sociolinguistic setting of Camfranglais in high schools.

In terms of origin, there is not much surprise that some studies such as Féral (2006) claim that Camfranglais has been in existence since the 1970s; while others, e.g., Kouega (2003), are convinced that it arose in the early 1980s when English was introduced as a subject in the high school educational system.

Studies on this language concur that it is consciously coined by high school students (Kouega, 2003; Vakunta, 2008), and is used as an anti-language by 'urban juvenile franco-phones' (Schroder, 2007) to signal rebellion and opposition against authority figures and norms (Ewané, 1989; Nchare, 2010; Stein-Kanjora, 2008). It therefore serves as an in-group marker of identity and urbanism. Kouega (2007: 34) explains that fluent speakers of Camfranglais are 'secondary school students, who eventually leave school and become soldiers and policemen, thieves and prisoners, gamblers and conmen, musicians and comedians, prostitutes and vaga-bonds, hair stylists and barbers, peddlers and labourers and, in a few cases, high-ranking civil servants and businessmen'. However, there is no indication of what language they use during and after transition from high school.

Many well-known studies in the field have provided a linguistic description of Camfranglais. They include Kießling (2005) who presents a detailed linguistic analysis and description of Camfranglais. Other similar, though restricted, studies on Camfranglais include Biloa (1999) who presents a syntactic description of the language; Efoua-Zengue (1999) and Fosso (1999), who give a morphosyntactic analysis of word formative processes; Kouega (2003) and Féral (2006) describe the general features and functions of the language, and Essono (1997) and Hecker (2009) discuss its relationship to French.

Foundational studies on the sociolinguistic profile of Camfranglais include Koenig et al. (1983) who laid the base via their study of the sociolinguistic profile of urban centres in Cameroon; Essono (1997) and Efoua-Zengue (1999) segmented Camfranglais from French, while, in a similar vein, Echu (2001) distinguished it from English. Vakunta (2008) took a different turn by describing the use of Camfranglais in Cameroonian literature. A more recent study is by Stein-Kanjora and Gardy (2015) who present views of Camfranglais in a metalanguage context on social media, and conclude that Camfranglais speakers (especially those living out of Cameroon) are well versed and aware of their linguistic repertoire. In a team spirit, they engage in intense discussions about the language and even invent new words and develop new elements of the language in online fora – a fact that is unique and unprecedented in other youth languages (Stein-Kanjora & Gardy, 2015: 261).

The main issue that currently surrounds Camfranglais is whether it has a potential for certification as a national language, or, for a start, if it can be approved and adopted as a medium of instruction in schools. These discussions are popular in the media with mixed views. I will discuss this further below (see page 421).

Ivory Coast

Nouchi is the AYL that is associated with Ivory Coast. It is referred to as the urban patois in Abidjan based on *Francais Populaire*. Nouchi has been used in Ivory Coast since the 1970s. Similar to some of the discussed AYLs, the etymology of the term Nouchi is not entirely clear. According to Kießling and Mous (2004), this term could be an inversion of the French *chez nous* (to/at our house) or it could be from Malinke language with the meaning of *moustache* (see details in Sande, 2015; Koffi, 2013).

Kießling and Mous (2004) explain that Nouchi is a combination of languages such as French, Dioula, Baoulé, Bété, Spanish, German, and English with French as the matrix language. However, studies such as Sande (2015) have shown that Nouchi has an independent grammar evidenced by 'derivational suffixes, both those borrowed from other source languages, and those original to Nouchi' (244).

In terms of origin, Nouchi was first used in Abidjan as the lingua franca of uneducated and unemployed youth, but over time it became the language of Ivoirian identity (Kouadio, 2005; Kube-Barth, 2009; Newell, 2009; Sande, 2015). It is currently spoken by a great majority of the population in Ivory Coast – and as a first language by some (Aboa, 2011; Ayewa, 2005; Kube-Barth, 2009). In fact, according to Koffi (2013), Sande (2015), and Kouadio (2005), Nouchi is already on its way to creolisation. This claim was made by Sande (2015) as a response to the question of whether Nouchi is the native language of a population. Sande explained that 'Kouadio (2005) addresses (the question) head-on when he states that Nouchi is the native language of the current generation of urban Ivoirians. My own consultants in Abidjan have confirmed this claim'. In as much as this could be the case on the ground, the collection of data and evidence to support such a strong statement is not credible in this case. The elicitation of data from consultants should be backed up by the actual observation of the ongoing practices in context, in order to keep it more objective.

Nouchi has not been studied much in comparison to other AYLs. Sande (2015: 244) explains that there are very few studies on Nouchi as a distinct language because '[w]ithin the academic

African youth languages

world, Nouchi is often treated as synonymous to "Ivoirian French," or has been referred to as "slang" Ahua (2008); Newell (2009), "an urban youth language" (Beck, 2010; Kießling & Mous, 2004), a "variety of Ivoirian French" (Kube-Barth, 2009), or a "sociolect'" (Kouadio, 2005). Perhaps this could be the reason why existing studies on Nouchi are still attempting to prove its existence as an independent language.

Kouadio's (1990) research is one such study that substantiates the existence of Nouchi in Abidjan. Sande (2015) presented an extensive morphological description of the language to prove that it exists as a distinct language and not as a French dialect. Koffi (2013) also describes Nouchi and provides evidence that Nouchi is neither an argot, nor a pidgin, but it is a creole in the making (though the evidence is somewhat incomplete). Ahua (2008) describes it in terms of vocabulary, phrases and syntax, and confirms that Nouchi's morphological features are not purely from French and therefore it is not a variety or dialect of French.

In terms of function, Ayewa (2005) expounds that Nouchi serves as a lingua franca because there is no other language in Ivory Coast that fits the role. French is not effective as a lingua franca because many people are not proficient in it. In addition, Nouchi is considered as neutral unlike French which has a colonial background. Newell (2009) also studied the functions of Nouchi and concluded that it is a symbol of modernity and city life. She claims that 'Nouchi indexes a new pan-ethnic Ivoirian identity based on the alternative modernity of cosmopolitan urban youth' (157). These are some of the reasons that make AYLs appealing to the youth.

Congo

Congo has several urban youth languages, such that it can be described as a melting pot for youth languages – it could easily be, and rightly so, referred to as a multi-youth languages community. The youth languages and varieties associated with Congo are *Indoubil*, *Indoubil ya kozongela* (also referred to as 'inverted Indoubil'), *Lingala ya bayanké*, *Langila* and, recently, *Yabâcrane*. With all these, it is surprising that not many studies have been done on these youth languages. Note that I will not discuss Langila since it is mainly spoken in the artistic industry, e.g., by entertainers such as musicians, painters, actors, choreographers, and dancers, and thus it is not a youth lingua franca per se).

Goyvaerts and Kabongo-Mianda (1988) posit that the etymology of the term Indoubil is based on an Indian magician Indou Sankara – who seems to have been an inspiration to the early speakers' style – and Bill (as a reference to a modern streetwise person).

Indoubil is widely used in Congo. It has varieties in close proximities, for example Indoubil ya kozongela in Mangobo district and the Indoubil spoken in the centre of Kisangani (see Wilson, 2015 for details). The foundational study on Indoubil was by Goyvaerts and Kabongo-Mianda (1988), who provided a historical background of Indoubil and also described the social context of the language. The variety of Indoubil in Kinshasa, which is known as Lingala ya bayanké, is based on Lingala as its matrix language, while the variety in eastern Congo, e.g., in Bukavu, is based on Swahili as its matrix language. Yabâcrane, also spoken in eastern Congo, e.g., in Goma, has been recently introduced in scientific literature by Nassenstein (2016) as a Swahili-based AYL. It is characterised by an aggressive and violent streetwise image.

In terms of origin, Indoubil was first traced in Kinshasa in the early 1960s amongst rebellious youths who wanted to represent an image of the 'cool guy in the hood'. This was not only through language but also through dressing and mannerisms (what Kießling and Mous (2004) and Wilson (2015) refer to as *meta-signs*, and Hurst and Mesthrie (2013), as styles). According to Goyvaerts and Kabongo-Mianda (1988), Indoubil disappeared for a while but later resurfaced amongst secondary school children, and, afterwards, it spread to other youths out of school. In Kinshasa it became known as Lingala ya bayanké. An elaborate sociocultural description of Indoubil has recently been extended by Wilson (2015) who did fieldwork in Kisangani culminating in an immersion of Indoubil into its social context of '*ngandas*' (Ngandas are food restaurants by day and pubs for chilling out at night – see Wilson, 2015 for details).

An interesting aspect from this multi-youth languages melting pot is that these languages too face a language contact situation and also tend to borrow from each other. For example, Nassenstein (2016) in his study on Yabâcrane discovered that this language borrows from other youth languages, especially from Lingala ya bayanké. This is somewhat similar to the Kenyan situation where Engsh borrows from Sheng (see Barasa & Mous, 2017 for details). Wilson (2015) also confirms that Indoubil ya kozongela spontaneously uses words from the mainstream Indoubil and manipulates them through inversion. Wilson also explains that speakers of Indoubil ya kozongela also speak the mainstream Indoubil. They mainly use Indoubil ya kozongela to maintain an in-group identity and secretiveness when in the company of 'outsiders'.

More studies should be done on AYLs in Congo to enable a comprehensive overview. For now, there are still many gaps and questions, for example, are there any other AYLs in Congo that have not yet been documented? What is the motivation for the flourishing of more than one AYL in the same region, with the same matrix language? What about rural urban migration? And what happens when speakers of more than one AYL (multilinguals) come into contact – what is the unmarked language choice and how is it used as an exploratory code? Research based on credible data is still needed to answer all the lingering questions.

Uganda

Luyaaye is Uganda's AYL spoken in Kampala, though now spreading to other parts of the country. It uses Luganda as its matrix language and borrows from English, Swahili, and, interestingly, the Kenyan Sheng, but hardly anything from Uganda's indigenous languages (Namyalo, 2015).

Similar to other AYLs, the etymology of the name has not been traced. Whereas some argue that the term Luyaaye is from a cry of despair that was repeatedly heard when small scale youth entrepreneurs were harassed by the security patrol agents of Idi Amin (the third president of Uganda, ruling from 1971 to 1979), others claim that the term is from the *Luhyia* language in Kenya where it denotes rebelliousness. The main agreement is that Luyaaye started as an in-group language used against those in authority by the uneducated young adults.

Luyaaye is believed to have emerged in the early 1970s, although there is no clear evidence apart from some sketch vocabulary from Nsimbi (1983) as cited by Namyalo (2015). Its origin has not been agreed upon. Some think that it was initiated in Kampala by young business people as an in-group language to exclude government officials during the political turmoil in the period of Idi Amin's rule. Others think that it may have originated from the Busia border town that is a hub of business between Kenya and Uganda. However, the majority believe that it was an in-group language used by criminals to evade the law by use of metonymy.

There are very few studies that give insight on Luyaaye. A promising foundational scholarly study is by Naluwooza (1995). This study proves the existence of Luyaaye and describes it as a social dialect for the economically less privileged community. So far, the most revealing study is by Namyalo (2015) who gives a brief introduction to the language and a detailed description of its dynamic linguistic strategies that are fast changing. Namyalo also reveals that Luyaaye has varieties based on the five regions (hills) in Kampala. She adds that each variety can be easily distinguished, and crossing to a different Luyaaye territory is risky. The (socio) linguistic implications of this strong in-group identity are yet to be unveiled.

Insights on AYLs

Nortier and Dorleijn's (2013) extensive and detailed universal overview of similarities and differences of what they call *multiethnolects* (language styles used by multi-ethnic adolescent groups) in Europe, Africa, Asia, and Scandinavian regions is an eye-opener for those interested in generalisations on youth languages.

This section outlines some common factors of AYLs based on this overview. Note that, in addition to the mainstream AYLs, this overview acknowledges the spread of AYLs in non-urban regions as well. Although not many studies have focused on highlighting the position of non-urban AYLs in general, I attempt to incorporate these varieties where applicable in order to provide a bigger picture on the whole phenomenon.

Etymology

An issue about youth languages is their etymological development. Most AYLs can be traced back to roughly half a century ago, though their history is mostly exogenous and somewhat uncertain. An example of this is reflected throughout in the naming of the languages. So far, perhaps only Engsh and Camfranglais are clear in terms of etymology. Even a language that has been studied relatively well like Sheng does not have a clear explanation of its name. Nouchi, Luyaaye, Indoubil and tsotsitaals are further examples, where the origin of their names is still uncertain.

Kerswill's (2010) observation is that 'all (AYLs) appear to have names. The assumption is that they are grassroots names, not imposed'. However, Beck (2010) contests this in her observation that AYLs are not named by speakers but by researchers and perhaps the media who impose the names. In addition to this, Beck (2010: 24) observes that the naming of AYLs is not associated to any cities of origin, or where they are majorly spoken.

Migration and socioeconomic factors

Migration is one main initiator of the original urban youth languages. Kerswill (2010: 38), captures this in the statement that all urban youth languages (worldwide) are 'the result of intense immigration to cities followed by the socialisation of young people in close-knit multilingual peer groups with little prospect of social and economic advancement'. In African contexts, migration is 'intra-national' or what Hurst (2008) calls 'in-migration', i.e., the movement from rural areas to big cities in search for some financial income. In the cities, these types of in-migrants are likely to work in the informal sector, earning minimum wages, and thus settling in poor neighbourhoods that are usually overcrowded with fellow in-migrants from different ethnic backgrounds. In a bid to communicate neutrally, but at the same time mark their identity, the youth initiate youth languages as lingua francae for in-group communication – for example, Sheng and Camfranglais – rather than use mainstream national languages. They also adopt metalinguistic features as part of the AYL culture e.g., dressing, body language, intonation, etc. (see examples of Tsotsitaal metalinguistic features in Hurst, 2016 and Brookes, 2014)).

The interesting fact is that it is this specific urban nature that makes AYLs appealing to the youth in non-urban regions because it gives them a sense of modernity. The non-urban youth acquire these AYLs and their metalinguistic culture from urban centres through contact with speakers perhaps through migration to and from cities, through contact with speakers in public spaces, e.g., in schools, and more-so through the media (Muaka, 2011).

These AYLs are well endowed with numerous vocabulary to comfortably discuss certain common urban themes such as entertainment, sexuality, alcohol, drugs, criminality, rebellion, etc. (Widawski, 2015: 90). It would be interesting to determine how they get adapted to fit the non-urban context as well. It is important to note that, as explained on pages 413–415, the origin and context of Engsh in Kenya is an exception to this migration concept.

Speakers

It is usually assumed that speakers of urban youth languages are young, yet the question that lingers is: how can youthfulness be qualified? So far, the majority of the literature claims that the AYL speakers are adolescents, teenagers, high school students, workers in informal sectors, etc. However, it is not uncommon to hear children (e.g., primary school children below their teens) speaking, for example, Sheng and Iscamtho. Hurst (2008) offers an explanation in her thesis that speakers of youth languages qualify themselves as young by 'excluding' the older generation. It now could be the case that the age bracket of speakers of these AYLs is growing on both ends of the scale so long as they have an older group to exclude.

Another aspect where studies in this field concur is that the majority of the speakers of youth languages are male (an exception is Engsh speakers whose majority are female youth). These male speakers 'define themselves in the sense of a particular masculinity (swag), which involves being "streetwise" or "clever" and tough' (Hurst, 2008: 250). However, such explanations are not generalizable because females are also exposed to similar conditions but are hardly reported to embrace the AYLs as do their male counterparts. It is notable that Githinji (2008) discusses the role of women in self-definition in Sheng, and Wilson (2015) acknowledges female prostitutes and hair stylists as speakers of Indoubil. However, in general, there is no satisfactory discussion of the role of women and children in AYLs. More on this is in the section below on Nativization.

Intelligibility

An observation of AYLs shows that they have varieties from within that affect intelligibility. This means that intelligibility of youth languages for non-speakers varies depending on the vocabulary continuum, where there is a variation between less dense ('basic') vs highly dense ('deep') (Barasa & Mous, 2017; Bosire, 2006; Githinji, 2009; Hurst, 2008; Samper, 2002). This means that, in some situations, speakers of the light variation might not understand the deeper variety because this deep variety is reserved for the inner circle.

Ethnicity

As already pointed out, ethnicity is a key player in AYLs. Most studies confirm this by tagging AYLs as eliminators of ethnicity. Contrariwise, in my view, ethnicity cannot be eliminated that easily. In reality, ethnicity is maintained in a 'neutralised and non-confrontational' form or what Newell (2009) refers to as 'pan-ethnicity'. The youth create a modern identity that is still embedded in their pan-ethnic and national culture. So far, the majority of AYLs display this. For example, the AYLs with a non-ethnic matrix language like Engsh maintain elements of ethnic languages and style, in this case, Sheng, Swahili and vernaculars, and manipulate them to fit in its schema. Even Luyaaye, which loans its lexicon widely but hardly from the Ugandan indigenous languages, has Luganda as its matrix language. This scenario in essence resembles a tree with pan-ethnic roots but with diverse branches.

Nativization

As already pointed out, the popularisation of AYLs has made them spill out from capital cities to smaller towns and even into rural areas. In addition, AYLs are no longer only a youth phenomenon but are developing into full-fledged urban lingua francae (Githiora, 2016a; Ntshangase, 1993). They are independent and can operate in many different contexts similar to other lingua francae.

There are many youth, for example in Cameroon, who can speak Camfranglais but do not have a good command of French or other indigenous languages. In such cases, is the youth language their native language? What about the second-generation speakers who speak the youth language at home, e.g., Sheng speakers who use it as a first language? And is there a possibility of empowering these languages at the national level? These are some questions that need to be addressed.

Beck (2010: 28) explains that there have been calls for Nouchi to be elevated to a national language. Similarly, Tsotsitaal has also been proposed as a national language mainly through public petitions, for example in Walton Pantland's blog on 'Let's make tsotsitaal the national language' (Hurst, 2013).

Kießling and Mous (2004) and Aycard (2007) have speculated that, with time, these AYLs might become first languages to some speakers. However, Brookes (2014) contests this in her claim that, from her naturally occurring data, Tsotsitaal is spoken by male youth only in specific contexts and thus it does not qualify for a vernacular. She continues that what is termed as their 'AYL vernacular' is not a tsotsitaal but an urban variety of a vernacular, e.g., urban Sotho or urban Zulu. In their discussion on tsotsitaals, Hurst and Buthelezi (2014: 185) claim that even though Tsotsitaal has been proposed as a national language, it is not standardised yet. They argue that 'it is not clear what features the different regional varieties share' – a fact that calls for further research before any decisions are made, especially concerning standardisation.

For now, it is difficult to project the future of AYLs in policy planning – though, given the current democratic era, there may be more tolerance of these languages than in the past. However, the question that needs to be answered is whether these languages are ready for this role given their fluidity, ever-changing nature, and lack of standardisation (Beyer, 2015: 9; Neuland, 2007: 26).

Nevertheless, perhaps these challenges are exactly what defines youth languages, i.e., their fluidity and 'un-standardness' are what define their standardness – that is, a youth language is standard in its own right if it exudes the mentioned features (Barasa, 2015).

Pending research on AYLs

For now, it is encouraging that research on youth languages in Africa is well underway. However, there still remains substantial ground to be covered, especially given the fluidity of these languages. In general, there are many areas that still need to be covered and I will mention a few in this section as recommendations for further research.

First of all, more studies need to be done on the less studied AYLs such as Yarada K'wank'wa in Ethiopia, and Rendók in Sudan. There is also a possibility that some AYLs or varieties of AYLs are in existence but have not yet been discovered. Local linguistics should be proactive in discerning them for further study.

A major recommendation that keeps recurring in AYL studies is to look further into the issue of national policies in regard to AYLs to determine whether they would be acceptable as national languages. This would mark a new era – and perhaps even lead to the development of new in-group rebellious youth languages to replace the gap left.

Longitudinal and generational studies on youth languages should also be investigated in order to observe how these languages are acquired by individuals and how they fade over time in the transition from youth. Such studies would give insights on the development and dynamics of these languages.

Research should also be done on speakers of more than one youth language (i.e., multilingualism in youth languages), and contact between youth languages. Such studies would be interesting as a way to find out how language choices and linguistic innovations are made, in a backdrop of different AYLs.

In terms of gender, why are AYLs mainly used by male youths? What do females use in similar contexts? Where would we place exceptions and variations (such as Engsh in Kenya) that are commonly used by females? In order to answer these questions, comparative studies based on spontaneous discourse between male and female speakers are needed.

Additionally, there should also be studies targeting the 'non-use' of these AYLs because, as much as the spread of these languages is stressed, there are still many contexts where they are not in use (yet), for example, Sheng is not used in some contexts, e.g., news in mainstream TV stations, in newspaper sections like in obituaries, etc. (Barasa & Mous, 2017).

Note that it is important for all these (and any other) AYLs studies to use research methodologies and data collection procedures that are systematic, streamlined and thorough in order to arrive at findings that can justify assumptions and generate credible conclusions and generalisations. Brookes (2014: 358) advises against using 'in situ' and out of context data. She observes that '[m]ost studies rely on a limited number of elicited decontextualized examples from informants or elicited conversations in which people are asked to "speak Tsotsitaal".' Credible research on AYLs therefore necessitates the collection and analysis of data based on the use of the languages in a natural context. It also requires extensive and well-calculated samples that can collectively support generalisations concerning AYLs. In addition, AYL research should take a wider scope with different perspectives other than only linguistic description – for example, writing and orthography in texts. Once all this is achieved, knowledge on AYLs would be elevated to a more advanced level which is crucial for all existing languages.

Conclusion

This chapter has shown that the phenomenon of AYLs is fascinating for many researchers.

In line with Comaroff and Comaroff (2005) I conclude that, be it in Africa or elsewhere, youth practices including language should be closely monitored and reported in scientific contexts, since the youths' voices need to be heard without being impugned by societal norms.

References

Abdulaziz, M. & Osinde, K. (1997). Sheng and Engsh: development of mixed codes among the urban youth in Kenya. *International Journal of the Sociology of Language*, 125, 43–64.

Aboa, A. L. A. (2011). Le nouchi a-t-il un avenir? Retrieved April 10, 2017 from www.sudlangues.sn/IMG/pdf/Le_nouchi_a-t-il_un_avenir.pdf.

Ahua, B. M. (2008). Mots, phrases et syntaxe du nouchi. *Le Français En Afrique*, 23, 135–150.

Aycard, P. (2007). "Speak As You Want To Speak: Just Be Free". A linguistic-anthropological monograph of first-language Iscamtho-speaking youth in White City, Soweto. MA thesis, Leiden University.

Ayewa, N. K. (2005). Mots et contextes en FPI et en Nouchi. *Actes Des 7ème Journées Scientifiques AUF-LTT*, 221–233.

Barasa, S. N. (2010). Language, mobile phones and internet: a study of SMS texting, email, IM and SMS chats in Computer Mediated Communication (CMC) in Kenya. PhD Dissertation, Leiden University, The Netherlands.

Barasa, S. N. (2015). Ala! Kumbe? "Oh my! Is it so?": multilingualism controversies in East Africa. In P. Smakman & D. Heinrich (Eds), *Globalising Sociolinguistics: Challenging and Expanding Theory* (pp. 39–53). New York: Routledge.

Barasa, S. N. & Mous, M. (2017). Engsh, a Kenyan middle class youth language parallel to Sheng. *Journal of Pidgin and Creole Languages*, 32(1), 48–74.

Beck, R. M. (2010). Urban languages in Africa. *Africa Spectrum*, 45(3), 11–41.

Beyer, K. (2014). Urban language research in South Africa: achievements and challenges. *Southern African Linguistics and Applied Language Studies*, 32(2), 247–254.

Beyer, K. (2015). Youth languages in Africa: achievements and challenges. In N. Nassenstein & H. Hollington (eds), *Youth Language Practices in Africa and Beyond*. Berlin: Mouton de Gruyter.

Biloa, E. (1999). Structure phrastique du Camfranglais: etat de la question. In G. Echu and A. W. Grundstrom (eds), *Official Bilingualism and Linguistic Communication in Cameroon* (pp. 147–176). New York: Peter Lang.

Bosire, M. (2006). Hybrid languages: the case of Sheng. In O. F. Arasanyin & M. A. Pemberton (eds), *Selected Proceedings of the 36th Annual Conference on African Languages* (pp. 185–193). Somerville, MA: Cascadilla Proceedings Project.

Brookes, H. (2014). Urban youth languages in South Africa: a case study of Tsotsitaal in a South Africa township. *Anthropological Linguistics*, 56(3–4), 356–388.

Brookes, H. & Lekgoro, T. (2014). A social history of urban male youth varieties in Stirtonville and Vosloorus, South Africa. *Southern African Linguistics and Applied Language Studies*, 32(2), 149–159.

Comaroff, J. & Comaroff, J. (2005). Reflections on youth: from the past to the postcolony. In A. F. Honwana & F. De Boeck (eds), *Makers & Breakers: Children & Youth in Postcolonial Africa* (pp. 19–30). Dakar: Africa World Press, Codesria.

Deumert, A. (2014). *Sociolinguistics and Mobile Communication*. Edinburgh, Scotland: Edinburgh University Press.

Echu, G. (2001). Le camfranglais: l'aventure de l'anglais en contexte multilingue camerounais. In *Ecritures VII : L'aventure* (Editions C, p. 207–221.). Yaoundé.

Eckert, P. (2008). Where do ethnolects stop? *International Journal of Bilingualism*, 12(1–2), 25–42.

Efoua-Zengue, R. (1999). L'emprunt: figure néologique récurrente du camfranglais, un français fonctionnel au Cameroun. In Z. Mendo (ed.), *Le Français Langue Camerounaise. Enjeux et Défis pour la Francophonie* (pp. 168–177). Paris: Publisud.

Essono, J.-M. (1997). Le Camfranglais: un code excentrique, une appropriation vernaculaire du. In C. Frey & D. Latin (eds), *Le Corpus Lexicographique Méthodes de Constitution et de Gestion* (pp. 381–396). Louvain-la-Neuve: De Boeck Supérieur.

Ewané, M. L. (1989). Transfert et interferences. Cameroun: Le Camfranglais. *Diagonales*, 10, 30–34.

Féral, C. de. (2006). Décrire un "parler Jeune": Le cas du Camfranglais (Cameroun). *Le Français En Afrique*, 12, 257–265.

Féral, C. de. (2012). "Parlers jeunes": une utile invention? *Langage et Société*, 3(14), 21–46.

Ferrari A. (2009). *Emergence de Langues Urbaines en Afrique: Le Cas du Sheng, Langue Mixte Parlée à Nairobi*. Louvain: Peeters.

Finlayson, R. & Slabbert, S. (2003). "What turns you on!": an exploration of urban South African Xhosa and Zulu youth texts. *Language, Culture and Curriculum*, 16(2), 165–172.

Fosso, F. (1999). Le camfranglais: une praxéogénie complexe et iconoclaste. In M. Ze (ed.), *Le Français Langue Camerounaise. Enjeux et Défis pour la Francophonie* (pp. 178–194). Paris: Publisud.

Gadet, F. & Hambye, P. (2014). Contact and ethnicity in "youth language" description: in search of specificity. In N. Robert (ed.), *Questioning Language Contact: Limits of Contact, Contact at Its Limits* (pp. 183–216). Leiden: Brill.

Githinji, P. (2006). Bazes and their shibboleths: lexical variation and Sheng speakers' identity in Nairobi. *Nordic Journal of African Studies*, 15(4), 443–472.

Githinji, P. (2008). Sexism and (mis)representation of women in Sheng. *Journal of African Cultural Studies*, 20(1), 15–32.

Githinji, P. (2009). *Sheng, Styleshifting and Construction of Multifaceted Identities: Discursive Practices in the Social Negotiation of Meaning*. Saarbrücken: Vdm Verlag Dr. Müller.

Githiora, C. (2002). Sheng: peer language, Swahili dialect or emerging creole? *Journal of African Cultural Studies*, 15(2), 159–181.

Githiora, C. (2016a). Sheng: the expanding domains of an urban youth vernacular. *Journal of African Cultural Studies*, 1–16, https://doi.org/10.1080/13696815.2015.1117962.

Githiora, C. (2016b). Urban youth vernaculars in Africa. *Journal of African Cultural Studies*, virtual special issue, available at: http://explore.tandfonline.com/page/pgas/urban-vernaculars-vsi.

Glaser, C. (1992). The Mark of Zorro. *African Studies*, 51(1), 47–68.

Goyvaerts, D. L. & Kabongo-Mianda, K. (1988). Indoubil: a Swahili hybrid in Bukavu (with comments on Indu Bill by K. Kabongo-Mianda). *Language in Society*, 17(2), 231–242.

Halliday, M. A. K. (1976). Anti-languages. *American Anthropologist*, 78(3), 570–584.

Hecker, A. (2009). *Das Camfranglais. Untersuchungen zur in Kamerun gesprochenen Varietät des Französischen*. Saarbrücken: VDN, Verlag Dr. Müller.

Hollington, A. (2016). Reflections on Ethiopian youths and Yarada K'wank'wa: language practices and ideologies. *Sociolinguistic Studies*, 10(1–2), 135–152.

Hurst, E. (n.d.). Tsotsitaal research. Available at: https://sites.google.com/site/tsotsitaalresearch/background-to-the-study.

Hurst, E. (2008). Style, structure and function in Cape Town Tsotsitaal. Unpublished PhD dissertation. University of the Western Cape, Capetown.

Hurst, E. (2009). Tsotsitaal, global culture and local style: identity and recontextualisation in twenty-first century South African townships. *Social Dynamics*, 35(2), 244–257.

Hurst, E. (2013, July 2). Youth shape the way we communicate. Available at: https://mg.co.za/article/2013-07-02-youth-shape-the-way-we-communicate.

Hurst, E. (2016). Metaphor in South African Tsotsitaal. *Sociolinguistic Studies; Galicia*, 10(1/2), 153–175.

Hurst, E., Brookes, H. & Ploog, K. (2012). Non-standard and youth varieties in urban Africa: language dynamics in rapidly modernizing cities. Thematic session at the Sociolinguistics Symposium, Berlin, 21st–24th August.

Hurst, E. & Buthelezi, M. (2014). A visual and linguistic comparison of features of Durban and Cape Town tsotsitaal. *Southern African Linguistics and Applied Language Studies*, 32(2), 185–197.

Hurst, E. & Mesthrie, R. (2013). "When you hang out with the guys they keep you in style": The case for considering style in descriptions of South African tsotsitaals. *Language Matters*, 44(1), 3–20.

Kariuki, A., Kanana, F. E. & Kebeya, H. (2015). The growth of Sheng in advertisements in selected businesses in Kenya. *Journal of African Cultural Studies*, 27(2), 229.

Kembo-sure, E. (1992). The Coming of Sheng. *English Today: English Studies*, 26–28.

Kerswill, P. (2010). Youth languages in Africa and Europe: linguistic subversion or emerging vernaculars? Available at: www.lancaster.ac.uk/fass/doc_library/linguistics/kerswill/Kerswill-African-Studies-19-10-10.pdf.

Kießling, R. (2005). bak mwa me do'-Camfranglais in Cameroon. *Lingua Posnaniensis*, 47, 87–107.

Kießling, R. & Mous, M. (2004). Urban youth languages in Africa. *Anthropological Linguistics*, 46(3), 303–341.

Kioko, A. N. & Muthwii, M. J. (2003). English variety for the public domain in Kenya: speakers' attitudes and views. *Language, Culture and Curriculum*, 16(2), 130–145.

Koenig, E., Chia, E. & Povey, J. (1983). *A Sociolinguistic Profile of Urban Centers in Cameroon*. Carlifonia: Cross-road Press.

Koffi, Y. (2013). El Nouchi: ¿argot, pidgin o criollo? *Estudios de Asia Y Africa*, 48(2), 537–556.

Kouadio, J. (1990). Le nouchi abidjanais, naissance d'un argot ou mode linguistique passagère? In E. Gouaini & N. Thiam (eds), *Des Langues et des Villes* (pp. 373–383). Paris: Didier Erudition.

Kouadio, J. (2005). Le Nouchi et les rapports Dioula-Français. *Le Français En Afrique*, 21, 177–192.

Kouega, J.-P. (2003). Camfranglais: a novel slang in Cameroon schools. *English Today*, 19(2), 23–29.

Kouega, J.-P. (2007). *A Dictionary of Cameroon English Usage*. Oxford: Peter Lang.

Kube-Barth, S. (2009). The multiple facets of the urban language form, Nouchi. In F. McLaughlin (ed.), *The Languages of Urban Africa* (pp. 103–114). London: Continuum.

Makhudu, D. (2002). An introduction to Flaaitaal. In R. Mesthrie (ed.), *Language in South Africa* (pp. 398–406). Cambridge: Cambridge University Press.

Mattiello, E. (2005). The pervasiveness of slang in standard and non-Standard English. In E. Lonati (ed.), *Mots Palabras Words: Studilinguistic* (Vol. 6, pp. 7–41).

Mazrui, A. M. (1995). Slang and code-switching: the case of Sheng in Kenya. *Afrikanistische Arbeitspapiere*, 42, 168–179.

Mbaabu, I. & Nzuga, K. (2003). *Sheng-English Dictionary: Deciphering East Africa's Underworld Language*. Dar es Salaam: Taasisi ya Uchunguzi wa Kiswahili.

Mbah, L. & Mbah, M. (1994). Le Camfrangais. *Diagonales*, 32, 20–30.

McLaughlin, F. (2009). *The Languages of Urban Africa*. London: Continuum.

Meierkord, C. (2011). U r ma treasure bila measure. Identity construction in Kenya's multilingual spaces. In E. A. Anchimbe & S. A. Mforteh (eds), *Postcolonial Linguistic Voices: Identity Choices and Representations* (pp. 25–50). Berlin: De Gruyter Mouton.

Mensah, E. (ed.) (2016). The dynamics of youth languages in Africa: an introduction. *Sociolinguistic Studies*, 10(1), 1–14.

Mesthrie, R. (2008). "I've been speaking Tsotsitaal all my life without knowing it": Towards a unified account of Tsotsitaals in South Africa. In M. Meyerhoff & N. Nagy (eds), *Social Lives in Language— Sociolinguistics and Multilingual Speech Communities: Celebrating the work of Gillian Sankoff*, 24, 95–109. Amsterdam: John Benjamins.

Mesthrie, R. & Hurst, E. (2013). Slang registers, code-switching and restructured urban varieties in South Africa. *Journal of Pidgin and Creole Languages*, 28(1), 103–130.

Mfenyana, B. (1977). *Isi-Khumsha Nesitsotsi: The Sociolinguistics of School and Town Sintu in South Africa (1945–1975)*. Boston: Boston University.

Mfusi, M. (1992). Soweto Zulu slang: a sociolinguistic study of an urban vernacular in Soweto. *Language Matters*, 23, 39–83.

Mitsch, J. (2016). The use of discourse markers among youth in Senegambia borderland. *Sociolinguistic Studies; Galicia*, 10(1/2), 67–87.

Mkangi, K. (1985, August 30). Sheng: flag of a people's culture. *The Standard*, pp. 17–18. Nairobi.

Molamu, L. (1995). Wietie: the emergence and development of Tsotsitaal in South Africa. *Alternation*, 2, 139–158.

Molamu, L. (2003). *Tsotsitaal: A Dictionary of the Language of Sophia Town*. Pretoria: Unisa Press.

Momanyi, C. (2009). The Effects of "Sheng" in the teaching of Kiswahili in Kenyan Schools. *Journal of Pan African Studies*, 2(8), 127.

Msimang, T. (1987). Impact of Zulu on Tsotsitaal. *South African Journal for African Languages*, 7(3), 82–86.

Muaka, L. (2011). Language perceptions and identity among Kenyan speakers. In E. G. Bokamba, R. K. Shosted & B. T. Ayalew (eds), *Selected Proceedings of the 40th Annual Conference on African Linguistics* (pp. 217–230). Somerville, MA: Cascadilla Proceedings Project.

Myers-Scotton, C. (1993). *Dueling Languages: Grammatical Structure in Code-Switching*. Oxford: Clarendon Press.

Naluwooza, V. (1995). Luyaaye: a social dialect of the underprivileged. Unpublished MA thesis, Makerere University, Kampala.

Namyalo, S. (2015). Linguistic strategies in Luyaaye: word-play and conscious language manipulation. In N. Nassenstein & H. Hollington (eds.), *Youth Language Practices in Africa and Beyond* (pp. 313–344). Berlin: Mouton de Gruyter.

Nassenstein, N. (2016). The new urban youth language Yabacrâne in Goma (DR Congo). *Sociolinguistic Studies*, 10(1–2), 235–239.

Nchare, L. (2010). *The Morphosyntax of Camfranglais and the 4-M Model*. New York: New York University.

Neuland, E. (2007). *Jugendsprachen: Mehrsprachig, Kontrastiv, Interkulturell*. Frankfurt am Main: Lang.

Newell, S. (2009). Enregistering modernity, bluffing criminality: how Nouchi speech reinvented (and fractured) the nation. *Journal of Linguistic Anthropology*, 9(2), 157–184.

Njogu, K. & Oluoch-Olunya, G. (2007). *Cultural Production and Social Change in Kenya: Building Bridges*. Nairobi: Twaweza Communications.

Nortier, J. (2008). Introduction. Ethnolects? The emergence of new varieties among adolescents. *International Journal of Bilingualism*, 1/2, 1–5.

Nortier, J. & Dorleijn, M. (2008). A Moroccan accent in Dutch: a sociocultural style restricted to the Moroccan community? *International Journal of Bilingualism*, 12(1–2), 125–142.

Nortier, J. & Dorleijn, M. (2013). Multi-ethnolects: Kebabnorsk, Perkerdansk, Verlan, Kanakensprache, Straattaal, etc. In P. Bakker & Y. Matras (eds), *Contact Languages: A Comprehensive Guide*. Boston: De Gruyter Mouton.

Nsimbi, M. (1983). *Kulya Nyingi Sikuggwa Maddu [Eating a lot does not stop one becoming hungry again]*. Kampala: Cranes Publishers Ltd.

Ntshangase, K. (1993). *The Social History of Iscamtho*. University of Witwatersrand.

Ntshangase, K. (1995). Indaba yami i-straight: language and language practices in Soweto. In R. Mesthrie (ed.), *Language and Social History: Studies in South African Sociolinguistics* (pp. 291–297). Cape Town: David Philip.

Ntsobé, A.-M., Biloa, E. & Echu, G. (2008). *Le Camfranglais: Quelle Parlure? Etude Linguistique et Sociolinguistique.* Frankfurt am Main: Peter Lang.

Ogechi, N. O. (2005). On lexicalization in Sheng. *Nordic Journal of African Studies*, 14(3), 334–355.

Osinde, K. (1985). Sheng: an investigation into the social and cultural aspects of an evolving language. Unpublished BA thesis, University of Nairobi.

Rudd, P. W. (2008). Sheng: the mixed language of Nairobi. PhD thesis, Ball State University.

Rudwick, S. (2005). Township language dynamics: isiZulu and isiTsotsi in Umlazi. *Southern African Linguistics and Applied Language Studies*, 23(3), 305–331.

Samper, D. (2002). Talking Sheng: the role of a hybrid language in the construction of identity and youth culture in Nairobi Kenya. PhD Dissertation, University of Pennsylvania.

Sande, H. (2015). Nouchi as a distinct language: the morphological evidence. In R. Kramer, E. C. Zsiga & O. T. Boyer (eds), *Selected Proceedings of the 44th Annual Conference on African Linguistics* (pp. 243–253). Somerville, MA: Cascadilla Proceedings Project.

Schroder, A. (2007). Camfranglais: a language with several (sur-)faces and important sociolinguistic functions. In A. Bartels & D. Wiemann (eds), *Global Fragments. (Dis)Orientation in the New World Order, (Cross/Cultures 90)* (pp. 281–298). Amsterdam: Rodopi.

Slabbert, S. & Myers-Scotton, C. (1996). The structure of Tsotsitaal and Iscamtho: code switching and in-group identity in South African townships. *Linguistics*, 35(2), 317–342.

Spyropoulos, M. (1987). Sheng: some preliminary investigations into a recently emerged Nairobi street language. *Journal of the Anthropological Society of Oxford*, 18(1), 125–136.

Stein-Kanjora, G. (2008). "Parler comme ça, c'est vachement cool!" or how dynamic language loyalty can overcome "resistance from above." *Sociologus*, 58(2), 117–141.

Stein-Kanjora, G. (2016). Camfrang forever! Metacommunication in and about Camfranglais. *Socio-linguistic Studies*, 10(1–2), 261–289.

Stroud, C. (2004). Rinkeby Swedish and semilingualism in language ideological debates: a Bourdieuean perspective. *Journal of Sociolinguistics*, 8(2), 196–214.

Tiayon-Lekoubou, C. (1985). Camspeak: a speech reality in Cameroon. Unpublished Maitrise Memoire (Master's Dissertation), University of Yaounde.

Vakunta, P. (2008). On translating Camfranglais and other Camerounismes. *Meta*, 53(4), 729–947.

Vierke, C. (2015). Some remarks on poetic aspects of Sheng. In N. Nassenstein & A. Hollington (eds), *Youth Language Practices in Africa and Beyond* (pp. 227–256). Berlin: Mouton der Gruyter.

wa Mungai, M. (2003). Identity politics in Nairobi matatu folklore. Unpublished PhD dissertation. Hebrew University, Jerusalem.

wa Mungai, M. (2013). *Nairobi's Matatu Men: Portrait of a Subculture.* Nairobi: Contact Zones.

Widawski, M. (2015). *African American Slang: A Linguistic Description.* Cambridge: Cambridge University Press.

Wilson, C. (2015). Kindoubil: urban youth languages in Kisangani. In N. Nassenstein & A. Hollington (eds), *Youth Language Practices in Africa and Beyond* (pp. 293–312). Berlin: De Gruyter Mouton.

Ze Amvela, E. (1983). The Franglais phenomenon: lexical interference and language mixing in the United Republic of Cameroon. *Bulletin de l'AELIA*, 6, 419–421.

22

GESTURES AND GESTURING ON THE AFRICAN CONTINENT

Heather Brookes

Introduction

Although the field of linguistics has focused mainly on spoken aspects of communication, language invariably involves both speech and bodily action in order to express ideas, intentions, attitudes, emphasis, and to manage interactions. Expressive actions with the hands and face are an integral part of spoken discourse, and increasing evidence suggests that gesture – the intentionally communicative actions that are part of spoken utterances – are integral to speech, thought, social interaction and cultural practices.

The field of gesture studies has expanded rapidly since its reemergence in the 1970s. Gestures have been studied from formational, structural, semantic, semiotic and functional perspectives (see Calbris, 2011; Kendon, 2004; Bressem & Müller, 2014; Ladewig, 2014). Gestures are also integral to thinking and conceptual processes (McNeill, 1992) and play an important part in learning (Goldin-Meadow & Alibali, 2012). Studies in language acquisition demonstrate that gestures are an essential element for language development (Capirci & Volterra, 2008; Colletta et al., 2010; Iverson & Goldin-Meadow, 2005). Studies in interaction show how actions with the hands produce symbolic meaning and become socially shared (Streeck, 2009) and how gesture, speech and body work together in human interaction to co-ordinate shared understanding (Goodwin, 2003; Mondada, 2016).

Like speech, gestures and gestural behaviour vary across linguistic and cultural groups (Kendon, 2004). Forms and form-meaning associations are not the same from one language group to another, and a number of studies have documented and compared repertoires of emblems/quotable gestures – conventionalized gestures that have established meanings independently of speech – across different language groups (see Brookes, 2004; Kendon, 1981; Payrató, 1993). However, co-speech gestures that are dependent on speech for their interpretation also vary across languages in their forms, meanings, functions and in how they are employed in relation to speech. These differences may in part be due to how differences in the structure of spoken languages encode meaning (McNeill, 1992; McNeill & Duncan, 2000; Kita & Özyürek, 2003; Kita, 2009). Gestures may also vary based on different conceptual systems across cultures such as the spatial construal of time (Núñes & Sweetser, 2006). Underlying norms and conventions relating to communicative and bodily conduct also shape gestures and aspects of gestural behavior (Kendon, 2004; Kita, 2009), and different sociocultural and material environments impact on the nature and role gestures play in the communicative economy of different speech communities (Brookes, 2014a; Kendon, 2004).

Africa, with its diversity of languages and oral practices, is a particularly rich source of data on gestures and gestural behavior. Gesture is a prominent feature in everyday interactions, in conversations, story-telling, song, dance, and other performative genres. Much of the initial work on gestures in African communities documented the conventionalized forms and meanings of gestures that could be used independently of speech among different linguistic groups. However, there has also been work on gesture typologies looking at form, meaning and function, and on the relationship between gesture and speech. More recently, studies have begun to examine how gestures function in interaction, the role they play in social differentiation, and how environment, including spoken language, material aspects, cultural practices and beliefs, shape gestures and gesture use. In this chapter I review this research across different languages and contexts providing an overview of gesture studies on the African continent and their theoretical contribution to the fields of gesture and linguistics.

The chapter begins with an overview of documentation studies of gestural repertoires among different cultural groups and work done on their forms, meanings, functions and processes of conventionalization and iconization (see Irvine & Gal, 2000). It then looks at co-speech gestures and how the structure of spoken languages and cultural conventions shape gestural forms and their deployment in relation to speech. It reviews work done on gesture and gestural practices in relation to different communicative genres and recent work on the importance of gesture in performance, linguistic style, social positioning and identity. It examines research on the relationship between the nature of gestures and gestural behavior and the communicative ecology shaped by social and material environments. Last, it focuses on the role of gesture in language development and what these studies tell us about the relationship between gestural development, spoken language and cultural practices. To conclude, I discuss the relevance of these studies in the African context for the field of gesture, their theoretical contribution, and highlight areas for further research.

Gestural repertoires

The earliest work on gestures in Africa begins with the documentation of Madagascan gestures by Sibree (1884) and Glauning and Huber's (1904) description of greeting gestures in East Africa (see Brookes & Nyst, 2014). Other early accounts of gestures are Westermann's (1907) description of Ewe gestures in Ghana and Tremearne's (1913) list of Hausa gestures.

With the reemergence of gesture studies in the 1970s, several studies were published documenting gestures among KiSwahili speakers (Claessen, 1985; Eastman & Omar, 1985), Hausa speakers (Olofson, 1974) and gestures in Central Africa (Hochegger, 1978). There were also two comparative studies. Baduel-Mathon (1969, 1971) described gestures in three West African language families: the Agni-Ashanti, the Manding, and the Yoruba, and Creider (1977) compared gestural repertoires across four Kenyan languages, three Nilotic languages spoken by Luo, Kipsigis and Samburu and a Bantu language among the Gusii. He then compared the gestures of these groups with Saitz and Cervenka's (1972) gesture repertories for North America and Columbia. Like research on quotable gestures/emblems in other parts of the world (see Morris et al., 1979), these comparative studies sought to determine the extent to which gestures might be universal given their iconic qualities. They found that gestures, for the most part, vary in form and meaning across different linguistic groups, although there are a small number of gestures such as calling or stopping a person that seem to be the same across many cultural groups.

Variation is also evident in studies of counting gestures (see Brookes & Nyst, 2014). Scholars have examined counting gestures among the Yao of Malawi and Mozambique, the Makonde of Mozambique, the Shambaa of Tanzania and Kenya, and the Sotho of Lesotho (Gerdes & Cherinda, 1993); the Nandi (Hollis, 1909), Arusha Maasai speakers (Gulliver, 1958), the Luo, Kipsigis, Gusii and Samburu (Creider, 1977); Central Sudanic languages in Chad (Caprile, 1995) and Samo in Burkina Faso (Siebicke, 2002). Caprile's (1995) study of counting gestures, in four Sudanese languages spoken in Chad, Central African Republic and Zaire (now the Democratic Republic of the Congo), expands documentation of counting gestures to consider how embodiment, cognition, gestures and spoken language are related. He demonstrates how speech and gestures are involved in complex mathematical operations and the manner in which spoken words reflect the gestural bodily construction of numbers.

More recent work on gestural repertoires has documented quotable gestures among the Yoruba in Nigeria (Agwuele, 2014) and urban Bantu language speakers in South Africa (Brookes, 2004). Agwuele (2014) describes Yoruba hand and facial gestures, their meanings and the contexts in which they are used. Brookes (2004) compares the semantic and structural nature of these types of gestures with those in previously published repertoires. Comparing Kendon's (1981) analysis of six repertoires in five different countries and work done on Italian quotable gestures (Kendon, 1992) with the South African repertoire, Brookes (2004) found, like previous analyses, that quotable gestures either convey complete speech acts or are equivalent to single words that may express different speech acts depending on context. She also found that several quotable gestures are polysemous in that a single form with variations in movement, orientation or location can express a number of different meanings all related to an underlying core concept. Semantically related realizations of a single gestural form can be considered to be a *gesture family* (Kendon, 2004). They appear to be similar to *recurrent* gestures (gestures that have a core form and meaning) identified by Bressem and Müller (2014), Ladewig (2011) and Müller (2010), although they consider quotable gestures to be a separate category from *recurrent* ones.

Quotable gestures: meaning, function and conventionalization

Why do certain concepts get encoded in gestural form and become conventionalized to the point where they are autonomous from speech? Examining the semantic domains of quotable gestures among Bantu language speakers in South Africa, Brookes (2004) found that most lexical gestures represent everyday objects and actions such as 'telephone' and 'sleep,' socially circumscribed items such as 'alcohol' and 'marijuana,' and taboo topics such as 'sex,' and 'HIV' (see Brookes, 2011 for an account of the emergence of the HIV gesture). Holophrastic gestures that convey complete communicative acts in this repertoire fall into four main categories similar to the semantic/functional categories of other repertoires of quotable gestures for different language groups (Kendon, 1981; Payrató, 1993). These categories are: (1) gestures of interpersonal control, i.e., commands, apologies, refusals, insults and promises; (2) evaluative comments about others; (3) expressions of personal states; and (4) expressions about general states. Based on these semantic domains, the concepts that become conventionalized in gesture and independent of speech appear to be related to: (1) practical matters when speech is impeded over long distances or because of noise, e.g., gestures for telephone and commands such as 'come here'; (2) when there is a need for secrecy due to illicit or taboo actions and topics, e.g., gestures for sex; (3) communicating a message without having the responsibility of having said it in speech, e.g., insults and comments about others; or (4) pragmatic purposes to emphasize a speech act or intention, e.g., insults or promises.

Brookes (2001, 2004) also noted that there are some gestures that have gained particular prominence in the gestural repertoire. These gestures are iconized symbolic expressions of particular ideological concerns emanating from the sociocultural and political circumstances of their users. One prominent example is a quotable gesture known colloquially as the *clever* gesture (Brookes, 2001). This gesture involves the index and last finger pointed towards the eyes and moved diagonally down across the face and back. Users gloss it with the word *clever* in the sense of 'streetwise/city slick.' Its underlying paradigmatic meaning is 'seeing,' and it can express a number of meanings including 'see,' 'watch out,' 'be alert,' 'he's clever/streetwise,' 'he's a trickster' and 'I see you' as a greeting. It is generally a sign of approval and an act of inclusion. Its most prominent meaning expresses the idea of the street-smart, city slick, modern, progressive and 'seeing' urban South African in contrast to their backward, tribal conservative and 'non-seeing' rural counterparts. It functions to include or exclude people who exhibit or do not exhibit an urban identity expressing a key social divide between urban and rural in South African society (Brookes, 2001).

The iconization of specific gestures has also occurred in other African contexts. One example is the development, in Nigeria, of the Afrobeat salute in which both fists and arms are fully extended upwards. Ayobade (2015) describes how the Nigerian musician Fela Kuti iconized the Afrobeat salute, a variation on the one-fisted black power salute, during his musical performances in which he used this gesture to signal black liberation and solidarity. Through his performative reiterations, it became symbolic of Afrobeat and its discourse of anticolonial ideology and African oppression. In 2012 the Occupy Nigeria Movement co-opted it as a symbol of resistance to economic oppression and corruption in Nigeria. This shift shows how gestural meaning can be appropriated and transformed for the expression of new ideological concerns and social purposes.

These studies show that quotable gestures do not all serve the same communicative functions. Some quotable gestures convey a single meaning or speech act, while other gestures develop multiple meanings, some of which undergo iconization to symbolize a particular ideological alignment or stance reflecting the social concerns and needs of a community. Both communicative needs but also wider social factors shape gestural meaning, use and conventionalization.

Co-speech gestures

While quotable gestures vary across different linguistic groups, there is also cross-cultural variation in co-speech gestures. Nyst (2016) demonstrates that there are language- and culture-specific conventions for the formation of co-speech iconic gestures in techniques of representation and the use of handshapes and movement. She compares size and shape gestures of Anyi speakers from the Ivory Coast with those of Dutch speakers from the Netherlands. Unlike Dutch speakers, Anyi speakers make use of body parts to represent size and shape. For example, one hand indicates the length of an object by demarcating or delimiting another body part such as the arm. Dutch speakers use more varied hand-shapes, orientations and movements when depicting size and shape in space. While several scholars argue that iconic co-speech gestures are idiosyncratic and primarily motivated by the object or action they represent (Padden et al., 2013; Sowa & Wachsmuth, 2002), this work on delimited body part gestures suggests that cultural conventions do play a role in the formational properties of iconic gestures.

Cultural conventions also play a role in shaping co-speech gestural forms, particularly in relation to handedness and hand shape. Sanders' (2015) work on ciTsonga speakers in Malawi, Orie's (2009) study of Yoruba speakers and Kita and Essegbey's (2001) study in Ghana demonstrate how cultural beliefs about the symbolic values and functions related to right- and left-hand use shape gestural practices, particularly pointing. Pointing with the left hand is taboo in many African cultural groups as is pointing with the index finger. Among the Yoruba, for example, the whole hand is generally used to point instead of the index finger (Orie, 2009).

Apart from the formational properties of co-speech gestures, there has also been work on the co-ordination of gesture and speech. Creider's (1978, 1986) studies in East African societies examine the co-ordination of gesture with intonation, tone and stress in Luo and compare it with the timing of gesture and speech among Kipsigis and Gusii. He notes that intonational structure and body movements are coordinated and that these vary cross linguistically depending on how stress is used in the different languages. Additional work on the functions and co-ordination of gesture and speech has been done in Zulu and South Sotho (Brookes, 2005).

Gesture and style

While it is now well established that gestures vary across linguistic groups, gestural variation as a marker of social class, gender and age has had little attention in gesture studies. Despite the move in sociolinguistics to understanding linguistic variation in terms of styles in which speakers combine semiotic resources associated with particular social meanings to express social distinctions, stance, attitudes, personae and identities (Eckert, 2012; Bucholtz & Hall, 2005), very few, if any, sociolinguistic studies have systematically looked at the role gesture plays in the construction of styles.

One exception is research on gestural behavior among urban Bantu language speaking communities in South Africa. In street corner groups that occupy local urban neighborhoods, male youth have developed different styles of talking and gesturing to differentiate social levels based on outlooks, attitudes, aspirations and orientations (Brookes, 2014a, 2014b). These styles are distinguishable primarily by the type of slang used, the density of slang words, patterns of intonation and gestural behavior (Brookes, 2014b). The features of gesture that distinguish these different styles are the frequency and speed of gestures, the kinesic movements of the hands and fingers, and the use of specific gestural forms. These gestural styles index different male identities from those youth with mainstream aspirations to youth who engage in anti-social activities.

Brookes (2014a, 2014b) describes how gestural behavior among young men is also part of expressing a persona. In their corner groups, young men constantly negotiate their status and place primarily through competitive displays of linguistic skill that involve skillful use of both speech and gesture in performances that both entertain and challenge their peers. Skillful co-ordination of speech and gesture expresses the core value of being streetwise and city slick, that is, of being a *clever*. Consequently skillful gestural behavior has become indexical of a 'cool' urban street-smart identity. However, too much gesturing indexes disrespectability and thuggishness.

Brookes (2014b) also notes that these styles among young men are instantiated and typified during performative moments in peer interactions. In their street corner groups, young men break into performance to demonstrate their skill and knowledge of the latest slang. These performances involve skillful co-ordination of gesture and speech to entertain and keep the attention of their peers. The young man with the most skill is always the leader of the group. The rest of the group takes up his way of speaking and manner of gesturing.

Across the leaders of these street corner groups, there are always one or two highly skilled performers whose use of gesture and the latest slang sets them apart from the rest. These young men use speech and gesture to create new spoken meanings that get taken up by their friendship groups and then by other groups because of the social status of the linguistic innovator and his group. This work points to the importance of gesture and its role in performance, in processes of meaning making during interactions and in creating linguistic change and spread.

Gesture and genre

While gestures are part of linguistic styles that differentiate social levels, gestural behavior also varies according to genre and communicative task. A rich area of gesture research on the African continent is the nature and use of gestures in performance genres (see Brookes & Nyst, 2014). Klassen (1999, 2004) describes the semantic, pragmatic and discursive functions of gestures in Shona storytelling in Zimbabwe. She details how storytellers use gestures to re-enact or diagram actions, situate the components of a story in space, pace the rhythm of the story to indicate the climax and express character, mood and attitude. Klassen shows that speakers use gestures and bodily movements as part of expressing both the form of the narrative and the moral message, and body positions can indicate the type of story, mark structure such as changes of scene, and act as a metaphor for social relations (Brookes & Nyst, 2014).

Calame-Griauel (1977) and Konrad (1994) find similar roles for gesture in Touareg storytelling in Niger and among Ewe speakers in Ghana. Sorin-Barreteau (1996) describes conventional gestures used among Mofu-Gudur speakers as part of storytelling in Cameroon. The role of gesture in other art forms includes Groß's (1997) study of gestures and body positions in the Adzogbo dance of the Ewe people in Ghana, and work by Thompson et al. (2002) who look at the use of conventional gestures and body postures of the Kongo culture in central Africa in dance and ritual interactions.

There have also been several studies of the relationship between ideophones and gesture in contexts of narration (Dingemanse, 2011; Klassen, 1999; Kunene, 1965; Zondo, 1982). Dingemanse (2011) looks at ideophones in everyday speech of Siwu speakers in Ghana including narratives. Klassen (1999) describes a case study of ideophones and gesture in the performance of the Ngano story-song genre in Shona. Kunene (1965) and Zondo (1982) give anecdotal examples of ideophones and gestures in South Sotho and Ndebele. Earlier studies make the claim that gestures invariably occur with ideophones (Zondo, 1982). However, Dingemanse's study of ideophones among Siwu speakers in Ghana demonstrates that co-occurrence occurs mainly in moments of telling and that the gestures that occur with ideophones are usually depictive. Dingemanse suggests that the experiential demand of narration motivates the occurrence and type of gesture. Here data from Africa challenges the suggestion that the coupling of ideophones and gestures is a universal phenomenon (Kita, 2001).

Gesture, culture and environment

To explain gestural variation from one cultural and linguistic context to another, scholars of gesture have also considered the role of the environment and how the communicative ecology of a community shapes the nature of gestures and gestural behavior (Kendon, 2004). Studying the communicative ecology involves examining the role different modalities play, how they work together in instances of communication, and how these are patterned differently across cultures because of communicative and social requirements (Kendon, 2004).

To explain the nature and prominent role of gestures among Bantu language speakers in South Africa, Brookes (2005, 2014a, 2014b) has undertaken ethnographic work looking at the communicative and social functions of gestures in urban multilingual communities. In these communities, gestures are often imagistic, depicting the content of what is said, and there is a large repertoire of quotable gestures in everyday use (Brookes, 2004). Brookes explores how the material and sociocultural environments have shaped what concepts get expressed in gesture, the nature of gestures and their communicative and social functions, as well as patterns of gestural behavior (Brookes, 2014a, 2014b).

Drawing on Kendon's (2004) analysis of the ecological environment of gesturing in Naples, Brookes (2014a) hypothesizes that overcrowding in urban communities in South Africa, where everyday activities take place outside homes and on the streets, has motivated the imagistic nature of gestures and the development of a large repertoire of conventionalized gestural forms. Imagistic types of gestures can be used to communicate in noisy environments and across multiple interactions and activities simultaneously. At the same time, she argues that gestures are particularly useful to hide messages in public spaces as speakers can play on the ambiguity between unintended hand movements and intended communication-making gestures, a useful resource in such environments.

In addition, cultural norms about appropriate communication among Bantu language speakers emphasize the aesthetic and performative value of communication in everyday interactions, and these beliefs may have also encouraged the prominent use of gesture as a form of display. Talk, in these communities, is not only a means to transmit information. Its manner of delivery must have aesthetic appeal and hold audience attention. The need for displaying ones performative skills and character would also be heightened in overcrowded conditions of constant visibility. In such situations, the body is an important resource for displaying stance, attitude and character.

In impoverished and volatile conditions in urban ghettoes/townships, with a lack of material resources and other symbols for creating and marking social distinctions, bodily conduct including gestures becomes even more important for expressing character and ones place in the urban milieu. With little protection from the police against criminal elements in these communities during apartheid, recognizing who was respectable and who might be a threat was of vital importance. Gestural and bodily conduct became indexical of respectability versus being disrespectable, enabling community members to recognize potential threats through their reading of bodily action and therefore to safely navigate their local environments. Hence the prominent role and importance attached to the gestural modality.

An additional perspective on the role of gesture in social life has been developed by Covington-Ward (2016) who examines the use of gesture in everyday performances among the Congolese. Placing the body at the center of her analysis rather than as marginal to the study of gesture, she analyzes how gestures are integral to social meaning in embodied cultural performances. She explores the interaction between gestures in everyday performances and larger social structures in the struggle for power and authority. Just as gesture in competitive interactions creates social positions in male street corner groups in South Africa (Brookes, 2014a), Covington-Ward shows how microinteractions of the body can frame and stake political claims in Congolese social life. For example, the use of gestures in greetings and other public symbolic exchanges can become emblematic of wider social struggles for power. She points out that the micropolitics of gesture in interpersonal relations can have much wider implications and impact. Gestures shape ideas, subjectivities and group consciousness and are part of: (1) embodying values, beliefs and ideologies; (2) social positioning; and (3) identity formation. In the field of gesture studies, the main approach to gesture has been to consider it separately from other bodily actions. Covington-Ward's (2016) bodily centered approach to gesture provides an additional and important dimension to understanding the relationship between gesture and environment.

Gesture and language development

Although there is now a substantial body of work on gestural development in children in different languages across the world, there is very little research on gesture and language development in African communities. At present, there are no studies on early acquisition of gesture in children below five years. However, there has been some work on gestural development in later childhood in Zulu, a South African Bantu language (Kunene, 2010; Kunene et al., 2016).

Kunene (2010) looks at gesture in narrative development from five to twelve years of age focusing on the intersection of cultural norms, language typology and their impact on gesture. It shows that Zulu-speaking children's gestures develop with age in similar ways to speakers of other languages. Gesture increases and the nature of children's gestures changes as they get older (Kunene et al., 2016).

When comparing gestural development in Zulu with other languages such as French, there appear to be some differences that can be attributed to the structure of the languages and cultural norms (Kunene et al., 2016). While gesture rate per clause among children increases with age in both languages, among Zulu-speaking adults the gesture rate is higher than for French-speaking adults. Zulu speakers give a detailed narrative remaining at the narrative level, while French speakers (as they get older) move towards a synthesis of events and switch between narrative and meta-narrative levels providing more commentary about the narrative. These differences impact on gestural production, with adult Zulu speakers producing more representational gestures that depict aspects of spoken content, while adult French speakers provide more discursive and framing gestures in line with moving more frequently between the narrative and meta-narrative commentary. The authors of these studies attribute these differences to cultural norms governing what is expected in an ideal narration.

Conclusion

In 1996, Adam Kendon outlined a research agenda for gesture studies (Kendon, 1996). He pointed out that, despite a longstanding interest in gestures, the field was relatively undeveloped, and he identified several key areas for investigation. These areas included: (1) kinetics – how gesture is organized as physical actions and in relation to speech; (2) morphokinetics – hand shapes, movement patterns, location and their compositionality; (3) the kinds of information gestures encode including typologies and functions of gesture; (4) the significance of gesture as to its role in communication, cognition and social regulation; (5) how gesture varies in relation to different communicative tasks and situations; and (6) how language, culture and the communicative ecology shape gesture.

Since then, there has been much progress in addressing this agenda, and studies in African contexts have made some important contributions. Several studies have contributed to knowledge on how speech, intonation, information units and gesture are organized in relation to each other and how this can differ based on language (Creider, 1978, 1986). Nyst's (2016) work on delimited body part gestures and work on pointing (Kita & Essegbey, 2001; Orie, 2009; Sanders, 2015) are useful additions to work on the morphokinetic properties of gesture and their relation to cultural norms. There has also been detailed empirical work on the nature of emblems/quotable gestures in their contexts of use (Agwuele, 2014; Ayobade, 2015; Brookes, 2001, 2005). Studies on story-telling, dance and other performative genres demonstrate how gestures vary according to task and cultural norms (Klassen, 2004), and work from South Africa and the Congo on gesture and its relationship to the material and social environments adds to knowledge on how gesture is both shaped and socially shaping.

A key theme throughout most of these studies is how communication is an embodied process embedded in material and sociocultural environments that shape the nature of gestures and gestural behavior (Brookes, 2014a; Covington-Ward, 2016).

However, much work still needs to be done, and the richness of languages and oral practices on the African continent is still largely untapped. In particular, there is a dearth of studies on the relationship between thought, gesture and culture and gestural development in language acquisition. Studies of gestural development in radically different linguistic and cultural environments, particularly comparative work across language groups, could provide rich insights into the impact of language and culture on gesture and gestural development.

References

Agwuele, A. (2014). A repertoire of Yoruba hand and face gestures. *Gestures*, 14(1), 70–96.

Ayobade, D. (2015). Fela's clenched fists: the double "black power" salute and political ideology. In Agwuele, A. (ed.), *Body Talk and Cultural Identity in the African World*. Bristol: Equinox, pp. 37–57.

Baduel-Mathon, C. (1969). Pour une sémiologie du geste en Afrique Occidentale. *Semiotica*, 3(3), 245–255.

Baduel-Mathon, C. (1971). Le langage gestuel en Afrique occidentale: Recherches bibliographiques. *Journal de la Société des Africanistes*, 41(2), 203–249.

Bressem, J. & Müller, C. (2014). A repertoire of German recurrent gestures with pragmatic functions, Chapter 119. In Müller, C., Cienki, A., Fricke, E., Ladewig, S.H., McNeill, D. & Bressem, J. (eds), *Body-Language-Communication: An International Handbook on Multimodality in Human Interaction. Vol. 2*. Berlin/Boston: De Gruyter Mouton, pp. 1575–1591.

Brookes, H.J. (2001). O clever 'He's streetwise.' When gestures become quotable: The case of the clever gesture. *Gesture*, 1(2), 167–184.

Brookes, H.J. (2004). A first repertoire of South African quotable gestures. *Linguistic Anthropology*, 14(2), 186–224.

Brookes, H.J. (2005). What gestures do: Some communicative functions of quotable gestures in conversations among black urban South Africans. *Journal of Pragmatics*, 37, 2044–2085.

Brookes, H.J. (2011). Amangama Amathathu 'Three Letters': The emergence of a quotable gesture. *Gesture*, 11(2), 194–218.

Brookes, H.J. (2014a). Gesture in the communicative ecology of a South African township. In Seyfeddinipur, M. and Gullberg, M. (eds), *Visible Utterance in Action. Festschrift for Adam Kendon*. Amsterdam: John Benjamins, pp. 59–74.

Brookes, H.J. (2014b). Urban youth languages in South Africa: A case study of Tsotsitaal in a South African township. *Anthropological Linguistics*, 56(3–4), 356–388.

Brookes, H. & Nyst, V. (2014). Gesture in the Sub-Saharan Region, Chapter 74. In Müller, C., Cienki, A., Fricke, E., Ladewig, S.H., McNeill, D. & Bressem, J. (eds), *Body-Language-Communication: An International Handbook on Multimodality in Human Interaction. Vol. 2*. Berlin/Boston: De Gruyter Mouton, pp. 1154–1161.

Bucholtz, M. & Hall, K. (2005). Identity and interaction: A sociocultural linguistic approach. *Discourse Studies*, 7(4–5), 585–614.

Calame-Griaule, G. (1977). Pour une étude des gestes narratifs. In Calame-Griaule, G. (ed.), *Langage et Cultures Africaines: Essais d'Ethnolinguistique*. Paris: Maspero, pp. 303–358.

Calbris, G. (2011). *Elements of Meaning in Gesture*. Amsterdam/Philadelphia, PA: John Benjamins Publishing Company.

Capirci, O. & Volterra, V. (2008). Gesture and speech: The emergence and development of a strong and changing partnership. *Gesture*, 8(1), 22–44.

Caprile, J.-P. (1995). Morphogenèse numérale et techniques du corps: des gestes et des nombres en Afrique Centrale. *Intellectica*, 1(20), 83–109.

Claessen, A. (1985). Investigation into the patterns of non-verbal communication behaviour related to conversational interaction between mother tongue speakers of Swahili. In Maw, J. & Parkin, D (eds), *Swahili Language and Society*. Vienna: Afro-Pub, pp. 159–193.

Colletta, J.M., Pellenq, C. & Guidetti, M. (2010). Age-related changes in co-speech gesture and narrative: Evidence from French children and adults. *Speech Communication*, 52, 565–576.

Covington-Ward, Y. (2016). *Gesture and Power: Religion, Nationalism, and Everyday Performance in Congo*. Durham, NC, and London: Duke University Press.

Creider, C.A. (1977). Towards a description of East African gestures. *Sign Language Studies*, 14, 1–20.

Creider, C.A. (1978). Intonation, tone groups and body motion in Luo conversation. *Anthropological Linguistics*, 20(7), 327–339.

Creider, C.A. (1986). Interlanguage comparisons in the study of the interactional use of gesture: Progress and prospects. *Semiotica*, 62(1–2), 147–164.

Dingemanse, M. (2011). The meaning and use of ideophones in Siwu. PhD dissertation. Nijmegen: Radboud University.

Eastman, C.M. & Omar, Y.A. (1985). Swahili gestures: Comment (vielezi) and exclamations (Viingizi). *Bulletin of the School of Oriental and African Studies, University of London*, 48(2), 321–332.

Eckert, P. (2012). Three waves of variation study: The emergence of meaning in the study of socio-linguistic variation. *Annual Review of Anthropology*, 41, 87–100.

Gerdes, P. and Cherinda, M. (1993). Words, gestures and symbols. *UNESCO Courier* 46(11): 37–40.

Gerdes, P. & Marcos, C. (1993). Words, gestures and symbols. *UNESCO Courier*, 46(11), 37–40.

Glauning, F. & Huber, M. (1904). Forms of salutation amongst natives of East Africa. *Journal of the Royal African Society*, 3(11), 288–299.

Goldin-Meadow, S. & Alibali, M.W. (2012). Gesture's role in learning and development. In Zelazo, P. (ed.), *Oxford Handbook of Developmental Psychology*. Oxford: Oxford University Press, pp. 953–973.

Goodwin, C. (2003). Pointing as situated practice. In Kita, S. (ed.), *Pointing: Where Language, Culture and Cognition Meet*. Hillsdale, NJ: Erlbaum, pp. 217–241.

Groß, U. (1997). Analyse und Deskription textueller Gestik im Adzogbo (Ewe) unter Berücksichtigung kommunikationstheoretischer Aspekte. PhD Dissertation, University of Köln.

Gulliver, P. (1958). Counting with the fingers by two East African tribes. *Tanganyika Notes and Records*, 51, 259–262.

Hochegger, H. (1978). *Le Langage Gestuel en Afrique Centrale*. Bandundu: Publications CEEBA.

Hollis, A.C. (1909). *The Nandi: Their Language and Folk-Lore*. Oxford: Clarendon Press.

Irvine, J. & Gal, S. (2000). Language ideology and linguistic differentiation. In Kroskrity, P. (ed.), *Regimes of Language: Ideologies, Polities and Identities*. Sante Fe, NM: School of American Research Press, pp. 35–84.

Iverson, J.M. and Goldin-Meadow, S. (2005). Gesture paves the way for language development. *Psychological Science*, 16(5), 367–371.

Kendon, A. (1981). Geography of gesture. *Semiotica*, 37, 129–167.

Kendon, A. (1992). Some recent work from Italy on quotable gestures (emblems). *Journal of Linguistic Anthropology*, 2(2), 92–107.

Kendon, A. (1996). An agenda for gesture studies. *Semiotic Review of Books*, 7(3), 8–12.

Kendon, A. (2004). *Gesture: Visible Action as Utterance*. Cambridge: Cambridge University Press.

Kita, S. (2001). Semantic schism and interpretive integration in Japanese sentences with a mimetic: Reply to Tsujimura. *Linguistics*, 39(2), 419–436.

Kita, S. (2009). Gesture and culture. *Language and Cognitive Processes*, 24(2), 145–167.

Kita, S. & Essegbey, J. (2001). Pointing left in Ghana: How a taboo on the use of the left hand influences gestural practice. *Gesture*, 1(1), 73–95.

Kita, S. & Özyürek, A. (2003). What does cross-linguistic variation in semantic co-ordination of speech and gesture reveal? Evidence for an interface representation of spatial thinking and speaking. *Journal of Memory and Language*, 48, 16–32.

Klassen, D.H. (1999). "You can't have silence with your palms up": Ideophones, gesture, and iconicity in Zimbabwean Shona women's ngano (storysong) performance. PhD dissertation, Indiana University.

Klassen, D.H. (2004). Gestures in African Oral Narrative. In Peek, P.M. & Yankah, K. (eds), *African Folklore: An Encyclopedia*. New York, NY/London: Routledge, pp. 298–303.

Konrad, Z. (1994). *Ewe Comic Heroes: Trickster Tales in Togo*. New York, NY: Garland Publications.

Kunene, D.P. (1965). The ideophone in Southern Sotho. *Journal of African Languages*, 4(1), 19–39.

Kunene, R. (2010). A comparative study of the development of multimodal narratives in French and Zulu children and adults. PhD dissertation, University of Grenoble 3.

Kunene, N.R., Guidetti, M. & Colletta, J.-M. (2016). A cross-linguistic study of the development of gesture and speech in Zulu and French oral narratives. *Journal of Child Language*, 1–27, doi:10.1017/S0305000915000628.

Ladewig, S.H. (2011). Putting the cyclic gesture on a cognitive basis. *CogniTextes* 6.

Ladewig, S.H. (2014). The Cyclic Gesture, Chapter 121. In Müller, C., Cienki, A., Fricke, E., Ladewig, S.H., McNeill, D. & Bressem, J. (eds), *Body-Language-Communication: An International Handbook on Multimodality in Human Interaction. Vol. 2*. Berlin/Boston: De Gruyter Mouton, pp. 1605–1618.

McNeill, D. (1992). *Hand and Mind: What Gestures Reveal About Thought*. Chicago, IL: University of Chicago Press.

McNeill, D. & Duncan, S. (2000). Growth points in thinking-for-speaking. In McNeill, D. (ed.), *Language and Gesture*. Cambridge: Cambridge University Press, pp. 141–161.

Mondada, L. (2016). Challenges of multimodality: Language and the body in social interaction. *Journal of Sociolinguistics*, 20(3), 336–366.

Morris, D., Collett, P., Marsh, P. & O'Shaughnessy, M. (1979). *Gestures, Their Origins and Distribution*. New York, NY: Stein and Day.

Müller, C. (2010). Wie Gesten bedeuten. Eine kognitiv-linguistische und sequenzanalytische Perspektive. *Sprache und Literatur* 41(1), 37–68.

Núñes, R.E. & Sweetser, E. (2006). With the future behind them: Convergent evidence from Aymara language and gesture in the crosslinguistic comparison of spatial construal of time. *Cognitive Science*, 30, 401–450.

Nyst, V. (2016). The depiction of size and shape in gestures accompanying object descriptions in Anyi (Côte d'Ivoire) and in Dutch (The Netherlands). *Gesture*, 15(2), 156–191.

Olofson, H. (1974). Hausa language about gesture. *Anthropological Linguistics*, 18(1), 25–39.

Orie, O.O. (2009). Pointing the Yoruba way. *Gesture*, 9(2), 237–261.

Padden, C.A., Meir, I., Hwang, S-O., Lepic, R., Seegers, S. & Sampson, T. (2013). Patterned iconicity in sign language lexicons. *Gesture*, 13(3), 287–308.

Patrick, P.L. & Figueroa, E. (2002). Kiss-teeth. *American Speech*, 77(4), 383–397.

Payrató, L. (1993). A pragmatic view on autonomous gestures: A first repertoire of Catalan emblems. *Journal of Pragmatics*, 20, 193–216.

Saitz, R.L. & Cervanka, E.J. (1972). *Handbook of Gestures: Columbia and the United States*. The Hague: Mouton and Co.

Sanders, K.W. (2015). The convergence of language and culture in Malawian gestures: Handedness in everyday rituals. In Agwuele, A. (ed.), *Body Talk and Cultural Identity in the African World*. Bristol: Equinox, pp. 111–132.

Sibree, J. (1884). Notes on relics of the sign and gesture language among the Malagasy. *The Journal of the Anthropological Institute of Great Britain and Ireland*, 13, 174–183.

Siebicke, L. (2002). Die Samo in Burkina Faso: Zahlen und Zählen im San im Vergleich zuseinen Nachbarsprachen. *Afrikanistische Arbeitspapiere/AAP (Köln)*, 69, 5–61.

Sorin-Barreteau, L. (1996). Le langage gestuel des Mofu-Gudur au Cameroun. PhD dissertation, University of Paris V.

Sowa, T. & Wachsmuth, I. (2002). Interpretation of shape-related iconic gestures in virtual environments. In Wachsmuth, I. & Sowa, T. (eds), *Gesture and Sign Language in Human-Computer Interaction*. Berlin & Heidelberg: Springer, pp. 21–33.

Streeck, J. (2009). *Gesturecraft: The manu-facture of meaning*. Amsterdam/Philadephia: John Benjamins.

Thompson, R.F., de Dieu Nsondé, J. & Dianteill, E. (2002). *Le Geste Kongo*. Paris: Musée Dapper.

Tremearne, A.J.N. (1913). *Hausa Superstitions and Customs: An Introduction to the Folk-lore and the Folk*. London: Bale, Sons and Danielsson.

Westermann, D. (1907). Zeichensprache des Ewevolkes in Deutsch-Togo. *Mitteilungen des Seminar für orientalische Sprachen*, 10(3), 1–14.

Zondo, J. (1982). Some aspects of the ideophone in Ndebele. *Zambezia*, X(ii), 111–126.

23

TENSE AND TIME-DEPTH IN THE MABIA LANGUAGES OF WEST AFRICA

Testing the philosophy of linguistic relativity

Adams Bodomo

Introduction: the Sapir-Whorf hypothesis

This chapter[1] re-examines the philosophy of linguistic relativity in the light of some linguistic data gathered in northern Ghana. Linguistic relativity (Lucy 1997) or the Sapir-Whorf hypothesis (Crabtree and Powers 1991), as it is normally called, raises fundamental issues about the relationship between language, thought, and reality and has attracted the attention of linguists, philosophers, anthropologists, and psychologists. Does the structure of the language we speak influence or even determine our thought or the way we conceive of reality? And, if so, can an analysis of the lexical, grammatical, and pragmatic structure of a spoken language enable researchers to capture the way a group of individuals think about their environment? At least proponents of the Sapir-Whorf hypothesis think this is the case.

Indeed, Benjamin Lee Whorf, who is known in the literature (e.g., Crabtree and Powers 1991) as a mechanical engineer turned philosopher of language, based his claims on a comparative study of the differences between the way the English language and the Hopi Indian language categorize time and space, claiming that the verbal systems of the two languages show that speakers of English have a more structured or "calibrated" way of categorizing time and space than speakers of Hopi. Whorf's greatest contribution has been to analyze the interrelationship between the linguistic structure and world-view of a non-Western linguistic group and to compare it with the "Standard Average European" world-view and their linguistic categorizations (Stewart and Vaillette 2001). One of Whorf's conclusions is that since the Hopi verbal structure does not distinguish clearly between past, present and future as does English and other "calibrated" languages, the Hopi people do not have a concept of time as a linear progression, only being able to distinguish between the manifested and the un-manifested (Stewart and Vaillette 2001). As a result, the Hopi (and presumably other people whose languages do not exhibit such a calibration) tend to be unconcerned with exact dates and records.

The validity of the Whorfian hypothesis remains in question to date for at least two reasons. The first is that there are strong and weaker versions of the hypothesis, which I alluded to earlier when I raised the question of whether language *influences* or completely *determines* our thought. Strong versions or proponents of linguistic determinism (such as espoused in Agar 1994) claim that language can completely determine our thoughts and subsequent actions.

438

Weaker versions (such as espoused in Boroditsky 2001; Boroditsky, Fuhrman, & Mc Cormick 2010; and Li & Gleitman 2002) claim that language only influences the way we think and categorize reality. The other reason, probably due to these differing versions of the hypothesis, is that it is difficult to test this philosophy of linguistic relativity, especially across various languages (Lucy 1997).

Various studies have used various methods, including a comparison of color terms (e.g., Lucy 1997) from language to language and the analysis of the way different languages express time and space (e.g., Bodomo 1997b; Boroditsky 2001; and Boroditsky, Fuhrman, & Mc Cormick 2010). In terms of other African languages besides the Mabia languages (Bodomo 1997b, 2001), studies exist that have attempted to test the hypothesis in languages such as Somali (Laitin 1977), Yoruba (Agwuele 2010; Adekunle 2015), and Zulu (Adekunle 2015). There may be a few others but surely a more comprehensive programme of research to test the hypothesis in many more African languages using various approaches is a rather viable research endeavor.

One suggestion (Crabtree and Powers 1991: 416) for testing a version of the theory would be the investigation of a non-Western culture (such as in Africa) speaking languages with quite elaborate tense systems. What would be the differences between the way these people and English speakers express time? In what ways would speakers of such non-Western languages be preoccupied with time?

The Mabia languages[2] of northern Ghana and adjoining areas of Burkina Faso, Togo and the Ivory Coast constitute just one such group of non-Western languages with an elaborate tense system, even more elaborate than that of English and several other Indo-European languages such as French and Norwegian. Quite apart from exhibiting a structured tense system divided into past, present and future tenses, Mabia languages such as Dagaare and Dagbane have an additional system of tense marking that has been termed time-depth (Bendor-Samuel 1971; Bodomo 1997b), metrical tense (Chung and Timberlake 1985) or remoteness (Schwenter 1995), raising an additional philosophical question about the universality of the linguistic category "tense".

Before investigating Mabia tense structure, we give a further exposition of the Whorfian hypothesis. Benjamin Whorf declared in 1935 that linguistics "is fundamental to the theory of thinking, and in the last analysis to all human sciences" (Whorf 1935). His 1935 unpublished manuscripts of the structure of the Hopi language mark an important milestone for the development of the philosophical idea that the structure of a person's language is a factor in the way he or she thinks of and understands reality and behaves with respect to this reality. This relationship between language and thought gives birth to a new theory of relativity that can roughly be stated as follows:

> All observers are not led by the same physical evidence to the same picture of the universe unless their linguistic backgrounds are similar or can in some way be calibrated.
> *Carroll 1956: v*

Earlier on, another linguist cum philosopher of language had laid the groundwork for such a view in the following way:

> Human beings do not live in the objective world alone, nor alone in the world of social activity as ordinarily understood, but are very much at the mercy of the particular language which has become the medium of expression for their society. It is quite an illusion to imagine that one adjusts to reality essentially without the use of language

and that language is merely an incidental means of solving specific problems of communication or reflection. The fact of the matter is that the 'real world' is to a large extent unconsciously built up on the language habits of the group . . . We see and hear and otherwise experience very largely as we do because the language habits of our community predispose certain choices of interpretation.

Sapir 1929

Having now provided a short exposition of the Whorfian hypothesis, let us discuss this in the light of natural language systems. Natural languages have various ways of referring to event, space, time, and other conceptual categories. A typical example of conceptual categorization is time. In the next section, we shall investigate how this conceptual category is expressed in the Mabia languages of northern Ghana and adjacent areas in West Africa.

Mabia temporal system: the concept of "metrical tense"

Tense in the Mabia languages (including Dagaare, Dagbane, Gurenne (Frafra), Mampruli, Kusaal and Moore) is expressed by means of a system of preverbal particles in conjunction with the lexical verb(s) in the clause. Apart from tense, these particles can also express a wide range of other verbal systems in this language group. Table 23.1 below lists the main preverbal particles and the verbal systems they express in Dagaare and Dagbane.

Together with the changing forms of the verb (whether it is in the perfective or imperfective aspect) and some other (postverbal) particles, these preverbal particles both individually and in combination express a large range of verbal systems in Mabia. Such verbal systems include tense, aspect, polarity (positive and negative systems) and mood (indicative, imperative or subjunctive). The following sentences in Dagaare illustrate these aspectual, modal, polarity and tense systems.

(1a) *Ǹ dà gàá lá   à   wèé*
 I past go foc. def. farm (foc. = focus particle; def = definite particle)
 'I went to the farm' = past, perfective, positive, indicative sentence

Table 23.1 The main preverbal particles and the verbal systems they express in Dagaare and Dagbane

Tense, aspect, modal particles	Dagaare	Dagbane
today; also: once upon a time	dà	dì, dáá yì
one day away	zàá	sá
two or more days away	dáá	dáá
habitual	máng	yì
still, yet	nàng	ná
once again, as usual	yàà	yáá
suddenly, just	déè	díí
non-future negative	bá	bì
future particle	nà	ní
future negative	kòng	kú
imperative subjunctive negative	tá	dí
again	là	láh

(1b) *Ǹ dà gè-ré   lá   à   wèé*
I past go-imperf. foc. def. farm
'I was going to the farm' = past, imperfective, positive, indicative sentence

(1c) *N   nà gáá lá   à   wèé*
I fut+pos go   foc. def. farm (pos = positive particle)
'I will go to the farm' = future, perfective, positive, indicative sentence

(1d) *Ǹ bá   gàà   à   wèé*
I past+neg go def. farm (neg = negative particle)
'I did not go to the farm' = past, perfective, negative, indicative sentence

(1e) *Ǹ kòng   gàà à   wèé*
I fut+neg   go def farm (fut = future particle)
'I will not go to the farm' = future, negative, indicative sentence

(1f) *Gàà   à   wèé!*
Go+imperative def. farm
'Go to the farm' = perfective, positive, imperative sentence

(1g) *Gè-ré   à   wèé!*
Go-imperf. def. farm
'Get going to the farm !' = imperfective, positive, imperative sentence

(1h) *Tá   gàà à wèé!*
Neg+imperative go   def. farm
'You should not go to the farm' = negative, imperative/subj. sentence

(1i) *ó   gàà à wèé*
s/he+subj. go   def. farm
'She or he should go to the farm' = positive, subjunctive/imperative

While the major grammatical systems within the verb phrase as shown above are aspect, mood and polarity (Bodomo 1997a; Dakubu 2005), other important secondary ones are tense and time-depth and it is these we will focus on in this chapter.

Metrical tense in Dagaare

The above exposition of the preverbal particles in Dagaare and Dagbane indicates already that the Mabia languages exhibit a quite structured, "calibrated" system of expressing tense, divided mainly into the past and future, each with its independent preverbal particle (e.g., the Dagaare past tense particle *dà* and the future tense particle *nà*).

In addition to this calibrated system of expressing time in the verbal system, the Mabia languages also express a still more calibrated system known variously as 'time-depth', 'remoteness' and 'metrical tense' (see references above). This last designation, 'metrical tense', underscores the structured nature of temporal expressions in this language group and will be the preferred designation in this chapter. Table 23.2 below shows the various preverbal particles used in expressing metrical tense in Dagaare and Dagbane. Following Dahl (1985) and Schwenter (1995), we will refer to the finer categorizations of metrical tense as hodiernal (from the Latin *hodie* 'today'), hesternal (from the Latin *hesternus* 'related to yesterday') and pre-hesternal.

Adams Bodomo

Table 23.2 The various preverbal particles used in expressing metrical tense in Dagaare and Dagbane

Time depth/metrical tense	Dagaare	Dagbane
hodiernal	dà	dì
hesternal	záà	sá
pre-hesternal	dáà	dáá

The following sentences from Dagaare exemplify the occurrence of the particles.

(2a) *Áyúó dà   mɔ̀ŋg lá sááó ko má*
     Ayuo past-hodiernal make foc. food give me
     'Ayuo made food for me today'

(2b) *Áyúo záa   mɔ̀ŋg lá sááo kò má*
     Ayuo past-hesternal make foc. food give me
     'Ayuo made food for me yesterday'

(2c) *Áyúó dáá   mɔ̀ŋg lá sááó kò má*
     Ayuo past-prehesternal make foc. food give me
     'Ayuo made food for me two or more days ago'

The hodiernal particle in Dagaare, *dà*, designates not just the past tense but, in addition, gives a restricted time interval within which the action designated by the sentence is supposed to occur. It primarily refers to past within today. In addition to this primary restriction, many speakers extend it to express past tense beyond today, especially if it is used in conjunction with hesternal and pre-hesternal particles. Furthermore, it may be used to express very remote tense, i.e., the 'long ago' or 'once upon a time' tense.

(3) *Kɔ̀ŋg dà   lè-è   lá*
    hunger once-upon-a-time fall-perf. foc.
    'Once upon a time, there was famine'

The particle with the most specific meaning is the hesternal preverbal particle, *zàà*. It refers specifically to yesterday past and, contrary to the hodiernal tense particle, can never be extended to prehesternal use. It can, in addition, occur concurrently with only the hesternal adverb, *zààméŋg* 'yesterday'. This particle must appear when hesternal reference is intended, with or without the adverb, *zààméŋg* 'yesterday'.

The prehesternal verbal particle, *dáá*, is also quite specific in that it can never be used to mark hodiernal and hesternal tenses. It is used to express actions which take place between two to six days or thereabouts in the past. The limits of this particle correspond more or less to the limits of the traditional Dagaare six-day week. Like the hesternal metrical tense particle, it can occur together with the prehesternal adverb, *dááré*, which it resembles very much phonologically. This is shown in (4) where (4a) is very natural while (4b) is a bit quirky or even ungrammatical given that a hodiernal particle is used with the prehesternal adverbial.

(4a) *Dááré, Áyúó dáá   mɔ̀ŋg lá sááó kò má*
     adv.   Ayuo past-prehesternal make foc. food give me
     'Two or more days ago Ayuo made food for me'

Tense and time-depth in Mabia languages

(4b) *?Dááré, Áyúó dà   *mɔ̀ŋg lá sáóó kò má*
  adv. Ayuo past-today/remote make foc. food give me

In the next section we compare this metrical tense system in Dagaare with that of another Mabia language, Dagbane, spoken mainly in and around northern Ghanaian towns like Tamale and Yendi.

Metrical tense in Dagbane

Dagbane (also sometimes spelt as Dagbani or Dagbanli) has an even more complicated metrical tense system than Dagaare in terms of the way it uses its three hodiernal, hesternal and prehesternal preverbal particles. In addition to most of the intricate gradations of the past that we saw in the Dagaare verbal system, Dagbane also has the same intricate gradations into the future with more or less varying forms of the same metrical tense particles. The hodiernal particle, *dì*, which expresses past tense within today, also has another form, *dì n*, which expresses future within today, as shown in the following sentences.[3]

(5a) *Ń di [dən]* *kyáng shíkùrú zúŋɔ̀*
  I past-today go school adv.
  'I went to school today'

(5b) ? *Ń di ní [dən]* *kyáng shíkùrú zúŋɔ̀*
  I future-today go school adv.
  'I will go to school today'

The next is the hesternal particle, *sá*, which expresses past actions that took place only within yesterday. In addition to that, however, we have a form of this particle, *sá ní*, which expresses future actions taking place only within tomorrow, as exemplified below:[4]

(6a) *Ń sá*   *kyáng shíkùrú*
  I past-hesternal go school
  'I went to school yesterday'

(6b) *Ń sá ní*   *kyáng shíkùrú*
  I future-tomorrow go school
  'I will go to school tomorrow'

The third metrical tense particle in Dagbane is *dáá* and it expresses past actions taking place two or more days ago. But again this Dagbane prehesternal tense marker has a form that expresses future actions taking place only two days or more from today:[5]

(7a) *Ń dáá*   *kyáng shíkùrú*
  I past-prehesternal go school
  'I went to school two days ago'

(7b) *Ń dáá ní kyáng shíkùrú*
  I future-two days away go school
  'I will go to school in two days'

Figure 23.1

Summary

The above characterization of metrical tense in Dagbane shows a lot of similarities with the Dagaare system in as far as the basic system is concerned. This tripartite additional segmentation of the common past, present and future tenses into hodiernal, hesternal and pre-hesternal seems to be a general Mabia pattern,[6] and indeed recent studies involving Kusaal (Abubakari 2016) and Gurenne (Atintono 2013) grammatical analysis are confirming this general trend. There may be some Mabia-internal variation from language to language or dialect to dialect but it is possible to generalize onto what I will call a basic Mabia "tempometre" having the following gradations as in Figure 23.1.

What can this tempometre tell us about the world view and the behavior of the Mabia-speaking people, as far as time and temporal categorization are concerned?

Testing the Whorfian hypothesis

Having presented the basics of the Sapir-Whorf idea of linguistic relativity in the first section and then a quite detailed description of Mabia temporal systems, we will now proceed to test the validity of one or two aspects of linguistic relativity in this section.[7]

The Whorfian hypothesis, as we have seen, does not consider language *merely* as a tool for expressing the world-view and general cultural behavior of its speakers but as *shaping* this world-view and the way these people behave towards it (Carroll 1956; Crabtree and Powers 1991; Lucy 1997). With respect to the topic of the study reported in this chapter, and following a careful study of the temporal systems of Mabia, even if we didn't interact with these people before, the hypothesis could be said to claim that it is possible to predict, to a large extent, not only the temporal world-view of its speakers but the way these people would behave with respect to time.

Some supporting evidence

In order to support the observations that have been made, the following questions could be raised and addressed. Are these tempometric categorizations pertinent and observable in the day-to-day activities of the Mabia? Do the Mabia describe and relate to events, taking into consideration these categorizations? To some extent, yes. First of all, among the Mabia, especially the Dagaaba (speakers of Dagaare), the limits of the tempometre from the 'now' point correspond roughly to the traditional week, which is six days long, among the Dagaaba. The upper reference point of the particle, *dáá*, corresponds roughly to this six-day-week limit. Now, this six-day week is very central to the Mabia every-day and periodic activities. Markets come after every six days.[8] Multiples of the six-day week are used to locate events both in the past and in the future. This pertinent verbal category then seems to predict a pertinent real-world metaphysical calibration among the Mabia.

More importantly, finer gradations of time than the above are not important among the Mabia. It is commonly believed that Africans, including the Mabia, are less concerned about exact times and punctuality as compared with Europeans, for instance. The above gradations show that the concept of punctuality may in fact be a bit different between the two groups. The Mabia tempometre is a series of *time intervals* and not *time points* as may be found among other cultures. Thus, punctuality is defined not in terms of time points but in terms of time intervals in the traditional Mabia society. As a result, if a Mabia is told that a function is to begin at 4 pm, he or she is likely to interpret it as a time interval (four-ish) and not as a time point. He or she would therefore aim at being 'punctual' within his or her conceived time interval into which 4 pm falls. The gradations or calibrations of the Mabia tempometre thus seem to shape or influence this 'interval' approach to events.[9] If this conclusion is right, this could count towards confirming some aspects of the Whorfian hypothesis: that the structure of the language we speak determines or, at least, influences how we conceptualize our environment.

Problems for the Whorfian hypothesis

Unfortunately, however, the Whorfian hypothesis runs into problems in the light of some pertinent universals in the way human beings, irrespective of their linguistic backgrounds, behave with respect to time. It seems to be true that, irrespective of differences in the linguistic dissections of reality, there are certain situations in which human beings, wherever they may be in the world, would react in more or less the same way with respect to time. Whorf has argued that, given the differences between Hopi and English with respect to the expression of tense, Hopi speakers do not regard time in terms of a linear progression while English speakers do. As a result Hopi speakers are often less concerned with exact times, dates and written records. English speakers, on the other hand, attach a lot of importance to these issues and usually seem to be very conscious about time points and punctuality in real life. Granted that this observation is right, one may still wonder what would happen in cases of urgency and emergency such as accidents and hospital situations where the difference between staying alive and dying is time. It seems to me that whether we speak Hopi, English, or Dagaare we are all likely to suspend our peculiar world-view of time and react in the same, universal way to save life or reach our urgent goals. It is quite evident that, faced with such universal behavior in the light of some situations, the Whorfian hypothesis has to be abandoned altogether or a weaker version taken to account for these universals.

As a second reservation about the Whorfian hypothesis or linguistic relativity in general, I will discuss briefly the issue of politically correct language, a phenomenon that has become quite prominent in our time. A particularly strong view of linguistic relativity would be to state that world-view is so dependent on language that it is possible to change public opinions and behavior about some real-world issues by altering the linguistic structures, including vocabulary structures, used to refer to such issues.[10] Politically correct language, in the sense I use it here, consists of using milder vocabulary items and other euphemisms to describe some minority groups in our society. In politically correct speech, one is called upon to be sensitive to the plight of a group of people by using more pleasant language that would mitigate any negative world-views about these people. Hence, we use terms such as "underprivileged class" for the poor class and "mentally disabled" for mad-men and other mentally sick people. If this linguistic purging always succeeded in giving positive world images to these groups of people, it would constitute some evidence in support of a strong version of linguistic relativity.

The problem with politically correct speech however is that, sooner or later, even these milder terms and other euphemisms used to refer to some minorities become offensive and must themselves be replaced. Such is the case with cripples and other physically distorted people. The expression "physically handicapped" was probably a politically correct term for physically distorted people. However, at least in everyday English language press, both in traditional print and social media, people are beginning to question this term and, aided by members of physically handicapped associations, are beginning to suggest terms such as "physically challenged" for physically distorted people. This itself has been challenged and now we often hear what is supposed to be a better term "people living with disabilities". It is not clear if this term in turn might not be challenged in the next five or ten years. The failure of politically correct speech to alter the world-views of language users seems to me to be strong evidence against the validity of linguistic relativity.

To lay bare a final problem for the Sapir-Whorf hypothesis, let us return to our Mabia data. The Whorfian hypothesis, it seems to us, cannot explain why some cross-linguistic differences and similarities do not result in corresponding alternations in world-view. From the data about the expression of tense in the Mabia verbal system we realize that Mabia is just as "calibrated" as English and other "Standard Average European" temporal systems. English and Mabia on the one hand thus have a calibrated temporal structure while Hopi does not. It would follow from the Whorfian hypothesis, if it were really valid, that speakers of English and Mabia would behave in similar, though not the same, ways with regard to time in real-world situations while Hopi, as a consequence of their different linguistic structure, would behave quite differently from these groups. It seems to me, however, that from the descriptions Whorf provides about the Hopi attitude to time, the Mabia speakers of northern Ghana share a lot more in common with the Hopi than with the "Standard Average European" speakers Whorf describes. It may be said that, while the "Standard Average European" is more concerned (not to say stressed) about fitting into temporal precisions in their day-to-day activities, the Hopi and Mabia speakers are more concerned about fitting into larger chunks of time intervals, which makes them less concerned or even stressed when compared with Whorf's Standard Average Europeans. We thus see a case in which cross-linguistic similarities do not mirror into world-view similarities. This is certainly a problem for any version of linguistic relativity that claims that linguistic structure is a factor in determining a people's *weltanschauung*.

Conclusions

This chapter has discussed the Sapir-Whorf hypothesis with evidence from the structure of a group of languages in northern Ghana. The hypothesis, as has been encountered throughout the chapter, claims a certain amount of governing relationship of the structure of language over the structure of thought or the way reality is conceived of by speakers of the languages in question. Stronger versions of the hypothesis would claim that the structure of a language spoken by a group of people completely determines the way these people view their environment. Weaker versions would however maintain that linguistic structure influences the world-view of its speakers and that a careful study of the language of a people can lead us to an understanding of their culture and world-view.

This hypothesis has been tested by using the rich temporal systems of the Mabia languages, especially the concept of metrical tense that employs verbal particles to calibrate time into various gradations or intervals. Our discussion brought certain counter-evidence against the

Tense and time-depth in Mabia languages

Sapir-Whorf hypothesis, including evidence from some universal cognitive behavior in the face of some situations, the inability of politically correct speech to change a people's view of reality and the inability of the hypothesis to explain why cross-linguistic differences and similarities do not correspond to differences and similarities in world-view. This and other evidence would generally tend to negate the Whorfian hypothesis, especially its stronger versions.

There has been evidence to show however that the calibrations of the metrical tense in Mabia corresponded to the interval approach to time as practiced by the Mabia in real-life situations. The metrical tense system of the Mabia also rightly predicted the market-week culture of these people. This is evidence that tends to support the Whorfian hypothesis, especially its weaker version.

We would therefore conclude by saying that our study supports only a weak version of linguistic relativity. It is our opinion that, independent of the language they speak, all humans are capable of going through the same thought processes. Language does not determine or structure the logical thought process. What the structure of language does is to influence the way we express thought and not determine the way we reason about reality. We would thus conclude with Steinfatt (1989: 60) that "language affects representational thought, not logical operations."

Notes

1 An earlier version of the work discussed here was originally presented as a philosophical essay to the doctoral committee of the Faculty of Arts, NTNU, Trondheim, Norway in May 1996. Versions of this research write up subsequently appeared in *Cahiers Voltaiques/Gur Paper*, a collection of conference and other papers on Gur Linguistics (Bodomo 1997b) and in an abridged form in 2001 (in *The Journal of Cultural Studies*). The present version has been thoroughly updated with new data and theoretical re-examinations. I thank people in all these various fora for their very useful comments and suggestions. I am, however, responsible for any errors that may be detected in the chapter.

2 In previous works (e.g., Bodomo 2005, Bodomo and Abubakari 2017) I have used the term Mabia as an alternative to the Oti-Volta sub-group of the Gur languages, but increasingly I have used it as a complete replacement of the entire membership of the Gur language family. Previous works (e.g., Naden 1989) on these languages have used the term Gur languages (or Langues Voltaiques for French-speaking writers). The claim has been that there are many language names in this group beginning with the syllable "Gur" such as Gurma, Gurunshe, or Gurenne or that there are many "gur" syllables in this language. However, in many works, beginning with Bodomo (1993), the author has argued against these reasons for calling the linguistic group "Gur". There are many more languages in the group that have non-Gur names: Dagbane, Kusaal, Buli, Kasem, Dagaare, Sisaali, etc. We have instead used the term Mabia (coming from *ma* – "mother" and *bia/biiga* – "child", which are recurrent lexical items in most of these languages) as an appropriate genetic classificatory term for these languages.

3 I thank Salifu Yakubu, a native speaker of Dagbane from Tamale, Ghana, now resident in San Jose, California for providing me with these Dagbane sentences.

4 The particles *dƏn* and *sƏn* are actually compound particles comprising *dƏ* (in the case of *dƏn*) and *sƏ* (in the case of *sƏn*) and the future particle *nƏ*. The particles *dƏ* and *dƏn* also have the variants *tƏ* and *tƏn*. I am grateful to Salifu Nangtoma Alhassan, a native speaker of Dagbane from Tamale for this information. There are, however, opinions that suggest that this could alternatively be an instance of apocope where the final vowel segment of the second particle is deleted rather than compounding involving these functional items, since compounding is more usual with lexical items. I am grateful to Samuel Alhassan Issah for this discussion. I will however leave the debate open in this chapter.

5 It is not very clear whether such a regular system of hodiernal, hesternal and prehesternal metrical system exists throughout all the Mabia languages. Dakubu (1991) reports that Guruni uses *daa* as hesternal particle and this is contrary to what Dagaare and Dagbane do:

Dáárí, `n dáá dóósì      lá `n   kéémà
day   I past following foc. my elder-sibling
'Yesterday, I was following my elder brother'

It would be necessary to do further research on metrical tense systems to discover the exact nature of the phenomenon. However, what has been attested for Dagaare and Dagbane is probably enough to make plausible generalizations for Mabia.

6 This generalization seems to have been confirmed by a preliminary survey of data in the Mabia languages by Naden (1996).

7 At this point we draw attention to the fact that the Whorfian hypothesis is quite comprehensive and would involve many more issues than can be adequately handled here. We would thus briefly relate it to the specifics of time categorizations among the Mabia.

8 Some Mabia have a three-day market week and this corresponds to the lowest limit of the *daa* interval.

9 It is of course possible that Mabia speakers who speak different languages and who have experienced different cultures' views about "punctuality" would acquire world-views that over-ride the Mabia worldview about punctuality and would thus not behave exactly as a mono-lingual Mabia speaker who has not experienced other cultures.

10 Whorf probably did not espouse this strong view but it can still be used to expose the shortcomings of even milder views of linguistic relativity such as the Whorfian hypothesis.

References

Abubakari, H. (2016). Contrastive Focus Particles in Kúsáàl. Paper presented at the 47th Annual Conference of African Linguistics (ACAL). Berkeley, CA.

Adekunle, O.T. (2015). A linguistic relativity appraisal of an African drama: The Lion and the Jewel. Master's thesis, Durban University of Technology, Durban, South Africa.

Agar, M. (1994). *Language Shock: Understanding the Culture of Conversation*. New York, NY: Morrow.

Agwuele, A. (2010). Linguistic relativity: Lexical understanding across languages. *TRANS*: www.inst.at/trans/17Nr/2-2/2-2_agwuele17.htm (last accessed April 12, 2017).

Atintono, A.S. (2013). The semantics and grammar of Gurene positional verbs: A typological perspective. Manchester: University of Manchester dissertation.

Bendor-Samuel, J. (1971). Niger Congo, Gur. In *Current Trends in Linguistics, Vol. 7: Linguistics in Sub-Saharan Africa*, Thomas A. Sebeok (ed.), 141–178. The Hague: Mouton.

Bodomo, A. B. (1997a). *The Structure of Dagaare*. Stanford Monographs in African Languages. Stanford, CA: CSLI.

Bodomo, A. B. (1997b). Linguistic relativity in the light of Mabia temporal systems: Evidence from Dagaare and Dagbane. In *Cahiers Voltaiques/Gur Papers* I. 95–103. Bayreuth, Germany.

Bodomo, A. B. (2001). The temporal systems of Dagaare and Dagbane: re-appraising the philosophy of linguistic relativity. *Journal of Cultural Studies*, 3(1), 43–55.

Bodomo, A. B. (2005). Moore and the Gur languages. In Philip Stranzy (ed.), *Encyclopedia of Linguistics* (Vol. 2; pp. 709–711). New York, Oxon: Taylor & Francis Group.

Bodomo, A. and H. Abubakari (2017). Towards the harmonization of a writing system for the Mabia languages of West Africa. In Prah, K. K. and Miti, L. M. (eds), *The Myth of an African Tower of Babel: The Typological Fragmentation of African Languages*. Cape Town: CASAS Book Series No. 120.

Boroditsky, L. (2001). Does language shape thought? English and Mandarin speakers' conceptions of time. *Cognitive Psychology*, 43(1), 1–22.

Boroditsky, L., O. Fuhrman and K. McCormick (2010). Do English and Mandarin speakers think about time differently? *Cognition*, 118, 123–129. doi:10.1016/j.cognition.2010.09.010.

Carroll, B. J. (ed.) (1956). *Language, Thought and Reality: Selected Writings of Benjamin Lee Whorf*. Cambridge, MA: The MIT Press.

Chung, S. and A. Timberlake (1985). Tense, aspect and mood. Language typology and syntactic description, Vol. III. *Grammatical Categories and the Lexicon*, ed. Timothy Shopen, 202–258. Cambridge, Cambridge University Press.

Crabtree, M. and J. Powers (compilers) (1991). *Language Files: Materials for an Introduction to Language*. Columbus, OH: Ohio State University Press.

Dahl, Ö. (1985). *Tense and Aspect Systems*. Oxford: Basil Blackwell.

Dakubu, M.E. (2005). Dagaare (*Collected Language Notes, Vol. 26*). Legon, Accra, Ghana: Institute of African Studies.

Dakubu, M.E. (1991). Notes of the particle la in Northwestern Oti-Volta, ms., Language Centre, University of Ghana, Legon, Accra.

Laitin, D. (1977). *Politics, Language, and Thought: the Somali Experience*. Chicago, IL: The University of Chicago Press.

Li, P. and L. Gleitman (2002). Turning the tables: Language and spatial reasoning. *Cognition*, 83(3), 265–294.

Lucy, J.A. (1997). Linguistic relativity. *Annual Review of Anthropology*, Vol. 26, 291–312.

Naden, T. (1996). Western Oti-Volta comparative dictionary, ms., GILLBT, Tamale, Ghana.

Naden, T. (1989). Gur. In *The Niger-Congo Languages*, ed. J. Bendor-Samuel. Lanham, MD: The Universities Press of America.

Sapir, E. (1929). The status of linguistics as a science. *Language*, Vol. 5, 207–219.

Schwenter, S.A. (1995). Dagaare remoteness in functional and typological perspective, ms., Stanford University.

Steinfatt, T. (1989). Linguistic relativity: Towards a broader view. In *Language, Communication and Culture: Current Directions*. New Park, CA: Sage Publications.

Stewart, T. and N. Vaillette (eds) (2001). *Language Files: Materials for an Introduction to Language and Linguistics*. Columbus, OH: Ohio State University.

Whorf, B. (1935). The Hopi language, unpublished ms.

INDEX

Note: References in *italics* are to figures, those in **bold** to tables.

Abasheikh, M.I. 273, 279n1
Abdulaziz, M. 396, 409, 413, 414
Abels, K. 279n5
Abney, S. 286
Aboh, E.O. 111, 286
accretion zones 49–50
Acooli 73
Acoustic Invariance Hypothesis 122
acoustic representation 62
Adamawa-Eastern **36**
Adamawa-Ubangi 99, 111
Adegbija, E. 57
Adele 151
Adger, D. 282
Adika, G.S.K. 346–7
Adioukrou 77, 151
African language studies 1–4; maps of African
    languages *3*, *37*, *44*; number of languages 2,
    4, 244; some issues 4–8; *see also* history of
    African language studies
African Linguistic Association 124
African linguistics 8–10
African urban youth languages (AUYLs) 409–10
African youth languages (AYLs) 7, 391, 409–11;
    approaches to study of youth languages 403–5;
    AUYLs 409–10; Cameroon 400–1, 404–5,
    415–16, 421; Congo 417–18; Ethiopia 421;
    ethnicity 420; etymology 419; intelligibility
    420; Ivory Coast 398–400, 404–5, 416–17,
    421; Kenya 395–8, 403–5, 413–15, 420;
    language practices compared 401–3;
    matrix languages 411, 412; migration and
    socioeconomic factors 419–20; nativization
    421; pending research 421–2; South Africa

392–5, 411–13, 420, 421; speakers 420; Sudan
    421; Uganda 418, 420; conclusion 422
Afrikaans 394, 395, 411, 412
Afro-Asiatic phylum 2, 35, **36**, 49, 73, 81, 246
Agbedor, P. 381, 386
Agbozo, G.E. 346
Aghem 111, 156, 247
Agwuele, A. *et al.* 7, 8, 124, 133, 144, 145, 429
Ahan 110
Ahua, B. 398–9, 417
Aikhenvald, A.Y. 208–9
Akan 19; ATR-harmony 182–4, **183**, **185**, *188*,
    188–9, *189*, 190; clausal connectives and focus
    markers **256**, 256–8; demonstratives 282–3,
    292; focus 250, 252–3; MOOD systems 94,
    103–4; serial verb constructions 209, 211–12,
    213, 214, 215; topic marking 254–5
Akinlabi, A. 8
Akinlabi, A.M. 125, 130
Akortia, P.T. 255
Algeria: Kabyle 178n2; Tadaqsahek 47, **47**;
    Tamashek (Touareg) 178n2
Alsina, A. 265
Ameka, F. 51, 249, 255–6
Amekor, K.C. 346
Amfo, N.A.A. 244, 254, 255, 292
Amharic 6
Ancient Egyptian **36**
Andersen, T. 42, 254
Anderson, S.R. 162
Anderson, V. 62
Andreas, H. *et al.* 156
Angi-Ashanti gestures 428
Anglo-Romani 48

450

Index

Angola: Kwadi **36**, 41; Portuguese 344
anti-languages 410–11
Anyidoho, A. 386
Appessika, K. 399
Appiah, K.A. 332
applicatives *see* Bantu applicatives; Chimwiini
  instrumental applicatives
Arabic 46–7, 170, 178n1, 178n4; *see also*
  Moroccan Arabic
Articulatory Compensation 122
Articulatory Phonology 122
Atangana, K. 27
Atintono, A.S. 284
Atlantic-Congo 247
Attié 82, 87
audio representations 62
Auditory Enhancement 122
Augustine 326
Autosegmental Phonology 90, 125, 162, 182, 184
Autosegmental Theory 5
AUYLs (African urban youth languages) 409–10
Avatime 150
Avoid Pronoun Principle 229–30
Aycard, P. 421
Ayewa, N.K. 417
AYLs *see* African youth languages
Ayobade, D. 430
Aziza, R.O. 329, 335–6

Ba Mambila 64, 65
Baale 46
Baart, J. 85
Baduel-Mathon, C. 428
Bafut 246
Baka 151
Baker, M. 262, 263–4
Bakker, P. *et al.* 47
Balmer, W.T. 207
Bamgbose, A. xiv, 3, 125, 379, 385
Banda 99
Bantoid 106
Bantu applicatives 262–3, 279n2; Chimwiini
  instrumental applicatives 269–75; expanding
  the landscape 268–9; history 263–8; locative
  DP merged above the agent 278; multiple
  applicatives: BEN + INSTR 276–7; Zulu locative
  applicatives 268, 277–8; conclusions 278
Bantu languages 49; borrowing 45, 48; citation
  form 83; classification 34; coarticulation 124;
  culture 25; depressor consonants 81; dialects
  43; focus 245, 246, 247, 248–9; MOOD systems
  111, 114; noun classification 67; research 19,
  21; South Africa 394, 395, 429, 431, 432–3;
  tone 73, 82, 88; translation 361; verbs 362;
  writing systems 373
Barasa, S.N. 396, 414, 415
Bari **39**, 43, 46

Bariba 152
Barnwell, K. 327, 334
Barrows, S. 27
Bassa 401
Batibo, H. 345
Beach, D.M. 73, 80
Beck, R.M. 409, 417, 419, 421
Becker, D. 34
Beekman, J. 333
Bench 81
Benes, T. 17
Benin: Ewe 344; Foodo 252, **256**, 256–8;
  French 344
Bensoukas, K. 171
Benue-Congo **36**, 94–5, 106, 109, 110–11
Berber languages 34, **36**, 47, **47**, 178n2; *see also*
  Moroccan Berber
Berlin Conference (1884-5) 29n6
Berlin Missionary Society (BMS) 17
Berry, J. 182–3, **183**, 201n5
Bert, Michel 68
Berta 35, 38
Beyer, K. 412
Beza, T. 330
Bhat, D.N.S. 281
Bhele 81
Bible translations *see* translations of Scripture
Bickel, B. 217
Bila 44–5, 80–1
Biloa, E. 415–16
binding theory 224, 231–2
Bismarck, O. von 20, 29n6
Bissell-Doggett, T. 265, 266
Black, R. 353
Bleek, W.H.I. 19
Blench, Roger M. 55, 61
Blommaert, J. 344
Blust, R.A. 33
BMS (Berlin Missionary Society) 17
Boadi, A.L. 282–3
Boadi, L.A. 152
Bodomo, A.B. 7, 284, 378, 380–1, 383, 386,
  447n2
borrowing 41, 45–6
Bosch, T.E. 346
Bose, P.B. 43
Bostoen, K. *et al.* 49, 156
Boudlal, A. 171
Bouquiaux, L. 64
Bowern, C. 60
Bowra, C.M. 339
Bresnan, J. 263, 264, 265, 268
Bressem, J. 429
Broohm, O.N. 251, 256
Brookes, H. 7, 393–4, 405, 409, 412, 413, 421,
  422, 429, 430, 431, 432–3
Brown, D.R. 250

Bryan, M.A. 160
Bucholtz, M. 405
Budu 79
Buell, L. 268, 277–8, 279n11
Buli 161, 281, 286
Bullom 20
Burkina Faso: Dyan 87–8; Lyélé 77; Samo 429;
   see also Mabia
Burundi 246
Bushman 34
Buthelezi, M. 412, 421
Büttner, C. 20, 21
Buxton, T.F. 18

C-command 232–3
Cahill, M. 150, 154, 157, 160, 163, 240
Calame-Griaul, G. 432
Callow, J. 333
calquing 46
Calteaux, K. 393
Calvet, L.-J. 59
Cameroon: Aghem 111, 156, 247; Bafut 246;
   Camfranglais 400–1, 404–5, 415–16, 421;
   colonialism 21; Fulfulde 58; language use 58;
   Mofu-Gudur storytelling 432; Pidgin English
   400, 401; Sawabantu languages 156
Camfranglais 400–1, 404–5, 415–16, 421
Campbell, L. 41
Caprile, J.-P. 429
Carnie, A. 287
Carpenter, S. 59
Carroll, B.J. 439
Carstens, V. 240
Casali, R.F. 161
Castells, M. 400, 401
Central African Republic: counting gestures 429;
   Kaba 77, 78–9; Yaka 86
Central Khoisan 36, 40–1
Central Saharan 35
Central Sudanic 35, 38, 43, 429
Cervenka, E.J. 428
Chad: Dazaga (Tubu) 39; gestures 429; Laal
   36–7; Mambila 247
Chadic experiencer predications 297–9;
   abbreviations 319–20; Chadic languages 298;
   definition 299; Gidar (Central Chadic) 317–19;
   Hdi (Central Chadic) 314–17; Lele (East
   Chadic) 299–303; Mina (Central Chadic)
   309–11; Mupun (West Chadic) 311–14; Pero
   (West Chadic) 308–9; Wandala (Central
   Chadic) 299, 303–7; conclusions 319
Chadic languages 36, 73, 81, 156, 247–8, 298
Chafe, W. 243–4
Chai 46
Chari-Nile branch 36, 38
Chennoukh, S. et al. 130
Chichewa 245–6, 263, 264–5

Chidigo 159, 161
Childs, G. T. 67, 68
Childs, T. 253
Chimwiini instrumental applicatives 279n1;
   explanation 272–5; instrumental vs.
   benefactive/recipient applicatives 269–71, **272**;
   object agreement 273–4; passivization 274–5;
   279n9; questioning the applied object 275;
   topicalization/relativization 275; word order 273
Chinese 233, 234–5, 236, 237, 240
Chitumbuka 245
Cho, K. et al. 362
Chomsky, N. 89, 162, 164n3, 286, 287, 294n6
Christaller, J.G. 18, 19, 207, 209
Chumburung translation of the Bible 329, 334–9,
   340, 341n1–2; calques, transliterations, loans
   338; functional equivalence 336–9; implicit
   information made explicit 338–9; natural
   idioms and expressions 337–8; problems of
   non-equivalence 336; proverbial names 339
Church Missionary Society (CMS) 16, 17, 18, 19
Cicero 325–6, 331, 333
Cinque, G. 285, 286, 291
ciTsonga 430
Clements, G.N. 163, 163, 184, 187–8, 230
Cleve, G.L. 25, 26
Click 35, 41
clicks 40, 52n2
coarticulation 5, 121–2; African languages and
   coarticulatory studies 123–4; anticipatory
   coarticulation 122, 123–4; auditory/acoustic
   perspective 122; co-production 122; gestural
   accounts 122; Locus Equations 122–3, 124;
   non-invariance problem 121, 122; tone 125–6;
   see also Yoruba segmental/suprasegmental
   interaction
codemeshing 52
codeswitching/codemixing 47, 346, 396
Cole, P. et al. 222, 223, 233, 236, 237, 239, 240, 241
Coleman, J. 175
colonial linguistics 2, 19, 34, 344, 379
colonialism 18, 20–4
Coman 36
Comaroff, J. and J. 19, 422
communication and development 380
community profile questionnaires 57
comparative approach 1
Comrie, B. 263
Congo: gesture 433; Indoubil 417–18, 420;
   Langila 417; Lingala ya bayanké 418; urban
   youth languages 417–18; Yabâcrane 417, 418
Connell, B. 58, 59, 67, 150, 151, 152, 153, **153**,
   156, 157, 160
Cook, J. 33
Cook, T. 160
Cooper, J. 60
Cooper, R.L. 59, 376, 377

Index

Côte d'Ivoire *see* Ivory Coast
Coulibaly, A. 398–9
Coupland, N. 344
Courtenay, K.R. 125
Covington-Ward, Y. 433
Cowie, M. 325
Crazzolara, J.P. 73
creative expression 7
Creider, C.A. 428, 431
creolization 47, 48
Crowley, T. 60, 68, 69
Crowther, S.A. 19
Cunliffe, D. *et al.* 344, 345, 347
Cushitic languages **36**, 46, 48, 73, 249–50
Cust, R.N. 19

Daats'iin 35
Dada, S.A. 335
Dagaare 94; interpersonal clause structure *94*;
    MOOD systems 98–9, 100, 101, 104, 105, 106,
    108; temporal system 439, 440, **440**, 441–3,
    442, 444–5
Dagbani: aspect 284; basic grammatical features
    283–7; focus 250; labial-velars 160, 163,
    164n6; MOOD systems 101–3, 111–12; sentence
    structure 284; temporal system 284, 439, **440**,
    442, 443–4; tones 283–4; word order 284–6
Dagbani demonstratives 281–3, 287,
    294n2; abbrevations 295; data sources
    283; demonstrative determiners 287–9;
    demonstrative pronouns **289**, 289–91;
    locational/demonstrative adverbs 291–3;
    summary & conclusion **293**, 293–4
Dahl, Ö. 441
Daju languages 50
Dakubu, M.E.K. 215, 217, 218, 219n8, 244,
    447–8n5
Dalrymple, M. 290
Dan 64, 152, 155
Dangme 250, 252, 255, **256**, 256–8, 346
Dante 340
Davies, D.W. 286
Dazaga (Tubu) 39
De Lacerda, A. 122
De Waard, J. 334
Defaka 155
Defina, R. 214
Dell & Elmedlaoui (1985, 1988, 2002) 175
Democratic Republic of the Congo: Bila 44,
    80–1; Budu 79; counting gestures 429; dialect
    variation 43; Lendu 77–8, 82, 85; Lingala 86;
    Mayogo 79; Ngiti 85, 86; Zimba 86–7
Demolin, D. 150
demonstratives 281–3, 292; *see also* Dagbani
    demonstratives
Denya 106
depressor consonants 79–81

Deumert, A. 411
development 377–8; ingredients of development
    378–9; sustainable development 378
dialectological studies 42–5
Dibone, N. 21
dictionary compilation 371
dictionary testing 372
Diessel, H. 281–2, 289
Digo 88
Dik, S.C. 244
Dimmendaal, G.J. 40, 41, 42, 45, 46, 49, 50
Dingemanse, M. 67, 68, 432
Dinka 254
Dinka-Nuer-Atuot cluster 41–2
Direct Realism 122
Dixon, R.M.W. 281
Doke, C.M. 114
Dolphyne, F. 3
Donzo, J-P. 156
Dorleijn, M. 410, 419
Downing, L.J. *et al.* 245, 246
Dowty, D. 298
Dresser, C.A. 286
Dryden, J. 325, 326, 331
Dryer, M.S. 281, 284
Duala 21, 27, 401
Durban Zulu 245
Durie, M. 212
Duruma 164n4
Dyan 87–8
Dynamic Specification 122
Dyula 73, 399

Eastern Nilotic 38–40, **39**, *40*, 41, 43, 48, 49
Eastern Sudanic 35, 38, 39, 49
Eaton, H. 253
Ebobissé, C. 156
Ébrié 77, 79–80
Eckert, P. 410
Edo 250–1
education 6–7
Efe 151
Efik 153, 158–9, 160
Efoua-Zengue, R. 416
Ega 164n1
Egon 160
Ehret, C. 73
Elderkin, Edward D. 41
Embick, D. 269
endangered languages 68, 343
Engenni 152, 155
English: African dictionaries and grammars 17,
    20; demonstratives 282, 283, 288, 289; Ghana
    346, 381–2, 383; globalisation 344; Kenya
    361, 365, 395, 396; as official language 6, 344,
    359, 361; pronouns 224–5, 226–7; translation
    326–7, 329, 330, 332, 334–6, 338, 339

Engsh 396, 397, 398, 413, 414–15, 420
Erasmus, D. 330
Eritrea 246
Esahie 250, 251, 256
Esan 335
Eshun, E.S. 346
Essegbey, J. 51, 430–1
Essono, J.-M. 416
Ethiopia: Amharic 6; Baale 46; Bench 81;
   colonialism 18; Daats'iin 35; Gamo 254;
   Ge'ez 16; Komo 255; language in the market
   59; missionaries 17; Ong'ota 50; Oromo
   249–50; Shabo 50; Tigrinya 246; Yarada
   K'wank'wa 421; youth languages 421
Ethnologue 344
ethnonyms 52n1
European Union: translation applications 360;
   translation policy 328, 360
Ewe: Benin 344; gestures 428; Ghana 255, 344,
   345, 346, 428, 432; labial-velars 152, *152*,
   158; pronoun *ye* 230; research 27; Serial Verb
   Constructions 207; Togo 344, 345; topic
   marking 255
Ewe use on Facebook 343, 345, 346–7; adaptation
   of Ewe fonts 351, **351**; bilingual practices,
   codeswitching, translanguaging 351, 352;
   COD model and data 347–8, **348**; competence,
   opportunities, desires 353–4; linguistic features
   351–2; socio-cultural features 348–50, **349**;
   conclusions 354–5
Ewondo 27, 164n2, 401
experiencer predications 297–8; *see also* Chadic
   experiencer predications
Eyamba, B. 3

Fabri, F. 20
Facebook *see* Ewe use on Facebook
Fagles, R. 339–40
Feature Geometry 156, 162–3
Fennig, C.D. 244
Féral, C. de 410, 415, 416
Fiedler, I. 245, 252, 256
fieldwork *see* linguistic fieldwork in Africa;
   surveying language knowledge and use;
   tone and tonology fieldwork
Fillmore, C.J. 291
Fink, C. *et al.* 345
Firth, J.R. 62
Fishman, J. 376, 377
focus 243–4; clausal connectives and focus
   markers 256–8; data sources 244–5; linguistic
   strategies for encoding 245 (lexical strategies
   250–1; mixed strategies 251–3; morphological
   strategies 247–50; phonological/prosodic
   strategies 245–6; syntactic strategies 246–7)
Foodo 250, 252, **256**, 256–8
Fosso, F. 416

Frafra 153, *153*, 440, 444
Frajzyngier, Z. 299–300
Francke, A.H. 17
Fraternité Matin 399
French 46, 58, 76, 169, 297; Ivory Coast 344, 359,
   398, 399, 400, 417
Fresco, E.M. 161
Fromkin, V. 184, 189
Fula 249
Fulani 73
Fulfulde 58
Fur 35, **36**, 51, 77, 78, 86

Ga: clausal connectives and focus markers
   256, 256–8; MOOD systems 97, 100–1, 106,
   107, 110, 113; preverbs 210; serial verb
   constructions 213–14, 215–16, 218; topic
   marking 255–6
Gairdner, W.H.T. 25
Gamo 254
Gardy 416
Garrigues-Cresswell, M. 302, 303
Gbadi 95
Gbe languages 286
Ge'ez 16
generative phonology 89–90, 124, 125
genetic classification of African languages 33–7,
   36, *37*, **38**; metaphorical representation 48–9, *49*
genetic research 23
Gerdts, D. 266, 279n4
German: Low German and social media 345–6
German-East African Missionary Society 20
German Lutheran Church 16
Germany 16–18, 20–4
gesture and gesturing 7–8, 427–8; co-speech
   gestures 430–1; counting gestures 429; culture
   and environment 432–3; and genre 432;
   gestural repertoires 428–9; gesture families
   429; and language development 434; quotable
   gestures 429–30; recurrent gestures 429; and
   style 431–2; conclusion 434–5
Ghana 7, 18; Adele 151; Akan 254–5, **256**, 256–8,
   346; Buli 161, 281, 286; codeswitching and
   translanguaging 346; Dangme 252, 255, **256**,
   256–8, 346; English 346, 381–2, 383; Esahie
   251, 256; Ewe 255, 344, 345, 346, 428, 432;
   Ga 255–6, **256**, 256–8, 346; gestures 430–1;
   Ghanaian Pidgin English 346, 353–4; Kwa
   157; Likpe 249; multilingualism 346, 380–5;
   Nawuri 161, 164; proposed late-exit policy
   381–3; proposed localized trilingualism
   380–1, 383; Siwu ideophones 432; *see also*
   Chumburung translation of the Bible; Dagbani;
   Ewe use on Facebook; Mabia
Ghavami, G.M. 123, 145
Gichuka 111
Gidar (Central Chadic) 317–19

Gikuiyi 395
Gippert, J. *et al.* 61
Giryama 164n4, 395
Githinji, P. 397, 405, 413, 414, 420
Githiora, C. 396, 397, 398, 403, 411
Glaser, C. 413
Glauning , F. 428
globalisation 343–4
Goldie, H. 159
Goldsmith, J. 90
Gonja 152
Good, J. 67, 248
Google Translate (GT) 359, 360
Google Translate (GT) and SALAMA 362–3;
  assessment of translation tests 368–70;
  English–Swahili translation 365–7, 369–70;
  structure of tested translation systems 363;
  Swahili–English translation 363–5, 368–9
Gorgoryos, Ä. 16
GoSheng 398
Government Phonology 169, 171; Proper
  Government 172; vowel harmony 184–9, **185**
Goyvaerts, D.L. 417
Gragg, G.B. 246
grammar 5
grammaticalization theories 51
Grant, F.C.F. 207
"Great Lakes" group 38
Greenberg, J.H. 34–6, **36**, 38, 41, 52n2, 244, 284
Gregory 326
Grey, Sir G. 19
Grimm, J. 17, 18
Grinvald, C. 68
Groß, U. 432
GT *see* Google Translate; Google Translate (GT)
  and SALAMA
Guerssel, M. 169, 171
Guinea: Kisi 253; Loma 152
Güldemann, T. 41, 252, 257
Gumuz 35
Gundel, J. 244
Gungbe 286
Gur **36**, 184, 447n2; citation form 83; clausal
  connectives and focus markers 256; MOOD
  systems 94, 98–9, 101, 106–7, 111; time depth
  particles 284; *see also* Dagbani; Dagbani
  demonstratives; Mabia
Gurenne 440, 444
Gurindji Kriol (Australia) 47
Gurune 96–7, 447–8n5
Gùrùntùm 247–8
Gusii 428, 429, 431
Gutt, E.-A. 330, 332
Gwari 159, 161

Haacke, W.H.G. 246, 253
Hadza 36, **36**

Hajek, J. 154
Hall, K. 405
Halle, M. 89, 162, 164n3, 187–8
Halliday, M.A.K. 100, 244, 410–11
Hamburg Colonial Institute Phonetics Laboratory
  21–3, 28; kymograph 27; pedagogy and
  research 24–7; *Taubstumme* (deaf-mutes) 25
"Hamitic" languages 21
"Hamito-Semitic" languages 34, 35
Hammarberg, R. 121
Hansford, G. 341n1
Harries, P. 16, 19
Hartmann, K. 247–8
Hastings, A. 18
Haugen, E. 376
Hausa 18, 21, 27, 34, 73, 428
Hawkins, J.A. 51
Hdi (Central Chadic) 314–17
Hecker, A. 416
Heepe, M. 27
Heine, B. *et al.* 8–9, 51, 244
Hellan, L. *et al.* 209
Herault, G. 150
Herder, J.G. 17, 18
Herero 20
Hermon, G. 222, 239, 240
Higham, T.F. 339
Himmelmann, N.P. 61, 64
historical linguistics 4, 33; abbreviations 52;
  accretion and spread zones 49–50; area
  spreading of innovations 42–5; comparative
  method 38–42; dialectological studies
  42–5; metaphorical representation of
  genetic relationships 48–9, *49*; multilateral
  comparisons and genetic classification 33–7,
  36, *37*, **38**; other language contact phenomena
  45–8; structural properties of language change
  38–42; prospects for future research 50–2
history of African language studies 15;
  German colonialism, nationalism, inherent
  racism 20–4; missionaries and the written
  word 15–20; pedagogy and research 24–7;
  conclusion 28
Holmes, J.S. 329
Hombert, J.-M. 66, 124
Homer 339
Honeycutt, C. 344, 347
Hopi (Native American) 438, 439, 445, 446
Horace 326, 333
Hottentot 34, 73
House, J. 334
household surveys 57
Huang, C.-T.J. 223, 233, 235, 236
Huber, M. 428
Humboldt, W. von 17, 18
Hume, E.V. 163, *163*
Hungarian 184

Hurst, E. 393, 409–10, 412, 413, 417, 419, 420, 421
Hyman, L.M. 64, 89, 189, 200

Ibibio 151, 153
Ibo 73
Icelandic 238
ideophones 67–8
Idiatov, D. 245
Igbo 19, 152, **153**
Igo 161
Ikalanga 79, 164n3
individual surveys 57
Indo-Europeanists 48
Indoubil 417–18, 420
Infl parameter 223, 239–40
information structure encoding 243; clausal connectives and focus markers 256–8; data sources 244–5; focus 243–4, 245–53; topic 244, 254–6; conclusion 258
Innes, G. 155
intelligent language learning systems 372
intonation 74
Irvine, Judith T. 34
Iscamtho 392, 395, 412, 420
isiXhosa 411
Isoko 150
Ivory Coast (Côte d'Ivoire): Adioukrou 77; Anyi gestures 430; Attié 82, 87; Dyula 399; Ébrié 77, 79–80; French 344, 359, 398, 399, 400, 417; Kwa 157; Nouchi 398–400, 404–5, 416–17, 421; Vata 251; *see also* Mabia

Jacobs, J. 244
James, Z.L. 100
Japanese 238
Jeong, Y. 262, 266–7, 268, 272, 277, 278, 279n5
Jernudd, B.H. 376
Jerome 326, 333
Jita 76
Johnston, H.H. 19
Jones, W. 1
Joos, M. 122
Juba Arabic 46–7
Judah ben Quraysh 34
Judaeus, P. 326

Kaanse 161
Kaba 77, 78–9
Kabbaj, O. 169
Kabiye 345
Kabongo-Mianda, K. 417
Kabyle 178n2
Kadu 50
Kalinowski, C. 247, 248, 250, 256
Kandybowicz, J. 108, 251
Kanerva, J.M. 246

Karanja, L. 396
Kariuki, A. *et al.* 397
Katamba, F. 85, 188
Kaufman, T. 47
Kaye, J. *et al.* 169, 170, 171
Keenan, G. 263
Kelly, J, 60
Kembo-Sure 9
Kendon, A. 429, 433, 434
Kenya: Digo 88; English 361, 365, 395, 396; Engsh 396, 397, 398, 413, 414–15, 420; Gikuiyi 395; Giriama 395; Luhya 395; Luo 45–6, 395; Masai 395; missionaries 17; Oromo 249–50; Rendille 86; Shambaa 429; Sheng 395–8, 403–5, 413–15, 420; Swahili 43, 361, 395, 396, 398, 410; Taita 395
Kerswill, P. 419
Khoekhoe 246, 253, 257
Khoisan phylum 2, 35, **36**, 40–1, 52n2; depressor consonants 80, 81; focus 246; tone 73
Kichaga 263, 264–5
Kiessling, R. 396, 400, 401, 409, 411, 415, 417, 421
Kimenyi, A. 266, 267
Kinande 279n9
Kinyarwanda 109–10, 194–5, **195**, *195*, 265–6, 267–8
Kioko, A.N. 415
Kipsigis 428, 429, 431
Kisi 250, 253
Kisseberth, C. 88, 273, 279n1
Kiswahili 6
Kita, S. 430–1
Klassen, D. H. 432
Klein, J.S. 17
Kloss, H. 376, 377
Koelle, S.W. 4, 17, 18, 26, 34
Koenig, E. *et al.* 416
Koffi, Y. 416, 417
Köhler, O. 38
Koko Wachi 88–9
Kolonialsprachen 16, 19, 24
Koman 35, 50
Komo 81, 255
Kongo gestures 432
König, E. 244
Konkomba 154, 250
Konni 152, 153, 164n2
Konrad, Z. 432
Koopman, H. 251
Korana 80
Kordofanian 35, **36**
Körner, E.F.K. 23
Koromfe **185**, 188, 190, 195–7, **196**, *197*
Koster, J. 223
Kouadio, N.J. 399–400, 416, 417
Kouega, J.-P. 401, 415, 416

Kpololo **185**
Krachi 108
Krakow, R.A. 124
Krapf, J.L. 17, 18
Kresh 250
Krio 210
Kroeger, P. 216, **217**
Kube-Barth, S. 417
Kukú 161
Kulango 94, 95, 97, 107, 112, 113
Kulango-Lorom 94, 107, 108–9
Kultursprachen 16, 22, 23
Kunama 35, 38, 51
Kunene, D.P. 432
Kunene, R. 434
Kuno, S. 238–9, 244
Kurmuk 254
Kusaal 154, 440
Kuti, F. 430
Kutsch Lojenga, C. 44
Kwa **36**, 68; clausal connectives and focus markers 256–8; interpersonal clause structure 94–5; labial-velars 157; MOOD systems 94, 97, 103, 106, 107
Kwadi **36**, 41
Kwanyama 373

La Velle, C.R. 124
Laal 36
labial-velars 5, 150–1; historical development **155**, 155–7, **157**; phonetics 151–5; phonology 158 (labial-velars as labials 161–2; left-sided phonology 158–9; other patterns 160–1; representational models 162–3, *163*; right-sided phonology 159–60); concluding remarks 164
Labov, W. 404
Ladd, D.R. 64
Ladefoged, P. 60, 61, 62, 63, 133, 150
Ladewig, S.H. 429
Lagowa 50
Lahrouchi, M. 171
Lakoff, R. 281, 283
Lambrecht, K. 243, 244, 245
Langila 417
language change 26, 38–42
language documentation and revitalization 2–3, 6; phonetics 60–2
language in the market 59
language planning and policy 6; acquisition planning 377; corpus planning 377; status planning 377
language planning for sustainable development 376; communication and development 380; definitions of language planning 376–7; development 377–9; multilingualism, education and development 379; proposed

solutions to multilingual problems in Ghana 380–5; sustainable development 378; conclusion 386
language shift 46
language typology 51
Larson, M.L. 333
LDRs *see* long distance reflexives
Lebanese Arabic 170, 178n4
Leben, W.R. 90
Lefevere, A. 339
Leggbo 153, *154*
Lehmann, C. 61, 62
Lekgoro, T. 412
Lele (East Chadic) 299–303
Lendu 77–8, 82, 85
Lepsius, K.R. 34
Lepsius, R. 26
Lesotho: Sotho 429
Levinson, S.C. 282
Lewis, M. *et al.* 52n4
lexical phonology 90
Liberia 34; Loma 152
Libyan Arabic 178n1
Likpe 249
Linda 99
Lindblom, B. *et al.* 123, 124, 125, 130, 144, 145
Lingala 73, 86, 418
Lingombe 156
linguistic determinism 438–9
linguistic fieldwork in Africa 4–5, 55–6; ideophones 67–8; nominal classification 67; phonetics 60–3, 65–7; salvage linguistics 68–9; surveying language knowledge and use 56–9; *see also* tone and tonology: fieldwork
linguistic isolates 35, 36–7, **38**
linguistic relativity *see* Sapir-Whorf hypothesis
linguistic taggers 371
linguistics 5
linguograms 62–3, *63*
lip positions 63, *63*
literacy 6
Liu, C.S.L. 235, 236
Lobe-Ewane, M. 401
Local, J. 60
localized trilingualism 380–1
Locus Equations 122–3, 124
logophoric pronouns 230–1; C-command 232–3; variable binding and co-reference 231–2
logophoricity: definition 230–1; and long distance reflexives (LDRs) 235–6
Loko 155
Loma 152
London Missionary Society (LMS) 16
long distance reflexives (LDRs) 222, 233; binding theory 224; blocking effect 234–5; categorical status 222; derivation 223, 236–9; and the Infl parameter 222, 239–40; logophoric account

238–9; and logophoricity 235–6; mono-
morphemic 233; movement analysis 236–7;
pronouns, reflexives and binding theory 224–5;
subject oriented 233–4; types 236; variable
binding interpretation 235; *see also* Yoruba
anaphor *òun*
Lorentz, J. 162
Lotuxo 39, **39**, 40, 43
Lowenstamm, J. 169
Ludolf, H. 16
Luganda **185**, 188, 190, 194–5, **195**, *195*
Luhya 395
Luo 45–6, 395, 428, 429, 431
Luyaaye 418, 420
Lyélé 77

Maa 43
Ma'a 48
Maasai 38, **39**, 49, 395
Maban 35, **36**, 51
Mabia 94, 115n2, 447n2; Dagaare 439, 440,
    440, 441–3, **442**, 444–5; Dagbane 439, **440**,
    442, 443–4; MOOD systems 96–7, 98–9, 101–3,
    104, 105, 106, 112; temporal system:
    "metrical tense" 8, 439, **440**, 440–4, **442**,
    444; Whorfian hypothesis 438–40, 444–6;
    conclusions 446–7
McConvell, P. 47
McGetchin, D. 17
McGinnis, M. 265, 266, 279n4
Mackail, J.W. 339
Mada 160
Madagascar 74, 428
Maddieson, I. 60, 63, 81, 124, 133, 150,
    152, 153
Ma'di 250
Maganga, C.M. 88
Maho, J. 244
Makhudu, D. 412
Makhuwa 248–9
Makonde 429
Malagasy (Austronesia) 74, 282
Malawi: Chichewa 246; ciTsonga 430; Yao 429
Mali: Tadaqsahek 47, **47**; Tamashek (Touareg)
    178n2
Mambila 66–7, 247
Mande languages **36**, 83
Manding gestures 428
Manfredi, Stefano 46, 47
Manuel, Y.S. 124
maps of African languages *3*, *37*, *44*
Marantz, A. 262, 263, 264
Marchand, S. 17
Maribe, T. 394, 405
Marlo, M.R. 82
Masai 395
Mathangwane, J.T. 164n3

Matras, Y. *et al.* 48
Matrix Language Frame (MLF) 411
Matthews, P.H. 297
Max Planck Institute, Nijmegen 68
Maxwell, M. 181–2
Mayogo 79, 161
Mazrui, A.M. 396, 413, 414
Mbugu 48
Mchombo, S. 3, 265
Meakins, F. 47
Mebitaghan, R.O. 329, 335–6
Mednyj Aleut (Aleut region) 47
Meeussen's rule 87, 88
Meierkord, C. 415
Meinhof, C.F.M. 15, 21, 22, 23, 24–6, 27, 28,
    28n2, 28n4, 38
Mensah, E. 411
Menzerath, P. 122
Merino, B.J. 382
Mesthrie, R. 393, 409–10, 412, 417
metatypy 46
metrical tense *see* Mabia: temporal system
Mfusi, M. 412
Microsoft Translator 360
Mills, E. 151
Mimi (of Nachtigal) 35
Mina (Central Chadic) 309–11
Minimalism 286–7, 294n6
minority languages 345; and social media 344,
    345–7
missionaries 15–21, 34, 38, 376, 398
Mitsch, J. 410
"mixed languages" 47
MLF (Matrix Language Frame) 411
Mofu-Gudur 432
Mohanan, K.P. 90
Molamu, L. 411, 413
mood, defined 94
MOOD systems of Niger-Congo languages 93–4;
    abbreviations 114; elemental interrogative
    103–11, **105**; imperative 111–14; indicative:
    declarative 98–100; indicative: interrogative
    100–11; interpersonal clause structure 94–5;
    polar interrogative 100–3; typology of MOOD
    systems 96–8, **98**; conclusion 114
Mòoré: tense 440; vowel harmony 184,
    185–8, **186**, *186*, **187**, *187*, *188*, 194, 201n8,
    201n10–11
moribund languages 68–9
Moro 50
Moroccan Arabic syllable structure & vowel-zero
    alternations 168, 169: CVCV model 171–3,
    173–4; syllable-based approaches 169–71;
    conclusion 177–8
Moroccan Berber syllable structure & vowel-
    zero alternations 168–9: causative formation
    176–7; CVCV model 171–2, 173–4; syllabic

consonants 175–7; syllable-based approaches 171; Tamazight 169, 171, 173–4, 175, 176, 177, 178n2; Tarifit 178n2; Tashlhiyt 168, 169, 171, 174, 175–7, 178n2; conclusion 177–8
Moshi, L. 263, 264, 265, 268
Mosse, G. 17
mother tongue instruction 7
Motor Theory 122
Mous, M. 48, 396, 400, 401, 409, 411, 414, 415, 417, 421
Mozambique: Makhuwa 248–9; Makonde 429; Portuguese 344; Yao 429
Mufwene, S.S. 3
Mugane, J. 9
Muhammed Ali 46
Müller, C. 429
multilingualism 51–2, 379, 380; Ghana 346, 380–5; localized trilingualism 380–1
multiverb constructions (MVCs) 217, *218*
Mupun (West Chadic) 311–14
Mutaka, N.M. 156
Muthwii, M.J. 415
Myers-Scotton, C. 411

Nafaara 154
Nakagawa, H. 41
Naluwooza, V. 418
Nama 80
Namibia: Herero 20; Khoekhoe 246, 253; Korana 80; missionaries 17, 20; Nama 80
Namyalo, S. 418
Nassenstein, N. 43, 409, 414–15, 417, 418
Nawuri 161, 164
Ndayiragije, J. 246
Ndebele gestures 432
NeighbourNet representations 48–9, *49*
Neogrammarians 39
neural machine translation (NMT) 359–60
Newell, S. 417, 420
Ngano story-songs 432
Ngbaka 160
Ngemba 246
Ngiti 85, 86
Ngoboka, J.P. 267
Nichols, J. 49
Nicolas of Hereford 326
Nida, E.A. 331, 332, 334
Niger: Tamashek (Touareg) 178n2; Touareg storytelling 432
Niger-Congo (Niger-Kordofanian) phylum 2, 35, **36**, 42, 49, 50; depressor consonants 81; interpersonal clause structure 94–6; labial-velars 150, 156, *156*; noun classification 67; tone 73; *see also* MOOD systems of Niger-Congo languages
Nigeria: Afrobeat salute 430; Edo 250–1; Ewe 344–5; Gùrùntùm 247–8; Ibo 73; Koko Wachi

88–9; languages 4, 55, 61; missionaries 17; Nupe 251; official languages 6; social media 345; Yoruba 429
"Nigritic" languages 21
"Nilo-Hamitic" group 38
Nilo-Saharan phylum 2, 35, **36**, 38, 39, 42, 49, 50; labial-velars 150, 161; tone 73
Nilotic language family 38, 39, 41, 73
NIng 252
Njogu, K. 415
Nkore-Kiga 101
NMT (neural machine translation) 359–60
Noon 248
North German Missionary Society (NMS) 17
Northern Khoisan **36**, 41
Northern Sotho 373
Nortier, J. 410, 419
Nouchi 398–400, 404–5, 416–17, 421
noun classification 67
Nsimbi, M. 418
Ntshangase, D.K. 392, 394, 395
Ntsobé, A.-M. *et al.* 415
Nubi Arabic 46
Nubian languages 50
Nupe 154, 251
Nupe-Oko-Idoma 94, 95–6
Nurse, D. 8–9
Nyam 156
Nyangiya 35
Nyangumarda (Australia) **185**, 190, 201n7
Nyländer, G.R. 17, 20
Nyo 106, 107
Nyst, V. 430
Nzema 160, 163

Och, F. 360
official languages 6, 344, 359, 361
Ofoe, L.C. 252
Ogechi, N.O. 398
Ohala, J. 162
Öhman, S. 122
Òkó 94, 102, 113–14
Olawsky, K.J. 284
Oluoch-Olunya, G. 415
Omoruyi, T.O. 250–1
Omotic languages 46, 73, 81
Ong'ota 50
Optimality Theory 91, 124, 125, 163, 200n3
!Ora 40–1
Orie, O.O. 7, 430
Origen 326
Oromo 249–50
Oropom 37
Osam, E.K. 209
Osinde, K. 396, 409, 413, 414
Osituemu, E.O. 335
Osofisan, F. 334–5

Index

Otero, M.A. 255
Owoeye, K. 335
Owoeye, O.K. 334–5
Owu-Ewie, C. 346, 380, 381–2, 383, 386
Oyelaran, O.O. 125

Painter, C. 152
palatograms 62–3, *63*
Pallas, S. 34
Panconcelli-Calzia, G. 15, 23, 25, 26–7
Pantland, W. 421
paralexification 48
Parkinson, F. 163
Pawlíková-Vilhnová, V. 18
Pero (West Chadic) 308–9
Petrollino, S. 46, 47
phoneme correspondences 39
phonemic inventory 61, 62
phonetics: experimental phonetics 26–7; labial-velars 151–5; *see also* coarticulation
phonetics in fieldwork: importance of training 60; investigation of tone 65–7; language documentation 60–2; presenting phonetic structures 62–3
Phonological Development 122
phonology 5–6, 50, 61, 158–63
phylogenetic relationships 48
pidginization 46, 47, 400, 401
Pietism 17, 18
Pike, K.L. 73, 81, 89
pitch 74
Poliakov, L. 17
politically correct language 445–6
Ponelis, F. 156
Pool, J. 379, 385
Portuguese 16, 344, 359
Poser, W.J. 41
Praat 85, 127
Pratt, M.L. 26
Prince, A. 91
Progovac, L. 223, 233, 236
Pugach, S. 2
Pulleyblank, D. 90, 130, 229–30
Purvey, J. 327
pygmoid groups 50
Pylkkänen, L. 264, 265, 268, 279n3

Quantal Theory 122
questionnaires 56–7, 58
Quintilian 326

racism 16, 21, 34, 38
Ramirez, J. 382
RBMT *see* rule-based machine translation
Recasens, D. *et al.* 127
Rédei, K. 184
Reershemius, G. 345, 355

Register Tier Theory 87, 91
Reh, M. 244
Reindorf, C.C. 19
Reinhart, T. 223, 236, 244
Relevance Theory 244, 330, 332
Rendille 86
Rendók 421
Rennison, J. R. 186, 199
reticence in surveys 58
reticulation 48
Reuland, E. 223, 236, 241
Reynolds, B. 340
Rhenish Missionary Society (RMS) 17, 20
Ridouane, R. *et al.* 171
Ritter, E. 291
Rizzi, L. 240
RNN Encoder-Decoder 362
Robert, S. 249
Robinson, D. 325, 326
Roboredo, M. 16
Romani (Europe) 48
Romanticism 17–18
Rotimi, O. 334–5
Rubin, J. 376
rule-based machine translation (RBMT) 361–2; applications derivable from rule-based approach 370–2; problems in detecting translation errors 370; SALAMA 363; *see also* Google Translate (GT) and SALAMA
Rundi 246
Runyakitara 373
Rwanda 246
Rybarczyk, M. 281, 282
Ryder, M.E. 150, 159, 162–3

Sabel, J. 287
Sacleux, C. 18–19
Saeed, J. 252
Sagey, E. 159
Saharan **36**, 51
Saitz, R.L. 428
SALAMA (Swahili Language Manager) *see* Google Translate (GT) and SALAMA
Salffner, S. 62
salvage anthropology 1–2
salvage linguistics 68–9
Samal (Philippines) 282
Samarin, W. 60, 68
Samburu 428, 429
Samo 429
Samper, D. 405
Sandawe **36**, 41, 250, 253
Sande, H. 416–17
Sanders, K.W. 430
Sands, B. 244
Sango 73
Sapir, E. 7, 439–40

460

Index

Sapir-Whorf hypothesis 8, 438–40, 444; problems 445–7; supporting evidence 444–5, 447
Sawabantu languages 156, 164n5
Sayers, D.L. 340
Schachter, P. 184, 189
Schadeberg, Th.C. 35, 88
Scheer, T. 176
Schiller, E. *207*, 214, *214*
Schleicher, A. 1
Schlenker, C.F. 17
Schneider-Zioga, P. 275, 279n9
Schnoebelen, Tyler 48, *49*
Schön, J.F. 17, 18, 19
Schroder, A. 415
Schuchardt, H. 45
Schwarz, A. 245, 256
Schwenter, S.A. 441
Seargeant, P. 348, 353
segmental/suprasegmental interaction *see* Yoruba segmental/suprasegmental interaction
self-reporting in surveys 58
Sells, P. 230
Semitic languages 34, **36**, 46
Senegal: Fula 249; Noon 248; Wolof 73, 249
Senufo: labial-velars 157; Supyire 157; Tyebaara dialect 151–2, 159
Serial Verb Constructions (SVCs) *see* West African Serial Verb Constructions
Sesotho 412
Shabo 50
Shambaa 429
Shaw, J. *et al.* 171
Sheehan, J. 18
Sheng 395–8, 403–5, 413–15, 420
Shilluk 28n3
Shimizu, K. **199**
Shona 124, 432
Shryock, A. *et al.* 155
Shuttleworth, M. 325
Sibree, J. 428
Sierra Leone: Kisi 253; missionaries 16–17, 34; Susu 16; Temne 16; Vai 16
Sievers, E. 122
Silverstein, R.O. 161
Simons, G.F. 244
Sisaala-Pasaale 154
Siwu 68, 432
Smith, N.V. 154
Smolensky, P. 91
SMT *see* statistical machine translation
Snider, K. 64, 91
social media 343–5; language use: COD model and data 347–8; and minority languages 344, 345–7; Web 2.0 343, 355; *see also* Ewe use on Facebook
sociolinguistics approach 4, 55, 56
Somali 251–2, 439

Somalia 251–2
Songhai/Songhay 35, **36**, 47
Soninke 250
Sorin-Barreteau, L. 432
Sotho 412, 429; Northern Sotho 373; South Sotho 431, 432
Souag, L. 47, **47**
Soukka, M. 248
sound correspondences 39
South Africa: Afrikaans 312, 394, 395, 411, 412; Bantu 394, 395, 429, 431, 432–3; Iscamtho 392, 395, 412, 420; NIng 252; official languages 6; Tsotsitaal 392, 393, 395, 411–13, 421
South Sudan: Bari languages 46; Juba Arabic 46–7; Komo 255; Nilotic languages 38
South West Africa *see* Namibia
Southeastern Tunisian 178n1
Southern Khoisan **36**, 41
Southern Nilotic 38, 39
Soyinka, W. 335
SPE (*Sound Pattern of English*) theory 89, 125, 182
Speech Analyzer 85
spelling checkers 371
Spener, P.J. 17
Sperber, D. 330, 332
Spivak, G.C. 9
spread zones 49–50
Spyropoulos, M. 396
Standard Sudanese Arabic 46–7
statistical machine translation (SMT) 359–61; problems in detecting translation errors 370; *see also* Google Translate (GT) and SALAMA
Steere, E. 18
Stein-Kanjora, G. 401, 416
Steinfatt, T. 447
Steinkopff, K. F. 16
stem tree (Stammbaum) theory 1
Stephanus, R 330
Stewart, J. 207
Stewart, J.M. 184, 189
Strawson, P.F. 244
stress 74
stressed syllables 74
Stroud, C. 410
Sudan 46; Fur 78, 86; Komo 255; Kresh 250; Kukú 161; Kurmuk 254; Nuba Mountains 50; Rendók 421
"Sudanic" languages 21, 38; Central Sudanic 35, 38, 43, 429
Sulemana, A. 281, 286
Sung, L. 223, 233, 236, 239
Supyire 157
Surkum 42
Surmic 39, 46

Index

surveying language knowledge and use: administering a survey 57–8; knowledge and training 56; language in the market 59; pitfalls and problems 58; questionnaires 56–7; utility of surveys 56

Sussman, H.M. *et al.* 121, 123, 124, 127, 130, 133, 145

sustainable development 378; *see also* language planning for sustainable development; sustainable language technology

sustainable language technology 359–60; applications derivable from RBMT 370–2; bootstrapping rule-based approach to other languages 372–3; dictionary compilation 371; dictionary testing 372; distrust between SMT and RBMT developers 362; Google Translate and SALAMA compared 362–70; hybrid approach 362; intelligent language learning systems 372; linguistic taggers 371; neural machine translation (NMT) 359–60; problems in detecting translation errors 370; RNN Encoder-Decoder 362; rule-based machine translation (RBMT) 361–2, 370; spelling checkers 371; statistical machine translation (SMT) 359–61, 370; vocabulary compilers 372; conclusion 373

Susu 16

Swahili 43–5, *44*, 73, 124; colonialism 21; Kenya 43, 361, 395, 396, 398, 410; missionaries 18; research 21, 27; sound shifts 25–6; stress 74; Tanzania 43, 361; *see also* Google Translate (GT) and SALAMA

Sweet, H. 121

syllable structure: CVCV approach 171–2; *see also* Moroccan Arabic; Moroccan Berber

syncretic languages 47, 48

Tabain, M. 123

Taber, C.R. 331, 332

Tadaqsahek 47, **47**

Tagg, C. 348, 353

Taita 395

talking drums 74

Tamanji, P.N. 246

Tamashek 178n2

Tamazight *see* Moroccan Berber

Tang, C.-C. 223, 233, 236

Tano 94, 103

Tanzania: English 361; Jita 76; Kiswahili 6; Luo 45; Ma'a 48; Sandawe **36**, 41, 250, 253; Shambaa 429; Swahili 43, 361

Tashlhiyt *see* Moroccan Berber

Taylor, W.E. 19

TBU *see* tone-bearing units (TBU)

Temeinian languages 35, 50

Temne 16, 152

Teso-Turkana 43

theoretical linguistics 2, 5

Thomas Aquinas 326

Thomas, J.M.C. 64

Thomason, S.G. 47

Thompson, R.F. *et al.* 432

Thorne, L.S. 353

Thrainsson, H. 241

Tiayon-Lekobou, C. 401

Tigrinya 246

Tima 50

Tirma 46

Tlingit (North West America) 282

Togo: colonialism 21; Ewe 344, 345; French 344; Kabiye 345; missionaries 17; *see also* Mabia

Tollefson, J.W. 376

tonal polarity 87, 88

tone analysis methodology: acoustic analysis 85; aim 82; data gathering 82–3; further analysis 84; listening for surface tonal melodies 83–4; neutralization 84–5; organizing the data 83; theories 89–91

tone and tonology: coarticulation 125–6; contour tones 64, 75, **75**, 76, 77; declination 64; depressor consonants 79–81; downdrift 88–9; downstep 64, 76, 88–9, 91; floating tones 78–9; function of tone 85–7; grammatical tone 64; level tones 75, **75**, 76; lexical tone 64; mora 76–7; register tone 64; research 50; surface structure 76; syllables 76–7; tonal processes and register phenomena 87–9; tone-bearing segments 77–8; tone defined 74; toneless morphemes 78; typology of tone systems 81–2; underlying structure 76, 78–9; upstep 76, 89, 91

tone and tonology fieldwork 5, 72, 91; basic considerations 64–5; listening and mimicking 74–5, 82; phonetic investigation 65–7; transcribing tone **75**, 75–6

tone-bearing units (TBU) 74, 76

tone languages 72–3; defined 73–4; pitch, tone, stress, intonation 74

tone shifting 87, 88

tone spreading 87–8, 124

tonogenesis 80

topic 244; aboutness 244; marking 254–6

Torrence, H. 108

Tosco, M. 252

Touareg 178n2, 432

Toury, G. 329, 335

Traill, A. 41

transaction analysis 59

translanguaging 52, 346

translation 325; abbreviations 340–1; accuracy and fidelity 331–2; close translation 331; cultural translations 332, 333–4; direct translation 332; dynamic equivalence 333, 334, 340; formal equivalece 332; free translations

332–3; functional equivalence 334, 336–8; gloss translation 331; Greek and Latin poetry 326; idiomatic translation 333–4; imitation 326, 333; interlinear translation 331; linguistic translation 331–2; literal translation 331; metaphrase 326, 331; modern theories 327–30; paraphrase (paraphrasis) 326, 333; Romans translating from Greek to Latin 325–6; sense-for-sense 333; Source Text 327; Target Audience 327–30; thick translation 332; word-for-word 331; conclusion 340; *see also* sustainable language technology; translation, non-Scripture; translations of Scripture

translation, non-Scripture: business correspondence 328; descriptive translation studies 329; European Union legislation 328; IT instructions 328; machine translation 329; novels, operas, films, plays 328–9, 334–6; poetry 339–40; pragmatics 329; Relevance Theory 330, 332; secular literature - West African examples 334–6; Target Audiences 328–30

translations of Scripture: Bible 19, 326–8, 329, 330, 331, 332, 333, 334–9, 340, 341; functional equivalence 334, 336–9; Geneva Bible 327; Hexapla 326; indirect translation 330–1; intra-text explanatory material 330; King James' (Authorised) Version 327–8; Koran 330; machine translation 329; New International Version 328; paraphrase (paraphrasis) 333; poetry 340; quality 327; sense-for-sense 326, 327, 333; Septuagint (LXX) 326; Source Language 330; Source Text 326, 330; Target Audience 326, 327–8; Vulgate 326, 327

Tremearne, A.J.N. 428
Trubetzkoy, N.S. 184–5
Trudgill, P. 43
Tsotsitaal 392, 393, 395, 411–13, 421
Tucker, A.N. 45
Turkana 39, **39**, 40, 52n1
Turku Arabic 46
Turner, G.S. *et al.* 125
Twi 207
Tyndale, W. 327
Tzika, M. 62

Uganda: Acooli 73; Luo 45; Luyaaye 418, 420; Runyakitara 373
Ugorji, C.U.C. 335
Ulfsbjorninn, S. 174
UNESCO 343
United Nations: Declaration on the Rights of Indigenous Peoples 359; translation policy 360
Urhobo 150, 329, 335–6

Vai 16
Vakunta, P. 416

Van de Velde, M. 245
Van der Wal, J. 249
Vata 104, 251
Vater, J.S. 28n2
Vaux, B. 60
verb serialization 51
vocabulary compilers 372
Voeltz, E.F.K. 9
Volta-Comoe languages 152
Voorhoeve, J. 81
Vossen, R. 38, 39–40
vowel harmony 50
vowel harmony (beyond ATR) 181–2; advantages of 189–90; advertising *vs.* alms 190; as aid to identification of word structure 194; ATR-harmony in Akan 182–4, **183**, *188*, 188–9, *189*, 190; autosegmental analyses 184; within Government Phonology 184–9, **185**; harmony domain 190; as last-stage checking mechanism 194–7; Mòoré 184, 185–8, **186**, *186*, **187**, *187*, *188*, 194, 201n8, 201n10–11; parsing 191 (morphological 181, 192–3, *193*; phonological 191–2); SPE theory 182; suicidal vowel harmony: Yukuben nouns 190, 197–200, **198**, *198*, **199**; conclusions 200
vowel-zero alternations 169; *see also* Moroccan Arabic; Moroccan Berber

wa Thiongo, N. 6
WALS *see World Atlas of Language Structures*
Wandala (Central Chadic) 299, 303–7
Wang, W. 89
Ward, I.C. 73, 158–9
Watters, J.R. 246, 247
WCED (World Commission on Environment and Development) 378
Webb, V. 9
Wedekind, K. 81, 82
Weibegué, C. 303
Weinstein, B. 376, 377
Weitzenauer, S.M. **199**
Welmers, W.E. 73, 81, 152, 158, 159
Welsh and social media 345
West Africa xiv, 65, 150
West African Linguistic Society 125
West African Serial Verb Constructions (SVCs) 51, 207–8; methodologies and further research 216–18; properties *207*, 208–12 (composition 209–10; contiguity 209, 210, *211*; marking 209, 211–12; wordhood 209, 211); prototypical features 216–17, **217**; syntactic and semantic 'unity' 212–14, *214*; Twi 207; valency of verbs 215–16, **216**; conclusion 218
West Atlantic **36**, 73
Westermann, D. 21, 38, 160, 207, 428
Western Nilotic 39, 40, 41, 45
White Fathers 18

Whorf, B. 438, 439; *see also* Sapir-Whorf hypothesis
Wilberforce, W. 16
Wilhoit, L.K. 152
Williamson, G. 17
Wilson, C. 409, 417, 418, 420
Wilson, D. 330
Wilson, J.G. 37
Wilson, W.A.A. 152
Witzlack-Makarevich, A. 252, 257
Wolof 73, 105–6, 110, 249
Wolter, K.L. 288
Wondimu, H. 254
World Atlas of Language Structures (*WALS*) 93, 94
World Commission on Environment and Development (WCED) 378
Wundt, W. 25–6
Wycliffe, J. 326–7

!Xun 248

Yabâcrane 417, 418
Yaka 86
Yao 429
Yarada K'wank'wa 421
Yerima, A. 335
Yevudey, E. 346
Yip, M. 73, 89
Yoruba: Bible translations 19; gestures 428, 429, 430–1; labial-velars 158, 161, 164; MOOD systems 109, 110, 111; pronouns and binding theory 225; Sapir-Whorf hypothesis 439; source for English plays *et al.* 334–5; tone 124, 125

Yoruba anaphor *òun*: and 3rd person sing. pronoun *ó* 227–8; Avoid Pronoun Principle 229–30; and English *him/her* 226–7; as logophoric pronoun 230–3, 238–9; as long distance bound anaphor 233–5; and reflexive *araàr* (herself/himself) 228; conclusion 241
Yoruba segmental/suprasegmental interaction 122, 123, 126; instrumentation 127; Locus equations 123, 127; method 126–7; results and observations: (Euclidean distance 130, *131*, 131–2, *132*; higher Locus Equations for sentence form 130; Locus Equations and tone effects 132–3; Locus Equations parameters/ Yoruba stop place categories by tone 127–9, **128**, *128*, *129*; Modified Locus Equations analyses 134–8, **135**, **136**, **137**; second order Locus Equations 130, *130*, *131*; three-dimensional diagram of F0, F1 and F2 of V2 *142*, *143*, 144; tone effect: citation form *138*, 138–9, *139*, **140**; tone effect: connected speech (sentence form) *140*, *141*, **142**; vowel space in F2/F1 coordinate: Low vs Mid tone 133, *133*, *134*); tone 125–6; discussion 144–5
Yukuben vowel harmony **185**, 190, 197–200, **198**, *198*, **199**

Ze Amvela, E. 401, 415
Zeijlstra, H. 294n6
Zeller, J. 246, 248, 254
Zimba 86–7
Zimbabwe 432
Zimmerman, M. 247–8
Zondo, J. 432
Zulu 112, 245, 268, 277–8, 412, 431, 434, 439